Main Street Forest looking North 1900.

SCOTT COUNTY
· 1830 ·
· 2002 ·
Forest
MISSISSIPPI

TURNER PUBLISHING COMPANY

Main Street Forest

West side of Courthouse, Forest MS.

TURNER PUBLISHING COMPANY

Turner Publishing Company Staff:
Publishing Consultant: Keith R. Steele
Designer: Peter Zuniga

Copyright © 2002
All rights reserved
Publishing Rights: Turner Publishing Company

This book or any part thereof may not be
reproduced without the written consent of the
publisher and Scott County Genealogical Society

Library of Congress Control No.
2001097758
ISBN:978-1-68162-534-8

Additional
copies may be purchased directly from the
publisher. Limited Edition.

Table of Contents

Cook Motor Company, Forest, MS

3

Preface

Mary Grace Haralson Schwab, Chairperson Book Committee

The purpose of this history book is to preserve our heritage and the heritage of the many families that have made Scott County their home since it was founded. The county history as well as the histories of the town and communities, businesses, schools, homes and interesting facts and legends was researched by the book committee. Information was obtained from articles in the state archives, citizens and articles at the Forest Public Library.

Every effort has been made to represent all sections of the county. It is not our intention to leave anyone or anything out.

The book committee would like to thank everyone that has submitted his or her family histories and photos. Mr. Marion McCrory was real helpful in letting us use his photo collection. The family histories were sent to the publisher as submitted.

I would personally like to thank Dorothy Vance, Marcia Estep, Shawna Alexander and Delores Sanders for helping in this project. A special thank you goes to Ike Crudup Jr. and Mary Vance for helping with the project in its final weeks and Mr. Sid Salter and employees of the *Scott County Times* Newspaper for publishing our press releases and making photos for us when we needed them.

I hope future generations will look at this book and be proud to know that their family was from Scott County, MS.

Mary Grace Haralson Schwab
Forest, MS

Introduction

Committee Members L-R: Shawna Alexander, Dorothy Vance, Mary Schwab (Chairperson).
Not pictured: Marcia Estep and Delores Sanders

On August 9, 1997 a group of people interested in forming a genealogical society in Scott County came together at Forest Public Library. By-laws and a mission statement were adopted. Scott County Genealogical Society was accepted as the name with membership open to anyone wishing to join. Dues and meeting times were set. Officers were elected with A.D. Boykin as our first president, Steve Watkins as vice-president, Dorothy Vance as secretary/treasurer and Linda Harvey as program chairman. Officers at this time are: Mary Schwab third term as president, Marion McCrory third term as vice-president, Dorothy Vance secretary/ treasurer and Shawna Alexander program chairman. Over the last four years membership has steadily grown. We now have 78 members all over the United States. Our quarterly newsletter *The Tree Climber* is also traded with other societies. In 1999 the society decided to put together a cookbook of family recipes to include photos of ancestors, it took a year but as of now we have had three printings. In 2000 the society put together a Pedigree Chart book that includes over 900 names and is indexed. In 2000 we got permission to name the Genealogical Collection at Forest Public Library in honor of the late Richard S. Lackey; a plaque was presented to the library and Mr. Lackey's daughter, Ellen attended the presentation.

In October 1999 Mary Schwab the president of Scott County Genealogical Society was contacted by a representative of the publishing company. The purpose of the contact was to see if the society would be interested in publishing a book on the history of Scott County and its families. The society discussed the idea and in January 2000 the contract was signed. A book committee was formed with volunteers. It has taken two full years and a lot of work but we feel it will be well worth our efforts.

Scott County History

Abram M. Scott

Abram M. Scott, seventh governor of Mississippi (1832-1833). He was a native of South Carolina, but at an early age went to the Mississippi territory. Mr. Scott became a leading planter of Wilkinson County and was one of its five representatives in the first state constitutional convention of 1817. He served two terms as lieutenant governor, during the first and second administrations of Gerard C. Brandon, and in January 1832 succeeded the latter as chief magistrate of the state. His term was rendered conspicuous by the assembling of the constitutional convention in 1832, which reconstructed the whole organic law of the state. The principle feature of the newly adopted constitution was the increased power given the people through the ballot box in making the election of legislators and state officers, including the judges, by direct vote and by doing away with the property qualifications. Mississippi was thus the first state in the union whose constitution provided for a judiciary elected by the people. Gov. Scott did not live to complete his term of two years, having fallen a victim to Asiatic cholera, which raged throughout the Mississippi Valley in 1832-1833. He died in Jackson, MS June 12, 1833. Scott County was named for this well respected leader of the great state of Mississippi.

Scott County

Scott County was organized from land acquired from the Choctaw Indians September 27, 1830 by the Treaty of Dancing Rabbit Creek. This treaty stipulated that the Choctaw Indians would leave the area of the Choctaw purchase as quickly as they safely could. The number of Choctaws who immigrated to the Choctaw nation west of the Mississippi River was reported by the Commissioner of Indian Affairs of 1838 to have been 15,177. The county, along with 15 others, was organized about three years after this treaty. Scott County was organized December 23, 1833 and was named in honor of Abram Scott, seventh governor of Mississippi.

The act of the legislature creating the county defined its borders as follows: beginning four townships, or 24 miles, north of the Choctaw base line and four townships east of the Choctaw Doak's stand line; thence northward 24 miles, westward 24 miles, southward 24 miles and thence eastward to the starting point. The county was originally square and contained 576 square miles. There was however a strip on the east side of the Doak's Stand boundary line which had not been granted to any county. Four years after its creation Scott County was enlarged by the addition of all that portion of territory east of Pearl River and the old Choctaw boundary line, describing the dividing line between the Indian and white settlements prior to the Dancing Rabbit Treaty of 1830 from the point where the same boundary line crosses Pearl River to the point where the same intersects the western boundary line of the county. This additional territory contained only eight square miles, making a total of 584 square miles, or 373,760 acres in the county. With this exception the boundary lines of Scott County has not been changed since its creation. It is situated in the south central part of the state, about halfway between Jackson and Meridian. The principal streams in the county are Strong and Leaf rivers; Tuscalameta, Tala Bogue, Nutuckala, Schocklala and Coffee Bogue creeks. The bottom and prairie lands produce well and the hill lands by fertilization give remunerative crops. It is now in the Fifth Congressional, the Eighth Circuit Court and the 13th Senatorial Districts. The county is bounded by Newton on the east, Smith on the south, Rankin on the west and Leake on the north with a very small portion touching Madison on the northwest. The commissioners appointed to organize the county were John J. Smith, Gilbert D. Gore, James S. Jolly, Samuel Hawthorn, Morgan McAfee, F. Carr, Joe Bogan, John R. Dunn, D.W. Hopkins Sr., John P. Smith, Robert Laird, James Boykin and James Furlow. The following persons were appointed by said commissioners as members of the first board of supervisors, known as the Board of Police, John Dunn, James Russell, Wade H. Holland, Stephen H. Berry and Jeremiah B. White. The board met on April 7, 1834 and organized by electing John Dunn, president and Stephen Berry, clerk pro tem. The first election held in the county was on

Abram M. Scott

the 18th and 19th of April 1834. John Smith was elected sheriff and Nicholas Finely was clerk of the probate court and William Ricks was elected the first probate judge.

By 1840 the white population was 1,184. The following were among the early settlers of the county, to wit: Maj. R.W. Roberts, who is remembered as a prominent and worthy citizen and elected to Congress before the formation of congressional districts; John J. Smith, Landon Butler, Duncan Smith, George D. Keahey, S.J. Denson, Stephen Berry, Jonathan Summers, Alfred Eastland, Abner Lack, Mesback Patrick, Joseph Hunt, William Ricks, J.B. White, J.M. Finley, Cullen C. Coward, Thomas Segreath, Gabe Fields, Thomas Slay, Isaac Carr; the late A.B. Smith, familiarly known as "Dick Smith," son of John J. Smith was the first white child born in Scott County; he was regarded by his professional brethren as an excellent criminal and land lawyer; he was the father-in-law of Col. Thomas B. Graham, who was for 14 years chancellor of the 8th Chancery District.

These settlers came into the county by way of the road, which came from Winchester in Wayne County, MS and passed through the southern part of the county and the stage road from Montgomery, AL which passed from Union in Newton County to Hillsboro in Scott County. From Hillsboro the stage followed a route to Vicksburg. A stage stop was located down this latter stage road near the present town of Morton. The road was in use by 1836.

According to the first census taken after the organization of the county, there were only about 200 white families with an average of two sq—ves to the family. During the next 10 years the population almost tripled. Many settlers in the Scott County area came from or were descendants of people from France, Ireland, England, Germany and Scotland. The first white child born in Scott County was A.B. Smith. He was born in Hillsboro but moved to Forest in 1869. He was a lawyer and a leading Democrat of the time.

The first county seat of the county was located at the now extent town of Berryville. It remained there until 1836, when the county government was moved to Hillsboro, where it remained for 30 years. Volney E. Howard, a gentleman of varied accomplishments, by profession a lawyer

Scott County Courthouse ca. 1910

Scott County Courthouse ca. 1950s

1846, 48, 50	A.H. Metcalf
1852	David R. Jones
1854, 56	S.J. Smith
1857	E. Rush Buckner
1858	J.W. Wofford
1859-1861	David R. Jones
1861-1862	Mathew Lyle
1865-1867	Thomas B. Graham
1870-1871	John G. Owens
1872-1873	John Gaddis
1874-1875	J.G. Crecelius
1876-1877	Green B. Huddleston
1878	A.C. Farmer
1880-1882	Mathew Lyle
1884, 86, 88, 90	Joseph H. Beeman

Scott County Government

Scott County's government is made up of the sheriff, circuit clerk, chancery clerk, tax assessor and collector, board of supervisors, constables and the justice court judges.

During most of the reconstruction period, the office of sheriff was held by most of the Owen family. John G. Owen was sheriff at the close of the war. Federal authority appointed John R. Owen in 1867 and by election until 1875.

Sheriffs	
1875	R.T.M. Simmons
1897	J.M. Stephenson
1900	J.C. Mize
1903	J.M. Nichols and J.C. Mize
1912	A.L. McKenzie
1916	W.T. Robertson
1919	Frank F. Mize
1931-1935	George J. Taylor
1935-1939	Duff Austin
1939-1943	O.D. Loper
1944-1947	Howard B. McCrory
1948-1951	Otis Myers
1952-1955	Johnnie Williams
1960-1963	Dewitt Simmons
1964-1967	Hubert Fitzhugh
1968-1975	Clell Harrell
1976-1979	W.C. "Pete" Wall
1980-1987	Glen Warren
1988-Present	William Richardson

History Of The Scott County Courthouse

The Scott County Courthouse is clearly a 1950s style structure, its strict lines and austere appearance an example of the architecture of that period. There was little romanticism in architectural design, buildings were meant to reflect efficiency and moderness. The structure that stands on the town square today has been more fortunate than the ones that stood before it. The 1950s efficiency may be the best thing that has ever happened to a Scott County Courthouse.

The courthouses of Scott County have been somewhat ill fated. The present building erected in 1955 was built to replace the one that had to be torn down due to a faulty foundation. The troubles go past that, to the very beginning of Forest as county seat. Forest was made county seat in 1873. When the county was formed in 1833, the no longer existent town of Berryville was the county seat. In 1836, Hillsboro was made the county seat because it was nearer the center of the county. Hillsboro was the political and social center of the county until the close of the Civil War. For years after the organization of the county, Hillsboro was the only community of importance in Scott County.

The county seat remained at Hillsboro for 30 years. Sherman's soldiers destroyed the courthouse at Hillsboro on their march to the sea. For-

and a native of Maine, was the second member of the legislature from Scott County. After the adjournment of that body, he remained in Jackson and in connection with his brother, Bainbridge Howard, purchased the *Mississippian* and edited that journal for some time. During the Civil War, Yankee soldiers during Sherman's march to the sea destroyed the courthouse at Hillsboro. In 1865, the Mississippi Legislature passed an act giving the Board of Police power to authorize a county election to determine the location of the county seat. The act also provided for the erection of a courthouse at Forest should it be chosen as the site. The election was held and a large majority selected Forest. This caused one of the largest controversies in county history. Scott County has had numerous senators and representatives during its history. Here are a few:

Senators	
1837-1839	Oliver C. Dease
1840-1843	John C. Thomas
1844-1846	Simeon R. Adams
1848, 50, 52	O.R. Singleton
1854	William McWillie
1856-1858	S.J. Denson
1859-1861	J.R. Davis
1861-1862	Oliver A. Luckett
1865-1867	Mathew Lyle
1870-1871	Thomas J. Hardy
1872-1873	John Watts
1874-1876	T.B. Graham
1877	H.C. McCabe
1878, 80	Asa R. Carter
1882, 84	Thomas Keith
1886, 88	R.P. Austin
1890	A.M. Byrd

Representatives	
1835	Jeremiah White
1836	Volney E. Howard
1837	John Dunn
1838-1843	Robert W. Roberts
1844	John J. Smith

est was chosen as county seat in 1865 by the state legislature and a courthouse built, the records were moved there in 1866. However, Hillsboro citizens did not want Forest to become the county seat. Before the courthouse at Forest could be completed the roof was almost torn off by a crowd of citizens who did not favor the location at Forest. Forest citizens kept watch at night after that but sometime later the courthouse was partly burned. Feelings ran so high that the military district suspended the act of legislature that made Forest county seat and another election was ordered. Hillsboro charged that the first election was carried by fraud and wanted the Lake and Forest precincts thrown out. The second election held in November 1867, declared Hillsboro the selected site. But a December issue of the *Forest Register* said that election was carried by fraud. Military troops were sent to Forest and camped on the square until 1868. Part of the records were at Forest and part at Hillsboro. The courthouse at Hillsboro had been destroyed and the one at Forest badly burned. In June 1869, the board of police ordered the records removed from Forest, but the attempt was stopped by threats of violence from counsel and leaders of Forest. Another attempt to destroy the Forest building was made in January 1870. Forest citizens and sympathizers stood guard over the courthouse, which had been rebuilt by contributions from the townspeople. On the night of February 2, the building was burned so badly that it was nearly useless.

The remains of the Forest building were moved to Hillsboro and the new courthouse there was completed in February 1872. It remained there for less than a year. The Forest people were not satisfied and demanded another election. The election was granted in May 1873 with Forest the winner.

A $5,000 two-story wooden building was built on the square in Forest in 1875 and a one-story brick jail was located west of the square. The courthouse building at Hillsboro was sold and converted into a schoolhouse. After 1875, there was no question as to the location of the county seat, but ill feelings continued to exist for many years.

In 1900 a fire that burned much of the Forest downtown area burned the courthouse and many valuable records were lost. It was replaced by a $20,000 brick structure. The courthouse eventually cracked so badly because of the yazoo clay soil in this area, that it had to be replaced in 1924. (The same thing happened to that two-story building also.) A $55,000 courthouse and jail project was approved in 1938. The cost covered the building of a new jail adjoining the north side of the courthouse and repairs for the courthouse. In July 1939 the new jail addition was turned over to Scott County officials. By 1953 the old courthouse had begun to show strains of the moving clay ground syndrome. It was decided that it would cost just as much to repair the building as it would to replace it with a new structure. A $300,000 bond issue was passed to construct a new building. During the demolition of the old building, a roof fell in on Chancery Clerk Taylor Tadlock and his wife as they were leaving his office. A steel filing cabinet and a heavy desk held the falling debris and probably kept the Tadlocks from being crushed. This courthouse remains today. In 1998 parts of the courthouse were remodeled to give us the beautiful building we have today.

Scott County In The Military

It is impossible to name all the men of Scott County that served in the different wars, but we can mention the ones that gave their lives to help protect this nation and state. The following are names of the men that died in the Border Skirmish with Mexico, WWI, WWII, Korea and Vietnam:

Elsie Fisher, Harry F. Banks, Andrew Franklin Webb, Bryan Webb, Sidney Ford Lewis, Lemuel Jackson Lewis, Lambert Lane, Edwin Pope, Louis Davis, Lexie Horn, Ira Evans, W.B. Hensley, Glen Hickebein, T.C. Hudnall, George Roberts, Simeon Rush, William Silvey, Olen Sims, Jozef Stewart, Rufus Tubby, James Winstead, Ralph Burroughs, Rufus Matthews, Cecil Crimm, Billy Graham, Henry Goss, Lewis W. Harmon, James Cox, Robert M. Stroud, James W. Squires, Clarence R. Chambers, Ethan Lowe, Leslie Greer, James Buntyn, Charles Powell, Paul Weaver, X.O. Carpenter, James A. Askin, Wilson Cater, Morrell Hughes, Robert L. Waldrip, George Green, Felix Henderson, Roger Pace Vance, Kenneth McCullar, Mack Tyner, Lester Braddy, Buford Hall, Robert N. Wright, James G. Jones, Prentiss Moore, Farris Edwards, Melvin Dennis, Harry Roebuck, Atley Coward, A.C. McCurdy, Onnis Sharp, Linnell Neely, Woodrow Carter, A.Q. Davis, Percy Norman Bowie, Edward Chambers, Wilson Griswell, Roosevelt Gray, Chester Longmire, Max Ralph Idom, Eric Ficklin, Excell Ficklin, Canoy Lewis Sistrunk, Terah A. Ursy, James Fitzhugh, Harvey Lee Register and Delbert Goodman

Chester Longmire

Lambert Lane

James Aubrey Askin

X.O. Carpenter

Scott County Courthouse 2000

Andrew Webb

9

Harry C. Roebuck

Leslie Greer

Max Idom

Lt. Mack O. Tyner

Lt. Robert M. Stroud

Lexie Horn

Lt. Wilson C. Cater

Bryan Webb

Sgt. Roger Pace Vance

Ethan Lowe

Lewis W. Harmon

Robert L. Waldrip

Notable Scott Countians

If Virginia can be called an American cradle of presidents, then Scott County may be termed a Mississippi cradle of leadership. Few sections of the state can claim so many families whose members have distinguished themselves in the Magnolia State as Scott County. A list of prominent men and women in Scott County at once makes one aware how true this statement is. This is just a partial list, there are far too many to name in just one book. We are very proud of each and every one of you.

Dr. Lamar Weems - Head of Urology Dept. at UMC

Admiral Roy L. Johnson - Commander of Pacific Fleet

Lewis Easom - Formerly with US State Department in Tunis

Hederman Brothers - Former owners of *Clarion Ledger* and *Jackson Daily News*

Mr. and Mrs. Dan Ott - State and National leaders of Eastern Star

Burnam Lee - Professional baseball player for Philadelphia and Red Sox

Jack Stuart - Past director Mississippi Dairy Commission

B.C. Rogers - Founder of Rogers Poultry

Atlee Donald - Professional baseball player

Claude Passaue - Professional baseball player

John M. Rogers - Vice-president Mississippi Manufacturing Association, Secretary National Broiler Council, President Mississippi Southern Industrial Board.

BGen. Glen Walker - Brigadier General in Vietnam

Roscoe Simons - Guerrilla warfare in China during WWII Bronze Star

Therman Patrick - Pilot Soldiers Medal WWII

Dr. Walter Gordy - Head of Science Dept. Duke University

Dr. Atlee Kitchens - Professor of Greek and New Testament

Fred Davis - Head of IBM at MSU

G.W. Harrison - Inventor of Harrison's Lotion

George M. McIlhenny - Engineering Scientist Chemist

Van McCombs - Formerly at Cape Kennedy in computer section

Guy C. McCombs - Manager of a test center at Redstone Arsenal

Joe Lee Mitchell - Manager of Tactical Radar Program for Westinghouse

Robert Weems - Head of Mississippi VA 1943-1959

James Harvey - Professional Football Player Oakland Raiders

Mr. E.T. Hawkins - Head of Negro Mississippi Education Association

Miss May Haddon - Former Head of Home Demonstration Dept. for State of Mississippi

Col. Claude Sanders Jr. - Past Director Selective Service System and Department Director

Big Bill Broonzy - He had a recording career that spanned five decades. He was a songwriter, vocalist and guitar hero. Recorded over 250 songs prior to WWII.

Arthur "Big Boy" Crudup - Big Boy wrote the song *That's All Right Mama*, the first song that Elvis released.

Johnny Littlejohn - Born John Funchess at Lake Mississippi April 16, 1931, he was one of Chicago's best blues slide guitarists.

Joe Chamber - Chambers Brothers Rock Group

Sylvia Howell Krebs - She scored 4,205 points in four seasons at Forest High School and won 150 of 164 games in the 1952-1955 seasons.

Jim Ashmore - Scored 1,023 points averaging 35 per game in a red and blue uniform of Forest High School.

Carla Lowery - In Carla's senior year, 1957 at Forest High, she scored 1,045 points in basketball.

Richard S. Lackey - Mr. Lackey was a leader in and teacher of scholarly research and the recording of it. He wrote *Cite Your Sources* and co-wrote *Write it Right*, both books on genealogical research. Mr. Lackey died at the early age of 41 on January 16, 1983.

Senator James O. Eastland - He was reared, attended school and practiced law in Scott County and later went on to become the US Senator from Mississippi.

Governor Paul B. Johnson Sr. - Governor from January 16, 1940-January 26, 1943. He died while in office December 26, 1943.

Percy M. Lee Sr. - Supreme Court Justice Attorney 8th Circuit Court District 1929-1938. Judge Circuit Court 8th Judicial District 1939-1950.

Judge Roy Noble Lee - Son of Percy M. Lee, elected to Mississippi Supreme Court June 1976. Elevated to Chief Justice of Mississippi Supreme Court 1987.

Judge Tom S. Lee - Son of Percy M. Lee. Attorney for Scott County Board of Supervisors, Scott County Prosecuting Attorney, Attorney Scott County School Board, Scott County Youth Court Judge, City of Forest Municipal Judge, former commissioner of Mississippi Bar Association, former president Scott County Bar Association and a member of the Mississippi Association of Trial Lawyers.

Sidney L. "Sid" Salter - Although not born in Scott County, Sid is by all standards a native son. He is a John C. Stennis Scholar in political science at MSU and also has a BA in political science. Sid is former editor of our local newspaper *The Scott County Times*.

Rashad Anderson Burgess - Graduate of Forest High, he was recently drafted by the NFL football team Carolina Panthers.

Todd Pinkston - Graduate of Forest High, he was recently drafted by the NFL football team Philadelphia Eagles.

Milo Perry - Graduate of Scott Central School, he was drafted by the NFL team Buffalo Bills.

Constance Iona Slaughter-Harvey - The first Afro-American female to graduate from the University of Mississippi School of Law.

Though this list is large for such a small county it is no way complete. How many have left Scott County and have accomplished great things for their state and nation only is known by God.

First Child Born In Scott County

written by Sonny Renfroe of Forest, MS

Two colossal oak trees stand near the central portions of Forest's Eastern Cemetery. A bit west of the northern most oak there is a weathered and discolored monument which bears this inscription:

Anderson B. Smith
Born
In Scott County Miss.
August 14, 1828
Died
October 23, 1879

One would infer from the non-descript inscription and the modest size of the monument that the one whose life is commemorated was of no greater or lesser consequence than most of the others who rest in the cemetery. There are clues in the inscription that hint at an attribute that is unique in both the life of A.B. Smith and of Scott County.

Scott County was not organized until 1833. Lands lying east of the Choctaw Line were not ceded to the US by the Choctaw Tribe until the signing of the treaty of Dancing Rabbit Creek in 1830. Thousands of Choctaws and a few scattered Chickasaws roamed the woods of east central Mississippi. Diffused among the Indians and spread over great stretches of lands lived a few scattered white settlers and their slaves. It was in this setting that Scott County was organized. If one looks at the date of Smith's birth and takes note of the fact that Scott County was not organized until 1833, Smith's unique place in our local history emerges: he was the first child born to pioneer parents in the lands that became Scott County. This fact is substantiated by the Indian Census of 1831, the WPA

Anderson B. Smith Gravesite

file for Scott County and the obituary notices of the 1879 issues of the county newspaper.

Census data for 1860 indicates that A.B. Smith was one of the county's richest residents. By 1860, Smith owned extensive land holdings in Scott and Neshoba counties. He was practicing law at Hillsboro, the county seat. According to the assistant US Marshal, A.W.W. Metcalf, Smith held personal assets valued at $15,000 and real property valued at $10,000. His holdings in real estate had to have been extensive in view of the low assessment of taxable land. Within the newly chartered town of Forest, Smith owned out-right blocks 52, 54, 57 and 58. His land holdings in the countryside were often in partnership with Lod Moore, one of Forest's pioneer settlers and merchants. Moore, incidentally, was the individual who chaired the original board for Forest's town cemetery (now Eastern Cemetery).

Smith's household at Hillsboro included the following persons; Mrs. A.B. "Lucy" Smith, age 27; Elizabeth Smith, age 3; Margaret Smith, age 6; Bena "Birdie," age 3; Albert Eastland, age 53, occupation, gentlemen net worth $3,000; Oliver R. Eastland, age 26, occupation: merchant's clerk; Milton Eastland, age 16, student, net worth $2.50. Elizabeth Smith would later be known as Lizzie Graham and would own the house, which occupied the present site of the Forest Baptist Church.

After the onset of the Civil War, Smith used his influence to help organize and equip the Forest Guards, an unenumerated company attached to the 20th Mississippi Infantry Regiment. Oliver R. Eastland of the Smith household was elected as the company's second lieutenant. As in most of the rest of the south, the Civil War and reconstruction played havoc with the Smith fortune. Oliver Eastland, the administrator of the Smith estate, stated in his report to the probate court that as of late 1879, Smith's fortune had fallen to less than $6,000.

Anderson B. "Dick" Smith's rise to prominence is characteristic of many other successes in the ante-bellum rural south. Men like Smith who were born on the frontier established a transitional prototype in the shift from an agrarian rural economy to the more commercially diverse economy that evolved after the Civil War.

A.B. Smith deserves not only the title "first pioneer child" but additionally, Scott County's "first citizen."

Anderson B. Smith claimed to be the first white child born in Scott County. He was born here five years before the county was formed. This grave marker is located in about the center of the Eastern Cemetery, Forest.

Scott County

County Administrative Complex
Courthouse/Chancery Offices
100 Main Street
Forest, MS 39074

Visit these lovely communities in Scott County: Forest, Morton, Lake and Sebastopol.

Scott received its name for the seventh governor of Mississippi, Abram Scott. Located east of Rankin County, Scott was established in 1833 - the 14th county by that year.

Scott is a rural county, with two-thirds of its population living in a rural setting and boasting the most farms of any county in central Mississippi save Hinds. It is the state's largest poultry producing area and is recognized by the annual Mississippi Boiler Festival held in Scott.

One of the state's finest state parks, Roosevelt State Park, is located here.

Native Sons/Daughters: Legendary bluesmen, Arthur "Big Boy" Crudup and Big Bill Broonzy were both born in Scott County along with rockabilly legends Alton & Jimmy (Alton Lott and Jimmy Harrell).

County Seat: Forest
Estimated 1998 Population: 25,750 (32)
Estimated annual population growth rate: 1995-2000: 1.00% (12)
County size (sq. miles): 609 (31)
Median Household Income (1990): $17,040
Total employment: 16,520
Unemployment rate: 4.4 (March 1998)
Leading employment sectors: Manufacturing, service, farming
Business establishments (1995): 507
(Parenthesis represent ranking among 82 counties in Mississippi)

Board of Supervisors

District 1
Jackie Bradford

District 2
Tim Sorrey

District 3
Buford Palmer

District 4
Jack Gordon

District 5
Bruce McMillan

County Board Meetings

First Monday of each month, 10:00 a.m., Chancery Offices

Departments

Chancery Clerk
Billy Frank Alford

Circuit Clerk
Joe Rigby

Sheriff
William Richardson

Tax Assessor/Collector
Myra Murrell Davis

Justice Court Judges
Robert G. Wilkerson
Wilbur McCurdy

Circuit Court Judges
Marcus Gordon
Vernon Cotton

County Attorney
Rick Clark

District Attorney
Ken Turner

Coroner
Joe Bradford

Superintendent of Education
Bingham Moncreiff

Constables
Bill Wilbourne
Richard Prestage

Indians In Scott County

written by Sonny Renfroe of Forest, MS

If history teaches any lessons, one that may be observed is that of geography and its influence on patterns of settlement. The first inhabitants of our area were of course, the Indians. By the time Indian tribal structure had evolved, a pattern of settlement had become apparent; the Indians almost always settled near a creek.

The most important tribe in the Scott County area was the Choctaw. They belonged to a larger classification of North American Indians, the Muskhogeans of the Eastern Woodland group. Never a real threat to the settlers who entered east-central Mississippi, the Choctaws quickly became willing allies of the US during the War of 1812. By far the most serious threat to settlement in the central part of the Mississippi Territory was the Creek Nation and its allied tribes.

Under the command of Andrew Jackson, the Choctaws participated in the decisive Battle of Horseshoe Bend in 1814 and in the Battle of New Orleans in 1815. In addition to helping Jackson crush the last Indian threat to settlement, the Choctaws assisted in the construction of the Jackson Military road, one of the oldest roads in Mississippi. As a reward for their loyalty, the Choctaws were eventually forced to cede their remaining lands to the US government in 1820 and 1830. Andrew Jackson, no friend of the Indians of the southeast, insisted on a policy of removal after becoming president in 1829.

This policy of removal meant that the Indians of the southeast would be forcibly removed to the Indian Territory in the west (Oklahoma). Few policies in US history have been as callous or as cruel. Indians by the thousand died along the route, the Trail of Tears. The actual Choctaw "Tribe" now lives in Oklahoma.

Those Choctaws who now live in this vicinity were either allowed to remain by special permission of the US authorities or hid in the numerous swamps until things cooled off. By 1833, when Scott County was officially organized, the Indian removal had largely been completed.

Nearly all of the Choctaws who lived in what is now Scott County, as late as 1831, have at least had their names preserved thanks to a thorough Indian Census. Data from the 1831 enumeration reports that hundreds of Choctaws lived on lands that are now ours. Near the headwaters of the Leaf River there was an Indian settlement governed by Capt. "Chief" Tishbahoma. He farmed several acres of land and was the head of a family of eight. Among those whom he governed were Nockahcheyahbe, Holahtubba, Hotenah and their families.

In the northeastern corner of Scott County near Sebastopol a large settlement of Choctaws prospered along the shores of the Young Warrior River (Tuscalameta Creek). More than 20 families inhabited this village. Chief Tobala farmed eight acres and had fathered 14 children, 13 females and one male. Other prominent residents of the settlement included Onatubba, Nockawahou and Snakebone. Snakebone holds the distinction of having the largest family in the Young Warrior Region: 15 children.

Slave ownership was common among the Choctaws. Cornelius Kearney, a Choctaw half-breed was the largest single slave holder in the Young Warrior Region. He owned 12 slaves.

Little physical evidence remains to remind us of our Indian heritage. When we cross a creek, the odds are that the stream was once the home of our first inhabitants. These place names are more enduring than any monument or book and through the oral tradition they will always serve as a permanent reminder of our early Indian settlers.

Railroad And Telegraph

About 1855 when the Mississippi and Alabama Railroad was mapping out a route through the state in an east-west direction, the route through south central Scott County was selected. This was an extremely important event in the history of Forest because it was the first step in Forest's becoming the county's trade center. The railroad was laid through the county in 1858. It was built mostly by slave labor. Railroad contractors in Scott County were E. Gresham, James P. Clark and Warren Clark. An exciting day in the history of the railroad occurred September 20, 1860 when the first train reached Newton. Railroad officials, headed by Mr. Vossburg, gave all the crowd gathered there a ride to Forest and back. The railroad was first called the Southern Railroad, then the Vicksburg and Meridian Line and later the Alabama and Vicksburg Railroad. In connection with the railroad there were soon two telegraph lines, the Western Union which ran parallel to the railroad and the Postal Telegraph.

Sherman's Men Met Opposition By Civilians

Reprinted with permission of Mr. Ovid Vickers

For five days in 1864, the armies of Union Gen. Tecumseh Sherman marched through Scott County. In February 1864, Gen. Sherman decided to move his armies across Mississippi from Vicksburg to Meridian. His objective was to cut the communication and transportation lines across the state and to destroy the rail yards at Meridian. His march through Scott County was not easily accomplished.

On February 7 as northern forces moved toward Morton, the Confederates positioned themselves two miles west of the town and began the construction of earthwork fortifications. These fortifications began at Tank Hill and made an arc around Morton, along the west side of Ridge Road to the top of Nathan Hill. Why a stand was not made here by the Confederates is not known, but just before dark the order was given to retreat north to Hillsboro.

After a quick skirmish with a column of Rebel Calvary, a brigade of Union soldiers marched into Morton shortly after noon on February 9. They immediately set fire to most of the buildings and scattered in all directions to search for food. They soon returned laden with hams, poultry and plunder from nearby homes and smokehouses.

As the Rebel Army moved from Morton to Hillsboro, the county seat of Scott County at that time, they burned bridges across creeks and confiscated food from farm houses along the way.

On the morning of February 10, the Union soldiers moved through Hillsboro. When they reached the town, civilians fired upon them from the windows of several houses. According to accounts in Civil War diaries kept by both Union and Confederate soldiers, the entire town of Hillsboro was put to the torch in retaliation for the citizens killing or wounding several Union soldiers. The fire was so intense that the wagon train traveling behind the Army had to stop because the wagon masters and mules could not tolerate the heat and smoke. Falling sparks set fire to the canvas covers of the supply wagons.

The retreating Confederates burned bridges to the east of Hillsboro spanning Little Beaver Creek and Tallabogue Creek. The advance of Union troops was slowed considerably when these bridges had to be reconstructed before artillery pieces and supply wagons could continue to advance.

One Union solider observed that the roads were generally good as long as they were on high ground. He lamented the fact that travel through the Tallabogue swamp was slow and required the felling of trees to "corduroy" the road. This soldier also remarked that the county was not thickly populated east of Hillsboro but those farmers who did live along the route of march were busy breaking land to plant as soon as the weather warmed.

A soldier named Lucius Barber who was serving with the 15th Illinois mentioned in his diary how surprised he was that the people of Scott County had managed to raise a good quantity of meat, good cured hams and much bacon. Barber goes on to say that he never ate such sweet cured ham. He speculates that the people of Scott County cured their meat with just enough salt and molasses and without over-smoking.

At Hontokalo Creek, sticky mud clung to the soldiers' shoes. Four miles distant they came to the Tuscalemeta swamp where they found another bridge burned by the retreating Southern Army. While the body of the Union Army moved from the main body and pillaged the town of Lake before rejoining their comrades just east of Box Creek.

At one point a scouting party raked up a pile of leaves on which to sleep. During the night, the fire they had made to cook and warm by was blown about by a small wind igniting the piles of leaves. One soldier lost his shoes and another had half his overcoat burned away.

From February 7 until February 11, Northern soldiers were in Scott County. Their foray through the county had not been easy. Although they met with little organized resistance, the citizens of the county had acted as snipers, felling a man here and another there. Bridges were burned by the retreating Confederates and the weather that February was apparently cold and very wet.

Some sections of the roads that Sherman's men followed remain almost unchanged since 1864. Parts of some roads have been abandoned or rerouted, but most stretches can be traveled 131 years after an invading army marched across Scott County.

Roosevelt Park

The Lions Club of Morton, with the help of the American Legion and the Jackson Lions Club, made plans for Roosevelt Park in 1933. A very successful drive for funds was launched and in 1933 Representative Elwin Livingston was appointed to go to Washington to confer with park officials. A little more than 500 acres at $10.00 per acre was purchased from W.R. Rogers for the park site. The citizens of Morton, town officials and the Scott County Board of Supervisors purchased and donated the land. It was then deeded to the state and Governor Conner officially accepted it. The park is owned and operated by the state of Mississippi. The National Park Service declared it a State Park in the early part of 1935. The CCC camps of the county furnished labor. A 140-acre lake, as well as overnight cabins, assembly hall, caretakers cabin, bath and boathouses and nice gravel roads were also constructed. Trees were also planted. Mississippi Power and Light Co. furnish the lights and the park furnishes their own water supply. Scott County has one of the nicest parks in the state.

Scott County Hospital

The Scott County Hospital at Morton opened October 15, 1937 with Dr. O.J. Burnham and Dr. J.M. Townsend as owners and Dr. George G. Townsend, surgeon; Dr. J.M. Townsend, assistant surgeon; Dr. W.A. Jones, anesthetist. All had private practices and had their offices in the hospital including Dr. O.J. Burnham, dentist.

Mrs. Charles Boykin was the first operating room nurse. The hospital consisted of 16 beds at that time and later increased to 22 beds. In September 1956, the hospital closed and was reorganized under the same name in September 1957 with 26 beds. On May 26, 1963 a new wing was added, making a total of 36 beds.

Mrs. Charles Boykin and Miss Eula Laird helped open Scott County Hospital in 1937 and are the two most outstanding nurses of that time. The doctors on the staff in 1966 were Dr. Alex Gordon Jr., Dr. Howard D. Clark, Dr. Charles Crenshaw and Dr. Liles Nelson Williams, dentist, who was born and reared in Morton.

Dr. W.A. Jones, born in Scott County at Sebastopol, MS February 11, 1878, attended high school in Harperville and attended medical school at University of South Sewanee, TN. He began practicing medicine in 1906, seven miles south of Morton at Pulaski, MS. Dr. Jones married Cleo Sanders in 1910 and moved to Harperville in 1918. He lived there until 1919 when he moved to Morton and practiced medicine until 1948 for a total of 42 years.

Dr. Junius Massey Townsend, born November 4, 1878 in Scott County, MS, northeast of Harperville in the Malco Community, lived there until he was grown and attended school at Harperville and graduated from Memphis Hospital Medical College in 1904. He first practiced in Harperville, then a little over two years in Forest. He moved to Morton in 1912. Dr. Townsend married Lilla Dale of Forest.

Dr. O.J. Burnham was born January 11, 1880 in Scott County at Branch and attended school at Harperville. He went to dental school in New Orleans, graduating in 1906. He practiced dentistry in Branch, Ludlow, Pulaski, Leesburg and Morton. He practiced in Morton for 53 years. Dr. Burnham died in 1956.

Roster of Doctors

Physicians were not licensed in Mississippi until 1882 and therefore, no records are available prior to that time. Here is a listing of doctors

Forest Register Newspaper, E.E. Butler editor

that have practiced in Mississippi. There are several from the Scott County area. This is just a partial listing.

Dr. John Gaddis
Dr. L.R. Moore
Dr. George Booth Pickle
Dr. A. Polk Sims
Dr. Lewis T. Edmonds
Dr. Fields
Dr. Brooks
Dr. Robert Coats
Dr. Will Porter
Dr. Albert McCoy
Dr. Isaac Edwards
Dr. J.B. Patrick
Dr. W.E. Peek
Dr. O.J. Burnham
Dr. H.O. Lee
Dr. J.M. Townsend
Dr. Stagg
Dr. Webb
Dr. Stephens
Dr. W.A. Jones
Dr. L.W. Willey
Dr. Lamar Russell
Dr. W.F. Johnson
Dr. G.G. Townsend
Dr. H.L. Cokerham Jr.
Dr. Jack King
Dr. Lowell V. Ozment
Dr. John R. Edwards
Dr. Alex Gordon
Dr. J.W. Hudson
Dr. Jim L. McLain
Dr. Baker G. Nagle
Dr. Ralph Dunn
Dr. Liles N. Williams
Dr. Howard Clark
Dr. Charles N. Crenshaw Jr.
Dr. Alma Rowe
Dr. Ellis Rowe
Dr. John Paul Lee
Dr. Archie Howard
Dr. Bill Austin
Dr. R.B. Austin
Dr. Bill Lewis

Early Scott County Newspapers

In 1867 a wagon full of printing equipment arrived in Forest and was set up in a small frame building in the yard of the Simmons and Peavy Hotel. Forest's first newspaper, *The Scott County Weekly Register*, was owned and published by James P. Dement. The editor was Joe Blackwell and a young employee of the newspaper was R.H. Henry who was hired to work as a printer's devil for $11.00 a month.

In 1868 upon the resignation of Mr. Blackwell, James A. Granville became the editor of the weekly *Register*. Mr. Blackwell later served Scott County in the State Senate. Mr. Granville purchased the newspaper from Mr. Dement March 1, 1869. Dr. Stephen Davis, who had moved from Alabama to Forest, purchased the paper May 29, 1870 and retained ownership until May 1880 when he sold the paper to Mr. F.W. Blackwell. Mr. Blackwell in turn sold the paper to his brother, Pat Blackwell, and his sister, Stella Blackwell.

Miss Blackwell eventually married a Mr. Butler, a printer who came to Forest from the North and she and her husband edited and published the paper.

Mr. W.H. Joyner had established another weekly paper, the *Scott County News*, in Forest. Mr. Joyner purchased the Butler's paper and combined it with the *Scott County News*, under the name of *The News Register*. In 1920 John Harmon bought the paper; in 1921 Mr. Joyner and Mr. H.A. Schmidt became co-owners. Mr. Schmidt took over sole ownership March 1922.

Employees of Scott County Times during the ownership of Erle Johnston

The Progress Herald

In July 1937, Walter Scott Busick and his wife, Minnie, purchased the *Progress Herald* from Walter N. Everett, who had established it in Morton April 22, 1936. Mr. Busick was editor and co-publisher for almost 30 years until his death in 1965. Mr. Busick was a native of Arkansas and his main policy through the newspaper was always to build up and not tear down, and this he did in many ways. His love for God, family, town, country and his fellowman was seen each week in his editorials and his special column of "The Editor Says."

An era of progress has been recorded in the pages of this newspaper, with service to the entire community foremost in all things.

County Newspapers Merged, *Scott County Times*, 22 April 1970

Erle Johnston, publisher of both weekly newspapers, announced merger of the *Progress Herald* of Morton with the *Scott County Times* of Forest the week of April 15, 1970. Johnston, who purchased the Morton paper in October 1970, said the change became necessary because costs exceeded revenues, even though the paper had more than tripled its circulation with a press run of 1850. The *Progress Herald* was launched 34 years ago and the *Scott County Times,* youngest of the three papers, was established in 1939. The *News-Register* folded in 1948.

Bienville National Forest

The Bienville Ranger District of the Desoto National Forest was organized in 1934 and the US government proceeded with the acquisition of this tract, which includes lands in Scott, Smith, Newton and Jasper counties. In 1936 approximately 75,000 acres had been purchased and set aside by the government as a National Forest. In 1936, by proclamation of President Roosevelt, this area was named the Bienville National Forest. These lands, which were set-aside as National Forests were to be administered by the US Forest Service so as to produce the greatest benefits to the largest number of people. The main objective of this forest is timber production and other land uses as are correlated with this main use. Grazing allowed under permit and regulated so it will not interfere with other uses to the exclusion of those other uses. Recreational developments were made to be enjoyed by all.

In 1936 there were four CCC camps on the Bienville National Forest, two of which are in Scott County, one north of Morton and one south of Forest. The men in these camps were working under the direction of the Forest Service and all their work was aimed at accomplishing the tasks, which needed to be done in order that the aim of management might be reached. The first step was protection from fire. In 1936 there were seven lookout towers in the forest and three more to be built during the next year. Roads built in Scott County include a road from Morton to Ludlow. This road is 20 miles long and will be graveled by the end of October 1936. Road from Homewood east to Roberts was being worked on and was to be complete by the summer of 1937. Road from Highway 35 southwest to Trenton and Heater was to be completed in the near future. Approximately 40 miles of road in Scott County nearly completed in 1936 with more to be finished. 180,000 trees planted in 1935 with 5,000,000 more planted in 1936. Benefits of Bienville National Forest to the county include: free firewood, fire protection, new and better roads, new recreational areas, 35 percent of receipts from grazing permits, sales of timber, etc. go to the county and scientifically managed grazing area. Eventual aim: a permanent supply of timber, giving permanent industry.

Early Afro-American Families

Wade Needham and Anderson Jennings operated what was probably the first black business in the town of Forest, an Afro-American barber shop. Other older black families of the Forest area were Burks, Hoods, Lambs, Loveladys, Battles, Moores, Bodys, McLaurins and Garretts. Allen Lightfoot was an herb doctor, who went into the forest and gathered herbs to make medicine. Miss Nettie Lovelady was a midwife who was much sought after by the people of the Forest area.

Scott County Times

The *Scott County Times*, the successor newspaper to *The Hillsboro Argus* (1863), *The Forest Register* (1867), *The Forest Weekly Register* (1869), *The Scott County Register* (1897), *The Scott County News* (1915) and *The Scott County News-Register* (1918) was founded on November 30, 1939 by L.G. Agard and Lewis Henderson. Agard and Henderson sold the newspaper to Erle E. Johnston in 1941.

The Johnston family, including Faye Johnston, daughters Carol L. Lindley, Lynn J. Catalina and son Erle E. (Bubby) Johnston, owned and operated *The Times* from 1941 until July 15, 1983 when they sold the newspaper to a group of investors that included Mildred T. Dearman, S. Gale Denley, George H. Keith, Jerry C. Mooney, Sidney L. (Sid) Salter and W.C. (Dub) Shoemaker.

Johnston served as president of the Mississippi Press Association in 1949.

Salter was named publisher and editor on July 15, 1983. Salter, Denley and Dearman bought out their partners in 1989 and consolidated ownership. Salter assumed the additional duties of president of the newspaper's parent corporation, Scott Publishing, Inc., in 1989. Salter served as the president of the Mississippi Press Association in 1993.

In 1998, *The Times* was named Mississippi's best large weekly newspaper by the Mississippi Press Association.

On December 15, 1998, *The Times* was acquired by Emmerich Newspapers, Inc., Mississippi largest home-owned newspaper company, a third-generation Mississippi news organization that publishes 21 daily and weekly newspapers in Mississippi, Louisiana and Arkansas. Salter was named vice-president of ENI and continues to server as publisher/editor of the Forest newspaper.

The Times is also the headquarters of Mid-Mississippi Publishing, LLC, a joint-operating newspaper printing company that serves *The Times*, *The Neshoba Democrat* and *The Union Appeal* weekly newspapers in east central Mississippi.

In 2000, the newspaper held a paid circulation of 5,641 and a *Times Plus Shopper* free circulation of 12,895 for a total of 19,536.

Erle Johnston

Scott County Times publisher Sid Salter (center) and managing editor Leilani Pope (right) accepted the General Excellence Award for large weekly newspapers in Mississippi in 1998 and 1999 and community Service among all Mississippi weekly newspapers in 1998, from Mississippi Press Association president John Carney of Crystal Springs, left. Salter was the third publisher of the Times, serving from 1983-2001. He succeeded the late Erle Johnson, who served from 1941-83

Forest County Seat

Forest

Forest the county seat of Scott County is located near the geographic center of Mississippi on the Illinois Central Gulf railroad, Interstate 20, US 80 and state highways 35, 21 and 501. It is 45 miles east of Jackson and 45 miles west of Meridian.

People who came to the central Mississippi area in the mid 1800s found a land of towering pines so thick that the sunlight could barely penetrate to the ground. A ridge which rises in the Chunky River Swamp passes through the Forest and Scott County area before disappearing into the Pearl River near Jackson. Because of this ridge some of the local streams actually flow northward. The coming of the railroad was in 1858. Settlers arriving in this beautiful forested area soon began to congregate in the area of the railroad. Forest was incorporated as a town in 1860 and was being settled rapidly when the Civil War began. During the war; with Forest almost a deserted village, the charter was dropped. Another charter was granted to the town of "Forrest" on November 21, 1865 with a one square mile radius, the depot occupying the central spot. It is interesting to note that the town was no where spelled with the two "r's" except on this charter, recorded with the Secretary of State. No doubt the misspelling was due to the popularity of Gen. N.B. Forrest of the Confederacy.

Forrest of the Confederacy
Charter CCVII

An act to incorporate the Town of Forrest in the County of Scott

Section l. Be it enacted by the legislature of the State of Mississippi, that the Town of Forrest, in the County of Scott, be and the same is hereby incorporated and the corporate limits of said town shall run to the four cardinal points of the compass and form one mile square to be laid off in such manner that the depot of the Southern Railroad Co. in said town, shall form the center of said corporate limits (Copy of 1865 Charter).

Forest City Government

Forest's first government was established when it received a special act charter from the state legislature in 1865. This charter provided the board of alderman with the power to appoint a clerk and treasurer and declared that the elected constable was to serve *ex officio* as assessor and collector of taxes. The town officers were elected by every free white male, 21 years or older, residing in the town for one month or more. Forest operated under this form of government until 1892. In that year, the Mississippi Legislature provided municipalities with the option of retaining their private charters or adopting the new so-called "code-charter." Twenty-two cities exercised the option of keeping private charters while all others adopted the new "code-charter." Today there are approximately 237 "code-charter" cities in the state. Forest selected the "code-charter" option as set forth in Article II, Title 16 of Sections 3374-34-46 of the Mississippi Code.

The pertinent sections of the code under which Forest operates today, include the following provisions:

3374-35. *Elective Officers*. The elective officers are the mayor, police justice, marshal or chief of police, the tax collector, tax assessor and city clerk. (Offices of the clerk and marshal may be combined with office of tax collector or tax assessor and any or all offices except mayor and alderman may be appointed.)

3374-36. *Number of Aldermen and Wards*. The council consists of five aldermen, elected at large or by four wards with one elected at large. The mayor is elected at large.

3374-37. *Appointive Offices*. The council can appoint a person (in cities of less than 10,000 population) to any two or more of the appointive offices; a member of the board of aldermen may be appointed to the office of street commissioner.

3374-40. *Duties of Mayor*. The mayor presides at all meetings and may cast the deciding vote in case of a tie; he has the superintending control of all the offices and affairs of the municipality.

Former Mayors:

1866-1870	J.M. Brassell
1870-1873	Capt. George E. Hassie, W.A. Lack
1873-1874	A.H. Briscoe
1875	H.C. McCabe
1900	R.D. Cooper
1905-1908	O.R. Singleton
1909-1912	J.A. Huff
1912-1918	Oliver McIlhenny Sr.
1918	J. Knox Huff
1919-1920	O.B. Triplett
1921-1924	Percy M. Lee
1925-1926	W.H. Joyner
1927-1930	E.S. Palmer
1931-1934	J.M. Wadsworth
1935-1936	E.S. Palmer
1937-1939	Dallas Stewart
1939-1948	H.E. Bishop
1949-1950	Joe Lee Smith
1951-1957	Hugh Lee
1957-1961	J.E. Calhoun
1961-1973	Fred L. Gaddis
1973-1977	G.B. Beard
1977-1981	Fred L. Gaddis
1981-1985	Erle Johnston
1985-2001	Fred L. Gaddis
Present	Nancy N. Chambers (first woman mayor)

Forest Depot

Church Street Forest, MS 1920 Main structure in center is Forest Methodist Church, church in left distance is Forest Baptist Church

The only qualifications for office for the mayor and members of the board of aldermen are that they "shall be qualified electors of the city" and that the aldermen be residents of their respective wards.

Chamber of Commerce

Forest for many years has had an active and alert Chamber of Commerce which plans and carries out a variety of programs during the year. The charter for the Forest Chamber of Commerce was granted June 3, 1949. The Chamber is supported by many firms and individuals through their contributions for the work that must be, and is being done, to secure better living conditions and employment for the people of Forest. A pleasant and sincere invitation is extended to prospective newcomers to make Forest their permanent home, joining with its citizens in building a community that excels in livability and neighborly affection.

Forest Today

Forest is a thriving city that has balanced its social, religious and educational activities with its agricultural and industrial development. Industry has found this area to have many factors favorable to successful plant operation. The most important factor is the availability of an excellent, easily trained labor force.

Forest was one of the first cities in the state to fluoridate its water to reduce cavities and its sewage lagoons have been inspected by representatives of many other cities from several states. The city operates its own water system. Forest is served by electricity from Mississippi Power Co. and gas from United Gas.

Chief farm products are cotton, corn, cattle, hogs and poultry. Just south of Forest is one of the last remaining stands of loblolly pines. Pine tree farming has been greatly developed in the Forest area. Diversified industrial activities include the manufacturing of pine lumber and a pulpwood-loading yard with automatic unloading equipment. Forest is also the home of a Raytheon plant and the future home of Unipres a supplier for the new Nissan plant being built in Canton, MS.

Transportation

Transportation developed from horses and wagons on dirt paths to buggies and later surreys. Eventually a few people in Forest acquired cars. Mr. Bob Noblin, Mr. Rob Robertson, Mr. Ollie Eastland owned four of the first cars in town and Dr. W.H. Pevey. At first there were only dirt roads to drive on. The first gravel road ran from Forest to Tallybo Creek. People would get in their cars and ride from one end of the road to the other. A car could be purchased at this time for about $325. Gasoline sold for 20 cents a gallon.

Fire of 1900 Destroys Downtown Forest

The most disastrous fire in history swept through the Forest business district shortly after midnight May 22, 1900 causing damage estimated at over $60,000.

Will Dowling, prescription clerk at Eastland's drug store, first discovered the blaze in the camp room of Story and Smythe's storehouse and sounded the alarm by firing pistols. A huge crowd gathered shortly afterward and joined in fighting the flames. Merchants near the fire began evacuating their merchandise just before the walls of the Story-Smythe building crumbled.

The blaze licked hungrily across a vacant lot to Sones and Dansby's Store and then threatened the building occupied by the *Register* weekly newspaper. A total of 20 business houses were destroyed including the A&V

Depot and the Peavy Hotel, with the hotel and its furnishings almost a total loss. The John L. Farmer livery barn was saved by the volunteer fire fighters, even though it caught fire at least 15 times during the night. Estimates of the losses included:

Story and Smythe, stock, goods and building, $12,000; Hi Eastland Jr., stock of drugs and building, $5,000; Dr. J.J. Haralson, office fixtures, books and instruments, $1,000; Dr. G.A. McIlhenny, dentist, $250.

Sones and Dansby, merchandise, $10,000; Percy Lowry storehouse, $1,500; M. Gardner, stock of goods, $2,500; building and office of Miss Ida Gardner, $1,500; G.H. Banks, merchandise, $1,000; Mary Harper building $500; B. Wolf, merchandise, $10,000; Lod Moore building, $1,000; Postal Telegraph and Cumberland Telephone Co., $300; Percy Lowry building and drugs $5,000; G.C. Rew, merchandise, $8,000; Mrs. Harriet Moore building, $900; T.B. Smythe, storehouse, $1,000; Jeff Kent, attorney, office fixtures, $200; Miss Millie Peavy, millinery goods and building, $800; Peavy and Hood building with two buggies, $860; Will Hi Earbee, dry goods and groceries, $1,700; Pevey Hotel, including furniture, $3,000; Lolla Idom storehouse, $1,500; M.D. Graham & Co., goods and storehouse, $11,000; A&V Railroad and Southern Express Co., $6,000 (only loss fully covered by insurance); post office building, $200, including fixtures and $80 in two-cent stamps.

In addition Wade Needham lost everything in his barbershop, but Anson Jennings saved his chair and a few articles.

Most of the losses were partially covered by insurance, although many buildings had no insurance at all.

Fire of 1910

The most destructive fire to occur in Forest since May 21, 1900 when the entire business section of town was destroyed happened in February 1910. The fire was discovered upon the roof of the Farmer Hotel about 2 o'clock but how it originated was only a matter of conjecture. The only plausible theory was that sparks from the chimney or kitchen flue ignited the building. The hotel was a three-story frame structure owned and operated by J.L. Farmer who was on a prospective tour in Texas at the time of the fire. All efforts to save the buildings were utterly hopeless and the entire west side was doomed to destruction. The two-story frame building adjoining the hotel was owned and occupied by W.L. Jones as a grocery, restaurant and soda water factory. Next to it was the two-story frame building owned by Dr. J.J. Haralson and occupied by J.L. Jackson as harness and saddlery. Leman Green, who with his family occupied the upstairs, lost his entire household effects and much wearing apparel.

The iron corrugated building belonging to Mrs. Eleanor Walker, Mrs. Nettie Miller and the latter as a feed store occupied G.H. Story. Goodwin and Walker, who represented the Forest Mercantile Co., lost

Main Street fire ca. 1970s

Forest Post Office Building Feb. 26, 1938

Forest Post Office

fertilizer and wagon material. C.H. Noblin lost his two-story frame building. Meridian Fertilizer factory loss of building and T.M. Steele lost merchandise in this same building. G.G. Beamon lost mercantile stock, caused by water damage.

There was a slight damage to the west side of the Courthouse caused by the intense heat from the fire. The burning brands flew all over the eastern and southern part of town, igniting the old Womack Hotel, the office building at Mrs. Lizzie Graham's, the Presbyterian Church, J.R. McCravey's residence and the buildings on the east side of the square among them being the office of the *Scott County Register* which caught fire several times. The total loss was estimated to be between $16,000 and $20,000.

Forest Post Office

The first charter was granted to the town of Forest February 17, 1860, but the Forest Post Office had already been established nearly two months prior to the time of the charter.

Louis Runge, a cotton buyer at the time petitioned the US government for a post office in Forest to enable his firm to receive information daily from the cotton markets in New Orleans.

Although there were telegraph lines and railroads here at the time, Runge foresaw the growth of Forest and envisioned the importance of a post office in the city and county.

The government agreed to establish a post office if Runge would accept the job as postmaster. He undertook the job; thus the post office was established on December 31, 1859.

Runge served as postmaster for a year then Jonathan Crouch became postmaster for one year. The post office was discontinued in 1861 and re-established in 1886, leaving Forest 15 years without a post office.

Since 1886, the Forest Post Office has had 12 postmasters. They were William A. Lack, Jabez M. Brassell, George E. Hasie, Hiram Eastland, Bettie S. Greer, Charles D. Graham, James H. Owen, Lynn E. Crane, Malcolm S. Graham, John E. Nordan, Mrs. Ida E. Ormand and Prentiss Loper.

Construction began on a new building in 1938 by contractor

Algernon Blair and is still in operation today with Steve McFarland as postmaster. The post office was located on West Main Street before that time.

The US Post Office at Forest is on the National Register of Historic Places. Built in 1938, it is significant for being one of the 32 post offices constructed in Mississippi during the Great Depression with funding from one of the New Deal Public Building programs. It is a locally important work of mid-20th century colonial revival architecture and is a well-executed and well-maintained example of the colonial style post offices.

An oil-paint-on-canvas mural entitled "Forest Loggers" by Julien Binford was created under the Treasury Department's section of Fine Arts Program and installed in the Forest Post Office in 1941 at a cost of $650. It was restored in 1991. The mural depicts three African-American loggers straining to fell a tree while a fourth drives a team of mules pulling a large log. It is not known if Binford painted murals for any other Mississippi post offices. One of his murals hangs in the Saunders Postal Station in Richmond, VA.

"Forest Loggers" was an appropriate mural for the Forest Post Office. The town acquired its name from the dense forest surrounding it in the 1850s when it was initially being settled. It became a sawmill town with an economy based on lumber.

Modern Hospital Established

The S.E. Lackey Memorial Hospital was planned, constructed and equipped under the Hill-Burton construction program and was opened October 1, 1951.

The total cost of construction for the hospital building and equipment was $360,000. Beat One Scott County did the financing, with a bond issue in 1948 in the amount of $120,000 representing one-third of the cost of construction. The state and federal government financed the remaining two-thirds of the cost under the provisions of the Hill-Burton Hospital Act.

In 1962 another bond issue was passed to construct the S.E. Lackey Memorial Convalescent Home. This facility cost a total of near $400,000 and provides extended care for cases that cannot be cared for at home, yet are not sick enough for hospitalization. Cecil P. Ramer was the first administrator of the hospital and served for one year. Surry A. Grafton served as administrator for 15 years from 1952 until 1967 when resigned to take on similar duties in Picayune, MS.

The S.E. Lackey Memorial Hospital Corp. came into being as a direct result of a proposition presented to a group of business men by Mrs. S.E. Lackey Sr., in which she proposed to purchase the T.B. Graham property, the lot on which the Baptist Church is now located, for the purpose of constructing a hospital. On July 15, 1945 a trust agreement was entered into between Mrs. S.E. Lackey Sr. and Dr. R.B. Austin, R.L. Goodwin, R.M. Christian, V.R. Lackey and J. Knox Huff acting as trustees. It was agreed that Mrs. Lackey would purchase the property mentioned for the establishment of a hospital, to be called the S.E. Lackey Memorial Hospital, provided the trustees would obtain a charter and secure subscriptions of not less than $10,000 upon which to inaugurate said hospital. The cash subscriptions of $10,000 were raised as agreed and in early 1946 a charter was granted to S.E. Lackey Memorial Hospital Corp. The original directors were Dr. R.B. Austin, V.R. Lackey, R.L. Goodwin, R.M. Christian and J. Knox Huff. S.E. Memorial Hospital has been operated by Independent Health Care Management for the past 13 years. They have 44 licensed acute care beds and 30 long term care beds. Donna Gail Riser is the present hospital administrator.

First Radio Station Started

WMAG Forest's first radio station went on the air September 9, 1955. Under ownership of Judge W.E. Farrar, R.E. Hook and Hugh Hughes, WMAG began serving a 50-mile radius on 860 kilocycles, 500 watts, daytime power. Mr. Hughes was station manager and Willie Weems was employed as an announcer, later Mr. Weems purchased Mr. Farrar's interest in the station. Other early employees were Mrs. Barbara Goodwin, Tom Estes, Billy Ray Strebeck and Warren Jones. The station was located upstairs behind Ott and Lee Funeral Home on First Street in Forest. The station operated in this location until 1959 when it moved into a new building on Hwy. 80 east of town.

Towns And Communities

Beach

Beach is located 14 miles northwest of Forest. It was settled in 1876. It was named for the nearby creek which, although a small stream, has built up occasional broad sandy beaches. Beach, generally known as Old Beach is mentioned in a publication of 1891 as a post office and trading post but the post office was moved without changing the name to Forkville, which left no remaining stores here.

Two of its pioneer residents were Dr. Wade Lovett who came here from Neshoba County and B.C. Ponder, a US traveling postmaster.

Berryville

Berryville, now extinct, was about four miles south of the present site of Forest. It was the first county seat of Scott County. The town was formed about 1830 from what was known as the Gray Place and named for a nearby creek. The house of Stephen Berry was appointed for holding the courts and all county business April 7, 1834, the day that Scott County was formed. The board agreed to hold court at his home until such time a courthouse could be established. The streets of Berryville were laid out and then it was abandoned within 12 months, when in the Fall of 1836, the county seat was moved to Hillsboro where it remained for 30 years.

Balucta

Balucta was situated about 13 miles northwest of Forest and eight miles northeast of Forkville on the Morton and Canton Road. It was formerly a post office. It was named for Balucta Creek, a creek that runs through the northern part of the county. The town was formerly known as Beach. It was formed in 1900 from a settlement. It is near the Yalabushaa River. The region is a flat sandy clay area that was known for raising livestock and cotton. In the early days it had a one-teacher school house with a school term of 3-1/2 months long until it was consolidated with Lena.

Arch Rigby, who was born there, and his brother, Lee Rigby, were among the early settlers of Balucta.

Blanch/Ball Hill

Blanch is located four miles southwest of Lake. It was settled prior to 1886 and was known as Ball Hill. A post office was established here in 1886 and named Blanch for Blanch Singleton but the place became extinct along with the closing of the post office in 1905.

Branch/Groveton

Branch is located 10 miles northwest of Morton. Branch was established prior to 1900 and named for its location on the banks of a small branch or creek. There was once a post office at this site named Groveton, but it has long since been discontinued.

Broach/Lowery Mill/Donohoe

Broach is located about five miles east of Forest. Broach was settled in 1888 by W.W. Briggs of Wisconsin. The place was never more than a sidetrack on the Y&MV Railroad, but before becoming extinct about 1914 the place was also known as Lowery Mill, Fairchild Mill and Donohoe.

Buckleytown/Sherman Hill

Buckleystown or Buckleytown was once known as Sherman Hill. It is seven miles from Forest and about five miles southwest of Lake in the southeastern part of Scott County. It was formerly a post office in 1870 that was named for John Buckley. The name was generally forgotten when the post office was closed in 1900. There was a Negro settlement in this neighborhood. It was an area isolated and widely scattered with residents. The region was in the black prairie, very fertile and the pasturage exceptionally fine.

Coffeebogue Neighborhood

from the files of the Scott County Library

In the mid-1840s, perhaps earlier, Robert Powell Chambers moved his family to the vicinity of present day Forkville, where he was a charter member of Bethlehem Church in 1847 and later pastor. His son, Luke, told his children that he grew up in Coffeebogue, a name commonly used for the area near Coffe Bogue Creek, in this case the area between Morton and present day Forkville. They lived there at least 15 years before moving to Hillsboro just before the Civil War.

Cash

Cash was once a post office nine miles east of Ludlow, extinct by 1890. Cash was established in 1871 with a storekeeper named Lyle who served as postmaster. There is a Cash Baptist Church and a Lyle Family Cemetery presently in this area.

Clarksburg

Clarksburg is located two miles west of Morton. The date of this settlement and the name origin is not generally known. A post office located here was discontinued in 1920 while a man named Champion was serving as postmaster.

Clifton

Clifton is 10 miles northwest of Forest. It is located on the Hillsboro-Clifton Road, which was also known as the old Thornhill Road. In the early days before Clifton became a community, it was a stage coach stop known as Buckhorn Tavern.

Clifton was organized in 1861. I.R. Ealey was the first postmaster and operated the first store in the community. Clifton was the center of a prosperous farming community of considerable size. The soil was of post oak variety, fertile and difficult to work. The area contains much black prairie land and the bottoms are rich alluvial.

Among the outstanding personalities of those early days was J.T. Calhoun, a Confederate soldier who lived most of his life in this community.

The Clifton Community consisted of a consolidated grade school, school library, Baptist Church, Macedonia Methodist Protestant Church and other buildings. The old log home of Joe Rolin built in 1863 was mentioned in a WPA report of the 1930s.

The Clifton School first started as a one-teacher school house with Mrs. Missouri Smithart as the first teacher. Later it was consolidated with several neighboring schools. The community eventually lost the school and also the post office, which was moved to Hillsboro.

Contrell

Contrell is located 16 miles north of Forest in an old and well-known neighborhood that was established in 1883. It is in the extreme northern part of Scott County. It is situated at the junction of the Hillsboro-Lena and the Morton-Lena (Hwy. 13) and the road to Ludlow. Homes are scattered and the community was built around the old Contrell Methodist Church. A school was located there at one time. There is a cemetery at this church.

R.M. Roberts who lived from about 1818 to 1884, son of R.W.

Roberts, was a congressman who was from this area. His home stood one-half mile east of the church on Hillsboro Road. The home was built of heavy hewn slabs between 1840-1850. The front walls were of split logs about two feet wide which were mud packed giving the appearance of bricks. The settlement was extinct by 1900.

The surrounding region is low and nearly level, traversed by small creeks and covered with dense undergrowth. J.M. Thomas was a good farmer of the Contrell Community. He was born near Lake but moved to Contrell in his early life. He attended school in a log house.

Cooperville Community

Cooperville is located nine miles southwest of Morton. Cooperville was settled when the Amberr Gipson family moved here in an ox-driven wagon from Alabama. These were the parents of Mrs. Green Raspberry Sr., whose husband was killed in the Civil War. Some of the original homestead was in the family seven generations and was owned by Mrs. W.B. Everett.

The Wiggins family moved into the community not long after the Gipsons. They too came by ox-wagon, but started in Georgia.

Another early Cooperville family was the Cicero Wesleys, who donated land in the community on which the first one-teacher school house was erected. Teachers who served the school were Marion Palmer, H.W. Bradshaw and later Miss Kate May. These all taught in the 1900s.

About 1890, a post office was opened by Will Cooper whom the town was named after. Two years later, Will Raspberry took it over and ran it for 15 years. After these two postmasters were Tinny Raspberry, Will Mize, Marion Palmer, Lera Lewis and Polk Sheeley.

The Cooperville store was begun by Will Cooper and later taken over by the Rasberrys, to be followed by Will Mize, Lera Lewis, Edd Phillips, Leach Wesley, J.W. Gray, Tellman Raspberry, Marion Palmer, Dolan Raspberry, S.L. Varner, Mrs. Bob Thorne, M.H. Thorne Sr., C.L. Bradshaw, La Rue Cooper, James Lee Everett and Mrs. Roy Everett.

Other industries in the community have been a sawmill, cotton gin, grist mill and feed crusher. The post office was abolished in 1901 and Cooperville became extinct.

Damascus

Damascus is near Walnut Grove and is 12 miles from Forest in the northwest part of Scott County, three miles from Sebastapol. It had a store, a small school, a Primitive Baptist Church and a few scattered houses. In about 1877 the Golden School stood on a blackjack-covered hill about two miles northeast of the present site of Damascus. This school was so named for Dr. William Golden. About 1890 a post office was opened and named Damascus for the old Baptist Church where the Sacred Harp concerts, an all day singing event, was held on the fourth Sunday in May each year. The post office was later discontinued for RFD from Walnut Grove.

Eley

Eley, nine miles northwest of Harperville in the northern part of Scott County on the Ludlow-Lena Road 11 miles from Forest. It was formed in 1884 and named for Bill Eley who operated the post office along with a store, sawmill, cotton gin and grist mill in 1884. Eley became extinct in 1922.

Forkville

Forkville is located on Highway 13 north of Morton. It was established in about 1890 and was named for its location in the fork of two roads eight miles north of Morton. The post office here retained the name of Beach when it was moved from the settlement of that name. It is for that reason Forkville is often called New Beach or Beach as distinguished from Old Beach located to the south. The Scott County Fair was established here in 1930-31 but in 1932-33 it moved to Clarksburg, then to Forest. Calvin Beavers and Jim Armstrong are listed as early settlers of Forkville.

Gail/Salmon

Gail or Salmon was eight miles east of Forest, near the Tusealmoice River on a dirt road. It was first called Gail but with the establishment of a post office in 1896 its name was changed to Salmon. W.W. Lewis served as postmaster but in 1906 the post office was closed. Lang's Mill, owned by Uncle Billie Lang, and a cotton gin were located there, now extinct for many years.

Gum Springs

Gum Springs was located four miles east of Hillsboro. It was named for sweet gum trees and springs that were located there. Its location was at the site of a group of seven mineral springs along the Old Jackson Road which in early days was the stage line from Livington, AL to Brandon, MS. Travelers for many years rested and drank of the water from the spring. It was said that Sherman, in his raid through the country, camped there. At one time the water from the springs was sold for its medicinal properties. It was an ideal camping site and a tabernacle was located there. Church services and singing meetings were often held by Mr. Eady, a Baptist preacher and owner of the springs. A man named Mack Warren who lived to be about 80 years of age and lived a good clean noble life, settled Gum Springs. The town was formed in 1865 and became extinct by 1900. Children there attended the Harperville School. A post office was established at Gum Springs in 1922 operated by A.A. Eady.

Harperville

Harperville is located nine miles north of Forest. It was formed in 1861 and was named for George C. Harper, an early settler. A flour mill was established at Harperville about 1868 by Mr. Harper. The Harperville College was established in 1870 with Capt. Charles A. Huddleston as president. The first Board of Trustees were George C. Harper, Dr. H.H. Haralson, C.B. Hadden, Dr. R.B. Austin and R.H. Campbell. In 1913 an Agricultural High School was established and considered one of the best schools in the state until the advent of the Smith-Hughes School in 1930. Harperville at the present time has a grocery store/gas station and two churches.

Hays

Hays is two miles south of Sebastapol, on the Forest-Sebastapol Road, 13 miles from Forest. Hays was a farming community with one store and was named for John Hays, a Methodist preacher, who formerly resided there.

Heatherly

Heatherly was 12 miles north of Forest and six miles west of Harperville. Heatherly was at one time a post office on a local dirt road. It was formerly known as Branch, formed in 1910 and was extinct by 1920. It was situated in the prairie region but the soil in the immediate vicinity was sandy and rather sterile, said a WPA report of the 40s. It was on the Tallabogue Creek. It was a very fine farming community. They raised cotton, corn, sugarcane, potatoes, peanuts and all kinds of vegetables. They would bring all their surplus to Forest for market. Later cattle and hogs were raised for a time. Presently the same area is used for pine timber and cattle raising. Children attended school at Clifton.

Hall Gatewood came to this settlement when a young man, married and reared his family here. He and his wife were leading citizens of the community along with John Lyle Sr., Joe Ealy, pioneer settler and Jody Parker, pioneer merchant.

The road that presently runs through this area has been named Hattie Lyle Road in honor of the wife of Troy Lyle, a brother of John Willis Lyle. Both homes still stand along this road, both being around 100 years old and both still being owned by descendants of the original Lyle families.

The Lyle families were formerly from the Cash area and are buried at the Lyle Family Cemetery at Cash.

A Mr. Lyle owned and operated a store in Heatherly and was also the postmaster. Another early resident was G.W. Talbot, who raised a family there. It was said in the 1940s that there was an old colonial home of A.M. Lyle that was still standing and occupied by Ray Lyle, his son.

At present the area is still occupied by some of the decedents of the original settlers, those of Gatewoods, Milners and Lyles.

Hillsboro

Hillsboro is eight miles northwest of Forest. It was named for its elevation on a range of hills, while not great, is well above that of the surrounding country. It was formed in 1835.

Hillsboro was originally the county seat of Scott County from 1836 to 1856. It is said to be one of the three oldest towns in the county and is located on the old stage coach route.

With the abandonment of the town of Berryville, which was briefly the county seat, the courthouse was established at Hillsboro in 1836 and remained there until it was moved to Forest in 1856. The honor was not surrendered without a struggle and bitter rivalry existed between the two towns for a number of years. It was said that the first courthouse built in Forest was demolished by citizens of Hillsboro and removed piecemeal to the latter place. However, the rapid growth of the town of Forest after the coming of the railroad soon established its permanence and the feeling gradually died down.

When the town of Hillsboro was incorporated it was specified as being one mile square with the courthouse in the center. Abner Lack, Jeremiah B. White, William Chambers, Thomas M. Petty and Alfred Eastland were authorized to hold an election in the town thereafter.

The courthouse at Hillsboro was sold at public auction May 22, 1873 and was bought by H.P. Chandler and a school house was made out of it. In 1873 a $5,000 wooden frame building was built. In 1898 it burned and was replaced by a $20,000 brick building. In 1924 it was torn down and replaced by a larger building in the same place.

The editor of the first paper at Hillsboro was a man named Farris. He established *The Argus*, the year of the war.

A grist mill was operated by E.C. Scott, located in an old building that was constructed by Dr. Barber soon after the Civil War. There was one chair factory operated by Parks Brothers.

In the early days a pond called Babbits Pond was built for the purpose of watering the stage horse. It was located on the old stage coach road, one mile east of Hillsboro. The pond was named for Mr. Babbit who owned the land.

The Methodist Church at Hillsboro was the first church organized in Scott County, being organized in 1836. A Baptist church is nearby. The Methodist Church Cemetery contains the monuments of six soldiers who fought in the Civil War. Col. Hi Eastland, saved the record books from the courthouse when it was burned by Sherman's Army during the Civil War. He hid them in the woods, it is said.

Hillsboro presently is a quiet residential community with a combination gas and grocery store. Other buildings include a fish house, laundry mat, car wash and beautiful churches.

Homewood

The town of Homewood is located nine miles south of Forest in the southern part of Scott County at the intersection of State 35 and the old Paulding-Brandon Road. Homewood has a post office and had postal and Western Union telegraph and Southern Bell telephone service. It is not on any railroad. Homewood was established first as Bucksnort July 14, 1849 and then its name was changed to Homewood May 30, 1850. It has also been referred to as Hells Half Acre. It has had a post office since March 6, 1940. Mrs. Ruby Boykin ran the post office at the beginning.

Andrew Jackson Boyles, writing for the Homewood Methodist Church Circuit, had the following to say about the town known now as Homewood:

"During the War of 1812, the white man started urging the Indians to go west. In 1830, Congress promised lands to all eastern Indians who would move west. In Mississippi and other sections, the white man soon began to occupy their lands. In 1833, the federal government of the US promised to sell their lands and hold the money in trust for them. The government paid the cost of moving the Indians to their new lands in the west. In 1834 Congress established the Indian Territory in the fertile valley of the Arkansas River, where each family or nation was to have its own lands. They were further promised never to be molested again by the white man. By 1842, nearly 125,000 Indians had crossed the Mississippi River to their new territory where the government was to distribute free rations and blankets and to regulate all trading with the Indians. Many small clans of Choctaws did not go west, but instead remained on their hunting grounds in south Mississippi. The name Homewood came through one of these small tribes, known as the Turkey Creek Indians, the Homewood area. This section was a very rich fur trading center with the Indians at that time. To the east were Little and Big Talleybogue, Turkey Creek, Leaf River, the Talleyhalleys and Talleyhouma. To the south were Okahay and many other small streams. To the north was Tusklameter and a vast flatwooded wilderness, a real paradise of wild life. We note that many of our streams have Indian names today.

Lickskillet was the first name of the Homewood area. White fur traders established a trading post near the center of this great section of country and during fur season they traveled among the Indians. They made camp and left a tent keeper who served as cook for the traders. When the cook fried meats he would sop the gravy out of the skillet and eat it. This being the custom, he was referred to as the "Sopper," or "Skillet-licker." Soon his tent and then the trading post was known as "Lickskillet."

Bucksnort was the second name of the Homewood area. After a few seasons the white men brought their families with them during the fur season. One newly-wed couple moved into the camp. One day when the young wife was at her cabin door some dogs ran a deer by her shack. When the hunters came along they asked if she had seen the deer. She replied that she saw a big buck which went by "just snorting." Very soon the trading post was known as "Bucksnort."

On Turkey Creek east of Bucksnort lived a tribe of Choctaws, known as the Turkey Creek Indians. The chief of the tribe had a son who was a famous turkey hunter. He had killed a turkey and skinned it and stretched the feathered skin over his cap and dried it for a hunting cap. When he went turkey hunting he would crouch on the ground among the brush, move his head and yelp. The turkey would take him for another turkey and come close to him and he would kill the turkey with his bow and arrow. One day as this fine hunter was calling to a turkey among the bushes some white men from Bucksnort camp were also turkey hunting. One saw the feathered cap moving among the brush and fired the rifle at his head, killing the chief's son.

The firing of this old muzzle loading cap-and-ball rifle thus led to the Turkey Creek Indian War, which lasted for several weeks.

During the troublesome days following the war, some fur-trading white men caught one of the Turkey Creek Indians in the trading post of Bucksnort and forced him to stretch himself across while they whipped him. As soon as they ceased to whip the Indian he ran east into the direction of Turkey Creek. After he had gone a mile or so from Bucksnort he met other white fur-traders coming back to the trading post. They insisted that he go back to Bucksnort with them and that he would be treated better. He ran from them still going east, while rubbing himself where he had been beaten and shouting, "No! No! No! Me go to me home in de woods." These traders came into Bucksnort and told the story of how the Indian ran and shouted "Me home in de woods." Soon Bucksnort was known as "Me home in de woods." For some time the trading post went by that name.

Finally Homewood, later when one of the white men applied for a post office at "Me home in de woods's," the name was spelled "Homewood." The old trading post took on a new name and soon grew into a village that has been Homewood ever since.

Homewood thus means a place of refuge, of healing, rest from physical and mental disturbances and fears, in short, another chance in life.

The above legend of Homewood was told to the writer in 1910 by Squire Sam Noblin, then an old man, a Justice of the Peace and member of the Board of County Supervisors. He lived at Homewood near where he was born and reared. He said this legend was told to him when he was a boy. Thus having come from the mouth of the law, this legend was taken for the truth by the writer and as he passes it on no one has disputed it.

Homewood was recognized as a settlement, though not formally named, in the early 1840s. In 1847 Col. Bob Hooper, who with two broth-

Patrons Union, Lake MS

ers moved to Forest in 1840 and built a home there, took up land at Homewood and built a log house. The first store of record was a small frame structure built in 1851 by a Mr. White and was later used as the post office. In 1847, Mr. Melton homesteaded a farm in the then dense forest and called it "Homewood," which was adopted by later comers as the name of the settlement. Homewood was on the old stage route which connected with the Vicksburg Road (A&VRR) at Brandon and Mr. Melton cared for travelers in his home.

In the 1930s Homewood was reported to have two good general stores and two churches, Methodist and Baptist. It had a fine, modern, brick consolidated school (grammar and high), with an enrollment of 180 pupils. The school served a large and thinly populated territory. School buses, or "tallyhos" as they are called in this section, operate over four routes, with "wagon routes" as feeders from by-roads impassable for heavy motor vehicles. Homewood lies on the dividing line between the fertile central prairie region and the great Long-leaf Pine Belt which stretches away southward to the shores of the Gulf. In the richer soil lying north and east of town, widely diversified agriculture is practiced and the community is a prosperous one. Cotton is, of course, the main crop, but corn, oats, sugarcane, alfalfa and sweet potatoes are grown in quantity as are also soybeans, vetch and other soil-building crops. Fruit growing and stock raising are of increasing importance, with steady improvements of breeds in the latter industry.

The surrounding surface is gently rolling, intersected at intervals by wet, thickly wooded bottoms but without any streams worthy of note. Lowland forestation is mainly black gum and silver bay with some white oak and magnolia.

Uplands are mostly cleared and under cultivation or in pasture, but there is a scattered growth of black-jack, post and Spanish oak, hickory and loblolly pine. Flowering shrubs are dogwood, azalea, crabapple and several species of haw. Field flowers are mainly composites; daisies, erigeron and various sunflower types in spring; asters, golden-rod, iron-wee and eupatorium in the fall.

Homewood profited but little from the forest of long-leaf pine which once covered its site, as this was all cut out by mills at Forest and Laurel, but was an important cotton growing center until the coming of the boll-weevil. That disastrous event was followed by a long period of depression but better farming methods in recent years have done much to bring prosperity. Among early settlers whose families were still represented in the 1930s were Meltons, Tadlocks, Priors and Barnes.

A home built by Col. Bob Hooper was later owned by Will Guyse. It was originally a log and mud construction but was later sealed and weather boarded. Another home built by Mr. Hinton about 1857, on what was called the old Melton place, was later occupied by Mr. and Ms. Wardel on State 35 across from the post office. It was of log and mud construction. The post office was originally built in 1851, as a store, by Mr. White in the center of town on state 35. A Masonic Hall built with frame construction was in the center of town on State 35. First floor was built in 1861 by Jim Youngblood and used for a number of years as a one-teacher school. He built furniture that was used in this building. Later in the same year, a second story was built by the Masons and was used by the order.

Homestead Community

Homestead is a community about seven miles southwest of Morton.

In 1865, as war matters were still being settled, Allen Lindsey opened a Drug and Dry Goods Store in the community of Homestead. A few months later Will King, an itinerant, passed through the community and settled down. No one seemed to know anything about him and the general impression was that "he wouldn't stay around here very long." But Will King, perhaps strengthened by the trust that Allen Lindsey placed in him, did stay and furthermore operated Lindsey's Store with excellent management for many years and later became postmaster for the community.

A few years later Mt. Olive Primitive Baptist Church was organized with Marion Stuart, Fate Wade and Brother Ishie as some of the charter members. The first preacher was Jack Stuart.

In 1899, Wes Morgan gave land for a fine two-room school to be built for the 25 students in the area. The Rogers Mill cut the timber for the school and with donations from patrons, it soon became a very good center of learning, hiring Bro. William Cooper as its first teacher, followed by among others, Ace Husband and Bro. B.A. McCollough.

The Lindsey Store closed around this time and citizens had to ride horseback to Morton for their mail, for without Will King they had no postmaster.

From 1904 to 1910, Billy Palmer operated the second general store and post office. Again when he closed, no mail carrier was assigned to the area.

In 1921, Burley Cooper taught 35 to 40 students a year at the four-month school, which was built on the old Pelam Stegall place. A storm in this year blew away the school and destroyed also the homes of Jess Gray, Ez Gray, John Palmer and Will Stegall. The latter donated wood for a new school from timber on his land which had been cut down by the storm. In 1950 this school house, which had two rooms plus auditorium and stage, was torn down. The wood was used to build the Charles Clifford home, which was built on yardage adjoining that of the school.

Logging and farming were the main livelihood of the area which is located on the Brandon-Homewood Road, once the main route from Forest to Brandon.

Horseshoe

Horseshoe is five miles west of Sebastapol, 14 miles from Forest. It was a prepaid freight station on the railroad. Horseshoe was named for a horseshoe shaped bend in the nearby creek. In 1880 a post office was located here with W.L. Madden Sr. as postmaster. It is in a rolling sandy pinewood section.

Kalem/ Concord

Kalem is in the west central part of Scott County and is about five miles east of Morton. J.L. McCarry, who was born in Alabama in 1850, came to this section in 1879. The town was named for Caley Regeons, a railroad man who was an early citizen. Kalem was formed in 1911 from an old settlement called Concord for the Concord Methodist church. Kalem was a flag

Front Street Lake, MS Armstead Street and Frank Cox

Lake Depot

Cox Store

and water tank stop on the Y&MV Railroad. Kalem was noted for its corn, cotton, peanuts, sugarcane, potatoes and the finest of vegetables. During the 1930s it had two stores and filling stations owned and operated by Cleave Marlor and Joe Pickle. There also was a Methodist Church and a frame school building there. One of the earlier homes was built by a man, John Bowman, who built a home there in 1860. Kalem has been listed as extinct since 1921.

Lake

The flow of history moves inexorably onward, day-by-day, year-by-year. The town of Lake located about nine miles east of county seat Forest near the Newton County line, looks proudly, reverently to its past and hopefully to its future.

Since the early settlers began to gather back in the 1830s after the region had been opened for homesteading by the Treaty of Dancing Creek, Lake has been tested, literally, by war, fire, pestilence and hard economic times. The people of the town always rallied.

In the earliest years, there was prosperity. By the mid-1800s, cotton plantations had sprung up and were flourishing in the area of what was to become Lake. The War Between the States put an end to that.

In 1864, General Sherman encamped on a hillside near Lake and directed the torching of plantations and railroad facilities.

L.B. Wilkins, probably at some time in the 1850s (research is not clear as to the exact year) purchased land and decided to establish a town because he had heard "the railroad is coming."

He named the town Maryville in honor of his wife. Later, at the request of US postal officials concerned because there were other Maryvilles, the town was named Lake in honor of a railroad man, Robert Lake of Vicksburg, who had been instrumental in establishing the A&V Railroad line.

On September 20, 1860 the first train ran from Jackson to Newton and by 1861 the line was open all the way to Meridian.

Lake was very much a railroad town. A roundhouse, terminal and machine shop were located just west of the present site of the town.

A charter of incorporation was granted to Lake by the state of Mississippi February 9, 1867. Appropriately, a plat at that time had the railroad depot located at the exact center of the town.

In the coming years, Lake was to become a timber and mill town and a center for all manner of shopping and business.

At the turn of the century a large lumber milling business, The Muskegon Lumber Co. was organized and operating near Lake at a site being named Muskegon Spur. In 1904 a family named Merrill and John DuBois, both from Pennsylvania, bought the mill which then became Merrill's Mill. At one time the mill employed 200 people and ran 24 hours a day. About 1912, John DuBois took over the mill and the name was changed to DuBois Lumber Co. After a disastrous fire in 1927 and a bitter disagreement with Governor Bilbo the DuBois family sold its timber holdings and closed the mill. This dealt a severe blow to Lake's economy.

Later on Lake was the site of a number of other mills and timber operations. A large stave mill produced barrel staves for many years and

there were other sawmills and planer mills. A thriving pulpwood and crosstie business was developed in Lake.

Lake at various times was a center for trade and commerce for many people in the surrounding area. In its May 8, 1907 edition, a local newspaper reported: "Mr. McCombs, lately of Illinois, now living in our town, has put up a grist and feed mill which is a great convenience to our people." The newspaper also reported: "The section north, east and west of Lake is a fine farming section and thickly settled and gives the merchants a good nearby patronage ... Lake has a good upcountry trade. Our businessmen are planning for a wagon yard so as to offer someplace for them to camp."

Years later Lake was to become the first town in Mississippi to have dial telephones. The first dial exchange telephone call was made from the home of W.P. (Pat) McMullan, president of the local bank and mayor of Lake at the time.

Disastrous fires dealt setbacks to the town. Subsequent reports after each of these fires told of immediate efforts under way to rebuild.

A heavy blow of another sort had been dealt to Lake in 1878 with a disastrous outbreak of yellow fever. John P. Freeman wrote in an article: "All the annals of Mississippi's disasters can show nothing to compare in sheer horror with the yellow fever epidemic of 1878 ... One valiant solider of the Federal Prison Camp wrote in his diary: "August 10, 1878: Death visited again next door this morning ... Five coffins have been carried from the house this week ... War was sweet compared with this ... In war we knew our enemy and could fight back, here we are powerless and can only wait." By the time the wait was over and the epidemic had run its course, some 200 Lake people, roughly one-third of the town's population, had died of yellow fever.

Again the town worked its way back to recovery.

A bedrock of the town has always been its churches and schools. There are five churches in the heart of town. The first building for a school was built in 1865. A carpenter named Mr. Chester used lumber salvaged from the railroad shops destroyed by General Sherman's troops. It was also used for church services until a church building was built beside it about three years later. Other, larger school facilities were built in later years.

Lake was once the host every year for a large gathering of people and events known as the Patrons' Union. The campgrounds were located about three miles north of Lake. The Patrons' Union was organized in 1883 under the auspices of the Farmers Granges of Scott and a number of other area counties. Families would move to the campgrounds and reside for a week or more in what were called "tents" but actually were rough wooden structures. Activities at a large pavilion and elsewhere on the campgrounds included political speeches, talent contests, dances, much neighborly visiting, horse races and an annual knock-down-drag-out baseball series between Scott and Newton counties. The Patrons' Union was discontinued some time after the Depression years in the 1930s.

Or was it?

One of the annual projects of the people of Lake in recent years has been an annual one-day revival of the Patrons' Union on the grounds of the old Lake railroad depot. At the same time there is an ongoing effort to repair, restore and preserve the old Lake depot building.

Illinois Central Gulf Railroad records indicate the depot was built about 1890, probably as the first substantial replacement for the station that was burned by Sherman's troops. A spokesman for the State of Mississippi Department of Archives and History said: "The Lake Railroad Station is a symbol of the industry which was responsible for the founding and development of the town of Lake and is a rare example of the use of Queen Anne design for a commercial structure in a rural Mississippi town. It is the only known extant example of a Queen Anne style depot in Mississippi."

It would be difficult to think of a more striking link between the past and present. And that's why some of the people of Lake, honoring the past and looking toward the future, are working so hard to preserve it.

Lathamtown

Lathamtown was located six miles southeast of Ludlow and was founded in 1851. It was named for Dolpha Latham. There was once a post office here named Vera but it has been discontinued for many years.

Lillian

Old Lillian was located at a fork in the road, about a half-mile nearer Hillsboro than was the later community of Lillian. Lillian is 12 miles northeast of Hillsboro and was named for Lillian McCoy, formerly it was known as Mt. Olive. The Mt. Olive Baptist Church still stands at the former location. G.W. McCoy established Lillian. Lillian was a strictly agricultural community in the north central part of Scott County on the Hillsboro-Lena (improved dirt road, 12 miles north of Forest, four miles north of Hillsboro), presently the Hillsboro-Ludlow Road.

Lillian was formed in 1885. At one time the town had two general stores, a post office, barbershop, drug store, cotton gin, sawmill, gristmill operated by a gasoline engine, a blacksmith shop, millpond, a retired doctor and the Baptist church was used as a school house. Lillian was the trade center for five or six miles around.

H.C. Davis, Henry Calhoun and A.C. Farmer, father of B.U. Farmer, were some of the first settlers. A.C. served in the MS Regiment, was wounded very badly but lived to 78 years of age. Dr. F.H. Stubbs was a leading and successful physician. Bloxson Stubbs was the leading merchant who in later years moved to Leake County. His competitor was James Madison Lyle who also owned a store across the road from his; he later sold the business and moved to Texas.

James Madison Lyle purchased a house that once stood at the present location of the home of Vernon L. Gatewood operated a grocery store, gristmill and gas station at this location until his recent death. In previous years, Vernon and his brother, the late John D. Gatewood, were partners in farming interests and the V.R. Gatewood Cotton Gin. In 1973 after the death of his mother, Antoinette Lee Gatewood, Mr. Gatewood and his wife continued the operation of Gatewood Grocery together until 1999 when his health began to fail. The store had been in continuous operation by the Gatewood family since 1919. The original house at its location was an old historical place with an old-fashioned plantation type house and farm. James M. Lyle purchased the house at a time that it was in bad need of remodeling and was being referred to as a haunted house. It had been formerly called the Dossey place. After he remodeled the house he called it Sunnyside and lived there until his move to Texas. The house was later replaced with the present house.

According to a WPA report in the 1930s, Lillian had a population of 69 and it was stated that Lillian lies in that part of the central prairie region known as Bald Prairie and forestation is confined to the bottom lands, which are thickly wooded with white, water and willow oak, black gum, beech and scaly bark hickory. Flowering shrubs, such as dogwood, redbud and red male abound in the low ground, while yellow jasmine, iris and both red and white lilies are common in the same locations. On higher ground, wild roses, red begonia, helenium, ageratum and passion flower furnish abundance of bloom. While Chickasaw plums and blackberries are everywhere.

The ground is gently undulating and the soil is of high fertility producing heavy crops of cotton, corn, oats, hay and sugarcane. Pasturage is excellent through nine or 10 months of the year.

The town in later years in addition to the Gatewood's store and combination cotton gin and sawmill consisted of the Baptist church and other dwellings. Two or three small syrup mills were located in the vicinity. Lillian was a Postal and Western telegraph station. Mail was received on a route from Hillsboro.

Ludlow

Ludlow, 15 miles north of Morton, was established in 1847 and was named for James J. Ludlow, a pioneer in the area. Old Ludlow was located one-half mile north of the present site. The town of Ludlow was moved up to the station when the railroad was built through this section.

The first store built in Ludlow belonged to Judge Denson and was operated by John Burks. The second store at Ludlow was built by John L. Smith. It was burned by Sherman's Army and rebuilt by John L. Smith.

Miss Fannie Majors operated the post office. Dr. J.N. Denson had his headquarters at the store of Henry B. Lee.

Other early settlers included S.J. Denson and J.M. Smith.

Malco or Redtop Community

Malco or Redtop Community was four miles southeast of Harperville, 12 miles from Forest in the northern part of Scott County. It was formerly a post office established in 1895. It has been extinct since 1926. It was named for the infant son of Malcolm Beasly, the postmaster. It also had a rural school which was consolidated with Harperville.

Mashburn

Mashburn was two miles west of Morton. It was named for Will Mashburn. It was formed when a spur of the Y&MV Railroad was run to a sawmill that was owned and operated by Will Mashburn. The area was in the vicinity of Loftin and Broach. Mashburn was extinct by 1911 and the land became the property of Tip Stuart of Morton.

Morton

Morton is on US 80 in the west central part of Scott County.

Morton was originally established as Green Bush on September 15, 1849. Its name was changed to Morton on September 23, 1858.

In 1835 Caleb W. Taylor from Kentucky, patented land from the state and built a home. Later Col. Taylor laid out a town of 160 acres and named it Morton for his wife who was Mary Elizabeth Morton. Col. Taylor won his name by being one of the signers of the secession.

Caleb Taylor sold property to the Southern Railroad Co. for a depot and a rail right-of-way. The deed was signed October 24, 1859. Morton was built facing the railroad, which was toward the north.

Morton Agriculture Building

T.B. Gaddis Store

In 1847 the Academy was built on what we know now as "Tank Hill" and was used as a Union Church, school and Masonic Lodge.

In 1858 the railroad was completed through Morton and in 1860 Morton was made an incorporated town. During the war, Sherman's Army tore up all the railroad and burned most of Morton. They camped in the Academy during their stay in the town on their way to Vicksburg. In the 1930s, only three houses were standing that had stood before the war.

In 1879, the following businesses were a part of Morton:
Clowe, G.W., general merchandise
Crook, H.W., general merchandise
Flagan, W.J., grist and sawmill
Gaddis, John, general merchandise
Harris, John P., general merchandise
Keeton & Maynor, general merchandise
Manning & Co., general merchandise
McCaul, T.W., general merchandise
McGough, Morre & Co., general merchandise
McKineey, Busick & Co., general merchandise
Pettus, T.T. & Bro., general merchandise
Portor, X.O., proprietor of Portor's Hotel
Portor, X.O., druggist
Taylor, C.W. and Son, general merchandise

A Methodist church was established in 1882 and in 1888 a Baptist church was built, leaving the school and the Masonic Hall in the old Academy.

In 1890 a camping ground was built where later Bowman's store stood, called Camping Springs. It stood for 10 years.

Some other early settlers not previously mentioned were the Moores, Flanagans, Easterlings, Tibbs and Sims.

In 1898, the town was burned, then it was built where it now stands. The new buildings were built facing east and west, as they stand today. Later in 1900 the west section was destroyed by fire and was replaced.

A new frame school building and Masonic Lodge was built in 1911, north of the cemetery and stood until 1933. In 1931 a brick high school was built and in 1933 the old frame building was torn away and used to build a grammar school, which was a WPA project.

In 1912 the Hall-Legan Lumber Co. established in Morton as a result of a gift of land from the citizens in an effort to get an industry. Virgin forests for miles around became victims of the sawmill. The lumber company employed many people, thus raising Morton's economic standard and the town boomed.

A new school was built and stood until 1933.

Morton during WWI, was the second largest center of population in the county and still is. Morton had the largest merchandising house in the county. The store was owned by T.B. Gaddis, the Field Merchant Marshall.

The Hall and Legan Lumber Co. operated a 4,000 acre stock farm and a 200 acre agricultural experimental farm. Work was done on the farm and the native cattle were bred with a thoroughbred Hereford bull to raise the quality of the local cattle.

In 1914 and 1926, new Methodist and Baptist churches were erected in the same place where the old ones stood.

A new bank was erected of brick on the west side of the street in 1929. In 1930, a City Hall was built in connection with the Masonic Hall. It was made of brick and faced the east.

The depression cut timber demands in 1933 and the lumber company was bought by Adams and Edgar. The federal government bought the forest for an estimated $4.00 per acre. The 86,000 acres were named Bienville National Forest.

By 1949 the major business in Morton was the Stuart Co. which had been founded in 1900 by H.N. Stuart and Sons. The Adams-Edgar Lumber Co. became the A.B. Farris Lumber Co.

The poultry business was coming into its own. B.C. Rogers started the poultry business in this area. At that time Mr. Rogers was the largest Purina dealer in the world.

Talon, Inc. was the first northern industry to locate here. The late Governor F.H. Wright worked hard to get the company located here.

Morton has been a prosperous town since 1960. Scott County is the largest broiler producing area in the world. Morton has been dubbed "Chicken Capital."

Muskegon

Muskegon, located about one-half mile west of Lake, was situated in the eastern part of Scott County on the Y&MV Railroad and a partly graveled road. Although only about a quarter-mile from US 80 it has no direct connection with it. It had a Postal Telegraph Station and a prepaid freight station.

The settlement was named for a mill that was built there by Michigan interests and was named for the well-known city in that state. The mill was a large hardwood sawmill and all of the buildings were company property. A large, two-story frame house formerly the residence of the proprietor is surrounded by extensive quarters but the mill discontinued operations many years ago and was abandoned.

Muskegon stood on a low knoll, surrounded by a wooded swamp and had no agriculture or industries other than the sawmill. It is very close to the town of Lake. The surrounding forestation was black gum, white oak, magnolia and hickory, thickly fringed with willow. Flowers were of the swamp variety, mainly iris, spider lilies and elder.

Nathan Springs

About one mile south of Morton on the Independence Road, Nathan Springs is situated just off the road on the west side under a hill. This place was named for an old Negro man who lived his life on that hill and enjoyed the best of water from the springs. It is here that Sherman's Army got ready to fight but Johnston's Army surrounded them on three sides and Sherman's men retreated.

Norris

Norris was a little village in the southern part of Scott County, five miles southeast of Forest, at the crossing of the Forest-Pineville and Lake-Homewood roads. It was named for Norris Williamson. Pioneer homes were built in this locality as early as 1840. One of the oldest schools in Scott County was established here in 1856. Among the early settlers were the Nemiah Harvey Jones, Halbert and Gatewood families. Norris was a prosperous community made up of well-to-do farmers. Norris had a postal and Western Union telegraph station. There were formerly two stores there but were closed many years ago. There was also a store and a small cotton gin about a mile south on the Pineville Road owned and operated by Harvey Jones. A Baptist church was located on a high hill in the area.

The region is hilly and the soil generally black prairie. Forestation is loblolly pine, hickory and various oaks. Little of the land remains in private hands, the greater part being incorporated in the Bienville Unit of the DeSoto National Forest.

Otho Moss Hill

Otho, a small settlement on the line of Smith and Scott 12 miles south of Forest, was named for Otho Gilbert and was formerly known as

Moss Hill, formed 1851. There was one portable gin, one mill owned and operated by the Gilberts. Early settlers were the Cars, for which the Methodist church was named. The Bethleham Lutheran Church was located here also. O.T. Gilbert had the post office there and owned a home that was built in 1851. The post office became extinct in 1910. Some of the early settlers were the Weems, Turners and McKenzies. It was a fine farming and pasture section. Beaver Dam was located one-half mile south of Otho and was noted for fine outings.

Otis/Harmond

Otis is 10 miles southeast of Forest. It was named for B.F. Otis. It is an old settlement formerly known as Harmond which was formed in 1841. There was never a post office at Otis and it became extinct in 1911. Sam Weems was born and lived his entire life of 100 years at Otis. He was a great cattle and hog raiser. Will Halleway and Frank Cox and the Ottis family were early settlers. The Sam Weem house was still standing in the 1930s, a house that was built before the Civil War.

Piketon/Piketown

Piketon is located nine miles northeast of Forest on the Tunclemeta River. Before the Civil War, the stage coach ran through Tunclemeta swamp making direct communication from Alabama to Jackson. The Hunt home which was built before the Civil War stood along this road. It was a large house called the caretaker home or inn. The Hunts took care of the traveling people and the stage changed horses at the place. The John Walters and T.J. Walters homes were also on this road. T.J. Walters was one of the first settlers and served as supervisor four years and circuit clerk four years. Piketon was formed in 1936 and Mose Price, an old settler, carried the mail from Piketon to Harperville in the earlier years before the post office was closed. The road was made into a pike road and from whence the name Piketon came. The settlement has also been referred to as Ringgold School which was just a half-mile southwest.

Pulaski

Before the Civil War, the community from which Pulaski originated was known as Porter Springs. It was first settled by X.O. Porter, who owned a small blacksmith shop and kept the post office in this shop. The Porter place is now owned and operated as a cattle farm by J.C. Johnson.

The first voting place of Porter Springs was held in a cow stable owned by Jimmy Brassell. He lived where the Brassell Cemetery is located.

During the Civil War or thereafter, this little town, Porter Springs, moved a mile west and was given the name Pulaski in honor of the Count Casimir Pulaski, a Polish soldier, who served as a general under General George Washington.

History tells us that he fought valiantly to help us gain our freedom from England. Count Casimir Pulaski camped at this small place called Porter Springs sometime before the Revolutionary War. He was on his way from Massachusetts to what is now the state of Florida. There are many other towns as well as counties and highways in the US that have been named in honor of this courageous solider that lost his life in the Revolutionary War in America fighting for our freedom. There was a book written by Mrs. H. Hostymaska, Redditch, England in memory of Count Pulaski. In the year 1959, George W. Miles, postmaster of Pulaski, MS received a letter from this lady asking for pictures and information about our town so that it might be published in her book. She also asked for a postmark of Pulaski Post Office for a souvenir.

The first house built was a log structure owned by the Robertson family. This family was among the wealthy people of that day. Most of the older members of this family are buried in a private cemetery on this property. One son, Billie Robertson, moved to Texas and carried with him his personal slave, Dumb Joe. In Texas he made a fortune and after the Civil War freed his slave. Dumb Joe came back to Pulaski to die. Mr. Robertson wrote the Pulaski postmaster seeking to obtain information concerning his original residence and his slave. Mr. Robertson was then living in Trenton, NJ and was 91 years old. The Robertson home in Pulaski was later owned and occupied by Sims Holmes, who was also a leading citizen and the father of Claude Holmes. This old log house has been torn down and replaced by a modern home now owned by Jack Miles.

The oldest house left standing is the home where A.E. Searcy lives. Its first structure of logs is still standing covered by new materials. It was built by J.W. Williams, first merchant of Pulaski.

The first church in Pulaski was a Primitive Baptist Church organized in the year 1842. It was a log structure with a mud chimney and a dirt floor. The first pastor of this church was Elder Hollon and the church clerk was W.W. Chandler. The first charter members were the Chandler family. These records, dating from 1842 are still intact and with fine quill pen writing, tell the story of the early church, which was located a few yards from the present post office. These records tell us of servants who worshiped in the same church with their masters in slavery days. Pews were provided for them in the back of the church. Minutes are recorded of a conference held to dismiss them to have a church of their own after they were freed. This site is now owned by Mack N. Miles. The Missionary Baptist Church was organized at Pulaski, August 20, 1894. Rev. T.J. Miley was the first pastor, R.D. Cooper, church clerk and A.F. Green, deacon. Some of the first charter members were R.D. Cooper, R.V. Dukes, W.T. Gaston, Fannie Sanders, A.F. Green and William Cooper. The church was located at its present site in a frame structure. The land was given by Mr. Saunders. The church has been replaced by a new building with Sunday school rooms and is now a full-time church with Rev. John Atchley, the pastor.

The Methodist church seems to have been officially started December 1892. C.M. McDonald was the presiding elder with Grandberry as bishop and Rev. K.S. Enoch the first pastor. There is a Bible in the church office, which was a gift from C.M. McDonald, dated in 1872. This would indicate that the church had a following at this date but records only officially show from 1892. It was the first Mutual Union Church, then known as the Methodist Episcopal Church South. In 1939 it became the Mutual Union Methodist Church. The first charter members were members of the Westberry family. The building was frame and was situated where the present Pulaski Methodist Church now stands. The new building was dedicated May 3, 1953. Rev. Warren C. Moffatt is now pastor.

In the Primitive Baptist Church the first school was organized. The teacher was Abb Rhodes. The little town began to thrive and in the year 1890, another one-room log house was built with a small shed on the side to take care of the beginners. John Davis, a leading citizen and politician in those days, had then become a teacher. The site of that building was located on Pulaski property now owned by Harold Loeb.

At this time there were many residents who influenced the progress of our town. Among these were Mr. Eady, Elder Jack Stuart, Sol Saunders and many others already mentioned. In order to accommodate the increasing population, a new school was planned by these men. Soon Pulaski had the only accredited school in the county. After completing the prescribed course of study in Pulaski, a student could take county examinations and become a teacher or enter the college of his choice. Professor Penn was the first instructor and was succeeded by Professor John Poole.

Students came from a radius of many miles to board and attend school. Some of the educated personalities of this school were Judge Bill Wade and Judge Lee Miles, both of Little Rock, AR now deceased. Others were Judge George Nobles, Jackson, MS and Luther Roberts, who was once superintendent of all city schools in Jackson, MS. The school now has been consolidated with Morton Attendance Center. The Pulaski school building is now used as a community center and voting place.

The first gin was owned by Elder Jack Stuart and pulled by mules. By beginning early and continuing past sunset two bales could be separated from the seed. In later years this antique machinery was replaced by a steam powered machine operated by Sim Holmes.

The first sawmill in this area was steam driven. Sim Holmes pioneered this establishment.

The first mercantile business was a small frame type store owned and operated by J.W. Williams; L.C. McLemore now owns this site.

The principle occupation of this small town was farming, with cotton as its major crop. Survival made the growth of vegetables a necessity.

The early means of transportation in Pulaski characterized by most pioneer towns were oxen. These oxen were later replaced by the horse

Main Street. Sebastapol Early 1900 Center building is the bank

and buggy, however as comparable to the history of the automobile of today, there were few who were financially able to own a horse and buggy. The highway was built from Morton to Pulaski in 1957. Since then new additions have been made.

Electricity was brought to Pulaski in 1940. This development gave the people the opportunity to progress as the beginning of the machine age was at hand. Telephones were added in 1950.

For entertainment, the early settlers enjoyed fox hunting, coon hunting and square dancing. A campground, known as Boozer Springs was located about two miles from Pulaski and served as a major point for gatherings. Tents sufficed as shelter and frequently straw beds were used for makeshift sleeping. People commuted for miles and enjoyed days of worship services and companionship with their neighbors.

Dr. Pope Sims pioneered medicine in Pulaski. He was always at the beck and call of his patients. Other doctors to follow him were Dr. Dukes, Dr. Burnham and Dr. W.A. Jones, whose widow, Mrs. Cleo Saunders Jones, was born here but now resides in Morton, MS. Pulaski has made an immense amount of progress. It now has two stores, a post office, the community center, three churches and two parsonages. The people are civic minded and susceptible to new ideas. Modern homes have replaced the older ones. Many have been known to remark all residents wish to become permanent residents. *Submitted by Martha Miles Nelson.*

Raworth/Mt. Vernon

Raworth is five miles west of Forest. It was formerly known as Mt. Vernon. It was formed in 1879 and was on the Y&MV Railroad on US 80. It was formerly a sawmill town with several stores and a water tank stop on the railroad. At the large water tank, located there, was an ideal place for an outing as they had boats you could use for fishing. The Bowman home was built there before the Civil War and was still standing with two large oaks in front and a kitchen off to the side of the house during the 1930s and was mentioned in a WPA report.

After the mill was moved the small settlement was destroyed by fire. The first sawmill was known as the Raworth Lumber Co., operated by the Fairchild Brothers and then by Wharbington. One store was owned by Taylor Taklock who was also a tax collector in 1908. W.T. Culpepper owned a sawmill, which was noted for its fine timber.

There was a school there known as Mt. Vernon which was used for church also, which was later known as Kalem.

J.L. McCrory was one of the first settlers and he lived to be a ripe old age. Howard McCrory who served as an officer of Scott County was from this area. Other leading men were the Westerfields, Vaughns and Bowmans.

When the timber was exhausted about 1911, the stores were abandoned and the water tank was moved two miles west to Kalem. Later the entire settlement, with the exception of one house, was destroyed by fire. This site has now been developed into a recreational area.

Ridge

Ridge was five miles north of Harperville and 14 miles north of Forest on Hwy. State 35. It was named for the contour of the region. It was formed in 1836. There was a one-room school-church used for grammar school there. The church was called Pea Ridge Baptist Church. Sol Clark was an early settler, as well as James Bailey and Jim Parker, who established the post office and was postmaster there. Oscar Shearman, one of Forest's successful businessmen, taught school at Ridge. Other residents of Ridge were the Jim Parker and Guss Calhoun families.

Ridge has been extinct since 1901 when the town of Walnut Grove in Leake County spread across the county line to envelope Ridge Community.

Ringgold Wolf

Ringgold is located seven miles northeast of Forest and five miles southwest of Harperville, the community was formerly called Antioch, then Wolf and then Robert S. Weems named the community Ringgold for a town in Georgia with a nearby consolidated school taking the name.

During late 1927 there was a growing concern for the children of the county because of a lack of a centrally located school for the advantage of a high school education. A special board meeting of September 7, 1928 formed a new school district to be known as the Ringgold Consolidated School District and was to be made up of the school districts of Steele, Piketon, Salem and Ephesus. The location of this school and the nearby area is referred to as the Ringgold Community.

The Ringgold Community Club was a group that was formed shortly after the school came into being. It provided for social needs of adults as well as for the children.

Sebastapol

Sebastapol is located 15 miles from Forest in the gently rolling red hills of the northeastern corner of Scott County. It has been called the little town that wouldn't die. The little town was taken from the Indians prior to the Civil War and was officially formed as Sebastapol in 1882. Sebastapol is an Indian name, the reason for the name is unknown. It was a regular station on the Jackson-Union Branch of the GM&N Railroad and was incorporated in 1917.

The early settlement had two churches, the Methodist and the Baptist, and a cemetery called Moors Hill. The post office was located in the Anthony store. Anthony owned a cotton gin and another man, Scarbroughs owned another cotton gin there. The bank of Sebastapol opened in 1920. A school was built in 1924.

Dr. T.L. Underwood settled at Sebastapol in 1884 and he practiced medicine there for over 55 years, being the oldest physician in Scott County. Another old settler was P.H. Underwood, a merchant. In the 1800s and early 1900s, the town depended on the pulpwood industry and cotton farming for its survival.

In the 1940s Sebastapol had 10 stores, five service stations and was a thriving little town raising cotton, corn, peanuts, oats and hay for the stock and had good cattle ranges.

The first small industry to spring up in the community was Maxim Manufacturing Corp., a lawn mower factory. It was established in January 1963 by A.G. Easom Jr. Three years later a second industrial corporation located in the town, Bishop Industries, owned and operated by the brother team of W.C. and L.L. Bishop. They manufactured tent liners for the government. Later Green Acres Farms, a poultry processing complex with a feed mill came into operation.

Presently the town is still thriving.

Sparksville

Sparksville is seven miles northwest of Forest and three miles southwest of Hillsboro. It was named in honor of Dan Sparks, a Civil War veteran who was the first postmaster in 1914 when the town was formed. He homesteaded a farm in the then dense forest and called it Sparksville.

It was located on the Shokaloo River. There was a Parksville Methodist Church which was also used for a school building. The town became extinct by 1917 when the post office was discontinued. Some of the early settlers were J.N. Sparks, a merchant at Hillsboro; Bob Bustin and the Sullivans. Edgar Wagener, owned and operated a sawmill there. In the 1930s it was reported to be a good farming community with the land being very fertile and level. There was an abundance of food supplies and several families had big chicken farms and raised cattle.

Stage/Track

Stage is six miles south of Morton and 13 miles from Forest. It was formed in 1889 and was on a gravel road. It was a small agricultural community of four or five farm houses, but for many years had a post office where Green Cooper was postmaster before the establishment of the RFD system and mail was then received through Morton. There was one sawmill owned and operated by Carven Morehead. Children went to Independence School one mile west of Stage's location. It was formerly known as Track. Stage for many years was a stop on the Old Paulding-Brandon stage road which passes through it and owes its name to that circumstance. The Independence School and Methodist church are one mile to the west and the old Springfield Baptist Church two miles southeast. The old Springfield Baptist Church had a pool built for baptism in 1901.

Important personalities were Edward Livingston of Stage, served as state representative for four years and W.C. Rushing, who settled at Stage in 1899. He was a prosperous farmer. Julia Rushing, elected in 1909 as clarinetist at Clark Memorial College in Newton, was from Stage. She had a home built there in 1899. Other leading citizens were the Ueetscheys, Merchants and Gaddies.

The area's surface was flat, well forested along stream courses with loblolly pine, gum elm, hickory and water oak. The soil is a fertile, sandy bottom land.

Steele

Steele is located nine miles northeast of Forest on what is now US 21. It was an agricultural settlement that was named for Tom Steele who settled here in 1887 and then later moved to another state. Steele was a widely scattered, strictly agricultural community with 20 to 25 farm houses surrounding two stores which formed the focal point of the community.

Sun

Sun is in the extreme southeast corner of Scott County, 12 miles from Forest. Sun was a very old community. It was named for the sun tower located on a high hill. The community was formed in 1896 on a local road. W.J. Stokes was an old settler from this area who served as county superintendent of education for four years. S.R. and W.L. Weems, other old settlers, did much for the upbuilding of the community. Mack Weems was serving as county superintendent of education in 1941 when a WPA report was made. The children attended school at High Hill. Sun was embraced by the Bienville Unit of the DeSoto National Forest and very little of the land remained under private ownership. At one time it had a post office which was said to be the smallest post office in the county, mail was brought to the Sun office three times a week from Bartlett. The post and store were owned by R.E.L. Weems. Very little farming was done in this area, except for the raising of watermelons for the market.

Taylor Place

The Taylor Place was a stage line stop, where the horses were changed. This place was called "Buck Horn" before Morton was originated. This place belonged to the grandson of Col. C. Taylor.

Other Small Communities

Here are some of the other small communities that have been in the Scott County area in the past: Crane Hill, Dennis settlement, Donohue settlement, Fikestown, Independence, Little Italy, Midway, Peagler Store, Singleton settlement, Salem and Usrytown.

If we missed any it was unintended. There are so many small communities that have come and gone over the years.

Colonel Caleb Taylor and J.A. Taylor his grandson.

Schools

Antioch School

Antioch was located near the present Antioch Primitive Baptist Church on Highway 21. The school building was in the edge of the present cemetery. It is known that the school was open in 1898. Families who attended were Walters, Warren and Reeves. Three of the first teachers at Antioch were O.D. Loper, Jeff Walters and Cooper Walters.

Bald Hill School

Bald Hill School, also called Blanche, was located four miles southwest of Lake. It was settled before the year 1883. T.F. Lloyd was the teacher in 1883; Miss Florence Hurst, 1897 and J.W. Faulkner, 1898. P.P. Hatch and Miss E.A. Roberts were also teachers.

Balucta School

Balucta School was just north of the W.F. Lyle place on what is known as the Balucta Road. It was consolidated with Clifton in 1926. Some of the teachers were Fontaine Lyle Caughman, Kate Denson, Lillie Lyle and Rose Taylor.

Bell School Class

Bell School

A group of the students and teachers of the old Bell School is pictured here. The school was located on Stage Road just south of where Edward McCaughn lives now. This photo was made around 1905 and was taken by Albert Ueltchey. L-R, first row: Birdie Lewis, Baxter Westberry, Frank Lewis, Mallie Bishop, Cleve Lewis, Emma Bell, Ossie Wade, Dora Lewis, Emma Westberry. Second row: Wallace Lewis and his dog, Ring; Mack Westberry with Bernice Westberry in his lap; Alfred Hooks, Geneva Lewis, Walter Wade, teacher; Thelma Ueltchey, Olga Bell, Neva Bishop, Mattie Westberry, Valdice Bell and Alma Ueltchey. Photo courtesy of Mrs. Percy Jones.

Bell School was also probably called Bellfield in the 1800s. In the booklet *Memoirs of Elwin Livingston 1776-1976*, he makes mention of Bell Schoolhouse, which was burned during consolidation. He also named these teachers: Mrs. Bob Brassell, Mrs. Bess McLemore, Mrs. Homer Thorton, Clyde Everett and Miss Bessie Cooper. Joe Roland was a teacher at Bell School just before WWI and Olga Bell taught there during WWI. Bell School was on Stage Road, just south of the Edward McCaughn place. The people in this area went to church at Independence Methodist Church. In the Superintendents Register of Pay Certificates book has teachers listed for Bellfield School. It could be the same school, those teachers are: H.J. Walker, 1891; P.T. Whitehead, 1893; D.J. Smoot, 1893; Nannie Anderson, 1895; P.T. Whitehead, 1895; H.P. Whitehead, 1896 and S.L. Moore, 1898.

Row 1: Lester Wallace, Nettie Duncan, Cora Hales, Temple Wade, Clinton Hales, R.J. Wade, Willie J. Wade, O.T. Rigby Row 2: Kate Denson (teacher), Lorene Duncan, Erma Lee Duncan, Erneze Lyle, Bessie Wallace, Bertha Hales, Claud Rigby

Branch School

The Branch School was begun in the early 1900s. The teachers for 1921 were Miss Ola Walsh, Miss Geneva Keeton and Claud Ponder. The old Branch School was on the site where Branch Baptist Church now stands.

In 1929, a new district was established. It was 3.5 miles wide and eight miles long. Cherry and Coffee Bouge Creeks bounded it on the east side. It ran north to the old Branch Community, west to the Rankin County line and south to Line Prairie. Charlie Thompson donated six acres of land to build a new school, which was a wood building that cost $5,000. This school offered classes for grades 1 through 12. Classes began in this building in 1930 with Peter Bennett as superintendent. The trustees were Rob Massey, Monroe Webb and Dan Lum. Other superintendents were Jack Waggoner, A.F. Kersch, George Cline, Paul Edwards, Jonathan Edwards, William Edwards, Tom Coward and a Mr. Gleason.

Beach School
Front Row: _, _, William "Bill" Miley Davenport,. Second Row: _, _, teacher, Jessie Mildred Davenport (Woods), _, Mary Elizabeth "Mollie" Davenport (#1 Lee, #2 Fewell), _, Lonnie Leroy Davenport, _. Third Row: _, _, Back Row: _, _, Bessie Mae Davenport (Evans), John Wesley Evans, _, _.

The Line Prairie, Prentiss and Liberty schools were closed and consolidated with Branch to make up the Branch Consolidated School. Line Prairie School goes back at least as far as 1874 when Mrs. Molly Lloyd was the teacher. During this time a school term could be as short as two months and no longer than four. The Line Prairie School was located on the west side of the present Line Prairie Presbyterian Church. Other teachers were M.E. Irby, 1877; J.M. Harper, 1880; John T. Pearson, 1882; J.H. Butler, 1883; Miss Sadie Ashmore, 1891; James A. McCoy, 1893; Mrs. Nola Barber, 1885; C.E. Burnham, 1898; Miss Gussie Kirkland, 1898 and Miss Marie Smith, 1921.

There are no records of Prentiss School in the 1800s, so it was probably started in the early 1900s. The Prentiss School was located on property owned by D.T. Measells Sr. Miss Agnes Franklin was the teacher in 1921. The Liberty (Groverton) School was located on the south side of the present Groverton Cemetery and goes back as far as 1881 when J.F. Martin was the teacher. Other teachers were S.C. Jordan, 1891; P.P. Hatch, 1891; R.E. Kelly and Miss Lillia Shepherd, 1921. Some of the other teachers that taught in these schools were Berry Slade, Fleta Kitchings Jones, Annie Bell Kitchings Boykin, Omega Denson, Betty Harp Coats, Ossie Lloyd, Florence Williams, Erma Strong, Lennye Thompson Peagler, Mildred Cooper Peagler and Ola Crapps Gordon.

On February 1, 1947 the school building was destroyed by fire. A community meeting decided that the school should be rebuilt. One year from the date of the fire, the new building was completed. At the conclusion of the 1956-57 school year, Branch closed the school doors. The students were sent to Morton in the 1957-58 consolidation, leaving only the many good memories of the life and times of Branch Consolidated High School.

Bustin School

Bustin was located on the Hillsboro-Harperville Road, what is now called South Little River Road. It was a log building. Mrs. Inez Askin Sigrest, Mrs. Sallie Simmons, Florence Bickham, Miss Mattie Owen, Lizzie Butler, Miss M.T. Bennett, Miss Emma Owen, Miss F.M. Tiner and Miss Ella Faulkner were teachers.

Center School

In 1901 the teacher was Miss Ollie Milling and in 1908 Center had two teachers, O.D. Loper and J.H. Finley.

Choctaw Indian School

There was an Indian school in Scott County until the late 1920s. We have not been able to get a name and exact location of this school, but believe it was in the area of the Pine Bluff Baptist Church in the northeast part of Scott County.

Clarksburg School

Clarksburg was located on the Scott/Rankin County line, west of Morton. Springfield School was discontinued and incorporated into Clarksburg Consolidated School. Clarksburg was a Smith-Hughes School for grades 1 through 8. In 1921, Clarksburg had four teachers. They were Miss Ruth Lay, Miss May Cloud, Miss Eva Lindsey and Miss Mable Cochran. Clarksburg had 102 students enrolled in 1931. With the push to consolidate in 1939, Clarksburg was discontinued and the students were sent to Morton.

Clifton/Myers School

The first school in the Clifton Community was named Myers School. The building was a one-room log building that was used for school and church purposes. The exact date when this building was constructed is not known, but the deed records show that E.H. Haralson on Aug. 2, 1892 deeded by donation two acres of land to the trustees of Myers School for

Myers (Clifton) School 1906-07
Row 1: _, Claud Calhoun, Ruby Sessums, Sharp Sessums, Estelle Sessums, Audrey Sanderford. Row 2: Edgar Waggoner, Clarence McCraw, Annie Roland, Jim Hall, Bryant Roland, Wilson Sessions, Mat Lasseter, teacher: Loti Sessums, Agnes Bailey, Lessie McCraw, Leola Norton, Velma Roland. Row 3: Willie Neal Hall, Emma Bailey, Ola Sessums, Tressie Waggoner, Ellie Jeffcoats, Lydia Roland, Versie Roland, Ida Roland, Evans Waggoner. Row 4: - Noel, _, Braxton Sessions, Jasper Roland, Luther Session, Bob Jeffcoats, Izona Sims, Joe Roalnd, Sapence Waggoner.

school and church purposes. This land was the only site for the Myers and Clifton schools.

When the name of the school was changed to Clifton is not known. The 1908 teachers' list still has Myers School, but by 1921 it was listed as Clifton. According to Eley Calhoun, son of Cliff Calhoun, the first framed school building was built in 1911 or 1912. This structure consisted of one large room that was divided by a curtain which was used to accommodate two classes. Some years later additional classrooms, with an auditorium on the second floor. was added to the building.

Information from the Scott County Board of Education minutes show that Heatherly School was consolidated with Clifton July 19, 1921. This school was located on land owned by Floyd H. Lyle in the Heatherly Community. Clifton's first frame building was destroyed by fire during March 1925. Classes were held in the Clifton Baptist Church, the home of Grady Sessums and two tenant houses located on the Atley Calhoun farm for the remainder of the year. A new school was immediately rebuilt. It was a one-story framed building consisting of six classrooms, an auditorium and a chemical storage room, which was later extended to include a science laboratory.

In 1926, Balucta School was consolidated with Clifton. This school was located on what is known as the Balucta Road immediately north of the W.F. Lyle place. In 1927 the Four Mile School was consolidated with Clifton. At the time of consolidation, the Four Mile School was located where the church in the Sparksville Community is now located. The school was also used for church purposes. The first Four Mile School was located east of and across Shockaloe Creek. In order to provide an adequate campus for the additional enrollment resulting from the consolidations, the board of trustees purchased four acres of adjacent land from J.A. and Emma Calhoun on Nov. 15, 1927.

The second frame building, which was built in 1925, burned in June 1943. Again pupils attended classes in the Clifton Baptist Church and the teacher's home until a new building could be built. The third framed building and the last school building was built very similar to the building it replaced. This building was used until it was closed in 1957.

Before consolidation the pupils walked to school. As consolidation occurred, they were first transported in covered wagons known as a tallyho. Later trucks with wood bodies were the mode of transportation. Buses with steel bodies replaced the wood bodied buses.

In addition to serving as the educational center of the community. the school was the center for social and political activities. These activities included fiddlers contests, basketball and softball games and speeches by politicians. Other school related remembrances include the wood-burning stoves, bringing in wood for the next day, going into the woods behind the church to cut and gather kindling for the wood heaters, the outside toilets, playing marbles, disagreements among boys that resulted in fights, marching by classes to the home of Billy Sessums and Angus Rigby's for a drink of water when the school pump was out of order, helping to push the school bus out of a bog, class picnics in the spring, eating lunch from a molasses bucket, going to school barefooted, wearing overalls to school, girls playing basketball in knee length bloomers, box suppers and cake walks.

Myers School's first teacher was Mrs. M.A. Noel. Others in the 1890s were J.C. Foster, Miss Dora Aycock, G.A. Park, Miss Lona Sigrest, Lilla Manning and M.B. Myers. In 1908, the teacher was R.L. Ware. M.L. Vance, Miss Pattie Stone, Miss Annie B. Chambers and Luther Harrell were the 1921 Clifton School teachers. The 1922-23 school year teachers were Eunice Weems, Peter Bennett, Myrtle Mapp, Luther Harrell and Gladys Burns. Clifton had many wonderful teachers through the years that served the school well.

Mrs. Lela Aycock Noel provided information in regard to a school that was operated in the Clifton Community. She stated that there was once a school on the road that intersects the Sparksville Road at the home of Mr. and Mrs. Talmadge Reeves. It was a one-room school. The last year of operation was probably the school year 1913-14. The last teacher was Miss Drucie Gilbert and the students were Fred Aycock, Homer Aycock, Lela Aycock, Otho Neal Aycock, Rob Aycock, Irvin Harvey, Otho Harvey, Tony Harvey, Margaret Miller and O.B. Sullivan.

Coffeebogue School

The teacher in 1878 was S.A. Burnett and Miss Lou Holmes in 1901.

Contrell School

The 1901 teacher was Miss Edna Moore. Contrell was located in the northwest part of Scott County.

Cooperville School

Cooperville was located in the southwest corner of Scott County. It was consolidated with Morton. Cicero Wesley donated the land for the one teacher school. Some of the teachers were Mr. Marion Palmer, Mr. H.W. Bradshaw and Miss Kate May.

County Line

County Line was located in northeast Scott County near Newton County. Miss Ada McDill was the teacher in 1901 and Miss Trudie Wilson was there in 1908.

Damascus School

Damascus was located in northeast Scott County, between Sebastopol and Walnut Grove. In 1916 Damascus provided an education for only grades 1 through 8. After completing these grades the students were sent to Sebastopol to finish their studies. In 1955, Damascus consolidated with Sebastopol, closing their school. In 1873 G.A. Park was their teacher. In 1901, D.S. Stewart and Miss Annie Lack were the teachers and in 1908, G.M. Golden and D.S. Stewart were the teachers.

Davis School

Teacher was Miss Gena Smith in 1908.

Dennis School

Dennis was located a few miles northwest of Lake. It was the first school to consolidate with Goodhope.

Ephesus School

Ephesus School was built around 1905 or 1907. It was located across from the present Ephesus Church. The first building was two-story. It had one classroom upstairs and two downstairs. There was a school bell to signal class changes. This bell was moved to the Ringgold School when Ephesus was consolidated with it. There was a well on the grounds to provide water and a cleared playground for basketball and other activities. There was a school wagon that provided transportation for the ones that lived a ways from the school. In 1915, the student body numbered 100. The school was destroyed by fire in 1918 or 1919. That school year was completed in the church and a new building was ready the following fall. It was a three-room single story building that was used until 1929. The parents had to build a desk for each of their children to replace the ones that burned.

Teachers at Ephesus were Annie Johnson, Bulah Johnson, Annie Lack, Ula Gainey, Cooper Walters, Cage Madden, Hubert Majors, Lloyd Clark, Nattie Walters, Bessie Stone, Jewell Hunt, Eural Guthrie, Annie Gardner, Thelma Lang and a Mrs. Hutchinson. Gus Johnson and J.C. Johnson were principals.

Equity School

Teacher was Miss Odessa Townsend in 1908.

Felder School

Teacher was R.Q. Kincaid in 1908.

Ephesus School student body, 1915. This school was located behind D.W. Saxon's new home just off Hwy. 21, north of Forest. It had a two-story building and went only to the ninth grade. The students were from L-R, first row: Hubert Brukes, Gardner Sr., Pete Harrison, Dovie Saxon, Luther Bounds, Edgar Harrison, Jimmy Riser, Arthur Harrison, Hugh Graham, Bryant, Aubrey Walters, Franklin Walters, McKenny Lashley, Hunt Walters, Floyd Massey, Ray Walls, Fate Riser, Lester. Second row: Hattie Bryant Cole, Clennie Harrison Lang, Jewel Wolf Smith, Lillie Burkes Shannon, Onie Patrick Madden, Effie __ Riser, Effie Riser Harrison, Albie Wynn Jolly, Tressie Gardner Matthews, Lalla Burkes Massey, Tressie Burkes McDill, Mattye Patrick Bishop, Estell Walker Bryant, Fern Huff, Chloe Neal Walters, Thelma Lang Harrison, Birdie Gardner Griffin, Blanche Pace. Third row: Mattie Stone, Duffie Neal Kilgore, Homer Wynn, Bernard Graham, Nonnie Patrick, Gertrude Gill Saxon, Allie Gorday, Veta Huff, Talver Walls, Lemmie J. Lang, Alvin Patrick, unidentified, Lee Wynn, Lavada Summers Creel, Nettie Walters, Stella May Walls, Fannie B. Culpepper, Mary Patrick, Margie Bell Riser. Fourth row: Decell Burkes Ellis, Francis Harrison, Flora Saxon McDill, Nannie Lou Lang Wolf, Bessie Gardner Walters, Guss Johnson, teacher; Alto Graham, Mrs. Johnson, teacher; Jewel Harrison, Beulah Johnson Reynolds, teacher; Ena Riser Harrison, Ellen Pace Guthrie, Ruby Wolf, Florence Wolf Williams, Jewel Gardner Thomas and Elois Ellis Warren. Fifth row: Weldon Harrison, Hubert Gardner, Jim, Levern Graham, Grady Riser, Walter Judge, Moody Huff, Manuel Lang, Eula Myers, Audrey Bryant Holifield, Daisy Judge , Sylvester Summers McNeal, Everett Patrick. Sixth row: Monroe Bounds, Make Dennis, Clois Riser, Annie Bell Lashley, Riser, Weldon Judge, Opal Wolf Hartman, Levera Patrick Bounds, Wade Ellis, Bill Summers.

1913 Girls' Basketball Team

1926 Boys' Basketball Team Row 1: Milton Wicker, John Epting, Rufus Howell. James Singleton. Row 2: Seaborn Ormond, John Singleton. Row 3: Seth Harris. Teddy Jones, Hilton Wicker. Standing is Coach Doss Fulton.

1926 Girls' Basketball Team L-R: Lois Anderson, Bessie Howell, Lola Holloman. Louise Parker, Ruth Wicker, Lois Wicker, Lillie Mae Boyles and Lila Harris. Center back is Coach Doss Fulton.

Forest Academy

Forest was established in 1866. The principal was D.W. Hamiter and the assistant was Miss N.C. Gresham.

Forest Female Academy

In 1869 the Forest Female Academy was established. The land was donated by Sylvester Pearls. The school was built of hune logs with a stick and mud chimney, which was seldom used. Miss Nannie Crenshaw was the first teacher and president.

The school was only open for about three months in the summer. Along with reading, writing, arithmetic, grammar and spelling, strict manners and morals were taught. Their daily practice was required. Some of the girls who attended this school made very useful and helpful women, such as teachers, musicians and milliners.

Forest High School

The first school in Forest was a two-room building, 30 by 40 feet. It had a few windows and a small front door. At the back of the building was a mud and stick fireplace. At this time the school term was four months. This building was located near where Lackey Convalescent Home is today. This school was probably built before the town was settled and was also used for religious services.

There was an unfinished school building in Forest during the Civil War. Early in the 1900s, there was a private school on the west side of town with a $2.00 a month tuition fee.

The second public school was a three-story frame building. When this building burned in 1917 the third building was constructed. It was a three-story brick building with a gymnasium on the west end and an auditorium on the east end. In 1933, this building was virtually destroyed when the boiler exploded. A new building was erected on the same location and was used until 1966. In 1955-56 the elementary school was built and is still in use today. In 1959 a new athletic field was built and is known as L.O. Atkins Field. In 1965-66, the new Forest High School was constructed beside the elementary school on Cleveland Street.

As early as 1913, sports were included in the activities with a girls basketball team. The girls dressed in bloomers that some of the townsfolk thought were indecent, but under Coach Bartly Fikes, they had one win after another to become the 1913 "Dixie" champs. Their basketball court was on the school yard, back of the present City Hall.

The first football team was organized in 1925. The coach was Doss Fulton, even though he had never played football. During this first year, a story in the *News Register* probably gave the Forest football team the "Bearcats" nickname. Their football field was in the fork of Hillsboro Street and Banks Street. In 1930, under Coach R.A. "Pop" Hartness, the undefeated Forest High School football team played Picayune for the South Mississippi Championship. At the end of five quarters, the score was still tied 0-0. The officials decided on a coin toss to determine the winner. Heads for Forest and tails for Picayune and tails it was. The Forest football teams have been champions many times through the years. In 1992, 1993 and 1999 under Head Coach Jack French, they were state champions.

The basketball teams also have been champions and for too many years to count, the Forest band was rated all-superior. The first band was organized in 1936. H.E. Cagle was the first band director. The first yearbook was published in 1943. A contest was held to decide on a name, the winning title was the *Rambler*, suggesting the idea of rambling through the school year. It was a paperback book of only about 12 pages. The editor was Joyce McKenzie.

The Forest Separate School has come a long way since the two-room log building with three large modern buildings to provide the students with an education that prepares them to be productive adults in the future.

Forest-Scott County Career & Technology Center

This school was established in 1973 to offer a variety of programs to prepare students for specific careers. In addition to teaching technical skills, good work habits and pride in work, respect for authority is also instilled in students. The land for the Vocational Center was provided by the Forest School District. An average of 340 students are in attendance each year.

Fork Line School

Fork Line had 27 students in 1931, these students had Pulaski addresses. Teachers: C.M. Chisholm, 1891; Alice Searcy, 1892; W.R. Madden, 1908; Miss Eunice Franklin and Miss Zola Miles, 1921.

Forest School 1928-29, 3rd and 4th Grades Miss Laura Filgo, teacher L-R, first row: Louise Windham, Dinah Singleton, Louis Singleton, _, Leona Smith, Elcie May Riser, Mildred Heflen, Peggy Gibson, Edwina Huff, Evelyn Cooper, Frances McDill, _, Alice Mosely, _, _. Second row: Boots Brown, - Border, Arnold Askin, Willie Lawrence Sawyer, Oscar Sherman, Jack Hopper, George Wynn, Titus Mapp, _, - Bryant, Mildred Looper, Johnnie Hazel Herron, Charlene Smith. Third row, three boys sitting on left side: Milton -, Willie Weems, Leon Border. Third row, standing: Kenny Weems, Bill Barner, - Rester, - Windham, - Weems, James Bassett, Wilford Wimset.

Four Mile School, 1919-20 Row 1: Willo Jones, Bertha Sullivan, Ruby Simmons, Ollie Sullivan, Mavis Simmons, Lloyd Sullivan, Robert Lovett, Jack Sanders, James Jones. Row 2: Clara Mae Jones, Glenn Sullivan, Bulah Mae Sparks, Eunice Alford, teacher; Wyatt Sullivan, Leon "Bill" Sparks, Henry Simmons, O.B. Sullivan, Laverne Tadlock.

Forkville School

On August 6, 1917 a bond issue of $2,500.00 was passed to provide the students with a better facility with a library and modern equipment. Forkville offered classes for 1st through 11th grades, being a three-year high school. The 1901 teacher's list names Miss Josie Hinkle as the teacher. Mrs. Virgie James was the 1908 teacher. By 1921 Forkville had four teachers: H.C. Anderson, Miss Dorothy Bassett, Miss Susie Bennett and a Miss Stegall. In 1931 Forkville had 190 students enrolled. In 1955 Forkville was consolidated with Morton.

Four Mile School

Four Mile Special School, also known as Sparksville, was located on the Sparksville-Hillsboro Road. It moved into the Mt. Zion Methodist Church. Some families who attended were Bustin, Lovett, Jones, Sullivan and Simmons. Some teachers were Ellen Williams, 1896; Miss Ola Askin, 1897 and 1908; Miss Lula Andrews, 1901 and Miss Olive Watson, 1921. Other teachers were Eunice Alford, Estelle Guthrie, Joe H. Roland, Homer

Aycock, Huel Donald, Elsie Jones, Hattie Kincaid, Lena Miles, Morris Milner, Effie Osborn, Lillie Mae Sessums, Vadie Shannon, Clara Sigrest, Marie Smith Sparks and Thelma Kelly. Four Mile was consolidated with Clifton in 1927. Board members of Four Mile were M.A. "Moaton Arnold" Askin, Daughton Jones, Toll Sullivan, G.D. Simmons and Jim Tadlock.

Frog Pond School

Frog Pond was incorporated into Sebastopol in 1905.

Garner School

Teachers: P.K. Moncrief, 1875; S. McCormick, 1881 and Miss Eula Gainey, 1908.

Gatewood School

Teacher was R.E.L. Kelly in 1908

Golden School

The Golden School stood on a black-jack covered hill in the northern edge of Scott County. It was about two miles northeast of Damascus. It was established about 1877. The Lang family attended this school. In 1883, Golden had two teachers, Paul Jones and Millie Sharp. C.S. Welsh was the teacher in 1891.

Good Hope School

A little one-room school called Good Hope was first in the corner where Walter Judge's pond is now. The teachers were Pearl and Lois Nichols, sisters. Eula Warren taught there too; she was a sister to Alice Usry.

There was a one-room school called Dennis, where Charlie Dennis' place was. Mr. Stead, Iwona Husband and Effie Brazel taught there.

There was also a one-room school called Usry, back of the Ezra May place. Around 1907 the Good Hope and Usry schools moved where we all went to school. It was a three-room school. Dennis was the first to consolidate with Good Hope. They beat Salem so much playing ball, they consolidated. There was an old Dummy Line that ran through the woods from Salem. All the children walked down it to school. Ethel Weger was a teacher. She stayed with the Lewis family, so she walked with the children.

Some of the teachers were Maggie and Fate Cloud (brother and sister), C.R. Johnson, better known as "Rip;" Maurice Hayes and Lawrence Ware. Lawrence's child burned to death while he was teaching there. Of course most of us can remember Mrs. Davis, Ora Robinson and Mrs. Rush. Irma Singleton taught there in 1919. She said she walked from Noblin Hill to Good Hope. One day a boy put a black snake on her. She ran all the way home. She said it was probably J.B. Usry. He was the most mischievous boy in school, but had such a sweet way until you would love him to death!

Ezra May drove a wagon to school and Eliza Waltman drove a wagon. Wesley can remember November 11, 1918 when WWI was over. They were in the wagon about a half-mile from school when the DuBois Mill and the Planer Mill started blowing the siren and horn and blew them for about 30 minutes so everybody would know "The War was Over!"

Bob Hunt taught there 16 years. The first year he taught, the school burned. Then it was built back with an auditorium and four rooms, with one on each end. Bob Hunt was supervisor in Beat 1 at that time. The supervisors would have a board meeting the first Monday of every month. He would leave Mrs. Rush in charge. That was always the "Boy's Day!" One Monday they knocked the stove pipe down, leaving one pipe going from one room to the other. They took Perry Davis' crutch and knocked it through into Mrs. Rush's room; she shot out of there like a cannon! One Monday all the boys went rabbit hunting. They made it up that no one would take a whipping. All chickened out but Frank Davis, so he was sent home. Mrs. Davis brought him back and made him stand up and apologize.

They just had an 8th grade school for many years. Then they went to the 11th grade and finally in 1935 went to the 12th grade. The last school year was 1956. In 1957, Floyd Hollingsworth took his school bus and others took cars and 70 students went to Ringgold and the rest went to Lake. *Submitted by Virginia May Cook.*

Graham School

Teacher was G.N. Johnson in 1908.

Grange Hall Line School

The 1879 teacher was Annie Lloyd, M.E. Owen was the 1880 teacher, T.D. Graham was the 1881 teacher and Miss Kate Denson was teacher in 1901.

Harperville College ca. 1907

Agriculture High School

Agriculture High School 1919

Green College School

This was an elementary school located off Highway 21 between the Pete Harrison home and the Allen Hegwood home. It opened around 1909. Ula Gainey, Carrie Whaltey and Bert Eady were some of the teachers.

Haley School

Haley was located north of the Clifton area. Teacher: Miss Nettie Eley, 1908. Miss Eley was from Harperville.

Harmony School

Harmony was located in the southeast part of Scott County. Teachers: A.B. Presberry, 1880; W.R. Foster and Miss Pearl Fergerson, 1908; A.L. Weems, Mrs. Mary L. Wilkins and Mrs. O.T. Gilbert, 1921.

Harperville

Education in Harperville has carried many different names through the years. W.R. Chambers came to Scott County along with two other teachers, Mr. Cox and Mr. Galloway and established the Chambers Business College in 1874. Chambers Business College was located in the upstairs of the school. It was also called the Stonewall Jackson Institute for a short while. In 1878, Capt. Charles A. Huddleston came and was made president of the school. Capt. Huddleston was a Confederate solider and a graduate of Emery University. Early in his administration the school began to operate as Harperville College. G.C. Harper, Dr. H.H. Haralson, C.B. Hadden, Dr. R.B. Austin and R.H. Campbell made up the first Board of Trustees.

In 1879, Harperville College was purchased by Professor Huddleston and Dr. F.M. Hunt of Griffin, GA. Under their direction the Harperville Collegiate Institute was chartered in 1881. The collegé grew into one of the most excellent schools of higher learning, the second best in the state. It was coeducational and offered military and religious studies. The first class graduated in 1883. They were F.W. Woodly, Kate Harper, Lizzie Butler, Helen Graham, Hattie Miles and Sue Beaman. Students could get six years of education at Harperville College, three preparatory and three college. Students who successfully completed the requirements could earn a bachelor of science degree. Tuition ranged from $9.00 to $12.00 per term. Laundry was 25 cents a week, with a 12 piece limit. Board was $8.00 to $10.00 a month for a furnished room. Students had to provide their own toilet articles, towels, lamps and oil.

The school burned in 1904, but with the help of former students, a new two-story building was constructed on the six acre campus. It cost approximately $4,700.00. In 1913 the Scott County Agricultural High School took over the education facilities in Harperville. This was a boarding school for grades 9 through 12. It was considered one of the best schools in the state. The Agricultural High School operated for 17 years. In July 1928, a bond for $5,000.00 was issued to give Harperville the honor of having the first Smith-Hughes School in the county. Opening in 1930, it continued until 1936-37 when the public school took over the building. Now it was known as Harperville High School. Harperville continued to educate its children until 1964, when it graduated its last seniors. The following year, Harperville merged with Ringgold into the new school called Scott Central.

Some of Harperville's teachers were Miss C.E. Hightower and J.W. Turner, 1873; A.L. Summers and Mrs. T. Torchenburger, 1874; C.A. Huddleston, W.S. Huddleston and Miss Lizzie Butler, 1901; C.A. Huddleston, H.A. Stovall, P.M. Jones and Miss Marion Huddleston, 1908. Two sets of teachers are named for the 1921 school year. Harperville Consolidated School (for grades 1 through 8): Mr. and Mrs. O.L. Stewart, Miss Emma Hannah and Miss Annie Lee Lewis. The Harperville Agricultural High School (for grades 9 through 12): J.B. Edwards, Charles A. Huddleston, J.L. French, R.P. White, C.A.

Lowe, Miss Katie Mae Dear, Miss Clair Stedman and Miss Eula Dampeer.

Harrison School

Harrison was located east of Homewood. It provided an education for the Harrison, Gatewood, Wicker and Johnson children. Lowery Harrison provided the land for the school to be built on and he ran the school bus. He and his wife, Allie, boarded the teacher also. In 1931 there were 23 students attending school at Harrison. Some of the teachers were Rossie Hawkins, Herman Anderson, Eunice Franklin and Wydell Golden.

Harvey School

Harvey was located in front of the present Oak Grove Baptist Church on the Lake-Norris Road. It was named for the Harvey family that lived in the area. This was a very nice one teacher school, with double desks and a stove in the middle for heat. The boys sat on one side of the school and the girls on the other. A spring outside provided water for the children. The children carried their lunches to school. Harvey School provided a book-case full of books for the children to read. They taught classes 1st through 8th grades; to finish the students had to go to a boarding school. Some of Harvey's teachers were R.E.L. Kelly, Miss Tennie Day, Miss Lee Boozer, Miss Ola Boozer, Mrs. R.L. Thompson and Mrs. Bertie Thompson. Harvey School closed in the early 1920s. Mrs. Pennye Merle Fikes Gatewood attended this school.

Heatherly School

Heatherly School was on land owned by Floyd H. Lyle. It was consolidated with Clifton in 1921. Some of the teachers were Ethel Barbour, Jewell Henkel, Minnie Holliday and Hattie Stone.

High Hill School

One of the oldest schools in Scott County was located at Norris, a prosperous village thickly settled and made up of well-to-do farmers who always had plenty to eat and nice comfortable homes.

High Hill School was established about 1856 by leading citizens interested in the education of their children. The school was located at the top of a high hill were High Hill Methodist Church is presently located. Patrons of the school paid a sum for each child sent to this private school. Teachers were paid $12.00 to $15.00 per month plus board. Ms. Robertson was one of the first teachers. Some of the early students were Nemiah and William Harvey, J.L. McCrory. Later in the early 1900s some students were George Gatewood, Ep Wilkerson, Nettie and Eddie Crout. One of the teachers around 1910 was Ms. Eris Crudup, who was well liked by the students. She road a buggy to school. Charlie Sanders took children to school by wagon to help increase attendance.

Three other schools in the area were Harvey School located on Lake Norris Road near Oak Grove Baptist Church; Equity School located on Lake Homewood Road on the hill above the Youngblood residence and Harmony School located on Mudline Road near the present landfill site. These schools all were consolidated into High Hill School in the early 1900s.

High Hill School was relocated about 1914 to Highway 501 where the present Community Center is located. This school went through the 11th grade. Students were then bused to Lake some years and to Forest other years. The first school at the new site was a two-story building which was torn down and the last building was erected at the same site in 1924. High Hill operated through the 11th grade during most of the 1920s. It then operated through the 8th grade until 1949.

Most of the present residents of Norris attended High Hill School. Some of the teachers during the later years were Robert Weems, Mack Weems, Waddy Weems, Flora Beaty, Neal Putnam, Delia Hollingsworth, Perry Davis, Mary Lou Wilkerson, Mabel Carr, Lenora Fikes, Pennye Merle Gatewood, Vera Palmer, Fannie Fikes, S.T. Roebuck, Grace White, Eloise Sansing, Mary Houston.

Row 1: _, Lucy Lyle, Troy Lyle, Mary Lyle. Row 2: Annie Bowman, _, Justus Myers, Waller Myers, Morris Milner, Sim Lyle. Row 3: Jemel Henkel, teacher, Fannie Mae Bowman, _, Lyle Milner, Reese Bowman, Zebb Milner, Clyde Myers, _.

Harvey School 1917-18
Front row: Jim Harvey, Atley Durr, Shelby Durr, James Halbert, Mildred Halbert, Pennye Merle Fikes (Gatewood). Second row: Fayrene Durr, Delene Harvey, Lozelle Halbert, William Price, Crout Halbert, Winston Halbert, Lula Belle Harvey, Thelma Harvey. Third row: Barber Harvey, Verassie Warren, Allie Kate Price, Gladys Warren, Cleat Harvey, Howard Fikes, Homer Durr, Jewell Halbert, Geneva Harvey. Standing in door, teacher Miss Lilla Carr; standing in back, Alfred Usry.

High Hill School

Ms. Pennye Merle Gatewood gave me most of the history written about High Hill School which she and I both attended and she was one of my teachers at High Hill School.

Hillsboro Academy

Before the Civil War, Hillsboro was the county seat. It also claimed the distinction of having one of the finest academies in the county. The academy was established by citizens of the community who had it built with slave labor in 1859. It was incorporated by the state of Mississippi in the county of Scott with 15 trustees to make regulations for the school.

These trustees had the power of electing and displacing teachers at will. Some of the trustees were the following: John K. Clower, William Graham, W.W. Lowery and Dr. Abraham. The school also received help through the Peabody Fund.

The students were offered all the usual subjects taught in academies of that time: reading, writing, arithmetic, grammar, geography and spelling. In addition they were given lessons in strict manners and morals.

Hillsboro School

Before the Civil War, Hillsboro was the county seat of Scott County and it was a growing town. When Sherman's troops came through during the war, the school was burned along with most everything else in town. In 1880 the old courthouse was being used for the school. In 1906, Miss Annie Antley and Miss Hattie Mae Uletchley were the teachers. They boarded at the home of Mr. and Mrs. Will Russell. The Russells' 4-year-old son, Duff, was allowed to attend school that year so the school would have enough students to qualify to keep two teachers. Since 1913, Hillsboro has had a graded consolidated school. It offered all the standard subjects for grades 1 through 8. A new two-story school was built in 1918 in a pine grove on the south side of town. It cost $4,000.00 to build. The top floor was the auditorium with a stage and dressing rooms. The first floor consisted of four classrooms. Through the years as the schools were upgraded, the high school students were sent to Forest to complete their education. In 1931, Hillsboro had 171 students enrolled. The Hillsboro Elementary School was open until the late 1940s, when it was also consolidated with Forest and closed.

Miss Martha Russell worked several years in the Hillsboro School lunchroom. She prepared lunch for the whole school, often baking the same tea cakes she baked for her family. She worked several more years at Forest after the consolidation. Some of the teachers for Hillsboro were Mrs. M.F. Chandler and J.C. Foster, 1874; Mrs. M.O. Sims and Miss Annie Hederman, 1893; G.A. Park, principal and Miss Roberta Thompson, 1896; W.R. Hunt, Miss Ola Boozer and Miss Vadie Shannon, 1921; Miss Gurtrude Austin, R.A. Thorn, Mrs. W.O. Griffith and C.L. Beard, 1800s; R.L. (Lawrence) Ware, Jim Sparks, Lamar Rigby, Mr. and Mrs. Floyd Franklin, Mr. and Mrs. Roy Harmon, Mrs. Flora Scott, Mrs. Lillie Mae Aycock, Mrs. Ernest Simmons, Miss Annie Bell Chambers, Mrs. Winnie Waldrop, Miss Clara Noel and a Miss Gunn.

Homestead School

Homestead School, also called Stage, was located about seven miles southwest of Morton on the old Stegall place. The school was open from 1911 until the early 30s when it was consolidated with Morton. They had 35 to 40 students attending each year. In 1921 the teachers were Glover Clark, Mrs. Marie Clark and Miss Iris Clark. Burley Cooper also was a teacher. He was teaching when a storm blew the school away. Will Stegall donated wood from timber that was blown down to rebuild the school. The school building was torn down in 1950.

Homewood School

Homewood School was located about nine miles south of Forest. It was established in 1859. The one-room building was crude and small. A stick and dirt chimney took up the entire back of the room. Dr. Van Hendon, Dr. Hardner, Tom Melton, Jack Pryor and Joe Beaman helped organize the school. The usual subjects were taught here. At recess and the noon hour, the children played games. Homewood averaged 20 to 30 students per year. There were several buildings through the years, the last one built in 1927. It only offered grades 1 through 8, the high school was sent to Forest to finish their education. There were 192 students in Homewood School in 1931. At the end of school, Spring of 1956, the school was closed. Some of the teachers were Miss E. McClennechan, 1873-74; Mrs. E.M. Windham, 1875; C.C. Campbell, 1879; E.T. Melton, 1880; J.D. Davis, 1881; Hanice Walk, 1882; Miss Bettie Holmes and Miss Iola Askin, 1898; C.D. Risher and Miss Bessie Boyles, 1908; R.L. Edwards, Mrs. Flora Scott, Miss Ora Baker and Miss Edwards, 1921.

Independence School

Independence was located west of Pulaski in the area of the Independence Methodist Church. The teacher in 1881 was R. Franks. In 1901 W.H. Mize and A.E. Searcy were the teachers. In 1921 A.L. Davis, Miss Cleo Windham and Caughman were the teachers. In 1931 Independence had 131 students attending school.

Hillsboro School 1930
Row 1: Leon Bustin, Travis Chambers, Erskin Eure, Mason Sparks, Cedrick Horn Jr., Marvin Simmons, Margaret Myers, Jack Eady, Juanita King, Clarence Chambers, Marion Artis Jordan, Delois Bustin, Leona Bustin, Ernestine Carpenter, Emanuel Hatch, Floyd Burkes, Tom Glaze. Row 2: Lexie McMurry, Helen Tadlock, Johnny Harrell, Catherine Chambers, Lamar Russell, Mary Lee Warbington, Annabel Chambers, Frances Sparks, Miriam Tadlock, Flora Scott, Mae Sparks, Mrs. Slay, Juanita Eure, Mrs. Waldrip, W.D. Russell, Lexie Horn, Ellis Sparks, Rowe Britt Sparks, Marcus Roland. Row 3: Raymond Riser, Tucker Sparks, B.C. Freeman, McClain Hatch, Hilton Bustin, Dennis Eure, Ewart Simmons, Elvin Simmons, Elton Myers, Gilbert Chambers, Violet McClenahan, Nannie Ruth Slay, Winifred Scott, Peggy Harrell, Clotile Brogdon, Valda Roland, Mildred Horn, Helena Clower, James Howard Sparks. Row 4: Frances Horn, Elaine Warbington, Eva Dee Eady, John Henry Freeman, Virgil Dean, Buster Brogdon, B.T. McMurry, Etna Jean Carpenter, Myrtle Myers, Ima Lee Burkes, Wilbur Myrick, Snowdie Chambers. Row 5: Rex Eva Barber, Lewis Eure Jr., Louise Tadlock, Billy Joe Carpenter, J.C. Hatch, Herman Dean, Dallas Glaze, Gladys Horn, Wesley Burkes. Row 6: Annie Jean Glaze, Hazel Ruth Brogdon, Thelma Carpenter, Christine Chambers, Janice Eure, James Westal Simmons, George Gann Sparks, Minnie Lou Harrell, Gladys Myrick, Frances McClanahan, Dorothy Sparks, Neppie Bustin, Malcolm Burkes. Row 7: Bernard Burkes, Leroy Bustin, Marcus Eure, Ollie Henry Houston, Trudie McMurry, Mamie Glaze, Polly Carpenter, Charlene Hatch, Lexie Warbington.

Hillsboro School 1909
Row 1: Earl Chambers, Joe Smith, Vinton Chambers, Martin Stallings, Roy Harvey, Ozie Jones, Myrtie Park, Maggie Clower, John Chambers. Row 2: Vera Jones, Alita Rowe, Bryant Clower, Mollie B. Graham, Mr. Hendricks, Odie Russell, Verna Park, Tressie Chambers, Luther Bounds, John Sim Clower. Row 3: Martha Russell, Willie Lay, Eddie Jones, Merle Rowe, Elsie Simmons, Earl Rowe, Jewel Eure, Lela Bounds, Otis Eure, Mary Russell, Louie Jones, Mary Belle Sigrest. Row 4: Clyde Lay, Hunter Bustin, Clois Park, Lonnie Eure, Claud Park, Willie Chambers.

Graduating Class of 1938, Homewood High School
Front Row: Polly Thornton, Buelah Bell Wicker, Cornelia Wicker, Mildred Wardell, Mildred Horsely, Georgia Mae Craig. Back Row: Dara Davis, teacher; Lucien Foreman, Will Harrison, Marzelle Stokes, Royce Windham.

Hygiene Class at Homewood High School ca. 1936
First row: Buelah Bell Wicker, Vera Craig, Cornelia Wicker, Mildred Wardell, Evelyn Morehead, Vermiel Johns. Second row: Mary Neal Wardell, Lucille Craig, Zilphia Boyles, Elna Hannah, Georgia Mae Craig, Hazel Wicker, Sue Wicker, Audrey Brown, teacher. Third row: Mattie Beth Barnes, Peggy Black, Mavis Stokes, Alma Pryor, Marium Barnes, Lora Black, Mildred Horsley. Back row: Mae Neal Tadlock, Iva Craig, Sue Barnes, Cornelia Barnes, Cornelia Boyles, Effie Bruce, Marie Tadlock, Clare Boyles.

Homewood School Classes ca. 1926
First row: Iva Craig, _, _, Walter Tadlock, Mildred Wardell, Zilphia Boyles, - Boozer, Marium Barnes, May Neal Tadlock, Sue Barnes, Cornelia Boyles, Mattie Beth Barnes, Georgia Mae Craig, Clara Moore Windham, John S. Crosser, Alma Pryor. Second row: Tom Noblin, Marzelle Stokes, Billy Barnes, _, _, Clara Boyles, _, Cornelia Barnes, Ed Lane, teacher; - Burns, teacher; _, teacher; Royce Windham, _, Buck Craig, _. Third row: Lottie Bell Herron, Mae Bell Moore, Bertha Mae Younce, Burnice Wardell, Ruth Tadlock, Pat Boyles, - Barnes, _, Ester Tadlock (in front of post), _, Ruth Windham, Jessie Mahaffie, _, (face behind person), _, Roger Pryor. Fourth row: _, _, - Craig, - Herron, Lucille Windham, Clara Tadlock, - Craig, H.M. Foreman (at post), Martha Pryor (at post), - Herron, Clemmie Tadlock, - Pryor, - Craig, _, _ (with heads together), - Boyles, - Barnes, -Cooper (behind Barnes), Walter Foreman, - Craig, _, _. Fifth row: - Boyles, _, - Craig, - Herron, Lucille Windham, - Tadlock, - Craig, - Foreman (next to post), Martha Pryor (next to post), - Herron, Clemmie Tadlock, Mozelle Craig, - Boyles, - Cooper, - Craig, _. Back row: Waldo Pryor, Clay Noblin, _, _, - Craig, _, Eady Windham, - Boyles (by post), Bob Dan Moore (by post), Sheely Barnes (with basketball), _, Mize Windham, Woodard Tadlock, _, - Boyles.

Keeton School 1928-29
L-R, front row: Hurlie Owens, Frances Jones, Virgie Ruth Jones, Lula Belle Jones, Elmer Horrell, Walter Owens, Ray Chestnut, Doris Jones, Lorris Smith, K.B. Lum. Second row: Winnie Lum, Maggie Dee Jones, Loy Jones, Mary B. Chestnut, Retha Bishop, Connie Lum, Lamar Massey, Albert Jones, Marion Smith, Catherine Horrell. Third row: Mrs. Carrie Horrell, teacher; Irene Keeton, Grace Jones, Raphael Bennett, J.T. Jones, Jimmy Bishop, Nat Chestnut, Jack Jones, Miss Bertha Boyles, teacher.

Judge School

This school was built and operated as a private school. It was located west of the Pete Harrison place on Highway 21 north of Forest. It only lasted about four years.

Kalem School

Kalem/Concord had 110 students in 1931. Teachers: Elbert Gainey, 1908; E.B. Guthrie, Mrs. Guthrie and Miss Bessie Cooper, 1921. Also Mr. and Mrs. D.T. Measells, Mrs. Maggie Myers and Lucille Eichelberger. The school was a large wood frame building. It consolidated with Morton in 1929. The Kalem Methodist Church met in the Concord School until they could get their church built. It was about 100 yards from the school.

Keeton School

Keeton was located in a community known as Frog Town, northeast of Pulaski. Keeton was established around 1893. The first school bus was not a bus at all, it was a covered wagon. Mrs. Grace Jones Faulkner said her grandpa (Thomas N. Jones) drove this wagon and picked the kids up. Keeton's grades 1 through 8 were sent to Pulaski and the high school to Kalem for one year. Peek Jones drove the bus that carried the Keeton students to Kalem. The next year, they were all sent to Morton. Some of the teachers were Pattie Robertson, 1893; Nelie Miles, 1894; Miss C.A. Miles, 1895; Zola Saunders, 1896; P.M. Jones, 1897; John D. Davis, 1898; Miss Florence Hurst, 1901; W.J. Smith, 1908; Miss Ruby Morehead, 1918; W.J. Smith and Mrs. Ida Murphy Tait (Tate?), 1921.

Lake School

The first Lake School was built by a carpenter named Chester. It was built with used lumber that was salvaged from the railroad shops destroyed by Sherman's troops. A small one-room school, it was located about where the Methodist parsonage is. This building was also used for church services. The bell used for the school and church had been on a train engine that was destroyed in Sherman's raid.

The second school was a two-story wood frame building and was used until WWI, when it was torn down. The first graduating class was in 1913 when Corrie Lee McKenzie, Viva E. Brooks and Eva Street, dressed in long white dresses and carrying bouquets of flowers, received their diplomas.

Lake High School Football Team 1924
Front row: Stanley Youngblood, Mark Rape, Howard Fikes, Preston Ware, Ernest Gould, Harold Monroe, Loyce Davis. Back row: Troy Morgan, Frank Cox, Frank Brooks, Travis Hollingsworth, Edward Mabry, Cleon McClenahan, Taylor McClenahan, Frank Gibbs, J.D. Harris, Elmer Freeman, Loomis Monroe.

Lake High Bus

The third school was a three-story brick building. It had no running water. The top floor was the auditorium and the two other floors were classrooms. On April 1, 1937 this school was completely destroyed by fire. Lake's first gym was built as a WPA project in 1934. The front part of it was the lunchroom. Another WPA project paid the lunchroom ladies to can vegetables that the parents brought in from their gardens. The students were given credit for the vegetables their parents provided. They could trade home canned food for lunches. Before the days of school lunchrooms, students brought baked sweet potatoes, biscuits and molasses cookies in a lard or syrup bucket for their lunches. Some years school began with half days because many students had to pick cotton. During the depression, some of the teachers were offered land as their pay. The land was valued at 50 cents an acre.

About 1932, the football coach, C.C. McClenahan wanted new uniforms for the team. One student suggested green and white, as that had been the colors of the last school they attended. Until this time the Lake School colors were purple and gold. The diplomas were encased in purple and gold until 1932. The 1927 boys basketball team, with a 14-2 record, won the county championship. The coach was Billy Moore. Under Coach Granville Freeman, the football team was Cherokee Conference champs for six years with a 59-1 record. This being the years 1973 through 1978. The 1974 team was undefeated, untied and unscored on with a 12-0 record. Lake Attendance Center averages 450 students a year and the middle school has approximately 300 students.

Lang Line School

Lang Line was about one mile south of the center of Sebastopol. It was located in front of Walter McCann's home. A.M. Woods was the teacher in 1901. When the Sebastopol School was built in 1905, Lang Line School was closed and combined with it.

Langs Mill School

This school was located off the Forest-Piketon Road. The name Langs Mill still identifies a voting precinct. Some of the teachers boarded in the home of Will and Lou Russell. Some families who attended were Lang, Russell, Gardner, Graham, Hall and Myers.

Lawrence Business College

The Lawrence Business College was located at Harperville. Immediately following the War Between the States, Harperville had one of the best schools in the county. In 1869, the Lawrence Business College was established with E.B. Lawrence, a graduate of Bryant and Stratton College, as president and W.R. Butler as vice-president and dean of the science department. This being one year before the public school system, the school supplied a long felt need. Mr. Lawrence was sent by the government under the Peabody Fund, which at this time was being granted to only one other school in the county, Hillsboro.

All boarding students were in private homes with the boys in the home of Mose Lack and the girls in the home of G.C. Harper. Board was $15.00 per month and a scholarship cost $60.00.

At this time the school building was very crude. It was long and straight with only one-story. However, it had several rooms. The subjects taught were very unusual, such as Latin, French, German and bookkeeping. These were quite different from the subjects taught in the private schools and academies.

Liberty School

Teachers: J.F. Martin, 1881; S.C. Gordon, 1891; P.P. Hatch, 1892; R.E. Kelly and Miss Lillia Shepherd, 1921. Consolidated with Branch in 1929.

Lillian School

The teacher in 1891 was __Tolbert; Miss Effie Moore was the 1901 teacher; and Miss Nona Moore was the teacher in 1908.

Line Creek School

Line Creek was located about eight miles northwest of Morton. It was established in 1866 with Kinsy Winstead donating the land to build it on. Some of the first teachers who taught there were Miss Nancy Cavner and Mr. Shrumpherd. Miss Mollie Lloyd was the teacher in 1873. In 1908 it was Miss Eva Nordan and Miss Allie Mangum.

Line Prairie School

Miss Marie Smith was the teacher in 1921. Line Prairie consolidated with Branch in 1929.

Lone Star School

Lone Star, also called Sulphur Springs, was located on the Scott/Newton County line, about 15 miles northeast of Forest. In 1924 a building was erected at the cost of $4,500.00 and again in 1933 some improvements were made at the cost of $2,800.00. Teachers: T.M. Crocket, 1880; T.L. Denson, 1883; A.G. Pettey, 1891-92; Miss May Cloud, 1908 and Nick Johnson, 1921. In 1931 Lone Star had 148 students and in 1955 it consolidated with Sebastopol.

Longview School

This school was located northwest of Morton. The 1874 teacher was L.T. Edmonds and the 1908 teacher was T.M. Peagler.
Lovett School

Lovett was located south of Forest near the Hopewell Baptist Church. Some teachers were A.E. Clark, 1882; B. Wilkins, 1891 and 1892 and Mrs. Rubye Bassett, 1921.

Lucy School

Teachers: Lucy Slay, 1892 and Miss Maggie Rigby, 1908.

Ludlow School

The town of Ludlow was established in 1847, it's not known exactly what year the school was organized. In 1873, Ludlow had two teachers: F.H. Lee and J.H. Grady. Most schools had only one teacher, Ludlow had to be a larger school to qualify for a second teacher. Ludlow High School began in the fall of 1901. This was a boarding school for grades 1 through 10. The school had a music department and offered the usual studies. The 1901 teacher's list names R.H. Pate as the only teacher. During the 1904-05 session, Ludlow had 95 students enrolled. The teachers for 1905-06 were Reverend Tom Tomlinson, principal; J.B. Pool and Miss Fannie Halbert. A dormitory consisting of 15 rooms was to be completed for this session. Tuition per month ranged from $1.50 for first through third grades, $2.00 for fourth and fifth grades, $2.50 for the sixth and seventh grades, $3.00 for the eighth and ninth grades and $3.50 for the 10th grade. Music education was an extra $3.00 a month. Board and a light with fuel was $6.00 a month. The teachers for 1908 were J.M. O'Briant (Bryant) and Miss Maggie Lee.

A frame building was constructed in 1917 at the cost of $1,120.00 on land provided by Mr. and Mrs. T.H. Lee for the price of $145.00. Ten years later, the community saw fit to improve the school. They issued bonds in the amount of $18,000.00 to erect and equip a brick school building. The son of Mr. and Mrs. T.H. Lee, Dr. H.O. Lee, donated six acres of land for the school, free of cost to the district. In 1931, Ludlow had 245 students enrolled in classes. In 1936-37, it was one of six accredited schools in Scott County. Ludlow was consolidated with Morton in 1957 and the doors of their school were closed. Some other Ludlow School teachers were J.A. McCoy, C. Black, F.H. McMurphy, Miss Katie McMurphy and Mary Foster in the 1800s; S.C. Wallace, Miss Lois Windham, Miss Myrtle Cater, Miss Corzell Anderson and a Miss Lee in 1921.

Lyle Line School

Teachers: L.B. Lyle, 1880; Miss Bettie Townsend, 1908; Miss Josie Smith and Shellie Bailey, 1921.

Malco School

Malco was located between Steele and Harperville in what is known as the Red Top Community. The school closed in the 1920s. O.D. Loper, L.O. McClendon and Mrs. Minnie McClendon were teachers here.

Many Roads School

Many Roads was located northeast of Forest. A family named Champion attended this school. In 1891 the teacher was T.A. Steele.

Marler School

Teacher was Miss Autense Liles in 1908

Midway School

Teachers: A.B. Bisley, 1880; Miss Euna Bates, 1901 and Mrs. Nola Rushing, 1908.

Morton Academy

The Morton Academy was located on what is now called "Tank Hill," the highest hill in a hilly community.

In 1847 the citizens of the community interested in the education of their children, met to organize a private school. J.J. Smith donated the land and immediately a schoolhouse was constructed. It was built in the early California style, with unplaned planks nailed in a vertical position. Benches of split logs were arranged along the walls on each side, facing the long stage that filled the whole back side. This stage was used for various activities, such as Thanksgiving and Christmas entertainment, concerts and spelling matches.

A few subjects were deemed essential for educating boys and girls, mainly the three "Rs" (Reading, 'Riting and 'Rithmetic). The Morton Academy offered grammar and the blue-back speller.

Morton Christian Academy

The Morton Christian Academy began in 1993 to offer high academics to students with individualized learning. The school also offers team sports and computer technology. In addition to academics, biblically based character building is taught and all students must be involved in a bible-based church with regular attendance.

Morton High School

Morton has provided an education for its children from as early as 1847, when the Morton Academy, a private school, was organized. In the

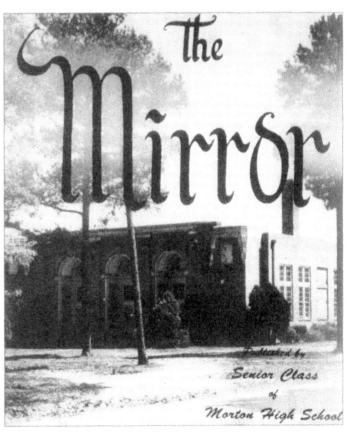

The Mirror

Morton Centennial Book it is made mention that the schools were shut down during the Civil War. The early school offered few advantages and few conveniences. The building and its furnishings were crude and uncomfortable, but most students who attended were eager to learn and learned rapidly.

In 1913-14, the first consolidation of schools began. There were three separate school districts in Scott County, one of which was Morton with 302 students. The school was on a 24 acre campus with two classroom buildings and 11 teachers. By the early 1930s, Cooperville, Independence, Kalem, Forkline, Pulaski, Keeton, Concord and Clarksburg consolidated with Morton to become the Morton Special Consolidated School. In 1931, a high school building was constructed. A scale model of this building was on exhibit at the 1933 World's Fair in Chicago. It drew nationwide attention in the Mississippi Exhibit as an example of our schools.

A bond issue for $50,000.00 was floated to construct a new high school, which was completed for the 1931-32 term. An elementary building was also constructed and lights were added to the football field in the 30s. In 1939, a principal's home was built by the National Youth Administration. They also built a brick canning plant in 1943. This building was later turned into a vocational shop building. Also in 1943, a WPA project built a new gym. The Panther Den started out as a lunchroom that was built in 1952. In 1955, Forkville School was consolidated with Morton and the Branch and Ludlow elementary schools came in 1957. A new elementary school and lunchroom was built in 1956.

Construction of new facilities continued through the decade of the 60s, with the construction of a new senior high building, vocational shop facilities, library and connecting covered walks for the elementary and junior high buildings. A new well lighted athletic field and a gymnasium with locker rooms were also added.

In 1934, Coach Hugh Lee's football team won the Middle Mississippi Regional Championship. From this team, Lonnie Tadlock and Teddy Sims were All-State players. The 1938-39 Middle and South Mississippi Championship winners were the girls basketball team under Coach Perry Davis. In the fall of 1939, a school band was organized under the leadership of F.E. Randle. This first band had 40 members. 1943 brought the first publication of a yearbook named *The Mirror*. The 1948-49 football team won the Region 6 play-off game against Byram 19-7 and they won the Region 5 and 6 play-off game beating Mozelle 33 to 13 but lost the South Mississippi Championship game to Magnolia by two points (14-12).

In the fall of 2000, Morton schools had a total of 1,652 students enrolled. Carrying on the tradition of over 150 years, Morton continues to work hard at providing its citizens the best education possible for their children.

Mount Carmel School

Teachers: Miss Mary Lack, 1894; Effie Moore, 1896 and Miss Johnnie Cloud, 1908.

Mount Pleasant Academy

Walter Roberts and his wife, Sara Jane Waters Roberts, gave two acres of land for the Mt. Pleasant Academy. The deed was recorded March 4, 1861 and names B. Hawkins, D.L. Waters and James S. Saunders as trustees. This land was in Section 29, Township 5, Range 7 which put it south of Pulaski.

Mount Vernon School

Mt. Vernon was located about five miles west of Forest at Raworth. The teacher in 1892 was T.J. Walters, Fannie Haley in January 1896 and M.R. Cooper in August 1896. In 1901 Miss Ella Faulkner was the teacher. This settlement was abandoned about 1911.

Mount Zion Free Public School

Mt. Zion was located south of Clifton, about halfway to Raworth. John S. Askin Sr. donated land in August 1891 to build a schoolhouse on. The school trustees in 1891 were C.N. Sigrest and J.B. McDonald. James Haley was the teacher in 1879, C.N. Sigrest in 1880, Winsie Moon in 1881 and Miss Merle Smith in 1896 and 1898.

Mutual Union School

Teachers: A.S. Summers, 1873; Miss Maggie Miles, 1901; Miss Ella Faulkner, 1908 and Miss Wilma Robinson, 1921. Mutual Union School/Church was located 2-1/2 miles north of Pulaski in the early 1880s. In the 1890s the church was moved into Pulaski and built beside the school.

Norris

Norris was located six miles southeast of Forest and had one of the first schools in the county. It was established in 1856.

Oak Grove School

Oak Grove School, also called Ridge and Pea Ridge, was located 14 miles north of Forest on the Leake-Scott line. In the 1800s the school was moved about two miles when Thomas L. Pettey purchased the land and moved his family into the building used for the school. Most of the

Morton High School
1937-38 Girls' Basketball Team
Row 1: Irma Lee Armstrong, Laverne Lindsey, Mary Baker, Mary Lee Gray, Mildred Jones, Grace Eichelberger, Mary Kathryn Buntyn. Row 2: Coach Leroy Brooks, Assistant Coach Sarah Paschal, Louise Crotwell, Xenobria Craig, Evelyn Evans, Statha Bennett, Elizabeth Lindsey, Assistant Marjorie Dearman.

Morton High School
1937-38 Football Team
Row 1: Morell Hughes, Miram Walker, Holt Walker Jr., Ralph Simmons, W.J. Lindsey, Mangum Crotwell. Row 2: Arthur Legan, James Jones, Billy Ray Lindsey, Maxwell Sessums, James Buntyn, Curtis Boozer, Dwight Lewis. Row 3: Caley Waldrip, Edward Huff, Ernest Hughes, Herbert Winstead, Roy Stone, Coach Leroy Brooks.

Piketon School 1919-20

Piketon School was located two miles from Forest on the Forest-Piketon Road, where the road forks between the home of Mr. and Mrs. Jack Shelly and Miss Lorane Gentry. All the students had to walk to school. There were two teachers. The students and teachers are left to right, bottom row: French Haralson, Edd Bell, Sarah J. Haralson, _, Clifton Hollingsworth, Hugh Bell, Ervin Hunt, Wilbur Massey, Aldean Tucker, Vernon Gentry. Second row: Minnie Lee Massey, Joe Bell, Lorane Gentry, Evelyn Hunt, Nettie Walter, teacher; Katie Lou Mann, Otha Massey, Thelma Lang, teacher; John Henry Gentry, Virgie Hunt, Leonard Massey, Melton Gentry, J.C. Haralson, Hunt Haralson. Third row: Lula Crimm, Roxie Crimm, _, - Bell Haralson, Allie Massey, Stella Mae Walters, Annie Lee Haralson, Edith Tucker, _, _, Lois Mann. Fourth row: Edwin Tucker, Clyde Mann, Roy Mann, Willie Mann, Otis Massey, Leon Haralson, Talva Walls, Clarence Crimm, Calvin Massey, Albert Mann, Elbert Bell, _, _, lady at top is Bell Gentry, a visitor. Photo furnished by Miss Lorane Gentry and Mrs. Tressie McDill.

area residents called it Pea Ridge or just Ridge School. It was a one-room school. Later the high school students attended Harperville to finish their education. In 1874, L.F. Lloyd was the teacher. In 1901 Miss Lula Curtis was their teacher and in 1908 it was A.A. Hester.

Old Union School

Teachers: Miss Clemmie Howard, 1901; J.L. Thomas and Miss Ethel Powell, 1908.

Piketon School

Piketon School, also called Pleasant Ridge, was located about 12 miles northeast of Forest between the Hontokalo and Tuskalameta Creeks. The first school was in the Pleasant Ridge Baptist Church and began in 1875. The first teacher was J.C. Elerbie. The first school building was constructed about a half-mile away from the church and Jeff Walters was the teacher. This school burned and was replaced with a two-room, two teacher school. Some of the other teachers were Otho Putman, Mrs. Lilla May Putman, Sussie Warren, Oscar Massey, Nattie Walters, Cooper Walters, Miller Sharp, Thelma Lang, Howard Clark, Marjoire Woods, Mary Patrick, Thomas Gentry, Blanch Pace and Mary Eichelberger. Piketon consolidated with Ringgold in the fall of 1928.

Prairie Hill School

Prairie Hill was located about three miles southeast of Forest. Some of the teachers were James Haley, 1880; Miss Nannie Thomas, 1901 and Miss Geneva Jones, 1908.

Prentiss School

Miss Agnes Franklin was the teacher in 1921. Prentiss consolidated with Branch in 1929.

Pulaski School

Pulaski's first school was organized in 1856 in the Primitive Baptist Church. Some of the teachers were: Abb Rhodes, John Davis, Miss Francis Miller and F.D. Davis. Before the Civil War the school was small. In 1890 a large two-room unplaned lumber structure was built. It had a few windows on the side with a door in the front. A large platform in back was used for concerts, Thanksgiving entertainment and Christmas trees. Reverend Penn was the principal and Miss Ida Morehead was the assistant. The next teacher was Orion Pittman. Pulaski High School was organized in 1895 and became the only accredited school in Scott County at the time. This was a boarding school which cost $6.00 to $7.00 a month and boarders were expected to furnish oil, lamps and toilet articles. Students came from miles around to attend. In the 1904-05 school year, 120 students were enrolled. The teachers in 1905-06 were George Nobles, principal; A.B. Millsaps, John Luther Roberts, Aida McCrackin and Abby Jewelle Bailey. At the cost of $7,000.00 a modern frame building was constructed in 1930, only to be consolidated with Morton, and their school closed shortly after.

Ringgold School

On September 7, 1928 the Ringgold Consolidated School District was formed. It was made up of the schools: Steele, Piketon (Pleasant Ridge), Salem and Ephesus. The school opened on September 2, 1929. The school bell was said to be the same one used at Ephesus School. It served to signal the beginning of class periods, recess, lunch and the end of the school day for almost 21 years. Walter Beeland was the first principal and the first teaching staff included: Ernest McDill, Mary Lyles, Myrtle Bishop, Oda Roland, Emma Walters, Harry Truitt and Edith Moore.

In the Spring of 1931, Ringgold proudly graduated its first senior class. The five people earning that distinction were Odell Wolf, Mary Grace Walters, Virge Hunt, Loraine Gentry and Flay Moorehead. Enrollment for the school year beginning in September 1934 was 246. This was an eight month school term. At times the school year would start in August and then would "let out" for a period of two to four weeks. This was done so crops could be harvested. But school spirit was high and basketball was the king sport. In 1934-35 the boys posted a 21-6 record under the coaching of M.S. Rowzee. The girls' team of 1937-38 was one of the best up to that time. Katie Maud Haralson Shelly was selected the best Scott County girl player that year. Nineteen thirty-eight was a year that brought joy to the basketball players and fans, for this was the year that the gymnasium was built.

In the spring of 1940, Ringgold graduated 19 students. This was the largest number to receive a diploma in a year since the school was begun. The years 1948 and 1949 brought another first (and only), the school's first yearbook. On the night of February 13, 1950 the Ringgold School burned. The main building was lost, with all of the contents. Makeshift classrooms were set up in every standing building. Even in the teachers' homes and the lunchroom. The new school was of modern design and much roomier than the old school. School start up, in the fall of 1950, was delayed a short time to allow for completion of the building.

Ringgold lost its title of "High School" with the graduation of the class of 1958. Most students would continue their high school education at Sebastopol. Ringgold would revert to elementary status. In November 1964, the school was closed. This was the end of an era, but the physical building would stand for awhile longer.

Rocky Creek School

Rocky Creek was located in southeast Scott County. Teachers: H. Langston, 1873; T.F. Laydo, 1877; R. Franklin, 1880; E. Myers, 1882; Nannie Lamb, 1892 and Miss Nannie Carr, 1908.

Salem School

Salem School was begun in 1859. Jack Lewis, Johnnie Graham, Ruben and Tom Milsaps, Alf Taylor, Berry Champion, Jim Futch and the

Sebastopol High School ca. 1947

Lay family were leaders in the movement to establish the Salem School. This was a small one-room log building. The light inside was provided by large cracks between the logs and crudely cut holes for windows, which had shutters to cover them. It had a door in the front and a chimney on the back wall. The school was rebuilt several times, at least one of those times was because it burned.

The usual subjects were taught: reading, writing, arithmetic, grammar and spelling. The children always seemed eager to learn. The average attendance was around 30 students a session. In 1873 C.H. Holifield was the teacher and Alice Ware was there in 1880. Miss Lizzie Butler, a graduate of Harperville College, was teaching in 1898; 1901 brought Miss Fannie Nichols and 1908, Miss Louise Howorth. In 1921 Salem had two teachers, Miss Mary Bell Sigrest and Mrs. Longino Rape. Some of the other early teachers were Dave Holmes, Fannie Ruth Lay, Thelma Lang, Unilea Clower, Onie Sessions, Vera Burns, Bessie Sanders, Ed Walker, G.A. Park and a Mr. Nicholson from the north.

In 1902 Salem was consolidated with Goodhope. This lasted only a few years, only to be consolidated in 1929 along with Piketon (Pleasant Ridge), Steel and Ephesus to make up the newly established Ringgold School.

Sand Ridge School

Teachers: Miss Ruby Simmons, 1901 and Miss Iva Nobles, 1908.

Sand Springs School

Teacher in 1901 was Miss Fay Hurst.

Scott Central School

Scott Central School opened in December 1964 to provide education for the students from the Ringgold and Harperville schools. The school is located on the Old Jackson Road between Highways 35 and 21. There was some trading of district lands to make this area available for Scott Central to build on. Scott Central was built to accommodate 500 students in grades 1 through 12. Scott Central students with the scholastic grades have the opportunity to be members of the Beta Club. In 1973, a band was organized and many times through the years the band has received All-Superior ratings.

The Scott Central girls' basketball team won the 1979 State Class BB title but lost to Duck Hill in double overtime (74-70) for the state title. Sammy Pace was the coach. In March 2000 with Chad Harrison as coach, the girls team won the Class 1A state title beating Durant 57-51. In December 1999, the Scott Central football team under Coach Mickey Bounds, were the Class 1A state champs. Scott Central is noted for being the high school where Marlo Perry got his education and played his first football.

Sebastopol High School

He now is a linebacker for the Buffalo Bills. His father, Jordan Perry, was assistant head coach at Scott Central and his mother still teaches there.

The principals for Scott Central have been: J.B. Henderson, William Stokes, Gerald Hollingsworth, Curtis Burrell, Maurice Harrison, Murphy Roberson, Rodney Tadlock (finished out the school year when Mr. Roberson passed away), Tommy Woodfin, Fred Yates and Leory Callahan.

Scott County Christian Academy

In 1969, the abandoned Harperville School was purchased by the Harperville Baptist Church. After a meeting of parents on June 5, 1970 the Scott County Christian Academy was chartered with school opening in September. Reverend Smith Sanders was named headmaster. The school offered a well rounded curriculum for its students. But once again in the spring of 1978, the school graduated its last seniors and closed its doors to students.

Sebastopol School

In 1873, Miss V.L. Lane was the teacher for the Sebastopol School and she was followed by Miss F.M. Pettey in 1874. The school building constructed in 1905 was a wood frame building. It was located in the area where the City Hall/Library is now. The principal was Dallas Stewart and the teacher was Ervin McClendon. A storm did considerable damage to this building and the people finished tearing it down. The school was rebuilt in the same spot. This second building was used until 1924, when a new modern designed brick building was constructed at the cost of $15,000.00 in the area of the present school. The principal was Bert Barnett. Part of this building was used until 1998 when it was torn down to make way for new construction.

Singing School at Ephesus Baptist Church before July 1927. William Robert "Bob" Harrison, teacher (the man on the second row from the back with the baton).

Steele School students in 1911. The Steele School was a two-story building with two classrooms on the second floor. On the first floor was the music room and the high school. This school was located behind Guthrie Stewart Wholesale on Highway 21 North. The children came from as far as 10 miles. Many of them walked. Pictured from left to right are: top row: Pollie Goss, Gracie Reeve Croxton, Bertha Sharp Cox, Lucell Edwards Stamper, Mary Sharp, Joe Brown Edwards, W.T. Edwards, O.C. Parnell, _, Wade Ellis. Second row: Milla Sharp, Wydell Guthrie Edwards, Cora Putnam, Bonnie Putnam, Lola Lewis Eason, Rusha Patrick Richmond, Necy Roberts, Fred Goss, Euel Guthrie, Eley Warren, Willy Putnam. Third row: Brasell Lewis, Lillie Roberts Bradford, Minnie Reeves Collins, Daisy Stewart Kayia, Esco Parnell, Estell Guthrie Riser, Bonnie Putnam, Odie Putnam, Odis Putnam, Grundy Reeves, _, Fourth row: Earl Putnam, Mary Reeves Barber, Jessie Warren, Harvey Posey, Linei Roberts Stone, Otha Putnam, Clifton Putnam, Norman Parnell, Sam Precelius, Sam Mulligan, Beaman King, Sam Posey. Fifth row: Harvey Posey, Lizzie Posey, Lizzie Putnam, Stella Myers Preculis, Velma Lewis Tolbert, Susie Warren Jones, Douglas Warren Jones, Ethel Parnell, teacher, Effie....CHECKING FOR MORE NAMES........

Steele School 1915
Front, left to right, row 1: Thomas Stamper, Mary Grace Waters, Clyde Waters, Mize Patrick, Macon Patrick, Milton Waters, Joe Warren. Row 2: W.T. Reeves, Billy Guthrie, Stella Townsend, Lizzie Putnam, Oleda Stamper, Lucy Perkins, teacher Emmet Pickles, teacher Miss Deannie Crecelius, Kathrine King, Etoval Patrick, Tiny King. Row 3: Willie E. Walters, Delos Warren, J.C. Reeves, Neal Putman, Douglas Warren, Floy Putman, Velma Lewis, Jessie Warren, Bob Stewart, Brazel Lewis, George Stewart. Row 4: Robert Warren, Milton Sharp, Varadon Croxton, Vernice King, Bee Bradford, Jannie Bradford, Eon Warren, Mary Lou Guthrie, Effie Stewart, Minnie Reeves, Odis Putman. Row 5: Lola Lewis, Mattie Putman, Hannie Bradford, _, Row 6: Estelle Stewart, Clemmie Warren, Onnie Woods, Alpha Reeves, _, Homer Woods, Otha Putman, Huron Croxton, Beamon King, Neal Bradford, Bobby Croxton.

As Damascus School only provided grades 1 through 8, the students in grades 9 through 12 were sent to Sebastopol to finish their education. A new school building was constructed in 1955 and is still in use today with a cafeteria and auditorium. In the fall of 1958, the Ringgold High School students began to attend Sebastopol, increasing the attendance.

In the 1958-59 school year, the first football team was organized. Their first coach was Riley Aimsworth. With no football field, the team practiced in a cotton patch beside the school. Their first opponent was Hickory High School, in this game the first Sebastopol points to go on the board were made by Billy Wayne Alexander. The following year, with a newly constructed athletic field, their coaches were Melvin Pulley and Marcus Moore. The first home field touchdown was also made by Billy Wayne Alexander.

Sebastopol averages just over 600 students a year. On October 14, 2000 the Sebastopol High School Marching Band received superior ratings in band, drum major, percussion and guard, making only the second time in the school history for the band to receive this rating.

Shepherd School

Shepherd was located in Pulaski/Wicker Mill area. In 1931, there were 31 students attending school. Teachers were J.C. Finley in 1908 and Miss Bessie Youce in 1921.

Sigrest School

Teachers: Miss C.A. Miles, 1891; Oliver Edwards, 1891; C.D. Black, 1893; Fannie Rayner and J.W. Wade, 1894; W.B. Cooper, 1896; Fred Laseter, 1901 and Miss Nettie Wade, 1908.

Simmons and Robert Schools

These two schools are not on any of the teachers' list, but according to Elwin Livingston they were somewhere around the Pulaski or Morton area

Singing School

Singing schools were held in most areas of the county where churches were located. The teacher was William Robert "Bob" Harrison, known affectionately as Uncle Bob to many. He taught from the Christian Harmony songbook. This was a shaped note songbook. In this kind of singing, the notes of the song were sang first, then the words. Christian Harmony had seven notes: do, ra, fa, sol, la, ti, do. There are places that still do this type of singing. These classes usually lasted from 10 to 14 days.

South West Corner School

Teachers: S.J. Barnett, 1879; A.L.D. Rhodes, 1882; H.W. Bradshaw, 1892; W.S. Searcy, 1901; W.B. Cooper, 1908; C.H. Bradshaw and Miss Rebie Franklin, 1921.

Spencer Hill School

Spencer Hill was located about four miles southeast of Morton. Near what we know as Sims Hill.

Springfield School

The school was in the Springfield Community about eight miles southwest of Morton. In 1868 the citizens met and organized a school. Some of the family names of those who took part in organizing the school were Manning, Cooper, Rushing, Miles, Merchant, Watkins and Wade.

The church building was used for the school for many years. A small one-room log hut was built, about 15 feet by 18 feet. The school year was about three months in the summer. The average attendance was 25 students. Springfield was discontinued and consolidated with Clarksburg School which was consolidated with Morton in 1929. Teachers: Tom Lee, Mr. Shrumpherd, D.S. Rushing, 1873 and A.M. Antley, 1879.

Steele School

Steele School was established around 1905/07 and was located on the west side of Highway 21 in Steele Town. The school had a large attic mounted bell with ropes extending down through the ceiling for ringing. In 1911, there was an enrollment of 65 students. Some of the teachers were J.W. and Dosia Pickel, Will Johnson, Lillie Mae Putman, Wadene Townsend, Ethel Parnell, Tim Thomas, Lennis Rhodes and Si Wallace. The school consolidated with Ringgold and the building was sold in 1929.

Sugar Bogue School

Sugar Bogue was located in northwest Scott County. Teacher was Ms. Druey Gilbert in 1908.

Union Hall or Hill School

Teachers: Miss Lula Quattlebaum, 1901; Miss Eula Risher, 1908 and Mrs. Lola Thornton, 1921.

Usry School

Usry School was located northeast of Forest on Old Highway 80. It consolidated with Goodhope.

Vaughn Grange School

Vaughn Grange School, also called Faulkner and Cedar Hill, was located in what was known as the Cedar Hill Community. The school was established in 1869 with Z.T. Faulkner as its first teacher. It was in the edge of the Faulkner Cemetery and as a usual rule the children played in the cemetery during recess. The school was a one-room unpainted wood frame building, about 18 feet by 20 feet. It had one door in front and a few windows with wooden shutters. Mornas and Bertie Askin boarded the teacher in the 1920s. Some families who attended were Faulkner, Stewart, Risher, Carpenter, McGee, Blossom, Brassell, Gray, Robertson, Hunter, Jones, Askin, Haralson and Sawyer. This school consolidated with Forest in 1928. Teachers: Mollie Harper, 1881; D.C. Linbough, 1882; Miss Ola Risher, 1908; Miss Lizzie Faulkner, 1921; Lola Brassell and Mrs. Lonnie Gordy.

Vaughn School

Vaughn, also called Pine Rosin, was located eight miles south of Forest. The school was established in 1859. The Vaughn School was consolidated with Homewood. Teachers were M.C. Smythe in 1883; P.M. Jones in 1896 and Miss Ida Faulkner in 1898.

Whiteweight School

Teacher was Miss Zella Stovall in 1908.

Wolf School

This school was northeast of Forest, on land near the Rube Bradford homeplace. Some of the families attending were Bradford, Wolf, Patrick and Walters. Cooper Walters, Olga Curry, Allie Mangum and Bell Thomas were some of the teachers at Wolf School.

Zion Grove School

Teachers: J.D. Sheely, 1874; Cliffie Sigrest, 1892 and F.M. Milling, 1901.

Vaughn Grange or Cedar Hill School 1910-11
Row 1, L-R: Leon Haralson, Annie Lee Haralson Pearson, Onie Bell Haralson Wolf, Lozell Risher Wall. Row 2: Jim Ward, Jim Faulkner, Joe Risher, Lamar Faulkner, "Ky" Hezekiah Risher, Abret Risher Sawyer, Roy Faulkner, Atley Risher. Row 3: Percy Hatch, Lizzie Faulkner Miles, Nellie Ward, Miss Ola Risher, teacher; Julia Faulkner Hawkins, Fred Harvey, Clarence Hatch.

Black Schools

Submitted by Ike Crudup

Anderson School

Anderson was located between Mar's Hill Church and Homewood about one mile off Highway 35. It was established in 1902 with 15 students and one teacher. This was a one-room wood frame building, built on land donated by Tom and Classie Anderson. It had a blackboard all the way across the room and had many teachers through the years. It was upgraded to classes 1 through 8. The Andersons had a large family that attended this school as did the Harper family.

Antioch School

Antioch was established in 1875 under the public school system. It was located about 2-1/2 miles northeast of Forest.

Armstrong School

Armstrong was located six miles north of Morton. It was established in 1900, with one teacher and 15 students.

Ball Hill School

Ball Hill was located south of Lake in a settlement where the Bells and Grays lived. This was a one-room school and provided classes for grades 1 through 8.

Balucta School

Balucta was located near the present site of Balucta Baptist Church near Ludlow, MS in the northwest corner of Scott County. The land was donated by Mrs. Odell Hollis. It was established in 1900. It was a one-room, unpainted wood frame building. There was one teacher and 40 to 60 students. The teacher had a table to sit at and teach. The students sat on benches. It had a blackboard that went all the way across the room. Tommy Ware was a teacher and principal and Zippa Ware Lofton was a teacher.

Beach School

Beach was established in 1900 and was located about three miles southwest of Ludlow in the Beach-Beach Creek Community.

Bellefield School

Bellefield, also called Mt. Carmel, was established in 1901 and was located two miles north of Morton on Highway 481. The name changed to Mt. Carmel in the 1940s.

Branch True Light

Branch True Light, also called True Light, was named after the community and the church that the school was located in. It was on Highway 491 north of Morton near the Scott/Rankin County line. It was a one-room schoolhouse that was established in the early 1900s.

Brusha Community School

Brusha, also called the New Mt. Calvery Church School, was located close to the Mt. Olive Community or about three miles from the East Scott Middle School (Lake). It was established in 1900 with 60 to 80 children in grades 1 through 8. Walley Needham was principal and his wife, Susie Needham and Mrs. Mary Keeton were teachers. Some of the students were Ollie Anderson and the Anderson family, the Dennis Amos family and Mint Williams. In 1960 this school was closed and the students sent to East Scott High School.

Cassidy School

Cassidy was an elementary school located in west Forest.

Cedar Grove School

Cedar Grove was established in 1873 and located in the northwest corner of Scott County, east of Ludlow. Tommy Ware and Marzella Donald were teachers of the eight grades that attended this school.

Clarksburg Line

Clarksburg was established in 1900. It was located three miles west of Morton on the Scott/Rankin County line.

Clifton School

Clifton was located west of Hillsboro.

Cooperville School

Cooperville was located south of Morton.

Crout School

Crout was established in 1901 and located two miles east of the Norris Community, southeast of Forest. It began with one teacher and 25 students.

Crudup Bottom School

The Crudup Bottom Schoolhouse was a one-room, one teacher public school for blacks in Forest, MS in the early 1880s. The school was located on the property of Wash Crudup, who having 10 children of school age allowed his old house to be converted into the school. The school was located on old Highway 35 between the area of Forest known as the Frog Bottom and the Mars Hill Church area, thereby giving the school its name. About 40 students from these areas went there.

The school was taught by Ms. Edith Butler, who divided the students into groups to teach the three Rs to grades 1 through 8, with the older students helping the younger ones. There were two recesses per day plus lunch. Each grade was given a day to cook lunch for the school on the wood burning stove. The government provided (commodities) powered eggs, powered milk, large cans of pork and beans, flour, etc.

The school was described as a wooden plank building about 40 to 50 feet long with a plank roof, plank floor and plank shutters for the windows. The school had a wood heater with pipes going out the side of the building. The school had benches and tables on which to sit and work on.

The Department of Education closed all of the community schools including the Crudup Bottom School in the 1940s. The students had to go to the Scott County Training School on the present site of the Head Start Center in Forest. Those students who could not walk there had to move closer with relatives. The new school went to higher grades than the community schools.

The students and families that attended the school were the 10 children of Wash Crudup, Annabell and Marzell Currie, the Anderson family, the Youngbloods, the Moores, the Harpers, Ida and Alexander Crudup, Ike and Martha Harper, Frank Battle, Hattie Watts, Gurtis Watts' parents, Duke and Rosa Robinson, Lottie Moore family and Pattie Robinson Ward. *Oral history as given to Ike Crudup Jr. by Annabell and Marzell Currie who attended 1930s to 1940, Naomi Wheeler, Addie Crudup, Joe Glover, Charles "Hubbard Neal" Glover.*

Dumas Line

Dumas was located in northwest corner of Scott County south of Lena. In 1943 there were 11 students and one teacher.

Ealy Chapel School

Ealy Chapel was located in the northwest part of Scott County, near the Scott/Leake County line close to Lena, MS. This was a one teacher, one-room, unpainted wood building. There were 40 to 60 students in grades 1 through 8. William Ware taught here.

East Scott High School

East Scott was built in 1960 near the site of Mt. Olive School for grades 1 through 12. Students from Mt. Olive, Brusha, Sebastopol, Sherman Hill, Glover Chapel and Union Grove were sent to this school. One three buses were allowed to get the students to school. Often students sat in other students' laps and students were standing from the back to the front of the bus to get on as many as possible. The buses would be so full until the driver could not stop, leaving many kids standing by the road. R.B. Dubouse was principal, Otis Evans was assistant principal and elementary principal was Idell Denham. Marvin Morgan became principal after Mr. Dubouse.

Ebenezer

Ebenezer, also called St. Peter, was located four miles southwest of Forest on land owned by Luther Moore. This school was established in 1879 as a school/church in Luther Moore's pasture. It began with one teacher and 25 students and the session lasted 3-1/2 months. The school was moved a half mile northwest of that site and then it was moved onto the Faulkner Graveyard Road (or CC Road), just off Blossom Hill Road across from present site of St. Peter MB Church. It was a one-room, unpainted wood frame school. It had a blackboard and glass windows with wood shutters. The students had to sit in chairs. In 1948 there were 74 students attending this school. Some of whom were Albert, D.L., Frank, Madison, Fannie and Teddy Moore, Margaret and Mable Hunter, Francis, Lizzie, Erma and Alex Parriot; Rebella Strong, Naomi Strong Wheeler and the Horton family. Some of the teachers who taught there were Mrs. Maggie Ware, Ms. Jewell Harvey, Ruth Ward and Dock Gray. When this school closed the students were sent into Forest.

Five Prong School

Five Prong was established in 1900 and was located northeast of Harperville off Highway 35 on the John Kelly family property. It began as a one-room wood frame building, with another room added later. There was no running water. A wood heater provided warmth for the children who had to sit on rough wood benches. Each room had a big blackboard and there was a platform stage in the back. There were wood shutters on the windows and out back there were outdoor toilets. The teacher had a desk to sit at. Ms. Hattie Lou Kelly, Ethel Mae Fortune, Professor Lee, Lella Sharp, Bertha Mae Wilson, Viola Fortune and Addie Lee Morgan

were some of the teachers. The Vivirette, Brewer, Wilson, Nix, Harrison and Kelly families were some of those who attended the school. The trustees were Joe Wilson, Belma Harrison and Frank Brewer.

Friendship School

Friendship, also called the Quarters School and the Hopewell School, was located on the present site of Friendship Baptist Church on Joe Street in Forest, just east of King Lumber Company on Highway 80 west. It was a one-room church/school building for grades 1 through 7. The students were given lunch and had two recesses a day. There were about 40 students attending this school. It was also called the Quarters School because the black children who went there mostly lived in the area of houses near the Bienville Saw Mill and Lumber Company where their parents worked. The Hopewell School was established in 1892 and was located about 1-3/4 miles west of Forest on land donated by Mr. Holbert. Hopewell Church also used this building. Some of the students were Fannie Proctor Bradford, Rutha Lee Brown, Missy Strong, Ester Strong and Deloris Glover Scott. This school consolidated with Scott County/Forest Training School.

Gaddis School

Gaddis was established in 1902 and located six miles north of Morton. It started with one teacher and 20 students.

Galilee Line

Galilee was established in 1886 and was located on the Scott/Smith County line. The building, a small one-room school, sat on the county line so the children from both counties attended. Students included Sylvester Parker, retired assistant principal of E.T. Hawkins High School; Alvin Parker, his brother and their other siblings, also the Gumbrell family.

Glover Chapel

Glover Chapel was located off Highway 21, north of Forest, north of the present site of the Union Grove Baptist Church. It was established in 1885 on land donated by Jim Denham. It started with grades 1 through 6 but later included grades 1 through 8. It was a two-room schoolhouse with 80 to 90 students. The principal from 1943-1953 was Alice Jackson. Some teachers were Idell Denham, Katie Eubanks and Alice Jackson. The school closed in 1960.

Gray School

Gray School, changed to Mt. Moriah School, was located in the southeast part of the county, near Pulaski in the Mt. Moriah Community. It was established in 1884; got its name from a very large family of Grays who lived there and had large numbers of children attending the school. Some of the students were Lonzo, Jack and Dock Gray. This was a one-room schoolhouse. During the time of this school, the community was called Gray Town. It was located off the Morton/Marathon Road, west of the present site of the Mt. Moriah Church and near the Moore Tower Road. It was on land donated by the Jack Gray Sr. family. The school was moved closer to the Mt. Moriah Church and graveyard. The name changed to the Mt. Moriah School, it was a school only, one-room, one teacher. It was an unpainted straight building about 20 by 16 feet. It had a wood heater, blackboard and only chairs for the students to sit in. There were about 30 students in grades 1 through 8. Some of the teachers were Professor Currie, Mrs. Mary Robinson, Professor Hopkins, Mrs. D.C. Lee and Willis Gray. Some of the students were James and Virginia Nixon, Wesley, Dessie S.D., Preston, Mertis, Cleveland, Major and Mildred Page;

Willie, A.B., Rebecca and Amos Crudup and nine members of the Gray family. The teacher sat at a wooden table with his/her books.

Green Grove School

Green Grove, also called West Green Grove, was located near the present site of Green Grove Baptist Church about four miles east of Homewood on the Norris/Homewood Road on the Loyd Moore plantation. This was a one-room, one teacher school. The trustee of the school was Ike Crudup.

Harrison School

Harrison was started by Richard Harrison, a black man who owned the land and built the Harrison Church/School. It was located west of Homewood about a half-mile just off the Morton/Marathon Road on Tadlock Road. It was an unpainted wood frame building with one-room and one teacher for grades 1 through 8.

Homewood School

Homewood was established in 1901 and located south of Forest. It began with one teacher and 15 students.

Johnson School

Johnson, also called Sebastopol, was located one mile east of Sebastopol on Highway 492. There were about 60 students in grades 1 through 8. The principal was Florine Johnson and the teacher was Mertis Lewis.

Jones Chapel School

Jones Chapel was located near Jones Chapel Church in the Norris Community. In 1942, 70 students attended and the teacher was Idell Denham and Luberta Forte was principal.

Kincaid School

Kincaid was established in 1886 and located near Midway. There was a large family named Kincaid in this area. This was a one-room, one teacher school.

Lake School

Lake, also called Antioch School, was established in 1886 and was located just south of downtown Lake, near the Antioch Church. A new building was finished in December 1949 and still stands today. It is used as a community building. Some of the teachers were Mrs. Alice Jackson, Mrs. Rosie Brown and Mrs. Katie Flowers-Eubanks. The students in grades 1 through 8 used homemade desks.

Liberty School

Liberty was located between Forest and Morton in the Kalem Community.

Lillian School

Lillian was established in 1885 and was located north of Hillsboro, near the Midway Community and present site of Sylvester Methodist Church. It provided classes for grades 1 through 8.

Little Rock School

Little Rock, also called Butlertown School, was established in 1884 in a community known as Buttlertown near Little Rock Church between Harperville an Steeletown. It was a one-room schoolhouse with two windows and a door on the front and one door on the back. The students sat on benches and the teacher had a chair. With no running water, the students used outdoor toilets. The board members provided water and also wood for heat. This school had classes 1 through 8.

Little Texas Special School
Lone Pilgrim

Lone Pilgrim was located about two miles northeast of Hillsboro, near the present site of the Lone Pilgrim Methodist Church. It was established in 1874 on land donated by Luke Smith. There was a large Negro settlement here. It was a Julius Rosenwald built school. It was an unpainted wood frame building with three or four rooms for grades 1 through 8 and about 90 students. The principal was Mr. Major and Estella Burks was a teacher. After the school closed, the building was left to rot down.

Ludlow School

Ludlow was established in 1901 and located two miles southeast of Ludlow. This was a one teacher, one-room school. Mrs. Zippo Ware Lofton was a teacher here.

Midway High School

Midway, also North Scott High, was started just after slavery in the 1860s in the Midway Community, northwest of Harperville. The school was started by the Odom family, with a couple of rooms. By the 1930s the school was a five to six-room white painted wood building with wood heaters. Later a Rosenwald Fund school was built. This was a modern brick building. From 1950 to 1964 the principal was Clell Ward and from 1964 to early 1970s W.L. Slaughter was principal. Two of the teachers were Viola Ware Doom and N.C. Eiland. This school closed in the early 1970s during integration.

Moore School

Moore was located in Forest.

Morton Vocational High School

Morton, established in 1900, was also called Morton Free Public School, Bettye Mae Jack High School and Morton Middle School after integration. A Rosenwald Fund school, it was a wood frame building with four or five classrooms and a principal's office. It also had a vocational shop, it was for classes 1 through 8. The school was located near the present site of Bettye Mae Jack Middle School. In the late 1940s, Mr. Golden was principal and Mrs. Zippo Ware Loften was the teacher. In the late 1950s a modern brick school was built and renamed Bettye Mae Jack High School and had classes 1 through 12. Newtie Boyd, Mrs. Annie Owens, Mrs. Barnes, Ms. Amanda Griffin, Mrs. McCoy, Ms. Claudett Holbert were teachers and Mr. Barnes was principal.

Mount Carmel School

Mount Carmel was established in 1918 and was located in Sebastopol. It began with one teacher and 25 students.

E.T. Hawkins High School, 1969

Mount Olive School

Mt. Olive was established in 1888 and located seven miles northeast of Lake. Later in the years a Rosenwald Fund building was constructed. It was a wood frame building finished on inside and outside with three classrooms. It had windows all the way around it but had no lights or running water. It had factory made desks and a stage. The blackboards separated the classrooms. It provided an education for grades 1 through 8. Otis Evans was principal and Essie Owens, Mezzy Freeman, Bertha Mae Wilson, Professor Gary and Pearly Mayes were teachers. Jack Wash, Neal Lay and Virgil Owens were school trustees. In 1960 Mt. Olive closed and the newly built East Scott High School was opened.

Mount Zion School

Mt. Zion was located eight miles southeast of Forest near Green Grove Church and established in 1884. This was a one-room wood frame building with no windows. In 1928-29 there were 80 students enrolled with one teacher, Ms. Idell Denham. The students were sent to Sherman Hill School when the school closed in the 1940s.

Pine Grove School

Pine Grove was located near Homewood.

Pine Ridge School

Pine Ridge was established in 1901 and located four miles south of Lake. It began with one teacher and 25 students.

Pleasant Gift School

Pleasant Gift was established in 1906 and was located about 12 miles north of Morton in the northwest part of the county.

Pleasant Hills School

Pleasant Hills was established in 1872 and located two miles southwest of Morton

Rasco School

Rasco, also called Thomas School, was located between Highway 35 north and Hillsboro. It was a one-room unpainted wood frame school with shutter windows for grades 1 through 8. Some of the students were Harvard, Walter, Ezekel, Jimmy and Jutus Rasco, also the Thomas family. Mrs. Cliff Jones and Alice Jackson were teachers there.

Scott County Training School/E.T. Hawkins High School Alumni Association

In 1990 former graduates of both Scott County Training School and E.T. Hawkins High School met to initiate the application of a chartered organization for graduates of the two former academic institutions. This meeting marked the estab-

E.T. Hawkins, Principal

lishment of the Scott County Training School/E.T. Hawkins High School Alumni Association, which would be later properly executed for incorporation by Attorney Constance Slaughter Harvey.

The following SCTS/ ETHHS graduates currently serve as officers for the association: president Pearl Clark, vice-president Abraham Buckley, secretary Juanita Jones, treasurer Carolyn Edwards Knowles, chaplain Albert Moore and sergeant-at-law Albert Pinkston.

The association has evolved into a family of schoolmates dedicated to improving the prosperity, welfare and enlightenment of its community's adults and youth. In reflection of its commitment to service, the association sponsors numerous community projects. Each year it awards scholarships to deserving high school students planning to attend a Historically Black College or University (HBCU); every two years during the second week of July it hosts a school reunion and it publishes a newspaper informing its readers about the positive things its graduates are doing not only for themselves, but for their communities. It also co-sponsors numerous programs, seminars and community service events.

Since the association's inception, it has reunited its former students with the historical legacy established by each institution and has rekindled the values of excellence that were instilled within the hearts and minds of its graduates.

Shady Grove School

Shady Grove had 65 students in 1924.

Shady Oak School

Shady Oak was established in 1874 and located near Pulaski. It had an average of 30 students.

Sherman Hill School

Sherman Hill, also called Pleasant Valley School, was established in 1901 and was located about 10 miles southeast of Forest off Highway 501, near the Pleasant Valley Church. This was a Julius Rosenwald Fund school. It was a three or four-room wood frame building with homemade desks for classes 1 through 8. In 1931 it had three teachers. Some of the teachers were Mrs. Jimmy Mae Ware-Walker and Ms. Idell Denham, with Robert B. Duboise as principal. The school closed about 1960 and the students were sent to East Scott High School.

Singleton School

Singleton, also called East End, East Forest and McMurphy School for the McMurphy family that lived near the school, was located two miles east of Forest, on old Highway 80 on the Bill Singleton plantation. It once served as a reform school. It was a one teacher, one-room, wood frame building for grades 1 through 6. It had plank benches for the students and a table for the teacher with a wood heater for heat. It had one or two windows and a sheet of plywood served as the chalkboard. The students brought their own lunches of roasted sweet potatoes, fatback meat and cornbread. Three of the teachers were Carrie Tucker, Velma Jackson and Roberta Turner. Some of the students were L.D. and Eva Durnham, Will Buckley, Elbert and Jordan Crudup. The school was in use in the 1920s and closed about 1948. The students then went to Forest/Scott County Training School/E.T. Hawkins High School.

Sparksville School

Sparksville was located three miles southwest of Hillsboro.

St. John

St. John, also called Davis and Bishop, was a school/church combined in the same building. It was located off Highway 80 west of Forest and two miles east of the town of Morton, near the International Paper Mill. It was a one-room schoolhouse; a plank building with black asbestos tar paper wrapped around to cover the planks. Mrs. Little Ware, the mother of Mrs. Robertha Ware Turner, was the teacher for grades 1 through 8. It was also called Davis School because of a very large family that attended the school, including Bilbo, Jacob and Esaw Davis. St. John was the name of the church when church services were held in the building.

Stage School

Stage was located south of Morton. In 1944 there were 32 students.

Strong School

Strong was established in 1904 and located three miles northeast of Midway.

Sylvester School

Sylvester was located near present site of Sylvester Methodist Church near Hillsboro. It was established in 1876 in a log building. Later a one-room, wood frame building was constructed with wood plank shutters to protect the glass windows. It began with grades 1 through 6 and later added grades 7 and 8. This school was packed with children. Three of the teachers were Gladys Lovelady, Mazolla Lamb and Annie Mae Mayes. The school closed in the 1940s.

Union Grove

Union Grove, also called Steele, Patrick and Hollow Grove, was established in 1882. It was located in the Steeletown-Union Grove area of

Highway 21 north of Forest. This was a wood frame building with more classrooms added on through the years. It had a blackboard across one wall with a stage in the back. The students had three recesses a day. The school's lunchroom was a shotgun shack, built separate from the school but close to the back of it. The cook was Eva Beamon. There were two outhouses for restrooms. The men of the community cut and donated wood for the heaters in each classroom. Students walked to school. Because of shortage of room and books, some students were not promoted. In large families two or three of the children could be in the same class. The students were sent to East Scott when the school closed. It was torn down about 1960 and Union Grove Methodist Church built on the site. Alice Jackson was a teacher and coach, Idell Denham was a teacher and principal from 1953 to 1960. Ora Day was a principal and Ruth Shepphard, Jeanette Stewart, Ethel Mae McClendon, Florence Johnson, Maud Fortune and Eula Crouther were teachers. Some of the students were Eudora, Henry Milford and George Peter Williams and Reverend Henry Patrick.

Walker School

Walker was established in 1896 and located 11 miles north of Morton. It began with one teacher and 20 students.

Zion Line

Zion was established in 1898 and located seven miles east of Little Rock. It began with one teacher and 24 students.

Betty Mae Jack
Morton, MS

Churches

Branch Baptist Church

The first service of Branch Baptist Church was held November 14, 1909. The congregation sat on stumps, logs and the ground while Reverend S.C. Gordon preached a sermon from Haggai. After the sermon, the church was officially organized and Miss Jennie Murray (later Mrs. Ernest Smith) offered land to the new church. The deed was executed the next day and the people of the community went to work on the first church building. People in the community gave the timber, which was hauled to G.B. Coward's sawmill. While the men of the community were working on the first building, the church met in a brush arbor.

During the church's first year, services were held on the fourth Sunday of each month. But the day before each fourth Sunday, a Saturday church conference was held with members from sister churches in attendance. Reverend Gordon was the church's first pastor. There is no mention of money for a preacher's salary in early church minutes, but notes do show that a "sacrifice offering" of $9.00 was given to Reverend Gordon at the end of the church's first revival.

That first church building, like the two buildings that succeeded it, had no baptistry. New members were baptized in nearby ponds. Marion Peagler's pond had white sand, so it was the one most often used for baptisms.

By 1932, the church was having Sunday School every week and preaching services on the second and fourth Sunday of every month. Leon Young was the pastor for that year and church records show that his salary for the month of April was $5.64.

Branch Baptist Church, 3997 Measels Road, Morton. This is the way the church looked in the late 1960s

First Baptist Church, 1948 Lake, MS

It was not until 1953, under the leadership of Reverend Homer Ainsworth, that the church began having preaching services every Sunday. Reverend Ainsworth was pastor at three different times during the church's history, in 1939, 1943, 1944 and from 1952 until 1954. Other pastors who served for five years to longer included Mack Hughes (1924-29), C.C. Cornelius (1960-63 and 1970-71) and T.W. Henderson (1974-80). James Watts was the pastor for slightly over 10 years, from 1988 until 1998.

The church's current brick structure, built in 1953, is the fourth building used by the church. A pastor's home was built in 1955 and a fellowship hall was built in 1972. New Sunday School rooms were added to the church in 2000.

In addition to Sunday School and discipleship training, the church members also enjoy their music ministry, which has been led by Norman Huggins since 1990. And its children are very important to Branch. The children and teenagers participate in Mission Friends, Girls in Action, Acteens and Royal Ambassadors. For more than 90 years, Branch Baptist Church has been an essential part of the lives of its members and the community.

First Baptist Church of Lake
Lake, MS

On June 22, 1867 three ordained Baptist ministers, the Revs. Nathon Clarke, L.P. Murrell and D. Fore, rode their horses into the community of Lake and met with the congregation of eight to organize the church. Reverend Murrell preached the first sermon and signed the church's charter with D. Fore and Nathon Clarke for whom Clarke College at Newton is named. The eight charter members of the church were T.J. Smith, L.R. Wilkins, Calvin Small, Armoda Simmons, B.F. Smith, Mary Wilkins, Mary A. Small and Mary Haskins. The first pastor called by the church was Reverend W.R. Butler. Prior to the organization, Lake Baptist met with the Methodist and Presbyterian in a Union Church located where the Methodist church is. In 1872 construction of the original Baptist church was begun on a lot donated by the Wilkins family. The building was completed in October 1873. Some repairs were made in 1908. In May 1924 the church purchased the Stovall home for a parsonage. The parsonage was destroyed by fire December 1955. A new parsonage was constructed in 1956. The present parsonage was constructed in 1973. In May 1961 the church begun construction of brick educational building which was completed in October 1961. Construction of the sanctuary was begun in December 1961. The dedication service for the new brick building was held April 1, 1962. The church began construction of a new auditorium in May 2000; construction which continues at this writing. *Submitted by Ken McLemore, Pastor.*

Forest Baptist Church

Forest Baptist Church was organized May 12, 1867 with Reverend L.P. Murrell preaching the organizational sermon. The organization committee was composed of Reverend N.L. Clark, chairman; Reverend W.R. Butler, secretary and Reverend L.P. Murrell. The first members were Alfred Eastland, Hiram Eastland, Elizabeth Eastland, W.W. Lowry, Mrs. Cornelia J. Lowry, J.L. Gresham, Mrs. Mary E. Gresham, Austin M. Gresham, Mrs. Flavela Harrell, M. Halestine, Virginia Harrell, Stephen D. Kennedy, Mrs. Mary Kennedy, Mrs. Francis Evers, James A. Lake, Bryant Harrell and Martha E. Harrell.

A. Eastland and J.L. Graham were requested to become acting deacons. W.W. Lowry, clerk and N.L. Clark, moderator. On July 1, 1867 Reverend W.R. Butler was elected as first pastor of the church.

The church made a petition to the Mount Pisgah Association on August 3, 1867 for membership into that body. A. Eastland and J.L. Gresham were elected delegates.

Forest Baptist Church, 1910 Forest, MS

Forest Presbyterian Church

On September 28, 1867 minutes show that the church received into membership Marcus Moore and Willey, his wife, by letter and Joseph H. Moore, Caroline James, Polly Conner and Molly Return for baptism. These were the first of 10 colored persons to be admitted to the church. These were excluded from the church in 1875 when they requested to be removed to join a church of their own people. The following is a list of the past pastors: W.R. Butler, J.B. Hamberlin, R.N. Hall, W.P. Carter, W.L. Skinner, C.M. Gordon, J.H. Grundy, J.A. Hackett, Clarence SanSing, W.N. Nathan, G.S. Jenkins, W.H. Thompson, Owen Williams, J.C. Richardson, D.A. Youngblood, W.C. Howard, A.B. Wood, B.W. Walker, W.L. Holcomb, L.E. Smith, N.F. Davis Jr., J.F. Brantley, H.D. Smith, Frank Gunn, Clyde Little, Charles Belt, S.A. Adkins and Gordon SanSing.

The church held services in the Presbyterian Church until April 4, 1874. The first church building was erected on property now occupied by Community Bank. Later a larger church was built. This building with the school nearby burned in 1919. The next building was a brick structure on the corner of Broad and Second streets. Property for a new church was acquired from the S.E. Lackey Memorial Hospital Committee. Ground breaking for the present building was May 16, 1948 with the cornerstone being laid October 17, 1948. Church services were held in the new building October 16, 1949. Many improvements have been made over the years to give us the church buildings we have today.

Forest Presbyterian Church

The Presbyterians early and steadily extended into and grew within the state. Their work began around 1800 in the Natchez region. The first church was organized in 1804. In 1816 a Presbytery of Mississippi was organized embracing all of Louisiana, Arkansas, Texas, much of Alabama and most of Mississippi. By 1830 Mississippi is said to have had 17 Presbyterian ministers, 15 churches and 634 communicants.

In 1866 the Presbytery of central Mississippi had 25 ministers, 38 churches, 978 members. In this post-war period conditions were worldly and somewhat discouraging and many had forgotten that the Lord is able and willing to prosper efforts to extend his kingdom even in destitute and relatively unexplored areas.

Reverend Richmond McInnis, a native of Greene County, MS began his ministry at Yazoo City. Before the war he served as editor of a religious periodical, residing and preaching in Jackson and later in New Orleans. When the denomination divided into northern and southern branches, McInnis was a commissioner to the First General Assembly of the Presbyterian Church in the Confederacy.

In the summer of 1866 he was employed as an evangelist of the Central Mississippi Presbytery. He preached first in Leake County as well as at several points along the Mississippi Central Railroad.

McInnis held evangelistic services in Forest at the end of January 1867 and on Monday, February 4, 1867 eight persons met to be organized by him into a Presbyterian congregation. They were William A. Lack, J.N. Jackson, Mrs. S.J. Lack, Mrs. E.C. Jackson, Mrs. E. Graham, Mrs. M.E. Jones, Miss Mary Christian and Mrs. L.L. Smith. Mr. Lack and Mr. Jackson were elected elders and that evening, after preaching, they were ordained and installed over the new Forest church.

Forest United Methodist Church

The earliest place of worship for the Methodist in Forest may have been a log school house located near the site of Lackey Memorial Hospital. Records from the Department of Archives and History describes the structure as 30 by 40 feet with few windows, a small door at the front and a large stick and mud fireplace at the rear.

It became apparent there was a need for the Methodist to build their own church and on October 18, 1871 four lots were purchased. These lots were located one block east of the courthouse and north of Fountain's Hardware. The purchase price was $25.00 per lot. This building was completed in time to host the Brandon District Conference in 1872.

With additional growth, the Methodist Congregation again purchased property January 29, 1910 from Ward and Mary Belle Jackson for $650.00 The resulting church building was on the site of the present church's location only facing south.

By the 1950s the congregation had out grown the facilities of the 1910 building. A building program was launched and the result was the construction of the present old English style church. Pieces of the beautiful stained glass windows from the 1910 building remain. One panel is now on display in the Memorabilia Room and other pieces were used in the Family Life Building located on the east side of the church. The first worship service in the present sanctuary was conducted May 5, 1957.

With the addition of a Family Life Building in 1994 the church continues to be a vital part of the community. During its 140 years of Christian service, the congregation has strived to live by the words of the founder of the denomination, John Wesley. "A Methodist is one who has the love of God shed abroad in his heart by the Holy Ghost given unto

Forest United Methodist Church East Third at Graham, Forest, MS

High Hill United Methodist Church

him; one who loves the Lord his God with all his heart and soul and mind and strength."

High Hill United Methodist Church

High Hill United Methodist Church, the building and cemetery are located at the intersection of Lake Norris Road and Hwy. 501.

The land was given for the location of a Methodist Episcopal Church to include the top of the hill for a church and graveyard. The deed is dated November 18, 1872 and is signed by Morris Emanuel. The deed is made to the trustees of the church at the time. They were Lindsey Harvey, W.M. Griffin, E.H. Walk, Philip McGee and John Price.

At some earlier date there was a school at this same location. The exact dates were not determined but there is a deed dated July 3, 1952 made to the Trustees of High Hill Methodist Church and their successors in office. The church trustees were Oliver Harvey, Melvin Boyles and George A. Eichelberger. The school trustees were Cliff Tadlock, Ray Moore, Oliver Harvey, Melvin Boyles and W.C. Eichelberger. It says that described land has long since ceased to be used as property of High Hill School and has for many years been used by High Hill Methodist Church as its property.

Then in 1952, the trustees were given some more of the land on top of the hill by Powell Jones, John and Lettie Daniels and E.C. and Mary Lou Wilkerson.

In 1976, the church and cemetery property was made separate entitles.

Mrs. Lodelle Eichelberger wrote in the membership register and church records book that it seems that no roll book was kept from 1872-1882, but in the program of dedication of the new church building in 1964, it states that the charter members of the church were the Harveys, McGees, Durrs, Chisolms, Griffins, Matthews, Joneses and Crouts.

In February 1960, a building fund was started. The first service in the new building was held May 21, 1961 with the dedication service held January 19, 1964.

Some of the families who are buried at this church are: Crout, Harvey, Eichelberger, McGee, Stokes, Fountain, Jones, Durr, Weems, Willamson, Boyles, Daniels, Usry, Wilkerson and Youngblood.

In the 1960s, the Home Demonstration Club started the Community Easter Sunrise Service held in this church. Later the Oak Grove Baptist Church, Hopewell Baptist Church and High Hill Methodist Church continued by rotating the program for this service at this picturesque location on Easter at sunrise.

Hillsboro Methodist Church

The first Methodist church in Scott County was organized in the home of Mr. and Mrs. Jesse McKay in 1836 with seven members in Hillsboro.

In 1847 John Chambers and James Chambers made a deed to Isaac Taylor, Abner Lack and Micajah Sigrest on the part of the Methodist Church South and John Owen, William Gatewood and Meschek Holoman, trustees for the Masonic Fraternity and Scott Lodge No. 80, for a parcel of land for the purpose of building a house; the lower story for a Methodist Episcopal Church and for a female school, and the upper portion to be used by Scott Lodge No. 80. This deed is recorded in Deed Book D, pages 439-440 on February 14, 1848. Alford Eastland, clerk.

The church grew, survived the Civil War and continued to grow. Several other buildings were built and land was donated for a cemetery. Margal Burkes gave land for the expansion of the cemetery, also Quention Mills.

In 1985 the membership had fallen, as young people moved away and older members died, it was decided to close the church.

A cemetery association was formed to meet each October for a homecoming and business. The church building and cemetery are well kept.

Old family names in the cemetery are Johnson, McClenehand, Askin, Sigrest, Burkes, Clower, Brodgen, Graham, Sparks, Eure, Dennis, Noel, Bustin, Westerfields, McCrory, Neal, Owen, Tadlocks and many more.

Hopewell Baptist Church

Hopewell Baptist Church was organized in 1849. The land, consisting of 3.7 acres, was donated by Mrs. Lula Gatewood Gay. The first church was a log building. Around the turn of the century a plank building was built.

Some records were destroyed by fire prior to 1903. Records are on microfilm at the Baptist Historical Commission, Mississippi College, Clinton, MS. Records show in 1903 there were 83 active members. The deacons were T.C. Youngblood, P.E. Jones and C.C. Sanders. The pastor was Reverend J.W. Rooker. At this time the church adopted Church Cov-

Hillsboro Methodist Church

Hopewell Baptist Church

enant, Gospel Order, Articles of Faith of Hopewell and rules on how the business should be conducted.

The present brick building was built in 1947. The pastor at that time was Bro. S.S. Kelly and there were 85 active members and the enrollment was 110.

In 1979 the church added a fellowship hall, nursery and two bathrooms. At present we are in the process of adding a larger fellowship hall, two bathrooms and two Sunday School rooms. Added to the cemetery is 1.2 acres of land donated by Mrs. Lloyd (Sara) Gatewood.

The deacons are Danny Harrison, Robert Ritchie, David Gunn and Joe Goodson. The church clerk is Mrs. Sara Gatewood. We have a total of 96 resident members and the enrollment is 128 members.

Lake Methodist Church

About 1865, shortly after Sherman's Army raided this country a carpenter named Chester moved a building from the bottoms at the railroad shops and rebuilt it as a school house. All church and Sunday School services were held in this building. It was located about where the Methodist parsonage was once located. The railroad shop foreman was Robert Haralson. The church and school bell was formerly on a railroad engine that was wrecked in Sherman's raid and is the same bell now in the Methodist church. The first church erected in Lake was a Union Church used by Methodist, Baptist and Presbyterians and is the main body of the present Methodist church. The boards were planned by hand and very few nails were used, as was the custom in those days. In 1875 or 1876, the Baptist sold their interest in the Union Church. During the pastorate of Reverend H.F. Tolle, December 1908-December 1912, the present building was rebuilt and in May 1928 was dedicated by Brother Tolle.

Lake Methodist Church

Liberty Baptist Church

The first frame building of Lynch Chapel United Methodist Church

Liberty Baptist Church

The Liberty Baptist Church was organized June 10, 1876 in a school house owned by Bro. David Adam Singleton.

W.R. Butler, moderator of the association presided. There were 16 charter members: W.H. Futch, B.J. Stuart, Margaret Alabama Sims, James Singleton, H.P. Stewart, M.J. Stewart, America McGowen, Charles Smith, T.H. Gould, Nepsy Singleton, David Adam Singleton, Luna Ann Smith, Martha Smith, John Myers, Pricilla A. Myers and E.B. Gould.

In 1893 Mr. Singleton deeded 3-1/2 acres of land to build a church. A one-room church was built called Liberty Missionary Baptist Church. During the early days the black people went to church there also. Mr. Singleton and his wife died in 1905 and both are buried in the cemetery behind the church.

Today a newer building still stands on the land deeded by Mr. Singleton and some of his descendants still worship there.

Lynch Chapel United Methodist Church

Lynch Chapel United Methodist Church is located at 504 East Fourth Street, Forest, MS. It is one of the oldest churches in the Mississippi Conference. It was organized while the Mississippi Conference was known as a Mission Conference. The church takes its name "Lynch Chapel" from its founding pastor, Reverend James Lynch.

In 1868, God sent a great spiritual leader, Reverend James Lynch to the Forest area. As his first endeavor in Forest, he organized a "Sunday School" in a small log hut. After that, the apparent need for an organized congregation was recognized. Reverend Lynch accepted a call from God to lead the congregation. On December 18, 1868 a deed was secured for the property where the present church stands. The trustees included Henry Harper, Samuel Carr and Lewis Graham. Shortly thereafter, the little log hut became a place of worship for the people. Later, a frame church and a parsonage were constructed.

The church and parsonage have been renovated and rebuilt several times during its history. In 1923, under the administration of Reverend R.N. Jones, the parsonage was destroyed by fire and rebuilt.

In 1957 when E.T. Hawkins High School burned, school was held in Lynch Chapel Methodist Church. Lynch Chapel was rebuilt in 1962 under the administration of Reverend H.C. Clay Sr. While the church was being constructed, services were held in the rebuilt E.T. Hawkins High School. Bishop B.F. Golden and Superintendent C.P. Payne participated in opening services for the new church March 4-11, 1962.

During the fall of 1964 under the administration of Reverend B.S. Thompson Sr., the mortgage on the church was burned with Cortez Lamb Sr., chairman of the Official Board; Mrs. Claudell Holbert, treasurer and Mrs. Carrie L. Moore, one of the oldest members participating. On December 13, 1964, the building was dedicated. Bishop M. Lafayette Harris and District Superintendent S.S. Barnett participated in this service.

The present Lynch Chapel

New Zion Baptist Church

Methodist Church Mission Team.

During the administration of Reverend Lewis, many dignitaries came and participated in church services. These dignitaries included bishops, district superintendents, city and state officials, college administrators and professors, foreign missionaries, television personalities, university and high school choirs, prison inmates, a medical doctor, a professional athlete and numerous ministers.

The ministers of Lynch Chapel United Methodist Church from 1868 to 2000 are listed in the order in which they pastored: Reverends James Lynch, Parks, Walker, O.C. Carter, Henry Handy, J.I. Garrett, Joshua, P.R. Crump, Mose White, J.K. Comfort, Nelson Tools, W.L. Lamb, W.N. Ross, H.E. Morgan, J.B. Brooks, N.N. Sidney, R.N. Jones, G.W. Adams, Harry Holston, J.N. Isabell, Finley Williams, P.A. Taylor, L.A. Bohannon, H.D. Smith, James C. Gaddis, Page, John Luther King, Roger McMillian, Henry C. Clay, Jackson, B.S. Thompson Sr., A.F. Nelson, Coleman Turner, A.L. Geralds, Harold Leverette, Tommie C. Greer, Elijah Henry, James F. McRee, C.P. Payne, Patrick Phillips, Arthur Lewis Jr., Dock Everett Jr. and Noah Moore.

Lynch Chapel continues to serve the community under the capable leadership of Reverend Noah Moore who has pastored Lynch Chapel since June 1999. Reverend Moore's vision is to increase current member participation, increase membership and reclaim the children and youth of our church.

New Zion Baptist Church

On August 24, 1924 New Zion Baptist Church was organized by G.W. Gardner and H.P. Yarbrough. The charter members were W.E. McGee, W.C. Wall, Lela McGee, Sallie Risher, Nannie Risher, Abret Risher. Reverend G.W. Gardner preached, W.C. Wall was elected church clerk and W.E. McGee was elected deacon. Mornas Askin, G.G. Risher, Wilber Brassell, James Chester Sawyer, Mrs. Bertie Askin, Lozell Risher, Jewel Faulkner, Cleo Risher, Minnie Lee McGee and Addie Jewel McGee were the first members received. In 1925, John Risher donated land to build a church on, then in the early 1950s a storm blew that church off its blocks. In 1954, J.T. and Ola Ree (Risher) Carpenter donated the land for a new church. Taylor Wallace, county missionary, W.H. and Glen Risher, deacons, led the effort to construct a new building. Bienville National Forest donated 20,000 board feet of standing timber. A lumber mill in Forest hauled the timber to the mill and sawed it for half of the lumber. Brother Wallace collected used bricks to build the piers and made mortar with sand taken from the road ditches and did most of the building with help from women, children and teenage boys. The total cost of the building, roofed, blacked in, with windows and doors, was $500.00 Many improvements have been made through the years but the pine lumber walls, floor and ceiling in the sanctuary have not been altered in anyway. In 2000, Brother Joe Crane is pastor with Billy Alexander, deacon.

In the summer of 1965, under the administration of Reverend B.S. Thompson, a new parsonage was constructed. Mars Hill and Green Grove, sister churches of the Forest Charge, shared this project. Later Sherman Hill became a part of the Forest Charge and shared in this project.

In the fall of 1974, during the administration of Reverend Harold Leverette, Lynch Chapel was renovated. This renovation was paid out under the 1976-80 administration of Reverend Tommy C. Greer Sr.

The present Lynch Chapel United Methodist Church was constructed in 1989. It is known as the "Miracle Church" because it was built and furnished within eight weeks. The church was built by Lynch Chapel Pastor Arthur Lewis Jr., Reverend Earl Greenough, members of Alta Woods United Methodist Church Mission Team of Jackson, MS; church members and many friends who volunteered free labor and services. The church was furnished by members and friends who donated pews, lights and other items.

The opening ceremony for the new church was held on the third Sunday in December 1989. Participants in the ceremony were Bishops Robert Morgan and Marshall Meadors Jr., administrative assistants to Bishop Henry Clay Jr. and Joe May; District Superintendents John Thomas, Charles Nickelson and Cecil Jones; Reverend Earl Greenough and members of Alta Woods United

Oak Grove Baptist Church

On a cold December Sunday 1902, in a one-room school building, Harvey School, a few yards in front of the original building, nine people were led by Reverend Z.T. Faulkner in the organization of the Oak Grove Baptist Church, Scott County, MS. Reverend Elisha Woods Sumrall and Reverend J.H. Gruney were the assisting ministers on this occasion.

The charter members were Mr. and Mrs. J.A. Fountain, Norris, MS; Mr. and Mrs. Levi (Victoria) Roland, Norris, MS; Mrs. Martha Halbert, Norris, MS; George Earls, Norris, MS; Mrs. Julia Earle Goulds, Lake, MS; Mrs. C.G. (Beadie) Hollen, Longview, TX and Robert L. Harvey, Lake, MS. All are deceased.

The church became affiliated with the Scott County Baptist Association and has continued in the association, as well as the Mississippi Baptist Convention and the Southern Baptist Convention. Oak Grove helped celebrate the 100th anniversary of the Scott County Association in the year 20000.

The present church building was built in 1908. Reverend Z.T. Faulkner, first pastor and Reverend Wayne Sutton conducted the first revival in 1908 with an ingathering of 18 members. There have been 28 pastors and Reverend Victor R. Vaughn Sr. has served as pastor from 1973 until the time of this writing.

For the past 98 years there have been good ones and slow ones, but in faith our forefathers struggled at times to meet the many challenges. In 1918, the Harvey School was consolidated with High Hill School and in 1912 the cemetery behind the church, became a reality with the first grave and the second grave. J.W. Fikes died August 15, 1924. Now there are several more graves with a cyclone fence.

The church's first paint job was done in 1914 by the efforts of the women of the church. The red and blue quilt which they made was embroidered in white with the names of persons paying 10 cents per name. It was quilted and later sold to Mr. J.W. Fikes for $3 and is now in possession of her grandson, Carl Jones of Grenada.

In 1927, under the pastorate of Dr. A.A. Kitchings, three Sunday School rooms were added to the building. A Sunbeam Band Organization in the 20s was under leadership of Mrs. Fanny Fikes. BYPU and Training Union organizations were active in the 40s, 50s and 60s. WMU women were active at intervals, as well as Vacation Bible School. Over the years, Brotherhood once had an organization, but briefly. In 1964 the church underwent a "Church Development Year," under leadership of pastor John Waid, with an award for completing the year's efforts.

Sunday School was organized in 1908 with W.T. Halbert, superintendent. *The Baptist Record* and *The Commission* have been in every home, with the latter being deleted. Contributions to The Children's Village annually have been ongoing many years, as well as a yearly donation to the Old Men's Home (now named The Homeplace, men and women). Under pastorate of Reverend Smith Sanders, the church went to half-time in 1953. Remodeling of the building was done in 1950 under pastor Reverend H.P. Dayton. New pulpit, porch and steps were added under the leadership of Reverend J.R. Chittum.

Physical aspects of improvements over the years include roofing several times, painting and washing down many times, erection of a steeple in 1990 in memory of Howard Fikes, walking ramp in the 90s, air conditioning in memory of Williford Fikes and Delene Barrett, pew cushions in 1989 in memory of Homer and Lenora Fikes, Communion table in memory of J.W. Fikes, pulpit chairs in memory of Mrs. J.W. Fikes and Bartley Fikes, a bell on a pole with plaque in memory of Daniel Youngblood, new heating and cooling system in recent years, amplified system in 1997, vinyl siding on church in 1999, cemented parking area in 2000, donation of an organ by Steve Lee and in 1996-97 a well furnished, beautiful Family Life Center was built for fellowship meals, bridal and baby showers, golden wedding celebrations and other multi-occasions.

Oak Grove Baptist Church

Oak Grove Baptist Church

Summer of 1946 Pleasant Ridge Baptist Church

Pleasant Ridge Baptist Church

Pleasant Ridge Church sets on a red clay ridge in the Piketon Community in beat five in Scott County, MS. Two acres of land for a church and school in the southwest corner of the south quarter of section three of township seven, range nine was given by William Walters August 3, 1874.

Soon thereafter, a large one-room building was built to be used for both church services and school. A public road divided the two acres and a cemetery plot was designated across the road from the church.

The first pastor was J.H. Grundy from Forest. He walked 12-1/2 miles once a month to preach to the people at Pleasant Ridge. After a few years a Mrs. McGowen felt sorry for him and gave him a horse to ride.

Some years later a two-room school house was built a half mile north of the church where two teachers taught grades one through six. This school remained through the Spring of 1928, then all the small schools were consolidated into Ringgold High School about five miles away.

Beginning January 1900, W.S. Ford was called as pastor of the church and remained pastor until October 1922. He preached once a month for $2.00 a month and had to quit because of old age. Early church clerks were L.M. Hunt, A.C. Walters and C.A. Hunt. Amro Walters was the first church treasure.

The appearance of the church building remained about the same for around 70 years. Weatherbeaten sides that had never been painted, wooden blocks for a foundation and a roof of hand riven boards. On the inside were crude looking benches. The floor was made of wide planks with cracks in-between. The simple made pulpit stood at the east end of the building with an outside door on each side. Directly behind the church was a path that led down the hill to a spring, where we could get water to drink at all day gatherings. A small outhouse, that we called the toilet, was the nearest thing to a bathroom. Travel was by horse and buggy, mules and wagon, horseback and on foot. The trees in the churchyard served as a hitching post.

After WWII electricity spread out into the rural area and improvements and additions were made on the church building. Some years later community water provided the opportunity to install bathrooms. Little-by-little, year-by-year additions and renovations have changed the appearance from the mid-40s until the present year, 2000.

The following names are most of the pastors that have preached through the years, but may not be in the order they served: Grundy, Ford, May, Thomas, Clark, Bufkin, Gardner, Beverly, Walker, Henderson, Byram, Fairchild, Durell Edwards, Wall, Nelson, Hollingsworth, Savel, Jenkins, E.E. McDill, Tucker, John Gardner, Ricky Edwards, Beaver, Jimmy McDill, Warren, Hawthorne and Latham. Robert Gardner has been pastor since December 1989.

Active deacons of the church, December 2000 are: Michael Gibbs, Toby Gibbs, Billy Gibbs, David Allen, Douglas VanEtten and Matthew Shelley. Inactive deacon K.C. Walters.

Church clerk, Ruby Shelley Fortenberry; treasure, Gwen Touchstone VanEtten; youth director, M'Lee Hamm Gibbs.

Most of the family names that were church members through the years: Walters, Hunt, McGowen, Thomas, Mann, Gentry, Lang, Tucker, Bounds, McDill, Summers, Haralson, Wall, Hollingsworth, Patrick, Burkes, Pace, Roberts, Croxton, Graham, Weems, Shelley, Posey, Arnold, Gunn, Bowles, VanEtten, Harrell, Abbott, Rushing, Rigby, Fortenberry, Gardner, Gallaher, Brown, Tadlock, Gibbs, Stroud, Beavers, Allen, Bryant, Rankin, Dugan, Bell, Barnes, Boykin, Warren, Strebeck, Sessions, Taylor, Rutlage, Massey, Stone, Collins, Wolf, Sanders, Lanthrip, Hodge, Mosely, Stewart and Clark.

Year 2000 Pleasant Ridge Baptist Church

October 1990 Pleasant Ridge Baptist Church

Ridge Baptist Church

Around 1900, a group of believers from northern Scott and southern Leake counties formed Ridge Baptist Church. Charter members were the R.L. Gomillions and the James Baileys. That same year, a church building was constructed on Hwy. 35, two miles south of the Scott-Leake County line. This agricultural region, named Pea Ridge, became home to many families who attended the new church.

In 1903, the congregation was part of Hopewell Baptist Association and later Scott County Baptist Association. Though largely Baptist, the community had a sizable Methodist population. As such, Ridge served both denominations with Baptist and Methodist ministers conducting services on alternating Sundays, a cooperative effort continued into the 60s.

Beginning with W.S. Ford in 1903, Ridge has been blessed with caring pastors. Ministers with the longest tenures are: Reverend J.L. Moore (1935-42); R.A Herrington (1943-47); Arlis E. Smith (1961-65) and I.L. Hill (1987-93).

Through selfless service, lay members filling leadership roles and providing behind-the-scenes support have greatly influenced the church's direction.

Led by volunteers, music services have always been a vital part of worship. Information since 1950 lists song directors Douglas Dodson, S.F. Barfield, L.E. Gomillion, Malcolm Green and accompanists Irma Jo Dotson and Janie Gomillion.

In the mid-60s, it became apparent that the original building was no longer adequate. Construction of the present building on Hwy. 35 began in 1973, with dedication May 12, 1974. Today, Ridge Baptist Church continues serving its community.

Old Ridge Baptist Church

Springfield Baptist Church

On Sunday, June 15, 1997 Springfield Baptist Church, Morton celebrated its 125th year of existence. The church was organized on Sunday, June 15, 1872 with 27 charter members.

The building where the members worship today was completed in 1950. Lumber from the old church was used in the new building and the pastorium that was built in 1951. The present pastor, Dr. Frank Lay resides in the pastorium built in 1972. A fellowship hall with education space was built in 1987. In the late 1990s the church auditorium was renovated and new pews installed in 1999.

The members of the church have supported mission causes through the years by their faithful giving and participation in long-term and short-term mission endeavors for the cause of Christ. Several individuals have been licensed and/or ordained by the church to preach the gospel.

The church has been led by some 35 pastors during its 128 years—many faithful men of God who have inspired us in various ways as we seek to serve Christ. It is our prayer that the progress which history records is only briefly noted by comparison with the importance of spiritual growth in the lives of all who have been touched by this church and its fellowship of believers.

Springfield Baptist Church

Organizations and Clubs

American Legion, Forest, MS

The first American Legion post organized in Forest was the Harry Banks Post No. 133. The post was organized March 21, 1921. R.L. Goodwin was commander and H.E. Bishop was adjutant. The post charter was canceled September 29, 1924.

Scott County Memorial Post No. 9 Forest, was organized June 22, 1928. Roy Stevens was elected commander and Hal Williams was adjutant.

The present Legion Hut is a concrete building constructed in 1968 with a separate meeting room for the Ladies Auxiliary. Regular meetings are held on the fourth Monday of each month and a meal is served.

The Legion prides itself on the community service it does, especially for the veterans. They sponsor boys and girls to the annually held Boys State and Girls State where the students learn about state government. Special recognition is given to high school seniors for outstanding work. Special programs are given for patriotic holidays, usually on the courthouse lawn.

Membership in the Legion in 2000 hovers around 300.

American Legion Auxiliary
Scott County Memorial Unit 9

This unit has been chartered twice. The first charter was in 1922 and was lost in the 30s. The records of this unit have been lost, but some of the early members were Mrs. Colbert Dudley, Mrs. R.B. Austin Jr., Mrs. Jeff Miles, Mrs. W.J. Gay, Mrs. Tom Wallace, Mrs. Grady Austin, Mrs. Stanley Bishop, Mrs. Roy Stevens and Miss Lillie Belle Hunt.

Our present charter was granted February 18, 1952. Our first president was Mrs. Willie Mae Mitchell and Mrs. Johnnie Loper was the first secretary. We still have two charter members on our rolls, Mrs. Dot Williams McGough and Mrs. Dorothy Lackey.

Mrs. Jean Eady served as state president 1984-85 from this unit. Numerous people have served on state committees. We strive each year to meet our membership goals. We participate in all programs that benefit the veterans in our county and state.

The aim and purpose of the American Legion Auxiliary is to help the veterans in all programs better suited for women to carry out.

All women who are wives, daughters, mothers, sisters, grandmothers, granddaughters and great-grands of veterans and who are the age of 18 years are eligible to become members.

The women of this unit raised the funds to buy the monument to all Scott County Veterans which is on the courthouse square.

Daughters Of American Revolution
Hontokalo Chapter, Mississippi State Society,

Hontokalo is an Indian word meaning "seven streams flowing north." In the northeast corner of Scott County the streams come together to form Tuscalameta River which flows into the Pearl River.

Hontokalo Chapter was organized May 20, 1976 in Forest, MS. Mrs. Oliver H. Hopkins served as organizing regent and also as first chapter regent. Other chapter regents have been Mrs. Elmer D. Evans, Mrs. Charles Stutts, Mrs. V.L. Smith, Mrs. Jack Stuart, Mrs. Charles Stutts, Mrs. V.L. Smith, Mrs. Peyton Eady and the present regent, Mrs. Joe. R. Clarke Jr.

The objectives of this organization are historic, educational and patriotic. The chapter motto is: "God, Home and Country."

Any woman over the age of 18 years who had an ancestor who fought in the American Revolution is eligible to join.

Each regular meeting includes devotions, patriotic exercises, the President General's message and a three minute National Defense Report.

Mid-Century Club Charter Members
Standing: Mrs. Stanley Peckham, Mrs. Prentiss Loper, Mrs. J.T. McAdory, Mrs. Don Wilkins, Mrs. W. B. Wall, Mrs. A.T. Cleveland, Mrs. Allen Roby, Mrs. Emmett Berry. Seated: Mrs. W. J. Dalrymple, Mrs. Fred Gaddis, Mrs. Earl Walsh, Mrs. Richard Meek, Mrs. Otis Redden, Mrs. Charles Sanders, Mrs. Guyton Idom.

Chapter meetings are held the first Tuesday of September, October, November, January, February, March and May at 2:00 p.m.

Forest Garden Club

The Forest Garden Club was organized February 1962 and became federated in November 1963.

The idea for organizing a garden club was first presented by Mrs. H.E. Bishop to two friends, Mrs. O.B. Triplett Jr. and Mrs. Fred Gaddis, while dining at the Gaddis lodge. All three ladies thought Forest should have a garden club. Interested ladies of Forest were called and the first meeting was held in the home of Mrs. O.B. Triplett Jr., Mrs. M.B. Latham and Mrs. John McLaurin from Brandon assisted in organization. Those attending the first meeting were Mrs. Jack Lee, Mrs. L.W. Willey Sr., Mrs. J.D. Allen, Mrs. Robert Weems, Mrs. R.E. Boyter, Mrs. H.E. Bishop, Mrs. T.G. McCormick, Mrs. Bill Huff, Mrs. Dick McCravey, Mrs. V.R. Lackey, Mrs. Horace Epting, Mrs. C.L. Brueck, Mrs. Fred Gaddis, Mrs. P.H. McLaughlin, Mrs. Frand Mize, Mrs. Dolly McNeill, Mrs. Bob Mize, Mrs. C.M. Ueltschey, Mrs. W.M. Christian, Mrs. D.G. Allen, Mrs. George Townsend, Mrs. Troy Hannah.

The purpose and objectives of this club is to further the artistic development of the members, to encourage their interest in gardening, to work for the conservation of our natural resources and to engage in the beautification of our civic community.

Month meetings are held on the third Tuesday of each month, September-May at 9:30.

Past presidents are Mrs. O.B. Triplett Jr., Mrs. George Townsend, Mrs. Ray Sturrup, Mrs. Robert Weems, Mrs. Hulon Blackwell, Mrs. William Huff, Mrs. R.O. Hannah, Mrs. Richard Meek, Mrs. Charles Sanders, Mrs. Henry Melicar, Mrs. James E. Jaggar, Mrs. Jim Brown, Mrs. V.R. Lackey, Mrs. Joe Anderson, Mrs. Ellis Sparks, Mrs. Lewis Eure, Mrs. James R. Wagner, Mrs. Wilson McGough, Mrs. Florene Rhodes, Mrs. Charles Palmer, Mrs. John Lynn, Mrs. Jimmy Lackey.

Forest Mid-Century Club

Under the guidance and sponsorship of La Petite Fortnightly Club, Forest Mid-Century Club was organized in November 1950 and admitted to full membership in Mississippi Federation of Women's Club, Inc. on December 9, 1950. Its objectives are the intellectual improvement of its members by systematic study, the promotion of a spirit of helpfulness to others and the organized effort for constructive public service. Over the last 50 years, Mid-Century Club has been at the forefront of projects designed to improve the quality of life in Forest, and members of the group have served in leadership roles throughout the community. The club's current budgeted projects include, but not are limited to, Penny Art, Adopt-A-Teacher, Mississippi School for Deaf, Hugh O'Brien Youth, Whitfield State Hospital, Forest Public Library and Habitat for Humanity. In earlier years Mid-Century sponsored and/or supported many projects which included preparation for the coronation activities for the Southeast Mississippi Livestock Show held annually in Forest, the Cancer Fund Drive, March of Dimes, Clean-Up-Paint Up-Fix Up Campaign, Red Cross, The Hemophilia Foundation, Inc.; Nurses Scholarship Fund, the Polio Fund, Mental Health Drive, United Givers Fund and countless others.

The club celebrated its 50th anniversary on October 15, 2000. Four of the 15 charter members remain active and were honored at the reception: Wilma Cleveland Bailey, Grace McAdory, Effie Ola Meek and Louise Sanders. Effie Ola Meek served as the club's first president. *Submitted by Martha Graham*

Forest Rotary Club

The Forest Rotary Club is affiliated with Rotary International and a member of District 6820. The club was founded in 1928. The Forest Rotary Club currently meets each Wednesday at noon at Penn's Santa Fe Restaurant on Highway 35 South in Forest.

The club currently has 38 active members.

Internationally, Rotary has led the private sector fight against eradicating polio, helping impoverished people get safe drinking water and has encouraged international cultural exchange around the world. Through the Paul Harris Fellowship Program, the Forest Rotary Club actively sponsors Rotary International Foundation activities each year.

The local Rotary Club's annual philanthropic project is the Dr. Bob Mayo/Mrs. Josephine Lackey Memorial Rotary Horse Show Classic, which over its history has raised over $50,000 for local schools, law enforcement agencies, health care facilities, orphanages and public awareness campaigns.

The motto of Rotary International is, "Service Above Self - He Profits Most Who Serves Best."

La Petite Fortnightly Federated Club

The La Petite Fortnightly Federated Club was organized in 1933 under the auspices of the Forest Fortnightly Club with the guidance of Dolly McNeil. The object of the club is "to enlarge our radius of mind and heart; and enlighten us to play a larger part in our community." Through the years, La Petite Club members have promoted many worthwhile causes.

The founding president of La Petite was Mrs. Sidney Doty followed by Mesdames: Frances Bain, Sam Howell, Frank Glick, Chester Mitchell, Oliver Hannah, Marjorie Williamson, William Pippin, James Fountain, Seymour Dalsheimer, Smith Tarrer, Oliver Ormond, Lamar Gatewood, G.C. Chambers, Sam Franklin, Joe Hunt, Bill Huff, Hamilton Stevens, Frank Stanton, Henry Melichar, Warren Jones, Meredith Mitchell, George Townsend, Marx Huff, John Bondurant, Roby Stegall, Marshall Carleton, Tip Bishop, Roy Noble Lee, Bill Dearman, Ray Sturrup, Guyton Idom, Bill Austin, Gordon Toudt, Lewis Eure, R.O. Hannah, Dan Thomas, Tom S. Lee, Jimmy Lovett, Richard Lackey, Jim Thompson, Bill Fortinberry, Marion Ueltschey, Wyatt Measells, Rhett Mitchell, David Gaddis, James Reed, John Smith, Grace Russell, Roy Fountain, Doug Woods, H.J. Hedgepeth, James Greener, Joe Townsend, Victor Hosey, David Dickerson, Troy Nettles, Allen Breland, John Mowrey, Billy Webb, Kevin Reynolds and Jerry Cook.

Morton Homemaker Volunteer Club

The Morton Homemaker Volunteer Club is a very dedicated, multi-talented, caring and service oriented group. With 17 active members they donated 2,167 hours to volunteer services in 2000.

In 1927, Miss Sidney Ann Standifer, Home Demonstration Agent, came to Scott County and began organizing Home Demonstration Clubs. These clubs met on a monthly basis. She taught cooking, canning, gardening, sewing and other things to help the homemaker. Today, we still have programs to educate, inform and enlighten the homemaker, as well as promoting volunteerism. Club members participate in the Cultural Arts Exhibits and Homemaker Fairs, bringing home many ribbons. Also, many awards are won at the Scott County Awards Luncheon by the Morton Club.

Some of the club projects are Blair E. Batson Children's Hospital (monetary gifts, personal size hygiene supplies); recycle old eyeglasses; card fronts for the St. Judes/Boy's Town project; Campbell's Soup labels for the Methodist Rehabilitation Center; We Care Mission (donations, workers); Faith In Action (delivery of meals to the homebound); magazines for waiting rooms; Friends of the Library; Ronald McDonald House (supplies); Camp Rainbow for children with cancer; Relay For Life Cancer Drive; Blue Ribbon Campaign to stop child abuse; Women's Correctional Facility (sewing supplies) and the delivery of Christmas boxes to the homebound.

Homemaker volunteers are always ready for service and assistance and share in a special fellowship of friends. Officers for 2000-01 are Katie Measells, president; Shirley Sawyer, vice-president; Bobbie Hodges, secretary; Alice Harris, treasurer; Shawna Alexander, reporter and Claudia Hollingsworth, telephone committee.

Norris and Scott County Club Activities
Past and Present

It's probable that I am as old as Home Demonstration work in the Norris Community, or that it is as old as I am here in our community, namely 88 years plus. My first remembrance was in the teens and early 20s when I was 8 or 9 years old.

Morton Homemaker Volunteers
Seated from left: Katie Measells, Maggie Willingham, Shirley Sawyer, Frisky Roland. Standing from left: Bobbie Hodges, Peggy Parkman, Claudia Hollingsworth, Lorene Moncrief, Lawanda Laird, Iris Holbert, Mary Nell Traxler. Members not pictured: Alice Harris, Doris Bedwell, Teri Burkes, Ann Owens, Shawna Alexander.

Members of the Norris Homemakers Club

Miss May Haddon was the first Home Demonstration Agent I can remember. She went from home to home, demonstrating, instructing, encouraging and advising the homemakers on methods of improvement for the rural family, especially in the preservation of foods. Everyone looked forward to her visits for she brought novel and practical ideas to share with the women. And how? By horse and buggy, of course. About that time, my mother bought an outdoor water-bath canner, which was heated by a wood fire underneath, as in a wood burning stove and held approximately eight to 12 half-gallon jars. Two large chinaberry trees in our backyard afforded an ideal place for the preparing and boiling of these large jars, filling them with snap beans, peaches, tomatoes, and blackberries. No other size jar was considered here at that time. They turned into yum-yum eating and sharing with the sick or otherwise in the community, such as "poundings," etc.

Before I finished high school in 1929, I had become a 4-H club member, probably when Mrs. Olga Magee, later Mrs. Olga Hughes, was the agent. Miss May Haddon had been promoted to a state assignment, namely, the first nutritionist in the state at State College. Our 4-H Club met once a month at the school and during the summer we met at the High Hill School building. Mrs. Magee did not remain long, maybe three or four years. I distinctly remember her teaching us to do patchwork neatly and correctly, for you recall a lot of patching and darning was done in those days.

About this time, late 20s, during the State Fair in Jackson, Friday was declared School Day and 4-H Club Day. We even paraded down Capitol Street, which was a highlight time of the year. Fun, then, of course. How did we get there? By train, of course, catching the 4:00 a.m. "Cannonball" in Forest and back on the regular 5:00 p.m. train. If it was wet weather and bad roads, we had to go around by Lake to get to Forest in time, for the "Cannonball." Passenger trains did stop in Lake.

I'm not sure, but I think there was another agent before Miss Sidney Ann Standifer came, but I'm not sure for I was away in school and cannot recall events of that period.

Then the vivacious, lovable, Miss Sidney Ann Standifer from Tennessee came on the scene in the late 20s or early 30s. She was a great leader, motivator, teacher, promoter and encourager. She put Scott County on a good, workable level as to organization, which stressed awareness of improvements in all areas of the lives of the homemakers, whether mother, grandmother, wife, or daughter. Clubs were duly organized in many communities in the county, Norris, being one. She arranged the monthly meeting dates of the clubs so that she could attend all the meetings and get all the members and potential ones to the meeting. Not unusual for her to make two, three to more trips around a community to gather up members for the meeting, even sitting four or five people to the seat with her in the center of the front seat driving. Even small children came with their mother to the homes of the hostess for the meeting; some even "played" sick from school on club meeting day to go with "Mama" to the meeting.

She enjoyed laughing at her own boo-boos and it was a joy to be in her company. At one meeting, she was reminded of having her dress wrong side out, to which she replied by telling the group she thought they ought to see how seams looked on the inside. She gave herself and her talents for the improvement and advancement of her fellow man. She remained in Scott County about 25 years and returned to Tennessee for retirement, making, however, two visits back on special occasions. When the primroses bloom in the spring, we think of her, as well as thank her, for having scattered the seeds along our highways and roads, far and wide.

Elizabeth Webb followed Miss Standifer in 1947-51, 3-1/2 years as agent and later married Vernon Lee Gatewood, now living in Scott County. Ruby Rone succeeded Elizabeth as agent from 1951-53 and later married Norman Fountain, living presently in Forest. After serving as the assistant agent with Ruby, Judith Kuykendall became the agent in 1953-64 and remained 11 years, now married to Richard Gatewood and living north of Forest. Mrs. Sarah Barr followed Judith for a term of service sometime in the 60s. Deborah Bennett followed Mrs. Barr, served many years, married Harold Harris and was promoted to a management position on the state level and is now deceased. By the way, Home Demonstration Agent name was changed to Home Economist in 1960.

Beverly Harden Maddox is presently in her 16th year as our efficient economist and has enhanced the progress of the original purposes of the extension service with many education advantages included. By her diligent efforts, she has succeeded in making the composite organization in Scott County urban as well as rural. Changes and more changes.

Another delightful experience in this reminiscing about the Norris Home Extension Club work was an afternoon visit recently in my home with Mrs. Carmen Ronken and her sister, Mrs. Annie Belle Murphey of Jackson. Carmen, who has retired from many years in extension work was Mississippi Southwest Leader for the District Extension Service, embracing 20 counties. She cited several instances of the highlights in her extension work and recalled with interest many areas of endeavors on the local and state level. I have the loan of her copy of *Our Heritage, 1909-1970,* an enjoyable informative history of Mississippi Extension Services.

Several members of the Norris Club, whom I do not have their names, have been in attendance at local, county, district, state and national meetings and have received 50 year and 25 year membership pins, as well as five ruby and three ruby pins for outstanding leadership over the approximately 80 years of existence.

It took me nearly 70 years, more or less, to earn a 25 year pin. Several years the Norris Club has been honored as the Scott County Club of the Year and Scott County Club Woman of the Year has been chosen on several occasions from the Norris Club membership. Several members were chosen at one time or other, president or some other officer of the Scott County Council. At one time, three generations were enrolled for many years, namely Alma Turner, Vallie Turner Burns and Zora Lana Burns, the last two still active members in 2001.

Various and numerous projects have been accomplished over the years, with a great one now pending, an Extension building for Scott County. *Submitted by Pennye Merle Gatewood*

Order of the Eastern Star

1921-2000

On April 20, 1921 Forest Chapter No. 168, Order of the Eastern Star was constituted with 24 charter members. The chapter continued to grow in membership until in 1932 the roll showed 75 members. However this being the year of the great depression, the chapter suspended 39 for NPD. Records show that in 1945 more interest was shown and membership increased.

The first lines of officers were Nettie Miller, W.M.; Dr. J.J. Haralson, W.P.; Odessa Allen, Asst. M.; Will H. Walker, Treas.; Louise Boyter, Sec.; Fredna Haralson, Cond.; Eleanor Walker, Asst. Cond.; Olivia Haralson, Adah; Ina Watkins, Ruth; Effie Little, Esther; Mary Christian, Martha; Ruth Huff, Electa; Tressie McCormick, Chap; Bertha Haralson, Org.; Hattie Mae Lee, Marshal; Tennie Haralson, Warder and Dr. W.C. Anderson, Sent.

We are still enjoying our chapter and presently the roll shows 85 members. The current officers are Doris Nanny, W.M.; Steve Russum, W.P.; Mary Thompson, Asst. M.; Johnnie Thrash, Asst. P.; Grace Faulkner, Sec.; Yvette Moore, Treas.; Patsy Leach, Cond.; Mildred Boykin, Asst. Cond.; Nadine Noel, Chap.; Colon Anding, Marshal; LaRue Barnes, Org.; Betty Gaskin, Adha; Gladys Williams, Ruth; Mary C. Culpepper, Ester; Sue Fortenberry, Martha; Joann Anding, Electra; Mavis Thrash, Warder; Udell Sessions, Sent; Maressa Russum and James Greener serving as pro tem officers.

Rose Garden Club

Lake, MS

The Rose Garden Club was organized in October 1930 as the Lake Garden Club when Mrs. Rose Harrison, Mrs. Vi Sanders, Mrs. Mae Mucklerath and Mrs. Ollie Kunes went to Laurel to a flower show, taking their best flowers to enter. Upon arriving they were told that it was Garden Club day and no individual entries could be accepted, so the ladies went outside and organized the Lake Garden Club with Mrs. Mucklerath, president; Mrs. Sanders, vice-president and Mrs. Harrison as secretary. They hurried back inside just minutes before the deadline for entering the show.

Their flowers were shown and the Lake Garden Club won second place. In January 1931, 18 women including the original four, met in the home of Mrs. Ida Wilkins to organize an official garden club. The four officers elected in Laurel were elected along with Miss Winnie Brooks as treasurer.

A constitution was adopted and by-laws written. In 1933, the name of the club was changed to the Rose Garden Club in honor of Mrs. Rose Harrison. The rose is the club's flower. In 1935 the garden club was affiliated with the State and National Federations. In 1980 Mrs. Mattie Ruth Evans was elected president, serving in that position until 1998. During the 18 years of her tenure, her focus was the restoration of the Lake Depot seeing the garden club receiving a Federal TEA Grant to restore this very important building from our historic past.

It is appropriate to pause and pay tribute to the founders of the Rose Garden Club and to the members, officers and committee chairpersons who throughout the 70 years have, with their enthusiasm and untiring efforts, kept the club going.

In this year 2000, the slate of officers are Ann Hall, president; Barbara Goodwin, vice-president; Louvenia Logan, secretary/treasurer and Peggy Pettey, committee chairman. Having completed its first 70 years, the Rose Garden Club now turns it attention toward the 100 year mark.

Scott County Library

The first library in Scott County was organized in 1933 by Reverend Jim W. Sells and has had a checkered but progressive history. It was first located in the home of Mary Katherine Knoblock who became the first director. At the beginning there were only a few books, some were donated and the Mississippi Commission at Jackson loaned as many as they could. Because of the efforts of Reverend Sells, collections were sent from Boston and other places. Later the library was moved to the high school and then to the County Agent's office.

In the beginning the going was rough and at times the very existence of the library was threatened. Funds were low and at times non-existent. The library was constantly being moved due to various reasons. The next location for the library was the Community House. Miss Knoblock worked for nine months at one time without pay.

After giving so much of her time and efforts, Miss Knoblock was asked to resign because of a ruling that the director must be a person on relief. At that time there were 1,200 books and 12 stations throughout the county.

The next director was Miss Emma Ryan Gresham and Mrs. Zula King was her assistant. During 1936-37 the town furnished lights, water, heat and janitor services. The library closed for several months in 1943. In the summer of 1945, Mrs. H.E. Bishop, Mrs. Ollie Ott, Mrs. V.R. Lackey and Mrs. Beamon Triplett met with the supervisors in the interest of the closed library. As a result of the meeting, $1,200 from county funds was made available for the reopening of the library. Complying with Senate Bill No. 166, a Library Board was appointed. It included Mrs. V.R. Lackey, Mrs. H.E. Bishop, Mrs. W.W. Gaddis, Beamon Triplett and Lamar Rigby. Mrs. Bishop was appointed as librarian August 29, 1945. In the next few years the library was located first over the W.F. Stephens Store on the corner of Main Street, then in 1948 it moved to the upper floor of the Masonic Building. During this time the library continued to grow and expand it's services to the people of Scott County. In 1950 the Mississippi Library Commission made their small bookmobile available to the library for periods of time. It was used to give even the most remote areas of the county better service. Sub-stations were located at Morton, Lake, Sebastopol and Ludlow. At one time the librarian used one of the county's school buses to carry books to and from the schools and the sub-stations. A number of improvements were made but the enlarged program made it necessary for the library to be on the ground floor. In 1953 an exchange of locations with the Masons became effective in February 1953 and it was moved downstairs in the Masonic Building. Beautiful new furniture was installed and the shelves were filled with books for every readers taste.

In December 1955 a colored library was started with a few shelves and a small book collection. Only 24 books were circulated in the first month. The first librarian was Jessie Mae Johnson. It was located in the old jail and was serviced by the work-

Forest Public Library

ers from the Capital Area Regional Library in the same way that it served the Scott County Library. Additional shelves were added and the collection of books increased year by year.

In 1967 with funds provided by the city of Forest and the Library Services and the Construction Act in cooperation with Mississippi Library Commission, the old band hall on the corner of Raleigh and Second Street was remodeled to become the library we have today. George Mason Construction Company of Jackson, MS and architects Cooke-Douglas-Farr of Jackson, MS did the work. The Board of Trustees for the library at that time was Jewell McMullan Smith, chairman; Sudie Thompson Allen, Opal Wilkes Austin, Myrtice Dearman Doty and Etoile Loper Hopkins. Marjorie Williamson was librarian. The Capital Regional Library of which Scott County had become a part, merged with the Jackson Library later to become the Jackson Metropolitan Library system. In 1986, this system split up and the Forest Library joined with Scott, Rankin, Smith and Simpson counties to form the current Central Mississippi Regional Library System. In 1988 the library was remodeled again. The library system offers a lot of different programs throughout the year for library patrons. They include story time for children, summer reading programs, Friends of the Library and Outreach to schools and clubs, both children and adults. There is also a good genealogical section with census records and materials to help people searching for their roots. Thanks to a grant from the Gates Foundation, the libraries in the Scott County area have computers that are connected to the internet that are available to the public. At present Tammy Jones is the head librarian, Dianne McLaurin is the children's librarian and Jan Hollingsworth is reference librarian.

"A public library is a necessary part of the educational equipment of every city and to it any man can go, feeling that he will find someone to help him."—William Greene

W.L. and O.K. Slaughter Memorial Foundation

The foundation was officially incorporated in 1982, one year following the death of W.L. Slaughter. The organization is an educational, non-profit entity funded entirely through private donations. One of the main programs is the library where more than 2,000 volumes are housed, along with artifacts, photographs and other precious memorabilia depicting African American lifestyle.

Another foundation project is the Boy Scout and Girl Scout Programs initiated in 1984. The foundation discontinued the Boy Scouting program in 1996. The Girl Scouting Program continues today.

The foundation also sponsors an Adult Reading Program and an Essay Contest in memory of its founder, Olivia K. Slaughter, who died in 1991. The contest challenges high school seniors to share their perspective or means of improving society.

The foundation's most recently devised project is the Slaughter Library-Todd Pinkston Tutorial Program. This program provides afterschool care and tutorial assistance for more than 35 young people. One of the financial co-sponsors is Philadelphia Eagle wide-receiver and former Slaughter Scout Todd Pinkston.

Additionally, the foundation works to provide assistance to residents of the W.L. Slaughter Subdivision. An annual Yard of the Season Contest is sponsored to encourage residents to decorate their homes and yards.

The foundation is governed by an Advisory Board and Board of Directors consisting of the six daughters of W.L. and Olivia K. Slaughter: Dr. Cheryl Ellis, Attorney Constance Slaughter-Harvey, Charlotte Moman, Alderwoman Cynthia Melton, Clarice Bell and Carolyn Fuqua. The board of directors also includes former coach L.T. Smith.

Olivia K. and W.L. Slaughter

Businesses

Bank Of Forest

Bank of Forest was organized at the turn of the century and observed their 100 year anniversary March 2000.

The bank was organized by a group of stockholders headed by the late Major R.W. Millsaps of Jackson, who appointed the late J.R. McCravey Sr., a young banker from Senatobia, as cashier. To young Mr. McCravey, the situation was a challenge and so firmly did he believe in the future of Bank of Forest, that he invested his savings of $2,500.00 and $1,000.00 borrowed from a sister in the purchase of $3,500.00 worth of stock.

One year after opening the bank, the deposits had grown to $42,389 and there was a net profit of $500.00 after paying the cashier's salary of $1,000.00 and other expenses.

Major Millsaps, who had served as president, died in 1916 and Z.D. Davis of Jackson was elected president. After Mr. Davis' death, Mr. McCravey was elected president in January 1921.

Mr. McCravey served as president until August 18, 1939 when his son, W.D. McCravey, became president. W.D. "Mr. Bill" McCravey assumed the title of chairman of the board in January 1981 when T.E. Walker was named president and CEO. Mr. Walker joined the bank in December 1979 as executive vice-president and chief executive officer. In January 1993, T.E. Walker was named chairman of the board and CEO and Allen Breland was named president and chief operating officer. Mr. McCravey remained on the board of directors as chairman emeritus until his death in December 1993.

Bank of Forest, Highway 80 Forest, MS

Antely Grocery

Antely Grocery, 1925 Forest, MS

Boutwell Butane

Sometime around 1940 D.W. Boutwell started Boutwell Butane. It was located at the corner of Wade and Walker streets in Forest, MS. Shortly after, John Boutwell went into partnership with his father. They operated in the same location until the untimely death of both men in 1978. At that time John's two sons, John Boutwell Jr. and Keith Boutwell took over the running of the business. Its present location is on Highway 35 South.

Bradley's Discount

Bradley Wolverton got his start in the food business when he began working for D.Q. Hunt at Hunt's Food Store in August 1949. This store was located on Highway 80 East. In 1952 he acquired Hunt's store and operated it as Bradley's Food Store. It was in 1959 that he opened Bradley's Red and White located north of the courthouse.

In 1962 Bradley opened his second store under the name of Wolverton's Grocery located on Highway 80 West.

He opened a Jitney Jungle Supermarket in Woodland Shopping Center in 1965. In 1974 the name was changed to Bradley's Discount Foods.

Businesses Around The Time Of World War I

Around the time of WWI, Fairchild's Grocery was located on the east side of the corner of South Main and First Street. It was later sold to Ace Burns. Ike Fleisman owned a store and W.A. Goodwin had a mercantile businesses. Mr. Goodwin once held a contest and gave away a piano. R.L. Noblin also owned a mercantile store. Some of the other business in Forest around this time were Lyle's Grocery, D.G. Allen's Hardware, Noblin's Hardware, Pevey Millinery and W.S. Vance and Company Drugstore. The druggist was Will Christian.

T.M. Steele's Department Store was one of the largest stores in Forest. Mr. Steele lived near where the Forest Baptist Church is located and he owned the hearse which was used for all funerals. Clyde Cater owned a bakery which was located on the west side of the corner of South Main and First Street; W.F. Stephen's Store was later in that same location.

In the bottom floor of the Kent Building was the Bienville Lumber Company Commissary. On the top floor were lawyer and dentist offices. Some of the lawyers were Mr. Kent, Mr. Nichols and Mr. Huff and Mr. Madden was the dentist. One of the activities that the young people enjoyed around this time was the Lyceum group that had concert pianists and singers who performed classical music. This group came to Forest three or four times during the school year. There was a Chautauqua Tent show, which had cultural and educational entertainment every night that

they were in town. Butler's Park was where the political rallies were held. A Mr. Schmidt, who was a Republican moved to Forest around this time. He was met with strange looks and many stares, most of the people had never seen a Republican before!

People also enjoyed the county field meets. Activities in these meets included races, games, literary events and contests in spelling, history and algebra. Back then the "big prize" was $1.00.

Local people who wanted to attend the State Fair in Jackson went on the "Number One Train" which left Forest at 4:30 a.m. There were no paved or gravel roads to Jackson at this time.

Businesses In The Early 1900s

Businesses of this time included Hill Gardner's General Merchandise, G.H. Banks' General Merchandise and Ben Wolf's General Merchandise, Liles Brothers Grocery, Pevey and Hood's Store, G.W. Rew's General Merchandise and Morgan Colbert Grocery. These stores were on the west side of South Main Street. On the east side of South Main was M.D. Graham and Company General Merchandise, which was one of the largest stores and provided for many of its farmer's needs. Next to Graham's was a camp yard. This was a vacant lot where farmers could camp out when they came into town. The next store was T.M. Steele's General Merchandise. Mr. Steele was also a cotton buyer. The only brick building in town was Eastland's Drug Store. It was a two-story building, which had offices for the town's doctors and dentist. The three doctors were Dr. Haralson, Dr. Pevey and Dr. Anderson. The dentist was Dr. McElhenny. The next building was J.F. Story's General Merchandise. Mr. Story was a Civil War veteran who had only one leg. Next was a camp yard and the W.W. Lowry's General Merchandise. Mr. Lowry's store was quite large. He was also a cotton buyer. Lee Gresham was a black businessman. His store was located on the eastern end of East Second Street. The stores usually opened very early in the morning and remained open until 8:00 or 9:00 p.m.

The original jail was located on the western end of East First Street. Most stores in town had cisterns behind them and people used dippers to get a drink of water. The first water works was located in front of the courthouse. People in town took up money and sank a well to provide water.

Businesses In The Late 1930s And Early 1940s

Some of the older businesses continued to operate in the same location into the 1930s and 1940s. There were however, many new businesses in the downtown area. Some of the new businesses on the east side of South Main Street were Ace Burn's Grocery, Barnes Clothing (later Ben Franklin Store) and R.M. Christian's (later Thomas Great M). On the west side of South Main Street were W.F. Stephen's Clothing Store, Walker Chain Store, Harrison Drug Store, Earl Noblin's Grocery, Sherman's Barber Shop and Stubb's Clothing Store (later Ott's Furniture). On the corner was Little and Ware Funeral Home, which was later sold to Ott and Lee. For a while Dr. Austin's office was located here. Later Certified Radio opened a business on this corner

New businesses and offices on the courthouse square were the Chevrolet Company (later Lott Furniture), Jitney Jungle, the post office (later Western Auto), Bill Mendum's Cafe (later Forest Shoe Repair and Carlton Drugs).

On the north side of Second Street were Irby's Drug Store, A and P Grocery and Mississippi Power Company. There was a vacant lot where the Town Theater was later built.

On the east side of the courthouse were the Standard Filling Station, Collier International Harvester, the Palace Theater, Drew Hunt's Grocery and Dinty Moore's Restaurant. Upstairs over the restaurant was the telephone exchange. Across First Street from Dinty Moore's was the Postal Telegraph operated by Mr. W.L. Jones. He also had a bottling works at the intersection of Broad and Jones Street. He bottled soda water at this location in the late 20s and early 30s.

Businesses, Past And Present

Scott County has been home to many different businesses, from the small, family owned mercantile to industry supplying goods all over the country. The county has evolved from the time of local dry goods stores and supplies arriving by train to a very prosperous area with eight banks, three newspapers and six schools. *The Scott County Times, The Lake Messenger* and *The Spirit of Morton*, published weekly, cover local news and interest. Many former Scott Countians throughout the US keep up with "news from home" with subscriptions or carefully cut articles mailed by loved ones.

The county also boasts of four public libraries, more than a dozen attorneys, two hospitals and a couple of dozen doctors. The Forest Public Library, being the oldest and largest in the county, houses the collection of the Scott County Genealogical Society. Lackey Memorial Hospital and Scott Regional Hospital offer state of the art health care and life saving emergency care to the citizens of Scott County.

Numerous restaurants, car dealerships, real estate offices and many locally owned manufacturers and retail stores can be found throughout the county. Poultry and lumber continue to be major industries in the area. B.C. Rogers, Inc., Choctaw Maid Farms, Lady Forest Farms, Peco Foods of Mississippi, Inc. and Tyson Foods, Inc., some of the largest employers in the county, make Scott County fondly referred to as the "Chicken Capital" of Mississippi. These companies have added much to the economy of the county and businesses have started as a result of this. Machine shops and poultry supply and hardware stores throughout the county are evidence of this.

From hardware to software to ladies wear, it can be found in Scott County! The 21st century finds Scott County ready for business.

C&R Auto Parts

C&R Auto Parts was organized in 1957 by Tom Culpepper and V.C. Rhodes. It was located on Highway 80 West. In 1971 Harry Culpepper became a partner with Tom. Tom retired from the business in 1984 and Harry took over. In 1995 C&R Auto Sales incorporated with Big Muffler and became Culpepper Sales. It is still located on Highway 80 West and is still owned and operated by Harry Culpepper.

Conditions In Forest In The Early Days

There was of course no electricity, no plumbing and no paving. Cattle, hogs and chickens roamed freely throughout the business and residential areas for a number of years. Eventually the business section had board sidewalks. Windows and window screens were unknown. When the hotel was built, its dining room had a large hinged ceiling fan. It was pulled by an attached cord and swung back and forth over the length of the dining room table. Travel was by foot, horseback, wagon, or stagecoach over rough dirt roads. Stagecoach passengers were sometimes in danger of being robbed. The Copeland Gang was said to operate in the Scott County area. The first stage line did not actually run through Forest. It ran from Alabama into Mississippi, through Hillsboro and Morton and on to Vicksburg. Later the stagecoach came into Forest on what is now Oak Street and stopped at the corner of Oak and Raleigh Streets. It also stopped at the Peavy Hotel.

In the early 1900s the people of Forest had few of the amenities that are enjoyed today. No running water, no telephones and of course no electricity. People bought kerosene that they used in lamps to light their homes. If they walked outside at night, they carried a lantern. At night people slept under netting to keep out mosquitoes and bugs. People used small tree limbs to kill flies. People had very little money, but almost every family had a garden, a cow and some chickens. Most people had to have these things to live because salaries were generally quite small. Railroad workers received $1.00 a day. A man who worked at a sawmill from sun-up to sundown was paid 50 cents a day. Bank clerks were well paid, receiving $30.00 a month, but they worked very long hours. Many of them stayed at a boarding house, which cost $12.00 a month.

Of course, prices on most items were much lower. Round steak sold for 10 cents a pound, sweet potatoes were 50 cents a bushel and corn was 35-50 cents a bushel. A barrel of flour that weighs 196 pounds sold for $5.00. A girl's used bicycle could be purchased for $2.00, 25 cents down and 25 cents weekly. George Antley, a young newspaper boy at this time, sold *The Times Democrat*, a New Orleans newspaper, for 5 cents a copy. The papers cost him 3 cents a copy. Coal oil was 10 cents a gallon. Postage was 2 cents. A haircut at the barbershop cost 25 cents and a shave cost 15 cents. Crossties for the railroad were 25 cents each and were hand hewn, not sawed. A hard worker could make 10 crossties in a day. Homesteaders could buy land for 50 cents an acre. People who came into Forest to conduct business would often camp out rather than pay 50 cents to spend the night in one of the three hotels. Meals at the hotel were from 25 cents to 50 cents for all you could eat. Sometimes these people came to town early and brought fresh meat to sell. They would kill the meat in the evening and build a fire to keep flies off it overnight. Many people cooked their meat to preserve it longer.

Plain food, much of which was raised in the family garden, was the main sustenance at this time. The only cereal people had was oatmeal. Fruit was not generally available during the year, but at Christmas most children received an orange, some raisins, or other fruit. Many children also received one Roman candle in their stocking. People did have plums, scuppernongs and persimmons, which grew wild. Hickory nuts and scaleybarks also grew in the forest.

Do You Remember?

Do you remember these places?

The Palace Theatre, Town Theatre when you could see the movie, get popcorn and a drink for a dollar, the Roxy Drive-In, Marlers Tasty Freeze, the Bus Station Café, Bill Mendums Café. How many remember when Forest had a public swimming pool? Do you remember shopping at any of these places: Ben Franklin, Walker Change store, the Soda Fountain at City Drug and six-cent cokes and coke floats, Dog and Suds when they had carhops, walking across Highway 80 to G.C. Chambers for candy when Forest High School was where the Community Bank is now; Anderson's Grocery, Tobe Ivy's Grocery, Milners Grocery, J.E. Noblin Grocery, Paul Chambers store at Hillsboro, Jim Pryor's gas station (coffee shop) and when Forest had an Ice House? When we had Stock Show Parades and when they had the stock show carnivals where the Tyson parking lot is now? Do you remember when Forest had a bowling alley? The Gunn's Dairy in Morton? There are so many businesses that have come and gone over the years. These are just a few that I remember

Cook Motor Company was connected to Kent Building West Main Street, Forest, MS

Cox Chevron Station

Raymond and Helen Cox opened the doors of Cox Chevron Station on October 17, 1963 as a full-service gas station and they have maintained their full-service line while adding self-service and in 1990 a well-stocked convenience store.

Before Raymond and Helen opened the station, it had been operated by Edward Rhodes as a Standard Station. The land was owned by the Hazel Lackey family from whom it was leased. After buying the station in 1963 and operating it as a Standard Station until the 1970s, the Cox's changed to Chevron. They purchased the land from the Lackey family in the 1980s. In 1990 they decided to upgrade their operation so they tore down the old station and built a new, larger more modern building.

Raymond and Helen moved their family from Columbus where they owned another service station. Raymond was from Sebastopol and Helen from Newton County so Scott County seemed like home. They have three children: Steve married Lisa Pittman and has a son Christopher, Vance married Amanda Agerton and has a son Briggs and another baby on the way; Steve and Vance help their parents operate the station and Judy, who is director of Cardiovascular Diagnostics at Baptist Hospital in Jackson; Amanda married Ron Henderson and has two children, Austin and Haley.

Cox's Chevron has been a family owned business since the beginning. It is only one of two full-service stations left in Forest and one of three of the oldest family owned businesses left in Forest.

"The customers are special to the Cox family," says Helen. "Some of our customers have been doing business with us since we opened. Many of our customers have become our friends. They really care about us and we care about them. That's the advantage of living in a small city like Forest."

Raymond semi-retired in 1993, but the goal is for the business to remain a family owned and operated business into the next generation.

The business hours are Monday-Thursday: 5:30-9, Friday-Saturday: 5:30-10 and Sunday 7-9.

Steve and Vance Cox

Helen and Raymond Cox

Forest Fish House

It all started with a dream in August 1984 when Willie D. and Jane Dennis started a Fish House in Jane's family home in Harperville, MS. It was known as "West Harperville Fish House." Willie also opened Hillsboro Snack Bar at Hillsboro in 1984 as takeout only, then on July 23, 1986, he opened the "Hillsboro Fish House."

On October 5, 1988 Willie rented a small space and started a carryout service in Forest. People started asking when they were going to have a place where they could dine in. So they started looking for a bigger place to move. On May 3, 1989 the "Forest Fish House" opened at 311 South Main Street. As Willie and Jane started Fish Houses in different towns in Scott and adjacent counties, the work became too much for just the two of them. Their children were in Florida, Willie called and asked if they would consider moving back to Mississippi and help with the businesses. When Willie decided to semi-retire his son Tom and his wife took over the Forest Fish House.

In 2000, it became clear that a bigger building was needed with more parking space. They acquired the old Sunflower/Aultman's building on Highway 80 and remodeled. They moved there in the last part of 2000. Willie D. Dennis loved people and it was his greatest joy to cook for them and make them laugh with his jokes. He also preached for 30 years. It was all a lot of work but it was well worth it. Everyone that has had one says there is nothing better than a "Willie Burger." Willie has passed on now, but the owners, staff and Mrs. Jane would love to thank everyone that has patronized any of the Dennis Fish Houses. The Dennis's have had Fish Houses in Harperville, Hillsboro, Lake, Newton and Carthage as well as the one in Forest.

Willie D. and Jane Dennis

Willie and Jane cooking at Hillsboro Fish House

Ed Davis Motors, Inc.

Founded December 10, 1986 with Edwin M. Davis, owner. Ed Davis started in the automobile business in 1957 working in Picayune, MS for GMAC. He worked there until 1968 when he bought interest in Rogers Davis Motor Company in Morton, MS. He owned that dealership until January 10, 1976. He purchased Service Chevrolet in Pelahathie, MS and changed the name to Ed Davis Chevrolet, Inc. He currently owns that dealership which has been renamed Don Davis Chevrolet, Inc. In December 1986 he purchased Lee Chevy-Olds from John Ed Lee and set his sights on building a new dealership. The land was purchased and the new dealership was erected at 835 Highway 35 South in Forest. It is currently known as Ed Davis Motors, Inc. At Ed Davis Motors we have a saying that "Price is only half the deal." We firmly believe this. We have great employees that truly believe that the customer comes first and will do what it takes to satisfy all of our customers. We treat them right. Ed Davis Motors, Inc. employs a great group of people that live in and around the Forest area. Ed Davis is committed to the Scott County area not only because he loves the area, but also because he was born in Pulaksi, MS.

First Homes And Businesses

George Brown partially constructed the first house in Forest, but before it was completed several other homes were started and completed. Although Mr. Brown's house was only partially complete, he provided food and lodging to the travelers and also cared for their livestock.

Captain David M. Womack, a prosperous merchant and Make D. Graham and their families came here immediately following Mr. Brown and built homes. Soon after Mr. Brown's house was begun, John C. Simmons and C.W. Pevey constructed a hotel here, the first building to be completed.

The first merchant to establish a business in Forest was a Mr. Briscoe. Other business men of the time were Lod Moore, who owned a mercantile store; W.W. Lowry; T.M. Steele, who owned a department store; Make D. Graham; Morgan Colbert; Ben Wolf; G.C. Rew; G.H. Banks and J.F. Story.

A Mr. Eastland operated the first drugstore and Tom Mitchell owned a jewelry store. Dr. Hillard Gardner was a merchant who was also considered to be one of the best doctors of his time. The first post office was located in his store. In 1873, Henry Garrett opened a blacksmith shop.

There was little cotton in the country, none worth mentioning being raised after the first year of the war.

Other early settlers in the Forest area included the Harpers, Smiths, Hogans, Manns, Clarks, Carrolls, Lacks, Singletons, Womacks, Hoods, Hendons, Granvilles, Millers and Mitchells.

Activities for young people involved games such as horseshoes, marbles, bicycle races, horse races, hunting and swimming at Crocker's gap, which was part of Dog River. A fallen pine log formed a pool in the river, which was then a clear beautiful stream. An older boy sometimes rented a buggy from the livery stable for about $2.00 a day and took the girl of his choice for a ride. One activity that many people enjoyed was watching the trains come into the depot. There were eight passenger trains; six carried mail. Townspeople would meet the trains to see who got on and off.

The townspeople had frequent parties, sometimes as often as once a week. Occasionally they had ice cream parties. The drug store would order 100 pounds of ice by express from Jackson.

Once a year 200 to 300 Indians would come into town to play a game of stickball. They would come the night before the game and the merchants of the town would give them food. The Indians would dance all night and play the ball game the next day.

Saturday night baths were a tradition. The water for people to bathe in had to be heated on a wood stove and poured into a tub.

Things sure have changed in the last 100 years

Fountain Ace Hardware

Fountain Ace Hardware was established in September 1946 by Carl S. Fountain and Laverne Fountain. The store has operated in the same location on East First Street since that time.

In 1968 the store joined the Ace Hardware group of individually owned stores.

In 1969 Carl H. Fountain joined the business at which time the Mendum Café building adjoining the store was purchased and the size of the store was increased. The business was incorporated in 1970 and the name was changed to Fountain Ace Hardware, Inc. The store is still run by the Fountain family in the same location.

Gum Springs Mineral Water

Located in Gum Springs, eight miles north of Forest in Scott County, was Gum Springs Mineral Water reported to relieve kidney and bladder trouble. Owned and operated by Reverend A.A. Eady, a boarding house was offered for visitors at $1.00 a day, $6.00 a week or $20.00 a month with children and servants one-half price. Analysis of the mineral water showed it to contain iron, calcium, magnesium, silita, chlorine, aluminum, sodium and potassium. Testimonials can be found of high praise for the mineral water and a stay at the boarding house:

"I have used Gum Springs water for drinking purposes almost exclusively for the past 18 months and have experienced excellent results from its use. Can heartily recommend its use to anyone." G.S. Stovall, Druggist.

Community Bank

On October 6, 1904, the charter of incorporation of Farmers and Merchants Bank was approved by then Governor James K. Vardaman and Secretary of State James W. Powers. The incorporators of the original charter were T.B. Graham, T.B. Smythe, Hi Eastland Sr., G.G. Beamon, J.D. Chadwick, D.G. Allen, S.E. Liles, T.M. Steele, G.H. Story, W.H. Pevey, B.F. Crook, H.O. Bland, R.H. Gatewood and Jeff Kent. On August 14, 1905, Farmers and Merchants Bank opened for business as a state bank with a paid-in capital of $20,000, one employee and 42 stockholders.

The first elected officers and directors included E.F. Ballard, president; T.B. Graham, first vice-president; Jeff Kent, second vice-president and attorney and C.H. Ferrill, cashier. The Board of Directors included the existing officers plus Jno. W. Rogers, W.A. Goodwin and G.B. Merrill.

By January 1955, total assets had grown to over $3.3 million with $60,000 in capital and over $3 million in deposits. Through the years, Farmers and Merchants Bank has had outstanding leadership from several Forest businessmen who guided the bank's growth, including H.E. Bishop who began his career at the bank performing a variety of jobs from cashier to bookkeeper and retired as its chairman of the board. Thomas Colbert joined Farmers and Merchants Bank as chief executive officer in 1968 and has overseen the bank's phenomenal growth since then.

At the close of business April 16, 1975 total assets had reached $17.5 million with $1.6 million in capital and over $15 million in deposits. Farmers and Merchants Corporation was formed in 1977 and acquired Farmers and Merchants Bank in 1978 to become Mississippi's first bank holding company. Farmers and Merchants Corporation changed its name to Forest Bancorp in 1986.

In May 1994, in an effort to reflect the bank's expansion beyond the borders of Forest, Forest Bancorp then changed its name to Community Bancshares of Mississippi, Inc., the name it holds today.

In 1995, Community Bancshares of Mississippi acquired M&M Bancorp, parent of Community Bank, Ellisville and merged with Community Bancshares of Indianola, parent of Community Bank, Indianola.

In 1996, Community Bancshares of Mississippi acquired Coast Community Bank in Biloxi. Community Bancshares issued its first cash dividend of $1 per share in 1997 and Community Bank, DeSoto County received its state charter. In 1999, Community Bank, Meridian received its state charter, as well.

Since the 14 original directors incorporated the bank in 1904, Community Bank has maintained excellent leadership, like today's directors who include Scott County residents George W. Taylor Jr., Freddie J. Bagley, Darrell Brown, Dink R. Gibson, W.C. Haralson, James V. Lackey, Dr. John P. Lee, Norma Ruth Lee, Charles W. Palmer and Sidney L. Salter.

In 1999, the *Mississippi Business Journal* named Community Bank one of Mississippi's fastest-growing private companies and Community Bank recently made the list of the *Top 10 Largest Mississippi Banks*. From the Tennessee border to the Mississippi Gulf Coast, Community Bank has grown to 20 offices, almost $1 billion in assets and more than 300 staff members statewide.

Despite its growth across Mississippi, the people of Community Bank still like to say, "It all started in Scott County."

Community Bank has called 323 East Third Street in Forest home since March 12, 1975

Gum Springs Mineral Water

For Kidney and Bladder Trouble

Located 5 Miles North of
Forest, Scott County, Miss.

RAILROAD STATION: FOREST. MISS.

A. A. EADY,
Gum Springs, Miss.

Gum Springs Mineral Water

Forest Hotel, ca. 1900s Forest, MS

"I have been a constant drinker of Gum Spring water for two years and can't say too much for Gum Springs water. I have been troubled with my kidneys for the past six years and have got a great relief from the use of this water." C.J. McComb.

"I suffered with indigestion for four years. I tried several doctors without any relief. I was not able to do my housework. Finally I began using Gum Springs water. I have been drinking the water about five months, I have gained 12 pounds and am now sound and well. I cannot say enough for Gum Springs water." Mrs. Ellie Parker

Lee Gray Chevrolet

The Lee-Gray Chevrolet Company was originally established in 1925 and its name was Joyner-Hannah Chevy Company owned by W.H. Joyner and William Hannah. A year later R.L. Goodwin, H.E. Bishop and J. Knox Huff purchased the company and the coporation of Central Chevy was organized for 25 years. Jack Lee and Caley Gray purchased it in 1951.

Mapps Florist

Mapps Florist originated in 1947 with Mrs. Dolly McNeil. Mrs. McNeil, calling the business Dolly's Flower Shop, had her shop located on Third Street, where the Old South Café once stood.

In 1950, Marcus and Elise Mapp bought the business and moved it to the Berry building on First Street, next door to Berry's Cleaners and changed the name to Mapps Florist.

Mrs. Bob Mize and Grace Buntin purchased the florist as partners in 1954 and in 1960 Grace purchased the other half of the business. Mrs. Buntin's son Tommy, ran the business until the early 80s when Pam Hollingsworth and Jimmy Rawson purchased it. Pam Hollingsworth then purchased Rawson's half and in the early 90s the shop was purchased by Tony and Samantha Wolf, the present owners.

Marler Auto Company

In 1945 B.E. Marler opened a new car dealership and a John Deere Farm Equipment business. The name of the new company was Marler Auto Company. They had a service shop for both cars and tractors. In 1947, he took J.D. Greener as a partner to serve as service manager. In 1949 James Archie Marler started to work after finishing college. The business operated in the partnership until 1960 when J.D. Greener died. Some years later a corporation was organized with B.E. Marler and James Archie Marler as principle stockholders. The corporation with James Archie Marler as president operated until 1987, when the property was sold to McCarty-Holiman in Jackson. They built the Jitney Jungle store on the property.

Poultry Packers

Poultry Packers was organized March 1, 1963 by Moore Farming Company, Inc. of Morton and R&R Milling Company of Carthage, this is now Tyson Poultry.

G.C. Chambers Gulf Station, now B.P. Station, Highway 80, Forest, MS

Gaddis Packing Company, now Tyson Forest, MS

Kent Building, now holds Lott Furniture West Main Street, Forest, MS

Lyles Woodworking Plant South Main Street, Forest, MS

Staff and employees Marler Auto Company 1960s Front row, L-R: Clyde Lay, Dale Burks, James Greener, Joddie Dudley, Louis Wilson, James Stewart, Hubert Walton, James Archie Marler, Violet Gaddis, Edgar Marler. Back row, L-R: Ray Haralson, Grady Hopper, Leroy Kidd, Lonnie Stephens, Edell Sessions, Jim Evans, Grady Sessions, Tim Bradford, Dallas Glaze, Willie Hurtt, Leon Sessions, Gerald Majors.

Lott Furniture Company

Lott Furniture Company of Forest, Inc.. opened in Forest July 1, 1936. This store was one of a chain of stores opened by Reuben Lott of Laurel, MS. Original stores that still use the Lott name are in Meridian, Jackson, Brookhaven, Forest and Laurel. The managers bought the stores from Mr. Lott and were told they could operate under his name as long as they paid their bills and operated the store in a reputable manner.

Mr. Lott was considered to be a rich man in his time. He knew how to manage money. He and his wife "Blondie" never had any children.

This store has always been on West Main Street in Forest. Hilton O. Boyles from Homewood came to work for Lott Furniture Company in June 1941. Later he became manager and bought the store in 1959.

The store was originally located between Fred's Dollar Store and Sturrup and Baddour Store on the corner. Lott Furniture is presently located in the "Kent" building, constructed in 1911. The Kent building once housed the Bienville Lumber Company owned by Loren, Harry and Chester Mitchell. They had a commissary in this building. They later closed the commissary and Jitney Jungle located in half of the building and Fred's Dollar Store occupied the other half.

Ray Sturrup bought the building from the Mitchells after Jitney Jungle left. Mr. Sturrup remodeled the building, replacing the floor and tin building on the back with brick and concrete floors. Hilton Boyles bought the store from Ray Sturrup in 1978 after Fred's moved to Highway 35 North, where it is presently located.

The original conveyor belt that Mr. Sturrup installed is still in use that leads to the upstairs. The upstairs is presently used for warehouse storage. It was originally divided into offices that were rented by different people in the early days. Some of the people who had offices upstairs were Dr. Madden's dental office, Kermit Reynold's dental office and Roy Noble Lee had an office there.

The original fireplaces are still there, along with a big safe. The petitions have been torn out and the upstairs is now open to storage.

The front of the Kent building originally had two entrances. When Ray Sturrup remodeled the front he moved the doors and made only one entrance after he acquired the whole building for Fred's Dollar Store.

Lott Furniture employees: James Goss, Jean Haralson, Frank Colbert Jr.

Ott And Lee Funeral Homes
Serving Scott County Since 1934

Photo ca. 1934, Ott and Lee Funeral Home located on corner of Highway 80 and Banks Street

Ott and Lee Funeral Home 2001 located on 1st Street, Forest, MS.

R.L. Noblin Grocery

R.L. Noblin Grocery, ca. 1896 Homewood, MS

Sherman's Barber Shop

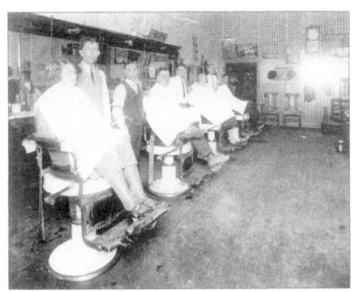

Sherman's Barber Shop South Main Street, Forest, MS

Six Cees Law Building

Constance Iona Slaughter Harvey, the first African American female to graduate from the University of Mississippi School of Law, officially opened her law office in January 1973 and worked in the Six Cees Office Building which housed her law office and her father's offices. She also conducted lay advocacy training programs (Southern Legal Rights Association) in that building. It has since been re-named the W.L. Slaughter Memorial Library Building. Attorney Harvey closed her office in February 1979 when she became executive director of East Mississippi Legal Services.

After spending 17 years as a state administrator (director of the Governor's Office of Human Development from 1980-84 and Assistant Secretary of State from 1984 until 1996), she re-established her practice in the old Six Cees Superette Building which she purchased from her parents in 1977. The building was renovated and refurbished in 1999 and still contains some of the original equipment such as a coke machine, bubble gum machine and benches.

Her practice includes a solo general practice with emphasis on family law, corporate and defense representation and some criminal work. The practice is located at 516 Jones Street, Forest, MS.

Southern Hotel

The old Southern Hotel stood across the street from the Forest Depot, on the corner of Oak and Main Streets. The proprietor of the hotel, beginning in 1913 was Mrs. A.S. Johnson. She believed that putting food on the table was the way to keep the hotel filled.

Mrs. Johnson was a shrewd businesswoman. She and her husband moved to Forest in 1913 and took over the old Womack Hotel. It was a 13-room structure with one bath. Nine years later in 1922, it burned to the ground. Mrs. Johnson was undeterred by disaster. She simply moved another building in to take the place of the destroyed one. She dismantled the Shubuta Hotel, which she had owned since 1921 and brought it to Forest.

The new building, built closer to Main Street was christened the Southern Hotel. Additions were made over the years which gave the hotel 22 rooms and 10 baths.

Mrs. Johnson ran the hotel until 1957 when she became ill, she turned the operation of the hotel over to her daughter, Mabel Johnson Bliss.

A 1958 Forest newspaper article boasted that the Southern Hotel had been patronized by people from "every state in the union and several foreign countries." The same article listed Mississippi governors and congressmen and their families who had visited the hotel to sample its fried chicken. The original price for a meal was 5 cents. The cost for rooms was $1.00 for one person and $1.50 for a couple.

Southern Hotel

Morton, MS March 20, 1923 T.B. Gaddis Millinery Store. Mrs. L.P. Roberts and customer

77

Steele's Department Store

T.M. Steele, Claude Steele, Clell Steele and Carl Steele organized T.M. Steele's Department Store in 1895. Its original name was T.M. Steele and Sons. In 1945 J.O. Freeman and F.H. Heide purchased the firm and changed the name to Steele's Department Store. It remained in business until the mid 1960s.

Thompson Motors

W.F. Thompson of Morton organized Thompson Motors, as a Mercury dealer in 1951. The American Motors line was added in 1958 and the Lincoln franchise in 1969. The company began in a building owned by Hillard McMillan and Red Smith (where J&R Sales was located) and operated there a year before moving to the Highway 80 East location. In 1963 James May and Tommy Sistrunk purchased the business. It operated for over 25 years in that location.

T.B. Gaddis Businesses

Morton, MS March 20, 1923 T.B. Gaddis Fertilizer and Feed Warehouse L-R: Ike Myers, Alongo Wilson, W.B. Tullos, F.H. Laseter

Morton, MS T.B. Gaddis Mercantile Store Will Howe and Laster Waldrip

W.F. Mapp Funeral Home

Mr. W.F. Mapp founded the funeral home in 1948. It was located in a building on East Fourth Street. Today it is in its third building and is still owned and operated by the Mapp family. Mr. Mapp's son, W.F. "Toby" Mapp Jr. operates it today

First funeral home ca. 1949

Second funeral home

Mapps Funeral Home, 2000

Legends

Bits And Pieces

from Old Newspapers

•July 17, 1901: Work on the deep well in the courthouse yard is being revised in order to put in an air pump, but a great deal of trouble is being experienced by the drill breaking into several feet below the surface. If suggestions counted for anything, Forest would have one of the best waterworks systems in the state.

•1901 Advertisement: Schoolbooks at J.H. Aycock & Co. Right kind of prices on everything; yes, get 5 cents worth of most anything you want.

•March 13, 1901: A bulletin has just been issued from Washington showing the amount of cotton ginned in Mississippi by counties in 1899, which showed that 618,833,461 pounds ginned in the state. The amount ginned in Scott County that year was 4,697,185 pounds.

•October 9, 1901: There are 16 licensed physicians in Scott County

•September 4, 1901: Supt. Lee Miles resigns: In the two years that I have been in office, we have decreased the number of schools from 105 to 91.

•January 6, 1904: The *Register* will give a year's subscription to the first couple to get married that results from the girls' leap year proposal. There are about 12 old bachelors in Forest and if they're not married before this year is out, the girls will have only themselves to blame. It's leap year you know.

•1927 ADV: Remote control door handles AC air cleaner amazing price reduction. The Coupe $625.00

•November 24, 1909: An Eastern Star Lodge is being organized in Forest. The wives and daughters of Masons are eligible to join.

•May 1, 1907, Teachers Examination: The following pupils of the Forest School made first grade licenses but have not reached the age limit for teaching, which is 17 years: Zula Banks, Ottis Buckley, George Rew, Graham Smythe and Forrest Cooper.

•May 8, 1907: The board of supervisors awarded the contract for enclosing the courthouse yard with a substantial and ornamental iron fence and lying of concrete walks within. The contract was let to the Colonial Concrete Co. at Meridian for $824.

•May 8, 1907: There are not many folks in Forest who can swim, so sidewalks have become a necessity. We must have them.

•October 5, 1904: Rolfe Stokes, a 16-year-old boy, who lives on Willis Stokes farm near Gilbert, picked 441 pounds of cotton September 20 and rested half an hour at noon.

•July 9, 1902: The deep well in the courthouse yard has now been equipped with a large pump and people and stock are being supplied with an abundance of pure water.

•August 1902: At the stockholder's meeting at the Patron's Union Wednesday morning, it was decided to lower the gate fee to 25 cents for gentlemen and ladies to be admitted free in the future.

•October 15, 1902: Official announcement of the census of educable children made this year - it is shown that Scott County has 5,303. By separate school district Forest has 296.

•August 23, 1918: It is very necessary that we have all our allotment of 57 pairs of socks knitted and ready for shipment to our soldiers by next week. Mrs. A.W. Cooper.

•The Spanish influenza epidemic of 1918 killed many people in Scott County.

•October 16, 1907: E. Cahn of Meridian, owner of the Forest Gin & Manufacturing Company has installed the electric light plant and the business houses of Forest can now be furnished with incandescent lights at the following rates: 1st light $1.00 a month, 2nd light $.75, all other at $.50 each month. The plant will run until 11:00 p.m.

Boiler Explosion In The Forest School

The morning of November 8, 1933 the school bell rang at 8:00 a.m. as usual in the Forest School. By 8:15 the students were in their desks in the three-story brick building, which was located where Community Bank now is.

The desks were bolted to the wooden floor and most of the students sat near the front of the room. However, in Miss Frances Bain's class, two boys, William Riser and John Boutwell, were sitting near the back of the room in the north corner. Directly underneath the back corner of Miss Bain's classroom was the boiler which provided steam heat for the building.

The two janitors did not know the boiler was empty and prepared to fill it with cold water. A tremendous explosion rocked the building. Students were thrown from their desks, many so high they hit their heads on the ceiling. The two janitors were killed, as was William Riser, who was sitting directly above the boiler. John Boutwell suffered a broken leg.

In Miss Annie Antley's second grade room, the force of the explosion had sealed the door shut. Soon townspeople appeared below the windows and the children were handed down to the waiting hands below.

The auditorium could still be used but a new classroom building had to be built. The school was rebuilt in the same location with the addition of a gymnasium. This building was used until May 1966. In September of that year classes began in the new building on Cleveland Street.

Broiler Festival

The amazing expansion of the broiler industry in Forest that rocketed this area to one of the top chicken producing counties of the US, involved tremendous foresight, willing financial assistance, energetic community cooperation and an unnerved test of confidence. In 1954 there were three chicken producing plants in the Forest area with a weekly capacity of 375,000 broilers; Cudahy, Gaddis and Forest Packing. The fourth processing plant, Southeastern, was about to begin operations.

In view of this outstanding progress and appreciation of this widespread interest in this area's accomplishments, the poultry dealers inaugurated the first Broiler Festival in Forest during June 1954. Fred Gaddis along with his brother Ed Gaddis were originators of the Broiler Festival. Fred Gaddis was the first president of the Mississippi Festival. Over 2,500 people attended, enjoyed a half-fried chicken with accessories and watched the judges select Vi Tarrer of Forest Bathing Beauty Queen and Kathy Bishop as Baby Chick Queen.

A crowd of 4,500 enjoyed the 1955 Festival. By 1956 the festival had reached giant proportions, becoming a statewide endeavor. In 1957, J.P. Coleman, Governor of Mississippi, delivered the welcoming address to a crowd of 13,000 people. Linda Lackey was the first girl from Forest to ever be chosen Broiler Festival Queen in 1958. The festival was held through the summer of 1959, when it was discontinued until the summer of 1982. It is still being held today, the first Saturday of June. It is presently held at Gaddis Park in Forest, MS.

Cemetery Receives Historical Notice

As a result of the efforts of a Forest native, Willie Horton, the Western Cemetery was awarded a Certificate of Historical Significance by the

The sponsors of the Forest Festival Chicken Dinner held on June 30, 1955 at the Community Center L-R: Fred L. Gaddis, Ed M. Gaddis (Gaddis Brothers); J.E. Calhoun (Calhoun Seed & Feed Store), W.L. Tate (Tate Hatchery), R.A. McAuliffe Jr. (Southeastern Hatcheries of Mississippi, Inc.), Jack Lee (Master of Ceremonies), Dennis Eure, D.W. Boutwell (B&E Feed Store); O.F. Waltman (Scott County Cooperative), Dr. Bob Mayo (Poultry Supply Company), R.F. Barnes (R.F. & J.W. Barnes), not in the picture J.B. Black (J.B. Black Company), J.W. Barnes (R.F. & J.W. Barnes), "Cooter" Hawkins (Black Brothers & Hawkins)

Graves of six confederate soldiers Western Cemetery

Western Cemetery 2000

Board of Trustees and the Department of Archives and History. The cemetery is located along side the railroad and almost under the overpass of Highway 35 in Forest. Horton, who worked as a projects officer in the Department of Planning and Policy for Federal State Programs, made the application with the department and included documents and information that led to the certificate. Mr. Hilliard of the Board of Trustees of the Archives and History Department asked the Scott County Board of Supervisors to see that the cemetery was repaired, rehabilitated and maintained as a national monument. A list of names on the headstones was also submitted. They are John B. Biscoe, 1841-1885 (one of the cities first merchants); A.H. Biscoe, 1814-1875; Fred Neill, 1883-1884; Mary Neill, 1876-1877; Emma R. Killen, 1872-1882; Martha Maranda, 1856-1882; Edmund Richardson Gresham, 1826-1875; infant of J.H. and K.C. Biscoe, 1879-1879; Allen A. Johnson, 1808-1866. There are six markers that read "Unknown Confederate Soldier." Another marker says "Six Brave Soldiers Sleep Here, In Memory of Confederate Dead."

Markers were placed many years ago by the federal government after the chapter of the United Daughters of the Confederacy applied for such recognition.

Dr. Howard Clark

What an honor it must have been for Dr. Howard Clark of Morton, MS to be named 2000 Country Doctor of the Year. Out of 501 nominations from 41 states, Dr. Clark won this most prestigious title.

For 44 years he has served the people of Scott County. He opened his Morton Clinic on July 1, 1956. A native of Richton, Dr. Clark graduated from Richton High School and Mississippi State University. He served during WWII in the Army. Dr. Clark has served 43 years as the Morton High team doctor, missing only one game to deliver a baby. A daily patient load of 60 plus, supervising the care of patients at Scott Regional

Hospital and 110 nursing home patients, he is on call nights and weekends at the SRH emergency room. At 73, Clark still makes house calls, even after having triple-by-pass surgery. Dr. Clark has delivered over 4,500 babies, the father of 13 himself. He still maintains 12-14 hour days. This is truly a dedicated doctor and we in Scott County are very proud of him.

Fact or Fiction

Whether more fact or more fiction, this is a story that has been around Forkville for many years. It was published in the *Morton Progress Herald*, December 8, 1949 as told by Mrs. Dora McCormick and it was reprinted in the *Centennial Edition* in 1966:

A well known story in the Forkville Community began at a Bethlehem Church revival which took place during the pastorate of William Robinson, probably about 1881. It seems that at the first service, Brother Robinson preached on "Crime Does Not Pay," a timely subject since the exploits of the Jesse James gang were being reported in every newspaper. Following the service, a stranger introduced himself as a minister and was invited by the pastor to assist in the remaining services. A great spiritual awakening occurred, with 75 applicants for church membership at the close of the revival, which probably more than doubled the size of the church's congregation. The visiting minister stayed in the home of the Sprouse family; after the revival he worked about 10 days in a sawmill at Ludlow and then disappeared.

Jesse James was killed April 3, 1882 in St. Joseph, MO; his brother Frank, surrendered, but was never brought to trial. Frank James became a clerk in a Dallas store and many people would go there just to see the once-notorious outlaw. A member of Bethlehem Church (one of the Ponder boys, son of a deacon), while in Dallas did just that and initiated a conversation with the former gangster. Frank James proved to be unusually interested in the fact that the store patron was a Mississippian and questioned him about a Scott County church, Bethlehem and it's pastor, Brother Robinson, only to learn that he was conversing with a member of that very church. Frank James then disclosed that he would never forget the good fried chicken he ate there many years before while assisting in a revival!

Local Woman Hanged

In the 1902s the Forest jail was located on the south corner of East Main Street. There was a gallows on the second floor of the jail. On November 4, 1921, a man and woman were hanged for murder on these gallows.

The pair was convicted and sentenced to be hanged for the murder of Alton Page. They had confessed to killing Page by hitting him on the head with a heavy piece of iron. They hacked the body to pieces and attempted to burn the remains. Two fireplaces and a stove were used, but all traces of the body were not eliminated. Part of the skull was found in one of the fireplaces and bloodstains were on the floor where the body had been. The trunk of Page's body was later found in the grave of Dave Ward, who had been buried only a few days before the murder.

The murder occurred on August 27 and separate juries found the two guilty on October 3, 1921. Judge J.R. East of Brandon presided over the trial. D.M. Anderson was the district attorney. The sheriff at this time was Franklin Mize and the deputy sheriff was W.T. Robertson.

At the trial the man testified that he killed Page but said that the woman had instigated the murder and laid the plans. The woman testified that she knew nothing of the murder until she was asked to help get rid of the body.

Some of the townspeople petitioned Governor Lee Russell to grant the woman a reprieve, but the governor would not do this. The gallows was a simple drop down type. The floor parted when the lever was pulled. The man was hanged first. When the woman was brought to the gallows she continued to beg for her life even as the rope was placed around her neck. So far as it is known she was the only woman ever hung in Forest.

Man Disappears, Then Found Dead After Seeing Mysterious Light

My great-grandmother was known as "Mammy" for miles around and when anyone got sick, they sent for her. She was always willing to go and do what she could to relieve suffering. In fact she would have felt quite hurt if they had not sent for her.

One night a neighbor living about three miles away sent word for Mammy to come right over. My great-uncle saddled the mule, put Mammy on it and leading the mule, set out to take her to the neighbor's house. On the way, they passed Mt. Olive Church where they worshipped on the days when the preacher could get there.

It took no time to get to their destination, as the mule was fresh and to them the journey was nothing. My great-uncle helped Mammy off, hitched the mule and went in to see if there was anything he could do and finding nothing, was soon on his way again.

As he came on down the road, this time riding the mule himself and whistling as he rode, he saw a light in the church which was dark only an hour ago when he passed the first time. He stopped, called out "Hello," as was the custom when hailing an unseen person. No answer. He called out again. Still no answer. He got down, hitched the mule and went to the door. He saw a candle burning on the table and no one to be seen in the church, which was only one small room. He called again, thinking that someone was camping there for the night and perhaps they had stepped out of the building for the moment. But he got no answer for the simple reason that there was no one there.

He would not go back to the church alone, so he remained at the neighbor's house throughout the night, going back next morning with Mammy. For several days he had been planning to go for a visit with relatives in Madison County and left that day, going from his home to Jackson where he was to catch the train. His people never saw him alive again. About a year later, the family heard that an unidentified man of about the age of their missing son had fallen under a train in Jackson and had been killed. No marks of identification were on the body, so after holding it for the required time, it was buried by the city.

Members of the missing man's family went to Jackson, got permission to dig up the unidentified man and look at him and found as they expected that it was their son who had been missing so long.

He was brought home and buried in the churchyard just across the road from where he saw the light, which warned him of his untimely death. For he was warned, no doubt about it. And to this day, people passing Mt. Olive Church during the night always half expect to see a lighted candle shining through the window and small boys surround the place if possible.

Mt. Olive Primitive Baptist Church is located just north of Cooper's Lake near the Homestead Community. The late P.B. Alford originally told this story on April 15, 1936. Until recently, it was deposited in the National Archives.

Several residents of the countryside near Mt. Olive Church deny ever hearing this story before. Mr. Alford's son who lives in Morton, reports he never heard his father tell the story. Mrs. Omega Marsh of Kracker Station said that she had frequently heard tales concerning mysterious lights in the cemetery but speculated that this was just a good old "tale." Mrs. Mattie Thorne, a resident of Cooperville, echoed Mrs. Marsh's sentiments. The names of people in the story have apparently been lost. Two interesting points may be illustrated in this little "tale." The art of storytelling in Scott County was a finely developed art. In the cemetery across the road from the church there are two headstones bearing the same inscriptions: B.W. Alford, January 10, 1843-October 20, 1877. *Written by Sonny Renfroe of Forest, MS.*

Quilting Party At Forest Library 1977

The Forest Library hosted a quilting party in the fall of 1977. The quilt is a flower garden pattern and was pieced by Mrs. Melba King. Mrs. Jean Eady joined them later in the afternoon and brought her two-year-old granddaughter, Deanna, to the party. A lot of people who had never seen a quilt in the frame stopped by. It was a most enjoyable day.

Scott Countian Stitched "Stars And Bars" Flag

Mississippi seceded from the Union on January 9, 1861. The Confederate States of America were formed at Montgomery, AL in February 1861 and on April 12 Confederate forces fired on Fort Sumter. This set into affect in one way or another the lives of almost every individual living in either the North or the South.

Left hand corner going left: Mrs. Jewel Smith, librarian; Mrs. Bertha Weems, Mrs. Ercelle Singlenton, Mrs. Melba King, Mrs. Mary Elizabeth McMullan, Miss Martha Russell, master quilter and Mrs. Lovie Wicker.

Two years before the outbreak of the Civil War, Carrie Clark had been sent by her father to live with her sister, Mrs. James Davenport in St. Louis. She was sent so that she could attend a young ladies finishing school there.

When it became apparent that a national struggle between the North and South was inevitable, Carrie begged for permission to return to her family in Mississippi. Her wishes were granted and on a May morning in 1861, the 13-year-old Carrie boarded the steam packet *S.J. Swan* on her way to Vicksburg.

Although she had been introduced to the captain of the steamer by Mr. and Mrs. Davenport when she boarded, she was somewhat startled when she heard her name called as she sat in a deck chair during the second day of her voyage.

Looking up from the book she was reading, she recognized the captain standing nearby. "Miss Carrie," he said, "can you sew?" "Of course I can sew," she said. "All girls my age can sew."

"Then I would like for you to help make a flag. You see we do not have a Confederate States flag to fly." "I shall be happy to help you," Carrie said.

Material for the flag, already cut and pinned together, was brought to Carrie's room and she began the task of constructing the ship's flag. The design of the flag was the first used by the Confederate States and was called the "Stars and Bars." It consisted of one horizontal white bar between two red bars. The field was blue with seven white stars. Many flags of this design were made during the first months of the war, loving hands sewing a prayer with every stitch, that the flag would not go down in defeat; that those who followed it would come home safely. Three designs were to follow.

At the first Battle of Manassas, July 21, 1861, the Confederate forces were said to have had difficulty distinguishing the "Star and Bars" from the "Stars and Stripes." To prevent a possible mix-up concerning the flags, a new design was ordered by the Confederate Congress. This flag, having a red field crossed diagonally by a cross of blue and 13 stars was called the "Battle Flag."

The third flag known as the "Stainless Banner" was pure white with the Battle Flag in the upper left hand corner. The fourth and last flag was adopted March 4, 1865. This flag had a broad red bar running the length of the unfurled end.

When it was time for supper to be served on the S.J. Swan, the dining room steward knocked on Carrie Clark's door and said, "The captain requests that you sit at his table at supper." Carrie had completed sewing the flag in the afternoon and sent it to the captain.

As the steward escorted her to her place at the table, the captain appeared with the flag and held it high over his head. Instantly the guests in the dining room gave a cheer. Then the captain asked the guests to give a cheer for the little lady from Mississippi who had worked so faithfully all afternoon to make the flag. Carrie was surprised and a little embarrassed, but she rose and acknowledged the cheers with a bow.

The next morning, Carrie noticed that the flag was lying from the boat's flagstaff. When the ship passed Cairo, IL the Federal soldiers fired on the flag but fortunately the boat was out of range of the guns. The captain had taken precautions changing his course and now sailed on the far side of the river.

The remainder of the trip was uneventfully. The Stars and Bars was cheered at every landing as the ship left the Northern states and proceeded down the river The boat was tied up every night because of a persistent fog, so they were nearly a week reaching Vicksburg, Carrie's destination.

Upon her arrival in Vicksburg, Carrie was met by a friend and escorted to a hotel to spend the night. The next morning, she departed for Forest where her brothers, Warren and Frank Clark, met her. Three of the Clark brothers would soon join the Confederate Army.

As is often true with family histories, there are conflicting accounts of the death of Warren and Frank Clark. One account records that Frank was killed at the Battle of the Wilderness in 1864 and that Warren came home at the end of the war and died in the spring of 1872. Another account states that Frank and Warren were both killed in the Battle of Shiloh and were buried by their brother in a nearby field the night after the battle.

Carrie Clark, who was the daughter of J.P. Clark of Scott County, married Alfred John Brown who wrote the history of Newton County in 1894. She died in Newton in 1940 at the age of 92. Throughout her later years, she entertained her grandchildren with the story of her trip from St. Louis to Vicksburg on the steamer "S.J.Swan." *Reprinted with the permission of Mr. Ovid Vickers of Decatur, MS.*

Sunset For Lake Dubois Lumber Company

About 1910, a man from Williamsport, PA named Merrill came to Mississippi and organized the Merrill Lumber Company and located a mill at Lake.

Mr. Merrill had borrowed money from the Dubois Coal Company in Dubois, PA to finance the sawmill operation. Merrill found living in Lake dull and uninteresting and attempted to run the mill from his Jackson hotel. In less than three years, Merrill was hopelessly behind with loan payments, and Mr. Dubois took the mill over and sent Eugene B. Nettleton down to run it.

They changed the name to Dubois Lumber Company a few years later. Young John Dubois, fresh out of Harvard, came down to help run the company. John had been a playboy and drove a Stutz Bear Cat around. Baston Louis, a younger brother, drove an Apperson Jack Rabbit. John took over the logging operations that had gotten behind. The log storage pond was empty. John decided they would have to haul logs on Sunday to catch up. The train had gotten deep into the log woods and they were firing up the skidder when about a dozen farmers appeared with shotguns and told John that he couldn't work on Sunday.

In disgust, he ordered the train back to the mill, muttering "these Mississippi rednecks will make and drink their moonshine whiskey on Sunday but they won't let me haul logs."

A fast talking chemist, by the name of Thomas from Chillicothe County, claimed he had a secret process whereby he could make white bond paper from southern pine. John and Mr. Nettleton agreed to build a paper mill if Thomas could prove his secret process would work. After piddling and dawdling with his pilot plant all one summer, he never came up with a sheet of white bond paper. Consequently, Dubois Lumber Company refused to build a paper mill.

Thomas brought suit against Dubois Lumber Company for one million dollars for breach of contract. Then Governor Bilbo appointed a crooked judge to try the case. Dubois panicked, sold their timbered lands to east Gar at Laurel and closed the sawmill. John returned to Dubois, PA and Mr. Nettleton set up a sawmill operation at Hickory.

Dubois Lumber was Lakes only industry and its economy was virtually destroyed. It never fully recovered. *Written by Milton McMullan*

The Yellow Plague

It was the year 1878, the month was July. This quiet little town and its people with dim memories of ancient glory, were picking up the pieces and trying to put it back together again. They had endured the ravages of war, the awful time of defeat, the humiliation and then the ultimate humiliation of reconstruction. But it was about over. The blacks, the carpetbaggers, the scalawags, no longer occupied the state house in

Jackson. The future was brighter. There was hope for better days. Then suddenly, without warning, disaster came. An itinerant peddler from Vicksburg had gotten off the train in Lake.

Within a few short months one-third of the people of this town of 600 would perish. Only days after the arrival of the peddler, the dread malady began to appear. It spread like wildfire. The onset of the disease was swift and terrible. It began with a severe headache followed by a raging fever. Destruction of liver cells brought yellow bile pigment into the eyes and skin of the victim. They called it yellow fever. Hemorrhaging in the mucous lining of the stomach and vomiting of dark altered blood followed. They called it black vomit. Soon the town's only two doctors were stricken and died. The Howard Association, an organization somewhat similar to the present day Red Cross, sent in several doctors and about 50 male nurses. The Federal Government sent quantities of medicine, whiskey and wine. The medicines of that time were completely ineffective in treating the disease. Bleeding and purging only added to the misery of the stricken. The male nurses, assigned to the homes of the sick, consumed the wine and whiskey and in many cases totally neglected their patients. Persons brought fresh food to the edge of town daily from surrounding communities.

Wagon loads of coffins, made in Conehatta, were brought to the edge of town. For some unknown reason the burying of the dead took place at night. Since most of the white men were attending the sick, the burying of the dead was entrusted to the Negroes. Of necessity there was lack of orderly arrangement of burial sites. Generally the whites were buried on the front or west side of the cemetery and blacks on the back or east side. But not always. In the confusion of the nighttime burials, whites and blacks were at times buried indiscriminately in the central part of the burying ground. Although crude attempts were made to provide markers, many of them disappeared. After the passage of years, many of the actual grave sites became indistinguishable. In later years, remains of skeletons have been turned up in newly dug graves. It is not known if they were whites or blacks. The bones are all the same color. Cold weather came early that year. There was a heavy frost in late October and bitter cold. There were no more deaths. The yellow fever epidemic had run its course.

Nearly a quarter of a century later, it would be known that the itinerant peddler had been bitten in Vicksburg by an Aedes Aegypti mosquito. In the year 1900 the Yellow Fever Commission under Major Walter Reed determined that the Aedes Aegypti mosquito transmitted yellow fever.

One out of every five persons died of the Black Death during the Great Plague in London in 1664. One out of three died of yellow fever in Lake in 1878. *Written by Milton McMullan, formally of Lake*

Yellow Fever Deaths Of 1878

Major J.J. Hood, who kept a diary of all the deaths of the epidemic in Lake, MS in 1878, recorded these names. Major Hood of Jackson did a noble job of aiding the yellow fever sufferers during the distressing sickness. Dr. J.J. Haralson and H.H. Watts of Forest, also helped.

Mr. and Mrs. W.E. Crowson, Mrs. R.A. Ray, Frank Tate, Adolphus Long, Mrs. Rachel Burge, Lee C. Scott, John R. Meader, George Jones' child-colored, Raney McGrorty, Dr. C.G. McCallum, W. J. Adams, George Jones-colored, Kate McCallum, Ann Bragg-colored, Richard Burge, Randall Flowers-colored, Henry Clay Atkins, W.H. Evers, Mrs. Joseph Stewart, W.Y. McFarland, Mrs. Stewart's daughter, Dr. J.J. Tate, Charley McCallum, L.B. Wilkins, Mrs. J.S. Yarbrough, John Clay, Corrie Evers, W.J. Crosby, Charles McFarland, Robert Davidson, Miss Lula Lowry, Semp Tate, Mrs. Evers, Mathew Young, Mary McFarland, Mrs. R.S. Hoskins, S.D. Kennedy, Reverend William Banks-colored, J.N. Couch, John Bragg's child-colored, John H. Crosby, Mrs. Martha Lowry, Jesse Long, George F. Lowry, Sarah Burge-colored, J.S. Yarbrough, Mrs. Hugh McFarland, Mrs. Thomas Ray, P. Saunders, Maurice Evers, Mrs. G.C. McCallum, Mrs. J.P. Snead, Mrs. M.P. Saunders, Oscar Long, Miss Fannie Sanders, Robert Hoskins, Mrs. S.D. Kennedy, Willie Weaver, Sarah Ann January, Lydia Adams Ritter (nurse), Miss Tate, Mrs. Evers baby, Mr. Schackelford, John Couch, Windem Moody-colored, Ella Burge, Mary McCallum, Mrs. Kittie Scott, Charles Banks-colored, Malide Burge-colored, Mrs. Sarah Wells, Lafayette Weaver, Tommy Weaver, Robert Tate, William Nichols, Albert Cole's child-colored, Stella Burge, Miss Nettie Burge, Richard Burge Jr., John D. Wells, Miss Annie Tate, Miss Julia Burge, Miss Lee, Thosman Price.

Homes

Lod Moore House

Harper Home

An ante-bellum home of unusual interest was the Harper home in Harperville. Harperville is on Highway 35, 10 miles north of Forest and Highway 80.

It was a lovely two-store square frame building, sitting about 50 yards from the road in a large grove of old cedar trees. With its colonial style of windows, blinds and doors, it was a picture of an old southern home that stood in the war days of the North and South.

This house was built by G.C. Harper, the founder of Harperville. Mr. Harper played a great part in the government of Scott County during the reconstruction period.

Sherman's Army came through the yards and raided the barns and pantry but did very little to the house.

Lod Moore House

The old Lod Moore house on Tower Road, south of Forest was constructed in 1871 on a 2,000 acre plot once known as Yockey Abbey. Lodric Moore and his wife Elizabeth and their two children, Lou and John, acquired the property several years before the War Between the States and after a journey from Alabama to Berryville in Scott County. They stopped at old Berryville to spend the night and heard about this place as being "one of the loveliest in the south, with natural beauty of hill, dell and woodland." When they looked at the site, they decided this was where they would settle and make their home. They first built a log cabin and cleared the land. When the war started, looms were setup on the place and clothing was made by hand for soldiers who were in service. It was after the war that the big house was built. Brickwork for the house was contracted by Martin Hederman of Hillsboro, father of the late R.M. Hederman Sr. and T.M. Hederman Sr. of Jackson, operators of Hederman Brothers Printing Company and the *Clarion-Ledger*. Woodwork for the house was handled by Patrick Henry of Ludlow, father of the late Colonel R.H. Henry who established the *Clarion-Ledger* and served as editor for many years. Originally, five fireplaces heated the home and water was drawn from a cistern.

Eventually, Lod Moore was known as one of the largest land owners and best planters in this area. The parents of the late R.M. Christian, prominent cattleman and cotton buyer, had their wedding supper in the new house in 1871, shortly after it was complete. Forest Country Club is on part of the original acreage. It was given by Lod Moore to two of his slavesOld Homes

T.B. Graham home and office, corner of Raleigh and Oak Street

Davenport Home, Forest, MS On site where Farm Bureau is

House built ca. 1897 by William Cornell, located in Lake, MS.

Home of R.L. Noblin, owner of Noblin Mercantile Company, a local merchant. This home was located on South Raleigh Street in Forest.

Wilkins House, Lake, MS

Street House, Lake, MS

This home located on East Second Street was built in 1900 by Mounger Jones. At one time or other it was occupied by the Carl Steele family and W.D. Cook family. William Moore Christian bought it from W.I. McKay of Vicksburg for $3,250. After Mr. Christian's death, it was occupied by his widow and his daughter and her family. Joyce Christian married Henry Melichar and they had four children: Randolph, Kenneth, Melinda and Alan. The house was sold to Hugh Haralson III in 1978.

Tributes

Captain George E. Hasie

Captain George E. Hasie was the first county superintendent of education and was appointed by Governor Ames. Hasie, a carpetbagger and Republican, spent his first day in Forest in jail for some disorder, probably drunkenness. Along with the office of superintendent of education, he was appointed mayor of Forest, postmaster, justice of the peace and president of the Board of School Directors. He was known as one of the greatest travelers that ever traveled Scott County. He was one of the hardest workers also, for it was told he worked 31 days in the month of February alone, quite a feat. Not finding enough money in his many positions, he left Scott County in 1871, never to return. He was not a friend to the county and had it not been for the Board of Supervisors he would have ruined this county. On May 6, 1871 the *Forest Register* told of his departure under the simple title "Gone."

Mr. L.O. Atkins

From 1953 until 1976, Mr. L.O. Atkins was the head man, "The Chief," of the Forest Separate School District. Luther O. Atkins attended public school in Kilmichael. He received his bachelor's of science degree, majoring in mathematics and science at Mississippi State University. In 1950 he received his master's degree from the University of Alabama.

Mr. Atkins served as principal of Kilmichael for 10 years and mayor for one four-year term. He married Miss Carolyn Applewhite. She was also from Kilmichael. The Atkins moved to DeKalb in 1944 where Mr. Atkins served as superintendent of the DeKalb Special Consolidated School for nine years. In 1953 they made their last move when Mr. Atkins accepted the position of superintendent of the Forest Separate School District.

Here in Forest, Mr. Atkins worked hard to improve the school facilities. Under his leadership E.T. Hawkins School, the Forest Elementary School, the Forest High School, the football field and stadium were built. As a tribute to his contributions to the community the L.O. Atkins Athletic Field was dedicated in the fall of 1963 by the Board of Trustees.

Mr. Atkins taught Sunday School for 23 years and served three terms as a deacon at Forest Baptist Church. Mr. Atkins lived the life of a dedicated Christian as shown in his love, guidance and interest in the young people of Forest.

Mr. Atkins retired in 1976 after 23 years as "The Chief." April 14, 1976 was set aside as L.O. Atkins Day in Forest and after a program at the school, he was presented with a new car. Luther O. and Carolyn Atkins had two children, John and Mary Jane. Mr. Atkins was born August 15, 1910 and passed away March 11, 1979 at Lackey Hospital in Forest. Mrs. Carolyn Applewhite Atkins was born December 2, 1913 and died March 15, 1999.

R.A. "Pop" Hartness

"Pop" Hartness is legendary in the history of football at Forest. He was hired in 1930 by Mr. Carter, superintendent and the School Board. He was a graduate of Mississippi State where he played end, playing at 140 pounds.

On the football field, he was tough, but off the field he was a lovable ole lamb. He spent a lot of his own salary on his "boys." The ones who lived out of town, he was known for carrying them home. He fed many of them at his own expense, even slipping the less fortunate spending money.

One heartbreaking moment in his career at Forest was the coin toss loss in the game with Picayune for the 1930 South Mississippi Championship. After five quarters, the score was still tied 0-0. The officials decided to get a winner, they would toss a coin. Heads, Forest won, tails, Picayune won. Tails it was.

"Pop" Hartness, also served as superintendent of Forest School, gaining the love and respect of the entire student body. After 12 years at Forest, "Pop" was called into the Army in 1942. In the first yearbook Forest published, the 1943 *Rambler,* a page was dedicated to him. "Pop" was quoted as saying "those 12 years (in Forest) were the happiest years of my life."

Mr. L.O. Atkins

"Pop" Hartness and the 1930 Forest football team. Kneeling: Charles Alexander, Bill McCormick, G.C. Chambers, Carl Steele, Harry McClenahan, Robert Allen, John McDill. Standing: Ernest Smith, John Farmer, "Pop" Hartness, Baker Austin, Hiram Anderson

Cloy E. Macoy

Cloy E. Macoy (b. Nov. 9, 1939), a native of Vicksburg, MS and son of John and Ethel Macoy, made Forest his home after his marriage in 1961 to Joanne Grantham (b. Feb. 22, 1946). Joanne is the daughter of Enoch and Mildred Grantham of Harrisville, MS. Cloy, the oldest of six children, worked with his father in the sawmill business. The young couple, Cloy age 21 and Joanne age 15, came to live in Forest near her foster parents, H.L. and Elise Lewis. Cloy worked as an apprentice plumber for H.L. until he started his own business in the 70s.

Cloy built his business, Macoy Plumbing, to include residential, commercial and industrial work. Cloy was known by all to be a man to come when he was needed. He volunteered his time to a lot of needy causes.

The Macoys were notorious for their love of renovating older homes and were often seen moving to a new home where Joanne would begin tearing out walls and adding new baths.

Joanne worked with Cloy in Macoy Plumbing, keeping books. She loved children and was known for organizing community activities for teens. All their four children: Lesia, Wanda, Cloy E. Macoy Jr. (Gene) and Salina are residents of Forest and the surrounding area.

Cloy, a loving father and loyal husband became a strong leader of his church, serving as deacon and active in the Masons until he died as a result of an industrial accident Aug. 18, 1997.

Cloy Macoy, son of John and Ethel Macoy, and Joanne Grantham, daughter of Enoch and Mildred Grantham

William Harrison Joyner

William Harrison Joyner was born near Cooperville, Scott County on Aug. 15, 1876, to Elder and Mrs. John Lee Joyner. His grandparents, John H. and Bettye Rushing Joyner, were natives of Georgia, coming to Mississippi in early life. John H. was a volunteer in the Confederate Army.

John Lee and Henrietta Goodman Joyner joined the Primitive Baptist Church at Mt. Olive, and John Lee was ordained to preach in 1887. At his death, he was the pastor of four churches: Mt. Hope, near Pelahatchie, New Chapel, near Pulaski, Mt. Olive, south of Morton, and Union near Chunky in Newton County. Ten children were born to John Lee and Henrietta.

Will attended school at Braxton Collegiate Institute and after graduating taught school a few years. He was the principal at Pelahatchie, where he taught the young woman who was to become his wife, Clem Mashburn. He was teaching school at Leesburg when he entered politics and won the race for Circuit Clerk of Scott County in 1903. From that time on, he made Forest his home and spent his time and energy helping build Forest and Scott County. He believed in their future. Forest is where he and Clem raised their three children: Alleene, Elsie and Clements. After graduating school at Forest, Alleene attended Blue Mountain College, then taught school for several years in Scott County before moving to Alabama. After graduation, Elsie married Marion Weems, and they remained in Scott County to raise their family. After his graduation, Clements left Mississippi and made the Border Patrol his career.

While serving as circuit clerk, Will became the manager of Forest Ginning & Mfg. Co. and opened a meat market. Also during this period he was a charter member of the Scott County Fair and Breeder's Association and was on the Board of Directors for the newly founded Farmer's and Merchant's Bank, becoming vice president in 1910 and president in 1911 and 1912. In 1911, Will sold his meat market to J.W. Tadlock & Sons and established a newspaper, *The Scott County News,* which he owned for several years before buying another newspaper in Forest, *The Scott County Register,* combining the two papers into one, *The News Register.* He later sold the paper to H.A. Schmidt who had become his partner. While in the newspaper business, Will became the secretary to Congressman Witherspoon. During his stay in Washington he wrote the news of the nation for several newspapers. In 1915, Congressman Witherspoon died in office and Will ran an unsuccessful race to fill the vacancy.

At one time, Will had a bottling company in the front part of his newspaper office. This gave Alleene and Elsie a welcome break from their newspaper chores.

Will was appointed Director of War Savings for Scott County in 1918, the year that Mississippi's allotment for WWI was four million dollars, Scott County's part being $336,000. This was a sacrificial year for every adult in the county, and the quota was met.

In 1924 Will took treatment for tuberculosis at Sanitarium, the State Tubercular Hospital and after receiving a clean bill of health he resumed his life, becoming active again.

Will served as a county election commissioner, taught Sunday school, and was a charter member of the Forest Business Men's Club, being an active participant in getting the street paving project started. During Will's term as Mayor of Forest in 1925 and 1926 the sewer system was a major project. He established the Joyner-Hannah Chevy Company in 1925 and later sold it to R.L. Goodwin, H.E. Bishop, and J. Knox Huff

Will believed in the need for Scott County to have other than a cotton economy and worked to establish a poultry and cattle industry. He traveled to Canada and purchased milk cows in his supportive efforts to secure a milk plant for Forest in the 1920s. Believing in his vision of Forest growing and becoming a focal point of the county, Will, along with others, bought land extensively. They plotted the streets, divided the land into lots and sold to people building homes. This resulted in several additions to the town which bear his and others names.

At the time of his death in 1929, he owned a hatchery and a wholesale distributor company, was president of the Scott County Poultry Association and president of the Board of Trustees of Forest High School. As a Mason, he received the Masonic rites and is buried in Eastern Cemetery.

W.H. Joyner, J. Knox Huff, W.A. Turner, Main Street, Forest, MS

William Harrison Joyner

Hunt-Haralson

In 1835 Joseph Hunt of Franklin County, MS purchased land in his name and the name of his son James Marion Hunt. The land lies in Northeast Scott County in what is known as the Piketon Community. They moved to Scott County in 1836. James Marion married Nancy Sue Walters, daughter of John Walters and Lucretia Thomas of Scott County in the mid-1840s.

Their first child was William Franklin "Babe" Hunt (b. 1846), followed by Sarah Elizabeth (b. 1847), Emanuel M. "Bud" (b. 1849), Lemuel Marion "Joe" (b. Jul. 27, 1855) and Martha (b. 1859).

James enlisted in Co. E, Lake Rebels on Aug. 24, 1861. This company was later made part of the Sixth Mississippi Infantry Regiment. His unit served in Kentucky, Battle of Shiloh, Vicksburg, Louisiana, Georgia and was in the battle of Nashville. In 1863 he was promoted to sergeant. While James was off at war, Grants troops moved East to Georgia along the Jackson Turnpike, which ran in front of the Hunt home place. While the troops forged for supplies along the way, usually leaving enough for women and children, Nancy cursed them. They took everything. The neighbors pitched in and helped Nancy and the children until James came home. James died about 1888 and was buried in Hunt Cemetery, located along the Jackson Turnpike. Nancy died in 1898, but had said she would not be buried with James. She is buried in the Summers Cemetery in the Piketon Community.

James Marion Hunt

Lemuel Marion their 4th child, Joe as he was known, received a very good education for the time. He married Sarah Olivia "Sallie" Singleton, daughter of David Adam Singleton Jr. and Nepsa White of Scott County, on Dec. 23, 1879. He purchased some of his father's land, where he farmed and operated a general store. On Nov. 1, 1880 their first child, Pearlie D., arrived and died Nov. 4, 1880. She is buried in Summers Cemetery. Other children: Nancy Maude (b. Apr. 12, 1882); James Singleton Hunt (b. Dec. 14, 1883); William Robert "Bob" (b. May 25, 1887); May Jewell (b. Jun. 9, 1889); Lilly Belle (b. Oct. 17, 1891); David Quincy "D.Q." (b. Nov. 12, 1893); Annie Clois (b. Sep. 15, 1896); Woods Eastland (b. May 17, 1899); and Drew Adam (b. Dec. 3, 1903). They moved to Forest, county seat of Scott County in 1910. He became a businessman and an influence in politics, although he never ran for office. They were members of the Baptist Church. Joe was a Mason as were all his sons. Joe died Mar. 27, 1926 and is buried in Eastern Cemetery in Forest. Sarah died Nov. 26, 1932 and is buried along side Joe.

Joe and Sallie Hunt

James Singleton Hunt became a mail carrier in Forest. William Robert owned and ran Hunts Frozen Food Locker in Forest. David Quincy, D.Q. as he was known owned Hunts Tourist Court. Woods Eastland, named after Senator James Eastland's father, became a Gulf Oil Distributor in Newton County. Drew Adam was one of Forest's City Marshals.

William Robert, May Jewell and Annie Clois were schoolteachers. Lilly Belle was deputy chancery clerk of Scott County for years. Nancy Maude climbed out a window, rode on a mule behind Tom Woods Haralson from Conehatta in Newton County and they were married the next day Jul. 7, 1900. On Apr. 2, 1901 their first child Allie Dee was born, the first of 11. Then came Leon, Annie Lee, Onabel, J.C., Hunt and French.

Tom and Maude lived in Newton County for a short time, then moved below Forest in Scott County. In 1914 they bought the old Hunt home place at Piketon, and Maude found herself looking out the same window she had slipped out in 1900.

Tom Haralson and sons

The old Hunt house burned and Tom and Maude built a new house where Sarah, Thomas, Ruby and Katie Maude (b. May 5, 1921) were all born. Their family was complete.

Allie Dee died at 6 years old with diphtheria. Leon married Sallie Bee Carson from Conehatta. They lived part time in Scott County and part time in Louisiana. Their first child, Leon Jr., died as a child, then Ida Maude, Ruth, Jack, Thomas and Keith were born. Keith married Carolyn Riser. They lived and raised their family in the Piketon Community, on part of the old Hunt homestead. Their children are Gordon, Peggy, Carl, Ronnie and Vicki.

Annie Lee married Howard Clark and had a daughter Dorothy Clark. Then she married Coyte Pearson and lived many years East of Forest on Hwy. 80.

Onabel married Lester Wolf and lived in the Ephesus Community. Their children were Theo, George, Eugene and Jerry. George lives at their home place with his wife Irene. They have four daughters.

J.C. married Mary Myers and raised his family in the Piketon Community, then moved to the Ephesus Community.

Hunt married Margaret Gouchie from New York and raised a son John and a daughter Margaret Ann. Hunt learned landscaping and tree surgery in C.C. camp at Vicksburg. He worked and owned his own business. He served in WWII and was in the Battle of the Bulge in Belgium. John joined the service fresh out of high school and served his country in many parts of the world. He and wife Sharon live in Virginia and he works for the State Dept. in Washington, D.C. Stacey and Derek are their children. Margaret Ann lives near John.

French married Tommie McDonald from Conehatta. French Jr. and Dudley Quincy are their children. French learned how to operate and mechanic on heavy equipment in C.C. Camp at Morton, what is now Roosevelt Park. He worked in many States and finally settled down near Fort Worth, TX. French Jr. lives at Bedford, TX, owns and operates Stonegate Pools. Dudley works for Delta Airlines and has lived in several states and in Germany. He now lives in Atlanta, where is an airline consultant. He and wife Virginia have two children, Holly and Dudley Jr. They have three grandchildren.

Sarah married Dwight Smythe. She was killed in a car accident at age 31.

Thomas left home and joined the Army at age 17. He was stationed in the state of Maine. After service he settled in New York, where he married Florence Kellor. They had two sons, Thomas Jr. and Donald. Thomas worked for his brother Hunt for a time, then went to work in a food service selling doughnuts. He worked his way up to manager of the business and later became district manager. His last days were spent in Tampa, FL. He was in WWII in the Navy.

Maude Haralson and daughters

Ruby was a beautician. She owned and operated a beauty shop in Newton, MS. Later she was manager of Mark Rothenburgs Beauty Salon in Meridian, MS. She married Walter Boykin from Demopolis, AL and lived most of her life there. She had one daughter Debra and lost a son a few hours after birth. Ruby has four grandchildren.

Katie Maude, the youngest of Tom and Maude Haralson's children, is the only one still living. She is the only one of the descendents of Joe Hunt that never left the old home place. She graduated Ringgold High School in March 1939, married James Matthew "Jack" Shelley from Kosciusko, MS and started her family. James Woods "Jimmy" was the first born, then Linda Darrell, Saralan Kay, Ruby Lee and Thomas Matthew. Jack farmed and helped his father-in-law operate a sawmill. He served in WWII. In later years he left the farm and worked in road construction. After Matthew started to school, Katie Maude went to work at Sunbeam Clock Company near Forest, where she worked for 19-1/2 years. After that she worked as clerk at a local clothing store. She is now retired and lives alone in the home where she raised her children.

Jimmy married Betty Lou Graham of the Sulpher Springs Community. They built a home and raised their family on the Graham homestead. Jimmy worked in maintenance at Sunbeam Clock Company and at US Motors in Philadelphia, MS while attending night school. He is an electrical engineer, owns and operates his own business, Shelley's Electric, near Sebastopol. Betty helps with the business and operates a large broiler farm. They have three children. Tammy has a doctor's degree in education. Pamela is a registered nurse and James Jr. is an electrician working with his dad. Jimmy and Betty have six grandchildren.

Linda Darrell married Robert Gardner from the Ringgold Community. They live on the site where her great-grandfather operated a country store and ran the Piketon Post Office. Linda Darrell has worked at several different factories over the years. Robert is now retired and is pastor of Pleasant Ridge Baptist Church. Their children are Joann, John and Sarah. Joann and husband live near Forest and operate a Broiler farm. Sarah and husband live at Petal, MS, and both are employed in Hattiesburg. John lives with his parents and is the 5th generation living on the Joe Hunt home site. John has a degree in poultry science and is employed as a chicken doctor. Linda Darrell and Robert have two grandchildren.

Katie and Jack Shelley and family

Saralan Kay married Charles Scott Brown from Sebastopol. They live in the Sulpher Springs Community. Saralan works at Peavey's in Decatur. Charles is a sewing machine mechanic in a factory in Sebastopol. Their children, Bobby, Mary and Charles Jr. "Chuck," are married and all live near their parents. Katie is married and lives near her grandmother Shelley. She is in her 4th year of college to be a physical therapist. Saralan and Charles have four grandchildren.

Ruby Lee married Van Fortenberry from Harperville. They live on part of the Joe Hunt Homestead. Ruby works as a desk clerk at Day's Inn in Forest. Van works for Tyson Food Inc. They have two children, Tony and Joy. Tony is a Baptist Minister and lives near his parents. His son Daniel is the 6th generation living on part of the Joe and Sallie Hunt homestead. Joy is married and lives and works near Jackson.

Matthew first married Joan McCraw from Harperville. They had two children, Heather and Amon. Matthew then married Marsha Garvin from Louisville. Marsha is a schoolteacher at Scott Central. They have a son Mason Grant. Matthew built a house across the Old Natchez Trace Road from the very spot his forefather James Marion Hunt built one of the first houses in the Piketon Community. Matthew worked off shore and for Shelley's Electric. He is now employed as an electrician and a maintenance man at Lazy Boy in Newton. Heather is married and lives near Sebastopol. She is a beautician and is going to college to become a teacher. Amon is a junior at Scott Central School. Mason is in the third grade.

AGNEW, My mother, Mabel Bedwell Agnew (b. 1907), thought herself a newcomer to Scott County in 1940 when she left the Federal Writers' Project in Jackson to marry into the Agnew family and live with James' parents between the railroad tracks and New 80, their house encircled by the houses of James' brother and five sisters.

Mabel's mother, Nanih-Lillie Williams Bedwell Mitchell (b. 1887, d. 1975) lived in back of her store beside the Kalem Methodist Church not far from James's aunt, Mary Agnew Strong. They and James' aunts, Lora (b. 1875, d. 1956) and Laura (b. 1875, d. 1961) Thompson Simmons (twins married brothers), liked to visit and Mabel's mother-in-law, Mandy Lee Thompson Agnew (b. 1873, d. 1953), liked to talk. So Mabel heard all about how Lewis Agnew (b. 1838, d. 1900) blacksmith, Mason and Episcopalian settled on Panther Hill in 1877, then sent for wife, Susan Grace (b. 1848, d. 1928) and children: Mary (Strong), Viola (Sims) and Mr. Jim (James Berry Agnew Sr.) (b. 1871, d. 1955). No mention of the children's brother, Leonard Agnew (b. 1869, d. 1936), dead five years before my birth, buried beside his parents. I would learn of his existence from a tombstone on Hodge Hill.

Othermama talked also of her father, Will Thompson (b. 1838, d. 1918) who starved out the potato famine in the wilds of western Ireland, then came over here, fought in the Civil War, married Susan Alice Cotton (b. 1843, d. 1917) while his leg mended and brought her to Scott County earlier even than Mr. Jim.

Mr. Jim liked to talk too. Age 6, moving from Texas to Mississippi, he stuck his head out the train window and lost his little red hat. Arriving at the depot, he saw his hat on a stranger's head. He grabbed it, put it on, got offered a new one and got threatened. But that hat was his. With both his hands he pulled it way down over his ears. Buy the new hat for Scott County.

Mr. Jim repaired watches while he talked, though having been a blacksmith in his youth, I don't know how he had the hands. His eldest son, Hollie William Agnew (b. 1898, d. 1956), owned fighting cocks and Agnew Hardware. Hollie's daughter, Christine McKay Searcy (b. 1923, d. 1992), had Hollie Archie McKay (b. 1943) of Brandon and Frederick Taylor Searcy Jr. (b. 1948) of Fort Lauderdale. Mr. Jim's youngest son, James Berry Agnew Jr. (b. 1906, d. 1968), owned Agnew Service Station (and general store). James and Mabel's daughters: Jo (b. 1941), Jean Agnew McKay (b. 1943) and Jimmie Dell Agnew (b. 1947), moved to San Antonio, Leesburg and Greensboro.

Only Mabel still lives in Scott County. And what "the newcomer" did not know back in 1940 was that this was her ancestors' hunting ground. When Choctaw villages dotted the banks of the Pearl to the north and west and were scattered to the east in what is now Neshoba, Newton and Jasper counties, these thick pine forests and sand clay hills (elevation 618 feet in the southeast corner) were Ouachito, Choctaw hunting ground. Mabel's great-great-uncle, Greenwood LeFlore (b. 1800, d. 1865), signed the 1830 treaty of Dancing Rabbit Creek, opening the way for European settlement in what is now Scott County.

ALFORD, Britton Washington Alford was born Jan. 10, 1843, to Spire Washington Alford (b. Oct. 1, 1807, d. prior to 1871) and Sarah "Sally" Brassell (b. Feb. 9, 1811, d. 1900) in Leake County, MS. By 1845 the family was residing in Scott County in the area south of Morton.

Britton W. Alford Family. Front Row, L. to R: Allen Alford, Emily Alford (mother) and Nannie Palmer. Back Row: Sarah Wesley, Linnie Stegall and Edna Joyner (later married Wesley).

Britton W. joined the Confederate Army Apr. 1, 1862 and served as a private in Co. C of the 39th Regt. of the Mississippi Infantry. He was captured at Port Hudson, LA, Jul. 9, 1863. On May 4, 1865, he was in the surrender at Citrionellia, AL and was paroled at Jackson, MS, on May 12, 1865.

On Aug. 1, 1866, Britton married Emily Lindsey (Lindsley?) (b. Feb. 27, 1850, d. May 17, 1935). She was the daughter of Allen Lindsey (b. May 9, 1822, d. Feb. 22, 1887) and Lucy Gaines (b. Dec. 29, 1826, d. Apr. 13, 1913). Britton died Oct. 20, 1887, leaving Emily with one son and four daughters. The son, the oldest, had just turned 10 and the youngest was less than 3 months old. Emily never remarried, but raised all the children to adulthood and saw them marry and have large families. In 1905 Emily made "Application for Pension for Indigent Widow of Soldier or Sailor of the late Confederacy under Chapter 132 Acts of 1904." At this time she was living with her daughter, Mrs. Edna Joyner. The family has copies of applications filed in 1905, 1911, 1916, 1923 and 1924. The 1923 and 1924 applications do not say "indigent widow" only "Application of Widow of Soldier or Sailor of late Confederacy."

These were Britton and Emily's children:

1) William Allen (b. Aug. 2, 1867, d. Oct. 20, 1930) md. Sally Paul.

2) Lucy Jane "Nannie" (b. Dec. 31, 1868, d. Feb. 6, 1942) md. Francis Marion Palmer.

3) Sarah Celia "Sally" (b. Nov. 25, 1870, d. Apr. 3, 1911) was second wife of Marion Leach Wesley.

4) Martha Perline "Linnie" (b. Nov. 15, 1873, d. Nov. 18, 1963) md. William B. Stegall.

5) Edna Ethel (b. Jul. 30, 1877, d. Dec. 4, 1955) md. first, Henry Joyner. After his death she became the third wife of Leach Wesley.

Britton is buried in the old Mt. Olive Primitive Baptist Church Cemetery across the road from the church. His parents are buried between his grave and the cedar trees. Emily died May 17, 1935. She is buried in the new Mt. Olive Church Cemetery beside her only son and surrounded by her children, their spouses, her grandchildren and great-grandchildren. *Submitted by Norma Earle Alford Idom.*

ALFORD, William Allen Alford (b. Aug. 1867, d. Oct. 20, 1930) was the only son Britton Washington Alford and Emily Lindsle He married Sally Paul (b. Jul. 28, 1872, d. Jan. 1923). They lived south of Morton in the Cooperville, Stage and Pulaski communities. They had 13 children with 12 living to adulthood:

Allen Alford Family. Front Row, L to R: Maudine, Allen, Margel, Sally holding Eloise and Horace. Middle Row: Penn, Rube and Major. Back: Anna, Luther, Britt, Ben and Eunice.

1) Edna Eunice (b. Aug. 29, 1891, d. Oct. 28, 1961) md. William R. Brett. They had no children. She is buried in Mt. Olive Church Cemetery, Scott County.

2) Paul Britton (b. Feb. 23, 1893, d. Jun. 11, 1965) md. Sudie Dowdle. They are buried in the Morton Cemetery. They had a son and two daughters.

3) Lucy C. (b. Apr. 17, 1895, d. Apr. 3, 1898) is buried in the family plot at Mount Olive Cemetery.

4) William Luther (b. Jan. 18, 1897, d. Mar. 10, 1954) md. Lilla Lotis Rushing. They are buried at the Springfield Cemetery. They had one daughter.

5) Anna Emily (b. Nov. 17, 1898, d. Sep. 17, 1961) md. Mack Miles. They are buried at Pulaski on land that Mack gave to a Primitive Baptist Church and at this time is an Independent Methodist Church. They had two sons and a daughter, all deceased.

6) Benjamin Milton (b. Oct. 6, 1900, d. Sep. 26, 1986) md. Claire R. Mapp. They are buried in the Loudon County Memorial Garden, Lenoir City, TN. They had a daughter and son who live in Tennessee.

7) Ruben Baxter (b. Jun. 14, 1902, d. Nov. 22, 1936) md. Ethyl Clark. He was killed in an automobile accident in Birmingham, AL. They had one son, now deceased.

8) Eddie Pennington (b. Mar. 2, 1904, d. Apr. 8, 1978) md. first, Clayton Weems. They are buried in the Carr Church Cemetery. They had three sons and a daughter.

9) Margel Mize (b. Oct. 29, 1905, d. Jul. 20, 1961) md. Carrie Belle Franklin. They had a daughter and two sons, one stillborn and the other killed in an auto accident returning to his Army base. All are buried at Mount Olive Church.

10) Major Henry (b. Jun. 22, 1907, d. Jul. 8, 1983) md. Wilma Winstead. They had no children. They are buried at Burns Methodist Church.

11) Florence Maudine (b. Nov. 13, 1909, d. Dec. 9, 1985) md. George William Miles and had three daughters and a son. They are buried at Pulaski. Two of the daughters married Miles brothers.

12) Samuel Horace "Red" (b. Sep. 30, 1911) Linnie Jackson. They had a daughter and sons. The daughter and one son are deceased.

13) Minnie Eloise (b. May 29, 1914, d. Dec. 1995) md. Sidney McClellan Crews and had daughters and a son.

Descendants still residing in Scott County with the Alford name are Horace "Red", Britt Jr., Robert "Bob" Shelby and his son. There are many other descendants not having the Alford name. *Submitted by Norma Earle Alford Idom.*

AMIS, My great-great-grandfather, John Woodson Amis was born Sep. 22. 1795, in North Carolina and grew to manhood there. Sometime about the year 1820, he went west across the Cumberland Mountains to some point on the Cumberland River. There he took passage on a flatboat down the Cumberland, Ohio and Mississippi rivers and landed at Natchez, MS. By occupation he was a millwright, a builder of grist mills, flour mills and cotton gins, to be operated by water power or animal power. He followed his trade of millwright in Adams, Copiah and Wilkinson counties of Mississippi. While engaged on a job of millwright he met Martha Wadkins who was living with her uncle, Seth Corley, in Copiah County. On Feb. 10, 1824, John Woodson Amis and Martha Wadkins were married. After their marriage they settled near Woodville in Wilkinson County, where they continued to reside until about 1838 or 1839. He became a land owner and a slave holder, as most other men of means were and was highly esteemed by the people of his community. About 1845 or 1846 they moved to Scott County and settled on the old stage road which ran from Jackson, MS, to Livingston, AL, at the eastern end of the old turnpike, across Tuscalameta Swamp. He died Feb. 4, 1849. He was buried on his own farm, in the old Amis graveyard, about five or six miles northwest of Conehatta.

Physically, John Woodson Amis was of sparse build and a little below medium height. He was a vigorous, active man and had considerable influence in his community. He was rather sensitive concerning the honor of himself and his family and not quick to forgive an injury to either. In politics he was a Whig and always voted the straight ticket. He was a Baptist, being a member of the Sulphur Springs Baptist Church at the time of his death. He was a royal arch mason, being a member of Hillsboro Lodge at the time of his death. His neighbors, widely scattered, in those days of sparse population, were the ancestors of the Graham, Brewer, Pettey, Eastland, Blalock, Keith, Carleton, Doolittle, Wilson and Johnson families of Newton and Scott counties. All of them were of the old pioneer stock; their like will never be seen again.

Five daughters and four sons were born to John Woodson and Martha Wadkins Amis: Ascension Lucrecy (b. Dec. 28, 1824) md. Samuel Blalock; Temperance Parisade (b. Sep. 18, 1826) md. first, B.O. Swinney and second, Charles W. Day; William Alexander (b. Jul. 24, 1829) md. Margaret Burleson; James C. (b. Jan. 20, 1832); Rankin Haywood Amis (b. May 25, 1834) md. first, Elizabeth Kimbell and second, Elizabeth J. Windham; Martha Jane (b. Mar. 11, 1838) md. first, E.A. Graham and second, James M. Parks; Albert Gallatin (b. Jan. 15, 1841) md. Augusta

Pettey; Mirnia Woodson (b. Feb. 27, 1844) md. J.D. Graham; and Frances M. (b. Jan. 28, 1848) md. W.H. Moore.

This article was adapted by Elvy Red Hammond from *"Sketches and Data of the Amis, Brewer, Pettey, Langford and Wilson Families of Newton County, MS"* by A.B. Amis Sr. *Submitted by Elvy Red Hammond.*

AMIS, Martha Wadkins Amis, familiarly and affectionately known as "Old Mother," was born at, or near, Macon, GA, Jun. 28, 1805. Her mother was a Curle. She had one sister named Tempe, but nothing else is known about her parents or other siblings. The parents died when the daughters were quite young. They were reared by their uncle, Seth Corley, in Copiah County, MS.

"Old Mother," Martha Wadkins Amis

On Feb. 10, 1824, Martha was married to John Woodson Amis and settled near Woodville, Wilkinson County, MS. By occupation, John Woodson was a millwright. About 1838 or 1839 they moved to Newton County and settled on a tract of land about halfway between Newton and Decatur. About 1845 or 1846 they moved to Scott County and settled on the old stage road at the eastern end of the old turnpike, across Tuscalameta Swamp. Five daughters and four sons were born to John Woodson and Martha Amis. In 1849, at the age of 44, Martha was left a widow. She never married again. After her husband's death, she took charge of the plantation and reared her family to manhood and womanhood. A few years before her death she went to live with her youngest daughter, Frances, on the old Ed Moore place, where she lived until she died Sep. 10, 1887. She was buried beside her husband in the old Amis graveyard.

She was a vigorous woman of strong personality and great courage. It is related that Sherman's army marched right by her place at one time during the Civil War and she knew that the soldiers would steal everything that they could lay their hands on. All her sons were gone to the war and there was no one at home except herself, her daughters and the farm helpers. So when she heard the army approaching, she had her few valuables and all her bacon, lard and other food brought in and piled in the middle of her room. She then got her daughters in, sat herself down in a chair in the open doorway and waited. When the soldiers arrived they went into the smokehouse, the corn crib, the dairy and some even tried to go past her into her room, but she calmly sat there and kept them back. In a little while she saw an officer approaching, whereupon she called to him, identified herself as a master mason's widow and asked for a detail of soldiers to guard her residence, which was immediately given her.

She was a member of the Baptist church and a devout believer in the ever ruling prov-

inces of God. She had a wealth of common sense and firmly believed that "God helps only those who help themselves."

"Old Mother" was of Scotch-Irish ancestry. She was a little below medium height. Her complexion at 70 years was ruddy. After each meal she smoked a clay pipe. She would sit and puff, the perfect picture of peace and contentment.

This article was adapted by Elvy Red Hammond from the original work *"Sketches and Data of the Amis, Brewer, Pettey, Langford and Wilson Families of Newton County, MS"* by A.B. Amis Sr. *Submitted by Kevin Ray Hammond, great-great-great-grandson.*

AMIS, My great-grandfather, Rankin Haywood Amis, was a son of John Woodson and Martha Wadkins Amis. He was born May 25, 1834, in Wilkinson County and died in Newton County Apr. 4, 1910. He was buried in the old Amis graveyard in Scott County.

On the Mississippi, Scott County 1850 U.S. census, Martha Amis, age 45 and seven of her children are listed: Parisade, 24; William, 20; Rankin, 16; Martha, 11; Albert, 9; Wootson, 6; and Francis, 2.

Rankin Haywood Amis

Rankin Haywood Amis married Elizabeth Kimball Dec. 21, 1854 and they had one son and five daughters: Frances Virginia, John Davis, Mattie, Eliza and Emma. Soon after they married they settled on a farm about half a mile from the White Plains Church and resided there until sometime after the Civil War. Then they moved to a farm they purchased from Uncle Charley Day, near the junction of the old Jackson Road and the Lake and Conehatta Road, where they resided the rest of their lives. About 1896 his first wife died and on Apr. 3, 1897, he married Elizabeth Windham. There were no children of this marriage.

He enlisted as a private soldier in the Confederate Army and served throughout the war. He was a master mason, being a member of the White Plains Lodge, at Sebastapol, at the time of his death. He was a consistent and devout Christian and was a member of Sulphur Springs Baptist Church. When there was sorrow among his neighbors and friends, he was there to aid and comfort them and when there was joy and gladness he was there to share it with them.

Uncle Tank, as he was known, was one of the finest and most lovable men in the community. He was jolly, even tempered and kind to everyone. He was frugal and industrious, but believed fully in the proverb that haste makes waste. So, no matter what the task, he never got in a hurry, worked steadily and deliberately until it was finished. His idea was, that if a man worked reasonably in the day time he was entitled to rest and sleep at night. He never tried to turn night into day to complete any task. No matter how pressing the farm work was, nor how fast the grass was growing in his crop, he never went to work until after sun up nor even until he had sat down after breakfast and smoked a pipe or two of tobacco.

He was of medium height, with a ruddy complexion and black hair and beard. He had a quick, ready smile, a short chuckling laugh and a sly wit that was often very amusing. In his later years he became almost blind, but that did not change his disposition or his outlook on life. Rankin Haywood Amis was buried beside both his wives in the old Amis "graveyard."

This article was adapted by Elvy Red Hammond, great-granddaughter, from *"The Amis, Brewer, Pettey, Langford and Wilson Families of Newton County, MS, Sketches and Data"* by A.B. Amis Sr. *Submitted by Virginia Elmyra Thompson, great-granddaughter.*

ANDREWS, John N. Andrews, son of Samuel W. and Annis Johnson Andrews, was first found on the 1860 Scott County census, Damascus area, with his mother, Ann Andrews and brothers, Jasper and Newton. Two brothers, William and Daniel, were not listed in this household. Also listed with them were Elizabeth, Henry and Benjamin Nelson. Elizabeth is believed to be a sister to Annis

John N. and Mary Elizabeth Chester Andrews

John N. was born in October 1841 in Butts County, GA and died Feb. 23, 1917. He married Mary Elizabeth Chester (b. June 1847, d. December 1900). Both are buried in Sulpher Springs Cemetery, Scott County.

John joined Co. I, 27th Regt. Mississippi Inf. CSA on Sep. 20, 1861, at Brookhaven, MS, for a period of three years. He was sent to the hospital after being shot in left heel Sep. 19, 1863. He filed for pension Sep. 2, 1912. John died of pneumonia and kidney trouble according to his death certificate. Jack Andrews of Conehatta gave information.

According to the 1900 census, John and Mary had 10 children, but only eight lived: Mattie; Louella M. (b. Mar. 31, 1873, d. May 12, 1952) md. Dec. 23, 1904, to John Bartlett Cater, brother of James Oscar Cater; William Austin (b. Mar. 7, 1875, d. Mar. 13, 1961) md. Mamie Georgia Turner; Francis A. (b. Aug. 18, 1878) md. Auther L. Beeland; John E. (b. 1880); Minnie Lee (b. Mar. 10, 1883, d. Jun. 16, 1961); Benjamin N. (b. 1886); Mary A. (b. Dec. 9, 1890, d. Sep. 9, 1973) md. Henry Ward Turner; Mattie (b. Apr. 7, 1871, d. Mar. 12, 1908) md. Sep. 18, 1898, to James Oscar Cater (b. Oct. 10, 1871, d. Nov. 29, 1927), son of John Lewis and Lucinda Weeks Cater, both are buried at Sulpher Springs Cemetery.

James Oscar and Mattie had five children:

Irma Estell (b. Aug. 7, 1899, d. Dec. 3, 1969) md. Warner Basil Turner; Lovett (b. Dec. 15, 1900, d. Jul. 12 1983) md. Golden Grace Vance; Mary Georgia; Vardaman (b. Mar. 16, 1904, d. Jan. 7, 1986) md. Bessie Haralson; and Elizabeth C. (b. Jan. 1, 1906, d. Jan. 17 1973) md. Marvin Vaughn. After Mattie died James Oscar married Alice Maybell Turner (b. May 31, 1884, d. Nov. 30, 1925, buried in Conehatta Methodist Church Cemetery, Newton County, MS). James Oscar and Maybell had three children: Petty (b. Oct. 15, 1913, d. Mar. 2, 1982) md. Lillie Vance; William D. (b. Jan. 16, 1921, d. Oct. 8, 1955) md. Lillie Bell Golden; and Lillian (b. Apr. 22, 1918, d. Feb. 10, 1958) md. Alton Leach.

After James Oscar and Maybell died, Lovett and Golden raised these three small children. Mary Georgia (b. Jul. 4, 1902, d. Oct. 4, 1878) md. Selby Vance (b. Mar. 25, 1905, d. Sep. 23, 1991), both buried Erin Presbyterian Church Cemetery, Newton County, MS. Selby and Golden were children of John Wesley and Mattie Ezell Vance. Selby and Mary Georgia had two children, Curtis Marlon (b. Jun. 18, 1924) md. Willie Ruth Butler and Helen Maurine (b. Dec. 26, 1934) md. Raymond Earl Cox of Sebastopol, MS, son of Wesley M. and Eula Mitchell Cox. Many descendants of John and Mary Elizabeth are still living in and around Scott County. Along with Andrews are McDills, Beelands, Turners, Caters and others.

ANDREWS, The Andrews family arrived in Scott County the latter part of the 1850s, from Butts County, GA. Annis Johnson Andrews was born 1823 in Georgia. She was the widow of Samuel Andrews. Annis and her five sons: William, John, Daniel, Jasper and Newton, were the first of the Andrews family to settle in Damascus, Scott County. She and her three younger sons,

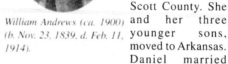

William Andrews (ca. 1900) (b. Nov. 23, 1839, d. Feb. 11, 1914).

moved to Arkansas. Daniel married Mary Madden, daughter of Josiah and Margaret Isabel Madden. Jasper married Sarah Wise, daughter of John and Emily Wise. Newton married Luella Dover, daughter of Lemuel and Clementine Dover. Sons William and John remained in Scott County. John (b. 1842) married Mary Elizabeth Chester.

Robert and Alma Andrews, 1940.

William was born Nov. 23, 1839. In 1860 William worked as a clerk in the general store in Damascus. Later he owned a watch repair shop in the Old Grange Hall in Sebastopol. He learned the art of photography while it was in its infancy. In 1860 William worked as a clerk in the general store in Damascus.

T.W. Andrews, 1943, WWII.

Aug. 24, 1861, William enlisted into Co. E "Lake Rebels," which later became part of the Mississippi 6th Inf. Regt. (The Bloody 6th). The 6th Inf. took part in many major battles, including Shiloh and Corinth. William later joined Co. K, 2nd Regt. of the Mississippi Cavalry, on Jan. 24, 1863. William married Sarah Catherine Stewart in 1868. Sarah was born Sep. 22, 1848, daughter of W.L. and Rebecca Stewart of Scott County. Sarah died Jun. 6, 1897; William on Feb. 11, 1914. They are buried in the Damascus Cemetery.

William and Sarah had nine children, only four lived to adulthood. They were: Elsie Andrews Goodwin, Sarah Frances Andrews, Alonzo and Robert.

Robert was born Mar. 2, 1884, Scott County. At a young age his mother died and his older sister, Sarah Frances, became his mother figure. Aunt Fannie, as she was known, was crippled at birth and never married. She was a kind and tenderhearted woman, who remained with Robert's family until she died May 25, 1967. Robert married Alma Burns Sep. 8, 1912. Alma was born Apr. 15, 1895, daughter of Noami Ofnal Burns and Cynthia Ann Elizabeth "Tennie" Gomillion of Leake County. Robert spent his life as a farmer in Scott and Rankin counties. He died Jan. 14, 1947; Alma on Oct. 9, 1976. Robert, Alma and Aunt Fannie are buried in Lodebar Cemetery, Rankin County. Robert and Alma had five children: Josie C. (b. Jun. 17, 1813) md. Lester Grantham; William "Billy" E. (b. Feb. 8, 1915) md. Ruby Winfield; Thellie W. (b. May 19, 1918) md. Mary Alma Brooks; Evelyn C. (b. Jan. 2, 1922) md. Delmar Balko; and Robert B. (b. Oct. 1, 1924) md. Betty Harpe.

These are the last descendants of William and his son, Robert Andrews, who lived in Scott County.

ANTLEY-PEVEY-SIMMONS, Perhaps no one has lived more years in Scott County then did the late George Brewton Antley, so I will use him as the connecting link between older and younger family members.

The first of the Antley name in Scott County was George's grandfather, the Reverend Joseph Smith Antley, who came to Mississippi from Orangeburg, SC, in 1850. Rev. Antley helped establish new churches in central Mississippi and for a time worked as an agent for Hillman Female College which was absorbed by Mississippi College. In a family Bible he inscribed his name followed by CSA. Whether he was a chaplain or just what his role was in the war isn't known at this time. His wife, Mahala Catherine Gambrel, also from South Carolina, came from a family of Baptist preachers including the famous J.B. Gambrel, who was four times elected president of the Southern Baptist Convention. Her grandfather, George Brewton, a Revolutionary soldier from Spartanburg, SC, became a Baptist minister somewhat late in life. John Gambrel, another Revolutionary soldier from South Carolina was also her grandfather as was her husband's grandfather, George Antley of Orangeburg, SC.

M.C. Gambrel Antley is buried in Forest but her husband, Rev. J.S. Antley, who wanted his tombstone to read "A Lover of Truth" is buried in Morton without a marker of any kind.

Again, the major connector for this narrative, George Antley (b. 1890), had a great-grandfather who completed the first building in Forest, the Simmons Hotel. It was built before the Civil War. This Simmons was John Christopher who with his wife, Frances Vineyard Simmons, came from Alabama. Her father, John, originally, I believe, from Virginia was also a soldier in the Revolution.

One of their two daughters, Frances Simmons, married Cullen Wade Pevey who took over the hotel, which overlooked the railroad in Forest, when J.C. Simmons died. Frances S. Pevey died at an early age but left 11 children including a daughter, Frances, who married George Brewton Antley Sr., a one time mayor of Lake, MS. Their marriage, by Mississippi standards, was a "mixed marriage" since George was a Baptist and the Peveys were Methodists. Their son in turn married a Methodist, Frances Nell Brevard from Natchez. Incidentally, even a very amateur psychologist would notice the prevalence of the name Frances for several generations.

While mention has been made of George Antley's ancestor who served in the American Revolution a book could be written about Frances' North Carolina Brevard ancestors who served in the 1770s and early '80s.

The tradition of military service begun by the first George Antley in the 1700s continued with "our George" in WWI and with two of his sons in WWII and the Korean War and in the military defense industry.

Besides having a number of worthy children, grandchildren and great-grandchildren, George and Frances Brevard Antley for years ran a business. The business, with the help of skillful associates such as Joe Lyles and George Williams, provided homes for low income families in Scott and neighboring counties.

This little history has to be brief but it would be inexcusable not to at least mention female members of the family like the Pevey sisters. Besides the small hotel they also ran a millinery shop in Forest for many years.

George's lovely sisters included Cornelia and Eleanor who moved to Texas with their husbands and Grace who moved to Moorhead, MS, with her husband. Then there was Annie who taught children in Forest for most of her long life.

The more I write the more I realize how much is left unwritten - but perhaps another time. *Respectfully submitted Eugene Brevard Antley.*

ALEXANDER-ASKIN, Billy Wayne Alexander and Shawna Lavonne Askin were

married in Scott County Mar. 14, 1982. Billy is a machinist working for R & L Tool in Burns, MS. Billy, the son of James Armos and Ila Mae (Smith) Alexander, was born Nov. 13, 1939, in Newton County. He attended school in Newton County the first eight years, changing to Sebastopol in 1956. Sebastopol had its first football team in the school year 1958-59. Billy scored their first touchdown in a game against Hickory. During his senior year of 1959-60, he scored the first touchdown on Sebastopol's home field. Billy joined the Marines in 1961 and in 1962, during the Cuban missile crises, he made nine trips to the U.S. Naval Base at Guantanamo Bay, Cuba. In 1963, Billy was sent to Okinawa, Japan for 13 months. After only six months at home, in September 1965, Billy went to Da Nang, South Vietnam when President Johnson sent in the Marines. He served there for 13 months, returning home with a National Defense Service Medal, Vietnam Campaign Medal, Vietnam Service Medal, Good Conduct Medal and a Sharpshooter Badge for five years

Joel, Shawna and Billy Wayne Alexander.

Shawna, the daughter of Marion Arnold Sr. and Frankie (Carpenter) Askin, was born Dec. 22, 1949, in Scott County. She attended Forest School and graduated in 1967. She worked many years at the Sunbeam Corp., but when it closed she retired, to being a full-time homemaker. This also gave her the opportunity to provide care and assistance to her father in his declining years.

Billy and Shawna live on the Askin homeplace, which her grandparents bought in 1919. They are active members of New Zion Baptist Church. Shawna has taught the Adult Sunday School class since January 1989. Billy was ordained a deacon in May 1994. Shawna is also an active member of the Scott County Genealogical Society and the Morton Homemaker Volunteers. Billy is the Quartermaster of VFW Post 4974 and past commander, senior vice and junior vice.

Billy and Shawna have a yours, mine and ours family. They are the parents of four children. Billy Wayne Jr. was born Feb. 17, 1968, in Hinds County. He married Tina Marie Harrelson Jun. 20, 1986, in Graham, TX. Wayne and Tina are the parents of David Wayne and Heather Nicole. James Robert was born Nov. 24, 1969, in Newton County. He married Joyce Campbell Apr. 4, 1986, in Graham, TX. James and Joyce are the parents of James Robert Jr., Meagen Rena and Ronnie Lynn. Shawna Leigh Harrison was born Oct. 3, 1972, in Scott County. Leigh is employed at Raytheon Systems of Forest. Joel Armos was born Nov. 2, 1983, in Newton County and attends Forest High School.

ASKIN-CARPENTER, Marion Arnold Askin Sr. was the third child of Arnold Mornas and Mattie Alberta (Sawyer) Askin. Arnold was born Aug. 6, 1917, in Scott County. He began school at Faulkner (Cedar Hill) School but after a couple years it consolidated with Forest. Arnold's favorite thing about school was playing football for "Pop Hartness." Arnold always regretted that he never got a diploma, but as one of the older children he was called on to quit school and work to help support the others. After spending four years in the Army, three of those years in Europe, Arnold married Cornelia Franks "Frankie" Carpenter on May 4, 1946. Frankie, the daughter of Ernest Leon and Mary Odessa (Russell) Carpenter, was born Sep. 22, 1926, in Scott County. Frankie began school at Hillsboro and went several years to Morton, but after the family moved to East Hillsboro, she attended Harperville School and graduated in 1945. Frankie was a member of the Hillsboro Methodist Church, making a profession of faith in 1941

Askin Family. Front: "Butch" Marion Jr., Sandra and Shawna. Back: Arnold and "Frankie."

On Oct. 22, 1947, Marion Arnold Jr. was born. Before long he was given the nickname "Butch," which he carried with him all through school. Eleven months after "Butch" arrived, their second child, Sandra Joy, was born on Sep. 25, 1948, followed by Shawna Lavonne on Dec. 22, 1949.

The years of hard work to provide for their family had begun. Arnold worked many years in the timber business with his brother, Nesba. After the children were all in school Frankie did public work. But in 1961, it was discovered that she had a heart problem, caused from having had rheumatic fever as a child. Four years later, Frankie had a fatal attack. On Nov. 20, 1965, at the age of 39, the Lord called Frankie home. She was buried in Faulkner Cemetery. Arnold never remarried. Whenever asked why he didn't, his answer was always the same, "I'll never find another Frankie."

In the fall of 1966, about to be drafted, "Butch" joined the Army and spent the next 29-1/2 years in the service. He married Karin Kollender Nov. 6, 1970. Butch adopted Karin's daughter, Silke and on Aug. 16, 1971, Stephanie Lynn was born.

Sandra married Warren Kerr Oct. 24, 1969. After a few years living in Jackson, they sold their house and moved to the hills of Eastern Tennessee. For Warren it was a move back home, for Sandra it was a move away from her family. Warren, an avid hunter and fisherman, spends many hours in the woods and on the lakes. Sandra, an avid collector, spends many hours in the antique shops. Dolls and Santas are some of her favorite collectibles. Sandra followed in the footsteps of her great-grandmother, Nancy Lou Lang Russell and great-aunt, Martha Russell. She inherited their crochet talent.

Shawna has two children, Shawna Leigh Harrison and Joel Armos Alexander. She is married to Billy Wayne Alexander. Her hobby is genealogy and she is very active in her church.

ASKIN-SAWYER,

ASKIN-SAWYER, Arnold Mornas Askin was born Dec. 27, 1888, in Scott County. He was the oldest son of John Sinclair Jr. and Juddie (Stokes) Askin. His father died in 1892, when he was 4 years old. In 1897, his mother married Jeff Faulkner. Tragedy struck again Oct. 5, 1904, when Mornas' younger brother, X.O., died. Within a few years, Mornas, his mother and step-

Mornas and Bertie (Sawyer) Askin

father, left Scott County and moved to Point, MS, where they lived on the banks of the Chunky River. After a few years at Point, they moved to Meridian, where Mornas worked for the railroad, laying tracks. Juddie and Jeff ran a mercantile store.

Mornas met Mattie Alberta Sawyer at the Fair. "Bertie" was the oldest child of William John and Mary Frances (Roberson) Sawyer. She was born May 12, 1891, in Lauderdale County. She worked at Kress's 10¢ Store and had saved up enough money to buy herself a piano. Mornas and "Bertie" married Feb. 8, 1914. Their first two children were born in Meridian, Nesba (b. Nov. 15, 1914) and Lois (b. Jan. 9, 1916). The railroad laid Mornas off in the spring of 1916, so he packed up his young family and returned to Scott County. Because of the deaths of her parents, three of Bertie's brothers (Carl, John and Chester) came with them. They moved to the Moore Tower Community, to what was known as the Smith Place. Three more children were added: Arnold (b. Aug. 6, 1917), J.D. (b. Apr. 25, 1919) and Ola (b. Oct. 17, 1920).

Mornas and Bertie purchased land from Z.T. Faulkner in 1919, in the Cedar Hill Community and began to build a house, moving in before the end of 1920. Her health bad, Mornas' mother, Juddie, also came back to Scott County to be with her family. Juddie died Sep. 13, 1922 and was buried in Faulkner Cemetery.

Mornas and Bertie had four more children: Clifton (b. Sep. 28, 1922), Aubrey "Cotton" (b. Apr. 1, 1924), W.J. (b. Jun. 15, 1926) and Ruby (b. Jul. 16, 1928). New Zion Baptist Church was organized in 1924 and the Askin family soon became involved in the church work. Mornas was ordained a deacon and Bertie was church secretary. All the boys were off in service when Bertie died Jul. 31, 1944, from tuberculosis. Aubrey "Cotton" was killed in France Oct. 15, 1944, less than three months after his mother's death. He was a 20-year-old young man caught in a World War. He just wanted to get back home to his family. With full military honors, his body

was brought back in a flag draped coffin, for burial at Faulkner Cemetery. "Cotton's" father was presented with the flag and a "Purple Heart" in recognition of his service to the U.S. Mornas died on Sunday morning, May 28, 1950, also from tuberculosis. New Zion Baptist Church canceled services that day because of his death. He was buried in Faulkner Cemetery between his wife, Bertie and his mother, Juddie.

ASKIN-STOKES, John Sinclair Askin Jr. (b. Oct. 26, 1864 in Mississippi) and Gabriella Juddie Stokes (b. May 29, 1868) married in Scott County Dec. 22, 1886. John was the oldest son of John Sinclair Sr. and Mary Ann Westerfield Askin. Juddie was the only child of Willis B. and Ann H. (Idom) Stokes. Ann Idom Stokes died in 1870, when Juddie was only 2 years old.

Juddie Stokes Askin

John and Juddie bought land from J.P. Harvey in the Clifton Community in 1888, just before their first son, Arnold Mornas, was born on December 27. Four years passed before John and Juddie had another son, X.O. (b. Jun. 19, 1892). John was a Methodist minister as well as farming and doing public work. Family history says that John was working in Morton, he would ride the train to Raworth. There he would get off and walk through the woods home. On a cold October night, John slipped off the log he was walking to cross the Shockaloo Creek. Soaking wet, he walked on home. Shortly after that John took sick, developing into pneumonia. John died the 17th day of October 1892, just nine days before his 28th birthday and two months before their sixth wedding anniversary. Juddie was left a young widow, with a 4-year-old and a 4-month-old to provide and care for.

Juddie married Fields Jefferson Faulkner in 1898. But tragedy struck again in 1904. Her youngest son, X.O., died on the fifth day of October. He was buried in the Hillsboro Methodist Cemetery beside his father. Juddie, Jeff and Mornas moved to Point and lived on the edge of the Chunky River. From there they moved into Meridian, where they ran a mercantile store.

In 1919, her health failing and her marriage to Jeff over, Juddie returned to Scott County. She moved into the house with Mornas and his family. Juddie gave marriage one more try. On Apr. 13, 1921, she married William Lewis "Bud" Norton. The mayor of Forest, Percy M. Lee, married them, but it was short lived. By July 25, she was back at Mornas and Bertie's in the Cedar Hill Community. Juddie lived out the rest of her days there with her son, daughter-in-law and five grandchildren. By the summer of 1922, Juddie's health took a turn for the worse. She was bed ridden for the last month of her life. Mr. and Mrs. Judd Jones, who were close neighbors, took turns helping Mornas and Bertie sit with Juddie. Juddie's life slipped away at 2:00 p.m. Sep. 13, 1922, at the age of 54. She was buried in Faulkner Cemetery.

ASKIN-WESTERFIELD, John Sinclair Askin, Sr. (b. Apr. 6, 1835 in Alabama) and Mary Ann Westerfield (b. Mar. 6, 1847 in Mississippi) married Dec. 8, 1863. They probably married in Kemper County, MS. John was the son of Samuel G. and Jane (Donald) Askin. Mary Ann was the daughter of Casparus and Rebecca (Billingsley) Westerfield.

John Sinclair Askin Sr.

John enlisted in May 1861, in Kemper County, MS. He joined the 13th Mississippi Inf., Co. F, under Col. William Barksdale and Capt. McLeroy. John was wounded in the arm Jul. 3, 1863, at the Battle of Gettysburg. I believe John and Mary Ann married during the time his arm was healing. He was discharged in May 1865.

John, Mary Ann and seven children came to Scott County around 1882-83. They bought land in 1884 from J.W. Tadlock, in what was called the Flatwoods. It was there, they settled to raise their children and live out the rest of their days.

Mary Ann passed away Sep. 11, 1905. She was buried in the Hillsboro Methodist Cemetery. John was to live 23 more years, staying on the farm and working it with the help of some of the children. At the age of 86, John was seriously injured when he was kicked by a mule, but he lived seven more years and at the age of 93 passed away Apr. 9, 1928. He was buried next to Mary Ann. Many of their children married and lived in Scott County, with many descendants still here today. All but four of John and Mary Ann's children were buried in the Hillsboro Methodist Cemetery around them. "Bessie" was buried in the Coy Cemetery in Neshoba County. Samuel was buried in Lawrence County, Ida in Lauderdale County and Martin was buried in Winston County.

John and Mary Ann had 11 children. Their children were: John Sinclair Jr. (b. Oct. 23, 1864) md. Juddie Stokes Dec. 22, 1886. John died at the age of 28 on Oct. 17, 1892. Ida R. (b. about 1866) md. first, John Smith in 1899 and second, Walter Myers. Ida died Mar. 27, 1931. Samuel H. (b. about 1868) md. Lula Brantly Mar. 8, 1892. Martin (b. about 1869) died after 1870 but before 1880. Moaton Arnold (b. May 1870) never married. He died Jun. 27, 1928. In less than three months, father and son were buried side by side. As close in death as they had been in life. Hattie Inez (b. Jul. 26, 1871) md. Willis Arthur Sigrest Feb. 24, 1892. She died Jul. 7, 1912. Iola (b. May 28, 1873) was a school teacher and never married. She died Apr. 8, 1959. Almeta (b. Jan. 23, 1878) also never married and died Apr. 10, 1911, at age 33. Naomi Estelle (b. Nov. 5, 1883) was a school teacher and married John Webster Tadlock Dec. 27, 1905. She died Aug. 22, 1969. Elizabeth "Bessie" (b. Oct. 10, 1885) also taught school and married Bennie Fulton Jan. 20, 1914. She died Dec. 15, 1926. Their last child was Pearl (b. Jul. 1, 1888). She married Grover Cleveland Tadlock Dec. 23, 1905. She died Aug. 18, 1914, at the age of 26.

AUSTIN, Jessie William Austin Sr. (b. Oct. 20, 1916, Osyka, MS, d. Feb. 12, 2001), son of Dr. Richard Baker Austin Jr. and Jessie L. Morse. His brother, Richard Baker Austin III, was born Apr. 28, 1915.

Dr. J.W. Austin and Opal Wilkes Austin

The family moved to Forest in December 1924. Dr. R.B. practiced medicine until he died in October 1967.

Bill graduated from Forest High School in 1934. He graduated from Mississippi State in 1938 and attended Tulane Medical School where he graduated in 1942.

He interned at Hillman Hospital (now UAB) in Birmingham, for one year. There he met and married Opal Wilkes from Huntsville, AL, Jun. 15, 1943.

He went on active duty in the Army Jul. 29, 1943. He arrived in Carlyle Barrack, PA, in August 1943. He landed in England and on to France with the 51st Ord. Bn. Bill was in five battles and received the Purple Heart, Silver Star and the Bronze Star. He was in the Battle of the Bulge.

Ms. Opal (as she is called) worked as office nurse for Dr. R.B. during the absence of her husband. Dr. R.B. was the only doctor in Forest during the war. Ms. Opal rode a bicycle to change dressings, etc. as cars were scarce.

Returning to Forest when the war ended, Bill began his medical practice with his father. He delivered 3500 babies, along with an active office practice. Dr. Bill and Ms. Opal, as everyone calls them, had five children: Sue Carole (b. 1944), Jesse W. Austin Jr. (b. 1946), Judith Anne (b. 1949), Richard Buford (b. 1952) and Terry Lee (b. 1954).

Both are active members of the Methodist church and school and sports activities. Their house was always open to welcome children, dogs, cats or anyone lonely. Some stayed a few hours, a few days or several months. Everyone felt free to come. They reared their children a block from the school and were available to help in any way needed. Dr. Bill retired from practice in 1984. He enjoyed playing golf and his grandchildren and traveling to Mississippi State for football games.

BARFIELD, The Barfields who lived in Scott County descended from John Barfield (b. ca. 1770, d. before 1800) and Dorcas __ (b. ca. 1774, d. ca. 1840) of the Barnwell Dist., SC, who married about 1790 to 1795 and had three children: John (b. 1794, d. 1841), Henry (b. 1795, d. 1844) and Ann Barfield (b. 1799, d. before 1950). About 1805 Dorcas Barfield, widow, married John Cherry and had three more children: William (b. 1807), Martha (b. 1812) and Allen Cherry (b. 1815). Before 1830 all of the Barfields and Cherrys, except Henry Barfield, moved to Mississippi. John Barfield, son of Dorcas, represented Perry County in the 1830s legislature, but he apparently moved to Copiah County where

he wrote his will in 1839, leaving to "brother Henry Barfield all the effects which I have in South Carolina" and asking his executors "to make an equal division of all my estate both real and personal between the children of my brother Henry Barfield, but should he have no children nor grandchildren living, then" he made provisions for the education of his executors' children. The will was probated in 1841, but Henry's children never did receive any part of their uncle's estate.

Meanwhile, Henry Barfield had married Sherett Elizabeth Sherett (b. 1802, d. 1873), daughter of James Sherett of Scotland and Jane Buckner and had five children, all born in South Carolina: Benjamin Henry who married Emma LaFar; Laura Ann; James Sherett who married Maude Hunter; Cornelia Jane; and Emma who married Dr. Thomas Hart Benton Williams. Family papers indicate that Henry Barfield died about 1844, after which Sherett Elizabeth Barfield came to Mississippi, but her name is not found in the 1850 census.

Laura Ann Barfield (b. Jun. 30, 1829), second child of Henry and Sherett Elizabeth Barfield, married on Feb. 20, 1849, Enos Rush Buckner, a lawyer living in Hillsboro, Scott County, MS. The 1850 census lists the young couple (ages 26 and 21) and 6-month-old son named for his father. Living with them is her younger sister, 17-year-old Cornelia. A few years later Cornelia Jane (b. May 1, 1832 in Robertville, SC) married William Whitehead Lowry, a druggist in Hillsboro. These two families lived on adjacent lots in the town of Hillsboro.

During the Civil War Laura Ann Barfield Buckner died of consumption on Mar. 3, 1864, just two years after her husband. The orphaned children were then taken into the Lowry household and cared for by Cornelia Jane and her husband. By 1870 Sherett Elizabeth Barfield was also living with the Lowrys, being listed there in the census along with Laura Ann's children, Ella, Ida and Eula Buckner. Cornelia's children were: May, Percy, Edgar, Lizzie and Lottie (twins) and Maud Lowry. After her husband died Cornelia eventually went to live in Texas and died in San Antonio Aug. 23, 1916.

Sherett Elizabeth Barfield died on Jan. 2, 1873 and was buried in Eastern Cemetery, Forest, MS, where she shares a tombstone with her granddaughter, Ella Florence Buckner, a schoolteacher in Forest.

BARNES-HARRISON, Nell Barnes Harrison was born Apr. 7, 1930, Homewood, MS, to William Lafayette and Erie Warren Barnes (b. Jun. 18, 1895, d. 1992). William (b. Jun. 24, 1890, d. 1972) was the son of William Wesley and Rebecca Ellen Noblin. William Wesley (b. Feb. 1, 1870) from Leake County, MS, a farmer and merchant. Rebecca (b.

Dr. William H. Barnes, soldier, physician and surgeon. Scott County, Homewood, MS.

Jan. 23, 1874, d. October 1951); William (b. Feb. 1, 1870, d. 1944), both buried Homewood Methodist Cemetery.

William Lafayette and Erie Warren Barnes had five children: Marium Barnes Kenney (b. May 3, 1919, d. 1970), John William Barnes (b. Sep. 23, 1920, d. 1998), James Cooper Barnes (b. 1924), Robert Lamar "Bob" Barnes (b. Apr. 23, 1927, d. 1990) and Nell Barnes Harrison (b. Apr. 7, 1930).

Dr. William Henry Barnes, father of: William Wesley, married Sara Jane Miller, daughter of Rev. David Laughlin Miller and Isabella (b. Jun. 18, 1847, d. May 19, 1920); William Henry (b. Sep. 5, 1845, d. Mar. 18, 1924, buried Homewood Methodist Cemetery).

William Lafayette and Erie Warren Barnes lived with Dr. Barnes and Sara until he died. They purchased the homeplace and lived in this home until they died. During this time Erie learned to aid Dr. Barnes with his patients by mixing medicines and helping to set broken bones.

Dr. William H. Barnes, soldier, physician, surgeon, was born Sep. 5, 1845, in Dale County, AL. He received the rudiments of his education in the public schools of his native state and graduated in medicine from the Alabama Medical College of Mobile. During the Civil War he was a soldier in the Confederate States Army in Co. D, 57th Regt., Alabama Volunteers, Scott's Bde., Loring's Div., Tennessee Army and was in numerous battles and skirmishes. He was a successful physician and surgeon of Homewood, MS. He was aide-de-camp on Gen. Cameron's staff U.C.V. of Mississippi with the rank of major. He was vice-president of the Scott County Medical Society; surgeon of the U.C.V. at Camp Lake, MS and filled various positions of trust and honor.

Nell Barnes Harrison married B. Alton Harrison, Homewood, MS, in 1951. They have two sons and seven grandchildren. Phillip Alton married Stacy Shaw of Forest, MS. They have three children: Ashley Rebecca (b. Nov. 3, 1983), Phillip Alton Jr. (b. Jul. 12, 1985) and Austin Michael (b. Feb. 8, 1991). They live in Louisville, MS and own the AM-FM radio station.

Dr. John Barnes Harrison married Lisa Loper in Laurel, MS. They have four children: John Brannon (b. Sep. 3, 1986), Nathan Barnes (b. Jan. 14, 1988), Andrea Williams (b. Aug. 9, 1989) and Erin Rebekah (b. Apr. 9, 1992). Dr. John graduated UMC School of Dentistry in May 1985 and moved to Newton, MS, opening the Newton Family Dental Practice.

BARRETT, John W. Barrett, son of Reubin Barrett Jr. and grandson of Reubin Barrett Sr., was born Feb. 22, 1822, in Alabama. He married Annria Bishop, May 31, 1863, in Itawamba, MS. They had two sons, Tom Barrett and Jack Barrett. Annria died about 1886 and John married Margaret W. Barrett in 1887. John W. Barrett died Mar. 26, 1892 and is buried in Ludlow Cemetery, Scott County, MS.

Tom was born in 1860 in Alabama and married Fannie (unknown). They had one child, Sudie (b. 1910, d. 1916).

Jack (b. Dec. 6, 1882 in Alabama) married Martha Ellen Holmes of Philadelphia, MS. They had six children.

Cordia Lee Barrett married Therl Burchfield. They had four children: William Therl, Margie, Lena Pearl and Doyle Henry Burchfield.

Viola Barrett married Ezra Burchfield. They had six children: J.B., Mary Lou, Louise, Jimmy, Floyd and Wade Burchfield.

Ed Barrett married Nina Jones. They had four children: Jackie, Florence, Ned and Jerry Barrett.

John Barrett married Willie Horton. They had six children: Peggy, Fredia, Jackie, Nancy, Glenn and John "Sonny" Barrett.

Davis Barrett married Annie Albright. They had one son, Davis Ross Barrett.

BENNETT-COCHERL,
Hiram Bennett (b. Georgia, d. 1903) married Mary Ann Cocherl (b. 1833 in Georgia, d. March 1897).

Their children were Drew Warren (b. Feb. 10, 1853, d. Apr. 25, 1926), Lawson Burton (b. Feb. 21, 1863, d. Jan. 18, 1955) and George Washington "Wash" (b. mid-1860s, d. 1932).

About 1932, Wash Bennett, along with his son, Harvey and his wife, Lessie Babb,

Lawson Burton Bennett with his wife, Ora Ellen Munday, at their home at Ludlow, MS (approximately 1950).

were living at Eudora, AR. During a very bad flu epidemic, Lessie gave birth to a baby, both died from the flu. Harvey and his father, Wash, died a day or so later with the flu. Harvey and Lessie's children were ages 9, 7 and 2. Rosa Bennett Sumrall (age 9) of Harvey and Lessie's children remembers snow being on the ground and her parents' bodies being taken away in wagons. They were buried in Eudora in the winter of 1932 or early 1933. After Lessie and Harvey's death, Lessie's parents brought the children back to Lena, MS.

About 1932, Maudie and Burton Bennett were also living in Eudora in an old boxcar with little or no heat. Joe Babb (Lena, MS) wanted to take their kids, but Burton would not let him. Maudie Babb Bennett also died with the flu.

Hiram Bennett brought his family from North Carolina to Georgia to Arkansas and then to Mississippi. They cut a road through to the Mississippi River and made rafts to go across the river. Hiram and his family would hold on to the horns of the ox while the ox would pull the rafts across the Mississippi. More children were born to Hiram and Mary, but some died with yellow fever and were buried on the trail except for the three children listed above.

Hiram would move his family back and forth from Arkansas to Mississippi due to crop failures.

After the Civil War, Lawson Burton Bennett said they ate wild onions and parched corn to keep from starving.

Lawson Burton Bennett married Ora Ellen Munday (b. Sep. 27, 1870, d. Jan. 5, 1957, buried Ludlow, MS). Their children were Loyd Milton (b. Oct. 15, 1891, d. April 1937), Peter

Jerry (b. Feb. 20, 1893, d. Apr. 23, 1948), Lewis Gordon (b. Feb. 2, 1895, d. Feb. 22, 1973), Susie Ellen (b. Jan. 22, 1899, d. Aug. 24, 1990), Lawson Eph (deceased), Calvin Washington (b. Jan. 8, 1901, d. Oct. 9, 1980), Clay Preston (deceased) and Carl Perry (b. Aug. 18, 1905, d. Jan. 8, 1983).

Hester Bennett Brogdon Gardner (Harperville, MS) remembers going to church in a wagon with her mother and father, Alma and Perry Bennett and remembers the wagon brakes as they would go down those long hills. Hester and cousin, Forrest Munday, remember Ora and Lawson's first car, Ora would run and get a pan of water to wash away the spit on the side of the car where Ora's sister, Julie, had spit. Hester and Forrest Munday said they never saw Ora get in a hurry "except those times to wipe the spit from Lawson's car."

BENNETT-MILLER,
Carl Perry Bennett (b. Aug. 18, 1905, d. Jan. 8, 1983) (born Ludlow, MS) married Nannie Alma Miller (b. Jan. 5, 1911, d. Jun. 12, 1988) (born Clifton, MS) Mar. 18, 1927). They are both buried at Ludlow.

Perry and Alma had five children: Hester Ellen (b. Aug. 17, 1928), Doris Carlene (b. Jan. 2, 1933), Lloyd Nolan (b. Aug. 3, 1938), Mavis Irene (b. Jan. 3, 1941) and Michael Perry (b. Oct. 24, 1952). Hester Gardner lives in the Harperville, MS, Community; Carlene Thrash and Mavis Withers live in the Morton, MS, Community; Mike Bennett lives in the Decatur, MS, Community; and Nolan Bennett lives in the Hazard, KY, area.

Carl Perry Bennett and wife, Nannie Alma (approximately 1977).

Perry and Alma were some of the hardest working people. They were not ones to just sit around, not even as they grew older. Perry was a carpenter most of his life, but farmed some. Alma had various jobs besides being a mother and wife.

Alma was on her way to church on the morning of Jun. 12, 1988, when she lost control of her car and went off the road. She died shortly after being taken to the Morton Hospital. She was a devout Christian and there was not even sitting room at her funeral.

Perry is the son of Lawson Burton Bennett (b. Feb. 21, 1863, d. Jan. 18, 1955) and Ora Ellen Munday (b. Sep. 27, 1870, d. Jan. 5, 1957), who lived in the Ludlow Community.

Alma is a descendent of Christopher Miller who was captured by Indians in the mid-1770s and held captive for some years. Christopher Miller's grandson, Thomas Edwin Miller, married Nannie Ellen Cooke Dec. 28, 1908, near Murfreesboro, TN. He brought his wife, Nannie Ellen, back to Scott County where they settled near Clifton, MS. They lived there until about 1929 and moved to the Long Creek Community in Lauderdale County. They are both buried at the Long Creek Baptist Church Cemetery.

BLOXSOM,
My great-grandfather, Daniel Edward Bloxsom, was born Feb. 20, 1848, in Macon, Bibb County, GA. From family letters and census records, it appears that the family moved to Lake, Scott County, MS, about 1863. His parents were E. Patrick Bloxsom and Anne Buxton Bloxsom. A sister, Anna, married Thomas Hamlin of Memphis, TN. After serving in

Daniel Edward Bloxsom

Mitchell's Co. of the Mississippi Cavalry Reserves, Daniel Edward moved to Houston, TX, about 1870; Clara moved to Houston in 1871; Omelia married Samford and lived in Washington County, MS; Sara Jane married Kimbrough and lived at Morton and Forest, MS; Alice Dellar married S.S. Greeney Jan. 6, 1878, with Elder J.H. Grundy officiating. (J.B. Blackwell was county clerk of Scott County.) They moved to Mount Pleasant, TX.

Daniel's father, E. Patrick, moved to Houston about 1868 followed by Daniel and Clara. Life was hard for Anne and the girls. They were seamstresses, housekeepers and baby-sitters. Anne died May 5, 1878, in Lake, MS.

In Texas, Daniel found work in Brenham and in Galveston. Then he became a master car builder for the Southern Pacific Railroad in Houston. He married Betty Milhop and had four children. He became a landlord in Houston and prospered. He was past master of the Masonic Gray Lodge, emeritus commander of Ruthven Commandery #2 and member of the Arabia Temple Shrine. He died May 9, 1929. Members of the Masonic order officiated, with services under the direction of all the funeral directors of Houston. *By Mary Aline Austin.*

BOOZER,
George Washington Boozer (b. Jan. 9, 1832 in Newberry County, SC) moved to Scott County, MS, in 1856 and married Mary Younce, daughter of William Younce. Mr. Boozer was a farmer. He enlisted in the Confederate Army Mar. 17, 1862, in Trenton, MS and died of pneumonia and typhoid in the hospital at Vicksburg Dec. 30, 1862. One child, Drayton Augustus Boozer, was born Dec. 25, 1861 (d. 1929).

Lloyd Clark Boozer and Elizabeth Mangum Boozer, around 1930.

Drayton Augustus married Elizabeth Vinzant (b. Nov. 5, 1864) of Burns, MS, Nov. 6, 1884. She died in 1949. Both are buried in the Luther Chapel Church Cemetery near Pulaski. Their children, all born at the home near Pulaski, were: George William Boozer (b. 1885, d. 1956), Mary Lee Boozer (b. 1887, d. 1963), Tinie Elizabeth Boozer (b. 1889, d. 1904), James Walton

Boozer (b. 1891, d. ?), Robbie Sue Boozer (b. 1893, d. 1978), Robert Grady Boozer (b. 1895, d. 1960), Ola Emma Boozer (b. 1897, d. 1968), Carl Davis Boozer (b. 1899, d. ?), Ellie Mae Boozer (b. 1903, d. 1989), Hilton Boozer (b. 1904, d. 1904) and Lloyd Clark Boozer (b. 1906, d. 1998).

From Left to Right: Lloyd Clark Boozer; son, Drayton Daniel Boozer; wife, Elizabeth Mangum; daughters: Brunell Boozer, Sadie Ruth Boozer and Mary Beth Boozer, around 1949.

Lloyd Clark Boozer married Elizabeth Mangum (b. Feb. 2, 1907), daughter of John Wesley and Susan Amanda Howorth Mangum, Oct. 9, 1926. Their children, all born at the home near Pulaski are: Brunell Boozer (b. 1927), Betty Sue Boozer (b. 1931, d. 1933), Sadie Ruth Boozer (b. 1932), Mary Beth Boozer (b. 1937), Drayton Daniel Boozer (twin) (b. 1944) and Nancy Clark Boozer (twin) (b. 1944, d. 1944). All of the Boozer children attended Pulaski Grade School and Morton Attendance Center. Mary Lee Boozer was principal of the Morton High School for many years retiring in 1950.

Lloyd Boozer lived all of his life on "Boozer Hill" in Scott County which is bordering on the Smith County line. The community became known as the New Good Hope Baptist Church Community. He was a farmer and cattleman. He died in Scott County in 1998 at the age of 92. Elizabeth Boozer (d. 1989) was a homemaker and a Sunday school teacher. She was a member of Luther Chapel Church and supported activities of the church throughout her life.

Drayton Boozer and wife, Beverly Beatty Boozer, of Albuquerque, NM, are now the owners of the family homeplace and farm known as "Boozer Hill." Brunell Boozer and husband, Carl Robert Howorth, live in Raymond, MS. They have two children, Pam Howorth Schmegel and Brian Howorth. Pam and husband Bill Schmegel, of Jackson, MS, have two sons ,Andy and Eric. Sadie Ruth Boozer Whitehead (husband, Eddie d. 1993) lives in Pensacola, FL. She has two children, Michael and Camille Whitehead, also of Pensacola. Michael and wife, Kathy, have two children, Christopher and Ginny. Camille Cutts Collins has three children: Heather Cutts, Blake and Joey Collins. Beth Boozer Churchwell lives in Memphis, TN and has two sons, Steven and Stanley Churchwell. *Compiled by Beth Boozer Churchwell.*

BOYKIN, Alva Dairel Boykin was born Apr. 11, 1927, the son of Alva Breland Boykin and Fannie E. (Webb) Boykin, in Smith County, MS. Alva grew up on a farm about nine miles northeast of Raleigh. He was one of six children: Allen Homes, Alva Dairel, Charles Ray, Doris Jean,

Annie Lois and Hebert Glenn. He attended Raleigh High School and after completing the 10th grade enlisted in the U.S. Navy in August 1944. He served aboard the USS *Schroeder* DD-501 in the Pacific, earning three service ribbons and three Battle Stars. After discharge from the Navy, Mar. 6, 1944, Alva took the GED test and entered college at Jones Jr. College. He received a BS degree from Mississippi Southern College with a major in mathematics in 1950. Alva taught high school math for three years (two in Scott County), then worked 30 years for the U.S. Air Force as a training specialist, then 10 years for Honeywell as a computer education consultant. He then retired and came home to Scott County in 1992.

On May 15, 1946, he married Mildred Lavern Duckworth, daughter of Hoye and Maude Duckworth. Mildred, one of nine children, grew up on a farm five miles south of Forest on Hwy. 501. This is the location where Alva and Mildred currently reside, 5254 Hwy. 501, Forest, MS 39074. They have three children: Delia Kaye Boykin, Roger Dairel Boykin and Millicent Lavern Boykin. All three are graduates of Mississippi State University (Kaye and Millicent as EEs and Roger as a forester). Kaye married Stephen Rankin of Poplerville, MS, Mar. 8, 1975. They reside in Warrenton, VA and have no children. Roger married Carolyn Marie Carter of Philadelphia, MS, Mar. 9, 1975. They have two children, Roger Benjiman Boykin and Stephanie Jane Boykin. Ben and Stephanie are currently students at MSU. Roger and Carolyn reside in Atlanta, GA. Millicent married John Wesley Brister Jr. of Jackson, MS, Jan. 10, 1986. They have two children, John Wesley "Tripp" Brister III and Margaret Kaye "Maggie" Brister. They reside in Madison, MS.

BOYD-HOLIFIELD, In 1942 Elijah "Son" Boyd and Lenzell "Len" Holifield, the first borns of Thomas "Sam" and Minnie Boyd and Joe and Ora Carr Holifield, were married. The bliss of marriage didn't last long because WWII was raging and young men were being called to serve. So, Elijah was called to serve leaving a wife and a young son.

Four years later he returned and moved his family to Pascagoula and later Laurel, MS. They lived in Laurel until the late 50s when they relocated to Scott County. By now the family had grown from the young son, Marvin, to include two girls, Eleanor and Idealia. Later in 1960 another girl was born, Maude Leverne, who passed away in January 1961. This was a very traumatic time for my parents. But together nothing was too difficult so this, like other difficult times, they rebounded and made it over. Daddy was not a very openly religious person but he was very well read and knew where to go for comforting scriptures. He knew which songs to sing to calm you during difficult moments. His beautiful tenor voice must be singing now.

During their younger days they both enjoyed sports. Daddy loved baseball and Mama basketball. Daddy had an opportunity to try out for one of the Negro League teams, but because of an injury to his shoulder that chance was lost. Daddy, along with his brother, Exso and some cousins formed a quartet and sang at local churches. Daddy's tenor voice caught the atten-

tion of a young boy named Wiley Denson. He would go to hear the group sing and the next week try to emulate my dad. He wanted so badly to sound just like him. Mama and Daddy at one time sang together in the church choir at Calvary Baptist Church, Laurel, MS.

Later, instead of sports and singing at family gatherings, we cooked and ate. Each holiday we got together and had a lovely time. Starting in July at my house (Eleanor), November (Daree), December (Mama), Easter (Aunt "Meat") and around again. Sometimes we had fish fries in the yard. Mama always remembered to get hot dogs for Renez because she didn't like fish.

They were the greatest people to be grandparents and they made their grandchildren feel like they were the only grandchildren. Charles and Cache' always felt like they were the only two grandchildren, but they actually had seven. Later when the great-grandchildren came they took on a new roll. They enjoyed the great-grandchildren and planned ways to be with them and to make them happy.

Daddy, a very quiet and loving man, always gave of himself to you as a friend, child, brother or stranger. Mama, his mate, very talkative was a perfect mate for him. At her death Oct. 9, 1999, the day after Daddy's birthday, our brother, Marvin, said "Daddy came into ICU to see about her and told her to come and go back with him, she smiled and said, yes." You see Daddy died May 31, 1992. Our mother died with a beautiful smile on her face.

BREWER, Wyche Brewer was born in Georgia Jul. 6, 1798. His wife, Flora McPherson, was born in North Carolina Dec. 1, 1803. The couple migrated to Scott County from Alabama where all 10 of their children were born. Wyche Brewer was living in Scott County during the 1850, 1860 and 1870 federal census.

Wyche and Flora Brewer's children were: Martha (b. Oct. 14, 1823, d. Jan. 15, 1911), Martha never married and is buried in High Hill Baptist Church Cemetery in Neshoba County; Christiana (b. about 1827) md. John W. Pettey; Lenora (b. about 1828); Mary (b. around 1830) married Romulous Day. Mary died during the Civil War; Eliza (b. about 1832); Nancy (b. about 1834); Henrietta (b. about 1836); md. William Owens; William Brewer (b. about 1840); Melissa (b. Jun. 15, 1840) md. Irvin Miller in Scott County Dec. 4, 1856. Melissa died Jan. 8, 1912 and is buried in Pea Ridge Cemetery in Scott County; Luvenia (b. Feb. 11, 1825) md. Albert Gallatin Pettey. Luvenia died Feb. 18, 1897. Both Luvenia and her husband, Albert, are buried in Amis Cemetery on the Scott and Newton County lines.

Wyche died Mar. 17, 1877 and Flora died Feb. 6, 1866. Both of them are buried in Amis Cemetery.

BROGDON-BENNETT, Buster Brogdon (b. Dec. 20, 1919, Hillsboro, MS), son of Conley Hatch and Jones Brogdon of Hillsboro, married Mar. 13, 1945, Hester Ellen Bennett (b. Aug. 17, 1928, Ludlow, MS), daughter of the late Perry and Alma Miller Bennett of Morton, MS. Buster died Jul. 25, 1964, from lung cancer, buried Harperville Cemetery, Mississippi.

Their children are Jones Perry (b. May 3, 1946, Hillsboro, MS); Roselyn Jo (b. Oct. 11, 1947, Hillsboro, MS); and David Wayne (b. May 21, 1959, Lackey Memorial Hospital, Forest, MS). Jones and Rose attended Harperville School and then they, along with their brother, David, all three graduated from Scott Central High School.

Hester Ellen and Buster Brogdon at Aunt Daisy Sessum's House, Harperville, MS (approximately 1946).

Both Brogdon/Bennett families have been genealogically traced by their daughter, Rose McCullough.

Buster (WWII veteran) fought in the Aleutian and Marshall Islands and was a heavy gunner on amphibious boats; he also fought on the islands. His feet and hands froze during the war and he was sent to Hot Springs, AR. After the war, Buster and Hester moved to Mobile, AL, where he worked as a mechanic and Hester worked at Woolworth's Dept. Store. He then decided THIS was NOT what he wanted and they came back to Harperville where he farmed. Buster was mostly a farmer, but also worked at a poultry plant in Forest, MS.

In 1982, Hester Brogdon Gardner worked at the Walnut Grove Manufacturing Co. Since approximately 1983, Hester has worked with Scott County Home Health, Forest, MS, as an aide. She is a member of the Harperville Baptist Church. Hester was a devoted wife and is a devoted mother and grandmother and loves her family very much.

As a child, Rose remembers Saturday nights going to Harperville - to the "show." There was a little store called "Snookie's." To the side of the store was a gristmill at the front and at the back were benches and the BIG screen. Many a Saturday night were spent watching Roy Rogers, Flash Gordon and many others. She and her brother, Jones and cousins and aunts enjoyed the good country life of riding bicycles up and down dirt roads, looking for muscadines in the woods and playing in the back pasture on their farm. Rose also remembers baby-sitting her younger brother, David, in the summertime while their mama and daddy worked. They played cars in the dirt and usually always walked down the road to Aunt Daisy Sessum's store to buy a bag of goodies, 10 or 15 cents got all kinds of goodies. Back then (1962), you could get about three cookies or three pieces of candy for five cents and a Coke for five cents.

Jones and Rose, along with cousins: Frances, Thenetia and Shirley Brogdon, would walk "way back in the woods" for their Aunt Mary Brogdon to get guinea hen eggs.

At Christmas time, Jones and Rose would get on their new bicycles with their Aunt Mavis Bennett Withers and ride up and down the roads. They also enjoyed shooting fireworks.

Jones Brogdon married Emma Jean Turner (divorced). They have two children, Angela Dawn (b. Sep. 9, 1968) and Mark Jones (b. May 19, 1970). Angela married Denis Kelley

Kennedy (b. Aug. 22, 1960, Biloxi, MS). Angela teaches at Three Rivers Elementary School, Gulfport, MS. Mark is a foreman for B&B Tree Service, Gulfport, MS. Jones has been city councilman in Laurel, MS, several years and also owns Brogdon Construction Co.

Jones married Robin M. House McKee (b. Mar. 23, 1966, Mobile, AL). They have two daughters, Amanda Michelle McKee Brogdon (b. Dec. 5, 1985) and Jennifer Renee McKee Brogdon (b. Sep. 7, 1987).

Rose started her working career (June 1966) at the U.S. Army Engineer Waterways Experiment Station (renamed U.S. Army Engineer Research and Development Center), Vicksburg, MS, where she was employed nine and one-half years. The remainder of her working career has been with the U.S. Army Corps of Engineers, Vicksburg Dist. On May 29, 1993, Rose married Percy B. McCullough Jr. They have no children. Rose is a member of Calvary Baptist Church in Vicksburg. Percy owns Red Carpet Cleaning; is a Vietnam veteran (U.S. Army); and is a mason (W.H. Stevens Lodge No. 121).

David Brogdon married Norma Yvette Rainey (b. Jun. 21, 1962, San Pedro, CA) (divorced). They have three sons: Michael Austin (b. Oct. 24, 1981), Buster Wayne (b. Jul. 9, 1984) and Darrell Ervin (b. Dec. 10, 1985). David is in construction and also owns Brogdon's Training Kennels at Harperville.

Michael Brogdon attends Otero Jr. College, La Junta, CO and plans to further his education at Colorado State University. Buster and Darrell Brogdon attend Scott Central High School.

BROGDON-BROWN, Noble Jim Brogdon,

son of Willie Jones Brogdon and Conley Hatch, was born Jun. 6, 1917, in Scott County. He married Florria Ogustia Brown (better known as "Shine") (b. Dec. 13, 1915, d. Dec. 8, 1986). He and Shine had four sons: Noble Jim "Jimmy" Jr., Bobby Ned, Michael Glen and Tony Nathan.

Jim's other siblings were: R.P. Stanley, Jack, Hazel Ruth, Buster and Clotile Voncille. After Jim's father's death, his mother, Conley, married Barney A. Simpson and had two daughters, Dorothy Ellen "Elna" and Bessie Helen. They had one baby girl who died very young. Conley and Barney Simpson are buried at the Baptist cemetery at Hillsboro.

In Jim's early teenage years, he moved to Vicksburg, MS, where he joined the Civilian Construction Corps (CCC) during which time he met and married Shine.

Following the CCC years, Jim and Shine moved back to Harperville, MS (Scott County), to work on a farm as a sharecropper and foreman. He told his oldest son, Jimmy, that the year of his birth (1938), after settling up with the company store, he cleared $50. He worked for the farm owner several years, but following an argument with the owner, he moved his family to Pascagoula, MS. Jim was employed in the shipyards as a carpenter. Soon after moving to Pascagoula, he was drafted into the Navy during WWII. He took his basic training in Detroit, MI, but was given a medical discharge prior to active duty.

Following his military duty, Jim and his family moved back to Vicksburg where he got a job as a carpenter at the U.S. Army Waterways

Experiment Station (CEWES) (currently renamed the U.S. Army Engineer Research and Development Center). During his 36 years at CEWES, the last 15 years he served as foreman of the carpenter shop. CEWES was and continues to be the largest engineering research laboratory in the world, employing more than 1,500 engineers and scientists.

During this period of time, Jim purchased a small farm and enjoyed buying and selling livestock. During the last 15 years of his life, he was also a homebuilder and contractor, building or supervising the construction of approximately 25 homes in Vicksburg. Jim loved to trade and would buy almost anything from a truckload of watermelons to a herd of cattle. His philosophy in life, as he often related to his sons, was "Always tell the truth and pay your debts." He was a very genuine person and gave away a large portion of the money he made. Jim was a Christian and belonged to a small Methodist church in Vicksburg. He always said, concerning his generosity, "Don't let the left hand know what the right hand does." He was always helping people and the color of the person's skin did not matter.

Jim died of lung cancer Nov. 6, 1979 (the 18th birthday of his first grandson, Perry Lee Brogdon). Jim most likely contracted the cancer while working around asbestos at the shipyards.

BROGDON-CLOWER-FARMER, James

"Jim" Franklin Brogdon (b. 1848, d. 1925) was the son of Peterson Gideon Brogdon (b. 1805, d. 1880) and Talitha D. Turner (b. 1805, d. 1861) of Alabama. Peterson and Talitha had 10 children: Emily Jane (b. 1828), Teletha Ellen (b. 1830), Mary Ann (b. 1831), Elizabeth (b. 1833), William J. (b. 1837), Caroline L. (b. 1840), Asberry (b. 1842), John R. (b. 1844), James

James "Jim" Franklin Brogdon, son of Peterson Gideon Brogdon, reading on his front porch (approximately 1906).

Franklin (b. 1848) and Sarah E. (b. 1852).

After Talitha's death, Peterson married Francis Lyons Oct. 6, 1862, in Tallapoosa County, AL and they had three children: Mary F.L. (b. 1865), Peterson (b. 1869) and Delila E. (b. 1874).

Peterson Gideon was a farmer and school teacher, a very well educated man.

We have been told that Jim Brogdon came to Mississippi with the Henry Jefferson Moreman family. Jim was young and worked for Mr. Moreman.

Jim Brogdon built a log cabin and filled in between the logs with clay dirt. After that, he married Mollie Burna Clower (b. 1879, d. 1902). They had one daughter, Florence Burna Brogdon (b. 1876, d. 1957). During childbirth of their second child, both mother and child died.

Florence Burna Brogdon married Charlie William Graham (b. 1873, d. 1962). Some of their descendants are around the Hillsboro, MS, area.

After his wife's death, Jim married Fannie Jane Farmer (b. 1863, d. 1934). They had four sons: Warren Alston, Jesse, James Gordon and Willie Jones and one daughter, Maude (see Brogdon-Hatch information).

The Moreman farm connected to the Farmer Plantation. That is how Jim met Fannie Farmer.

One day, Alexander Cecil "Mart" Farmer, who owned Farmer's Plantation at Harperville, came home and told his daughter, Fannie Jane Farmer (Good Ma as she would be later called), that he was bringing an eligible bachelor home that night who she was to marry. This bachelor was Jim Brogdon. Jim was about 32 years old and Fannie was 17. Jim asked her a lot of questions that night and afterwards, Fannie ran out of the house. They were married for approximately 54 years. Jim and Fannie made their home at Hillsboro, what was known as the Old Brogdon Place. Jim cut his own wood to build their house. To a lot of the family he was known as Uncle Brogdon. Jim, we have been told, was a very peculiar man and some people even said he was harsh and cruel, but Fannie was devoted to him. Jim died of tuberculosis and Fannie later died of cancer.

When Buster and Hester Brogdon's children were very young, they would always go to the Old Brogdon Place to cut down Christmas trees which was so much fun and such a great memory.

BROGDON-HATCH, Willie Jones Brogdon

(b. 1889, d. 1923) married Conley Hatch (b. 1894, d. 1966) (see Hatch-Street information).

Their children were R.P. Stanley, Jack, Hazel Ruth, Nobel Jim, Buster and Clotile Voncille.

Willie Jones Brogdon was 17 and Conley (Mama Conley to her family) was 13 when they married. Press Chambers (a cousin) took them in a buggy to get married. They went to several different places, but no one would marry them. After about three places, Conley told them if they could not find someone to marry them to just turn the dern buggy around and take her home!

Willie Jones Brogdon (approximately 1905, age 16, maybe).

Willie Jones was a farmer and also a logger at a sawmill, he was 34 years old when he died. He had a tooth pulled and infection set in. They took him to the old Baptist Hospital in Jackson, MS, where he died. Buster Brogdon was only about 4 years old, but he remembered playing on a hill of dirt outside the hospital. Willie Jones' last words to his son, Jack (age 12), were "son, go home and feed my mules." Willie Jones liked to keep his mules fat.

When Willie Jones died, they put his body on a train and brought him back to Forest. From there, they put him on a flat-bottom truck and brought his body to his home at Hillsboro. Willie Jones is buried at the Methodist cemetery at Hillsboro.

After Willie Jones' death, Conley Hatch married Barney A. Simpson and had two daughters, Dorothy Ellen "Elna" and Bessie Helen. They had one baby girl who died very young. Conley and Barney Simpson are buried at the Baptist cemetery at Hillsboro.

Also, Mama Conley's grandchildren remember she never had grass in her front yard. She would always hoe it up, I assume so she would not have to cut grass. Memories of Mama Conley are walking through the back woods to Paul Chambers' store at Hillsboro, walking to church and the cemeteries and eating her "tea cakes."

BROOKS, Brothers, Henry and William

Brooks immigrated from Bedfordshire, England, to Harper's Ferry, VA and later continued westward. Their descendants lived in Kentucky, Indiana (Orange County), Bible Grove, Illinois (Clay County) and finally Lake, MS. Henry W. Brooks first came to Lake in 1900 following the lumber business which his family had followed, along with farming across the frontier since arriving from England. By 1904 the wife of Henry W. Brooks, Caroline Chenoweth Brooks and several of their family established and operated lumber mills at Lake, Sturgis, Calhoun City and Quitman, MS.

Eight of the 10 children born to Henry W. and Caroline C. Brooks lived to adulthood. They were: Hattie, Chester, Susie, George, Maben, Winnie, Clyde and Stella. Hattie Brooks Webster and family lived at Lake for a brief time. Chester Brooks and wife, Edith, lived at Lake at the close of their lives in the late 1930s. Susie Brooks Richards and family never lived at Lake but lived in Lilbourn, MO. George Adam Brooks and wife, Martha Olive Smith, lived at Lake where they reared their six children, although they lived for brief periods in both Sturgis and Calhoun City. More will be said about them. Maben E. Brooks, wife, Mellisa and daughter, Blance, lived at Lake and Sturgis. Winnie Brooks and Stella M. Brooks trained at Vicksburg and became registered nurses. Winnie lived at Lake and late in life married J.A. Cox. Stella lived in New York City until she retired, at which time she returned to Lake and lived there until her death. Clyde Brooks married Augusta McKnight and they and their children lived at Meridian. He and his nephew, Clorus G. Brooks, operated the mill at Quitman.

Descendants of George A. and Martha Olive "Ollie" Brooks still live at Lake in 2000. Their oldest child, Viva, married George Neal McIlhenny of Forest. Having no children they lived at Lake until their deaths. Their second child, Clorus George Brooks, married Nell Morgan of Sturgis. Having no children they lived at Quitman until his death. Then she moved to Starkville. Their third child, Henry Dale Brooks, died at age 19 from complications arising from an appendicitis operation. Their fourth child, Frank Ardath Brooks, married Ida Laura Bonelli of Vicksburg. They were the parents of three children: Viva Francis Brooks who married James Paul Tadlock of Homewood; Frank A. Brooks Jr. who married Jo Anne Biggers of Corinth; and Ava Ann Brooks who married Ted L. Monk of Lake. Frank and Ida Laura lived at Lake all of their adult lives with the exception of a few years at the time of WWII in Greenwood, MS and Panama City, FL. The fifth child of George and Ollie was Mary Caroline "Carolyn" who married Barry R. Doolittle of Calhoun City. The sixth child was Dorothy Joyce who married Paul Vance of Neshoba.

Family descendants living at Lake in 2000 are the two sons of Viva Brooks and James Paul Tadlock. They are Paul Franklin Tadlock and George Neal Tadlock. Paul F. married Patricia "Tricia" McCoy of Morton. Paul and Patricia had two daughters, Laura and Paula Elizabeth "Beth." Laura married Jacob "Jake" La Rue Wilson of Foley, AL. George N. married Joan May of Newton. George and Joan had two sons, Nathanial "Nathan" George Tadlock and Neal Patrick Tadlock.

BROOKS, Burwick Bunyon Brooks (b. Feb.

12, 1889, Leake County MS) was the son of Zacheus Byron Brooks and Mary Ann Virginal Ellis. Burwick married Annie Maude Hudson Dec. 9, 1915, daughter of W.L. Hudson and Mary Alma Henderson.

In 1921, Burwick, Annie Maude and their three children: Billy Burwick "B.B." (b. Jul. 31, 1917), Nolan H.

Burwick "B.B." Brooks, circa 1920.

(b. Sep. 8, 1918) and Mary Alma (b. Aug. 23, 1921), moved to Sebastapol.

Burwick was a professional baseball player. His career started while attending Mississippi College. Gaining fame by striking out 24 of 27 men, while pitching against the University of Alabama. He pitched in the Georgia-Alabama League, the Cotton States League, South Atlantic Association and was player-manager of the Jackson Senators. Retiring from baseball in 1924, he had two automobile repair garages in Sebastapol. He was a member of the Masonic Lodge in Sebastapol.

Burwick and Annie Maude had three more children born in Scott County: Charles D. (b. Aug. 17, 1925), an infant son (b 1927) died at birth and Wm. Judson Brooks (b. Feb. 8, 1929). Their oldest and beloved son, B.B., died in 1927, age 10.

In 1940 the family moved to Jackson, where in October 1949, Burwick passed away in his home. Followed by his sweet wife, Annie Maude, on Jan. 10, 1970.

BROOKS, "B.B. Brooks, Our Hero" written

by a fan, in the 1920s.

Now, in the ninth, with two men down and Roberts at the bat

Most pitchers would have let him walk, we are sure of that

But, Brooks, the hero, was made of sterner stuff

For his kind get the medals and the long newspaper puffs

He knew the time had come for him to play the winning role

He heard the fans a-yelling and it was music to his soul

He saw the gleam of confidence in Mighty Roberts' eyes

He then resolved, "I'll strike him out. I'll do it or I'll die."

Now, Brooks whirled his body, in truest cork-screw plan

And threw a swift in-shot, that cut the corner of the pan

But, Roberts thought the first ball pitched would surely be a ball

And did not try to strike at it, to the greatest joy of all

Again, our twirler figures the dope on our visitor's pride

He thinks the next will be out and will throw it wild

But, Brooks shot through a straight one, cross the center of the plate

While Roberts waited for the curve until it was too late

And now the mighty slugger is hanging on a string

And if another good one comes over, it's up to him to swing

Brooks, then saw the jaunty smile had faded from Roberts' face

And a look of straining agony was there to take its place

One moment, Brooks pauses, hides the ball behind his glove

And then he drives it from him, with a sweeping long-arm shove

Now, the air is rent in twain before the slugger's split

For Roberts, Mighty Roberts, had not figured on the spit.

BUCKNER, Enos Rush Buckner (b. May 4, 1824, Hardin County, KY), son of Horace (b. 1799, d. 1835) and Nancy Purdy Buckner (b. 1800, d. 1890), came to Mississippi about 1844 and married 20-year-old Georgiana Letcher (widow Hann) on Jan. 15, 1845, Jasper County. Their son was born and died Apr. 10, 1846 and three months later on July 27 Enos was left a widower when Georgiana died of consumption in Columbus, so they are buried there in Friendship Cemetery.

Writing in 1857 to his brother-in-law, James D. Culley in Kentucky, from his Hillsboro, Scott County residence, Enos indicates he is still single, a practicing lawyer with aspirations to the judicial system in admiration for "an uncle of judicial fame in this state" (which judge? Eliphalet Frazier Buckner, Robert Hawes Buckneer or William Aylett Buckner?) as well as "two Judge Buckners in Kentucky." He also mentions suffering a recent illness due to "pulmonary symptoms."

Two years later Enos was married again to Laura Ann Barfield of Charleston, SC, on Feb. 20, 1849 and they had five children: Enos Rush Jr. (b. Jan. 20, 1850, Hillsboro, d. Dec. 8, 1869, Hardin County, KY), Ella Florence (b. Apr. 12, 1852, d. Sep. 14, 1886), Laura Ida (b. Mar. 28, 1854, d. Feb. 28, 1887), Reubenia Emma (b. Sep. 23, 1855, d. Oct. 14, 1857) and Eula M. (b. May 5, 1859, d. Feb. 4, 1896). The 1860 census adds

another occupation for Enos, farmer, with real and personal estates valued at $23,790. Writing to his sister, Ellen, this same year, Enos spoke of just having returned from a long political tour making speeches (he had represented Scott County in the 1857 legislative session), mentions severe droughts devastating his crops, this financial loss making it difficult to feed his family as well as impossible to visit his mother and family in Kentucky. He is also distressed at not hearing from his brother, Edmund, a minister, who often sent him copies of his sermons.

Two years later Enos died "of consumption" on Feb. 25, 1862, followed by his wife's death of the same condition in 1864. Except for baby Reubenia dying "of croup" as noted in the Buckner family Bible, all other members of this family died of tuberculosis. Only Reubenia's tombstone marks the Buckner burial plot in Baptist Church Cemetery, Hillsboro. Enos Rush Jr. is buried in a cemetery in Elizabethtown, KY, where he died at the age of 19.

Only two of Enos' daughters married. Laura Ida married Frank Lawrence of Vicksburg and had two children, Stella and Frank Lawrence Jr. Eula, the youngest child, was married at age 20 at the home of her uncle, James Sherett Barfield, in Jackson to Edward Minnick Scott, a 37-year-old widower with three sons: Julienne, Charles and Edward Scott Jr. Their marriage resulted in eight more children: Laura, Elizabeth, George (who died at birth), Frank, Ida, Malcolm, Georgie (girl) and Norbert Scott. Eula outlived her siblings, dying at age 37 in the Scott residence in Rosedale but buried in the Scott-Pointer plot in Greenwood Cemetery, Jackson. She is survived by numerous descendants in subsequent generations.

BURKS, Horace O. "Don" Burks and his wife, Ercel Carter Burks, made Forest, MS, their home in the late 1940's for about five years. We bought a home from John Boutwell in Forest. We have fond memories of our time in Forest, such as Don making music with Genny McCoy and Bill Ladd for the dance once a week. Don worked for Maurice Mitchell Jewelry Store in Forest.

Horace O. "Don" Burks and wife, Ercel Carter Burks and family: Melissa Burks Dearman, Melinda Burks Lick and Horace O. "Don" Burks II.

Don and Ercel have three children: Melissa, Melinda and Horace O. "Don" II; five grandchildren; and one step grandchild.

Don's great-great-grandfather, James Lyons Burks moved from Tennessee to Georgia and married Miss Martha Robinson. Afterwards he fought in the war of 1812. He ended up in New Orleans and was later moved out by way of Mobile, AL and back into Georgia. He then left

Georgia to go to Arkansas and en route passed through Ludlow, MS. He and his company camped at Coffeebogue Creek west of Ludlow. Judge S.J. Denson visited him there. They later learned that their first wives were first cousins. This fact led to a change of mind, which caused him to stay in Mississippi. Later James Lyons Burks' son, Milton H. Burks, married S.J. Denson's daughter, Susan Denson. Milton H. Burks was a member of Harperville Creek Baptist Church. He also fought in the Civil War. Thomas J. Burks, son of Milton H. and Susan Denson Burks, was born near Harperville, MS, in 1851. He was 16 years old when he left this Harperville Community. During his lonely life he often went to Hillsboro, the county seat of Scott County. He brought mail to his friends, which came in on the stagecoach. He later moved two miles north of Ludlow in Leake County.

William M. Burks and Annie Hurst Burks are my grandparents. William M. Burks was justice of the peace in Scott County until his death in 1896. He is buried in Ludlow.

William H. Burks and Colie Jane Whinery Burks are my parents. My father was born about one-fourth mile south of Bill's Catfish Restaurant, west of Ludlow on River Bend Road at Highway 25. My mother was born near Remus Church in Leake County. My grandmother, Anna Hearst Burks, moved the family to Hickory, MS, in 1896, after my grandfather, William M. Burks, passed away.

BURKS, James Lyon Burks migrated with his large family about 1845 to Scott County. He was born in 1791 in Edgefield Dist., SC, the relative of two adjacent landowners, Billy Burks and John Lyon, who appeared on the 1800 census. He became a successful attorney in Talbot County, GA and served four years in the Georgia state legislature.

He married first, Martha Robinson.

1) Daughter, Margaret, died as an infant.

2) Son, John Robinson Burks, married May Amazon Pope.

3) Daughter, Lydia Jane Burks, married Thomas Jefferson Harris. After her death in 1861, Harris, while serving as a captain in the Confederate Army, married her younger sister, widow Elizabeth Burks Traylor. Lydia's grandson, James Lyon Harris, married Birdie Lou Lowery, daughter of Robert Lowery, governor of Mississippi.

4) Son, William Carroll Burks, was a minister in the Primitive Baptist Church and married Sarah Weathers. Their sons, Daniel and William Milton, died in the Confederate Army.

5) Son, James Madison Burks, married Narcissa Jane Holmes.

6) Son, Milton H. Burks, married Susan Denson, daughter of Judge S.J. Denson. Susan was a granddaughter of Luke Robinson, brother to Martha Robinson. Milton helped muster one of the first military units in Scott County before he died in 1863.

7) Son, Abel Robinson, married Frances Wofford. He published the Hillsboro *Argus* newspaper, then served and died in the Confederate Army.

8) Daughter, Martha R. Burks, married first, William R. Milton and second, Chesley C. Bonds.

9) Son, Simion B. Burks was born in 1826.

10) Daughter, Elizabeth Burks, married first, Champion Travis Traylor and second, her widowed brother-in-law, Thomas Harris. Her daughter, Martha Frances Traylor, married Byron Lloyd McCabe who was born in Scott County in 1844.

11) Son, Benjamin Franklin Burks, married in Scott County Emily Smith, daughter of John Jackson Smith.

12) Daughter, Mary Ann Frances Burks, married Josh Whitehead.

13) Son, Thomas Jefferson Burks, married Exah Jane M. Lassiter. He served in the Confederate Army. In 1866 he joined the Primitive Baptist Church in Damascus, Scott County, MS.

14) Daughter, Nancy A. Burks, was born in 1835.

James Lyon Burks married second, Nancy Hutchinson. Their children were:

15) Emily H. Burks.

16) Lemuel Andrew Burks.

17) Silas Wright Hutchinson Burks.

Both sons served in the Confederate Army. James married thirdly, Eunice Fleming.

18) Son, Berry Maximilian Burks, married Nancy Burns in Scott County.

19) Son, Rufus Lot Burks, served in the Confederate Army.

20) Daughter, Eunice Jane Burks, was born in 1851 in Hillsboro, Scott County, MS. She married M.J. Sander and in 1890 was living in Ludlow, MS.

James Lyon Burks married a fourth time to Sarah Horne of Scott County.

James Lyon Burks died in 1966 in Damascus, Scott County, MS. He was 75 years old. His estate showed that James owned two plantations on the north boundary of Scott County, each containing about a section of land. His youngest child, Eunice, said that he had a fair complexion, blue eyes and sandy hair.

BURKS, Milton Henry Burks was born Apr. 8, 1821, in Talbot County, GA, to James Lyon Burks and his first wife, Martha Robinson. He was married in the late 1840s to Susan E. Denson who was born in 1832 to Shadrach James Denson and Alethia Chambers. The Burks family had removed to Scott County, MS, from Georgia in the mid-1840s. The decision to settle in Scott County was based largely upon the fact that first wives of James L. Burks and Shadrach J. Denson were cousins. Alethia Chambers Denson's mother was neé Christian Robinson.

Primarily a farmer by profession, Milton H. Burks owned, in 1850, four slaves and a 106 acre farm. Ten years later his operation had more than doubled, consisting of 240 acres valued at $2,500 and five slaves worth $7,000. In addition to being a farmer, Milton H. Burks served Scott County as a justice of the peace.

He died in 1863 and his widow 11 years later.

Children of Milton Henry Burks and Susan E. Denson:

1. Martha Elizabeth Burks (b. Mar. 15, 1847, d. Dec. 19, 1930) md. James Andrew Jackson Chambers;

2. James Shadrach Burks (b. 1849, d. after 1880);

3. Thomas J. Burks (b. Sep. 14, 1851) md. (1) Elizabeth Morgan, (2) Anna Vaughn;

4. Mary Ann Frances Burks (b. Feb. 3, 1853, d. Mar. 8, 1880) md. Andrew Walker McDuff;

5. William Milton Burks (b. Apr. 30, 1856, d. Nov. 16, 1896) md. Anna Elizabeth Hurst;

6. Margaret L. Burks (b. February 1860) md. Green M. Raynor;

7. Emma Burks (b. 1862) md. Henry Majors.

BURNHAM, Walter le Veutre went to England at the Conquest (1066) with William of Normandy; and at the survey (1080) was made lord of the Saxon villages of Burnham. From these manors he took his surname of de Burnham, becoming the ancestor of the family by that name. Spelled Burnham, Bernham and in Norse, Bjorn, the name means "bear" (chief, lord). "Ham" signified "a town, village or meadow"; when applied to a person it signified the lord of a town or village.

Irene Burnham Martin with parents, John Raymond and Fannie Burnham (ca. 1945).

The American Burnham family springs from three brothers: John of Ipswich, Thomas of Ipswich and Robert of Dover. In 1635 they sailed from England aboard the *Angel Gabriel* which was shipwrecked, thereby losing the coat of arms presented to Sir William Burnham in 1571 by Queen Elizabeth I. They settled in Cape Ann near Boston.

Burnham homeplace. Center of house is two-story log cabin built in early 1800s. Remainder of house and surrounding buildings, pre Civil War.

In 1694 Benjamin Burnham died in England, leaving approximately 150 acres, including Burnham Road (now Regent Street in London) for the Burnham heirs of America. Years of efforts to recover the property culminated with a trip by Scott County resident, Dr. Jones Burnham, to Boston and New York just prior to the Civil War to look into the matter. He ascertained that the chain of lineage was incomplete.

The Scott County Burnhams are apparently descended from Thomas of Ipswich. D.J.

Burnham, son of Elijah and Sallie Burnham, was a successful planter in Camden County, NC. He and his wife, Parthenia Spence, removed to Scott County, MS, in 1837. They settled in Ludlow and had 13 children including William (md. Sallie Spence), whose son, Oscar, was a dentist in Morton; Thomas Plutarch, the grandfather of Dr. Van R. Burnham, Clarksdale, a recent trustee of the Mississippi Dept. of Archives and History; Margaret (William Spence); Mary Jane (Cary Spence); and Newton Edney, married to Sarah Irene McCabe.

During the Civil War encampment in Scott County, the Burnham seal ring signifying property ownership in England was taken off the finger of Parthenia Burnham by Gen. William T. Sherman. Upon seeing this crude act, her daughter, Mary Jane, dumped the milk she was churning on Sherman's head. His officers commanded that she be shot, but the general said, "Any child who loves her mother that much, I adore. Let her live!" The ring is said to be in the Sherman Family Archives and one of Mary Jane's descendants has petitioned the Archives for the return of the ring to Burnham heirs.

Our more current story begins with George McCabe, married to Obedience Julia Denson. With slave labor, McCabe built a two-story log cabin on land approximately 12 miles north of Forest. McCabe was a successful businessman and substantial landowner in Scott County. He founded a millseat on Tallabogue Creek in Harperville and erected the first grist mill in the county. His wife preceded him in death; and at his death, his estate was put into trust for his minor heirs: Sarah Irene, Mary Scott, Henry Clay, Florence Antoinette and Harriet. The children were reared by their uncle, Thomas Denson and their grandparents, Shadrach and Alethia Chambers Denson, saw to their education. Sarah Irene and Mary Scott were sent to a finishing school in North Carolina while Henry, educated at Mississippi College, later became a candidate for governor of Mississippi.

In 1868 Newton Edney Burnham and Sarah Irene McCabe were married. Thus began Pleasant Valley Plantation on land deeded to them by Irene's siblings including Florence McCabe Butler and on land grants to Benjamin and Landon Butler from President Martin Van Buren.

Newton and Irene Burnham's 12 children were: Minnie; Charles, a physician in Bay Springs; Florence; Henry "Hal," a physician in Pearl River, LA; Hattie May; Blanche; George, who was in charge of building on to the two-story log cabin; Kirk, owner of Burnham Drugs, Moss Point and supervisor of Jackson County for 26 years; Kate Antoinette, married to Troy Townsend of Morton, a music teacher who studied at the Cincinnati Conservatory of Music; Samuel; Edgar; and John Raymond.

During their medical studies, Charles and Hal kept a skeleton in a closet. The rumor among the field hands was that the house was haunted and one of the bodies was in the closet. "Haunted" or not, from time to time, the house is visited by "past" residents!

On land comprising acreage from what is now near Highway 21 to Tallabogue Creek, the Burnham plantation was worked by 26 families. The black families were the Hunts and the Butlers. Presumably Abe Butler, a slave, was brought here from Texas by Florence McCabe and her husband, George Butler. After the Emancipation Proclamation, Abe's son, Sam, was chief cook for the Burnhams. His wife, "Miss Jessie," and their descendants settled land about three miles north of the Burnhams. The friendship between the two families has been so close that many times they refer to each other as Cud'n (Cousin) Robert, Cud'n Raymond, etc.

The house proper was all bedrooms except for a parlor. A breezeway connected the kitchen. Outer buildings included a storehouse with supplies for the families living there, barn and corncrib, smokehouse, blacksmith shop and several cotton houses. Running water and lights were operated from a carbide tank still in the yard.

In 1917 John Raymond Burnham married 17-year-old Fannie Woods and she moved one mile north to Pleasant Valley. Fannie was the 11th of the 12 children of Nancy Selinda Croxton and A.W. "Andy" Woods. Bro. Woods was a Primitive Baptist minister and farmer. He also was justice of the peace for Dist. Five, a title conferred on him in 1916 by Gov. Theo. G. Bilbo. Andy and Nancy Woods' children were: Adolphus, Edward, Stella, Willie, Lillie, Wilson, Marjorie, Winnie, Abner, Homer, Fannie and Onie. They also reared their grandchild, Stella Townsend, whose mother, Stella, died in childbirth.

After the death of Raymond's parents, he and Fannie bought the place from his siblings. They were active members of the community with membership in Union Baptist Church until the early '50s when they moved their membership to Harperville Baptist Church.

John Raymond attended Harperville A & M College in Harperville and Mississippi State. When his father died, he returned home to manage the place. He was a very successful farmer. Erle Johnston, former owner and editor of the *Scott County Times*, called him Scott County's prognosticator. Every March 22, he would make a special trip to the paper to forecast, according to the direction of the wind, the upcoming crop year.

Even though he has been dead since 1974, he was such a colorful character that his descendants talk about him almost every day. He and Fannie had not owned a car since their 1941 Chevrolet as a pickup was more feasible on a farm, but she finally persuaded him to buy a car, a 1957 Plymouth Fury. It was an appropriately named model since he thought the "R" button meant "rev," and he drove the car "like a bat out of hell," (his expression). Having been deaf since childhood, he had a hearing aid which he seldom wore, except to hear the preacher, since he did all of the talking. On a trip to Forest a highway patrolman finally got him to stop and said, "Mr. Burnham, I clocked you going 75 MPH." "You must have been, too, young fella," he responded, "or you couldn't have caught me." His daughter, Helga, had to go to the courthouse and "explain" Mr. Burnham to keep him from being arrested.

Family and field hands alike worked hard Monday through Friday; Sunday was for church, but Saturday was going-to-town day! Everyone piled in the pickup and headed for Forest. While Raymond talked politics on the Courthouse Square, daughters, Irene and Jackie, went to the Palace Theater and for 10 cents saw a movie, newsreel, a serial, next week's preview and a short feature! Then they visited Mrs. Audrey Stevens at her store and she treated them to a milkshake at Vance's Drugs.

Fannie was best known for her sense of humor, her wonderful attitude toward life and her cooking. Her visitors from all over the world raved about her chicken and dumplings. She often would expect 10 and wind up with 40 for dinner (noon meal). Unperturbed, she would simply set more tables. She was a friend and a provider to all who were less fortunate than she. In her early married days, she not only had outside but also household help and nannies for her children; but when times changed, she did most of the work herself with her ever cheerful attitude.

The children of Raymond and Fannie Burnham are: Roy (deceased) md. Martha Van Dyke (deceased), New York. Children: Joey (deceased), Bob, Gary, Roy Jr., Thomas and Darlene Scorzelli); Doris (deceased) md. James Gallaspy (deceased), Jackson. Children: Bettye Stewart and Jim); Helga md. Hubert Watson, Forest. Children: Linda Wiggins, Gleda Williams and William); Reba md. Claude Jackson (deceased), Jackson. Children: Claude Jr., LaWanda Hynum and Kerry); Nancy md. Donald Freeman (deceased), Gadsden, AL. Children, ADonna Hunter and Jim); John md. Martha Ansley, Forest. Children: Belinda Barnes, Kathy Lee and Anne Steptoe); Irene md. Joe Martin, Forest. Son, Steve); Jackie md. Karl Noel (divorced), Pensacola, FL. Children: Randy, Danny, Antoinette Wiedemann, Raymond and Chris). Of their grandchildren, Kathy Burnham and David Lee (Joni and Jacob), Anne Burnham Steptoe (Sains, Connor, Logan) and Steve and Karon Martin (Russell, Tara) have remained Scott County residents. As of December 2000 the Burnham family totaled 119.

Fannie was lovingly cared for by her children and grandchildren until she died peacefully at home May 26, 2000, a few days after her 101st birthday. At her death daughter, Irene, inherited the house, believed to be the oldest in Scott County. Restoration has begun on the upper two rooms of the log cabin, the center of the house, built in the early 1800s. Irene's son, Steve; his wife, Karon Russell (granddaughter of W.J. "Red" and Sula Cochran of Harperville); and their children, Russell and Tara, live on the home place. They are three of the six generations who have lived in and loved Pleasant Valley, Scott County, MS. And life goes on ...

My appreciation to Cary Spence, Jackson; to John Smallwood, author, *The Denson Family of Scott County, Mississippi* and to Dr. Van Burnham Jr., Clarksdale, for some of the information contained herein and to Dr. Gene Wiggins, University of Southern Mississippi, for editorial assistance. *By Irene Burnham Martin.*

BURNHAM, I remember the wood frame house facing the road that ran south to Morton, the pink blossoming crape myrtles at the roadside and, farther back in the yard, two giant black walnut trees shading the house. Pah (Thomas Plutarch Burnham), my grandfather, let me use his beautiful claw hatchet to crack the nuts underneath the trees. Across the road was the barn and the large pond where Mur (Margaret Jones Denson Burnham) loved to sit by the hour in her outdoor chair with her fishing pole. On the north side of the house was a brick walled cistern with bucket and windlass beneath a cedar shingled roof that sheltered cabinets filled with dairy produce. About 20 yards north of this was a small general store facing the road where Pah, with his white goatee, held sway. I'll never forget the large folding key that he let his 6-year-old grandson use to lock and unlock the thick wooden door at the store's entrance.

On the left end of the gallery (front porch) that extended across the entire width of the house was a shelf with a bucket of water from the cistern, a dipper, a basin for washing and towels hanging on nearby pegs. Just inside the door to the parlor attached to the wall above the top of my head was a telephone box with an earphone hanging on the side and a mouthpiece with a long neck protruding from the front of the box. I think their party line ring was two longs, followed by two shorts. Behind the parlor and the bedrooms was a 10 to 12 foot passageway, with breakfast table and chairs that connected to the kitchen built that far behind the house because of fire hazards. In back of the house were a wood shed, a smokehouse always filled with hams and sausages, a corn crib full of golden ears, one or two other storage buildings and, of course, to the other side, the outdoor toilet.

This was in general a picture of my grandparents' place at Branch in Scott County, MS, in the 1920s. Tom and Margaret Burnham were natives of Scott County, children of Doctor James and Parthenia Spence Burnham and of William Howard and Jane Jones Denson, respectively. They had 11 children, five of whom lived to adulthood: Margaret P. Burnham Stuart, James P. Burnham, MD, Maude Burnham Cochran, Van R. Burnham, DDS and Tommie Louise Burnham Nichols. Their descendants are scattered over Mississippi and elsewhere. *By Van R. Burnham Jr.*

BUTLER, Burnall B. Butler, son of John Butler of Virginia, a Revolutionary War soldier and Mary Ann, daughter of Seaborn Jones, was born 1806 in Graves County, KY. Burnall was one of nine children: William M., Fanny, Ruth, Suzanna, Elizabeth, Landon Carter, Margaret, Burnall and Martha.

Burnall B. Butler, son of John Butler and Mary Ann Jones and Sarah Ann Ricks, daughter of William Ricks and Martha Ward.

When young, Burnall was left deaf and mute by a childhood disease. In 1811, Burnall and other siblings accompanied their parents to Washington County, AL. By 1816 the family moved into Wayne County, MS, where John Butler died before 1820.

Burnall married in 1826 in Wayne County, Sarah Ann Ricks, daughter of William Ricks and Martha Ward. Burnall's family and his mother, Mary Ann, moved into Scott County in 1834. They were followed by his brother, Landon and his sister, Margaret, the wife of John J. Smith a member of the Commission that organized Scott County.

When the Antioch Primitive Baptist Church was organized in 1835, Burnall, Sarah, Landon, his wife, Elizabeth and Mary Butler became members. The church congregation built its first church in 1836 on Burnall Butler's land. Both he and his brother, Landon C., were Masons and farmers. Mary Ann Butler died before 1850 in Scott County at Landon Butler's home.

Burnall's children: Susan Collier (b. 1828 in Wayne County, MS); John Woodward (b. 1830), James J. (b. 1832 in Rankin County, MS); William Green (b. 1834), Mary Ann (b. 1836), Ruth (b. 1838), Robert and Elizabeth, twins (b. 1841), Albert (b. 1844), Hulda (b. 1846), Pleasant Burnall (b. 1848), Washington and Lafayette, twins (b. 1851 in Scott County) and Daniel and Burnall Jr., twins (b. 1858 in Karnes County, TX).

Burnall and his brother-in-law, Robert Ricks, moved their families by ox-cart to Goliad County, TX arriving on Christmas Eve, 1852. Burnall cleared land, began ranching and helped develop this area which is now Karnes County. In 1855, he and William took 100 cows to hungry, newly arrived Polish immigrants to feed them through the winter. Burnall died in 1870 after a fall from a cliff overlooking the San Antonio River. He and many of his descendants are buried in the Butler Family Cemetery which has a Texas historical marker.

Burnall's son, William Green "Bill" Butler, married Adeline Riggs Burris, daughter of Benjamin Burris and Susan Riggs in 1858. Bill Butler served in the Civil War in the Trans-Mississippi Dept. He was captured at the battle of Arkansas Post in 1863, but escaped and served the rest of the war in Arkansas and Missouri.

After the war, Bill Butler became one of the largest and most influential ranchers in Texas, owning some 75,000 acres. He took many herds of cattle up the Chisolm Trail to Kansas. Adeline Butler died in 1908 and Bill died in 1912. Some of his 75,000 acres are owned by his descendants today.

William Green Butler's children: Newton married Mary Elder; Louisa married Joseph Adams; Emmett was killed in a shoot-out at Helena, TX; Sykes married Emma Seale; and Hemis married Ida Bright.

Burnall B. Butler helped to form and develop Scott County in 1834. In 1853, he helped create and developed Karnes County, TX. His many descendants live in Karnes County, the rest of Texas and much of the USA.

BUTLER, The Mississippi census in 1845 shows Landon Carter Butler and Burnell Butler with three other Butlers, probably cousins from Edgefield Dist., SC, where their grandfather, William Butler, a North Carolina Regulator, had died in 1790. Their father, John Butler, died in 1820 in Wayne County, MS and their mother,

Mary Ann Jones, is known to be with the two men in Scott County in 1836 when they all joined the Antioch Primitive Baptist Church.

The children of John Landon Butler and Mary Ann Jones: (1) William Butler md. a Miss Sarah. (2) Ruth Butler md. William Calley. (3) Suzanne Butler md. Jesse Goodwin. (4) Fanny Butler md. James Kidd. (5) Elizabeth Butler md. John K. Rankin. (6) Landon Carter Butler md. Elizabeth Byrne and they were pioneer settlers in Scott County. (7) Margaret Butler md. John Jackson Smith who was on the commission to organize Scott County. (8) Burnell Butler md. Sarah Ann Ricks and they were early settlers of Scott County. (9) Martha Butler md. William Porter.

Landon Carter Butler's children were all born in Scott County: Benjamin James, William C., Mary Ann, Reason, Jane, Emily, Wade and George W. The youngest son married Florence Aleathea McCabe, daughter of George W. McCabe and Obedience Denson. In 1850 Landon was elected to the Mississippi state legislature.

Burnell Butler's children were all born in Scott County: Woodard, James J., William G., Mary Ann, Ruth, Robert Andrew, Elizabeth Hulda, Pleasant Burnell, Emily, George Washington, Marcus Lafayette, Daniel Webster and Albert Brown. William G., known as Bill and Pleasant Burnell, called Pleaz, became well-known Trail drivers, moving thousands of heads of cattle from Texas to Kansas before the railroads were built.

BUTLER, W.R. Butler was born in Rankin County, MS, in 1828. His father, Landon C. Butler, was a native of Kentucky (b. Apr. 14, 1800); his mother was Elizabeth Burns (b. in North Carolina in 1806). They were married in Wayne County, MS, in 1822 and had nine children, of whom W.R. was the third in birth order. Mr. Butler was a planter who located in Rankin County in 1828 and moved to Scott County in 1831, remaining there until 1856 when he moved to Texas.

W.R. received a common school education, then read theology and became a preacher in the Baptist church in 1849. He was instrumental in establishing Union, Ephesus, Pleasant Ridge, Ringgold and Forest Baptist Church. He preached in Hillsboro as assistant pastor in 1857 and as pastor from 1859-88. W.R. also preached in Hopewell Baptist in 1886, 1888, 1889 and 1890. In his latter years, he was moderator for 16 years of one of the largest Baptist associations in the state.

W.R. married in August 1854 to Miss Julia E. Long of Hinds County, MS, who has borne him 12 children: Eugene H. married; Laura E., wife of W.E. McGee; and Edward J. married. Hiram J., Mary E., William L., George L., Lucy E., Anderson S., Alice M., Eula B. and Julia remained single.

He was successful as a planter, owning 360 acres, of which about 65 acres being under cultivation. He was a member of the Masonic Order and served a number of years as missionary of the General Association of Mississippi.

CAMERON, John Andrew Cameron was born in 1844 in Greene County, AL. He died in 1928 in Scott County, MS. He served as a private in

Co. C, of the 43rd Regt., of the Alabama Inf. serving throughout the War Between the States. He was wounded and lost one eye. He was present when Gen. Robert E. Lee surrendered. When he returned home to Alabama he found his stepmother and father had died. The land and home had been mortgaged during the war and been foreclosed. His brothers and sisters were scattered. He came to Scott County, MS, to be with an aunt about 1868. About 1870 he married Henerietta Victoria Harmon, born in South Carolina in 1850. She died in November 1933, in Scott County, MS. She was the daughter of Jesse and Eliza Harmon. She came to Mississippi with her family in a covered wagon and buggy sometime between 1855-56. John and Henerietta moved to Otho, MS, which is located in the southeast corner of Scott County.

John Andrew and Henerietta Cameron. Made in the front yard of Laura and Henry Gaskin in the early 1920s.

John was a farmer. He and Henerietta had six children. Walter Pickens Cameron was born in 1871 and he died in 1948. He was married to Kate Brooks. John Albert Cameron was born in 1874, but was killed by a falling tree limb at age 7. James Frank Cameron was born in 1876 and died in 1920. He was married to Ella Idom. Laura Cameron was born in 1878 and she died in 1959. She was married to Madison Henry Gaskin. Virginia Frances Cameron was born in 1880 and she died in 1974. She was married to Virgil Thaxton. Herbert Archibald "Arch" Cameron was born in 1887 and he died in 1960. He was married to Julia Margaret Whatley.

The Arch Cameron Family: Arch, Julia, John Raye, Lucille and Viva Jewell. Made at the Jackson, MS, zoo, Easter 1947.

Frank, Laura and Arch remained in Scott County their entire lives.

Frank and Ella were farmers. He also worked in area sawmills. They had six children: Hubert, Estelle, Felton, Myrtis, Zelma and Albert.

Laura and Henry were farmers. They had 13 children: Cleo, Glover, Mattie, Vera, Aubrey, Bessie, Blanche, Woodrow, Annie Laura, Harold and Howell (twins), Billie and Dorothy Ellen.

Arch and Julia had three children: Viva Jewell, Mary Lucelle and John Raye. Arch worked in timber, sold livestock and was a salesman for Ford Motor Co. in Lake, MS. He also worked part-time for the sheriff of Scott County and he worked for various oil companies buying oil leases and was a farmer.

Several family members are buried at Carr Methodist Church, Highway 501 South, Smith County, MS. These include: Jesse and Eliza Harmon; John and Henerietta Cameron; John Albert Cameron; James Frank Cameron; Laura and Henry Gaskin (including several of their children); and Arch and Julia Cameron and one of their daughters.

CARPENTER, Ernest Leon Carpenter (b. Jan. 19, 1894 Leake County, d. Oct. 13, 1973 Scott County) md. Dec. 23, 1916, in Scott County, Mary Odessa Russell (b. Mar. 26, 1895 Scott County, d. Feb. 26, 1940 Scott County). They're buried in Hillsboro Baptist Cemetery.

Ernest Leon Carpenter and Mary O. Russell Carpenter.

Ernest and Mary had nine children: William Joseph "Billy Joe" (b. Nov. 19, 1918, d. Jun. 5, 1985 in Yazoo County, buried in Hillsboro Baptist Cemetery) md. and divorced Dorothy Clark. He retired from the Army after 25 years.

Etna Jean (b. Jan. 7, 1920) md. Peyton Victor Eady (b. Jan. 11, 1912 Scott County, d. May 25, 1962, buried in Eastern Cemetery Forest). They had one son, Peyton Victor Jr. "Shot" (b. Apr. 14, 1945 Lauderdale County). He married Jul. 11, 1970, Mary Deloise Sessums (b. Sep. 15, 1952 Scott County). They have one daughter, DeAnna (b. Feb. 5, 1975 Hinds County). DeAnna married Shawn Rowe Sparks Mar. 6, 1999, in Scott County.

Leon Ellis (b. Oct. 30, 1921, d. May 30, 1923) is buried in Hillsboro Baptist Cemetery.

Ernestine Faith (b. Jan. 30, 1925, d. Dec. 17, 1996, buried in Mt. Olivet Cemetery, Yazoo County) md. and divorced Dewitt Atchley. They had one son, Ernest Leland (b. Sep. 29, 1947 Scott County, d. Jan. 4, 1980, buried at Mt. Olivet Cemetery). On Sep. 9, 1950, she married Carl Rasco (b. Dec. 27, 1914 Scott County, d. Nov. 7, 1989, buried at Mt. Olivet Cemetery). Their children were: Carlene Elizabeth (b. Nov. 20, 1952 Yazoo County) md. Jun. 1, 1972, Hal David Gober (b. Oct. 7, 1950 Hinds County). Carlene's son, Kristoffer David was born Apr. 20, 1978. Thomas Edward (b. Sep. 20, 1957 Yazoo County) md. Jan. 20, 1996, to Annie Catherine Nelson in Yazoo County.

Cornelia Franks "Frankie" (b. Sep. 22, 1926, d. Nov. 20, 1965) md. May 4, 1946, Marion Arnold Askin (b. Aug. 6, 1917, d. Nov. 4, 1995), they're both buried in Faulkner Cemetery, Scott County. Their children were: Marion Arnold Jr. (b. Oct. 22, 1947) md. Nov. 6, 1970, Karin Kollender (b. Nov. 26, 1942). Their daughter, Stephanie Lynn, was born Aug. 16, 1972, in

Germany. Sandra Joy (b. Sep. 25, 1948) md. Oct. 24, 1969, Warren Jerrell Kerr (b. Nov. 24, 1944 in Mississippi). Shawna Lavonne (b. Dec. 22, 1949) md. and divorced Edwin Harrison. They had one daughter, Shawna Leigh (b. Oct. 3, 1972). Shawna married Mar. 14, 1982, Billy Wayne Alexander (b. Nov. 13, 1939). They have one son, Joel Armos (b. Nov. 2, 1983).

Xavier Otis "X.O." (b. Apr. 19, 1928, d. Jul. 31, 1951) was killed in Korea, fighting with the U.S. Army. He's buried in Hillsboro Baptist Cemetery.

Marion Douglas (b. Oct. 17, 1929) md. Letha Cole (b. May 28, 1921 Simpson County).

Kermit Dandee (b. Sep. 11, 1932) md. Ruby Travis in North Carolina, they divorced. Their children were: Mary Jane (b. Jun. 30, 1952 in Catawba County, NC) md. Dale McDonald and died Dec. 24, 1995, in Hattisburg. Ruby Ann (b. Nov. 6, 1954 in Catawba County, NC) md. and divorced Jessie Paul Hollingsworth. They had one daughter, Cory Ann (b. Mar. 6, 1984). Kermit Jr. (b. Sep. 9, 1957) md. Kathryn Forshee in 1998. Kermit md. Jun. 24, 1967, Nancy Williams Holland (b. Aug. 31, 1928).

Wilburn Lang (b. Dec. 14, 1934) md. Jul. 6, 1984, Minnie Mae Gant (b. 1935 in Choctaw County). All of Ernest and Mary's children were born in Scott County.

CARPENTER, In 1910 Joseph L. "Lee" Carpenter (b. Nov. 16, 1869, Leake County MS, d. Apr. 4, 1958, Scott County) moved with his three sons: Ernest Leon (b. Jan. 19, 1894 Leake County, d. Oct. 13, 1973 Scott County); Otis Clyde (b. Jan. 7, 1896 Leake County, d. Oct. 11, 1983 Scott County); and Wilburn Carpenter (b. Apr. 17, 1898 Leake County, d. Sep. 28, 1933 Yazoo County). They are all buried at Hillsboro Baptist Cemetery, Hillsboro, MS.

They brought their live-in housekeeper, Ann Manning, with them. Ann was known to all of the family as Black Mammy. She and her mother were sold in the slave market in Charleston, SC, to a man named Cotton, who owned a plantation in Yazoo County. He rode a horse and the slaves all walked to Mississippi. Mammy said when she would get so tired walking, he would let her ride behind the saddle. She and her husband moved to J.H. Carpenter's plantation in Leake County when Lee was 9 years old. Her husband left and she remained with the family. When Lee's wife, Mary Etna Chestnutt, became ill with cancer, Mammy moved in to take care of her and remained there with the family until she died in March 1944. Mammy is buried in the Sylvester Church Cemetery.

Lee married Mrs. Lula Lee Jordan Royals on Feb. 18, 1912. She was born Apr. 2, 1886, in Leake County and died Jul. 17, 1961, in Brandon, Rankin County, MS and is buried in Hillsboro Baptist Cemetery. This union produced two sons and three daughters: Buford Wilson (b. Dec. 31, 1912 Scott County, d. Dec. 6, 1976, at the Veterans Hospital in Hinds County, MS). Buford is buried at Hillsboro Baptist Cemetery. Audie Lee (b. Aug. 13, 1921, d. Sep. 18, 1989, Picayune, MS) is buried at Hillsboro Baptist Cemetery. Marcella Ruth was born Feb. 14, 1915, in Scott County. Thelma Christine (b. Feb. 12, 1917, Scott County, d. Jul. 28, 1937, Hinds County, MS) is buried at Hillsboro Baptist Cem-

etery. Mary Eliza (b. Jun. 27, 1919, Scott County, d. Jul. 29, 1980 in Hinds County, MS) is buried in Hillsboro Baptist Cemetery.

All of these children are deceased except for Mrs. Marcella Bell. Numerous grandchildren still live in Scott, Leake and Hinds counties. All children and grandchildren are buried in Hillsboro Baptist Cemetery except for Nancy Smith, daughter of Thelma Carpenter Smith, who is buried in Vicksburg; Frankie Askin, daughter of Ernest and Mary Carpenter, is buried in Faulkner Cemetery in Scott County; and Ernestine Rasco, daughter of Ernest and Mary Carpenter, is buried in Mt. Olivet Cemetery in Yazoo County, MS.

CHAMBERS, GC and Lizzie Mae Chambers were residents of Scott County all their married lives. GC was a fourth generation Chambers from Hillsboro, MS, whose great-grandfather, Robert Powell, settled in Scott County in 1840. His paternal grandfather, Luke, fought for the Confederacy in the Civil War against his father, Robert Powell's, wishes since he did not vote for secession. GC's grandfather, Luke and his father, Preston, were both brick masons, his grandfather having built chimneys and fireplaces in some of the oldest homes in Scott County. Luke also helped to tear down the Forest courthouse when the county seat was moved from Forest to the original county seat of Hillsboro in 1872 for about a year. Luke's nephew, Robert Hiram Henry, also became the founder and editor of *The Clarion Ledger*.

Gulf Service Center in the early 1950s, managed by GC Chambers. It is still located at 234 Third Street, now known as Roberts BP. It is a third generation business, in 2000 becoming over 50 years old.

GC's maternal grandfather was Percy P. Hatch, a school teacher who would retreat to the corn crib with a book when his grandchildren would come to visit. His daughter, Gertrude Hatch, married Preston Chambers. Eleven children were produced out of that union. Before Gertrude's death at 95 in 1978, she was the oldest living member of the Hillsboro Baptist Church and had 10 living children, 27 grandchildren, 47 great-grandchildren and eight great-great-grandchildren. Marion Austin Chambers and Pearlie Mae Chambers Hudson, both of Brandon, MS, are now the only two living children of the Preston Chambers family.

As a young businessman, GC operated the Standard Service Station when he met and married in 1939 a Newton County native, Lizzie Mae Scarborough Austin, who worked next door at Collier Implement Co., where he formed a daily habit of bringing her coffee. Around 1948, he became manager of the Gulf Service Center, now

Roberts BP, which became a landmark known as GC's in the 1950s as high school students across the street made it a frequented place. About this same time, he and Lizzie Mae gave birth to a fifth generation Scott Countian, a daughter, Janis.

GC and Lizzie Mae Chambers. March 1941, 18 months after they were married.

In 1959, GC became a Gulf Oil distributor, with his office in Newton, MS. In 1974, his business passed to his son-in-law, Stanley Roberts, whose great-great-grandfather, Jeremiah Roberts, settled in Scott County in the 1830s and the business was renamed G. Stanley Roberts Distributor, Inc. In 1997, the office was moved to Pearl, MS and the name was again changed to Capital Oil, Inc. With the move to Jackson, GC's grandson, Stan Roberts, became the sixth generation Scott Countian to enter a three generation business, which became over 50 years old in 2000.

CHAMBERS-WILSON, Robert Powell

Chambers was born to Josiah and Christian (Robinson) Chambers in South Carolina in 1805. He was about 12 when they settled in northwest Washington County, AL. About 1819 the Chambers met the Thomas Wilson family, recent migrants from Kentucky. The Wilsons had three daughters, who eventually married Chambers sons. Robert Powell married Huanna Sep. 25, 1825.

Gravestone markers of Robert P. Chambers and Huanna W. Chambers, close relatives and loving supporters of Susan Virginia Chambers Hederman and her four small children following the death of Martin Hederman in 1879.

Robert and Huanna owned land in several counties before settling in Scott County. It is probable that they settled near Bethlehem Baptist Church in present-day Forkville. Robert was one of 11 charter members of Bethlehem Church in 1847, as indicated by his position as a del-

egate to the Mt. Pisgah Baptist Association in October. In 1850 Robert's brothers, Henry and John, were the delegates from Bethlehem. In September 1856, Robert is named as the pastor of the then 12-member church. Six of Josiah Chambers' children settled near Bethlehem: Silas, Robert, Obedience (Robinson), John, Henry and Susan (Byrn). Upon the arrival of all these families, the neighborhood was filled with at least 19 double-first cousins. Robert and Huanna had seven children: Mary Ann (b. 1826), Christian (b. 1827), James Andrew Jackson (b. 1837), Sarah Jane (b. 1839), Luke Robert (b. 1842), Susan Virginia (b. 1843) and William Marion (b. about 1846).

When the Civil War came Robert apparently did not support secession. Nevertheless, his sentiments did not prevent his sons from joining the Confederate Army. In early 1864, Sherman made a quick eastward strike from Vicksburg. Troops were issued two days' rations and therefore foraged. On February 10th, advance Union cavalry skirmished in Hillsboro with Rebel troops covering the Confederate retreat. The Yankees were fired on from several houses as they entered Hillsboro about 9:00 a.m. In immediate retaliation, they set fire to the town. Union foragers cleaned out Robert that morning. In 1872, Robert testified that he lost two horses, a mule, 20 sheep, six hogs, five bee stands with honey, 1,100 pounds of pork, 80 bushels of corn, 800 pounds of fodder, a buggy, a saddle, bedding and clothing.

Sarah Jane is shown on the 1860 census as wife of E.G. Skinner. Early in the 1860s, Christian is believed to have married William H. Rogers, who was a farmer as well as tax assessor/collector and sheriff of Scott County. James married Betty Burks, granddaughter of his Aunt Alethia Denson. They settled in Morton where James ran a store and was appointed mayor by Gov. Alcorn. Luke, a carpenter and brick mason, married Mollie Price by 1866. They lived in Hillsboro.

Mary Ann and Patrick Henry moved to Forest in 1867. Their 16-year-old son, Robert Hiram, got his first newspaper job as an apprentice at the *Forest Register*. In 1872, he was owner and editor of the *Newton Weekly Ledger*. Susan married Martin Hederman Feb. 28, 1874 and on Aug. 15, 1877, William Marion married Malinda Jennie Skinner in Newton County, where most of the family had moved. At their deaths, Robert and Huanna were buried in the Baptist Church Cemetery on Church Street in Newton.

CLARK-KILGORE, Nancy Caldonia

"Donie" Clark was born Apr. 1, 1858, in Scott County, MS. She died May 5, 1953, in Fort Worth, Tarrant County, TX and is buried in Mount Olivet Cemetery.

Her parents were William "Wig" Clark and Martha Caroline Finely. They are listed in the 1860 census of Scott County, P.O. Damascus, dwelling 61.

Martha was the daughter of John M. Finley, a farmer, born in Georgia and Nancy, born in Georgia.

I believe William "Wig" Clark was the son of David Clark, born in Kentucky and Celia, who was born in Georgia. They are listed in the 1850 census of Scott County. There were three chil-

dren listed in the census and there may have been more: John, 7; Mary, 4; and Nancy, 2.

Mary Jane Clark married Franklin Kilgore and Nancy C. "Donie" Clark married Alney Dozier Kilgore, cousins.

J.S. Record and Mary Ann "Mollie" Kilgore Record and baby, Bertha L. Record, 1906.

The marriage for A.D. Kilgore and N.C. Clark was in Scott County, MS, Jun. 5, 1879. Alney's father M.T.G. Kilgore was born in 1817, Covington County, MS. He died around 1863. He was a blacksmith by trade, but he was also a Confederate soldier. He enlisted Sept. 10, 1861, by A. McLemore, in Jones County. He was hospitalized in Shelbyville, TN and also Chattanooga Hospital with frozen feet. He was sent home to recuperate. When he was returning to his unit he was murdered by a gang of outlaws. This left Alney and his siblings orphaned.

Their mother, Nancy Ann Stafford, had died shortly after the 1860 census. Alney, Henry and Elizabeth, were brought to Sebastopol by their sister, Mary Francis Kilgore Lang, who had married William Jackson Lang.

When Alney and Donie married, they moved to Texas. Her sister, Mary Jane and her husband, Franklin Kilgore, went to Texas also.

Alney and Donie settled in Ellis County. They were farmers and cattle people, like most of the settlement at that time. On Jan. 5, 1892, Alney froze to death while taking care of his cattle. Donie was left with six children to care for. She returned to Mississippi to her father's home to get some help. Her father gave them out to family members, keeping the youngest child and Donie with him. Donie was unhappy with this arrangement and gathered her children up and came back to Texas to raise them. Before Alney died, they were one of the few families listed in the 1890 census that were not destroyed.

They had seven children, six living in Ellis County, TX, Dist. 3 and Mountain Peak. These children were: Beatrice Florence 10 Kilgore (b. Oct. 10, 1880, d. after 1958 in Melissa, TX) md. Charles Douglas Record Dec. 1, 1896, in Ellis County, TX. Source: Vol. H, page 571 Ellis County marriages.

Virginia Elizabeth Kilgore (b. Aug. 6, 1883, d. 1965, Mabank, TX) md. William Autry Dec. 15, 1898, in Waxahachie, Ellis County, TX. Vol. J, page 263. William Alney Kilgore (b. Feb. 8, 1885, d. Mar. 31, 1936 in Kaufman, TX) md. "Tek" Sexton.

Mary Ann "Mollie" Kilgore (b. Oct. 10, 1886 in Files Valley, TX, located just outside of Itasca) is my grandmother. She died Sep. 14, 1958, in Fort Worth, TX and is buried in Mount Olivet Cemetery. She married Joseph Sian Record in Kaufman County Jul. 16, 1905 and she used her nickname of Mollie on the marriage certificate.

Luke Midleton Kilgore was the fifth child. He was born Apr. 16, 1888, in Texas and died in

1959 in the Methodist Hospital in Dallas, TX. He married Minnie Mae Baldwin.

The last child was Joseph Henry Kilgore Sr. (b. Nov. 9, 1889 in Waxahachie, d. Jun. 25, 1975 in Fort Worth). Buried in Mount Olivet Cemetery. He married Winnie L.C. Young Feb. 6, 1912, in Kaufman County.

My mother was the oldest living child of Mary Ann "Mollie" Kilgore and J.S. Record. She was Bertha Lorena Record. She married Lovell Raymond Britt Jul. 8, 1925, in Fort Worth. She died Jan. 20, 1999.

CLEVELAND, Patrick H. Cleveland and Martha Molds Cleveland moved to Forest in September 1974 with their 10-month-old son, Patrick Brian. In 1976 Melanie Ann was born to this family. We are members of Forest United Methodist Church.

Patrick H. and Martha both have Irish ancestors. They both were born and grew up in Newton County. They were educated in public schools, East Central Community College, University of Southern Mississippi and graduate work at Mississippi State University. Patrick has taught school, coached and worked for the Dept. of Human Services for 30 years. Martha earned National Board Certification and has taught school for 30 years.

Patrick and Melanie were both educated in Forest public schools. Patrick earned his DVM from Mississippi State University. Patrick is associated with Newton Animal Clinic. Melanie earned her RN from University of Mississippi Medical Center. Melanie is associated with Central Dialysis Unit of Forest.

CLOWER-GRIFFITH, Simeon, son of John Kager Clower and Nancy Clarke Hayley, was born Dec. 3, 1863, in Hillsboro, Scott County, MS. He married Helena Harper Griffith Aug. 18, 1889. She was the daughter of Edward Wallace Griffith and Mary Thompson Park. She was born in Alabama Sep. 19, 1867.

Simeon Clower and Helena Harper Griffith.

Simeon operated the family farm in Hillsboro inherited from his father. In 1897, his sister, Johnnie, deeded her part of the estate to him. The farm prospered under "Mr. Sim's" management and "Miss Lena" gained the reputation of 'setting the best table' in the county. From their wealth they shared generously with their neighbors and when cause arose, they expected the same from them as one recalled story points out.

Miss Lena had a fiery temper and a sharp tongue which she used effectively to accomplish her goals. A grandchild states that on one occasion she accompanied her in a wagon driven by Son Gaston (descendant of a Clower Plantation slave) to procure food for a young widow with several small children. A merchant offered five pounds of flour to help, Miss Lena stamped her foot and belittled him until he increased it to 25 pounds and added five pounds of sugar, much obliged to get rid of her.

Miss Lena was a devout Baptist believing that to be the only road to salvation while Mr. Sim was a God fearing man who never attended church.

Despite the deflated economy, the family strived to preserve the culture and refinement enjoyed by their ancestors and for which the area was known. Education was considered a priority and the three girls became teachers while the boys maintained the farm.

Before his death, Simeon divided the land between the boys. John Sim got the house and was to care for Miss Lena until her death. Simeon died Aug. 6, 1936, in Hillsboro and Helena "Miss Lena" died Jul. 14, 1945, also in Hillsboro. They are both buried in the Baptist cemetery in Hillsboro.

They had six children: Flora L. "Big Sis" (b. Nov. 17, 1891, d. Feb. 13, 1974), Mamie Park (b. Oct. 28, 1893, d. Feb. 2, 1896), Bryant Barber (Sep. 13, 1897, d. Apr. 17, 1977), Margaret (Apr. 1, 1900, d. in Silver Springs, MD), John Sim (b. Oct. 16, 1902, d. Mar. 24, 1961) and Edna Earl (b. Oct. 4, 1905, d. Sep. 18, 1992). All children, with the exception of Margaret, are buried in the Baptist cemetery at Hillsboro, Scott County, MS, in the family plot.

Flora L. married Erskine Coleman Scott Sep. 13, 1919, in Jacksonville, Duval County, FL; Bryant Barber married Euna Lee Burkes Mar. 20, 1920, in Hillsboro, Scott County, MS; Margaret "Maggie" married Clyde Farrell Clark Jun. 29, 1924, in Hillsboro, Scott County, MS; John Sim married Louise Lloyd May 8, 1926, in Scott County, MS; and Edna Earle married Robert Margel Burkes May 3, 1931, in Scott County, MS.

CLOWER-HAYLEY, John Kager Clower and his wife, Nancy Clarke Hayley, moved from Alabama to Hillsboro, MS, in 1857 and became one of the pioneer plantation owners of Scott County.

By 1860, John's acquired estate, consisting of land holdings, slaves, livestock, farm implements, pleasure carriage and other personal properties, was valued at over $30,000.00. It was during this year that one acquisition of land from a Charlotte Wiggins of London, England for $360.00 is of interest. (240 acres more or less in Section 14, Township 7, Range East.) It required that Robert Morse and Charles Rolfe appear before the Lord Mayor of the city of London, John Carter, Feb. 8, 1860, for swearing to the signature of Charlotte Wiggins. It was then given to Robert B. Campbell, consulate of the USA at London on Feb. 9, 1860, for swearing to the seal and identity of the Lord Mayor. The affidavit was then presented to James D. Jones, clerk of the Probate Court, Hillsboro, Scott County, MS, Mar. 20, 1860, for recording.

History books show that "Hillsborough" was on a route used during the Civil War by Gen. Sherman. Family legend states that Gen. Sherman used the Clower Plantation as headquarters when he stopped there. Upon leaving, Sherman ordered that the house not be burned but orders were disregarded and it was set afire. When he learned of this, he made the men return to extinguish the fire and repair the damage. Among cattle confiscated was a cow whose milk was used to feed John's sickly infant son, Simeon and this caused much concern for his welfare. However, the cow escaped and returned the next day.

John Kager, was born in Harris County, GA, Aug. 24, 1812 and died in Hillsboro, Scott County, MS, Nov. 28, 1883. His father was Thomas Clower and his mother's last name was Bryant. He married Nancy Clarke Hayley Dec. 22, 1837. She was born Jul. 17, 1820, in Georgia and died Nov. 19, 1889, in Hillsboro, Scott County, MS. They are both buried in Hillsboro.

John Kager willed most of his estate to his wife, daughter, Johnnie and son, Simeon. Simeon was to remain on the property and care for his mother and sister.

Seven of the 10 children born to John and Nancy traveled with them to Mississippi from Lee County, AL. They were Thomas Holiday (b. Oct. 1, 1838, d. Nov. 13, 1906), Louise Jane "Lula" (Sep. 28, 1840, d. Jul. 30, 1913), Laura A. (Dec. 17, 1842, d. Oct. 1, 1928), Jesse W. (b. Aug. 27, 1845, d. Sep. 18, 1871), George Demosthenes (b. Feb. 19, 1849, d. Oct. 3, 1924), Nancy Aderson "Addie" (Nov. 3, 1852, d. Nov. 15, 1911) and Mary Bryant Burma "Mollie" (b. Mar. 14, 1853, d. May 17, 1879). While in Hillsboro, Johnnie O. (b. Oct. 2, 1857, d. 1907 in Purvis, MS), Josiah Cager (b. Nov. 21, 1859, d. Jan. 30, 1930) and Simeon (b. Dec. 3, 1863, d. Aug. 6, 1936) were born.

Thomas Holiday married Mary Jane Robbins Sep. 18, 1879, in Hillsboro, Scott County, MS. Laura A. md. William Addison Lynn Feb. 11, 1877, in Wilkes County, GA. George Demosthenes md. Salena Flanagan Nov. 9, 1882, in Morton, Scott County, MS. Nancy Aderson md. Vandy Marcellus Neal, MD in 1880 in Auburn, Lee County, AL. Josiah Cager md. Mary Georgia "Poca" Thornton May 10, 1888, in Hattiesburg, Perry County, MS (Perry County later was split and Hattiesburg now lies in Forrest County). Simeon md. Helena Harper Griffith Aug. 18, 1889, in Hillsboro, Scott County, MS.

CLOWER-SCOTT, Flora Lydell Clower was born in Hillsboro Nov. 17, 1891, as the first child of Simeon Clower and Helena Harper Griffith.

She was known as Big Sis to her siblings, Aunt Coda to her nieces and nephews and Miss Flora or Mrs. Scott to her many students during her 45 years of teaching.

In 1913 she obtained a "Mistress of Pedagogics" from the Mississippi Industrial Institute and College. Two years later she received her professional license from the state of Mississippi. She also received de-

Erskine Coleman Scott and Flora Lydell Clower.

grees from MSCW in Columbus and State Teachers College in Hattiesburg.

The first teaching assignment was in Harperville where her brothers, Bryant and John Sim, were among her first students. Other early teaching assignments included positions at an Indian reservation in Oklahoma and as a home economist in Starke, FL. It was while in Florida that she met and married a young telephone company employee, Erskine Coleman Scott.

While on assignment in Florida she was driving through the marshlands of Bradford County and came upon an alligator stretched across and blocking the road. Intent on keeping her assignment, she shot the alligator and found someone to load it in her car. She later had shoes and a purse made from the hide.

Erskine and Flora moved to Mississippi when he began to have problems with his health. They lived in Homewood where Flora taught school. They soon moved to Hillsboro and bought a home near her parents.

At Hillsboro, Flora taught and served as principle where her duties included coaching a boy's basketball team that advanced to play in the state championship tournament. After teaching one year at Ringold, she was forced into retirement from the Forest City Schools by state retirement laws. Her 45 year career included teaching a class of 65 enrolled students and another class that she followed to the next grade at parental request.

Erskine, aka Skinnye, because of his tall, thin frame, was born Apr. 4, 1893, in Giles County, TN, to John Calvin Scott and Lizzie Barnett. He served in the U.S. Army 7th Signal Bn. until he received a discharge to return and help with telephone problems in Florida. While in Hillsboro, he managed a farm and worked briefly as a cotton grader until poor health forced his retirement.

Erskine died Jun. 13, 1953. at his home in Hillsboro and Flora died Feb. 13, 1974, at the Methodist Hospital in Hattiesburg, Forrest County, MS. They are both buried at the Baptist cemetery in Hillsboro, Scott County, MS.

Erskine and Flora had one child, Winifred Ellen, who married John David McElhaney Sr. of Hattiesburg, MS.

COOPER-RUSHING-DABNEY,

William Greene Cooper and Josephine Rushing were married and homesteaded acreage in Scott County in 1878, in what was then called Stage, MS. It was located at a crossroads where Woodrow Rushing's brick home now stands on Morton-Marathon Road. To this union were born 11 children, one of who was my dad, Andrew Richard Cooper (b. Sep. 8 1888). Once a month a stagecoach would bring mail, hardware supplies, canned goods, materials and accessories for the ladies to buy to make clothes for their families, salt by the pound or in 100 pound sacks for the farmers' livestock to lick, for preserving meat killed on their farms and for table use. There was a mail slot for each family living in the postal area. People would ride horseback or walk to get their mail. For family supplies they would come in mule or horse drawn wagons. The family operating this mail-store business had living quarters behind the store. My dad, Richard, met and married my mom, Harriet Lahrea Parker, in

Colorado Springs, CO, Sep. 8 1927. Then they came home to Mississippi to live. My grandpa, William Greene Cooper, deeded to my mom and dad 42-1/2 acres of this homestead where they lived the remainder of their lives. My dad, Richard, passed on Jan. 11, 1962 and my mom, Harriet, on Mar. 8, 1989. My dad told me some about his childhood. They all got shoes once a year at Christmas time. One apple, one orange, one peppermint stick, three nuts, raisins dried on their own vines. Many times he told me of his getting up at 4:00 a.m., walking barefoot in the snow to their family sawmill, which was run by steam, by water pumped from a small pond they had dug and that was fed by a spring. He would fuel the fire with coal to get the steam engine going good enough to run the sawmill. One time he told me that his dad, William Greene Cooper, laid by his corn in July while wearing his overcoat, while it was snowing. The children got only a minimal amount of schooling as they could only go during the winter months when they weren't out working in the fields. The school was located where the Independence Methodist Church is now on Independence Road in Morton. Dad was an educated man for his time. He finished ninth grade, was excellent in penmanship, letters and numbers. Most of the children walked to school; a few got to ride horseback. Stage, MS, was later named Morton, MS.

Wedding party of Timothy Dabney and Marie Gerdel. Left to Right: Janet Dabney, Marie Dabney, Timothy Dabney, Lucille Dabney, David Dabney and John Cooper.

To the union of my dad and mom were born Daisy Lucille Cooper (b. Jul. 19, 1928) and John David Cooper (b. May 31, 1925). John never married but Lucille married Fitzhugh Y. Dabney whose parents were Fredrick Yeamons Dabney and Elizabeth Fitzhugh on Feb. 14, 1924. They lived on Raymond Road in Jackson for the greater part of their lives. Fitzhugh and Lucille were married in the First Baptist Church in Morton Aug. 14, 1948. To this union were born Timothy Andrew Dabney (b. Apr. 4, 1958), Jonathan David Dabney (b. Jul. 31, 1959) and Janet Lucille Dabney (b. Jun. 30, 1961). In early July 1962 a few days past Janet's first birthday, the children's dad and Lucille's husband left them for parts unknown. On Sep. 8, 1964, Lucille got a divorce on desertion charges. Lucille and the children lived there until the children were grown and left for collage. If there had been a father in the home, none of the children would have gone to college, because they would have been ineligible for grants and loans, etc. Lucille still lives there on property inherited from her parents, Richard and Harriet Cooper, on 23 acres which were deeded to her two sons, Timothy and

David Dabney, by Harriet Cooper, John D. Cooper and Lucille Cooper Dabney in December 1967.

Timothy Andrew Dabney and Bonnie Marie Gerdel formerly from League City, TX, was the first wedding to take place in the newly built Alfreda Lodge at Roosevelt State Park, Morton, MS. Both Timothy and Marie had temporary jobs at the park prior to their wedding on May 23, 1981. Grandmother Harriet Cooper was not able to attend due to ill health. To this union was born Erica Leigh Dabney (b. May 31, 1986) and Casey Nicholas Dabney (b. Jan. 14, 1988).

Jonathan David Dabney and Jennifer Ann Little were married Jun. 16, 1990, in Houston, TX. Ricky Latham, from Morton, performed the ceremony.

Janet Lucille Dabney received a MA degree from Mississippi State University and did her internship to work with the visually impaired. Before she got a job she got too sick to work. This began when she was 25. It was a blood disease later diagnosed as Aero Plastic Anemia. She is now waiting for a bone marrow transplant, hopefully to be done in June 2000. Her brother, Timothy, is to be the donor. Her doctor is Lawrence Rice.

COOPER,
James Leon "Lynn" Cooper (b. Mar. 17, 1884, d. Jun. 18, 1953) was the son of William Green and Josephena Saphronia Rushing Cooper. He was married the first time to Minnie E. Bowman (b. Dec. 26, 1890, d. Dec. 17, 1913). They had a son, Vilous Spurgeon Cooper. Minnie died when Spurgeon was 9 months old of pneumonia. After her death, Leon and Spurgeon lived with his parents until Spurgeon was 6  years old, when he married Betty Elizabeth "Bessie" Winstead. They had three children: Mazie Marie, James Winstead and Audrey Griselda.

Children of James Leon Cooper. First Row: Mazie Marie Cooper Dye and Audrey Griselda Cooper Wood. Second Row: Vilous Spurgeon Cooper and James Winstead Cooper.

In his early years, Lynn was a school teacher at Cooperville. There is where he met and married Minnie. He was very good in math. He built a home in the Springfield Community and there is where he raised his family. He was a farmer. He was a deacon in the Springfield Baptist Church and served as church clerk for many years. Bessie was a Sunday school teacher. They took their family to church in a wagon pulled by horses. Most of their church services were only on Sunday and only had preaching twice a month. There were a lot of dinners on the ground with another service in the afternoon. Revival always began on third Sunday in July and each day each family took lunch. There was a service in the morning and after lunch. During this time of the year all their crops were laid by and they had a few days that they could take off for the revival.

Since they did not have a car and most of the neighbors did not either, their children walked to most of their activities. They lived close to Independence School and walked to school each day. During planting and harvest time school was dismissed so the youth could help with the crops. Many get-togethers were in homes where they got together to sing. The young people walked to these homes in groups. Many of the people married people in their community.

In 1949 Bessie developed cancer and died. Lynn then made his home with his oldest son, Spurgeon and family. His health was failing. He had what they called then hardening of the arteries. He could not remember present things but his memory of younger years was good. One special memory of the time he lived with Spurgeon and family is that he always said the blessing at meal time. The family had better be ready because soon as everyone was seated he asked the blessing. There were five grandchildren in the family: Minnie Jean Cooper, Sudie Frances Cooper, Betty Joye Cooper, Sarah Elizabeth Dye and Marshal Leon Dye. This has always been a close family, even after Lynn and Bessie's death. Many good memories were made in this family.

COOPER, Vilous Spurgeon Cooper (b. Mar. 14, 1913, d. Nov. 30, 1981) was born to James Leon and Minnie E. Bowman Cooper in Scott County near Morton, MS. He attended Independence School and graduated from Morton High School. He married Roberta Wade (b. Jul. 13, 1918) Feb. 15, 1936. They were schoolmates and when they married they had a large sum of $20. They rented land to farm in the

Vilous Spurgeon and Roberta Cooper, taken about five months before his death Nov. 30, 1981.

Springfield Community for four years before they could find some land they could buy. Their daughters, Minnie Jean and Sudie Frances, were born here.

In 1943, Spurgeon purchased 200 acres on Hwy. 13, eight miles south of Morton. The land was all in woods and they had to clear the land before they could build their home. It seemed they were carving a home out of the wilderness. On Jul. 18, 1944, a daughter, Betty Joye, was born. He sold 80 acres to family. Spurgeon grew corn and cotton for several years along with raising chickens. They were one of the first families in Scott County to go into the poultry business that is now one of the county's most important businesses. In 1953, he went into the dairy business to help supplement the chicken production. Dairying became more important than the poultry and he went into the dairy business completely.

Spurgeon and Roberta are lifetime members of the Springfield Baptist Church where both were active members. He served as music director, a deacon, leader of RAs, Sunday school superintendent and teacher. She taught a Sun-

day school class, Training Union Class, GA counselor, extension worker and member of WMU. Minnie Jean and Joye served as pianist for the church. All three daughters attended or graduated from Mississippi College.

Spurgeon had a dream of turning his land into something more than a dairy farm. He bought 40 acres of additional land with the idea of building a catfish pond. He contacted the Soil Conservation Service and with their help, Cooper Lake was on its way to being a recreation area with fishing, camping, swimming and picnicking. At the time it was built in 1969, the dam was the largest dam in Scott County and probably the largest dam of an individual landowner that was built in the state. In August that year, Spurgeon received "Outstanding Conservationist of the Year" award. The lake contains 55 acres of water with approximately four miles of shoreline. A giant slide that was new to the area was built which was a favorite of all visitors in the swimming area. Camping was good with overflow crowds. There were 37 campsites with water and electricity and a few with sewer hookups.

On Nov. 30, 1981, Spurgeon died from a massive heart attack. Roberta operated the lake for a while but found it too much for her. Her daughters were married and two of them lived out of state. Now concentration is on fishing with permits and rental of sites on a monthly basis. Although Cooper Lake is not as busy as it once was, people still enjoy it and in the future it could be everyone's favorite place again.

COX, About 1914 J.A. Cox and his wife, Ella Blanche Simpson Cox and family: Tom, Clifton, Myrtle, Ruth, Edna, Sadie, Elizabeth (Love) and Frank, moved to Lake from Rankin County. J.A. Cox worked at the Dubois Mill for a time and then they owned and operated J.A. Cox Store on Main Street in Lake. Clifton, Elizabeth and Frank ran the telephone company in Lake for a

Frank and Marion Cox

number of years. All of the family moved off and married, except for Frank.

Frank went to school in Lake, played on the football team, was offered a scholarship to Mississippi College, but instead stayed home to marry Marion Holloway. Three children: Barbara, Frank Jr. and Billy, were born while they were living south of Lake at Bartlett. In 1941, the family moved to Mobile, where Frank worked as a paint superintendent at the shipyard. Betty was born while they lived in Mobile. In 1946, the family moved back to Lake into the Cox home that he had bought from his family.

He made his living as a painter, raised cattle and hogs. He was town marshal in Lake and tended to the Water Works for a number of years. During those years, the mail came to Lake on the train, which did not stop; the conductor would hang a pouch containing the mail and then grab the outgoing pouch from another hook. Frank

hung the mail and carried the mail to the post office for a while. He was a security guard at Southeastern Poultry Plant and at McCarty Feed Mill before he retired.

After he retired, he operated Kim's Quick Tan during the day. He said that was the job he enjoyed the most. His name for it was "The Barbeque Pit."

Frank Cox was well-known for his quick, unique wit and his generosity to others. In Lake, he's one of our legends.

CRANE-WILKERSON, In the late 1960s a young mother moved back to Forest, MS, to be closer to her family after her husband left her. The middle of those five children was named Joe.

Sandra and Joe Crane with daughters: Rheannan, Deana and Kayla

Joe grew. His mother, Dollie, married Junior Kirkpatrick, the man who became Joe's father in every sense of the word. He taught Joe the value of hard work at an early age. He and Dollie brought up their children with love tempered with discipline.

Joe, as a teenager, became rebellious as many teenagers do. He decided to leave school before his senior year and enter the Job Corps in Kentucky. After a brief stay there he came home to work in the poultry business. He joined the National Guard. After his basic training he came home. Shortly thereafter he met Sandra Wilkerson, an event that would change his life forever.

Sandra was the daughter of O.B. and Geroldean Parker Wilkerson. She was the fifth of six children born to this hard working couple from the Two Mile Community in Morton, MS.

Sandra attended school at the Morton schools. She was an excellent student and graduated third in her class in 1977. After a failed engagement in 1978, she went to work at Scott County Hospital in Morton. She worked in the radiology department there. In 1980 she met Joe Crane, an event that would also change her life forever.

In 1981, Joe and Sandra married. They settled down on land in the Two Mile Community. To this union three daughters were born: Rheannan, Deana and Kayla.

Life was good although sometimes hard. Joe continued to work in the poultry business and Sandra was a stay-at-home mother after the death of her mother in 1983. She cared for her father and brother until their deaths.

They attended Two Mile Baptist Church until the mid-1980s. Another life changing event was about to happen.

Joe was called into the ministry. He spent several years as a supply pastor. In 1990, he was called as pastor of New Zion Baptist Church. He and his family still serve there today.

God has blessed this couple many times. They have reared their family in the same place for 20 years. They are looking forward to many more with God's blessings.

CRECELIUS, Jesse Crecelius was born in Washington County, TN, Jan. 22, 1815 and died Jul. 10, 1900, in Scott County. He married Drucillia Turner (b. Jul. 12, 1838, d. Nov. 29, 1895). They are buried in Antioch Cemetery. She was the daughter of Littleton and Oliff Turner. Jesse and Drucilla had nine children. Jesse was a Primitive Baptist minister. He was ordained as a minister Aug. 10, 1850, in the Antioch Primitive Baptist Church in Scott County. He preached at several churches. There is a plaque in the New Bethel Primitive Baptist listing ministers from 1851-53 and 1886-91. Jesse was elected to the Mississippi legislature in 1874.

Jesse and Drucilla Crecelius

He served on both the Committee on Agriculture. Three of his sons served in the Civil War: Elias Cline Crecelius, my great-grandfather; Albert Galitan Turner Crecelius; and Adam D. Crecelius. They all served Co. F, 20th Mississippi Inf. Jesse and Drucilla's children were: 1) Elias Cline (b. Jul. 1, 1839, d. Nov. 17, 1893) md. Mary Caroline Fleming before 1869, five children. 2) Albert Galitan Turner (b. Sep. 23, 1840, d. Nov. 15, 1876) md. Mary Elvira Saxon before 1870, three children. 3) Adam D. (b. Mar. 6, 1843, d. Jan. 12, 1887) md. Martha F. before 1871, five children. Martha Ann (b. Aug. 2, 1846) no further info; Sarah Rebecca (b. Nov. 22, 1848) no further info; John Randolph (b. Dec. 17, 1850, d. 1910) md. Matilda M. Baldwin before 1873, eight children. William W. (b. Sep. 24, 1854, d. Jul. 19, 1940) md. Nancy A. Thomas Feb. 6, 1879, 11 children; Mary T. (b. Dec. 26, 1856, d. Sep. 21, 1898) md. Green Sanderson Jan. 30, 1879), eight children and Margaret Naomi Crecelius (b. Dec. 26, 1859, d. Jul. 2, 1908) md. John Bishop Stewart in September 1877, seven children.

Elias Cline and Mary Caroline Fleming Crecelius' second child was Martha Olive Crecelius (b. Jun. 15, 1869, d. Oct. 21, 1943) md. James Presley Stone (b. August 1848), the son of David and Mary Stone. They were married Dec. 7, 1884, in Scott County. They had 11 children.

CRAIG, George Pickney "Pink" and Slonia Kitchings Craig had a teenage marriage in 1898. They were blessed with 13 children. Three died as infants. Both parents and children were born and reared in Scott County, MS, in a 10-mile radius of Forkville and Ludlow communities.

Of the nine surviving children, seven lived to celebrate their 50th wedding anniversaries. Two sons lost their wives in death after 40-plus years of marriage. The names of Pink and Slonia's children and spouses are: Walter and Maggie Craig; Nannie Craig and Thomas Price;

Ruby Craig and Grady Merchant; Tressie Mae, single, who died at age 24; Leola Craig and Joe Wallace; James Edward "Eddie" and Mary Baker

George "Pink" and Slonia Kitchings Craig

Craig; Clifton and Odell Davis (deceased) and Mavis Wall Craig; Merle Craig and John D. Latham; (twins) Mary Craig and James Denson; and Gary and Fannie Carroll Craig. As of Jul. 1, 2000, only Merle, Mary and Gary survive.

Since that marriage about 100 years ago, there have been 243 descendants who are now living in 12 states. How proud our parents would be to learn of their descendants' contribution and dedication to the Craig Family. From data reported, the following professions were noted: doctors, ministers, educators, bankers, administrators, entrepreneurs, pharmacists, firemen, secretaries, appraisers, barbers, therapists, policemen, engineers, accountants, plumbers, mechanics, armed services, farmers, housewives, carpenters and computer specialists.

Although our parents were limited in schooling, they shared wisdom and Christian values. Our dad was a good, honest, hardworking man. As a master carpenter, he built homes all over Scott and adjoining counties. His sugar cane syrup was the best to be found! He was also a blacksmith. He enjoyed entertaining visitors, working a garden, playing dominos and checkers. But his favorite leisure time was rocking grandchildren. He was industrious and believed in raising obedient children. He knew how to use his razor strap for things other than sharpening his razor. He died in Morton Hospital with a heart attack Mar. 21, 1948 and was buried in the Forkville Cemetery.

Our mother was compassionate, peace loving and tender hearted. Living was giving for her. Although we were poor as "Job's Turkey," we never knew it for Mama found ways of helping someone who was less fortunate than we. She was happiest when she had her family together. She was a Christian who lived what she taught. Primarily, "Trust in the Lord and your prayers will be answered, but don't pray for anything you don't want for you might get it." Another of her favorite sayings was, "If people are coming to see my house, I don't care if it is messed up. But if they are coming to see me, I want it to be cleaned up." Although Mama was crippled with rheumatoid arthritis for 42 years, she was cheerful and wanted to go and be involved in everything How she loved family reunions! She died in Hinds General Hospital Jul. 19, 1967, with heart failure. She was also buried in the Forkville Cemetery. *Written by Mary Craig Denson.*

CRAIG, In 1789/90, Robert Craig, his pregnant wife, Catherine "Katy" Craig, along with

their children: James, Thomas, John and Jane, left County Antrim, Ireland for Charleston, SC. While making this journey, the father, Robert, died and was buried at sea. Also on this journey, his son, Robert, was born. The Craigs and Chestnuts of present day Scott County descended from the younger Robert who was born at sea.

Craigs from Northwest Scott County descended from John Craig and the Craigs from Homewood and Morton descended from his younger brother, Robert Craig (born at sea). The Chesnuts from Morton descended from the same Robert Craig.

The Craig family, headed by Catherine "Katy," widow of the original Robert Craig, landed in Charleston, SC, in 1789. They moved up country to Fairfield County, SC and resided there about 10 years, then most of them moved to Humphries County, TN and after the war of 1812, they moved from Tennessee to Dallas County (Selma), AL.

Robert Craig married Martha Hayes in Tennessee ca. 1812. They had eight children: Catherine, Elizabeth G., Thomas C., James C., Robert M. (b. 1823, d. 1900), Jane "Jennie" B., Nathaniel Henry and Martha Hayes.

Two of these siblings, Nathaniel and Martha, died in 1865 of typhoid fever in Alabama; three of the siblings settled in Houston and McLennon counties in Texas, Catherine, Thomas C. and James C.; and two ended up in Scott County, MS, Robert M. and Jane "Jennie" B.

Robert M. Craig married Mary Elizabeth McCraw in 1868 in Alabama and in 1873, they left Dallas County, AL, for Texas by wagon train. By this time, Robert had died in 1863 and Martha, his wife, had died in 1867. Both are buried in Prosperity Presbyterian Cemetery in Dallas County, AL.

On the trip west, Mary Elizabeth "Lizzie" Craig, who was pregnant, lost the child she was carrying and they had to leave the ox wagon train in ca. 1873 in Scott County. They had relatives already in Scott County, a son of John Craig also named John had settled in NW Scott County, so they stayed in Scott County, MS. Robert M.'s sister, Jane, stayed in Scott County with them. They lived around the Clifton/Hillsboro area for a while. The sister, Jane "Jennie," then married Mr. George Marler and she, her husband, her brother and his family moved to Homewood. Jane and George Marler who married late in life had no children. The remainder of Robert M.'s and Lizzie Craig's children were born in Homewood. Robert M. and Mary Elizabeth McCraw Craig lived out the rest of their lives in Homewood, MS and are buried in the cemetery of the Homewood Methodist Church.

All of Robert M. and Lizzie's children are buried there except John, who is buried in Kemper County, MS.

Their children were: Martha Caroline "Mattie" (md. Bob Tadlock); Robert William "Rob" (md. Lizzie Moore); Nathaniel Henry (md. "Haley" Moore); Catherine Jane "Kittie" (md. Leslie Herran); John (md. Etheldra Lake "Lakey" Moore); "George" Young (md. Ida Moorehead); and James Palmer "Jim" Craig (b. 1881, d. 1942) married in 1902 to Bessie Jane

Huggins (b. 1886, d. 1964). (Jim and Bessie Craig were the grandparents of the writer, Sue Shuttleworth Coats.)

From the Craig-Huggins union came Ollie Pearl (md. L.E. Graham); Eula Mae (md. Claude R. Shuttleworth); Emma (md. Tommy Graham, brother of L.E. Graham); Bill (md. Mildred Rennick); John Sharp (md. Marie Yelvington); Audie (md. Harrell Mason); Walter "Buck" (md. Marion McEwen); and Iva Cornelia (md. W.L. Lott).

At the date of this writing, Eula Craig Shuttleworth, widow of Claude Shuttleworth, is 95 years old and is the only living member of the Jim Craig family from Homewood, MS. Claude R. Shuttleworth had by his first wife, Mary Alford (d. 1930), two sons, William Martin "Billy" Shuttleworth (b. 1917, d. 1991) and Claude L. Shuttleworth; then a daughter and son by his second wife, Eula Mae Craig. These later children were Sue Shuttleworth (Coats) and Robert Glen "Bob" Shuttleworth.

Elizabeth G. Craig, daughter of Robert and Martha Hayes Craig, married John Chesnut Jan. 20, 1841, in Dallas County, AL. Their children were: Robert Craig Chesnut, John William Chesnut, Margaret Alabama Chesnut, Nathaniel Presley Chesnut, Martha Hayes Chesnut, John Young Chesnut and Elizabeth Catherine Chesnut.

Nathaniel Presley Chesnut married Mattie Jo Tadlock who was a sister to Mr. Bob Tadlock (who took for his second wife, Mattie Craig, daughter of Robert M. and Mary Elizabeth McCraw Craig). Nathaniel Presley Chesnut died in 1882 in Alabama and was buried in Dallas County, AL.

Mattie Jo Tadlock Chesnut, his wife, was left with four little children so she moved to Scott County, MS, to be near her Tadlock relatives (MDC Tadlock, Bob Tadlock, John Webster Tadlock (md. Maggie McCraw, a sister to Mary Elizabeth McCraw Craig!). Mattie Chesnut never remarried and is buried at Sims Hill Cemetery in Scott County near Morton. Her children were: Josephine Alabama "Bama" Chesnut (md. James Garrett Risher); John Allen Chesnut (md. Mollie Camilla Green); Robert Nathaniel Chesnut (md. Annie Dubose); and Irvin Young Chesnut, who to my knowledge remained in Alabama.

CRAPPS, The first time we have record of the Crapps family they were living in the vicinity of Columbia, SC. The name is spelled Crapps, Craps, Crapse and Kreps. The name changed from Craps to Crapps after the Civil War.

George and John Jacob Crapps were brothers living in Columbia, SC. George had a large farm and raised cotton. Most of his family remained in South Carolina but some moved eastward to Georgia and Monroe County, AL. George Crapps lived near Monroeville, AL, in the 1840 census.

Crapps family members that came to Mississippi were: Jacob (md. Dedemiah); Jeremiah (md. Martha); Daniel returned to Monroeville, AL.

Crapps sons born in Alabama: 1) Yancy md. Elizabeth Walker from Rehobeth Community; 2) Jeremiah md. Martha; 3) Jim remained single, he served in the Civil War and is buried in The Beauvoir Soldiers Cemetery in Gulfport, MS;

4) John moved to Attalla County; 5) Shepard Riley Crapps moved to north of Canton, MS.

Yancy Crapps, son of Jacob, md. Sarah Elizabeth Walker. Their children were: 1) Will, lived and is buried at Ludlow, MS; 2) George, lived and is buried in Canton, MS; 3) Mack, md. Pearl Thompson, lived north of Morton and is buried in Old Branch Baptist Church Cemetery; 4) Charlie "Babe" md. Allie Jackson (first) and Pearl Jackson (second), lived and is buried at Old Branch Cemetery. His daughters are Amanda Crapps Bates and Angie Crapps Bates.

John Jacob Crapps, 25 years of age, landed in Charleston, SC, in November 1754 accompanied by a girl, Margaret Catherine, 13 years of age, who was indentured and with an Anna Marie Zimmerman. The ship was the *Snow Princess*.

CRIMM, Clarence Pickens Crimm was born in Newton County, MS, in 1875. Nora Headrick was born in Newton County in 1874. They were married in Newton County and started a family there. Their first four children were born in Newton County in the following order: Mamie, Ola, William and Effie. They moved to the Piketon area shortly after 1900. Five more children were born in Scott County in the following order: Spivy, Willie, Clarence, Jewell and Lula.

Aerial photo taken in 1942. The numbers 1 to 13 are the names of the people in that area. 1. Dock Arnold; 2. Ina Hollingsworth; 3. Roy Regester; 4. Tom Burns; 5. Will Gunn; 6. Leonard Massey; 7. Lee Massey; 8. Tom Harelson; 9. Cupper Walters; 10. Albert Posey; 11. Bill Gentry; 12. Magg Walters; and 13. Summers.

C.P. Crimm had teams of oxen that he used in the logging business. The 1910 census showed C.P. Crimm was employed at the stave mill, where he used his oxen to haul logs for the mill, then the mill would turn the logs into wooden barrels, shingles, etc. Ola told me that he lived in a tent during the summer months while he was hauling logs for the mill; he called the place where they camped out Indian Town. Couchata Indians were living there at that time and still are today as far as I know. During the winter months, he would come back and live at the homeplace.

C.P. and Nora are buried at the Piketon Cemetery. C.P.'s brother, William W. Crimm and his mother, Martha J. Crimm, are also buried there.

Doc Arnold was born in Hickman County, TN, in 1878. He came to Scott County to work at the Chase & Weiman stave mill in the early 1900s. The stave mill was located approximately two miles east of Pleasant Ridge Church in Tuscalometta Swamp at a place called Jeff Walter Lake. There was a narrow gape railroad that

came through the area in 1922. There was also a spoke mill in the general area.

Doc Arnold bought land approximately one-half mile east of Piketon Church on a road that ran along the west side of the Tushatata Swamp. It started at the old Jackson Road and ran south to the Ringold Conehatta Road. This road is no longer in use and ends up at the old Arnold homeplace. The road is now called the Ola Arnold Road.

Doc Arnold and Ola Crimm were married in 1912. They had nine children beginning with Etoile (b. 1914), Milton (b. 1916), Myrtle (b. 1917), Wilson, known as Wig, (b. 1919), Lorene (b. 1922), Altonin (b. 1924), Albert (b. 1927), Monroe (b. 1933) and Maxine (b. 1935).

Doc Arnold died in 1944 and Ola continued to live at the homeplace until she broke her hip in 1986.

All of the children of Doc and Ola moved from the area except Alton who never married and lived on the farm until his death in 1993.

Doc, Ola, Etoile and Alton are all deceased and buried in the Piketon Cemetery.

I left the Piketon area in 1955 and I have returned to visit the area as often as I could. I have many good memories of the good people I grew up with in the Piketon area and the Ringold School Community. *Submitted by Thomas Monroe Arnold.*

CRYE, James Benjamin "Ben" Crye of Scott County was a businessman from the last decade of the 19th century through four plus decades of the 20th century. His land and timber holdings throughout that period covered much of Scott County and neighboring counties.

He owned cotton gins and sawmills in Pelahatchie, Ludlow, Morton and other neighboring towns and communities. He also owned and operated gristmills.

Born in Scott County to William Mathison Crye and Maryland Elizabeth Waldrip, he became independent at a young age when his family moved west to Louisiana and he stayed in Mississippi.

Ben purchased a marriage license and married Betty Miles, daughter of Robert and Nancy (Stuart) Miles.

The Cryes' firstborn, a daughter, Ina Merle was born Jul. 3, 1900. Her marriage to Irven Young Chestnut was in March 1917. Their daughters were Nannie Elizabeth and Bonnie Fay.

Nannie married James Clinton Williams of Smith County and they had one child, Irven Summerall "Sonny" Williams. He married Sallie Sheilds and they reside in Florence, MS.

Nannie, Irven and Ina Merle are buried in Sims Cemetery in Scott County.

Bonnie Fay married Woodrow "Woody" Ivy of Smith County in 1958. Their children are Donald and Dana. Dana and her spouse, Jeff Pennington, have two daughters, Chandler and Courtlyn and reside in Columbia, MS. Donald is married to Charlette Fields and they reside in Raleigh, MS.

The second daughter of Ben and Betty, Birdie Ianthe "Nancy," was born Jul. 31, 1903. Her spouse was Jesse Lathan "Van" VanLandingham of Winston County. Their only child, a daughter, Bettye Ross VanLandingham, was wed to Hugh E. Davis. Van died Jan. 6, 1983. Ianthe "Nancy" died May 28, 1989. They are buried in Sherwood Memorial Park in Roanoke, VA. Hugh E. Davis died Mar. 5, 1989.

Bettye and Hugh Davis' son, Dr. Steve Davis, father of Rebecca and Hannah, is a cardiologist in Lynchburg, VA. Their daughter Linda and her spouse, Dan Frith, parents of sons Bo and Davis, are both attorneys in Roanoke, VA.

The last child of Ben and Betty Crye, Bennye Beatrice was born Nov. 24, 1907. Bennye married Harold McRae "Happy" Loeb in Jackson, MS, Dec. 25, 1932.

Harold was born Aug. 2, 1900 and raised in Atlanta, GA, the son of Cohen Loeb and Franceska Lorch.

Bennye and Harold had one daughter, Franceska Lorch Loeb "Frisky." Franceska married Melvin Thomas Roland, the son of Jesse and Flora Roland and they settled in Morton in 1972.

Their children Harold Melvin "Hal" married Bobbie Sue Ditcharo Apr. 30, 1983. They reside in Harvey, LA. Franceska Kyle resides in Bellevue, WA. Alben David resides in Cincinnati, OH. Brian Jess resides in Morton. Harold Loeb died and is buried in Floral Hills Cemetery in Pearl, MS.

"Ben" Crye survived Betty who died Sep. 21, 1927 and a second wife, Miss Cooper, who died a few weeks of their marriage. He was survived by his third wife, Ida Moore Crye. He died Mar. 16, 1960. He and Betty are buried at Brazwell Cemetery in the Pulaski Community on Morton-Marathon Road. Ida died in 1972.

CRUDUP, Arthur "Big Boy" Crudup was born Aug. 24, 1905, in Forest, MS, on Hwy. 21 North. His mother was Minnie Crudup; his father was Rev. Tools. His siblings were: Jessie Mae Whittington, Pocahontas Whittington, Marie Tools, Willow Tools and Tim Williams.

Big Boy Crudup, 1905-1974. Great Mississippi bluesman.

As a young boy Arthur attended the Union Grove Church where he sang in the choir and with the quartets at age 10. He attended the Scott County Training School through the fourth grade.

His family moved to Indianapolis, IN in 1916 to work. He returned to Forest, MS, in 1926 to work at Lackey Lumber Co. He married Nemie Harper Apr. 13, 1929 and moved to the Belzoni/Clarksdale area to sharecrop in the 1930s. He later returned to Forest around 1938 and continued to work with the lumber company.

Early in 1939 his older second cousin, Malcolm Banks, gave him a black guitar trimmed in white (his first guitar) with the promise that Arthur would buy strings for it. That same day Arthur and Hubbard Neal Glover went to the W.F. Vance Drug Store on Main Street Forest and bought four strings. That same day Arthur

started teaching himself how to play. He started playing in Juke-Joints and House-Parties.

In 1939, less than a year after starting to play, Arthur recorded his first records, Coal Black Mare/Black Pony Blues, Death Valley Blues and If I Get Lucky. Lester and the RCA Co. gave him the nickname "Big Boy" and put it on the label of his first record. The record was played on jukeboxes all over the country and Big Boy was in high demand, recording and writing well over 40 records from 1939-74.

In 1942 he became one of the first blues singers to record with an electric guitar. He recorded and wrote famous songs like: Hound Dog, Blue Suede Shoes, Younder's Wall, That's all Right Mama, Dust My Broom and See See Rider, but received very little royalty payments. He was supposed to receive 35 percent.

His work was recorded by Elton John, Elvis Presley, Marty Robbins, B.B. King, Rod Stewart, Elmore James, James "Son" Thomas and Carl Perkins.

In between his recordings he bought a bus and carried seasonal migrant farm workers from state to state. He toured Europe, the U.S. and Australia before his death in March 1974 in Virginia. He and his mother are buried in Delray Beach, FL, where he was living with his wife and 13 children.

Arthur's whole children include: Percy Lee Crudup, Fred Allen Crudup, Johnnie Lee Crudup, Jonas Crudup, James Arthur Crudup Jr. and Angie Dale Crudup. His other children are: Hattie Ruth Crudup, Joe Willie Crudup, Annie Pearl Crudup and George Allen Crudup.

Here is a short list of some of "Big Boy's" records: Roebuck Man, I'm Gonna Dig Myself a Hole, Big Boy, Rock Me Mama, If I Get Lucky, Coal Back Mare/Black Pony Blues, Death Valley Blues, Look On Yonder's Wall, So Glad You're Mine, Who's Been Fooling You, Keep Your Arms Around Me, That's Alright Mama, My Baby Left Me, She's Gone, Going Back to Georgia, Mean Old Frisco (Trip), Harping On It, Crudup's Mood's, The Father of Rock and Roll, Ethel Mae, Mean Old Frisco Blues, Dust My Broom, Cool Disposition, You Ain't Nothing But a Hound Dog, Pearl Harbor Blues and Blue Suede Shoes.

CUPIT, James Alfred Cupit Sr., a Franklin County, MS, native and Doris Mae (Perkins) Cupit, a Neshoba County, MS, native came to make Forest, MS, home in 1960.

The couple came from Bude, MS, with their son, James Alfred Cupit Jr. (b. Sep. 16, 1959). The Cupits came to Forest and went to work with "Gaddis Industries."

James A. Cupit Sr. and Doris Cupit.

James Sr. served four years in the Army. He served in the Korean Conflict 1950-54.

Doris graduated from Walnut Grove High School. She worked at Lackey Hospital in For-

est from 1969-85. She then went to work at the Scott County Health Dept. from 1985-98.

James and Doris were married in Decatur, MS. They moved to Jackson for a year and a half before coming to Forest. James Jr. was born in Union while they were living in Jackson.

Their daughter, Charlotte Ann (Cupit) Harris, was born in Forest. Charlotte is the mother of three daughters: Jessica Ann Harris (b. Jun. 26, 1983), Janet Elizabeth Harris (b. Dec. 14, 1989) and Kristen Abigail Harris (b. Jun. 15, 1997).

James Jr. is the father of two daughters, Carrie Nicole Cupit (b. Oct. 8, 1987) and Lindsay Leigh (b. Nov. 11, 1998).

James Sr. is the son of Cyrus Henry Cupit and Anna Wallace of Bude, MS. Doris is the daughter of John Henry "Bud" Perkins and Lena Pearl Barrett of Walnut Grove, MS.

The Cupits live in the Ringgold Community and are active members of Ephesus Baptist Church where James is a deacon and Doris sings in the choir.

DAVENPORT, Lancelot Davenport was born in Werowocomoco, England in 1599 and had at least one son, Martin Davenport (b. 1625 in England). Martin sailed to Virginia in the 1600 and died there.

L.-R: Caroline A. Thomas, Wilson A. Davenport, Sarah Eliza Rushing

L.-R. Top: Bessie Mae Davenport, Lucy Caroline Davenport and Jessie Mildred Davenport. Second Row: Wilson A. Davenport, Sarah Eliza Rushing, Jessie M. Pearson, Lucy Emmy Waggoner, Rushing and Pearson. Third Row: Lonnie Leroy Davenport, Emmit Nathan Davenport, William Miley Davenport and Mary Elizabeth Davenport

Martia's son, Davis Davenport, was born in King William County, VA, before 1680 and died there before 1735. Wife unknown, but had three children: Martin Davenport married Dorothy, Thomas Davenport and Richard Davenport.

Davis's son Thomas Davenport was born in King William County, VA in September 1775. Wife unknown. They had seven children: James Davenport (md. Jane Hart), Thomas Davenport (md. Jane), Henry Davenport (md. Ann), Julius Davenport, William Davenport (md. Sallie Holt), Stephen Davenport and Drucilla Davenport. They were all born in Halifax County, VA.

Thomas's son James Davenport was born in Halifax County, VA about 1742 and died in 1823. He fought in the Revolution War. Married Jane E. "Jincey" Hart Dec. 2, 1796. Jane was born about 1779 and died Dec. 28, 1849. James and Jane had six children: (1) Wilson Davenport married twice, first Polly Lowry and second, Jane Gooby; (2) Elizabeth T. "Eliza" Davenport married Charles Mayse or Mayes; (3) James H. Davenport married first, Margaret Loftis and second, Reany Vanghan; (4) Joseph A. Davenport married Lucy A. Carter; (5) Thomas T. Davenport; (6) Benjamin F. Davenport married Jane. The first four children married in Halifax County, VA.

James's son, Wilson Davenport, was born 1799 in Halifax County, VA and died about 1850 in Scott County, MS. He married first, Polly Lowry on Jan. 17, 1820 and had two children, R.H. Davenport (md. Martha J.) and a female (name unknown). Married second, Jane Gooby on Jul. 5, 1830 and had three children: Wilson A. Davenport (md. Carolina A. Thomas), Sarah J. Davenport (md. Thomas Jefferson Patrick) and Mary B. Davenport. All born in Virginia.

Wilson's son, Wilson A. Davenport (b. 1833 in Virginia) md. in 1849 in Scott County, MS to Caroline A. Thomas (b. 1831 in South Carolina). They had five children: Nancy "Nan" Davenport (md. L.A. Searcy in Scott County); John Wilson Davenport (md. Sarah Eliza Rushing in Scott County); Sarah Davenport; Robert Davenport; and Mary Davenport.

Wilson A.'s son, John Wilson Davenport (b. Jul. 12, 1861) md. Jan. 13, 1880 in Beach, Scott County, MS to Sarah Eliza Rushing (b. Aug. 27, 1863, Springfield, Scott County MS). John died Jul. 26, 1934 and Sarah died Dec. 21, 1933, both in Jackson, Hinds County, MS. They had nine children:

1) Leona Davenport died young.

2) Lucy Caroline Davenport married Bennett Compton Ponder; four boys and three girls.

3) Bessie Mae Davenport married John Wesley Evans; four boys and two girls.

4) Jessie Mildred Davenport married Albert Spencer Woods; seven boys and five girls.

5) Mary Elizabeth "Mollie" Davenport married first, Mr. Lee, one girl; married second, Ernest B. Fewell July 28, no children.

6) William Miley "Bill" Davenport married Clara Johana Schmalz in Louisiana; four daughters.

7) Lonnie Leroy Davenport married first, Bonice Haley, children one boy, one girl; married second, Gladis, no children.

8) Emmitt Nathan Davenport married Mrs. Sladen; one stepson.

Most of the children were born and married in Scott County and some are buried there.

John Wilson's daughter, Bessie Mae Davenport (b. Sep. 5, 1885) married Sep. 6, 1903 to John Wesley Evans (b. Oct. 25, 1882). His parents are Joseph Tillman Evans and Mary Francis Patrick. Bessie and John were born and attended the same school and married in Beach, Scott County, MS. John died Mar. 20, 1960, 12 days before Bessie died Apr. 1, 1960. They are buried in Richland Cemetery, Rankin County. They had six children (five were born in Morton and one in Rankin County):

1) Louvenia Wydell Evans married William Henry Wilson, children: four boys and one girl.

2) Herman Roscoe Evans married Helen Maderia Jones, no children.

3) Percy Leroy Evans married Lola Belle Hutson, one son.

4) Sally Ruth Evans married first, Gus Wansley Dear, one son. Married second, Bill Hardy McAlpin, no children.

5) James William Evans married Laverne Odam, one daughter.

6) J.T. Evans married Helen Hazel Steverson (Loveless), one stepson.

DAVIS-LOPER, In 1900, Tommy Davis met Lula Loper of Conehatta, MS. Lula was teaching school in a Newton County community known as Garlandsville. Tommy was a successful farmer. They married and lived with his parents until they moved to Scott County near Lake, MS. This couple raised seven children. Their names in order of birth were

Tommy and Lula Davis

Earl, Loyce, Fred, Frank, Perry, Wynona and Marjorie. The whole family became members of Good Hope Baptist Church.

Mrs. Davis taught school at Good Hope for years. She and her children walked three miles to school through the woods. When it rained or snowed, Papa Davis would hook up the buggy and drive them to school.

Mr. Davis was a Justice of the Peace for many years. Marjorie remembers people coming to their house on occasion to ask Mr. Davis to perform their marriage ceremony.

Lula Davis was well known as a local artist. She loved to create oil paintings on any scrap piece of wood, syrup can lids, card board, etc. that she could find. Many people in the community still have the hand-painted pictures that she gave them for graduations, weddings, anniversaries and many other occasions.

Frank, Perry, Wynona and Marjorie all finished college and became school teachers. Earl became a successful business man. Loyce ran a gasoline station in Lake. Fred stayed home to help Papa Davis on the farm and also served in the Army.

DAY, Romulous W. Day was living with his parents, Orlton Day and Elizabeth Bullock, during the 1850 Newton County federal census. "Rum" was 20 years old. Rum married Mary Brewer around 1852 and moved to Scott County before the 1860 federal census. They were living close to Mary's parents, Wyche Brewer and Flora McPherson.

Rum served as a private in the Confederate 11th Mississippi Calvary, Co. K. He enlisted Dec. 20, 1863 in Newton, MS for a period of three years. On the muster roll dated from Oct. 6, 1863 to Apr. 30, 1864, he was absent without leave since Apr. 14, 1864. Since Rum's wife, Mary, died during the Civil War he may have returned home to bury her or house their children with relatives. He returned to his unit by the time of the muster roll dated July and August 1864.

Rum and Mary had four children: Melvina Day was born about 1852 and married Phineas E. Bailey. Fleta Irene Day (b. Jul. 18, 1856) married James M. Smith on Oct. 15, 1879 in Scott County. Fleta and James are both buried in the Neshoba Baptist Church Cemetery in Neshoba County. Almanza Helen Day was born Nov. 25, 1857 and married George W. Underwood on Dec. 3, 1879 in Leake County. Almanza died Aug. 24, 1940 and is buried in the Cude Cemetery in Conroe, TX. Mary Day was born about 1861.

Rum was still living in Scott County during the 1870 federal census. By this time he had remarried and had two more children. His wife's name was Elizabeth and their children were William or Aldon (b. 1867) and Sarah (b. 1869).

Rum was widowed again by the time the 1880 Scott County census was taken. Rum later married at least two more times. He next married Mrs. N.A. Pinkston on Nov. 27, 1880 in Scott County and next to M.S. Evans on Nov. 29, 1895 in Newton County.

Rum was thrown from his buggy by a runaway mule near Philadelphia, MS on Jul. 30, 1908. He suffered a broken leg and internal injuries. Rum died on Aug. 5, 1908 from these injuries. He is buried in the Neshoba Baptist Church Cemetery in Neshoba County next to his daughter, Fleta Smith.

DEARMAN, William Abner Dearman purchased farm and timber property near the Clarksburg Community in the late 1880s. He and his wife, Leta Jane Hitt Dearman, were both children of Baptist Ministers. Even though not blood related they were reared in the same home as stepbrother and sister. They married in 1870 and were the parents of nine children. Five generations of Dearmans lived in Scott County. Four daughters: Alice Gresham, Mattie Noblin, Emma Nordan and Dolly Noblin McNeill married Scott Countians and lived in Forest all of their married lives. Jim remained on the original property as a planter, Cleveland moved to Tampa, FL and pursued a career in real estate. Bob, Sol and Henry were partners in the timber and cross tie business. Bob was also in insurance. Henry enjoyed music and sang in a quartet that regularly participated in Gospel music. He also served as tax assessor. Sol owned a farm north of Forest and engaged in the construction of houses in Forest.

William Abner and Leta Jane Dearman - 1915

Sol married Eula Nordan and Eula's brother, John Nordan, married Sol's sister, Emma Dearman. The five double first cousins: Myrtice, Marjorie, Elise, Bill Dearman and Delois Nordan always had a great time explaining their "close family ties."

The youngest of the Dearman children was always called Miss Dolly. She was a businesswoman and very active in civic affairs. She and her first husband, Bob Noblin, owned and operated Noblin's Hardware until his death. Miss Dolly continued this operation for many years before marrying Hugh McNeill, Manager. After his death she sold the business and opened a florist and gift shop which she operated until selling it to her niece, Elise Dearman Mapp and her husband, Marcus Mapp, in 1954. The Mapps now reside in Monroe, LA.

While a member of The Fortnightly Club, Miss Dolly organized La Petite Fortnightly Club. Her niece, Myrtice Doty served as charter president and another niece, Elise Mapp was a member. It was under the chairmanship of Miss Dolly that the Fortnightly Club sponsored Forest's first Miss Hospitality.

Myrtice Dearman Doty taught Speech both in the Forest schools and privately until her retirement. She still resides in Forest. Marjorie Dearman began her teaching career in the Morton Schools and then taught in Gulfport until her retirement. She died in 1985.

Elise and Marcus Mapp wrote and published a family cook book in 1980 that is entitled "Treasure Tree." It is composed primarily of family recipes inclusive of three generations. One of their first autograph parties was in Forest at the "Calico Corner."

Bill Dearman was president of Southern Lumber Company, president of the Mississippi Lumber Manufacturer's Association, board member of the Pearl River Valley Water Supply District and on the Board of the Community Bank in Forest. He was a Veteran of WWII having served in the South Pacific. He lived in Forest following retirement until his death in 1998. His wife, Edna Earl Dearman, still resides in Forest.

DENSON, Shadrach James Denson was born Apr. 23, 1800, in Anson County, NC to Shadrach Denson and Jane Conner. In 1818 his family removed to Washington County, MS Territory where they settled among a large contingent of relatives and friends from Anson County.

Of particular interest to the young Shadrach James Denson was Alethia Chambers, eldest daughter of Josiah Chambers and Christian Robinson, whom he married Aug. 11, 1820.

About 1827 the Denson and Chambers clans migrated to central Mississippi, most settling in the soon-to-be formed Rankin County. The exception being Shadrach and Jane Denson who removed to Bond County, IL. They would later remove to Houston County, TX where they both died in the 1840s.

While in Rankin County Shadrach James Denson and his wife helped organize the Mt. Pisgah Baptist Church, where he served as its first clerk. In 1834 they moved Scott County, settling on the Coffee Bogue. In 1838, Shadrach J. Denson helped establish Jerusalem Baptist Church now Ludlow Baptist Church.

It was in Scott County that Shadrach J. Denson acquired his first slaves. In 1850 he operated an 800-acre farm valued at $3,400, which was worked by 25 slaves. Along with his farming enterprises, Shadrach J. Denson established the first store in Ludlow. He was later joined in business by two of his sons-in-law, George W. McCabe and John Lane Smith.

From 1836 until 1840, Shadrach James Denson served as president of the Scott County Board of Police (i.e. Board of Supervisors). While serving in this capacity he oversaw the founding of the then county seat of Hillsboro. Other offices held were justice of the peace and probate judge, hence, his being called "Judge Denson." In the 1840s he was appointed by the governor as commissioner to oversee construction of the railroad from Jackson to Brandon.

In 1854 the Democratic Party was divided over the "Know-Nothing Question." The seat of state senator for Leake and Madison counties was vacant and due to the great uproar caused by this division, no candidate could be found to satisfy both factions of the party. A joint senatorial meeting was held at Ludlow and Shadrach J. Denson was chosen as the Democratic candidate. Shadrach J. Denson served with distinction from 1856 until 1859, refusing re-nomination at the expiration of his term.

In early 1860 Alethia Chambers Denson suffered a stroke and died on February 6 at their home on the Coffee Bogue. In that year S.J. Denson was ordained to the full ministry, serving the church in that capacity until his death. During the Civil War he was pastor of the Hayes Creek Baptist near Harperville.

It has always been maintained in the family that Shadrach J. Denson met the arch-villain and arsonist, Gen. William T. Sherman while he was in the area of Ludlow, camping on the grounds of S.J. Denson's home. At Ludlow, on hearing that the invading forces were in route, preparations were made to save what could be. Silverware was buried and the livestock was driven into the swamp. Shadrach J. Denson lost much of his cotton, which was burned by the Yankees.

Shadrach J. Denson was married twice after the death of Alethia (Chambers) Denson. His second wife was a widow, Eveline (Eley) Perry, who died in 1868. Going blind in the latter part of that year, Shadrach J. Denson found that he needed someone to care for him in his declining years. In 1871 he was married to Martha Frances (Lynn) Lyon, who survived him.

During the 18 years between 1870 and his death, Shadrach J. Denson retired from active farming and devoted his life to the ministry. Although he maintained his home at Ludlow, he also resided in Leake County, near the home of his youngest son, Dr. James N. Denson, in Pensacola (now Tuscola). He died Jan. 14, 1888, at his home on the Coffee Bogue at the age of 87 years, eight months and 21 days. He was interred in the Ludlow Cemetery between his first two wives.

Shadrach James Denson and Alethia Chambers were the parents of 10 children: William Howard Denson (b. Dec. 18, 1822, d. Aug. 20, 1892) md. Jane Elizabeth Jones; Josiah Conner Denson (b. Jan. 24, 1825, d. Jul. 14, 1899) md. Harriet Burnham Small; Thomas Jefferson Denson (b. 1826, d. 1897) md. first, Sarah L. Smith and second, Mary Mildred Ledbetter; Obedience Julia Denson (b. 1828, d. before January 1859) md. George W. McCabe; Mary Denson (b. Mar. 4, 1830, d. Jan. 6, 1876) md. John Lane Smith; Alethia A. Denson (b. Feb. 28, 1831, d. Mar. 3, 1870) md. Joseph Luther Denson; Susan E. Denson (b. 1832, d. 1874) md. Milton Henry Burks; Jane Henrietta Denson (b. February 1834) md. James Henry Lee; James Nathaniel Denson (b. Jun. 17, 1836, d. Mar. 20, 1907) md. Mary Foster Lee; Margaret A.H. Denson (b. 1839, d. 1906) md. first, Francis C. Smith Jr. and second, William Pagan Gill.

DENSON, Shadrack "Shade" Denson was the son of Rev. William Jordan Denson and his wife, Amelia Lyles Denson. Rev. Denson was elected to Mississippi Legislature in 1860 and served one term. Several years before the war, Rev. Denson served pastorates in Scott, Madison, Rankin and Hinds counties. He organized a Baptist association composed of these counties. He also served as president of the Board of Trustees of Mississippi College. In Scott County, he organized and served as pastor of Jerusalem Baptist Church at Ludlow. The church was later named Ludlow Baptist Church. In 1873, Rev. Denson decided he was too old and feeble to continue his ministry. On the day that he preached his farewell sermon at Jerusalem Church, his horse ran away with him and after going downhill from front of the church, he was thrown from his buggy and killed instantly. He was buried at Old Pisgah Cemetery. Rev. Denson and wife Amelia Lyle had three boys: Shade, William L. Shadrack and Jessie Rufus Denson.

Shadrack married Bessie Webb and they had 13 children. Their oldest son, William Henry, married Dovie Peagler and they had seven children: Henry and Dovie lived to celebrate their 50th wedding anniversary; oldest daughter, Katherine md. Ray Massey; Alma Evangeline md. Leroy Bustin; William James md. Mary Craig; the fourth child, D.Q., md. Janie Sumrall; Maggie Jean md. Royce Lindsey; Annie Mae md. Wayne Andrews; the seventh child, Yvonne "Bonnie," md. Truitt Calhoun.

Jim, Shadrack's second son, md. Vada Thompson and had two children. Charlie Ray md. Arletha Franklin and Jack Lee md. a Kyzar. Vonette md. Michael Latham and their last child, Mayola, md. Eugene Burnham.

Kate, Shadrack's third child, md. Marion Peagler. Kate and Marion had two children, Wayne and Katie Ethel. Wayne md. Marie Calcote and Katie Ethel md. W.J. Measels. The fourth child, Jennie, md. Earnest Crapps and they had five children: Charlie, Otis, Haywood, Ernestine and Billy. Charlie md. Helen Measels. Otis md. Marie Armstrong. Haywood md. Judy Beth Walsh. Ernestine md. Kenneth Pigg. Billy md. Glenda Presley and later md. Ann Allen. Nannie md. Asher Warren Davis and they had four children: Bessie Lee md. G.D. Barrow; Asher Warren "Junior" md. Betty; L.J. md. Charlene Horn; and Nannie Ruth "Ruthie" md. Douglas Brown. After his death, she married Robert J. Kockovich. Erie md. J.C. Robinson. Nethel md. James Monroe Warren and they had two children: Robert and Hilda Jean. Robert md. Ellie Mae Phillips and Hilda Jean md. James

Beasley. Flora, the eighth child of Shadrack, md. Jesse Roland. They had three children: Jimmy, Melvin and Shirley. Jimmy md. Nancy Nutt; Melvin md. Frisky Loeb and Shirley md. Chester Sawyer.

David married Thelma Simmons and they had seven children: Dallas, Marty, Sotty, Dorothy, Barnie, David and Daphine. S.J. married Arlene Renfroe and they had five children: Mary Merle, Raymond, Don, Larry and Pauline. Ollie married Emma Maude "Sue" Stewart and they were the parents of Rick and Brenda. Rick married Jean Holloway and Brenda married Wayne Melohn.

Shadrack and Bessie Denson have over 250 descendants who live in Mississippi, Tennessee, Texas, North Carolina, Louisiana, Alabama, Oregon and Alaska. They are engaged in 43 different occupations and professions. How proud they would be today to learn of their descendants' contribution and dedication to the Denson Family. We salute the future generation and challenge them to love their relatives and to uphold the Denson name!

DENSON-WARREN, Nethel Lou Denson was born Jun. 10, 1911 and spent all her life in and around Scott County, MS. Nethel and Monroe were married in 1934. They celebrated their 50th wedding anniversary at Roosevelt State Park in 1984. Family and friends from as far away as Illinois and the Mississippi Gulf Coast honored them. It was a proud day and a testament of the strength of their marriage. What God had joined together would only be separated by death, which sadly came for Nethel two years later. The Lord called her home on Mother's Day 1986.

Nethel became a homemaker upon marrying and gave birth to two children. Her son, Robert Hulon Warren, was born in 1936, while her daughter, Hilda Jean, was born in 1940. Nethel continued raising her family during WWII and after that took on an additional job in Morton as a Poultry Plant worker. Although Nethel and Monroe lived in Morton most of their life, they both enjoyed traveling. When their son, Robert, was at Greenville Air Force Base, they visited him. They would only stay for a day or two at a time as "the garden" was sure to need something picked or weeded.

When Robert was stationed in Austin, TX, they flew to visit him. While there, they toured President Lyndon Johnson's ranch. They also made a trip to Shreveport to visit their daughter, Jean, who had married an airman in the USAF. Nethel and Monroe remained at home in Morton while the children kept passing through to assignments in Japan, Germany, Vietnam, Arkansas, Louisiana, South Carolina, Texas, Illinois, Nebraska and Biloxi, MS.

Their son, Robert Hulon, married Ellie Mae Phillips of Polkville, MS. They have two children. His son, James Robert Warren, lives in Petal, MS, with his wife Kathleen, their three children: Matthew, Kristen and Russell. His daughter, Sherri, lives in D'Iberville, MS, with her husband, Scott Seymour. They have two daughters, Jerika and Kelli. After retirement with the U.S. Air Force, Robert and Ellie Mae reside in Biloxi, MS.

Their daughter, Hilda Jean and her husband, James G. Beasley, Jr. live in Biloxi, MS. Jean is employed in Gulfport with Mississippi Veteran's Administration Hospital. Jean has two children: James G. III who is married to Stephanie Wood and they reside with their daughter, Emily Anne, in Carbondale, IL. Jean's daughter, Sonya LuAnn, is married to Andrew Moore and they live in Sicily with their two children, Joshua and Carli.

Nethel's children and grandchildren are far-flung but they know about her. Nethel and Monroe never met anybody they didn't like and no one has to look past them for a role model.

DENSON, Flora Grace Denson was born on Sep. 2, 1913 in Branch, MS. Her parents were Shadrack and Bessie Webb Denson. She grew up in Branch during the depression years on a farm. She remembers having to walk to school in bad weather.

In 1932, she met and married Jesse Roland of the Clifton Community. They moved to Clifton on a farm to live with his mother. His father had recently passed away. Jesse farmed and held various other jobs including driving a school wagon and being a barber in Hillsboro to supplement their income. In 1942, they moved to Branch. In Branch, Jesse farmed and worked at the local saw mill in the winter. In the late 1940s, they moved to Morton. In the early 1950s, Jesse and Flora went to work for the Morton School System. They have three children.

James L. Roland was born on Mar. 27, 1933 in Clifton, MS. He married Nancy Nutt in 1958 and they have two children. Tammie Ann Roland (b. Nov. 6, 1959) is married to Tim Taber and they have two children, Tyler and Taryn. Tim Roland (b. Sep. 8, 1964) and his wife Stephanie have two children, James and Jacob. Both Tammie and Tim live in Tupelo, MS with their families. Jimmy lives in Morton, MS.

Melvin T. Roland (b. Aug. 3, 1937 in Clifton, MS) married Franceska Loeb on Jul. 5, 1957 and they live in Morton, MS. They have four children: (1) Harold Melvin "Hal" Roland (b. May 16, 1958) married Bobbie Ditcharo in 1983 and they live in New Orleans, LA. (2) Franceska Kyle Roland (b. Mar. 17, 1961) now lives in Seattle, WA. (3) Alben David Roland (b. Jan. 8, 1966) lives in Cincinnati, OH. Brian Jess Roland (b. Nov. 10, 1970) lives in Morton, MS.

Shirley Fay Roland (b. Oct. 31, 1941 in Hillsboro, MS) married James C. Sawyer Jr. in 1959 and now lives in Morton, MS. They have two children and one grandchild. Tommy Ray Sawyer (b. Oct. 31, 1960 in Jackson, MS) married Stephanie Johnson of Monroe, LA in 1988 and they live in Cropwell, AL. Suzanne Sawyer (b. May 12, 1963 in Jackson, MS) married Ray Meador of Forest, MS in 1988 and they have one child, Bryan. They live in Forest, MS.

Jesse retired in 1961 from the Morton School System due to ill health and Flora retired a few years later. Jesse died in 1968 and is buried in the Morton Cemetery. Flora now resides in the Mississippi Care Center in Morton, MS.

DENSON, James Nathaniel Denson, youngest son of Shadrach J. Denson and Alethia Chambers, was born in Scott County Jun. 17, 1836.

Hs early education was obtained at the male academy at Brandon, MS.

He began his professional life as a farmer, owning in 1859 four slaves and some 320 acres in Scott County. Prior to the Civil War he studied medicine under his elder brother, Dr. Josiah C. Denson. Following his return from the war he continued his studies at the University of Louisiana during the 1869-70 term, obtaining his medical license in 1882.

On Nov. 23, 1856, he was married to Mary Foster Lee, youngest daughter of Henry Bryant Lee and Margaret Bell Lee. The Lee family had only recently removed from Stewart County, GA.

During the Civil War he served in Co. F, 36th Regt., Mississippi Infantry as captain and Regimental ACS. He saw action at Vicksburg, where he was taken prisoner. His unit surrendered on Apr. 9, 1865 and he was interred at Ft. Massachusetts on Ship Island. From 1888-1890, he served as president of the Leake County Veterans Association.

In 1875 he purchased a large plantation in Leake County. In 1882 he made plans to sell this and move to Harperville. However, these plans were thwarted when the family's home burned in November 1883. James N. Denson represented Leake County in the Mississippi State House of Representatives from 1874 until 1878. He also served for

James Denson

many years as a delegate to the Harmony Association and the Mississippi Baptist Convention

Mary Foster (Lee) Denson died of cancer on Dec. 21, 1895 and her widower retired from farming and moved back to Ludlow. He resided with his brother-in-law, Thomas Hugh Lee and headquartered his medical practice at Lee's store.

He co-authored a history of Jerusalem (Ludlow) Baptist Church and served as a member of the Board of Trustees of Ludlow High School, as well as being its secretary-treasurer. James Nathaniel Denson died on Mar. 20 1908.

Children of James Nathaniel Denson and Mary Foster Lee:

1) Ida Jane Denson (b. Feb. 27, 1859, d. Dec. 6, 1936) md. Colon McMurphy;

2) James Oscar Denson (b. Feb. 13, 1862, d. Apr. 21, 1919) md. Dor Rebecca Blankinship;

3) John Denson (b. 1864, d. 1874);

4) Robert Lee Denson (b. Sep. 6, 1866, d. Jun. 18, 1947) md. Frances Olean Ethridge;

5) Richard Burr Denson (b. Apr. 2, 1869, d. Jun. 11, 1953) md. first, Effie Irean Hartness and second, Katherine Claire Denson;

6) Mary Ruth Denson (b. Mar. 28, 1871, d. Feb. 3, 1897) md. William Joseph McMurphy;

7) Josiah Hunter Denson (b. Nov. 3, 1873, d. Sep. 10, 1961) md. Phenie Estelle Ethridge;

8) Denson (b. 1875, d. 1875);

9) Claude Denson (b. Aug. 8, 1877, d. Apr. 30, 1879);

10) Denson (b. ca. 1881, d. ca. 1881);

11) Charles Hackett Denson (b. Aug. 26, 1883, d. Feb. 23, 1963) md. Bera Elizabeth Waggoner.

DENSON, Josiah Conner Denson, MD, second son of Shadrach James Denson and Alethia Chambers, was born in Washington County, AL Jan. 24, 1825. He was named for his maternal grandfather, Josiah Chambers and the family of his paternal grandmother. His wife was Harriet Burnham, daughter of Reddoch Small and Tamer E. Burnham. She was a kinswoman of his brother's wife, Jane Elizabeth Jones.

During his professional life he was a medical doctor, farmer and minister. His name first appears in the tax records of Scott County in 1846, when he paid on a Poll Tax. Four years later he was the owner of five slaves. In 1859 his wife was taxed on four of those slaves and he a watch and one pleasure carriage, valued at $150. In that same year Josiah C. Denson had a large two-story home built which was very similar to that of his father and his brother-in-law, John L. Smith. The home was still standing in the 1930s and belonged to the Stone family. He owned in 1870 a 364 acre farm, 129 acres of which was improved, valued at $830. The total value of farm products for that year was $1,300 (1870 US Census, Agriculture Schedule, Scott County, MS, p. 5, line 24).

Sometime after January 1895, Dr. Josiah C. and Harriet B. Denson moved, along with many of their kinsmen, to Franklin Par., LA. He died there in 1899 and she five years later.

Children of Josiah Conner Denson and Harriet Burnham Small: (1) Alethia Jane Denson (b. Sep. 21, 1848, d. Jul. 17, 1933) md. Thomas Hugh Lee; (2) Thomas J. Denson (b. Jul. 9, 1850, d. Nov. 13, 1920) md. Nannie Kuhn; (3) Shadrach James Denson (b. Jun. 25, 1852, d. Feb. 29, 1929); (4) Julia Guitella Denson (b. 1854) md. Absalom A. Ledbetter; (5) Josiah Buchanan Denson (b. Jan. 22, 1856, d. Mar. 19, 1930) married first, Mary Elizabeth Smith and second, Margaret Teresa Lee; (6) Newton Denson, b. 1857; (7) John Lane Denson (b. 1860, d. 1916) md. Geneva E. Latham; (8) William Alvin Denson (b. 1866, d. aft. 1906) md. Margaret _.

DENSON, Joseph Luther Denson was born Nov. 12, 1820 in Sumter County, SC to Joseph Denson and Martha A. Compton. By 1841 the family of Joseph Denson Sr. had settled in Scott County, MS. In 1850 Joseph L. Denson married Alethia A. Denson who was born 28 Feb. 1803 to his first cousin, Shadrach James Denson

Soon after settling in Scott County, Joseph L. Denson proved himself to be a successful farmer. In 1843 he was the owner of six slaves and by 1860 that number had risen to 16. Three of these slaves had been given to his wife by her father in 1854. In 1860, both his personal and real estates were valued at over $15,000 each.

During the Civil War, Joseph L. Denson served as a private in Co. G, 28th Regt., Mississippi Cavalry. Seeing action until becoming ill, he returned home on Jan. 17, 1864 for the duration of the war.

Following the Civil War, the family removed to Izard County, AR where Alethia Denson died Mar. 3, 1870. Joseph L. Denson returned to Scott County and was married in

1871 to a widow, Mary Frances (Frazier) Glaze. He died in Scott County on Mar. 23, 1893 and was buried in Contrell Cemetery.

Children of Joseph Luther Denson and Alethia A. Denson: (l) Eugenia Whitney Denson (b. Nov. 16, 1850, d. Jan. 27, 1893) md. first, James A. Keahey and second, James Madison Thomas; (2) Annie J. Denson (b. Mar. 28, 1852, d. ca. 1884) md. Samuel L. Yarrell; (3) Junius Judson Denson (b. Nov. 12, 1853, d. Dec. 5, 1904) md. Mary Rebecca White; (4) Betty Dulaney Denson (b. Jan. 5, 1856, d. Mar. 20, 1913) md. Thomas Johnson; (5) Edwin Clinton Denson (b. Oct. 31, 1857, d. Jan. 28, 1928) md. first, Mary Elizabeth Johnson and second, Martha Eliza Norton; (6) Martha Theodosia Denson (b. Jul. 18, 1859, d. Jun. 30, 1940) md. Wiley Warren White; (7) Lura E. Denson (b. Nov. 6, 1862, d. Jan. 6, 1953) md. James L. Johnson.

DENSON, Thomas Jefferson Denson, third son of Shadrach James Denson and Alethia Chambers, was born 1826 in Washington County, AL. Being primarily a farmer by profession, his name first appears in the tax records of Scott County in 1847. The following year he was married to 14-year-old Sarah L. Smith, a daughter of Francis C. Smith. Her brothers, John Lane Smith and Frances C. Smith Jr., married his sisters, Mary and Margaret, respectively. Their only child was born and died within a year of their marriage. She died two years later.

Three years after the death of his first wife, Thomas J. Denson was married to Mary Mildred Ledbetter, daughter of William Ledbetter and Cassandra Black. By the end of the 1850s, Thomas and Mary Denson owned a 600-acre farm valued at $2,500, a pleasure carriage and a store.

Thomas J. Denson was appointed on Aug. 19, 1845, Lieutenant of Co. A (or 1), 41st Regt. State Militia, Scott County. During the Civil War he served as captain in Co. F, 36th Regt., Mississippi Infantry, serving until the close of the war.

After his return Thomas J. Denson ran, unsuccessfully, for sheriff of Scott County. He also served on the Democratic Executive Committee in 1873. By 1880 he had moved his family to Leake County and later to Jasper County where both he and his wife are buried.

Children of Thomas Jefferson Denson and Sarah L. Smith: (1) Mary Elizabeth Denson (b. Jan. 19, 1847, d. Oct. 18, 1848).

Children of Thomas Jefferson Denson and Mary Mildred Ledbetter: (2) William Shadrach Denson (b. 1857, d. before 1870); (3) Leonidas Lycurgus Denson (b. Aug. 21, 1861, d. Nov. 9, 1932) md. Emma Jane Blankinship; (4) Ernest Absalom Denson (b. Jan. 3, 1864, d. Oct. 2, 1929) md. Hannah Jane Thigpen; (5) Teresa C. Denson (b. 1866, d. after 1910) md. G. Lee Kropp; (6) Wellington J. Denson (b. 1868, d. after 1880); (7) John Lane Denson (b. May 22, 1871, d. May 18, 1942) md. Eula Elizabeth Blankinship; (8) Thomas J. Denson (b. April 1875) md. Della Horn; (9) Joseph Edna Denson (b. Dec. 22, 1878, d. Mar. 7, 1880).

DENSON, William Howard Denson, eldest son of Shadrach James Denson and Alethia Chambers, was born in Washington County, AL Dec. 18, 1822. He was primarily a farmer by profes-

sion owning prior to the Civil War a successful 360 acre farm valued at $5,402 which was worked by eight slaves. He served for many years as a justice of the peace for Scott County.

His wife was Jane Elizabeth Jones, daughter of James R. Jones and Margaret Burnham, of Madison County, MS, whom he married about 1844. They were the parents of 14 children.

During the War Between the States he served as postmaster, as well as serving in the Confederate Cavalry, in Co. K, 2nd Mississippi Cavalry and later Co. D, 3rd Regt. Cavalry, Mississippi State troops.

Following the Civil War, William Howard Denson again became a prosperous planter. He died at Ludlow Aug. 20, 1892. His widow survived him until 1910.

Children of William Howard Denson and Jane Elizabeth Jones: (1) James William Denson (b. Jun. 27, 1845, d. Nov. 2, 1909) md. Emma Elizabeth Pearson; (2) Thomas Alvin Denson (b. January 1847, d. 1864); (3) Emma Gertrude Denson (b. Sep. 26, 1848, d. 1926) md. Horace Handy; (4) Margaret Jones Denson (b. Mar. 24, 1850, d. Oct. 26, 1927) md. Thomas Plutarch Burnham; (5) Mary Alice Denson (b. Sep. 4, 1851, d. Jul. 13, 1931) md. Richard Henry Lee; (6) Sarah Katherine Denson (b. Mar. 22, 1853, d. Dec. 29, 1915) md. first, John Campbell and second Andrew Walker McDuff; (7) Ella Jane Denson (b. May 1854, d. Jun. 12, 1945) md. Daniel Webster McDuff; (8) Lee Montgomery Denson (b. September 1855) md. Dorah Majors; (9) Harriet Virginia Denson (b. Mar. 3, 1857, d. Sep. 11, 1940) md. Elisha M. Davis; (10) Howard Alfred Denson (b. March 1861, d. in Texas) md. Ellen _; (11) Fannie Edney Denson (b. Nov. 24, 1863, d. Oct. 6, 1956) md. Alexander Stuart Handy; (12) Jessie Viola Denson (b. Jan. 13, 1866, d. Jun. 28, 1926) md. Spencer Armour Smith; (13) Eugenia Florence Denson (b. 1867, d. 1885); (14) Joseph Conner Denson (b. 1868, d. 1946).

DORSETT, The Dorsett family in Scott County began with the arrival of John Hezikiah Dorsett born Jan. 3, 1839 in Chambers County, AL. He was one of nine children of Hezikiah Dorsett and Jane Chapman. After the death of his mother his father married a widow with several daughters, Dorothy Lattimer Farrar.

His father died in 1847 when he was 9 years old and his step-mother when he was 13. His oldest sister, Maria married John Boyd of neighboring Troup County, GA. Whether he lived then in Georgia or remained in Alabama until he moved to Mississippi is not known for sure. The 1860 census shows him living in Scott County and his occupation was an overseer.

Also arriving in Mississippi before the 1860 census was William and Kasandra Black Ledbetter and three daughters and five sons. They settled in the old Cash Community. It is not known if John H. Dorsett traveled to Mississippi with the Ledbetter family.

John H. Dorsett enlisted in Co. G, 28th MS Cav. Regt. on Mar. 7, 1862. His unit surrendered May 2, 1865 in Citronelle, AL. He was paroled on May 12th and returned to Scott County. Later that year he and Aldoria Ledbetter were married. Born to that union in Scott County were daughter Wellie and sons, William McPherson "Mac," Jett, John and Jim.

Anxious for his children to have a good education he moved from the Cash area to Harperville where there was a junior college. He taught at the college while his sons attended school there. His daughter, Wellie, married Ezra Pruitt of Montrose in Jasper County. The sons also left after college and went to Greene County where they were educators, with Mac becoming the first Superintendent Education. Later Mac, Jett and John entered the business world while Jim studied medicine at Emory University. Mac settled in Richton, John in Wiggins and Jett and Dr. Jim in Lucedale.

While still in Greene County Mac went back to Rankin County and married Annie Laurie Ratliff whose family resided near Ludlow. She was the daughter of Jesse Denson Ratliff and Lenora Eleanora Little, one of three Little sisters to marry Ratliff brothers. Many of this family are buried in the Ludlow Cemetery.

By the turn of the century, all of the Dorsett children had moved from Scott County and when Aldoria became ill, John H. moved with his wife to Montrose to be near their daughter as she was a big help to her ill mother, who passed away Jun. 9, 1901. John H. remained in Montrose and visited his sons often, as they like Mac, had married. Jett to Harriet Ethridge, Jim to Lulu Roberts and John to Addie Smith.

The Scott County overseer, farmer, soldier and teacher passed away Feb. 16, 1913 and he and Aldoria are buried next to each other in Montrose.

When John H. came to Scott County he was the first of the family there. When he moved with his wife to Montrose, all of the family had left Scott County. Descendants now live in many Mississippi counties to include Scott, Pearl River, George, Stone and Forrest and in several states to include Louisiana, Georgia, Missouri, Arkansas, California, North Carolina, Texas and New Jersey.

Additional information on this family can be found in the book, By the Rivers of Waters *Vols. I and II by W. Harvell Jackson and in the book,* Four Centuries on the Pascagoula, *by Cyril E. Cain.*

DUCKWORTH, Christopher Columbus Duckworth came from England to America with his father, William, in the early 1860s. His mother (name unknown) and a sister Katie remained in England. William was a civil engineer. They lived in Whistler, AL. William indentured Chris to a teacher (name unknown) to learn his letters. William was killed while working on the railroad. When Chris learned his father had died he left the teacher, who worked him all day and would crack him over the head with a stick to keep him awake at night while he taught him.

Chris lived with the William Robert Harrison family and came to Scott County, MS with them. Chris (b. Jan. 3, 1856) married Sep. 26, 1878 Geneva Christian McGee (b. Aug. 23, 1860), daughter of Jacob McGee and Christian Jones. Chris and Jenny purchased 160 acres of land Oct. 10, 1885 located five miles south of Forest, MS on Highway 501. Chris was an industrious man who managed his resources well. He had peaches and cotton to sell and raised most of their food. Chris died Jun. 7, 1943 and Jenny died Dec. 6, 1951. They are buried at Hopewell Church Cemetery, Norris, Scott County, MS. Their children, all born at Norris, Scott County, MS are:

Maude and Hoye Duckworth with six of their children and spouses; Maude's sister Beatrice White with her four children; and Maude's brother Elton Lindsey

1) William P. (b. Oct. 1, 1881, d. Mar. 24, 1974, Pineville, LA) md. first, Drucilla Sims Jul. 28, 1901. Children: Percy, Eula Mae and Julia Merle. Married second, Merle Sims. William married in Louisana three other times. Other children: Mattie, Billie Merle and William.

2) Hattie (b. 1883) md. Jessie Sumrall, son of Elisha Woods Sumrall and Penny Hammonds. Children: Walter, Woods and Christopher.

3) Oscar (b. Feb. 13, 1885, d. Apr. 4, 1935 at Pineville, LA), wife unknown, no children.

4) Mary Christian (b. Apr. 22, 1888) md. Henry Rufus Wilkerson, son of Francis Shepherd Wilkerson and Mary Elizabeth Youngblood. Sons: Henry Marvin, Howard and Sam Ray. Mollie died Sep. 17, 1943 at Norris, Scott County, MS.

5) Lettie Geneva (b. Feb. 3, 1892) md. first, Henry McTyier Roberts and second, John William Daniels, son of John D. Daniels and Lenora Shirley. Children: John David, Tommie Ruth and Wilbur Lee. Stepchildren: Faye and Vermelle Daniels. Lettie died Jan. 23, 1962, Scott County, MS.

6) Katie (b. April 1897, d. October 1899, Scott County, MS).

7) Hoye Eugene (b. Dec. 29, 1899) md. Jul. 3, 1921 Maude Lee Lindsey, daughter of Franklin Povie Lindsey and Mariana Frances Tedford. Children: Mattie Geneva, Hattie Beatrice "Jackie," Hoye Frank, Celia Frances, Mildred Laverne, Sara Delois, Iris Lanelle, Virginia Lee, Tim Marler and Henry Lindsey.

DUCKWORTH-LINDSEY, Hoye Eugene Duckworth, youngest child of Christopher Columbus Duckworth and Geneva Christian McGee (b. Dec. 29, 1899, died Apr. 10, 1981), md. Jul. 3, 1921 Maude Lee Lindsey of Water Valley, Yalabusha County, MS. The daughter of Franklin Povie Lindsey and Mariana Frances Tedford and granddaughter of Mariana Frances Ivy, Maude was the oldest of three children. Her mother died when she was 7 and father died when she was 9. Maude, Elton and Beatrice were placed in the Methodist Orphanage in Jackson by an older stepbrother, James Marshall Lindsey.

At age 12 Maude was taken to Sun, MS on Highway 501 near the Smith County Line to live with Mrs. Mattie Gilbert. Maude always thought of her as Grandma Gilbert. She sent Maude to boarding school at Harperville. Maude and Hoye courted by buggy. He bought her jewelry and carried firewood, by wagon, to school for her use. They married and made their home with Hoye's parents at Norris Scott County, MS. Hoye felt responsible to care for his parents as they aged. They raised nine children during the depression years. Maude would not keep her children out of school to work the fields. This small woman of five feet and weighing less than 100 pounds did a lot of the field work. There was no electricity or indoor plumbing until after WWII. Food was cooked on a woodburning stove, they studied by an Aladdin lamp, bathed in a washtub and swept the dirt yard. Hoye worked as an electrician. He was known around Forest for hanging the Christmas light and as Night Marshall once.

In the early years they owned a Ford sedan and had a community phone. Later there was a battery radio. Most of the food was raised on the farm. Cotton, peaches, figs were sold to buy other needs. Hoye always bought special food for weekend eating. There was always food to eat and shoes to wear. He raised peanuts and sugar cane and made his own peanut butter and molasses. Maude canned the extra produce for winter use. Children:

Family picture of Christopher and Geneva Duckworth with five oldest children: William P., Hattie, Oscar, Mary Christian and Lettie Geneva

1) Mattie Geneva, housewife (b. Mar. 18, 1822), md. Ray Evans of Louisiana. Children: Richard, Rosemary, Sam, Noel, Johnnie and Patricia.

2) Hattie Beatrice (Jackie), Insurance (b. Jan. 10, 1925, d. Aug. 30, 1993), md. Milo Lincoln of Iowa. Children: Stanley and Christopher.

3) Hoye Frank: Computer programmer, USAF Retired (b. Jun. 18, 1926, d. Nov. 7, 1992), md. Nella Beasley of Wesson, MS. Children: Susan Dawn, Christopher Jay, Nella Gay and Abbie Gail.

4) Celia Frances, RN (b. Dec. 23, 1927), md. Aug. 4, 1953 William Eugene Tompkins of Utica Hinds County, MS. Children, Sherri Ann and Terri Lynn.

5) Mildred Laverne, seamstress/ housewife (b. Jul. 23, 1930), md. Alva Dariel Boykin of Raleigh Smith County, MS. Children: Delia Kaye, Roger Dariel, Millicint Laverne.

6) Sarah Delois, telephone operator (b. Jul. 9, 1932), md. Robert Montgomery Blue of Michigan. Children: Linda Diane and Robert Eugene.

7) Iris Lanelle (b. Jun. 14, 1934, d. 1934).

8) Virginia Lee, RN (b. Aug. 30, 1936), md. Blair (Buddy) Watkins of Neshoba County, MS. Children: Renae Watkins. Stepchildren: Marie, David and Bobby.

9) Tim Marler, regional sales manager (b. Jul. 21, 1938), md. Louise Card of Shuqualak Noxubee County, MS. Children: Kimberly Diane and Michelle.

10) Henry Lindsey: accountant (b. Aug. 27, 1944), md. first, Carolyn Runnels of Mississippi. Children: Andrew Lindsey, Karissa Erin and Joel Keith. Married second, Betty Williams of Jackson, Hinds County, MS.

DUDLEY, Sherwood Lee "Joddie" Dudley was born Mar. 30, 1917 in South Paris, ME to Harry Harrison Dudley and Eva Florence Allen. He was the oldest son of a large family. Sherwood grew up in and around South Paris, ME. In the early 1950s he came south in search of work. Sherwood worked for awhile in St. Charles, LA. Then around 1953 he came to Mississippi, stopping in

Sherwood Dudley and Mary Helen Jones Dudley

Forest. He lived in a boarding house owned by a Mrs. Farmer. It was located on the north side of Second Street across from the courthouse. Mr. Edgar Marler owner of Marler Auto the Dodge Chrysler dealer in Forest hired him as a mechanic.

In 1955 some friends introduced him to a local lady, Mary Helen Jones Haralson, daughter of Jeremiah Thomas Jones and Stella Estelle Horn. Mary Helen had a young daughter named Mary Grace. On Sep. 3, 1955 they were married. Nine months later, on Jun. 3, 1956, a son Leroy Joddie was born, giving young Mary Grace a little brother. In 1960 Joddie, as he was called, purchased some land on old Highway 80, east of Forest, in what was once known as Singleton Settlement and built a house. Joddie continued to work for Marler Auto until 1972 when he had to stop for health reasons. Even though he was unable to hold a public job, Joddie was able to do a little work at home. Every one came from near and far to have Mr. Joddie work on their cars. He was especially good on carburetors.

Mary Grace and Leroy went to Forest Public Schools. In later years Joddie returned to Maine to visit his siblings, but always came back to Mississippi. Joddie helped raise Mary Grace's son Robert Earl, who loved his papa very much. His health continued to fail and on May 11, 1993 he finally succumbed. He is buried in Liberty Baptist Cemetery, one mile from his home.

Mary Grace married Peter James Schwab April 1993 and lives in the home place, where she was raised. Mary Helen is still alive and in a nursing facility in Meridian. Leroy married Wanda Gail Maddox (b. Dec. 28, 1959, d. February 2001, buried in Leaf River Cemetery, Smith County, MS) and lives south of Forest on Hwy. 501. He is also a good mechanic in his own right. Robert Earl lives on old Hwy. 80 and works at Craft-Co in Morton, MS. Submitted by Robert Earl Haralson.

DUNCAN (1826-1904), This Tennessee native almost saw his family name die out before he did, save for the progeny of one son. But the name still lives. As do his descendants in Scott County and many other parts of the world.

After leaving Tennessee in the 1840s and after a brief sojourn in Kemper County, John Martin Duncan and his wife Margaret Elizabeth (Page) Duncan (b. 1829, d. 1891) continued their migration into the Mississippi "Indian Lands," and arrived in Scott County around 1855. They settled on a small farm on the Balucta Creek in the flatwoods area, north and east of present-day Forkville.

Of their 10 children, five died before they reached their mid-teens. One son, George, single at age 30, was struck by lightening and killed. And one daughter, Rose, was married to Mel Noel but died at 19 years, 10 months after giving birth to a son, Dan Noel, who survived and reared a family at Clifton.

John Martin found his wife-to-be, Margaret Elizabeth Page, the daughter of Thomas Andrew Page, in Kemper County. They were married there in 1848, when he was 22 and she was 19. Margaret was the sister of Mary Ada Page, second wife of Russell Thomas Rigby and the two families apparently moved to Scott County at the same time and settled in the same area.

The grave site for six of these early Duncans, including John Martin himself and his wife Margaret is located in a small plot on the Pat Jeffcoats place (T7N, R7E, Section 6) on the Hillsboro-Forkville Road.

Of their three remaining children one daughter, Amanda Duncan, married J.I. Rhodes and moved to Natchitoches, LA, where they produced four children. Another daughter, Virginia "Rhine" Duncan, married William M. "Pone" McCurdy and they produced several children and many of their descendants live in Scott County today. The remaining child, William Thomas Duncan (b. 1850. d. 1930), married his first cousin, Margaret Catherine Rigby (b. 1851, d. 1917), daughter of Russell Thomas and Mary Ada Page Rigby. They became parents to five sons and three daughters, all of whom are now deceased. Many of their descendants, however, are still citizens of the county. The children of W.T. "Will" Duncan and Margaret Catherine "Maggie" Rigby Duncan were:

1) George M. Duncan (b. 1874) who married Mattie Sprouse of the Forkville Community. They had three children, all of whom are deceased - no issue.

2) Lilla Margaret Duncan (b. 1876) md. Alfonso Warren "Doc" Gunn and they settled in the Pea Ridge Community. They had six children. Some of their grandchildren live in the area today.

3) Mary Ella "Ell" Duncan (b. 1878) md. Evander Tillman Britt. Their home was in Harperville where they produced eight children. Their numerous grandchildren live all over the United States.

4) William Franklin "Frank" Duncan (b. 1881) married Minnie Myrtle Wallace and lived in the Forkville Community. They had eight children and many grandchildren.

5) John Martin Duncan (b. 1883) md. Lou Etta Dodson. They made their home in Pulaski where they reared seven children. Two others died in infancy.

6) Joseph Benjamin "Joe" Duncan (b. 1886) md. Ruth Jeanette Haddon of Harperville. They had three children and made their home in Newton, MS.

7) Noah Clifton "Cliff" Duncan (b. 1890) md. a Miss Evelyn from Orange, TX, where they made their home. They had one son.

8) Rosa Jane "Rosie" Duncan (b. 1893) md. Albert Fulton Roberts of the Pea Ridge Community. They had two children. They lived their final years in Brandon, MS.

While all of these forbears have gone on to their final reward, the descendants who remain, hold them in fond remembrance—that to which Lincoln referred as, "The mystic chords of memory." We are bound, one to another, by these ties of memory. These "chords" confirm to us our brotherhood not only to each other but to all mankind.

DUNCAN, William Franklin Duncan (b. Jan. 8, 1881, d. Apr. 3, 1967) married Minnie Myrtle Wallace (b. Sep. 30, 1883, d. Oct. 25, 1941) on Mar. 5, 1905. It is believed they eloped in a horse drawn buggy. They lived in Balucta until around 1920 when they moved to a log home in Beach on Highway 13. There were already six children and two of the girls were born at Beach.

Farming was Frank's way of making a living. Each child was expected to help with the farming. At one time Frank had a timber scaling business. He was quite good at this work. When the depression hit, Frank moved his family to Ludlow bought the Charlie Rigby place and built his own home. Minnie was a strong Christian influence on each child insisting we attend Sunday School and church whenever possible. There was a great camaraderie in this family when we would all get together remembering the hard times we had as we grew up. Our life on the farm was not easy and we lacked for a lot of material things, but we had a great love for one another through it all. The children were:

L-R: Foch, Curtis, Jean, Raymond, Maggie Frances and Blumie

1) Blumie Field (b. Apr. 21, 1906, d. Oct. 16, 1987) md. Louise Walker and Daniel Field and William Douglas were born. B.F. and Louise helped all their brothers and sisters obtain some type of education.

2) O.T. Duncan (b. Mar. 23, 1908, d. Nov. 8, 1977) md. Katie Miller. Katie brought five sons to the marriage. One son, Alvin, was lost in the Vietnam War.

3) Iva Marie (b. Jan. 3, 1910, d. Dec. 24, 1940) md. Ernest Merl Kersh. Her life was lost after giving birth to Ernest Merl Jr. who did not survive.

4) Raymond Wallace (b. Sep. 14, 1913, d. Jul. 30, 1991) md. Linda Pigott from Tylertown. Their children were Shirley Jean, David Raymond and Lynn Ann. Most of their life was spent in Arkansas.

5) Curtis Hansel (b. Nov. 4, 1916, d. Jan. 10, 1992) md. Trudie May from Newton and had Charlotte Virginia. Trudie and Curtis made their home in Morton.

6) Marshall Foch (b. Sep. 15, 1918) md. Hilda Bates and Steven Wendell, Beverly Sue and Marshall Joe were born. This marriage was later dissolved and Foch married Christine Riser Gooch. Foch and his family made their home in Jackson.

7) Maggie Frances (b. Feb. 1, 1921) md. Robert Ray Nutt of Ludlow and to this union was born Diane Marie and Robert Randy. This marriage was dissolved and she married Raylon Pigg of Goodhope. This family made their home in Jackson.

8) Bonnie Jean (b. Nov. 19, 1923) md. Jesse Turbville of Kemper County and to them was born Jan Carol. They made Jackson their home. "Jack' died in 1977.

It is worthy to note that Frank and Minnie had five sons in military service at the time of Minnie's death in 1941.

EADY, The Rev. Eady bought the Gum Springs property from M.V. Warren and wife in 1907. The Warrens moved to Texas. Rev. Eady and some others built a tabernacle that was used for religious services, political picnics and other community gatherings. He operated the Gum Spring Water Co. He built some camp houses that people could rent by the week or month, to be able to drink the water.

Rev. A.A. Eady and great-grandson, Buddy Eady

He printed a brochure with these testimonials: "I frequently prescribe Gum Springs Water for my patients with good results. E.J. Rowe, M.D., Hillsboro, MS."

"I have been using the Gum Springs Water for 5 years for family use and in my practice as a diuretic. Think there is none better in the state for sluggish kidneys and Brights disease. J.P. Burnham, MD I have been using Gum Springs Water in my practice for 15 years and have found it to be the purest and lightest water I can procure. I use it frequently in cases of Brights disease on account of its purity and the large amount a patient can consume without discomfort. J.J. Haralson, M.D., Health Officer."

COPIED FROM THE BROCHURE: Terms: wanted From 5 to — all the time, at $1.00 per day, or $6.00 per week or $20.00 per month. Children and servants one half price.

Water placed on cars at Forest in 5 gallon carboys at 50 cents each. Send $1.50, P.O. money order or register to A.A. Eady, Gum Springs, MS. $1.00 will be returned when carboy arrives in Forest within 20 days in good condition all charges prepaid. There was a post office at Gum Springs, established on Jan. 28 1910 and closed Sep. 30, 1928 A.A. Eady was postmaster Sep. 13, 1911 to Sep. 30, 1928. The property was sold to grandson Peyton V. Eady in December 1949. Peyton V. Eady Jr. (Shot) and his family has lived there since 1971.

A.A. Eady lived 101 years, having been born Sep. 25, 1860 and died Dec. 22, 1961.

Rev. C.M. Crossley had this to say about Mr. Eady. This is to certify that I am personally acquainted with the Rev. Mr. Eady of Gum Springs, MS, "I heartily recommend him as a high-toned Christian gentleman, thoroughly reliable in every respect.

Gum Springs water is still being consumed by people in Scott County and surrounding areas.

EADY'S CAFE, In the fall of 1941 Peyton Eady built a Drive-in and Sandwich Shop on Highway 80 East in Forest, MS. It was opened for business on Dec. 5, 1941, two days before Pearl Harbor. He and his wife, Delona Reeves, had one son named Van Reeves Eady. The Cafe was called Van's Coffee Shop. That marriage ended in divorce and Van died in Las Vegas in 1988.

Eady's Cafe

Peyton was inducted into the Navy Dec. 30, 1943 was sent to the Great Lakes Training Center. From there he was sent to Camp Perry, VA, outside Williamsburg. He was discharged from there Dec. 10, 1945.

In 1944 he married Etna Jean Carpenter and they lived in Williamsburg until he was discharged. They had one son, Peyton V. Eady Jr. (Shot) who lives with his family at Gum Springs, MS.

That is the old family homestead in Scott County.

In January 1946 they reopened the Cafe as Eady's Cafe. In 1950-1951 it was leased to P.J. McDonald.

In September 1953 it was reopened and remained until 1981. Peyton died May 25, 1962 and is buried in Eastern Cemetery in Forest. Jean ran the restaurant until 1981 when she leased it to Evelyn Gould, six months later the building burned.

Jean had become very involved in the American Legion Auxiliary. She kept Unit 9 in Forest going for a number of years. She served Dist. 5 as president many times. In 1984-85 she served the State of Mississippi as president of the American Legion Auxiliary.

She has served two terms as Chapeau Departmental de Miss., 8et 40 a subsidiary of the American Legion Auxiliary. She also served as Demi Chapeau of the Southern Division, which is a National office. She joined Hontokalo Chapter, Mississippi State Society of the Daughters of the American Revolution in 1987 and has served as treasurer, registrar and three years as regent. She attends Forest United Methodist Church and is a member of the Gleaners Sunday

School Class. She is a member of the Scott County Executive Board of the Democratic Party. She is an elected member of the Election Commission for the city of Forest and holds membership in the Scott County Genealogical Society. Jean still lives in Forest in the home she and Peyton built in 1952. Her only grandchild DeAnna Eady Sparks and husband Shawn live nearby.

EASTLAND, James Oliver Eastland was born on the Eastland plantation at Doodsville, MS, on Nov. 28, 1904 and moved with his family to Forest in 1905 where he was reared and attended the local schools. He enrolled at the University of Mississippi and later attended Vanderbilt University and the University of Alabama. He was admitted to the Bar

James Oliver Eastland

in 1927 and began his practice of law in Forest. He represented Scott County in the House of Representatives 1928-1932. Married the former Elizabeth Coleman in 1932. They were the parents of three daughters and one son. Moved to Sunflower Country to practice law in 1934.

Appointed to fill the vacancy in the United States Senate in 1941 left by the death of Senator Pat Harrison, by Governor Paul B. Johnson Sr. He served 88 days. Elected to a full term in November 1942 and re-elected in 1949 and 1955. Named Chairman of the Senate Judiciary Committee in 1956 and was the youngest ever named to this post and served the longest. Re-elected 1961-1967. Elected President pro tempore of the Senate Jul. 29, 1972. Re-elected 1973. Became second in line to succeed the President with the resignation of Vice Pres. Spiro T. Agnew in 1973 and President Richard Nixon in 1974. He served three days as President at this time. Retired from the Senate in 1978.

He was honored on Aug. 9, 1985 as the Federal Courthouse in Jackson was named for him.

He died February 1986 and is buried in Eastern Cemetery in Forest by his parents.

These facts were taken from a Special Section, written by Erle Johnson, editor of the Scott County Times, *Feb. 26, 1986.*

EDWARDS, Joseph Richmond Edwards was born in Alabama on Mar. 9, 1839 and died in Newton County, MS on Feb. 19, 1907. He was the son of Joseph (b. 1799 in Georgia) and Missouri Edwards.

Joseph Richmond Edwards was a veteran of the Civil War (1861-1865). He served with Co. A, 35th Regt., Mississippi Volunteer Infantry, in Mississippi and Georgia. Joseph had a dark complexion, dark hair and gray eyes and was 5'11" tall. He was injured in battle and lived some 40 years with his injury. He was well respected in his community and the conduct of his life reflected credit upon himself and his family. The story he told about the injury was that a bullet went through his shoulder and into a comrade's mouth behind him; his friend did not survive.

Joseph Richmond Edwards was captured Jul. 4, 1863 at Vicksburg. He was released after he signed papers that he would not fight anymore. He was captured again Oct. 6, 1864 at Allatoma, GA by forces under Major General W.T. Sherman's commanding military division and forwarded to Captain S.E. Jones, additional A.D.C. Louisville, KY Oct. 20, 1864. He was sent to Camp Chase, OH Oct. 22, 1864. On Jun. 11, 1865, Joseph R. Edwards signed an Oath of Allegiance to the United States of America. After the war, he was so patriotic to his beloved southern homeland that he would not wear a blue suit ever again.

Joseph Richmond Edwards, wife Eliza Ann (Bryant) and their son, Earnest Zachery

After the war and his separation from service he returned to Kemper County, where he farmed. Due to civil strife in Kemper County during the reconstruction period, he moved to Newton County, MS during the year 1868.

Joseph R. Edwards's first wife was Sarah Jane Pace. They had eight children: Harriet Missouri, who married Jack Ponder; Jacob Miller, married Susan Bogie Boyler; Joseph Richmond married Annie L. Bruce; William Davis married Molly Bryant; Indiana died as a small child; Betty Elizabeth married Gus Easom and later Joe Edwards; George Quinton married Mamie Reeves; and John Lee married Alma Cole.

Joseph Richmond's first wife, Sarah Jane, died May 25, 1885. A number of years later he married Eliza Ann Bryant, daughter of Ira Bryant and Jane Ponder. From this marriage two children were born: daughter, Alma, died as a small child and son, Earnest Zachery Edwards, was born in 1898. He married Mary Ruthie Barnes (b. Apr. 15, 1896, d. Jul. 8, 1935), the daughter of John Barnes and Mittie Jane Smith.

The children of Earnest and Mary Ruthie are Dorothy Rudell, who married Roscoe Rowzee and later George A. Shepard; James Earl Edwards married Mary Sue Eaton; Joe Cortez Edwards; Mary Louise Edwards married Ozro Randall; Nellie Mae married Charles L. Gibson; and Marshall O'Niel married Martha Lee Dunbar.

Joseph R. Edwards died on Feb. 19, 1907. The following article appeared in the Meridian, Mississippi newspaper on Feb. 25, 1907: "Grim reaper calls good citizen to his reward."

On the 19th Inst, Joseph Edwards of Cooksey Community laid his implements of service and peacefully passed into the beyond. He was nearing his 68th birthday and for more than 35 years had been an afflicted sufferer. Yet amid it all, he manifested Christian resignation. He was a member of the Baptist Church from early manhood and his remains were laid to rest in the Poplar Church Cemetery, the funeral services being conducted by his pastor, Reverend Mr. Collins. A large concourse of friends and neighbors were present to sympathize with the be-

reaved family and to show love and respect for the beloved dead. He was a citizen of that community for nearly 40 years had reared a family of eight children and in all the relations of life was upright, faithful and true. In 1861 when the tocsin of war was sounded and his beloved Southland was invaded by marauding hordes or hirelings and adventurers, he early espoused the Confederate cause, enlisting in Co. A, 35th Regt., Mississippi Volunteer Infantry and was with that noted regiment in its campaigns in Mississippi and Georgia and did gallant service for the south on many of the battle fields of those states.

The Sleep
Soldier rest, thy warfare is o'er.
Sleep that knows no breaking.
Dream of battle fields no more.
Days of danger, nights of waking."
A Comrade
Feb. 25, 1907
Submitted by Sylvia A. Randall, great-granddaughter of Joseph Richmond Edwards, former resident of Scott County.

EMMONS, Henry Clay Emmons (b. Apr. 21, 1839) was the son of Loving and Mary Wilkinson Emmons and the grandson of Jonas and Rebecca Savill Emmons. He married about 1855 to a "Reeves" lady and had two children, Joel Lovern and Amanda Lee.

Joel (b. Apr. 20, 1856, d. Jan. 13, 1932) md. Elizabeth Tabitha Walton on Dec. 23, 1880. They had six children as follows: Zula Dell (b. Oct. 24, 1881) md. George C. Butts; Naomi Ruth (b. Oct. 25, 1884) md. Ike Brown; Johnie Perry (b. Jul. 13, 1886) md. Buena Vista Gomillion; Mary Alice (b. Sep. 27, 1888) md. James R. Bridges; Virgie Loucille (b. Mar. 8, 1891) md. James Thomas

Henry Clay Emmons

Crane; Robert Lee (b. Aug. 19, 1895) md. Elsie Lee Williams.

Henry's daughter Amanda Lee Emmons (b. Aug. 20, 1862) md. James W. Holliday on Apr. 2, 1885. They had eight children as follows: John W. Holliday (b. Feb. 8, 1886); Felix Wilder Holliday (b. Jan. 29, 1888) md. Margaret Lucille Peagler; Mattie Lou Holliday (b. Jan. 10, 1890) md. Theo D. Dowdle; Minnie Bell Holliday (b. Apr. 21, 1892); Lucy Ethel Holliday (b. Jan. 20, 1895); Owen Clay Holliday (b. May 15, 1897) md. Annie Lee McDonald; Mary Dee Holliday (b. May 13, 1900) md. William Yancey Thrash; Sophia Irene Holliday (b. Nov. 27, 1903).

Henry Clay Emmons joined for duty during the Civil War and was mustered in at Meridian, MS on Feb. 20, 1862. He was in Co. C (Harper Reserves) of the 36th Regt. of MS Volunteers. He was wounded at the Battle of Corinth and taken as a prisoner of war. He was paroled on Nov. 6, 1863.

After the war, Henry met and married Sophronia E. Murrell, the daughter of Rev. Lee Powell and Nancy Taylor Murrell. Sophronia was born Jan. 6, 1839 and died Jul. 18, 1920.

She and Henry married in 1864 and had eight children as follows: Henry Franklin (b. Jan. 10, 1867) md. Mary Ann Tillman; Nancy Alice (b. Feb. 14, 1868) md. William Kemp Johnston; Mary (b. Apr. 11, 1870) md. Marion Franklin Kelly; Charley (b. Apr. 31, 1871) md. Ada Valentine; Bessie (b. Mar. 1, 1874) md. Byrd Evans; Robert (b. December 1876, died young); Archie Lee (b. Dec. 3, 1877) never married; Lucille (b. Jul. 19, 1879) md. Noah Thomas Gould.

Henry Clay Emmons and Sophronia Murrell Emmons have many descendants in Scott County, MS. They are both buried at Salem Cemetery, Scott County, MS.

EMMONS, Oliver Lloyd Emmons, "Papa Tad" as he was called, was born Feb. 27, 1896, at Lake, MS. He was the grandson of Sophronia Murrell Emmons and a great-grandson of Rev. Lee Powell Murrell, a Baptist minister in Scott and Newton County.

At the age of 22, Papa Tad joined the army and served during WWI. On Sep. 21, 1919, Tad married Miss Eula Mae Clark, the daughter of Solomon C. Clark and Katherine Golden Clark. Eula was born in Leake County, MS on Dec. 27, 1892. They had five children as follows: Retha Emmons (b. Jul. 13, 1920) md. Lonzo Williamson; Evelyn Emmons (b. Jan. 31, 1922) md. Freeman Waltman; Oliver Birden Emmons (b. Feb. 12, 1924) md. first, Lena Everett and second, Jean Everett; Coyt Emmons (b. Jan. 29, 1926) md. Jimmie Mallick; William Clark Emmons (b. Mar. 22, 1931) md. Doreen Harriman.

Tad Emmons Family

Tad Emmons was a farmer by occupation and lived in the Goodhope Community, Scott County, for most of his life. He was also a Raleigh salesman for many years.

Tad loved to fish and hunt and trained all of his grandsons as soon as they were old enough to learn. Many people remember him for his very jolly laughter and for the fact that he was a friend to everyone.

He attended Salem Church and was an active member there all of his life. He died Feb. 27, 1969 and Eula died Sep. 1, 1956. They are buried at the Salem Cemetery.

EPHESUS QUILTERS, It all began about 18 years ago when we started our new auditorium at Ephesus. We were trying to raise extra money by getting together antiques, crafts and all sorts of things for an auction. One of the ladies, Desiree May, donated a quilt top, along with lining and batting. All we had to do was quilt it. This turned out to be very interesting and we decided to continue our quilting. It started with about six ladies and sometimes now we have as many as 18 to 20 each week. Some of our ladies are in their 80s.

This day of fun and fellowship means a whole lot to our quilters. We have some beautiful work done each week and we have some of the best cooks in the country. We also have a church cookbook called Country Cooking that has become

Kenneth and Theretha Jones and Carol Ann

pretty popular. Some of the recipes of the young and old alike are in this book.

The quilters are Trudy Jones, Mary Brogdon, Ellen Guthrie, Birdie McKinion, Hettie Driskel, Thenetha Jones, Elma Jones, Martha Matthews, Paula Bell, Mable Brittian, Margie Burkes, Mary Redd, Dorothy Lackey, Mary Lou Haralson, Nancy Myers, Wilma White, Karon Martin, Hazel Squires and Janet Everett.

Ephesus Quilters

We meet each Tuesday from 9 a.m. until whenever and around 11:45 a.m. the table is spread with each person's special recipe for that week. The fellowship is great, but the most important thing is that these ladies are feeling worthwhile and important. They are working to help pay for our beautiful new church building. Most of them have little income and this way they are serving the Lord too.

Besides all of this, we have learned to love, understand and appreciate our older ladies. We've not only learned how to make quilts, but we've learned new ways of cooking, how to handle family problems, how they reared their children, how people helped one another in trouble and lots of the old ways that are often forgotten today.

Not only is it a joy to quilt with these ladies, but also just to hear them talk about the "good ole days" is a real blessing. They tell of how they made soap by butchering hogs and cooking out the lard. They used the leftover crackling and red devil lye to make lye soap. They told of cooking sweet potatoes and parched peanuts in the fireplace. We have learned how to make homemade hominy from these ladies. They told of seeing their mothers use red clay dirt to dye quilt material and boil walnut bark to color fabric purple. They would boil chinaberries and string them for beads. They might walk a mile to the spring for a bucket of cold water and put a jar of milk in the spring to keep it cool

until needed. They go on and on with stories of old as we quilt away.

Now we are in a new year, 2001! We've been quilting since 1984. We've lost several of our ladies, but now and then a new one joins us and on with the quilting. Not many can drive themselves anymore so Bro. Jones makes his hour-long route to pick them up. He then returns home to prepare lunch for them. He brings the "fixins" to the church about 11:30 and spreads dinner with what the quilters brought and we all enjoy food and fellowship. What a blessing our Senior Citizens are!

As of now we have given $40,000 to the building fund, bought a refrigerator and stove for the kitchen, several tables and chairs and given quilts to needy people for various reasons.

The ladies enjoy company on "Quilting Day" and welcome anyone to come join us to quilt, eat or just visit for a while. They love the opportunity to show off their beautiful work.

In Joshua 14, we read that Caleb was strong and vigorous at 85. His cry was not for the easy places, but rather "Give me this Mountain." Not all elderly have this much strength, but we must never think of them as having lost their zest for life or having nothing left to contribute. God strengthens his children for service, no matter how young or old. Let's not underestimate our peppy Caleb generation. Remember, youth is not only a time of life, but also a state of mind. What you think, you look; what you think, you do; what you think, you are! Submitted by Thenetha Jones.

EVANS, Robert Evans born about 1726 in Cecil County, MD fought in the Revolutionary War. He married Sarah Hetty May (b. about 1749 in Hampton, SC) and they had seven children: Joseph Evans md. Amelia Hawkins; Ruth Evans md. William J. Reed; William Evans md. Luvisy Minson; Jabez Evans md. Rachael; Margaret Evans; Sarah Evans md. John Humphreys; Jacob Evans; and Charlotte Evans.

Joseph Tillman Evans and Mary Francis Patrick

Robert is buried in Evans Family Cemetery in Marion, Perry County, AL. Sarah is buried in Reed Family Cemetery in Birmingham, Jefferson County, AL.

Robert's son, William Evans, married Luvisy Minson Jan. 26, 1799 in Henrico County, VA. They had six children: Jane Evans md. Francis Whilcomb; Temperance Evans died young; Elizabeth Evans md. John Ricketts; Melton Jabez (John) Evans had three wives: first, Martha Elizabeth McKee second, Margaret Louise Harrison and third, Clarisa Louise Payne; Hetty Evans married Edward Hutchison; Robert William Evans married Emily Catherine Mitchell. William and Luvisy are buried in Kemper County, MS.

William's son Robert William Evans married Emily Catherine Mitchell in 1845 in Calhoun County, AL. They had 11 children: Sarah A. "Sallie" Evans md. John W. Britt (CSA); Rachael Evans md. Hewt Crosley; Mary "Mollie" Evans md. J.C. Gardner; Nancy A. "Nannie" Evans md. J. Andy Rigby (CSA); Joseph Tillman Evans md. Mary Francis

Bessie Mae Davenport, John Wesley Evans, child unknown

Patrick; William Edward Evans md. Eugenia Riley "Jennie" Bowling; James Henry Evans md. Hallie Lou Eley; Samuel Evans md. Lou Middleton; Robert Evans; Martha F. "Mattie" Evans md. Josephus H. "Joseph" Waggoner; John William Evans md. Jennie Johnson. Most of the children married and died in Scott County, MS.

Robert's son Joseph Tillman Evans married Mary Francis Patrick Dec. 14, 1876 in Morton, Scott County. They had eight children: Jessie Evans died young; Robert William Evans; John Wesley Evans md. Bessie Mae Davenport; Addie Mae Evans md. Sidney Johnson Wallace; Ida Bell Evans md. Otha Rogers Buntyn; Mary Francis "Frank" Evans; Lewis Tillman Evans md. Ira Vermelle "Imell" Gaddis; Lena Evans md. Lonnie L. Bradshaw. Most of their children married and are buried in Scott County.

Joseph's son, John Wesley Evans, married Bessie Mae Davenport Sep. 6, 1903. Bessie's parents are John Wilson Davenport and Sallie Eliza Rushing of Scott County. They had six children (five born in Morton and one in Richland, Rankin, MS):

1) Louvenia Wydell Evans (b. Dec. 14, 1904) md. William Henry Wilson Nov. 23, 1924. They had four boys and one girl.

2) Herman Roscoe Evans (b. Feb. 3, 1907) md. Helen Madeira Jones Feb. 3, 1929, no children.

3) Percy Leroy Evans (b. Nov. 8, 1909) md. Lola Belle Hutson Sep. 6, 1929, one son.

4) Sally Ruth Evans (b. Mar. 28, 1912) md. first, Gus Wansley Dear Jul. 15, 1933, one son. Married second, Bill Hardy McAlpin, no children.

5) James William Evans (b. May 14, 1915) md. Laverne Odom and they had one daughter.

6) J.T. Evans (b. May 10, 1921 in Richland) md. Helen Steverson (Loveless) Feb. 15, 1949, one stepson. John Evans family moved from Beach to Morton and he worked as a partner with his father in a general merchandise and mercantile business. The same building still stands today and houses Dan Ott's Drug Store.

EVERETT, Thomas Everett and Penelope Rogers Everett moved into Lawrence County, MS from Georgia about 1818. The 1820 Federal Census counted Thomas with a household of seven living in Lawrence County, MS. Records show that on Oct. 1, 1825 Thomas Everett purchased 160 acres of land in southeast Lawrence County Sometime after this land purchase, Thomas and his family moved to Hinds County, MS near Utica where he bought 159 acres of farmland.

Thomas Everett died February 1838, leaving his wife Penelope Rogers Everett and children: Elizabeth (b. 1798); Temperance (b. 1804); Cynthia (b. 1807, d. 1892); Henry Abner (b. 1810, d. 1890); John Aaron (b. 1813, d. 1879); Jackson (b. 1817, d. after 1880); Sarah Ann (b. 1819); Samuel Everett (b. 1821, d. 1908); Thomas Everett (b. 1825, d. about 1865). After the death of their father, the Everett children moved into Jasper, IN and Newton County, MS.

Samuel Everett lived in the southeastern part of Newton County, MS where he met and married Mary Ann Moore, daughter of Neil Monroe and Mary A. Dixon Monroe Feb. 27, 1945. Samuel was a successful farmer. He and his wife had 10 children, They were William Green (b. 1847, d. 1931); Cornelia Ann (b. 1849, d. 1927); John Columbus (b. 1850, d. 1919); Mary Ann Penelope (b. 1853, d. 1857); Clemenze Jane (b. 1855, d. 1934); Berry "Bennie" Clark (b. 1858, d. 1887); Mary Elizabeth (b. 1860, d. 1937); Thomas Neil (b. 1862, d. 1933); Samuel Bishop (b&d. 1864); James Sellers (b. 1866, d. 1946).

In 1873 John Columbus married Mary Ann Woodham, daughter of Aris Bryant Woodham and Hester Simmons. John and Mary had three children before she died of consumption September 1880. Their names were Mary Lillian (b. 1874, d. 1940); Lena Hester (b. 1876, d. 1928); John Aris (b. 1877, d. 1960).

After Mary's death John Columbus married Martha Jennifer "Jennie" Lacey and had four additional children: Mattie A. (b. after 1880); Kate (b. 1882, d. 1946); W.H. "Bud" "Redden" (b. 1887, d. after 1920); Minnie (b. 1888, d. 1955).

John Columbus Everett is listed in the 1892 Scott County, MS Tax Rolls, Lake Precinct owning three cows, one horse, one carriage. He and his second wife Jennie are buried in the Salem Baptist Church Cemetery, Scott County.

John Aris Everett married Lou Ella Usry, daughter of William Franklin and Mary Ann Lourcie Pickard Usry, on Jan. 28, 1899 in Scott County. John Aris and Lou Ella had 10 children: Tressie Edna (b. 1900, d. 1983) md. Walter Marion Dennis, issue 11 children; William Percy (b. 1901, d. 1973) md. Addie Leona Hollingsworth, issue 10 children; Annie Myrtle (b. 1903, d. 1971), married John Clark Smith, son of William Anderson and Julia G. Atkinson Smith, issue six children; Noel Columbus (b. 1906, d. 1992) md. Maudie Ethel Hollingsworth, issue four children; Allie Mae (b. 1910, d. 1974) md. Shelby Durr, issue three children; twins born in 1912, Nola L. (d. 1941) and Ola who married George Clemmons Boyles, issue one child; twins born in 1915, John Woodham (d. 1995) md. Inez Thrash, issue four children and Woodrow Wil-

Lou Ella (Usry) and John Aris Everett

son who married Katie Thrash, issue one child; Roy Carlton (b. 1920) md. Minnie Josephine "Jo" Jones, issue four children.

Descendants of this Everett family are scattered far and wide, however a few of them still live in Scott and Newton County.

FAIRCHILDS, After marrying in July of 1877, W.C. Fairchilds and Susie Rushing made their home in northwest Scott County, near Forkville, formerly Beach. They purchased land in Logtown, between Forkville and Morton and opened a general store. W.C. also began to clear land for farming. Their son, William Oliver was born Mar. 23, 1878. While Will was a

Will, Hattie and Children

very young child, his father died suddenly, leaving Will and Susie to work the land and the general store alone. When he reached the age of 18, Will married Hattie Zeola Roberts, daughter of Richard J. Roberts and Theodocia Dixon Roberts. Hattie later talked to her grandchildren of how her family had moved in a covered wagon to Scott County from Marengo County, AL, when she was only 2 years old and her sister Hassie was 5 weeks old. Her family had also settled in the Forkville area.

Will and Hattie purchased about 550 acres in the Forkville area where they reared a family of seven children. They raised cattle, turkeys, chickens, vegetables and cotton. Hattie kept a fruit orchard, preserved fruits and vegetables and loved to fish. She made quilts, clothing, soap and candles. She was a talented cook and filled the sideboard with a wide variety of cakes, pies and candies at Christmas time to offer visitors and neighbors, as well as family.

Will and Hattie's first child, Oliver Richard, was born Mar. 31, 1899. Then a daughter, Leola, was born on Sep. 28, 1902. The third child was another son, Jimmie Davis (b. Jun. 6, 1905). A third son, William Riley, was born on Sep. 14, 1907. Next was Clint Vester (b. Jun. 16, 1910); Hattie Mae (b. Feb. 21, 1913) was their second daughter and Grady Bassett (b. Nov. 16, 1915) completed the family.

Will died suddenly of a heart attack in 1935 and Jimmie came home to help support his mother and younger siblings. He married Mary Carroll, daughter of Jim Isaiah and LuElla Turner Carroll and they had four children: Marisue, Peggy, Janie and Jimmie Davis Jr. Jimmie was elected tax assessor of Scott County in 1950 and served 20 years in that office. Oliver married Mamie Beavers and settled in Forkville to make a living farming and logging. They had five children: Boncile, Wayne, Bobby, Elizabeth and Rita. Leola died of a lingering illness at the age of 28. Riley married Nannie Adcock and settled in Ludlow, where for many years he kept a general store. They had three children: Iwana, Riley Everett and Dinty. Clint served in the Civilian Conservation Corps during WWII and returned to marry Merle Boyd. Merle died of cancer at

the age of 28. Later in life he married Louise Collins. Hattie Mae received her degree from Mississippi Teachers College, now USM and later received a master's degree in education. She had a long, distinguished career and retired after more than 50 years as an educator. Hattie Mae married Louie Dobbs and had one child, William Louie Dobbs Jr. who lives in Forest. Grady served in the Army during WWII in the Pacific Theater. He met and married Gaye Morton in California and they settled in the Forkville area, also. They had two children: Brenda Gaye and William Grady.

After Will died in 1935, Hattie concentrated on her children and grandchildren, guiding them to a strong faith in God and enriching their lives with her gentle wisdom and patience. She died in 1967 at the age of 85.

FARMER-DAVIS, Urial Turner Farmer (b. 1812, d. 1840) Wilkes County, GA md. Rebecka Myers Davis (b. 1816, d. 1849) Wilkes County, GA. Urial Turner Farmer is buried at the Baptist Cemetery, Hillsboro, MS. Rebecka is buried near Thomson, GA. Rebecka's father, Mark Price Davis, is buried in an unmarked grave near what used to be called Quaker Hill near McDuffie County, Thomson, GA. His grave is near a stone wall made by Quakers in the 1700s.

Fannie Jane "Good Mall Farmer, granddaughter of Urial Turner Farmer and Rebecka Myers Davis, on her porch sewing. Fannie was wife of James "Jim" Franklin Brogdon. (Approximately 1906)

They had six children: Perry De LaFayette, Frances Foster, Alexander Cecil "Mart," Derias Clayton, James Daniel and Martha Jane "Mattie." Three of their sons: Perry De LaFayette Farmer (b. 1832), Mart Farmer (b. 1835) and Derias Clayton "D.C." (b. 1836), all fought in the Civil War.

Mart Farmer enlisted in Mississippi (see Farmer-Moreman information).

Perry enlisted at Loachapoka, AL, Co. F, 46th Alabama Infantry Regt., on Apr. 20, 1862. Perry was first sent to east Tennessee where he fought at Tazewell. He then fought a short while in Kentucky and then the regiment came back to Tennessee. Then they were ordered to Mississippi where they lost heavily at Port Gibson (1863); at Jackson, they lost heavily at Bakers Creek. The regiment was then ordered to Vicksburg. After the surrender at Vicksburg, he managed to join the Army of Tennessee where he fought at Lookout Mountain and Missionary Ridge in 1863.

According to Perry's family, he was wounded and captured and sent to prison in Illinois, although no records prove this. His family said after he was released or escaped, he joined a raider band and continued to fight another year not knowing the war was over. He then returned home.

Perry and his family moved to Mississippi in late 1870-1871. Perry was injured when a mule team ran away with him and the wagon overturned. He suffered a head injury and was taken to the Mississippi Mental Hospital at Jackson, MS, where he died sometime in 1877.

D.C. Farmer joined the Confederate Army on Feb. 22, 1862, at Vaiden, MS, where he enlisted in CPT Samuel Bains' Company known as the Vaiden Volunteers Artillery, Mississippi Volunteers—later became Co. L, First Regiment Mississippi Light Artillery. D.C. served as a nurse in the French's Division Hospital, Lauderdale, MS.

After the Civil War, D.C. farmed successfully, but felt the call to preach. Soon after he began his preaching career, he moved his family to Walnut Grove, MS. Later, in order that his six children might attend a better school, he moved to Harperville. Then, he was assigned by the Methodist Conference.

D.C. was a good Bible student, fluent speaker and had great faith in prayer. When he was 80 years old, he broke his hip. He prayed and after one week of being in a cast, he asked his daughter to call the doctor. Finally being persuaded to take off the cast, to the doctor's surprise and everyone else, D.C. was completely healed. D.C. died in 1920 at D'Lo, MS, from a stroke.

FARMER-MOREMAN, Alexander Cecil
"Mart" Farmer (b. 1835, d. 1912) md. Mary Frances "Mollie" Moreman (b. 1839, d. 1923). Mart Farmer is buried in the Harperville Cemetery and Mollie is buried in Newton, MS. Mollie and Mart were married in the home of her father, Henry Jefferson Moreman, near Opelika, AL. Mollie and Mart were members of the Baptist Church at Turnerville, Macon County, AL.

They had 10 children, four born in Alabama and the rest in Mississippi.

Alexander Cecil "Mart" Farmer standing by horse, his wife, Mary Frances "Mollie," sitting in chair and her father, Henry Jefferson Moreman. Unknown housekeeper in background. Taken at the Old Home Place in Lillian, MS. (Approximately 1903)

Mart Farmer served in Co. H, 40th Mississippi Infantry, during the Civil War. Mart enrolled on Mar. 7, 1862, in Jackson, MS. In 1865, his regiment was consolidated with the 3rd and 31st Regiments, Mississippi Infantry and about 1865 were formed the Mississippi Consolidated Regiment, Mississippi Infantry.

Mart was wounded in the knee in the Battle of Vicksburg and he walked all the way home to Harperville.

Mart Farmer was a staunch Baptist and did not believe in drinking. After Sherman came through and burned practically everything during the Civil War, the Baptist Church at Hillsboro, MS, was left standing. Mart told Pastor Ford, of that church, that he would keep up the church even if it was just the two of them there.

Mart would get up before day and walk to Forest (about 10 miles) to buy a plow or whatever he needed. He would throw the plow over his shoulder and be back home before noon.

Fannie Jane Farmer (b. 1863, d. 1934), daughter of Mollie and Mart Farmer, married James "Jim" Franklin Brogdon (see Brogdon-Clower-Farmer information).

FIKES-SUMRALL, Scott County, MS has
been home to the Fikes families since Jacob Ezra and Lucinda Price Fikes moved to this southeast area of the county in 1863 from South Carolina. They brought one little daughter with them, Lenora Fikes, after losing a small son, Paris, by death in South Carolina. Several of the Fikes families went to Lauderdale, Jasper and Smith counties in Mississippi, Illinois and Texas. Lucinda died in 1867 and Ezra in 1899. Both are buried in High Hill Cemetery.

Fikes home built 1910-1911

Sumrall Reunion, August 1923

Jacob Wesley "J.W." Fikes was born on Mar. 29, 1864 and died Aug. 15, 19_ in Scott County and several siblings in later years to the Ezra Fikes family.

J.W. and his half-brother, Mac Duff Fikes, married sisters from Jasper County, Sena and Elizabeth Sumrall, respectively, on Oct. 13, 1892. Wesley and Sena Fikes (b. Dec. 5, 1878, d. Feb. 7, 1961). Their children are as follows: Ruth Estelle (b. Aug. 22, 1898, d. Oct. 12, 1979) md. Lester "L.C." Jones, a Scott County native and both are buried at Oak Grove Cemetery, Scott County. Their family consisted of Ruth Evangeline "Eva" (b. August 1915) who married Mac McCormick, both of whom are buried in Lakewood Memorial Cemetery, Jackson; John Wesley Jones (b. Jan. 12, 1918) lives in Madison, MS; Lavonne Estelle Bates (b. Mar. 23, 1924) and her husband Tommy Bates, are both buried in Lakewood Cemetery in Jackson; Leon Caldwell Jones (b. Mar. 23, 1924), twin of

Lavonne's, lives in the Oak Grove Community, married to Merle Madden Jones (b. Jul. 18, 1924). Grandchildren of Ruth and Lester Jones are Ted Jones, Johnny and Rosa Lynn Jones, Carl Jones, Pennye Dees and Ann Klouria; great-grandchildren: Bailey, Brad and Davis Jones; Mick and Sena Ruth Dees; Amy Jones. Grandchildren: Sena Beth Bates, Angle B. Blanchard. Donna B. LaBlanc, Tammy Morrissey. Children of Lavonne and Tommy Bates; great-grandchildren of Ruth and Lester: Rob Wadley, Parker and Hayden Blanchard (twins), Jennifer Blanchard and Sophia LeBlanc.

Sherman Fikes, the first-born son of Wesley and Sena Fikes, died at the age of 4 and is buried at High Hill Cemetery, 1894-1898.

Bartley Baxter Fikes, second son (b. December 1896), married Flournoye "Noye" Henry, both residents of Scott County. He died at age 67, is buried at Oak Grove Cemetery and she lives in Clinton, MS, with her daughter, Barbara Sue F. Donahoe. His first marriage to Fannie McCormick, who died in 1927, did not produce any heirs. Clyde Donahoe, husband of Barbara Sue, is buried in Lakewood South Cemetery, Jackson. Two grandsons of Bartley and Noye live in Jackson with their families, Mike and Cynthia and Mark and Patricia Donahoe and great-grands are Jonathan, Blake Morris and Lauren Donahoe.

Glover McDuff Fikes (b. February 1900, d. January 1986) married Estelle Eichelberger (b. 1907) in 1924; he died at age 86 and is buried in High Hill Cemetery. Estelle lives at Forest Rest Home and was 93 years old on Jul. 21, 2000.

Glover Wesley Fikes, oldest child (b. June 1925, d. 1996), is buried in Fort Walton Beach, FL, where his widow, Sybil Stroud Fikes, still resides. Two daughters born to Glover and Estelle: Fanny Fikes, died at age 1 year and is buried at High Hill Cemetery and Myrtle Ruth F. Hutchison (b. in December 1930) of Littleton, CO, is married to Lebrun Hutchison, Neshoba County, MS, native. They reside in Littleton, CO. Grandchildren, Stephan Wesley Fikes of Virginia Beach, VA died Jul. 6, 2000 and is buried at Fort Walton Beach, FL, leaves one daughter, Lacey. Stephanie F. Hornback of Niceville, FL and Jerome Fikes of Bay City, TX. Other grandchildren are Sylvia Hutchison Ballinger, CA; Stella H. McCumber of Colorado; and Great-grand, Alexandra and Jack Ballinger, Kalley Fikes and three children of Stella's: Dale Jr., Sara and David McCumber.

Wesley Homer Fikes, fourth son of J.W. and Sena Fikes, was born in February 1902 and married Lenora McWhorten in 1927. She was born in August 1902. He died in 1969 and she died in 1989. They are buried in Oak Grove Cemetery. Their only child, a son, Williford Harold Fikes (b. November 1928) died in a tragic car accident in February 1950 at age 21, a junior at Mississippi State University.

Howard Berkley Fikes, fifth son (b. November 1903) married Mary Eloise Polson of Kilmichael, MS. She died in 1984 and is buried in Kilmichael Cemetery and he died in August 1989 and is buried in Oak Grove Cemetery.

Pennye Merle Fikes Gatewood (b. May 2, 1912), age 89, was the only surviving member of the J.W. Fikes family. She married George Gatewood in August 1933. He was born Aug.

3, 1904. Both are retired and are living in the family home where she was born. He will be 96 in August 2000. She taught school 45 years and ?e farmed and was a mail carrier. Submitted by *?ennye Merle Gatewood.*

?IKES-SUMRALL, The Mac Duff "Duff" and Elizabeth "Lizzie" Sumrall Fikes family consisted of three small children left orphans in 1899 and 1900. Eliza-beth "Lizzie" died in October 1899 and Duff in March 1900, she being born in 1873 and he in 1865. Both are buried at High Hill Cemetery. At their deaths, Zerate A., age 6, Felton Blakely, age 4 and Florence Hurst, age 9 months, became

The Duff Fikes family: Duff, Hurst, Felton, Lizzie and Zerate

wards of their grandparents, Elisha Woods and Pennye Elizabeth Sumrall.

Zerate (b. Aug. 29, 1893) md. Mason E. Walton, a Newton County native, in 1917. Their children were Margaret Bradley, deceased, buried in Mobile, AL; Eldred Walton, deceased, buried in Starkville, MS; Ruth Frances Gulledge, resides in Jackson, MS; and Iva Jean Lancaster, resident of Auburn, AL. There were a total of 10 grandchildren. Mason died in 1978 and Zerate died in 1979, both are buried in Newton, MS, Cemetery.

Felton B. Fikes (b. 1895, d. 1973) md. Iva Overstreet, both are buried at Lakewood, Jackson, MS. Their family consisted of two children, Bettie Floore Copeland, Houston, TX, married John Copeland, residents of Houston and a son, Bill, who died at age of 4 years and is buried in Jackson.

Florence Hurst Fikes (b. 1898, d. 1950) md. Oscar L. McWhorter and both are buried at Fellowship Cemetery in Smith County. Four children were born to them: Mary Ellen M. Barnes (b. 1916) resides in Jackson; Felton Gifford McWhorter (b. 1919) is deceased and buried in Jackson; Jim Ward McWhorter (b. 1925) is deceased and buried in Jackson; and Leon Clayton McWhorter (b. 1927) resides in Fort Worth, TX. Grandchildren are Carla Barnes Camp and Lisa Barnes Byron, both of Jackson; Hugh Carlton McWhorter, Alton Gifford McWhorter and Cindy McWhorter Ryan, all of Jackson; Jim Owen McWhorter and Janet McWhorter Windham, both of Jackson; Lea Ann McWhorter and Carol McWhorter Gonzales, both of Fort Worth, TX. Several great-grandchildren survive this family. Bettie Fikes Copeland, Houston, TX; Joanne Copeland, Houston, TX; Rebecca Copeland, Cairo, Egypt; Jennifer Copeland, Crockett, CA.

FINLEY, One of the earliest settlers in Scott County was John Middleton Finley in the Sebastopol Damascus Territory. He came into this region in 1830 on a hunting expedition. About three years before the signing of the Dancing Rabbit Treaty and before it was divided into counties. This county was known as the Choctaw Nation.

Mr. Finley was impressed with the beauty of the land and timber, also the same was so plentiful that after the Treaty of Dancing Rabbit was signed in 1832, he returned and laid out a location on this land for himself. This land is still in possession of descendants. It is now owned by Mr. and Mrs. Roy Jones, descendants of Ann Elizabeth Finley Jones.

The Finleys lived all their lives there and raised their 14 children and four nephews. John M. Finley was made guardian of these boys after their father James Guynes, died.

John was born in Georgia. Later his father moved the family to Louisiana, then to Amite County MS. When land was made available he moved to Copiah County MS. There John met his future wife, Nancy Guynes. They married in 1831.

On arriving in Scott County they lived for a short time in an Indian house that stood on a hill near Hurricane Creek, just behind the home they built. John was the first probate judge of Scott County and was known as Judge Finely. Here is a listing of all their children. Martha Caroline md. William Clark; Nicholas F.M. Finley md. Mary J. Spivey; Matilda Jane md. Elias Jack Madden; Mary Butler Finley md. Henry W. Lang; John Guynes Finley md. Susan Chiply; Elizabeth md. William Anderson Welch; Henry W. md. Charlotte Victory Henderson; Nancy A. md. Henry J. Johnson; Ann Eliza md. Dallas M. Jones; Sarah Angeline md. William Edwards; George B. md. Nettie O. Mosley; Narcisus Finley; Kittie Ann md. William Dawson; Jefferson Davis Finley.

Many of the Finley descendants live in Scott County and surrounding counties at the present time.

I am very proud to be a member of such a strong, law abiding and God fearing family. The book, Finley's of Damascus, Mississippi *is in the Forest Public Library.*

FISCHER, Rachel (McGee) Fischer's grandparents are Jhue Jackson McGee and Emma Harvey. Parents are Malcolm Daniel McGee (b. Oct. 12, 1896) and Eula Lee Westerfield (b. Sep. 30, 1900).

Children of Malcolm and Eula: Jhue (b. Dec. 24, 1916); James Otis (b. Dec. 17, 1919); Daris Marshall (b. Jul. 24, 1922); Malcolm Hubert (b. Mar. 14, 1925); Rachel Lee (b. Jan. 13, 1928); Clyde Jim (b. Sep. 19, 1930); Vernon (b. Apr 1, 1933); Clarence Talmadge (b. Jul 24, 1935); Roy Odom (b. Feb. 4, 1938); Bernice (b. May 30, 1940); Ottis Lefet "Pat" (b. Oct. 22, 1942) and Frances Earleen (b. Nov. 14, 1946).

Rachel Lee McGee married Eddie Fischer on Dec. 22, 1955. They have two children: (1) Charles Edwin (b. Apr. 8, 1958) md. Alice Ruth Jennings on May 27, 1977, children: Lauryn Hope (b. Dec. 7, 1983) and Joel Edwin (b. Apr. 4, 1987). (2) Donald Ray (b. Jul. 19, 1961).

FISHER, This tale of Scott County is offered by the family that left Sebastopol, MS in search of fame and fortune, or at least a decent living, out west. This family eventually settled in Sebastopol, CA. What a small world.

The story, for me, begins with the 1870 Scott County census. In that is listed Mrs. Mary L. Fisher, mother of John (15), Alfred (13), James

(10) and Mary Jane "M.J." (8). Family legend tells of a rider coming by in 1864 and telling 9-year-old John to tell his mother that her husband was dead, killed in battle. I have yet to find any more information on his demise.

Henry Jacob Fisher married Mary Lavinah Burns in Macon, AL on Jan. 1, 1852. How they came to Scott County is still unknown to me. That the family remained is clear. The local cemeteries are well populated with Fisher descendants.

John Henry Fisher (b. 1855, d. 1919) md. Alzada Arlene Finley (b. 1861, d. 1931), daughter of John Guynes Finley and Susan Augusta Chipley, on Oct. 23, 1880 in Scott County. Their children were Alvin (b. 1882); John (b. 1883, d. 1925); Elzie (b. 1885, d. 1957); Elvie (b. 1887, d. 1970); Alma (b. 1888); Floy (b. 1891, d. 1964), Myrtle (b. 1892, d. 1980); Dewey (b. 1896, d. 1973); Duff (b. 1899, d. 1902); Claude (b. 1901, d. 1972) and an infant daughter (b&d. 1906).

Alfred Fisher was born about 1857 and is said to have died young. I have no further information on him.

James Elzie Fisher (b. 1860, d. 1943) md. (unknown) and had Hortense and Elzie C. Fisher, the only Mississippian to die in the Battle of Vera Cruz (1914). James then married Olive Horton and had five children: Iris, Jack, Florence, Woodrow and Auzine.

Mary Jane Fisher (b. 1862, d. 1942) md. James Woods Beeland in Scott County Feb. 24, 1878. Their children were Arthur (b. 1879, d. 1965); James (b. 1882, d. 1955); Mary (b. 1855, d. 1977); Lula (b. 1887, d. 1949); Jessie (b. 1890, d. 1969); Earl (b. 1893, d. 1968); Nettie Mae (b. 1896); John (b. 1898); Walter (b. 1901) and Loyse (b. 1904, d. 1974).

Claude Middleton Fisher (b. Sep. 25, 1901), son of John Henry Fisher, met his wife, Leota Auto Lenord, in Texas and they were married in 1926. They had two daughters, Zemma Arlene (b. 1927) and Claudia LaVerne (b. 1929) in Fabens, TX. A son, Claude Middleton Fisher Jr. (b. 1930) and daughter, Leota Imogene (b. 1933), were born in New Mexico before their return

Claude Middleton Fisher

to Scott County in 1934. In 1936 Claude Jr. was accidentally killed by a horse while playing and is buried at Damascus Cemetery. Sidney Lenard was born in Sebastopol, MS in 1937 before the family left for the last time. They returned to Texas and remained until WWII when they moved to California to work in the shipyard.

In 1945 after the war ended, the family took a year off to travel and pack fruit. It was after this that they purchased a 20 acre hilltop ranch in Sebastopol, CA and settled, raising cattle (and the occasional grandchild) until they retired. Claude passed away Aug. 23, 1972 and Leota followed 18 years later Aug. 20, 1990. They both rest at Sebastopol Memorial Lawn, Sebastopol, CA. Submitted by Claude Fisher Jones.

FLEMING, William Thomas "Tom" Fleming, son of Thomas Samuel Fleming and Eugenia Thompson Fleming, was born on Sep. 21, 1891 in Neshoba County, MS. He married Mamie Zelma Lamkin of Ludlow, MS, on Dec. 6, 1913 and thereafter moved to Scott County. Three children were born to this union: Tommie Adell Fleming, Guy William Fleming and Clyde B. Fleming.

Adell Fleming (b. Sep. 29, 1918) md. Coy Shumaker on Oct. 12, 1935. They had one daughter, Velma Inez (b. Nov. 15, 1942). Adell and Coy were cattle farmers and owned both a country grocery and an egg farm. Adell may best be remembered for her love of flowers. Adell died on Apr. 23, 1993 and Coy died May 21, 1997. Their daughter, Inez, married Roy Marion Lawrence on Jan. 29, 1962 and together they have four children: Michael Roy, Matthew Coy, Mitzi Adell and Muffy Ann. Inez is a schoolteacher and she and Roy live in the Coal Bluff Community. They have six grandchildren: Austin Blake Lawrence, Leah Noelle Lawrence, Garrett Matthew Lawrence, Glenn Christopher Bryant, Kenneth Roy Bryant and Haley Paige Lawrence.

Guy Fleming (b. May 25, 1921) md. Ruby Inez Shoemaker on May 11, 1946. They have two daughters, Helen Jean (b. Oct. 22, 1947) and Hilda Dean (b. Jul. 27, 1953). Guy and Ruby currently live on the same property where Guy's parents once lived. Tom Fleming lost the property during the Great Depression and thereafter worked as a sharecropper, but Guy re-purchased the land in 1953. Guy has lived his entire life in Scott County, where he and Ruby raised cattle and chickens for approximately 50 years. Their older daughter, Helen, married Jimmy Lee Thrash on Apr. 9, 1966 and together they have two daughters, Cheryl Lynn and Chandra Leigh.

Helen retired from teaching school after 23 years. She and Jimmy presently live in the Leesburg Community and own Thrash Aviation, Inc. They have two grandchildren: John Elliott Jolley and Laura Alice Lee. Guy and Ruby's younger daughter Hilda married Randy Salmon on Jan. 16, 1980. Hilda is a schoolteacher and she and Rancy live near Hattiesburg, MS.

Clyde Fleming (b. Jan. 8, 1925) md. Betty Jean Holmes on Apr. 5, 1946. They had two children: Wanda Hope (b. Jun. 1, 1959) and Wendell Hugh (b. Aug. 24, 1963). Clyde and his brother Guy served in WWII and were discharged in 1945. Clyde was in the Battle of the Bulge. He was a farmer and a trim carpenter until his death on Oct. 25, 1988.

Clyde and Betty's daughter, Hope, holds a BS/BA degree from Mississippi College and is also a registered nurse. She is co-owner of Travel America in the Lake Harbor Community.

Clyde and Betty's son, Hugh, married Betty Lori Harvey on Jul. 6, 1986 and together they have two daughters, Lindsey Kristin and Courtney Brooke. Hugh graduated from East Central Community College and works as a trim carpenter. Hugh and Lori currently own Lights and More in Brandon, MS.

FORD, Willie Inez Ford (b. May 19, 1907 in Newton County, MS) moved to Forest, Scott County, in 1914 with her mother Ogenia Morris-Ford after the tragic death of her father Rev.

Carter Ford. She was the fifth sibling of the 10 children born to this family. They lived in Singleton-town Community. Her mother later married and they moved to Smith County. Willie eventually moved back to Forest where she worked for the Huffs, Judge Percy Mercer Lee Sr. and his wife Mrs. Hattie Mae Nutt-Lee and Mrs. Claudia Lee and also Dr. and Mrs. Kermit Reynolds.

Willie had four children: Walter Robert Lovelady (b. 1921), James Carter Robinson (b. 1922, d. 1924 of diphtheria), William "Pete" Robinson (b. 1927) and Carolyn Sue Edwards (b. 1947).

Her sons Walter Robert and William were noted for their athletic abilities. Both attended Scott County Training School and Alcorn A&M College. Walter Robert married Mae Doris Scott and William, noted for his talent of singing, married Annie Louise Patrick. Her daughter, Carolyn, married William Limbert Knowles and was noted for her singing talent.

Willie learned to play the piano and became well known for playing for churches throughout Scott County for more than 62 years. She was an active member of Concord Missionary Baptist Church. She attended the public school in Newton and Scott counties.

Willie married Eli Robinson and later Lewis Edwards. However, she chose to use her maiden name. Willie died Aug. 18, 1996 and is buried in Eastern (Lovelady) Cemetery in Forest, MS.

FORTUNE, Kermit Dale (b. Aug. 22, 1949) a native of Leake County, son of Henry Fortune and Wilma Herrington Fortune. Dale had one brother and one sister. Dale graduated Lena High School in 1969. He has always worked in the retail business. Dale started working in Scott County in 1987.

In 1999 he married Joanne Grantham Macoy, daughter of Enoch and Mildred

Kermit Dale Fortune and Joanne Macoy Fortune

Grantham of Harrisville, MS. Joanne was a widow with four grown children and 11 grandchildren.

Dale and Joanne make their home in Forest.

FOUNTAIN, Vera Gaskin "Aunt Vera" or "Miss Vera" as she was affectionately called by all who knew her, was born Vera Gaskin on Feb. 20, 1904 in Scott County. She was the fourth child of Madison Henry and Laura Cameron Gaskin, who had a total of 13 children. They lived on a farm in the southeast section of Scott County. The Post Office address was Sun, MS.

Vera's parental grandparents were Thomas George (who came to Scott County from South Carolina) and Mary Durr Gaskin. Her maternal grandfather, John Andrew Cameron, came from Greene County, AL to Scott County at the end of the War Between the States. Her maternal grandmother, Henrietta Victoria Harmon, came to Scott County with her parents from South

Carolina in a buggy and covered wagon sometime in the early 1850s.

Vera's father was a farmer and the entire family worked hard to make a living. Vera wanted to become a school teacher and help her family so that life would be a little easier for them.

During her 33 year teaching career, she taught at various locations. When she first began teaching at age 18, she had elementary school students. However, she taught high school English for much of her career. She was the first fe-

Vera Gaskin holding her cousin, Lucelle Cameron, on the left and her sister, Dorothy Ellen Gaskin, on the right, in 1924

male faculty member at Chamberlain Hunt Military Academy. Vera said the first thing she learned when she began teaching was, "You can't teach what you don't know and I've learned that it is what you don't know that is important." She ended her teaching career at Forest High School.

Vera married Osborne B. Fountain (who died March 1969) late in life. She had no children of her own, but had two stepchildren. Although she had no children, Vera had more children than anyone you will ever know. She loved all children and always had a treat for any child who came to visit. Vera and her husband built their home on the exact same location of the old home where she grew up.

Vera Gaskin during her teaching career in the 1940s

Vera was one of the most talented individuals one would ever meet. Every room in her home displayed a special talent; handmade bedspread and drapes in one room, embroidered pictures in another, ceramics and table runners in the kitchen and the wallpaper and paint throughout the house were her creations. She loved all kinds of handwork. Crochet was one of her favorite pastimes and everyone who came by for a visit usually left with a crochet doily or a towel with crochet edging. Vera loved giving gifts to all her friends, neighbors and relatives.

Vera also was an accomplished seamstress. She could see a dress or a jacket in a store, come home, cut herself a pattern from newspaper and create exactly what she had seen in the store. She was a wonderful cook. Those who visited her always had to eat something before they could leave. She always had "goodies" on hand and most often home made brownies for her guests to eat there or to take with them. Vera loved poetry and could quote "word for word" poems she had learned throughout her life. She was able to do this up until her death.

Vera Gaskin Fountain died Dec. 7, 1997 of cancer. She had gallantly battled the cancer for several years. Vera had a strong and complete faith in God. She loved life and all living creatures. Vera was a very special person, a great lady who always lived an exemplary life. She is sadly missed by all who knew her.

May her soul rest in peace and may light perpetually shine upon her.

GADDIS, Thomas Benjamin "T.B." Gaddis (b. May 21, 1862 in Morton) was the son of Dr. John Thomas "Jack" Gaddis and Laura Rawls Marion and married Mary Bryan Wooten on Jan. 23, 1884 in Forest.

Thomas Benjamin "T.B." Gaddis upstairs in his office area

Mary was the daughter of Graham and Carolyn Wooten. She was born on Mar. 21, 1864 in Forest. T.B. was the founder and owner of the T.B. Gaddis Mercantile Company, T.B. also had a millinery store and a fertilizer and feed warehouse. During T.B.'s lifetime he had the largest merchandising store in Scott County. People came for miles around to trade at the Gaddis store.

T.B.'s father also had a general merchandise store in Morton in 1879. T.B. and Mary had four children born in Scott County: Carolyn, Fannie Laurie, Minnie Zula and Watt Wooten. The Gaddis' lived in Morton until their daughters entered Belhaven College. At that time the family moved to Jackson but T.B. continued to operate the Gaddis Mercantile Company in Morton. After the death of Mr. T.B. Gaddis the store was liquidated.

Wooten Gaddis and his wife Eunice bought the store building from his sisters and reopened it. Eunice kept it open, after the death of Wooten, for five more years. She sold it to Charles Clifford III in April 1968. During the 1966 Centennial, Eunice Gaddis was the winner of the first prize for a store window display. She had on display some of the early fixtures from the Gaddis store. It was the oldest store in Morton at the time of the Centennial.

David and Rita French, French's Pharmacy, are now the owners of the Gaddis building. With much time and effort, they have restored the building to it's original splendor.

GARDNER-THRASH, Lonnie Gardner was born Jan. 7, 1874 to John and Sarah Gardner in the northern part of Scott County and died Aug. 17, 1964. Bethany Thrash Gardner was born May 31, 1875 to W.H. and Martha Thrash of Newton County, MS and died Sep. 4, 1964.

They were married Mar. 3, 1898. They were farmers and members of Sebastopol Baptist Church. Five children were born to this union: Dallas, Andrew, Elvie, Lelia and Oliver. Thirteen grandchildren including Laverne Sharp, Sebastopol; Billie Welch, Brandon; and Maxine Patrick, Morton, MS. Great-grandchildren include Julian Sharp, Lake; Travis Sharp, Sebastopol; and Margaret Rush, Union.

Lonnie and Bethany Gardner

GARNER, Mary Martha Sigrest (b. 1850, d. Mar. 29, 1934) was the daughter of Melvin Sigrest. In 1869 she married Americus Garner, a Confederate veteran from Jefferson Davis County. He died Jan. 10, 1878 in Jefferson Davis County leaving Mary with two young sons, Willie Zedora (b. Dec. 17, 1870, d. Jan. 29, 1929) and Jasper Wellington (b. Feb. 2, 1873, d. Apr. 21, 1960).

Family story says that three days after Americus was buried, Mary loaded her possessions and the 8 and 5-year-old boys in a wagon and came back to Scott County to claim some land. This land was in southern Scott County near the Smith County line—it was Strong River Swamp land with first growth forests. The sons grew up and reared their families on this land in the Springfield area known as Garnertown.

Willie Z. Garner family and mother. Standing in front: Louie and Celeste. Seated: Willie Z., Fannie Viola with Dola on lap. Mary Martha. Standing in rear: Mary and Nola

Willie Z. married Fannie Viola Rushing (b. Oct. 16, 1870, d. Jul. 21, 1950). He was in the logging/timber business. He used oxen to get the felled trees out of the swamp. A train came from the big mill at Morton and hauled the logs back to the mill; this was the Dummy Line. He also had a sawmill on the property. His sons grew up working with their father and kept the timber business until the early 1950s.

These are the children of Willie and Fannie: Mary (b. Feb. 5, 1894, d. Jul. 30, 1929) md. Forest Miles; Nola (b. Jan. 24, 1897, d. Jan. 13, 1977) md. Absolom Idom, his second wife; Louie (b. Jun. 30, 1900, d. Jul. 25, 1942) md. Anna/Annie? Horn; Pearly Celeste (b. Aug. 20, 1902, d. Jan. 2, 1962) md. Frank Idom; Dola Clester (b. Mar. 29, 1904, Dec. 19, 1979) md. Golden Kuhn; Thomas Jefferson "Jeff" (b. May 2, 1906, d. Oct. 24, 1964) md. Elma Copeland; William Fredrick (b. Mar. 29, 1907, d. Nov. 10, 1961) md. Wydell Fountain; Tonce Butell "T.B." (b. Jul. 5, 1909, d. Mar. 27, 1958) md. "Tot" Jones; Sudie (b. Dec. 3, 1911, d. Dec. 30, 1975) md. Bolen Stegall.

Willie, Fannie and all the children except Louie and Sudie are buried in the cemetery at Springfield Church.

Jasper Wellington "Welly" married Mary Josephine "Phenie" Winstead (b. Jun. 15, 1888, d. Jan. 20, 1954). Welly was a farmer. He was one of the earliest commercial chicken farmers in the area. There were five children in this family: Lennie md. Benjaman Cooper, both are deceased; Ray md. Ella Gray, both are deceased; Cleo never married and is in nursing home in Morton as of December 2000; Clara Bell (deceased) md. a Myrick; Joe David md. Ruthie Hawkins.

Willie and Welly married cousins, so the children always said they were first cousins and second cousins. There are still second, third and fourth generations of this Garner family living in the Springfield area of Scott County. Submitted by Frances Idom Cooper.

GIBSON-PALMER, Perry Franklin Gibson, a 22-year-old electric lineman apprentice and Bobbye Ruth Palmer, a 17-year-old senior at Forest High School, eloped to Mendenhall, MS, on Sunday afternoon Feb. 16, 1941 and were married by Rev. C.C. Jones, a prominent Baptist minister. Raymond Mapp was best man.

Perry Franklin and Bobbye (Palmer) Gibson

After a dinner in Jackson and delivering Bobbye to her home, Perry caught the 10 o'clock bus to Meridian where he worked for the Mississippi Power Company. There he found his draft notice waiting for him! Eight days later he was a $21 a month buck private at Camp Shelby.

Perry wrote Bobbye a postcard addressed to Mrs. Perry Franklin Gibson and since his dad and two of Bobbye's relatives worked in the post office, by the time she got to school, their marriage had been announced all over town.

The reactions were "crazy kids!" "cradle robber!" "give them 3-6 months!". "it will all be over in a year!" But with love for each other, the help of two sets of loving parents and caring friends, they made it through the war years.

Following are some of the things that has happened from then until now:

Perry graduated from Forest High School, Class of 1936, president of the class and captain of the "Bearcats" football team. He is a graduate of Coyne Electronic School and has completed studies in advertising and sales management from Lasalle Extension University. He was ordained as a Baptist deacon in 1956.

Retiring from the Mississippi Power Company after 42 years of service, January 1946-February 1968, he was their local manager in Richton, which also included Beaumont and New Augusta. This is where their children were born. His last 14 years were as manager of its Bay St. Louis operations.

With five years of military service, he spent 41 months of this time in the southwest Pacific during WWII. He graduated from the Signal Section of Officers' Candidate School in Ipswich, Australia, then was assigned to the 5th Air Force. He attained the rank of captain. His service included the campaigns of Papua, New Guinea, southern Philippines, northern Philippines and the Occupations of both Okinawa and Japan.

In 1972 he received a five year appointment to the State Park Commission, serving as its chairman in 1976; he was named a colonel and aid-de-camp in both the Waller and Finch administrations and was honored with an award for "Meritorious Service" to the State of Mississippi by Governor Finch.

In 1976 he was honored with an award for "Honorable and Distinguished Citizenship" by the city of Waveland. In 1981 he was honored by the Hancock County Chamber of Commerce as "The Outstanding Citizen" of the year.

His past civic involvement includes president of the Richton Rotary Club and chairman of the Trustees of the Richton Separate School District.

He was the disaster chairman for the Perry County Red Cross where he handled the relief for victims of a record flood of the Leaf River and a killer tornado in the Brewer Community.

He was a leader in which over 90 percent of the people of Perry County were vaccinated against polio in one day. He organized and was the first commanding officer of the National Guard unit in Richton. He was twice president of the Hancock County Chamber of Commerce, vice-president of the governing board of the Hancock Medical Center, a member of the Hancock County Port and Harbor Commission and the Hancock County member to the Gulf Coast Regional Wastewater Authority.

His fraternal affiliations include the Gulf Coast Chapter of the Sons of the American Revolution, the Sam Davis Camp of the Sons of the Confederacy and the Gulf Coast Chapter of the 31st Infantry (Dixie) Division Association. He is listed in the bicentennial issue of Notable Americans.

He is the author of a privately printed book, Gods Apprentice. *It contains 80 original, short, though provoking or inspirational messages he has delivered before various audiences. An autobiography titled "The Draftee," detailing his years of military service has been distributed to his descendants.*

During WWII, while Perry was overseas 3-1/2 years without coming home, Bobbye lived with her family and Perry's while working, for Mr. Taylor Tadlock as deputy tax assessor of Scott County. During slack times in that office, she also worked in the offices of the Sheriff, Chancery Clerk and Circuit Clerk and served as Clerk of Court during one session.

Mr. Tadlock led singing conventions and singing in churches during revivals. He encouraged his daughter Helen, Peggy Mapp and Bobbye to form a trio, accompanied by his youngest daughter, Miriam. They sang in churches, at funerals, high school graduations and other occasions.

After Perry's return and they moved to Richton, she was a full time mom and homemaker. She was active in the Baptist Church, teaching Sunday School and serving one year as president of the Women's Missionary Union. She was also a member of the Richton Woman's Club and Richton Garden Club.

The last year there, she had the unique experience of attending Jones Community College with her two oldest children, even taking English 101 in the same class with her daughter!

After the move to Bay St. Louis in 1968, she was an office employee at Hancock General Hospital, then as a medical secretary at Bay-Waveland Clinic, where one of the doctors was Dr. M.L. "Buddy" Dodson, formerly of Harperville.

The Gibsons had moved into their new home in Waveland when on Aug. 17, 1969, the worst hurricane (Camille) in history to hit the United States came. The eye passed over Bay St. Louis and the bay, blowing all the water out of it.

On preparing for the storm they had evacuated their daughters to Forest; their son was already married.

Perry, as local manager of the Mississippi Power Company, spent the night at his office two blocks from the bay, along with several other Power Company employees, ready to go to work as soon as the wind died down. Bobbye went to a school nearby, also two blocks from the bay, that had been opened as a shelter.

The screaming wind in excess of 200 miles per hour, the lowest barometer reading ever recorded anywhere in the world, the noise of buildings blowing away and other noises and sensations that long night were unbelievable.

The next morning everyone was in shock as they became aware of the damage. What had not washed into the gulf was piled 20 feet high on the beach and in the streets: smashed buildings, power and telephone poles and wires, trees broken in two or uprooted, furniture, dead people and animals.

No water, power, sewage, telephone, grocery stores, gas stations, etc. were too damaged to open; streets blocked so doctors and medical facilities were unavailable.

Their home, three blocks from the beach, had survived the winds with only minor roof damage, but the storm surge had broken open a door and destroyed all the appliances, furniture and other things. Water had settled at 30 inches for several hours leaving, silt, limbs, lizards and other debris.

Many of the power company employees had lost their homes entirely or had severe damage, yet they went to work with a will under very hard living conditions.

Line crews were sent from other electric companies across the south, but since there was no place for them to stay after work, they, along with Perry, were bused to New Orleans.

Perry worked late into the night and started again in the early morning hours for many weeks. He lost a thousand customers that took 10 years to regain.

Hancock General Hospital was so badly damaged the patients had to be evacuated by air. Many of the doctors and other personnel had lost their homes, some had been hurt or lost family members.

Bobbye found working conditions hard. After the most serious cases were again being admitted, a few dim lights powered by generators, no air-conditioning and charts missing.

The hours after work were spent getting the ruined furniture, clothes, etc. out of the house and it repaired, disinfected, repainted and new furnishings bought.

Food at home was plain bread and bologna sandwiches washed down with bottled water distributed door to door by the Salvation Army; candle light, baths in a pan, curfew from dark to daylight. The family was very grateful for all the help that came from New Orleans, the Red Cross, Salvation Army, family and friends.

While living on the coast Bobbye has been active in the First Baptist Church of Bay St. Louis. She was a charter member of the Bay St. Louis-Waveland Altrusa Club and is presently a member of the Gulf Coast Chapter of the Daughters of the American Revolution.

Bobbye and Perry have four children: Stanton Grimes, Perry Angela, Marie Paige and Leisa Jean.

Stanton (b. Feb. 10, 1947) was educated at Richton High, Jones Community College and the electrical apprentice training program at Ingall's Shipbuilding, Pascagoula. A 33-year employee, he is now foreman of supervisors in the electronic department. He first married Jeannie Walley. They are the parents of Kimberly Michele and Stanton Grimes Jr.

Michele is married to Vince Howard, employed at Ship's Furnishings in Pascagoula. She is a full time homemaker and mother of their three children: Amanda (12), Kendall (4) and Ethan (2).

Stan Jr. was educated at Gulf Coast Community College and a school for aircraft mechanics. He is now certified in the repair of jet engines. His wife, Kelly, is a registered nurse.

Stan Sr. married second Johanna "Jody" O'Brian who brought her two children, Joy and Jim, into the relationship along with four grandchildren: Jessica, Katie, Genna and Ian.

Angela (b. Apr. 7, 1949) is a graduate of Richton High, Jones Community College and the University of Southern Mississippi with a decree in speech pathology. She is a 28 year employee of Delta Airlines. Her husband, Bruce Jaildagian, is a marine biologist. They are the parents of Dylan (12) and Anna Leigh (11). Their home is in New Smyrna Beach, FL.

Paige (b. Mar. 9, 1952) was educated at Bay St. Louis High, Pearl River Community College and Southeastern Louisiana University. She is a registered respiratory therapist and lives in Novato, CA. Her husband was Robert A. McArthur Sr., a consultant on oil refinery construction. Their two children are Cynthia Marie and Robert Alison Jr. "Mac."

Cynthia received a bachelor of arts degree in political science from Louisiana State University, graduating cum laude. She is also a graduate of the School of Law. University of California at Berkeley (Boalt Hall), where she received her juris doctorate. She is employed as a corporate attorney in San Francisco. Her husband, Glenn Morelli, is a geologist. They live in Novato, CA.

Mac is a certified welder working in oil refinery construction and maintenance. His wife,

Yevette, brought two children into the union. Joshua (12) and Justin (10). They live in Gonzales, LA.

Leisa (b. May 28, 1957) is a graduate of Bay St. Louis High and William Carey College with a BS in elementary education. However, she is a reinstatement analyst with Equitable Assurance Company.

She married first Paul M. Skrmetti of Biloxi. They are the parents of Staci Leigh (20), Paul. Jr. (deceased) and Perry Joseph (18).

Leisa married second Thomas L. Blackwell, a specialist in the machinery that manufactures various concrete products. They live in Charlotte, NC. He brought two children, T.A. and Cynthia, into the marriage.

T.A. is a prison guard. He and his wife, Randi, have a newborn daughter, Laura Ashley.

Cynthia is a second year honor student at Gulf Coast Community College, Biloxi.

At this writing, Oct. 16, 2000, Perry and Bobbye have been married 59 years and eight months.

They have pre-placed their burial monument on the Gibson plot in Eastern Cemetery at Forest where they wish to rest until the second coming of their Lord and Savior, Jesus Christ.

GIBSON-RATCLIFF-GATEWOOD-GRIMES,

My family of Gibsons moved to Forest in the early years of the 20th century. They came from northwest Louisiana with the Bienville Lumber Company. My parents were Perry Henry Gibson and his wife Vera New Grimes. I was born in Forest on May 13, 1918. I have one sister, Ann Marie "Peggy" who married Titus Mapp, the son of Lorene and Charlie Mapp of Forest.

After Forest High School, Peggy attended Blue Mountain College. She was a secretary and worked for the Forest First Baptist Church and the local Chamber of Commerce. Titus, a WWII veteran was employed as a postal supervisor in Forest. Their only child, Molly, an X-ray technician, married Stan Prevost of Attala County. They are the parents of two sons, Shay and Noah.

In today's terminology my mother would be considered hyperactive. She was always busy. A great cook, artist, money manager, seamstress and landlord. She rented out two apartments in our big, old house on Hillsboro Street.

I was mostly reared by my Grandmother Grimes who lived with us. My father and his father were railroad engineers. After the mill cut out my father (Pop) became a deputy sheriff and was a long-time postal employee at Forest. He is best remembered as a Little League baseball coach and one of the great hunters and fisherman of his time. He was a veteran of WWI and was always active in the American Legion. One year he was named Woodman of the Year.

My father's nickname was "Pop." He was a very heavy smoker. Early on, when television was a novelty, a business placed a television out front so locals could watch as a remote crew went around town filming scenes. They focused on a group that showed volumes of smoke coming from one of them. Pop remarked. "That S.O.B. is on fire." The camera shifted, it was Pop!

My Gibson grandparents were Robert Henry and wife Eunice Eliza Ratcliff.

Robert was born in Courtland, AL, in 1869. Records show that his father, Robert, was born in Alabama and that his parents came from Kentucky. He was a shoe carpenter in the Confederate army. He and his family moved to Caddo Parish, LA. He was a farmer and his principal crop was tobacco.

Eunice, according to family legend, was related to President Woodrow Wilson through her mother whose maiden name was Wilson. Her Ratcliff line goes back to the year 1020 when Ivo de Tailbois of Normandy came to England with the invasion. The first Ratcliff of our line in America was Richard, a Quaker, lawyer, planter and weaver. He landed at Choptank, MD on Nov. 10, 1682. Her great-great-great-grandfather Joseph Ratcliff was a patriot of the American Revolution.

Her great-grandfather, another Joseph Ratcliff, was the captain of his company in the War of 1812. Her grandfather, Isaiah Ratcliff, was a member of the Minden Rangers, a Confederate cavalry unit who fought with Hood's brigade and with J.E.B. Stuart's division.

His brother Richard served in the same unit. After the war he went to Brazil as a Baptist missionary. He planted the seed and as of 1929 there were 450,000 members in 2,800 Baptist churches in that country.

Isaiah and Richard were great uncles of B.B. McKinney who composed many religious songs that can still be found in Baptist hymnals.

These grandparents brought three other children to Forest.

Allen, a WWI veteran and a plumber died in 1933. He and his wife, Blanche Barnes, reared south of Forest, had one son, Wayne. He was a good football player for the "Bearcats." Later he played fullback at Ole Miss when the whole squad volunteered for military service after the Japanese attack on Pearl Harbor. After the war he graduated from Temple University.

His wife was from Kalamazoo, MI and that is where he lived and worked as a fuel oil distributor before they decided to come South. His widow, Jean, lives in Long Beach, MS, near where he is buried. Their two sons, Steve and Tommy, make their home on the coast with their families. Blanche is near 100 years old. She is in a nursing home in Forest.

Another son, Stanton, returned to Louisiana where he was the captain of the Minden fire department until his retirement. He married Estelle Mozingo. He died at 94 years of age and is buried near his home.

Tessie Lee, a pianist and school teacher, was married to Orous "Ocie" Ellis from Leake County. He was a member of a quartet with Ross Barnett. He was a rural mail carrier. Tessie now widowed and 97 years old lives in Satsuma, AL, with her daughter, Rita, also a widowed, retired school teacher. There is, one son, Orous, who retired as a colonel, a helicopter pilot with extensive service in Vietnam. He and his family live in Alabama.

My mother, Vera, was the daughter of Benjamin Franklin Cleveland Grimes "Frank" and Mary Wall "Molly" Gatewood.

Frank came to Leake County shortly after the Civil War with his widowed mother, Amanda and five more small children. She came with the Gomillion family with which she had close ties.

They lived their first year in Leake County in their covered wagon.

Frank's father, James Grimes, a member of Co. B, 2nd Regt., Georgia State Troops, died in the service of the Confederacy.

James and his father, Lewis, lived in Stuart County, GA. The father of Louis, James and his grandfather, lived in Duplin County, NC.

Amanda and her three oldest sons established the Grimes family in Leake County and possibly in all of Mississippi. Amanda with her two youngest children who never married, are buried at Mt. Zion Church cemetery, a few miles north of Sebastopol.

Frank Grimes owned a general merchandise store in Harperville. It also housed the post office. Their home was next to the store.

Frank and Molly had one other daughter, Jewell "Judy." Both she and my mother finished school at the Harperville Agricultural High School. It was a boarding school. I can still remember those large wooden dormitories. A graduate from that school could get a license to teach.

Judy, a talented pianist and teacher, married Forrest Vernon McFatridge, a Baptist preacher. They served for years as home missionaries. Later, he was a pastor at Coldwater, at Lillian and at Springfield, South of Morton.

Their one daughter, Mary Bess, married Dr. Ralph Clayton of north Mississippi. They are the parents of six children. A son, Forest Vernon Jr., is married and lives in Nashville, TN. Judy and Brother Mac are buried in the Eastern Cemetery at Forest.

Frank Grimes had three children by a former marriage. Wilie married a Mr. Gresham. She and Frank Jr. "Bud" made their home in Bay Springs. Dessie married a South Scott County Gatewood. They remained in the county. Their children were Wayne and Dorothy.

Frank is buried in the Pleasant Hill Cemetery south of Carthage. Molly is buried in the Gibson plot, Eastern Cemetery, Forest.

Molly was the daughter of Richard Henry Gatewood and his wife Amanda Merrill of Carrol County.

Richard Henry and his brother William Andrew, with their mother, Lucy Dabney New Gatewood, relocated to Scott County from Kentucky before the Civil War.

William Andrew with their mother settled in south Scott County near Norris. Richard Henry who settled in north Scott County near Lillian was a pharmacist and a large landowner. He served the Confederacy as a private in Co. K, 2nd Regt., Mississippi Cavalry. He later transferred to hospital duty.

Richard Henry and William Andrew were the sons of Robert A. Gatewood and his wife Lucy Dabney New. Robert's father was Andrew Gatewood, a son of Isaac Gatewood. Andrew is on the patriot rolls of the DAR. Robert's wife came south with her sons because he had died from injuries due to being dragged by a horse.

Lucy Dabney New Gatewood was the daughter of Colonel Anthony New and his wife Nancy Wyatt. Colonel New served in the Revolution 1777-1781. He was colonel of the Virginia Militia 1780-1781. He was a member of the House of Delegates 1785-1790. He was a congressman from Virginia 1793-1805. He served in the 3rd, 4th, 5th, 6th, 7th and 8th Congress. Moving to Kentucky, he 17th Congress.

GILL-DENSON, Margaret A.H. Denson, youngest daughter and child of Shadrach J. and Alethia Denson, was born about 1838/9 at their plantation on the Coffee Bogue. Her first marriage occurred about 1859 to Francis C. Smith Jr., son of Francis C. Smith and brother of John Lane Smith and Sarah L. Smith. Francis C. Smith served in Co. F, 36th Mississippi Infantry during the Civil War. He died of disease in 1862.

In 1869, Margaret Denson Gill was married to Col. William Pagan Gill, moving with him to his place in the Pleasant Hill Community in Leake County. Colonel Gill died in 1880 leaving a young widow, five minor orphans and an estate heavily in debt. Margaret Denson Smith Gill later purchased her husband's estate at public auction. She died in Jackson in 1906.

Children of Francis C. Smith and Margaret A.H. Denson: Sarah Frances Smith (b. Jan. 20, 1862, d. Sep. 19, 1945) md. Charles Alexander Huddleston.

Children of William Pagan Gill and Margaret A.H. Denson: William Pagan Gill (b. 1870, d. 1935); Robert H. Gill (b. Jan. 1, 1872, d. Apr. 7, 1919); Mary Elizabeth Gill (b. _, d. aft. 1916); James Denson Gill (b. 1876, d. 1916), and John Marshall Gill (b. Apr. 27, 1879, d. Jul. 25 1957).

GOODSON, John Alexander Goodson was the sixth child of Robert E. Goodson, who purchased land in the eastern part of Scott County around 1854. John was born in Scott County on Mar. 1, 1860. He married Margaret E. Harrison who was born Sep. 12, 1859, in Marion, Perry County, AL on Dec. 23, 1881. This union produced 12 children: James Oliver, Tennie, Albert Franklin, William, Alice Naomie, Carrie Estelle, Nola, Leslie Benton, Mary, Chester Eli, Ruby Pearl and Roy Densmore. This was a very prolific family.

Harrison Town School Group (1910 or 1912). Front Row seated: George Johnson, Lula Johnson, Sallie Harrison with Sarah in lap, Dollie Harrison, Jim Harrison with Liles Harrison in lap, Margaret Harrison with James Harrison in lap, Allie Harrison with Larther Harrison in lap. Second Row, L-R, Seated: Ollie Goodson, standing Sidney Johnson, Eli Goodson, Robert Harrison, Lessie Harrison, School teacher (name unknown), Charlie Harrison, Ottis Johnson, Percy Harrison, Roy Goodson, Lowery Harrison. Back Row, L-R: Stella Goodson, Edna Johnson, Nola Goodson, Lonnie Johnson, Tom Harrison, Allie Harrison, Leslie Goodson and Allie Goodson. Note: Margaret Harrison is Joseph Goodson's grandmother. All others are his aunts and uncles.

James Oliver "Ollie" (b. Oct. 15, 1883) md. Ida Bonnie Harmon (b. Dec. 10, 1886) and had 10 children.

Tennie (b. May 16, 1884) md. John Apslum "Alps" Harmon (b. Feb. 22, 1871) and had seven children. Alps had been married and had two children by his first wife, Evie.

Albert Franklin "Didder" (b. Mar. 5, 1885) md. Mary Frances "Fannie" Robinson (b. Sep. 5, 1902) and they had 11 children.

William "Babe" (b. May 7, 1888, d. May 5, 1912) was the fourth child and never married.

Alice Naomie "Allie" (b. August 1889) md. Davis Leon "Lynn" Henry and had 11 children.

Carrie Estelle "Stella" (b. Feb. 12, 1892) md. Robert E.L. "Alphabet" Kelly (b. Jun. 4, 1874) and they had one child. Stella married W.L. Riser after Robert died.

Nola (b. Sep. 28, 1894) md. James Walter Cox (b. Feb. 25, 1884) and they had five children.

Leslie "Buddy" (b. Mar. 28, 1896) md. Rubie Lillie Slade (b. Apr. 16, 1900) and they had 10 children.

Mary (b. April 1898, d. as a small child).

Eli (b. August 1900, d. Oct. 15, 1981) was never married.

Ruby Pearl (b. Feb. 22, 1901) md. Walter David "Dave" Traxler (b. Jul. 27, 1894) and had two children.

Roy (b. Jul. 16, 1903) md. Ruth Evans Huff (birth date unknown) and had one child.

Margaret's father, Martin "Matt" Harrison was a private in the Civil War. He served in Co. 7, 17th Alabama Inf. Regt. and was killed sometime between 1860 and 1865.

The Goodson lineage is Scotch-Irish and has been traced back to their arrival in Virginia from Scotland.

John acquired 160 acres of land in Smith County, just over the Scott County line in 1906. Leslie purchased the land from his brothers and sisters in 1933 after his father's death. Joseph A. Goodson, along with a niece, Virginia Ann Goodson Batte and her husband Bennie, still own the original homestead.

John and Margaret are buried in the Carr Methodist Church Cemetery in Smith County. Submitted by Joseph A. Goodson.

GOODSON, Peter C. Goodson and Mary Harrison were married in Scott County, MS on Feb. 14, 1886. They had two sons, Arthur Lee and Horace and one daughter, Cordie. Peter bought land in southeastern Scott County and established a farm on the property. Peter built a log house and he and his family made it their home. Mary died in 1895 and Peter died in 1900 leaving the children as orphans. Mary's brother, Nathan Van Harrison, took the children and reared them.

Arthur was the oldest and was 12 years old when Peter died. During his growing up years,

Arthur Lee Goodson in about 1935

Arthur vowed that he would find a way to go to college. His education journey led him to Mississippi College in Clinton. He worked his way through college and graduated. With his college degree in hand, Arthur set about to become a school teacher. During his early teaching days, he met a teacher named Margaret Carolina Steele. On Jun. 7, 1915, they were married in Covington County, MS. In those days school teachers moved frequently and Arthur was no exception. All of his six children were born in a different place.

His six children were Margaret Owen, Robert Edward, Mary Lou, Arthur Lee Jr., Charles Morgan and Carolyn McCurdy. Finally, he moved to Collins, MS in Covington County. He bought a farm there and settled down.

The Depression years were hard years for Arthur and his family and most Mississippians. When the Depression came it was particularly devastating in the South because the South was still recovering from Reconstruction after the Civil War. During the Depression many people lost everything they owned including their home. Arthur and his family managed to make it through the Depression with home and farm intact. As America began to prepare for WWII the economy began to stir again in Mississippi. During WWII Arthur made his contribution to the war effort at the shipyards in Pascagoula, MS. After the war, he began teaching again but his renewed teaching career ended when he died on Jul. 7, 1947. He is buried in the Ora Cemetery at Collins, MS.

GOODSON, Bessie Cordie Goodson (b. 1890, d. 1935) was the daughter of Peter Goodson and Mary Harrison who lived in south central Scott County. At the death of her mother, at age 5, she was placed in the home of Mary's brother, Van Harrison and his wife Tempie who lived in Southwest Newton County three miles north of Lawrence. She and her two brothers, Arthur and Horace, were placed in the Harrison home. She lived with the Harrisons until 1905 when she married Floyd E. Parker in the same community. Their first child was Emmett Dean who married Jewell Carson and divorced. Then in 1909 Wallace Lee was born and later married Lavada Gibbs, then in 1912 Selby Clyde was born and married Earlene Gibbs. In 1914 Minnie Ola was born and the only girl among the nine children. She married Willie Davis "Bill" Gibbs. In 1916 Elton was born and died at 9 years of age. In 1919 O'Farrell was born and married Doris Young. Otell (b. 1924) married Katherine Deweese. In 1928 Glen was born and later married Fay Blackburn. In 1932 Jarvis Gordon was born and married first, Mary Gil and divorced, then married Lisa Roncolia. To date the marriage of Cordie and Floyd resulted in nine children, 21 grandchildren, 34 great-grandchildren and 23 great-great-grandchildren.

GOODSON, Leslie Benton Goodson (b. Mar. 28, 1896 in Scott County) was the eighth child of John Alexander Goodson and Margaret E. Harrison. In 1915 he went to work on the ICC "Dummy-line" Railroad in Branch, MS. He met Ruby Lillie Slade (b. Apr. 16, 1900) md. Jan. 3, 1916 and had 10 children: Myrtis Allene (b. Nov. 29, 1916); Leslie Willie Ray (b. Dec. 2, 1919);

Nova Ardell (b. Apr. 26, 1921); Milton Earl and Mildred Pearl (b. Oct. 15, 1924); Lillie Mae (b. Feb. 26, 1927); Winnie Juanita (b. Dec. 18, 1928); Joseph Austin (b. Sep. 4, 1931); Vinia Genevene (b. Aug. 3, 1933) and Samuel Benton (b. Apr. 1, 1938).

Daniel Larther Harrison (b. Mar. 6, 1910) md. Myrtis on Jun. 7, 1938 and had three children. Cora Mae Thrasher (b. Nov. 6, 1929) md.

Willie Ray on Sep. 7, 1943 and had seven children. Billie Jean Carr (b. Jul. 10, 1925) md. Ardell on Aug. 7, 1942 and had four children. Mary Allen Carr (b. Apr. 17, 1927) md. Milton "Brownie" on Feb. 23, 1943 and had two children. Mary Allen

Leslie Benton Goodson and Rubie Lillie (Slade) Goodson

and Billie Jean were sisters. Clarence Gerald Schuetzle (b. Sep. 18, 1921 in Fallen County, MT) md. Mildred "Sis" Feb. 5, 1946, while stationed in Jackson, MS and had one child. Clarence was a sergeant in the Military Police, U.S. Air Force. Stephen Jefferson "S.J." Sims (b. Jan. 2, 1924) md. Lillie Mae Jul. 9, 1945 and had two children. Morris Wandell Thrasher (b. Apr. 5, 1928) md. Juanita "Nita" on Dec. 4, 1943 and had four children. Wandell and Cora Mae were brother and sister. Vermelle Watkins (b. Jul. 1, 1931) md. Joe "Sonny Boy" on Mar. 31, 1950 and had three children. William Leslie Broadwater (b. Apr. 1, 1925) md. Genevene "Vennie" on Oct. 10, 1952 and had one child. Samuel "Sam" married Janie Eversell while in the Air Force in Arizona. Sam married Mary Ann Simpson and had no children. Thelma King (b. Jan. 4, 1953) md. Sam on Apr. 1, 1982 and had one child.

Leslie was a member of Hopwell Baptist Church. He served as teacher, deacon, Sunday School and Training Union Superintendent. Although he never served in the military services, patriotism was instilled in the family. Four children served in the Armed Services. Ardell and Milton served in the European Theater in WWII. Willie Ray and Ardell were in the CCC's. Sam served in the Air Force. Three grandchildren served in the military. Steve Sims and Douglas Schuetzle served stateside and Austin Goodson, U.S. Marines served in Vietnam.

In 1933, Leslie purchased the home place in Smith County. This homestead, purchased by his father, John Alexander Goodson in 1906, is still owned by Joe Goodson and niece, Virginia Ann Goodson Batte and her husband Bennie Batte.

Leslie (d. Dec. 10, 1955) and Ruby (d. Feb. 28, 1981) are buried in Carr Church Cemetery in Smith County.

GOODSON, The most common migration route for early settlers in the south was from Virginia to North Carolina to South Carolina to Georgia to Alabama to Mississippi to Louisiana and Texas. As they moved from place to place, some would put down roots and stay and others would move on. Such was the situation for Pe-

ter C. Goodson. His grandfather was born in South Carolina, his father was born in Alabama, Peter was born in Mississippi. Robert E. Goodson was Peter's father. While Robert was still a young man, he continued the migration by moving from Alabama to Newton County, MS. In the early 1850s, Robert bought land in Scott County near the Newton County line and settled down to raise his family there.

Peter was born in Scott County, MS in November of 1854. He was the third of 10 children. He grew up on a farm established on the land his father bought. When the Union Army came through Mississippi during the Civil War, they came close to Peter's home. Peter became a member of the Carr Memorial Methodist Church. Peter's brother, John Alexander Goodson, married Margaret Harrison. Peter met and fell in love with Margaret's sister, Mary Harrison. Mary's family also migrated from Alabama to Scott County. Peter and Mary were married in Scott County on Valentine's Day in 1886.

Peter bought land and established a farm in southeastern Scott County. Peter's home was at Gilbert, MS. He built a log house for his family to live in. Peter had two sons, Arthur Lee and Horace and one daughter, Cordie. Arthur married Margaret Carolina Steele. Arthur and Margaret Carolina had six children: Margaret Owen, Robert Edward, Mary Lou, Arthur Lee Jr., Charles Morgan and Carolyn McCurdy. Horace married Etta Nelson. Horace and Etta had two children, Evelyn and Alton Lewis. Cordie married Floyd Eugene Parker. Floyd and Cordie had nine children: Emmett, O'Farrel, Otell, Glenn, Elton, Wallace, Selby, Minnie Ola and Jarvis Gordon.

The married life of Peter and Mary was cut short by Mary's untimely death in 1895. Peter was left a widower with three young children to raise. Peter died in 1900. In the Carr Memorial Cemetery, there is a large vacant area with no grave markers. This large area remains vacant because people are buried there in unmarked graves. It is almost certain that Peter and Mary are buried there in an unmarked grave.

GOODSON, In 1854 Robert E. purchased land in the eastern part of Scott County, MS. He was born in 1828 in Alabama. His parents were born in South Carolina, names unknown. He moved to Newton County in 1845. He married Mary Ann Roberts (b. 1834 in Alabama, d. Jun. 3, 1898) Robert E. died in 1893. He served in the Civil War. Robert and Mary Ann had the following 10 children.

1) Andrew J. (b. 1850) md. Charity Price (b. 1849).

2) Cornellius (b. 1852) and died sometime after.

3) Peter C. (b. November 1854) md. Mary J. Harrison (b. 1859 in Alabama). Mary died in 1890 and Peter died in 1900.

4) Caroline (b. 1856) was married three times: Ben Griffith, _ Hellen and George Ritchie who was born 1848 in Alabama and died Jan. 11, 1916. At George's funeral, Caroline had a heart attack and died the same day, Jan. 13, 1916 and is buried in Louin Cemetery in Smith County.

5) Amanda (b. May 1858) md. Berry J. Everett (b. 1820 in Georgia, d. after 1870 in Mississippi).

Harmony School, 1926, Mud Line Road, Scott County. Top from left: Mrs. Mattie Roberts, Truett Stokes, Lilla Stokes, Blanch Gaskin, Bessie Mae Gaskin (principal), Myrtle Bell Harmon, Eula Mae Harmon, Woodrow Gaskin. Second Row: Harold Gaskin, Atley Harmon, Annie Laurie Gaskin, Etta Harmon, Avis Stokes, Viva Jewel Cameron, Frances Weems, Homer Turner, ___ Stokes. Third Row: Billy Gaskin, Dewey Horman, Mary Ruth Weems, Ardell Goodson, Jack Weems, Josephine Stokes, Myrtis Goodson, Will Goodson, Valley Turner, Herkania Stokes (torn off).

6) John Alexander (b. Mar. 1, 1860, d. Nov. 30, 1933) md. Margaret E. Harrison (b. Sep. 12, 1859 in Alabama). Margaret died Jan. 25, 1929 in Smith County and is buried in Carr Methodist Church Cemetery. She was the daughter of Robert Martin Harrison (b. 1829) and Melinda Caroline Horn (b. 1832). Melinda came to Scott County with her six children after her husband was killed in the Civil War in 1865. Melinda died Oct. 8, 1897 and is buried in Hopewell Baptist Church Cemetery.

7) Noah D. (b. 1865) md. Emma Robinson Dec. 8, 1889 in Newton County.

8) Katie (b. 1870) md. Walter McDaniel.

9) Caezor (b. June 1873 in Smith County). Robert E., his wife and family moved to Smith County sometime before 1880.

10) Sarah (b. 1879 in Smith County) and Caezor were living together in 1900 as brother and sister in Scott County. Neither was ever married. Submitted by Mildred Goodson Schuetzle, the great-granddaughter of Robert E. and Mary Ann Roberts. She was born in Scott County and presently lives in Scott County.

GOULD, Thomas M. Gould (b. Mar. 1, 1835 in Shelby County, AL) was the son of David and Rebecca McAdams Gould and the grandson of Michael Saunders and Elizabeth Post Gould.

Rev. Thomas M. Gould and wife, Elizabeth Kendrick

During the Civil War he enlisted in Co. E, 29th Alabama Inf. on Oct. 7, 1861, at Shelby County, AL. He was taken as a prisoner of war and paroled at Selma, AL during June 1865, by William R. Marshall, Col., 7 Mississippi Volunteers. He was wounded in battle and his right leg was amputated above the knee.

Thomas married Elizabeth B. Kendrick, daughter of Martin Kendrick, on Sep. 15, 1853. Elizabeth and Thomas had nine children as follows:

1) Gadson G. (b. Mar. 20, 1855) md. first, Elizabeth Williams and second, Julia Roland Earls.

2) Mary Elizabeth (b. Aug. 10, 1856) md. Jim Roberts.

3) Perry Franklin (b. Jan. 8, 1858, d. Aug. 3, 1951 in Scott County, MS) md. first, Lucy Flora Martin and second, Mary Louetta Williams.

4) Amanda E. (b. Jul. 1, 1859, d. Jan. 1, 1940) md. Oliver Felix Waltman.

5) Sarah Angeline (b. Aug. 15, 1865) md. John Wesley Baggett.

6) Emmagenia H. (b. Jun. 30, 1868, d. Dec. 8, 1969.)

7) Cornelia (b. Dec. 8, 1869) md. Fred Weaver.

8) Rebecca Sudan (b. Nov. 26, 1871, d. Sep. 26, 1875).

9) Thomas Scott (b. Mar. 27, 1874) md. Susan Arbena James.

Thomas M. Gould became a circuit rider preacher. His occupation, as listed in the 1900 census of Scott County, MS, was as a book agent. *He died Mar. 3 1902 and is buried at the Lake, MS Cemetery. His wife, Elizabeth, died in 1916 and is buried beside him.* Submitted by Martha Waltman.

GRAVES-HAYES, Mr. A.L. Graves was a native of Port Gibson, MS and grew up in Starkville, MS. He was born on Aug. 27, 1910. Odessa Valda Hayes Graves was born Nov. 7, 1914.

The couple met at Alcorn A&M College where Andrew received a degree in agronomy in 1934 and Odessa received a degree in elementary education in 1936.

Andrew worked as a Scott County Mississippi Extension Agent for 37 years in Forest as well as worked within the 4-H clubs. He retired in 1972. Odessa worked in the Forest Schools for 36 years, teaching a total of 39 years before she retired in 1974.

Both spent their lives devoted to working in and with the Forest and Scott County Community. The Graves were married for 59 years. Their children include Dr. Leroy Graves, Dr. Bobby Graves, Dr. Sheldon Graves and Maurita Graves Elam.

The Graves died together in a car-train accident just as they had lived for 59 years (together), in the community that they had lived, loved and worked for most of their lives.

GUTHRIE, In 1970, Benjamin "Ben" James Guthrie was born in Scott County, MS. He is the only son of Marion Pace Guthrie and Hazel Aline Guthrie, also of Scott County. Ben attended school from 1st through 12th grade at Scott Central School outside of Forest, MS. Upon graduation, he continued his education by attending East Central Community College (ECCC) in Decatur, MS. He completed his first two years of college there and received an associates degree in business. Ben was also recognized with multiple awards such as Outstanding Business Student,

Outstanding Phi Theta Kappa Member and the US National Achievement Award in Accounting.

Ben completed his formal education at the University of Southern Mississippi after graduating from ECCC. He attended after receiving one of only four USM Community College Scholar Award scholarships, awarded to candidates from across Mississippi. He also was active in various organizations while at USM and enjoys being a part of the USM family.

Ben and Cindy Guthrie

Upon graduation from USM, Ben moved to Dallas, TX in search of a job. He started his career as an auditor for Blue Cross Blue Shield of New Mexico, then moved into the technology industry at SHL Systemhouse as an accountant. He quickly moved up to a controller position by age 23 and over the next couple of years traveled extensively for work in New York City, NY; Houston, TX; Chicago, IL; Ottawa, Canada; and Toronto, Canada. Other travels during that time included Baltimore, MD; Montreal, Canada and Vancouver, Canada. It was on one of these trips to Chicago that he met his future wife; however, it was over a year later that they began their relationship.

In 1996, Ben and Cynthia "Cindy" Ann Mitchell began dating and Cindy soon moved to Dallas, TX from her home in Chicago, IL. They married on Oct. 17, 1998 in Dallas, TX. Ben was then employed at Proamics Corporation as a project manager and Cindy was employed at Compucom in Dallas as an accountant. They enjoyed their honeymoon in Hawaii. In the spring of 1999, they built a home in Frisco, TX (a suburb of Dallas).

At the turn of the new millennium, Year 2000, Ben worked as a project manager for the software developer, SAS Institute. Cindy worked as an accountant for Bombardier Aerospace; however, soon after started work with a software developer as a project accountant. They also together were building their own internet based business affiliated with Quixtar.com.

GUTHRIE, Gwyn Annette Guthrie (b. January 1962) was the second daughter of Marion Pace Guthrie and Hazel Aline McDill Guthrie, who are long-standing residents of the Ringgold Community of Scott County. Gwyn was born in the S.E. Lackey Memorial Hospital in nearby Forest. After graduation from Scott Central High School in 1980, she utilized a National 4-H Club scholarship for her work in the Consumer Education program along with other academic scholarships and savings to continue her formal education. Gwyn graduated from East Central Junior College (known today as East Central Community College) in 1982, then attended Mississippi State University where she graduated in 1984 with a bachelor's of professional accountancy degree. She later achieved a master's of business administration with emphasis in marketing, also through Mississippi State Univer-

sity. During the master's program, Gwyn worked as a co-op student in the accounting department of Northern Telecom Inc, a telecommunications equipment manufacturer located in Richardson, TX. Gwyn relocated each semester, fulfilling both the requirements of the master's program and of the co-op work experience.

Upon graduation, Gwyn accepted a full-time position with Northern Telecom, again in the Richardson, TX office. From 1986 until September 1997, Gwyn held a variety of positions with this same company, now known as Nortel Networks. During 1989-1991, she was assigned to the technology research division, known as Bell-Northern Research, also in the Richardson area. Although she was officing in the Richardson campus during these years, business travels afforded opportunities to visit such locations as Ottawa and Toronto, both in Canada; New York City, NY; Washington, DC; Raleigh, NC and Long Beach, CA.

In 1989, Gwyn completed the Texas licensing requirements and received formal designation as a certified public accountant.

During this same time span, Gwyn sometimes traveled with an ECCC travel group, including adventuresome and exciting trips to Italy, France, Greece, Hawaii, New Zealand and Australia and her favorite which was to Ireland, Scotland and England in 1994.

In September 1997, Gwyn accepted a position as senior manager of business operations with WorldCom Communications, Inc. in a division that is headquartered in Irving, TX and is an equipment distributor for Nortel Networks. In both 1998 and 1999, Gwyn received honors for her business contributions in that division of the company. Still an avid traveler, Gwyn visited southern Arizona and the Sonora Mountain region of Mexico in the spring of 2000. During July 2000, she traveled through the Rocky Mountain National Park of Colorado and was captivated by the beauty of that region of our country.

When not working or traveling, Gwyn can often be found participating in church activities at Valley Ranch Baptist Church, of Coppell, TX where she became a member and was baptized on Jun. 11, 2000. She also has a number of hobbies, including reading, genealogy research, crochet, sewing crafts and creative writing.

GUTHRIE, Marian Joyce Guthrie was the first child born to Pace and Hazel Guthrie on Jun. 12, 1960. Joyce loved country living and farm life in the Ringgold Community. She began driving a tractor at the age of 9 and was very active in 4-H. She particularly enjoyed showing Angus and Brangus calves that were raised on her parents' farm. In May 1978, Joyce graduated as valedictorian from Scott Central High School. Joyce attended East Central Junior College and earned her BS (with honors), MS and Ph.D. degrees in animal science from Mississippi State University, Oklahoma State University and New Mexico State University, respectively.

Joyce was employed as a research assistant at the Texas A&M University Agricultural Research and Extension Center in Overton, TX for six years before attending New Mexico State University. A few award highlights include first place presentation in the Western Section Graduate Student Research Paper Competition at the 1992 National Meetings of the American Society of Animal Science, New Mexico State University's 1992-1993 Gamma Sigma Delta Outstanding Graduate Student, 1998 Who's Who Among America's Teachers and 1999 semi-finalist in the International Library of Photography's photo competition.

Since July 1994, Joyce has lived in Commerce, TX where as an assistant professor at Texas A&M University-Commerce in the Department of Agricultural Sciences, she taught 17 different courses, advised two student organizations and four graduate students and participated in numerous service activities. Unexpectedly, in May 1995, Joyce was diagnosed with a rare type of sinus tumor. Most of the massive tumor was removed in August 1995 at the University of Texas Southwestern Medical Center in Dallas; this was followed by proton radiation therapy at Loma Linda University Medical Center in Loma Linda, CA during December 1995 and January 1996. Joyce was blessed with the presence of her mom and the support of her dad throughout this ordeal. To date, she is a very grateful cancer survivor. Her hobbies include reading, stitching counted cross-stitch and photographing people, animals and landscapes.

GUTHRIE-MCDILL, Pace was born in Scott County as the second child and only son of William Lang and Margaret Ellen Pace Guthrie on Sep. 13, 1936. The son of school teachers, he changed schools several times during his early education, attending Ringgold Community School through 7th grade, Sulphur Springs School in 8th Grade, Sebastopol School in 9th grade and Valliant High School in Valliant, OK during 10th through 12th grades, where he graduated in 1954. He continued his education and received a bachelor's degree in industrial arts in 1959 from the University of Southern Mississippi.

Hazel Aline McDill was born in Newton County and was the fourth of eight children born to Oliver Preston and Mary Alline Turner McDill of the Sulphur Springs Community of Scott County. A graduate of Connehatta High School in 1959, she graduated from East Central Junior College in 1970 and attended the University of Southern Mississippi.

Pace and Hazel Guthrie were married on May 2, 1959 in the home of Elder W.J. Sanders. They made their home in the Ringgold Community where they have resided for these past 41 years. El Ringo Farms was founded during 1959 as a cattle farm with registered Angus cattle. At the time of their marriage, Pace was employed as a bookkeeper for a Gulf Oil Corporation Distributor in its Newton, MS office.

After seven and one-half years in bookkeeping, Pace began a teaching career at East Central Junior College in the Technical Drafting program. In the summer of 1967, Pace studied in Oak Ridge, TN while working towards his master's of industrial education degree which he achieved from Mississippi State University. During this same time, Pace drafted custom home designs for many citizens of Scott County and the surrounding area and he and Hazel also worked continuously to expand the cattle farm-

ing operation, which by then included registered Brangus cattle. Pace achieved recognition as Conservationist of the Year in 1975 and as Cattleman of the Year in 1977 by the Mississippi Cattleman's Association. Hazel was active in the Mississippi Cow Belles Association, serving as 2nd vice president in 1974-1976 and then as 1st vice president in 1976-1978. She was recognized as Outstanding 4-H Leader in 1975 and was inducted into the Mississippi State All-Stars. She was quite active in 4-H Club projects with all of her children and contributed to the community through numerous service projects, which she helped organize and implement.

In 1979, the Guthries chose to move into a different career path. Pace resigned from his teaching position and began working full-time at the farm. He and Hazel began contract chicken farming with McCarty Farms, Inc. They were recognized as McCarty's #1 Grower for five years in a row within the Forest, MS division. They currently are contract poultry growers for Tyson's, which purchased the McCarty Farms business.

The four children born of Pace and Hazel were Marian Joyce (b. 1960), Gwyn Annette (b. 1962), Tina Carol (b. 1965) and Benjamin James (b. 1970).

GUTHRIE-PACE, William Lang Guthrie (b. Dec. 31, 1906) was the son of Benjamin Marion Guthrie and Ida Mae Lang Guthrie. On May 5, 1929, he married Margaret Ellen Pace, the younger of two daughters born of George Alfred and Naoma Harris Pace. They have two children, eight grandchildren, two great-grandchildren, four step-great grandchildren and eight step-great-great-grandchildren.

As a child, Margaret Ellen

William Lang "Billy" Guthrie, son of Ida Mae Lang and Benjamin Marion Guthrie and Margaret Ellen Pace, daughter of Sarah Naoma Harris and George Alfred Pace)

lived in Ringgold Community and later attended Forest High School, boarding with the Singleton family near the school. She was a 1946 graduate of the University of Southern Mississippi with an education degree.

Billy and Margaret Ellen enjoyed teaching careers throughout their marriage. In 1949, Billy served as Sulphur Springs School principal and taught 5th-8th grades in the three-room school. That same year, Margaret Ellen accepted a position with Bureau of Indian Affairs (BIA) and moved to Oklahoma where she began teaching at Wheelock Academy. In 1951, Billy and their son, Pace, moved to Oklahoma, leaving behind daughter and sister, Billie Margaret, who was married to Stites Gardner Jr. In 1954, Billy applied for a BIA teaching assignment and began teaching at Pinon, AZ in 1955. The closing of Wheelock Academy was announced in 1955 and Margaret Ellen was accepted for transfer to the Pinon school. The high altitudes of northern Arizona caused severe sinus illnesses for both Billy

and Margaret Ellen. At the school session's end, Billy, Margaret Ellen and Pace traveled throughout the southwest United States. Recalling the illnesses of the prior year, Billy and Margaret Ellen applied for teaching transfers and received reassignment to San Carlos, AZ for 1955's fall session. Later, they both received teaching posts at Bogue Chitto School near Philadelphia, MS and returned to their Ringgold Community homeplace.

Billy Guthrie died on May 14, 1968 and was buried at Antioch Primitive Baptist Church Cemetery in Scott County. He will be remembered for his musical talent and teaching skills.

Margaret Ellen retired that same year and spent her retirement years enjoying church activities with the Primitive Baptist Church community, gardening and quilting. She was recognized in a 1992 edition of Quilters Magazine. *She has completed over 100 quilts herself and has helped with over 100 others through the Ephesus Church Quilters Group, which she quilts with weekly. She recently celebrated her 93rd birthday on January 12 and resides on Lang's Mill Road of Scott County.*

GUTHRIE-THRASH, Derwin Neal Thrash and Tina Carol Guthrie were married on May 11, 1985. Tina is the third daughter of Marion Pace and Hazel Aline McDill Guthrie of the Ringgold Community. Derwin is the son of Frankie Viola Mullins Thrash of Harperville, MS and the late Earl Fletcher Thrash. They were both reared in Scott County and are graduates of Scott Central High School. Tina finished ECJC in 1985 with an AAS degree in drafting and design. Derwin began working for Milwaukee Electric Tool, while Tina worked for Southeastern Sprinkler System. They lived in Pearl, Clinton and Raymond from 1985-1988, Emily Michelle Thrash was born on Dec. 9, 1986.

After working for a year, Tina was able to work from her home drawing residential plans. In the summer of 1988 they moved back to the Ringgold Community. Their second child, Krista Alicia Thrash was born on Aug. 2, 1990. In the summer of 1996 Tina chose to return to college. She graduated with a bachelor's of science degree in elementary education in May 1999. Now employed by the SCSD, Tina is teaching 3rd grade at Sebastopol Attendance Center. Her hobbies include sewing, cross-stitching, crocheting and reading.

Derwin received recognition for 15 years of service with Milwaukee Electric Tool of Jackson, in the summer of 1999. He started working in the Steel Department on the armature shaft line in 1984. He is now working in the Machine Shop for the company. His hobbies include hunting, fishing and beekeeping. At the present time he has 43 hives of bees and has recently started selling pure honey in Scott County and the surrounding areas.

Emily will be in the 8th grade at Sebastopol Attendance Center (2000-2001). She plays the trumpet and the French horn with the high school band. Emily began playing in the band in the 5th grade. She has received the band's "Most Outstanding Student" award for the past three years. Emily also earned the first chair position (French horn) in the Scott County Honor Band in 1999-2000. Emily entered into the school's gifted program in the second grade and began participating in Chess competitions. She received the Chessmaster award for her division in 1999. Emily has held an all-A academic average since she began school. She enjoys singing, reading and playing the piano. Emily has a cat named Socks.

Krista will be in the 5th grade at Sebastopol Attendance Center (2000-2001). She will begin in band at Sebastopol playing the trumpet. She has held an all-A academic average since she began school. She loves the Tweety Bird cartoon character and also her cat Smokey. Krista likes to read, sing, draw/paint, play with her cat and ride the 4-wheeler.

The family would not be complete without mentioning the family dog, Gypsy. She watches over her family, her grandparents, her great-gran, the cows and the cats. We couldn't imagine life on the farm without her.

The Thrashes are members of Steele Baptist Church in the Steele Community.

HADDON, Columbus Bradshaw Haddon came to Mississippi when he was a boy of 10 years with his four brothers and his widowed mother. His mother died when he was 13, and he became a ward of his Uncle John Anderson.

C.B. Haddon's great-grandfather immigrated to America from England. He landed in Charleston, SC, fought and died in the War of Independence.

C.B. Haddon lived in various counties of the state - homesteading, clearing, making crops, moving on with the family of his Uncle John Anderson. He served four years in the Confederate Army during which time he was twice taken prisoner.

1992 picture of old home on Haddon Hill, used as hospital during the Civil War. On the steps are the three remaining grandchildren of C.B. Haddon, Mildred Duncan LaFoy, Margaret Duncan LaHatte, Marion Duncan Johnson.

On Jan. 1, 1878, he moved his family consisting of wife, Zilphia Sessums Haddon, and children: Benjamin Edward, Nancy Ann Beulah, and John William into Scott County. They moved into "the Old Lassiter Place" (the name he used for his home the 44 years he lived there). It is located approximately three miles north of the community of Harperville on what was then called Old Highway 35. The "Old Lassiter Place" is known now locally as Haddon Hill.

In his memoirs, written in 1922, C.B. Haddon states, "I had no thought whatever of making a permanent home here, but subsequent events have proven to my satisfaction that there was a Providential Hand in the matter, and looking back over the intervening years, I can be

thankful for the guidance of that Hand." In the concluding statement of his memoirs he writes, "the main thing that influenced me to remain here was that there had been a high school started at Harperville, and I thought I saw an opportunity to educate my children. So with that end in view, I started to reclaim the old place (Lassiter Place)."

Five more children were born to C.B. and Zilphia Haddon: May Ellen, C.B.

C.B. Haddon in Richmond, VA in front of the memorial to Gen. Stonewall Jackson. Mr. Haddon attended Civil War veteran's reunions as long as he was able to travel.

Jr., Ruth Jeanette, Una Gordon and Addie Ethel. By the time most of the children were through high school, C.B. had helped in the organization of a college. All eight of his children received a good education.

Community affairs were another of C.B. Haddon's concerns and he was a leader in the Grange and one of the organizers of the Patron's Union. His life in Harperville was devoted to his family, the church and the community.

There are now few, if any, who remember the Haddons as none of the children of C.B. and Zilphia made their home in Scott County, but their work and influence helped make the Harperville Community a place of culture. All of the Haddons mentioned in this history are buried in Harperville Cemetery with the exception of C.B. Haddon Jr.

HAMM, In 1740 a man by the name of John Hamm captured a girl by the name of Mary on the Irish coast, and took her to England. From there they came to the American colonies. Legend or truth? This started an ongoing search of my family roots 10 years ago (1990).

Jeremiah Hamm married Elizabeth Marie Rolph in Fleming County, KY in 1883. They had three children: Donna (b. 1884), Misty Iva (b. 1886) and Grover Cleveland (b. 1888). She died in 1888 or 1889 and is buried in Kentucky. Jeremiah married Elizabeth Windsor on Dec. 26, 1889 in Lewis County, KY. They had eight children: Annie Francis (b. 1891), Mina Overton (b. 1893), Riley (b. 1894), Robert Powell (b. 1896), John Otto (b. 1898), George Stanley (b. 1899), Gilbert (Gillie) (b. 1900) and James Calvin (b. 1903). Elizabeth died in 1905 and is buried in Kentucky.

In 1911 Jeremiah loaded his household possessions on a train boxcar and the family came to Mississippi because his daughter, Overton, had visited in Mississippi and went back home and told her father how rich the land was in Mississippi and that you could get rich raising tobacco there. The family settled near Lake and near the Dubose Mill. Jeremiah died Sep. 1, 1924. He is buried at Lake Cemetery in Scott County. George Stanley married Luddie Abbegail Braddock on Sep. 27, 1924 at Lake, MS. They had eight children: 1) Elizabeth married Frank Owens and settled in Vicksburg, MS and Baton Rouge, LA. They had two children Jerry and David. 2) Mary

Blanche married Jack Parks and had five children: Linda, Larry, George, Jeffery "Chuck," William Randall "Randy" and Donna Joy. 3) Barbara "Bobbie" married Earl D. Goodwin. 4) Minnie Lou "Inkey" married Albert Riddle and had two children, Kimberly and Mark. They settled in Vicksburg. 5) James "Buddy" married Joann Waltman and had two children, David Gregory and Karen Michelle. They settled in Florence, MS. 6) Baker married Mary Harrell and had three children: Jacquelene Lynn "Jackie," Baker Scott and Christy M'Lee. They settled in Lake, MS. 7) Jerry Stennet lives in Lake, MS. 8) Sandra "Sue" married Allen Waltman and has one child, Melissa Darlene.

HANNAH, Edward Eugene Hannah was born Feb. 23, 1879 in the Wicker's Mill Community of northern Smith County. His father was William L. "Will" Hannah (b. Apr. 1, 1855 in North Carolina) and his mother was Vernada Rhodes (b. Sep. 6, 1859 in Mississippi).

Eugene (b. Feb. 2, 1883, d. Mar. 6, 1972, buried in Eastern Cemetery, Forest) married Vallie Tadlock, the daughter of R.K. "Bob" Tadlock and Emma Weaver, on Feb. 8, 1900. They had six children: Emma Louise (b. Nov. 20, 1900, d. May 22, 1994, buried in Masonic Cemetery, Newton); Robert Oliver (b. Jan. 27, 1902); William Edward "Bill" (b. Feb. 22, 1904, d. Jan. 15, 1991, buried in Clinton Cemetery); Troy Howard (b. Jun 22, 1906, d. Mar. 27, 1963, buried in Eastern Cemetery); Eugenia Vernada (b. Jun 24, 1908); Floyd (b. Apr. 25, 1910, d. Sep. 9, 1997, cremated). Eugene worked in his father's gin/saw mill operations until 1909 when he moved his family to Forest. At that time he became an employee of Scott County and worked as a guard for prison road gangs. He later became town marshal for the city of Forest and held that position until 1917 when he began working for Bienville Lumber Company in shipping and sales. He remained with the company until it closed in 1930. After that he bought and sold cattle until 1933 when he became ill with heart problems. He died Aug. 20, 1934 in Forest and is buried in Eastern Cemetery.

Emma was born in Smith County. She was a teacher (High Hill and Clifton) and married Woods Eastland Hunt, the son of Lemuel M. Hunt and Sally Singleton, Jun. 30, 1924. They had one son, Harold Woods Jr. Woods Sr. was the Gulf Oil distributor in Newton where they lived. They were members of the Methodist Church

Robert Oliver was born in Smith County and moved to Forest with his family in 1909. He married Bertha Lavern Sullivan, daughter of Tolbert Boyles Sullivan and Lula Leona Lathum, on Oct. 4, 1932. The marriage produced four sons: Robert Oliver Jr., Ray Eugene, Thomas Edward and Ted Sullivan. Robert Oliver became the first superintendent of Roosevelt State Park in Morton in 1940 and Bertha managed the food service operations. They remained at the Park until they retired to their Newton County farm in 1960 and, following the sale of the farm in 1965, moved to Forest. They are members of the Methodist Church.

Bill was born in Smith County. He graduated from Forest High School, attended the University of Mississippi, and later married Elizabeth King, the daughter of Thomas Rivers King and Mary Helen Chatham, Dec. 20, 1928 in Magee. He helped organize Central Chevrolet in Forest and moved to Magee to open a branch where he met his wife who was teaching school there. The marriage produced three children: Dorothy Lynn, William Robert "Bobby," and Howard Barry. Central Chevrolet closed during the depression and Bill operated a service station in Forest until about 1941. During WWII he worked in Ingalls shipyard on the Mississippi Gulf Coast and later became an insurance agent for New York Life. He moved to Clinton in 1945, developed a highly successful insurance business and won many awards from New York Life. His family attended the Baptist Church.

Troy was born in the Homewood Community of Scott County. He married Launo Pearl Cook Jul. 22, 1938. No issue. Troy operated a cattle and poultry farm in Newton County and was a member of the Methodist Church.

Eugenia was born in the Lorena Community of Smith County. She married Wayne Sutton Alliston, son of Wayne D. Alliston and Sally South, on Jul. 20, 1934. The marriage produced three children: Wayne Sutton Jr., Brenda Catherine and Woods Richmond. Wayne was employed by the State Health Department and settled in Bay St. Louis. Eugenia is a member of the Methodist Church.

Floyd was born in Forest. He graduated from Forest High School and attended Mississippi State College. He married Bernice Lacey, daughter of Edward Walker Lacey and Adelina Hooper, in Attala County on Mar. 13, 1936. The marriage produced two children, Floyd Lacey and Mary Jane. Floyd worked for International Harvester and eventually owned the Ford Tractor dealership in Bastrop, LA. They were members of the Presbyterian Church.

HARALSON, In 1858 four Haralson brothers came to Mississippi from Alabama. They were William Franklin, Isaac Culberson, Eli Elias and James Marion, sons of Elijah Haralson II and Elizabeth Browing Culberson of Georgia and Alabama.

William Franklin (b. Dec. 4, 1815 in Green County, GA) md. Cornelia Hester Sep. 15, 1841 in Troupe County, GA. Their children: Sarah Elizabeth md. Robert Bruce Pace of Newton County; Martha "Patsy" md. G.D. Pace of Newton

John C. Haralson, son of William F. Haralson, and Emlie Haralson

County; John Culberson md. Emlie Smith of Newton County; Hugh A.; Mary L. md. J.M. Spivey in Scott County; William Franklin Jr.; Celeste America md. Lafayette W. Townsend of Scott County; Exene "Exie" md. Lewis Kennedy then Sam Shannon of Scott County; George Washington "Bud" md. Annie Caroline Finely of Scott County; and Clara Brownie "Bony" md. Thomas L. Read of Scott County.

During reconstruction William F. served on the Board of Police which is now known as The Board of Supervisors.

Cornelia died sometime after the 1880 census was taken. In 1885 William Franklin remarried Eliza Webster. He died Oct. 22, 1886, and is buried somewhere around Harperville in Scott County.

Isaac Culberson also had a large family. He was born Jan. 14, 1809 in Troupe County, GA. He married Jane Hardin Jun. 30, 1830 and. died Apr. 5, 1894. Almost all the Haralsons in Scott County today are descended from these two brothers. James Marion purchased land in Scott County but later sold it and moved to Conehatta in Newton County. He married Georgia Thornton. They were the parents of Dr. J.J. Haralson of Scott County.

Eli Elias lived in Scott County for almost 10 years. His wife Nancy Ann May must have died because he later moved to Newton County and remarried Charity West Thompson. They later moved to Texas.

HARALSON, James Clinton "J.C." Haralson (b. Apr. 23, 1909), son of Thomas Woods Haralson and Nancy Maude Hunt, was the fifth child in a family of 11 children. His grandparents were L.M. "Joe" Hunt and Sallie Olivia Singleton of Scott County and John Culbertson Haralson and Emily H. Smith of Newton County. He went to school at the Piketon Community School. J.C. loved to hunt with his dogs and to fish. In 1930, when he was 21, he married 14-year-old Mary Lou Myers, daughter of J. Lee Myers and Nancy Annie Harrison.

50th anniversary, November 1980. J.C. Haralson, Mary Lou Haralson, Billy Joe Haralson, Nancy Ann Myers, Darlene Gilmore and James Gray Haralson

They lived with J.C.'s parents for a while after they married. They went to church at Pleasant Ridge Baptist Church. In 1932 their first child, Robert Clinton, was born, then Billy Joe came in 1934, Nancy Ann in 1939, Tommie Darlene in 1943 and James Gray in 1947. The three older kids graduated school at Ringgold School. James Gray graduated at Scott Central. J.C. and Mary Lou farmed and raised what they needed to eat. Times were hard but they made a living and raised their family to be good outstanding people. Tragedy struck when J.C. lost his father and two brothers in March of 1961. In December 1961 they lost a grandchild and their son Robert was killed in a car accident. Mary Lou went to work at Sunbeam in Forest and J.C. worked at Southeastern Poultry Plant. They lost two more grandchildren in the following years, baby Randall Scott Gilmore in 1969 and Roger Earl Myers in a car accident in 1977. One of the grandsons started calling them "Big Pa and Big Ma" and it stuck. That is what everyone close to the family knew them as. The grandkids loved

to see Big Pa get down on the floor and do the rabbit dance—that would tickle all of them. As the years passed and J.C.'s hair turned white and his health failed, but he still kept his sense of family and love for his children, grandchildren and great-grandchildren. He died May 18, 1986 and is buried in Ephesus Baptist Cemetery in Scott County. Mary Lou still lives in the family home and is loved by all her children, grandchildren, great-grandchildren, and one great-great-grandchild.

HARALSON, Tom Haralson was the strongest and hardest working man I have ever known. His horses were his livelihood. They were his tractor, truck, bulldozer and whatever else they were need for, because his only horsepower was his horses. He used mules to cultivate the crops, but the horses did most of the heavy breaking of the land.

He was the father of 11 children and along with his faithful wife, Nancy Maude Hunt, raised 10 children to be grown and married. The oldest child, Allie D., died when she was 6 years old.

Tom and Maude Haralson

Tom was born and raised in Conehatta. Nancy Maude was born and raised in the Piketon Community. They were married in July 1900, both at the tender age of 18.

In 1915 when their eighth child was a baby, they bought the Hunt old home place and moved to Piketon. A few months later their home and most of their belongings burned. A house had to be built, crops to be raised, seven children to be fed and clothed and only man's power and his horses power to accomplish this great task. Tom and Maude worked and built this house and were blessed with two more children.

There wasn't much money back in those days, and survival was the main thought in people's mind. They lived off the land, raising vegetables, corn for bread, milked cows for milk and butter, hogs for meat and lard, chickens for eggs and meat. A calf was slaughtered once in a great while to have beef, and if time was available to go fishing—most of the time you could catch brim and mudcat out of the nearby creek. Everyone that was large enough had to work and the ones that were not large enough to go to the field, helped take care of the babies and helped Mama with the cooking and washing.

They were Papa and Mama to their children. Some of the grandchildren called them Papa and Mama and some said Daddy Tom and Mammy, but no matter what they were called, they were always there for any and all occasions. In their older years most everyone said Uncle Tom and Aunt Maude.

Papa only had a fourth grade education but you could not beat him in adding and subtracting on his fingers or make marks to count.

Papa wanted things done right. Don't half do anything. If a job is once begun, never quit until its done. Be the task large or small, do it well or not at all, was his motto.

Even though Papa did not have much education he wanted better for his children. He was one of the founding fathers of Ringgold School and served as trustee for 16 years.

He and his horses helped build the road over Hontokalo Creek, so the school bus could get across when there were heavy rains.

Papa had a tender heart and helped lots of people, but he would fight you at the drop of his hat, if you hurt or bad mouthed any of his family.

His children were Leon, Annie Lee, Onie Bell, J.C. Hunt, French, Sarah Jewell, Thomas, Ruby and Katie.

HARMON, Walter Preston Harmon (b. Feb. 11, 1898) married Lillian Cornelius Harrison in 1920. They had seven children: Walter Lewis, the oldest, was born Sep. 26, 1923. Lewis was in the military service and was killed Aug. 5, 1944; five girls, another son, Audrey Lee "Sonny" came later. All live in the state except Sonny, who lives in Huntsville, AL. Walter was a farmer, worked hard and loved life. He died at a very young age of 46 on Jan. 15, 1944. Lillian never remarried and died at age 75 on Feb. 2, 1980.

HARPER-GORDY, George C. Harper went to the gold fields of California in 1849 and met with fairly good success. He founded the town of Harperville in 1861 and was the principal spirit behind the establishment of Harperville College. George (b. Jul. 13, 1825 in Duplin County, NC, d. Mar. 17, 1903) is buried in Harperville in the old Lebanon Cemetery. His parents were Oliver and Mary Swinson Harper. The family moved to Leake County, MS when George was a small child. Other children were Edee (b. 1820) md. George W. Lee in 1837, Bibb County, AL; Catherine (b. Sep. 23, 1822, d. May 4, 1886 in Galveston, TX) md. James Whittington on May 4, 1866; Levi Harper (b. 1829) md. Sara Jane Putnam, daughter of Jeremiah Putnam and Elizabeth Smith Putnam. Jeremiah Putnam was related to Gen. Israel Putnam of Revolutionary War fame. George married Louisa Putnam on Jul. 25, 1847. Louisa was also a sister to Sara Jane Putnam. George and Louisa had one son, Hiram "Hi" Hinkle Harper.

Hiram (b. Oct. 8, 1852 near Hillsboro) md. Mary Elizabeth Shannon, daughter of Moses and Ellen Shannon, on Oct. 11, 1871. Hiram was a teacher, superintendent of Sunday school at Harperville College for a number of years, War Magistrate for 10 or 12 years, was in the mill and gin business for a

Hiram Harper

number of years and abandoned this and went back to teaching. He was elected and served as a member of the legislature from 1900-1904. Hiram was also a Mason, membership in the Lodge of Forest at Forest, MS. He was re-elected to the legislature in 1923 but died before his term expired and is buried in Harperville.

Hiram and Mary had four children: Thomas Braxton (b. August 1872); Neto (b. April 1874); Otho Tilden (b. May 28, 1876) md. Mary Elizabeth Foster on Jun. 19, 1901, daughter of Rev. J.C. and Jessie Trippe Foster; Eleanor (b. 1883) died in Jasper, TX.

Otho died Dec. 15, 1925 and is buried in Harperville. After Otho's death, Mary and her children went to five with her Mother and brother. Mary died Jun. 28, 1960 and is also buried in Harperville. Otho and Mary's children were Mary Elizabeth (b. 1904), Hiram Herbert (b. 1907), James Howard (b. 1915), Nellie "Nell" Odelle (b. May 22, 1917) and Otho Tilden (b. 1921). Nell married James "Jake" Edison Gordy on Apr. 13, 1941. Jake was born in Lake, Scott County, MS and was the son of William Walter Gordy and Bedie Usry. He was also a chief petty officer in the Navy during WWII and was stationed in the Pacific. Nell and Jake had three daughters: Carol Frances (b. 1942), Mary Lynn (b. 1946) and Elizabeth Anne (b. 1951). The family moved to Huntsville, AL in 1952 where Jake went to work at Redstone Arsenal. He died of a heart attack in December 1954. Nell and the girls still live in Alabama.

HARRELL, In about 1885, H.H. Harrell, or "Hartley" as he was called, and wife Lethia Jane Hayes moved from Smith County to Scott County, after coming to Mississippi from another state. They purchased 135 acres of land in 1886 in north central Scott County, MS. The area is now known as the Clifton Community. They remained there until their deaths. Hartley made a trip to Chattanooga, TN, where he became ill, died and was buried in Tennessee. Lethia died later and was buried in the Hillsboro Baptist Cemetery. Their children were John Cicero, B. Frank, William Henry, Neely P., Burl E. and L.P.

W.H. Harrell, Mattie Harrell Polk (daughter) and Mittie Moore Harrell

All the children except Frank and L.P. raised their families in Scott County. Frank moved his family to Louisiana. L.P. married a Mr. Hood and moved to Yazoo County, MS.

At the time of Lethia's death her son William Henry Harrell (b. Feb. 22, 1874) purchased the farm. William Henry, or "Will" as he was called, married Nannie Sessums on Apr. 17, 1899. W.S. Ford performed the ceremony. She later died in 1901 giving birth to a daughter

Nannie Omega Harrell. Nannie Sessums was buried in the Lebanon Cemetery just outside of Harperville, MS. Will later married Mittie Moore (b. Jul. 10, 1877, in Clarksburg, MS), daughter of Nick Moore and Rebecca Peagler. To this union was born Pauline, Louis Tendal, (died as a child), Haley B., Willie Sharp and Mattie Laverne.

Children of Willie Sharp Harrell Sr. and Eloise Lathem: Helen, W.T., Denzil, Willie Sharp Jr., Don and Sammie

William was a farmer, a brilliant man, who was self-educated, a jack-of-all trades. He was very well read in the Bible, and could quote scripture. He was a partner with Mr. Sam Turner, running a sawmill in his younger days. He also did blacksmith work, helped run a cotton gin, and was a basket maker. He was postmaster of Clifton Post Office from 1905-1907. He was also noted far and wide for being able to conjure warts. People came from everywhere to have him remove warts from their hands. William died on Jan. 1, 1960 and Mittie died Nov. 14, 1963. Both are buried at the Baptist Cemetery in Hillsborro.

William's children were married as follows: Pauline to L.Q. Reeves, Haley to Vera McCrory, Mattie Laverne to Carl Edward Polk, Willie Sharp to Margarette Eloise Latham in 1935.

Willie Sharp and "Eloise" had the following children: Helen Marie, W.T., Joseph Denzil, Willie Sharp Jr., Don Austin and Sammie Louis. Eloise died in 1954, after her death Willie remarried to Grace Smith Johnson. Willie farmed and later worked in poultry plants. Their children are David Earl, Beverly Diane and Nancy Louise.

W.T., Don and David live on the property originally purchased by their great-grandfather, Hartley Harrell. W.T. lives where the original house stood. In 1957 he married Alice Marie Williams. W.T. was a USDA Poultry Grader for 13 years, now retired. They are the parents of four sons: Victor Terrence, Jeff Lynn, James Mark and Todd Howard.

Victor married Kay Eure and they live in the Hillsborro Community. They have one daughter Megan Marie. Jeff married Cindy Craig and they are parents of Taren and Craig. Mark married Tina Thornton and they have one daughter Courtney. Todd married Renae Hollingsworth, and they have one son Toby. Jeff, Mark and Todd all live in the Clifton Community.

HARRISON-ALFORD, Ausbon Harrison was the youngest son of Robert Lowery Harrison and Mary Alice "Allie" Hawkins. He was born in Scott County on Dec. 4, 1920 and attended Harrison School. Just before being drafted into the Army during World War II, Ausbon married

Florence Wyvone Alford on Mar. 4, 1943. Wyvone (b. Dec. 30, 1925 in Scott County) was the daughter of William Alvie Alford and Florence Rosia Slade. Wyvone attended Forkville School through the eighth grade, then went to Morton High School.

Florence Wyvonne (Alford) and Ausbon Harrison

Ausbon and Wyvone had two children, Edwin Ausbon (b. Jun. 19, 1944) and Dinah Lou (b. May 6, 1954). Edwin and Dinah were both born in Scott County. Ausbon and Wyvone lived in the Harrison Town area east of Homewood on land that had been in the Harrison family since the 1870s. Ausbon worked as a carpenter and then for many years was employed at the Scott County Co-op. Wyvone was a homemaker and very active in Hopewell Baptist Church.

Edwin started school at Homewood and finished at Forest High School in 1963. He also worked for the Scott County Co-op for many years. Edwin married Shawna Askin on May 23, 1969 and they had one daughter, Shawna Leigh (b. Oct. 3, 1972). Edwin married Bobbie Johnston Shoemaker on Mar. 5, 1988. Edwin and Bobbie live at Sand Hill in Rankin County. Edwin works for Lampton Love Gas Company.

Dinah began school at Forest and finished at Scott County Christian Academy in May 1972. She married Guy McGee on Jun. 24, 1973 and they had one daughter Tammy Lou (b. Feb. 1, 1976).

Ausbon's mother, Mary Allie Hawkins Harrison, passed away on his and Wyvone's 20th wedding anniversary, Mar. 4, 1963. Ausbon died on Dec. 19, 1986, after suffering from Alzheimer's disease for many years. Wyvone quietly left this life on Apr. 6, 2000, at the beauty salon, while waiting to have her hair done. They are buried at Hopewell Baptist Church Cemetery.

HARRISON-BAILEY,

Dinah Lou Harrison is the daughter of Ausbon Harrison and Wyvone Alford. She was born on May 6, 1954 in Scott County. She has one older brother, Edwin. Dinah started school at Forest and finished at the Scott County Christian Academy in May 1972. Dinah attended East Central Junior College taking a business course. She married Guy McGee on Jun. 24, 1973 and they had one daughter, Tammy Lou. Tammy was born on Feb. 1, 1976 at the Woman's Hospital in Rankin County. Dinah and Guy divorced in 1991.

Dinah married Earl "Skip" Bailey Jr. on Mar. 22, 1997. "Skip" (b. Apr. 12, 1955 in Texas) is the son of Earl Bailey Sr. and Doris Cox. They live on the Harrison home place east of Homewood. This land has been in the family since the 1870s when Dinah's great-grandfather, William Robert "Bob" Harrison, purchased it. Dinah works for Tyson Foods as an inventory clerk. Skip was a truck driver before becoming disabled.

Tammy McGee, Dinah (Harrison) and "Skip" Earl Bailey Jr.

Tammy began school at Lake, then transferred to Pearl. She was chosen to attend the Mississippi School for mathematics and science, where she graduated in May 1999. She received her bachelor's degree from the University of Southern Mississippi in Exercise Science in May 1999. She now attends Belmont University in Nashville, TN to get her doctorate degree in physical therapy.

HARRISON,

Leigh is the daughter of Edwin Ausbon Harrison and Shawna Lavonne Askin. She was born on Oct. 3, 1972 at Lackey Memorial Hospital in Forest. Leigh attended Forest High School, graduating in May 1990. Leigh has one brother, Joel Alexander.

Leigh was employed at Hughes Aircraft from October 1992

Shawna Leigh Harrison

to September 1995, where she worked in the Prep department as an electronic assembler. She was employed at Southern Flow in Jackson, MS from September 1997 to April 1999 as an office clerk. She has worked at Raytheon since May 1999, also in the Prep department as an electronic assembler.

Leigh inherited a love for fishing from her father and her grandmother, Wyvone. She learned how to fish at an early age. Leigh also likes to go motorcycle riding and keeping in touch with family and friends. She is a member of Hopewell Baptist Church, where she taught Sunday School and was music director for one year. She lives on the Harrison home place that has been in the family since the 1870s, when her great-great-grandfather William Robert "Bob" Harrison purchased the land.

HARRISON-COLEMAN,

William Robert "Bob" Harrison (b. May 18, 1850 in Alabama) was the son of Robert Martin Harrison and Melinda Caroline Horn. Bob married Sarah Elizabeth "Sallie" Coleman on Jan. 5, 1869 in Alabama. Sallie was also born in Alabama on Apr. 17, 1845. We do not know the identity of Sallie's father or the maiden name of her mother. We do know her mother, Elizabeth, came to Scott County with Sallie and Bob. She was living with them at the time of her death in 1910. She is buried at Hopeful Baptist Church.

Bob and Sallie moved into Scott County in the early 1870s from Perry County, AL. Bob's mother, Melinda Horn Harrison, and all but one brother, also moved here at that time. Bob and Sallie had purchased land before

Sarah Elizabeth "Sallie" Coleman Harrison

1879 and this land is still owned by a great-granddaughter, Dinah Bailey, and a great-great-granddaughter, Leigh Harrison. Bob and Sallie got busy with clearing land and planting crops of cotton and corn. Bob had a brick kiln, making the bricks from clay and baking them. He also had a cane mill and cooked syrup for the public.

In his later years, Bob conducted Singing Schools, He taught from a shaped note song book. These schools lasted from one to two weeks. Bob could play the organ and taught his granddaughter, Nellie Weger, to play. His organ is still in the family, as is his cane mill.

Bob and Sallie were active members of Hopewell Baptist Church from as early as 1886, and many of their descendants have followed after them. It was said that Bob had been a Baptist since the age of 18.

Bob and Sallie's children were Lula A. (b. Feb. 10, 1871, d. Oct. 15, 1957) md. George Madison Johnson on Sep. 30, 1893. William James "Jim" (b. Oct. 11, 1873, d. Nov. 22, 1951) md. Liney Dora "Dolly" Johnson. John Wesley (b. Mar. 10, 1876, d. Apr. 20, 1948) md. Beulah Wicker. Robert Lowery (b. Dec. 24, 1878, d. Aug. 30, 1969) md. Mary Alice "Allie" Hawkins on Dec. 25, 1898. M. Elizabeth "Lizzie" (b. Sep. 26, 1880, d. Feb. 15, 1972) md. Dennis R. Austin on Jan. 16, 1902. Charley Thomas "Tom" (b. Jan. 8, 1884, d. Sep. 8, 1971) md. Nancy C. Arender. Nelia C. (b. Feb. 17, 1886, d. Jun. 23, 1984) md. Robert Frank Bailey on Jul. 21, 1910.

In a letter dated a year before his death, Bob told of being with his grandfather Jesse Horn when he died. Bob wrote, "Grandpa Jesse asked me to hand him his walking stick. I handed it to him, and he seemed to fold his arms around it and died." Bob was 10 years old and it made an impression on him. He also said that Grandpa Jesse spoke mostly the Dutch language and that he could not speak English very well. Bob's grandson Ausbon, at the age of 7, was present on Jul. 1, 1927, when his life slipped away. I think we could say this made a great impression on Ausbon as well, for he remembered it many years later. After 58 years of marriage, Sallie was left behind. She passed away on Nov. 2, 1936 and was buried beside Bob at the Hopewell Baptist Church Cemetery.

HARRISON-HAWKINS,

Robert Lowery Harrison (b. Dec. 24, 1878 in Scott County) was the son of William Robert "Bob" Harrison and Sarah Elizabeth "Sallie" Coleman. On Dec. 25, 1898, he married Mary Alice "Allie" Hawkins. Allie was the daughter of Benjamin Franklin "Frank" Hawkins and Mary Jane Moulder. She was born Jan. 30, 1879 in Smith County.

During the next 24 years, Lowery and Allie had 11 children. Lowery spent his life as a farmer and was Deacon of Hopewell Baptist Church for many years, as was two of his sons, Percy and Larther. Allie was a homemaker, car-

Robert Lowery and Mary Alice "Allie" Hawkins Harrison

ing for her family required many hours of hard work. She designed her own quilt patterns and made her batting from cotton that she gathered and combed. She also spun her own thread. Lowery and Allie boarded the teacher and ran the school bus for the Harrison School. They also provided the land where the school was built. Lowery inherited his father's cane mill, and in the fall he made cane syrup for the public. It was a treat for Percy to get a jar of cane juice every year.

Their children were Percy Lowery (b. Oct. 22, 1899, d. Dec. 18, 1998) married Verda Bailey on Mar. 26, 1932. They had no children.

Sarah Jane "Sally" (b. Jul. 12, 1901, d. Oct. 17, 1976) married George Aaron Johnston on Oct. 2, 1920. Sally and Aaron had three children: Marie, George and Noble.

Stuart Liles (b. Aug. 11, 1903, d. Jan. 17, 1973) md. Pearl Key on Feb. 16, 1923. Liles and Pearl had two children, Winston and Hazel.

Thomas Graham was born on Jul. 4, 1905 and died Sep. 25, 1905.

James Franklin (b. Jul. 3, 1906, d. Sep. 8, 1991) md. Eva Riser on Mar. 12, 1929. James and Eva had three children: Sue, Cleo and Lamar.

Daniel Larther (b. Apr. 6, 1910, d. Apr. 19, 2000) md. Myrtis Goodson Jun. 7, 1938. Larther and Myrtis had three children: Gwen, Jean and Danny.

Nellie Dora Adlene (b. Mar. 13, 1912) md. Delbert Weger on Sep. 22, 1934. Nellie and Delbert had two children, Virginia and Harrison.

Mattie Ola (b. Apr. 1, 1915) md. William Lee Culpepper on Aug. 3, 1935. They had one daughter, Carol.

Willie Alexander "Will" (b. Jan. 30, 1918) md. Margaret Hubbard on May 26, 1945 in London, England. They have two children, Martin and Charlene.

Robert Lowery Ausbon (b. Dec. 4, 1920, d. Dec. 19, 1986) md. Florence Wyvone Alford on Mar. 4, 1943. Ausbon and Wyvone were the parents of two children, Edwin and Dinah.

Mary Ellie (b. Jul. 4, 1922) md. Floyd Hollingsworth on Dec. 2, 1939. They had two daughters, Geraldine and Delores. Geraldine died as an infant.

Lowery kicked off the tendency of family events occurring on holidays with his birth on Christmas Eve, then his marriage on Christmas Day. Two of their children, Thomas Graham and Mary Ellie, were born on the fourth of July, 17 years apart and one child, Mattie Ola, was an April Fool's baby. Robert Lowery died on Aug. 30, 1968 at the age of 90 and Mary Allie on

Mar. 4, 1963 at the age of 84. They are buried at Hopewell Baptist Church Cemetery.

HARRISON, W.W. "Bill" Harrison (b. Oct. 1, 1856 in Mississippi) md. Lucy Sims (b. ca. 1865), daughter of James H. Sims and Nancy Moody, on Jan. 27, 1885, in Scott County Mississippi. They had three children: Nancy Annie, Frank and George.

Lucy died on Dec. 24, 1895 in childbirth with the fourth child. With three children to raise by himself, Bill had to find a new wife. He married Sallie Suttlers in 1901 but this marriage ended in divorce. In 1903 he married Jennie Earls and they had two children, Nola and Billy. W.W. died Oct. 23, 1929 and is buried in Salem Cemetery between Lucy and Jennie.

HATCH, The name Hatch, Hach, Hache, or Hetch originated in England, Amsterdam and Sweden. By the 13th century Geffery Hatch lived in Devonshire, England, with his eldest son John Hatch. John's descendant, William Hatch, was the first to migrate to America and settled in Connecticut. The family spread to New Jersey, Massachusetts and New York.

William's son, Jonatham Hatch, had a son, Timothy Hatch, who had a son, Moses Porter Hatch. Moses' son, John Porter Hatch (b. Jan. 9, 1822 in Oswego, NY) trained at West Point and served as a general during the Civil War, receiving the Medal of Honor.

Hatch Family: Theo, Percy, J.C., R.L., McClain and Emanuel

In the 1800s several Hatches held high positions: U.S. Senator, New York author, Massachusetts theologian and educator.

Percy Prescott Hatch (b. 1851, d. 1929), the patriarch of the Scott County, MS Hatches, was born in West Point, NY, a descendant of General John Porter Hatch. In his early 20s P.P. Hatch became disenchanted with Upper State New York; and, during the "Carpetbagger" era, migrated to Georgia where he met his wife, Anna Lee Street (b. 1861, d. 1937). Around 1890 they moved to Scott County, settled in the Ross (Raworth) Tank Community, and raised four daughters and four sons. P.P. and Anna are buried in the Hillsboro Baptist Cemetery.

Locals recall P.P. Hatch as a "great storyteller" and a "smart school teacher." When P.P. Hatch's house burned in 1928, they moved to Hillsboro, where he died in 1929, and Anna, a strong-willed woman, died in 1937.

P.P. Hatch's children are Charlie Patrick (Preston), Bessie Parks Simms, Gertrude Chambers, Fannie Harvey, Willie, Clarence, Percy and Conlee Brogdon.

Charlie Patrick (Preston) Hatch was P.P.

Hatch's oldest son and married Sally Chambers from Hillsboro. Their lifetime home was Hillsboro, Scott County, MS.

Charlie Hatch had eight children:

1) Minnie Lee, widow of Robert Earl Bustin, with two sons, Jerry Lee of Forest and William Earl of Brandon.

2) Walter Emanuel Hatch, married Rebecca McDill, with two children, Walter Emanuel Jr., Baton Rouge, LA, and Janice Fortinberry, Forest.

3) Howard McClain, deceased, married Annie Sue Walton with three children: Darwin, Hillsboro, Michael, Clinton, and Cheryl Parks, Philadelphia.

4) Charlene, deceased, married J.B. Harvey, deceased, with seven children: James, Memphis, TN; Randy, Statesville, VA; Richard, deceased; Debbie Waggoner, deceased; Vickie Hill, Seymour, TN; Valorie Griffing, Hattiesburg; and Camelia Noblin, Jackson.

5) R.L., deceased, married Ruby Lee Lyles of Morton. They had no children.

6) Theo, deceased, married Lousie Houston, deceased, with three children: Patricia Norman, Elouise Herrington and Doris Mears, all of Meridian

7) Percy, deceased, married Birdie Mae Graham, deceased, with three children: Rhonda, Long Beach; Aurelia Mae Hagin, Gulfport; and Phyllis Amelia Harbour, Cary, NC.

8) J.C. Hatch, deceased, married Betty Dale Stewart, deceased, with two children: Charles Gary, Jackson and Rebecca Stuart, deceased.

HATCH-STREET, Percy Prescott Hatch (b. 1851 in West Port, New York, d. 1919) married Anna Lee Street (1861-1938, born in Columbus, GA). Both Percy and Anna Lee are buried at Hillsboro, MS.

Their children were Conley, Gertrude, Clarence, Willie Prescott, Charles Preston, Percy James, Bessie and Frances Lee "Fannie."

Percy Prescott Hatch and wife, Anna Lee, with their son (early 1900s)

Percy Prescott Hatch was a small-framed man from New York. His family did not want him to come south because they wanted him to become a special somebody and well-known. He married Anna Lee Street, an illiterate farm girl from Alabama. They moved to Morton, MS, where Percy taught school at Raworth Tank.

Gertrude Hatch married Press Chambers (b. 1880, d. 1949) and two of their sons had stores around the Hillsboro Community: Paul Hunter Chambers and Noah Walter "Snowdie" Chambers.

Conley Hatch married Willie Jones Brogdon (b. 1889, d. 1923) (see Brogdon-Hatch information).

Fannie Hatch married Leonard Chester Harvey (b. 1886, d. 1967). Their son, J.T. Harvey, remembered visiting his grandfather, Percy Prescott Hatch, at Raworth Tank. Since his grandfather was always hollering at children at school, it seemed he hollered all the time. J.T. remembered sitting on the front porch of his grandfather's home and listening to him read over and over "very loud" books, newspapers, etc.

HAYS, Mr. and Mrs. Benjamin F. Hays and their son, Robert, moved to Forest in July of 1948 from Clanton, AL. They purchased the home located at 214 North Broad Street. Mr. Hays was a furniture salesman, and a couple of years after coming to Forest, he opened the Forest Furniture Market, a business which still exists as this is written in the year 2000.

Benjamin F. Hays, ca. 1951

Mr. Hays was a member of the Rotary Club. A popular and respected member of the community, he died after a long illness on Dec. 28, 1964. From the beginning, the family was active in the life of Forest Presbyterian Church, where Mrs. Hays (nee Martha Gladstone) served many years as organist and choir director.

A graduate of the University of Oklahoma, she was a teacher of English and music in the public schools. She began teaching in the Scott County system in 1951, first at Good Hope and then at Morton, before transferring to Forest High

Martha Gladstone Hays, ca. 1993

where she retired in 1974. Upon her retirement, Mrs. Hays was a member of the Fortnightly Club, the Hontakalo Chapter of DAR, MS Genealogical Society, Delta Kappa Gamma, Forest Garden Club and the Caledonian Society of Mississippi, and became active in the Scott County Retired Teachers Association.

Robert entered first grade in the fall of 1950, and graduated from Forest High in 1962. During

Robert Hays, ca. 1962, age 17

his high school days, he played first chair in the French Horn section of the band and was a member of various choral groups as part of the school's music program. After graduation from Belhaven College, he served two years in the Navy. One of two members of the class of 1962 to serve in a combat unit in Vietnam, he was a hospital corpsman attached to a Marine Corps infantry company. While there, in addition to receiving a Purple Heart and a Navy Commendation Medal, he received the Navy and Marine

Corps Medal, the highest award given for heroism in activity which is not directly due to enemy action.

He married the former Martha Emmons in 1968, and from the union came two children, Ben and Susan. After a brief career in business, he entered Reformed Theological Seminary in Jackson from which he graduated in 1977 with an M.Div. and received the D.Min. from there in 1984. After serving Presbyterian Churches in Arkansas and Oklahoma, in 1988 he returned to central Mississippi to pastor the Presbyterian church in Pearl.

Robert considers the privilege of growing up in Forest in the 1950s to have been one of life's great blessings. It was a culture and a time which can only be appreciated by those who lived through it and have lived long enough to value it. Though he has been away for several years as this is written, Forest will always be home.

HEDERMAN, Ellen Jane Hederman, the youngest child of Martin and Susan (Chambers) Hederman was born on Apr. 24, 1880, eight months after her father's death. She was 14 when the family moved from Hillsboro to Jackson where her older sister and brothers could work for their cousin's newspaper. Ellie entered the Jackson Graded Public School and graduated valedictorian of her class in 1898.

Ellen Jane Hederman (b. Apr. 24, 1880, d. Dec. 5, 1964), daughter of Martin Oliver and Susan Virginia Chambers Hederman. Sister of Robert, Thomas and Annie Hederman Rea. Postmaster, Jackson. Deputy State Auditor, Deputy State Banking Department, Deputy State Insurance Commission.

After one year at Belhaven College, for which she received a diploma, she taught school at Redmondville in Yazoo County and later at Poindexter Grammar School in Jackson. Probably in 1904 when her cousin Thomas M. Henry was elected state auditor, she began a career with that office, serving with four different auditors. She advanced from warrant and pension clerk to chief deputy auditor, the position she held for eight years. Ellie and her sister, Annie, walked together from their home to their respective workplaces. A neighbor observed that, as proper young women walking downtown, they crossed to the opposite side of the street if they needed to pass the saloon at the corner of Capitol and State Streets.

Upon recommendation of Mississippi Congressman Russell Ellzey, in the spring of 1934, Ellie was appointed Jackson's postmistress by President Franklin D. Roosevelt. At that time, the Jackson post office was in temporary quarters on the ground floor of the R.E. Hines Garage, behind the Edwards Hotel. A new federal building to include the post office was under construction. Six months after she took office, she supervised the big task of moving operations into

the new building so that no interruption of service occurred. She served four years, a period in which the post office department achieved a goal not since equaled—it operated within its revenues. In 1941, she became general secretary of the Mississippi Department of Bank Supervision, serving with two state comptrollers before her retirement about 1945. In each of her three public offices, she held responsibilities never given previously to a woman.

Ellie professed her Christian faith and was baptized in the First Baptist Church of Jackson in 1897. Soon after the turn of the century she began working with the Sunday School children. Before her death she was honored at a special ceremony for more than 50 years teaching in the Beginner Department.

Her favorite hobbies were genealogy and collecting dolls. When her five nephews married, each bride's gown was copied in minute detail to dress a bride doll. Her research into Hederman and Chambers family history spanned more than 50 years and was intense in the decade after her retirement until her health failed in 1956. Her dream of completing a family story for the sake of her nephews was not realized in her lifetime. She died Dec. 5, 1964 at the age of 84. She was buried in the R.M. Hederman lot in Cedarlawn Cemetery.

HEDERMAN-CHAMBERS, Martin Hederman (b. Feb. 3, 1834, in Bathhurst Township, Upper Canada), the third son of Michael and Catherine (Haugh) Hederman. At the conclusion of the American Civil War, in the late 1860s, Martin moved to Lake City, MN. However, Martin remained in Lake City no more than two or three years. For reasons not yet clear, he came far south to Mississippi, almost certainly traveling downriver on a steamboat.

Martin Hederman (b. 1834, d. 1879). Husband of Susan Virginia Chambers and father of Robert, Thomas, Annie and Ellen Jane Hederman. Born in Canada and moved to Hillsboro, MS in 1871.

Martin's skills as a builder would have been needed in any state the war touched, but, by design or accident, he came to Mississippi. Something as simple as the prospect of warmer winters may have been a factor. Whatever he was anticipating, it seems likely that he landed at Vicksburg and caught a train going toward Meridian. The greatest mystery is how he happened to stop in Scott County. As good a conjecture as any is that a fellow passenger may have known that another courthouse was planned in Hillsboro. That would be a promising opportunity for a bricklayer and plasterer with 20 years experience.

Nevertheless, Martin's first employment in Scott County seems not to have been on the courthouse, but on a house being built for the Lod Moore family about three miles south of Forest. It is believed that Martin made brick for the house from fire clay on the Moore property, built five brick chimneys, plastered the interior walls and stuccoed the chimneys. It would have been an eight or nine month's job, and was completed in August 1871. The completion date of the new Hillsboro Courthouse in February 1872, suggests that Martin possibly worked on the new Hillsboro Courthouse as soon as his work for Lod Moore was finished.

In November 1872, Martin paid $300 for a one-acre lot on Main Street in Hillsboro. Almost certainly, he knew Susan Virginia Chambers by that time.

Susan's brother-in-law, Patrick Henry, was contractor/carpenter on the Moore house and two of her brothers, Luke and William Marion, were bricklayers. Martin probably bought groceries at the store run by Susan's father.

Martin Hederman and Susan Virginia Chambers married Mar. 1, 1874. Susan, born Apr. 26, 1843, was the daughter of Robert Powell and Huanna (Wilson) Chambers. Within five years after their marriage, Martin and Susan had three children: Annie Catherine (b. May 30, 1875); Robert Michael (b. Aug. 13, 1877); Thomas Martin (b. Nov. 21, 1878). The fourth child was born eight months after his death. Martin died on Aug. 21, 1879 and Ellen Jane was born Apr. 24, 1880. Two stories have been handed down concerning his death: that his death resulted from a fall off the steeple of the Hillsboro Baptist Church on which he was working; that he died from chills and fever contracted while he and Luke Chambers were making tombstones. Martin was buried in the Hillsboro Baptist Cemetery. In 1988, Martin's remains were moved to Cedarlawn Cemetery in Jackson and re-interred near the plot of Susan, who died Aug. 28, 1911.

HEDERMAN-REA, Annie Catherine

Hederman was the eldest of the four children of Martin and Susan (Chambers) Hederman. She was born on May 30, 1875 in Hillsboro. Her father died when she was 4 years old, and the following year she started to school in the former courthouse which her father earlier helped construct. When her two younger brothers had to drop out of school at about age 10 to help their mother provide for the family, Annie taught them at home what she was learning in

Annie Catherine Hederman (b. 1875 in Hillsboro, d. 1953 in Jackson), daughter of Martin and Susan Virginia Chambers Hederman. Married William Oliver Rea. Sister of Robert, Thomas and Ellen Hederman. First lady member Board of Institutions of Higher Learning. First President Young Women's Christian Association.

school. Within a few years Susan and the boys accumulated enough funds to send Annie to the new Industrial Institute and College in Columbus, MS, the first public college for women in the nation. Costs for the eight-month term was about $85. She took courses in the newly devel-

oped skills of typewriting and shorthand, and in 1893 was hired by her cousin, Col. Robert Hiram Henry, to work for his Jackson newspaper, the Daily Clarion-Ledger. Col. Henry took great pride in Annie's ability to take long speeches in shorthand so he could report them in his newspaper sooner than competing newspapers.

Annie's family joined her in Jackson when Col. Henry offered jobs to her brothers. By August 1898, she was working independently as a "stenographer and typewriter" in a small office on East Capitol Street. While on a visit to her hometown, Hillsboro, she was "discovered" by former Governor Robert Lowry, whose speech she had recorded in shorthand. He recommended her to Judge Ed Mayes, who hired her as a stenographer—the beginning of her career as a legal secretary. Later she worked for the firm of Green and Green, At the time of her marriage in 1913, she had had a 20-year business career remarkable for a woman in that era. For many years she was "on call" to assist any editorial need at the Clarion-Ledger. It is not surprising that her brothers were supporters of suffrage for women.

Annie Catherine married William Oliver Rea on Jun. 18, 1913. Annie was dedicated to the Baptist church. Having been baptized in Hillsboro, she transferred her church letter to Jackson in January 1895. For 50 years she taught a Sunday School Class and her husband, Will, head of the Jackson Building and Loan Association, was equally devoted to the Presbyterian church. Annie took an active part in her church's support of war orphans during World War I.

A president and historian of the Research Club, a women's literary group, she was also chairman of its scholarship fund awarded to a Belhaven College student. Her interest in young people and their education was recognized by Governor Paul B. Johnson, who appointed her to the Board of Trustees of the State Institutions of Higher Learning.

William Oliver Rae suffered a long illness, but Annie predeceased him on Oct. 8, 1953, at the age of 78. She was buried in the R.M. Hederman lot in Cedarlawn Cemetery.

HEDERMAN-SMITH, Thomas Martin

Hederman (b. Nov. 21, 1878 in Hillsboro) was the third child of Martin and Susan (Chambers) Hederman. Thomas was not a year old when his father died.

He moved with the rest of the family to Jackson. Still only a boy, he became an apprentice typesetter in the *Clairon-Ledger* composing room under his cousin, Robert Hiram Henry. Thomas

Thomas Martin Hederman Sr. (b. 1878, d. 1948)

progressed to typesetting by linotype, at which he was exceedingly skilled, operating the first such machine to come to this area. In not to many years he was foreman of the composing room, then moved to the front office where he became bookkeeper then business manager. In 1920, Col. Henry sold the *Clarion-Ledger* to

Thomas and his brother "Bert" Robert Michael.

Thomas Martin Hederman was married Nov. 21, 1906 to Miss Pearl Smith, daughter of Arnold and Sally Smith of Madison. Pearl was a graduate of Blue Mountain College and an accomplished musician. This union was blessed with two sons, Thomas Martin Hederman Jr. (b. May 23, 1911) and Arnold Smith Hederman (b. Apr. 10, 1915).

Carrie Pearl Smith Hederman (b. 1882, d. 1971)

While Thomas was not a man who sought honors, many came his way, generally accompanied by responsibility. He was a member of the First Baptist Church of Jackson from his youth. He served on the Board of Deacons and on the building committee. He was a trustee of Mississippi College and president of the Jackson Chamber of Commerce, as well as a member of the Jackson City School Board for many years. He was president of the Mis-

Thomas Martin Hederman Jr. (b. 1911, d. 1985)

Arnold Smith Hederman (b. 1915, d. 1962)

sissippi Press Association and elected to its Hall of Fame.

Thomas Martin Hederman Sr. passed away on Feb. 25, 1948, while sitting at his desk composing an editorial. Interment was made in Lakewood Memorial Park.

HEDERMAN-TAYLOR, Robert Michael

Hederman, known to his friends and family as Bert, was the oldest son of Martin and Susan (Chambers) Hederman. Born Aug. 13, 1877 in Hillsboro, he was only 3 years old when his father died. Times were extremely difficult for the Hederman family. In order not to embarrass Susan, townsfolk would bring food anonymously and leave it for the family to find later. It became necessary for Bert and his brother, Tom, to quit school at an early age (after about the fourth grade) to assist their mother in providing for their family. When they were old enough to handle a pair of oxen pulling a wagon, they regularly took loads of railroad cross-ties, which they had cut and hewed, to Forest and sold them to Mr. Hi Eastland, who would always give them a fair price. While in Forest, they would pick up freight at the train station to take back to the Hillsboro merchant who ordered it. Such deliveries were tough work in good weather, but almost impossible in the rainy seasons.

Susan put her sewing skills to good use. Mr. C.W. Abraham, a Hillsboro storekeeper from whom Martin had purchased the land for his house, lent her a sewing machine for her own use and for demonstration to prospective customers. As she became proficient with the machine, she was able to "take in" sewing. Susan was truly a steel magnolia, pulling her family through 15 years of severe poverty with the precept of save a little, give a little, spend a little."

Robert Michael Hederman Sr. (b. Aug. 18, 1877, in Hillsboro, d. Feb. 28, 1944 in Jackson), son of Susan Virginia Chambers Hederman and Martin Hederman. Brother of Thomas, Annie Hederman Rae, Ellen Jane Hederman. Father of Robert Michael Jr., Zachary Taylor and Hiram Henry Hederman.

Jennie Bell Taylor Hederman, wife of Robert Michael Hederman and their children: Hiram Henry, Zachary Taylor and Robert Michael Jr.

Susan's nephew, Robert Hiram Henry, was in the newspaper publishing business. He moved his Brookhaven newspaper to Jackson in 1883 and named it the *State Ledger*. Four years later the *Eastern Clarion* and *State Ledger* merged, becoming the *Clarion-Ledger*. Bert was 18 when he and his brother accepted their cousin's offer to work at his newspaper plant in Jackson. Their determination to succeed became more intense when they arrived in Jackson. The family journey began by ox-wagon and was completed on the newly completed train from Forest to Jackson.

During their first year in Jackson, the Hederman family rented a "shot-gun" house on Congress Street. In 1895, Susan purchased a lot on North Jefferson Street and built a house. In 1898, Bert and Tom bought Col. Henry's job printing equipment and set up business as "Hederman Brothers." Under Bert's management, the business prospered and grew to become the largest commercial printing and bookbinding establishment in the state.

After a 13 year courtship, Bert and Jennie Belle Taylor, daughter of Zachary and Jennie (Strickland) Taylor, were married on Jun. 20, 1907. Shortly after their marriage, his bride accepted the responsibility of keeping books for the firm. Much of this was likely done at home because their first son, Robert Michael Jr., arrived in 1910, followed by Zachary Taylor in

1913, Martin Oliver in 1918 and Hiram Henry in 1920.

Bert was a deacon and chairman of the Finance Committee of First Baptist Church, Jackson, member of the Board of Directors of Mississippi Baptist Hospital, Mississippi Baptist Orphanage, Young Men's Christian Association, the School Board of Jackson, the Chamber of Commerce, Jackson State Savings and Loan, the Merchants Bank and Trust Company, the Kiwanis Club, *The Clarion-Ledger* and *Jackson Daily News* and manager of Hederman Brothers Printing Company.

On Feb. 28, 1944, God called Bert home. After a full and useful life, his passing was mourned by many. He was remembered as a kind and considerate Christian gentleman, who loved his family, his friends, his native state and the city of Jackson. His funeral service was held at the First Baptist Church, with burial in Cedarlawn Cemetery.

Bert's grandson, Zachary Taylor Hederman Jr., married Susie Lee, the daughter of Roy Noble, retired Chief Justice of the Mississippi Supreme Court, and Sue Lee of Forest. In 1982, all newspapers owned by the Hederman families were sold.

HENDERSON, James Monroe Henderson (b. 1886, d. 1951) and Arrie Hawkins (b. 1901, d. 1992) married in 1916, settling in Smith County. They were parents of 11 children. After moving to Forest in 1935 they operated a grocery store.

The James Monroe and Arrie Hawkins Henderson Family, ca. 1970. Men (l-r): Guy, Bobby, Howell, Troy, Roy, Ray. Women (l-r): Myrine, Ruby, Mother, Joanna, Mary Ellen.

Son Howell (b. 1918, d. 1975) married Frances Robbins. They have four sons: Larry, Tony and Billy. Howell served in the CCC and WWII, making convoy trips across the Atlantic into Mermansk, Russia.

Myrine (b. 1920-) married Maben Risher. They had two sons, Gary and David (b. 1944, d. 2000). Later remarried and had a daughter Vicki (b. 1954, d. 1998). Myrine resides in the Scott County Nursing Home.

Ruby (b. 1922-) married Raymond Viverette. They have one son Charles and a daughter Susan. They reside in Odessa, TX.

Ray (b. 1926, d. 1990) had three sons: Carl, Mark and Mike. He served in the Navy during WWII. Mark and family reside in Forest.

R.G. (b. 1924, d. 1930) was fatally injured by a car in Laurel.

Guy (b. 1928-) married Lois Robertson and they are parents of four: Rex, Melinda, Patricia and Angela. Guy served in the Navy and is a retired Army Reserve Chaplain. For 20 years

they were missionaries in Korea and the Philippines. Guy retired as editor of the *Baptist Record*. They reside in Clinton.

Bobby (b. 1931) md. Carol Breland and they had one son Ronald. Bobby served in the Air Force and retired from government service, living in McLain.

Troy (b. 1934-) md. Delores Underwood of Forest. They have three daughters: Pamela, Judy, Leigh. He served in the Air Force. His career was in education, retiring from Hinds Community College They reside in Raymond.

Roy (b. 1937-) md. Ann Taylor. They are parents of David and Kay. He retired to Arkansas after a career with Exxon.

Joanna (b. 1939-) md. Joe Hall. Their children are Sheila, Melanie, Sherry and Todd. She is employed by the State Personnel Board and lives in Clinton.

Mary Ellen (b. 1945-) resides in a nursing home in Jackson

The Henderson family cherishes its roots in Scott County because of the friends and associates made through the years.

HENRY, John M. Henry born 1824 in Alabama arrived in Madison County, MS in 1833. He married Anna Susan Lott and together with Anna's brother Solom J. Lott and Margaret Henry Lott moved to Scott County in 1845. John M. served in the 33rd Mississippi Infantry Regiment.

John and Anna's children were Elizabeth married William Cagle, Margaret H. Lott, Mary H. Babbs, Columbus W. married Millie Jane Irby, daughter of William Taylor and Susan Chambers Irby of Scott

Top Left: Columbus W. Henry Ela Beard, Leone Henry Birdie Henry. Standing. Fount Henry; seated: Jennie Accord, Millie Jane Henry; standing: Pearl Donald, the only survivor, 1901; seated: Taylor Henry, Van Henry, Earl Henry.

County. Millie Jane's mother was killed by runaway oxen near Line Prairie. Taylor Irby died of pneumonia. Millie Jane had one sister Mary who married John Bates of Scott County, and six brothers: Griffin (killed in Civil War at Perryville), Jeff, Wright, William, M.C.and Wesley.

Millie Jane and Columbus W. lived at Line Prairie five miles north of Morton where Millie Jane's family grew up. Columbus W. died in 1902 leaving nine children still at home.

Oldest son John was married, Birdie (19), Leon (16), Eula (14), Jennie (12), Fount (10), Earl (8), Taylor (5), Van (3) and Pearl (3 months).

Leon was left to support this large family. After the brothers and sisters grew up, he married Allie Goodson in 1911. They lived at Line Prairie where their first four children were born. Tray died at age 4, Vera was killed in a 1964 train and car accident near Presto in Jackson, MS. Van died in 1987 and is buried in Homewood Cemetery. Jennie married Norman Long. She died in 1997 and Norman died in November

1997. Leon then moved to Gilbert where their next two daughters were born, Visla Seton and Wedell Ballard.

Leon then bought the Sal Lott place in 1925. Sal was a distant cousin. The place was between Homewood and Pulaski, where their other five children were born. Otis, Macon died in 1986, Clara Wicker, Denson and Alice Hollingsworth.

Leon and Allie lived there until 1978, when they were admitted to Lackey Convalescent Home. Leon died Oct. 16, 1980. Allie died Jun. 16, 1981. They are buried in Hodge Hill Cemetery two miles north of Morton. This is the same cemetery that Great-Grandmother Annie Lott Henry is buried. *Submitted by Wedell Ballard.*

HODGES, Ailene Cox Hodges was the daughter of Wesley Marine and Eula Mitchell Cox of Sebastopol. Her immediate family included brothers: Melvin, Joe and Raymond, and sisters, Clotile and Mary Sue. She was a graduate of Sebastopol High School and Moler Beauty College in Memphis, TN. After receiving her hairdresser's degree in the mid-1930s, Ailene returned to Forest to begin her career in Myrtie Park's Beauty Shop located in Court House Square. She later opened her own beauty shop on the eastside of Court House Square. The shop was later relocated to George Street.

Ailene Cox Hodges

Ailene, a hairdresser for almost 50 years, was part of a family history of "Hair People" that included her grandmother, aunt, uncles, cousins, brothers and sister who all worked as barbers and hairdressers. Ailene was a role model for her sister Sue who also became a hairdresser. When it was time for Sue to go to beauty school, it was Ailene who took her to Memphis and enrolled her in school. Sue later moved to South Carolina and became a member of the National Cosmetologist Association of South Carolina, South Carolina Hair Fashion Committee, the National Cosmetologist Association and Hair America. Ailene was married to Kelly Hodges and they had one son, Kelly Hodges Jr. who married Kaye Smith.

Kelly and Kaye have two daughters, Krisanne and Kim. When Ailene began her career in the beauty profession, there was no legislature requiring the licensure for hairdressers. During the late 1940s and early 1950s, Ailene and the Fondren family from Jackson were instrumental in lobbying for the passage of legislation that required hairdressers and barbers to be certified and licensed. She worked hard for the Mississippi State Board of Cosmetology during her career, serving as a guest artist, platform instructor, teacher, and lecturer. Ailene was recognized as a leader in the beauty profession receiving many awards in styling and artistic competitions and for her dedication and commitment to establishing high standards for hairdressers in the state of Mississippi. *Submitted by Helen Vance Cox.*

HOLMES, It was in the sixth decade of the 19th century that the Holmes family was introduced into the Lake area. The original Holmes settler came to the area as a teacher and there was another who later served as Justice of the Peace.

There was a lady born as a slave, as most blacks were, in 1842 by the name of Lucy (maiden name unknown) who played a role in the building of the railway from Vicksburg to Alabama. She would later marry a man named George Montgomery, who according to sources was a Freeman, and together they had a daughter named Annie Louise. Annie Louise was born one of seven children in 1875, 10 years after the Emancipation Proclamation. Many years later she would be known and loved by many as Baby Ray.

The Burge's also came on the scene during this time. This family, originally from Germany, settled in the area. In 1861, John Thomas Burge was born who would later be known and loved as Big Daddy. Tom Burge fathered 16 children: 11 by a lady named Jane (birth date unknown) who took the last name of Holmes and five by a lady name Dote who was born in 1878 and took the last name of Denham.

George and Lucy (now a free woman) Montgomery raised their seven children (five girls and two boys). Annie Louise had six children of her own, the youngest, Annie Bell, was born in 1916.

Around the turn of the century, Tom Burge with Jane Holmes were raising their family and in 1906 John Thomas Holmes "J.T." was born.

Annie Bell was born in Sherman Hill, and at an early age she with her mother, Baby Ray, moved to Lake. Baby Ray and later Annie Bell worked as domestic help housekeepers for several white families as so many Blacks did in those days. During these times, it was not uncommon for people to walk the five to seven miles from Sherman Hill to Lake to work every day. Baby Ray walked the distance for many years until the opportunity to move to Lake became available.

Annie Bell, later met who was to become the love of her life and one month shy of her 19th birthday. Annie Bell Montgomery became the wife of J.T. Holmes. They were married on Oct. 15, 1935 and together they began a journey covering 39 years of marriage blessed with nine children. These nine children have ensured the legacy well into the next century with Annie Bell and J.T. having 22 grandchildren and 18 great-grandchildren.

HOPPER, Mabel Hopper with five children, twin daughters Lolita and Serena, Willie Mae, Grace and Jack, moved to Forest from Scooba in 1918. They lived in their new home on First Street among McKenzie relatives. Another daughter Dorothy "Dot" was born in Forest in 1922. They were all members of the Forest Methodist Church.

Four children began first grade in the Forest School and all six graduated from Forest High School.

All children married in Mississippi. Three couples were married in Forest. They all have made Mississippi their home and never lived in another state.

Six children of Mabel and Willie Hopper

Their mother, Mabel Hopper, worked many years in Stevens Department Store on Main Street in Forest.

Relatives of our mother are the McKenzies, Weems and Carr families.

Lolita Hopper married D.L. Harrison. Their children are Dr. D.L. Harrison Jr. of Grenada and MayBelle Beasley of Jackson.

Serena Hopper married Walter McGee "Red" of Louisville, MS. Their daughter is Ann Butler and granddaughter is Barbara Butler Pemberton.

Willie Mae Hopper married Chester Mitchell of Forest. They have a son, Joe Rhett Mitchell, named for his grandfather "Papa Joe." Rhett Mitchell married Patricia Burford "Pat" of Sara, MS. They have two sons, Dr. Joe Rhett Mitchell III "Mitch" and Stan Mitchell. Both graduated from Forest High School.

Grace Hopper graduated from MSCW in 1935. In 1937 she married Cecil Louie Allred of Hazlehurst. They have lived in Hazlehurst since their marriage. They have three sons: Cecil Louie Allred Jr. of Jackson, Chester Hopper Allred of Pascagoula and Dr. William Stanton Allred of Bedford, TX. They have five grandchildren and a great-granddaughter.

Jack Thadaeus Hopper married Vanda Nell Brent of Hazlehurst. Their children are Cheryl Payne and Jack Thadaeus Hopper Jr. "Thad" both of Jackson.

Dot Hopper Corbitt married Joseph Bernard Corbitt "Bunny" of Meridian. They have two sons and two daughters: Joseph Bernard Corbitt Jr. "Joe," Frank Leonard Corbitt "Leon," both of Meridian; Sandra Walker of Clinton and Carol Slye of Hattiesburg.

Kemper County and Scooba was home for our father, Willie Leon Hopper. Our father was in the grocery business in Decalb and Scooba. His mother was a Delchamps from Mobile, AL. Our great-great grandfather, Joseph Delchamps, was from France. He served in French Emperor Napoleon Bonaparte's wedding to Marie Louise of Austria. Our cousins have the gold buckles and medallions that he wore. Joseph was given the Montelou Island just south of Mobile, AL to grow Mulberry trees for the silk. Joseph Delchamps drowned in a oyster bed on Montelou Island. He was wearing a heavy gold belt and this weighted him down. His son Julius Delchamps was married to Sara Bancroff. The youngest son started the Delchamps grocery business in Mobile, AL. After a hurricane destroyed the home on Montelou Island the land was sold and our grandmother received a small inheritance.

HORN-TADLOCK, C.S.C. Horn (b. Sep. 18, 1855 in Greensboro, AL) md. Lula Tadlock on

Apr. 9, 1893 in Scott County, MS. Lula (b. Dec. 6, 1869) was the daughter of M.D.C. and Silena Tadlock.

C.S.C. and Lula were the parents of eight children: 1) Stella Estelle md. Jeremiah Thomas Jones and had four children: Edith Grace, Albert Eugene, Lula Belle and Mary Helen; 2) Ben Sedric md. May Mahaffey; 3) Willie Watson md. Leona Chambers; 4) Demmy Calip remained single; 5) Katie md. Henry Thomas Simmons; 6) Verona md. Albert E. Jones, brother of Jeremiah Thomas Jones; 7) Sam md. Merle Herring; 8) Lawrence Wesley md. Grace Fore.

They lived all their married life in Scott County. C.S.C. was a member of the Woodmen of the World. He died Apr. 28, 1911 and Lula died Jan. 26, 1940. They are both buried in Sims Cemetery in Scott County, MS.

HOWELL, Stephen Howell (b. 1782 in North Carolina, d. 1855 in Mississippi) appeared on the census in 1830 in Covington County, MS and on the census in 1840 and 1850 in Scott County, MS. He purchased 160 acres of land on Sep. 7, 1848 in E 1/2 of SE 1/4 S10 and W 1/2 of SW 1/4 S11 T5 R6E, Scott County, MS. He was married to Leah in 1804. Leah (b. 1785 in North Carolina, d. after 1861 in Mississippi) appeared on the census on Aug. 24, 1860 in Morton, Scott County, MS. Stephen and Leah had the following children: Charles Taylor; William Marion; Sallie, born between 1800 and 1810, married Peter B. Smith and died before 1835; Temperance (b. 1812 in Kentucky); a son born between 1815 and 1820; a daughter born between 1820 and 1825; a son born between 1825-30; ?Feriba was born between 1825-30.

Steven and Leah's oldest son, Charles Taylor Howell (b. 1806) resided, per Scott County, MS land deeds, between 1834 and 1857 in Scott County, MS. He appeared on the census in 1850 and 1860 in Scott County, MS. Charles married Mary Ann Evans on Jun. 30, 1831. She was born in 1815 in Mississippi. Charles and Mary Ann had the following children: Isaac E., Clarinda, Sarah A., Charles Taylor Jr., Thomas Jefferson, William, Leah Jane, Martha C. and Harriet.

Steven and Leah's next son, William Marion Howell, is the ancestor of this writer. William Marion (b. 1807 in Kentucky) appeared on the census in 1830 in Covington County, MS, p. 147. He resided in 1838 in Covington County, MS. He appeared on the census in 1840 in Covington County, MS, p. 140. He appeared on the census in 1860 in Smith County, MS, p. 112. He appeared on the census in 1870 in Covington County, MS, p. 405, hh #739/775. He died in 1875 in Mississippi and was buried in Ashley Cemetery, Rockport, Copiah County, MS. William Marion was married to Elizabeth McLemore (daughter of Amos McLemore and Equilla Byler) on Feb. 20, 1827 in Lawrence County, MS. Elizabeth (b. 1809 in Bedford County, TN) appeared on the census in 1880 in Salter's precinct, Copiah County, MS, ed. 28, pp. 9-10. She died after 1880 in Mississippi and was buried in Ashley Cemetery, Rockport, Copiah County, MS. Per notes of Alpha Jewel Sullivan, another descendant, Elizabeth, has no marker at Ashley Cemetery. William Marion Howell and Elizabeth McLemore had the following children: Leah J., a daughter born about 1829, Washington "Wash"

born about 1834 in Covington County, MS, Francis Marion, John T., Steven Marshall, Sara Elizabeth, Christianna L., Christopher Columbus and Jeniah C. *Prepared by Lisa R. Franklin, RN, BSN.*

HUBBARD, Thomas George Hubbard (T.G.) moved to Forest in 1942 to become superintendent of the Forest School, along with his wife, Ruth Dogett Hubbard and three children. Mary Jo, Dorothy Ruth and George Edward. They moved into the teacher's home across the street from the school. Two older children, Senie Beth and Sara Lee, lived and worked in Jackson.

They became active members of Forest Methodist Church. The three younger children graduated from Forest High School. In 1948 the family moved to Scooba, MS where Mr. Hubbard assumed the duties of Dean of Men at East Mississippi Jr. College, and Mrs. Hubbard served as girls dormitory hostess. She continued to serve in this capacity after Mr. Hubbard died in 1950. She moved back to Forest and lived on Banks Street until her death in 1990.

Senie Beth married James Greener and they had three children: Rodney, Kathy and Phyllis. Senie Beth died in 1988.

Sara Lee married Ward Gallman and they had two children, Gail and Sheila.

Mary Jo married James Archie Marler and they had three children: Brenda, Martha and Dave.

Dorothy Ruth married Robert Roth and they had three children: Laura, Tom and Joy.

George Edward married Brenda Pope and they had three children: Mike, Rowanna and Bonnie.

HUGHES, Lewis Cass Hughes (b. Oct. 31, 1843, d. Sep. 22, 1898) was the son of Joseph Hughes (b. Georgia ca. 1808) and wife Hincen H. (b. Georgia ca. 1804). Lewis' siblings were William, Thomas, Nancy, Sarah, Frances and James; the children were all born in Alabama. The family was farming in Newton County, MS in 1850. By 1860, they were living in Scott County, MS in the Hillsboro Community.

Lewis Cass Hughes was a Civil War veteran. He enlisted in Co. F, 20th Mississippi Inf., Confederate States Army, on Jun. 18, 1861, a private. On the company roll for Dec. 31, 1862, last on which his name appears, he was reported "absent with 4th Mississippi Cavalry." The records also show that L.C. Hughes, private, Co. K, 4th, latterly 2nd, Mississippi Cavalry (nickname: Mississippi Body Guards), Confederate States Army, enlisted Mar. 25, 1862, and that he was paroled May 16, 1865, at Columbus, MS.

After the war, he went to Texas and farmed in the counties of Leon, Bell and Williamson. He died in Leander, Williamson County, TX.

According to Civil War Widow's Application for Pension filed in Texas on Nov. 10, 1911, Lewis Cass Hughes married widow Martha Louisa (Sanford) May in Leon County, TX on Feb. 14, 1875. She was born in Scott County, MS on Mar. 15, 1833, the daughter of William D. Sanford (born Tennessee) and wife Sarah (born South Carolina). Martha's siblings were Wiiliam, Leroy, Burbary, Thomas, Erasmus, Edna, Rinda and Marshall.

Martha's 1st husband was James M. May

(b. 1840, d. 1869), also born in Mississippi. They had one son Joseph Nathaniel May (b. Jun. 1, 1867, d. Feb. 16, 1940).

The children of Lewis Cass Hughes and Martha include Luther; Annie (b. Feb. 7, 1876, d. Jul. 12, 1950); Thomas L. (b. Dec. 20, 1882, d. Aug. 26, 1957); William E. (b. Feb. 28, 1881, d. Aug. 26, 1957); and Sarah "Sallie" Henson (b. Jul. 14, 1878, d. Aug. 9, 1959). It is probable that Luther was the son of a previous marriage by Lewis Cass Hughes.

On the 1910 Texas census for Williamson County, Martha stated she had seven children born to her, with six still living.

Martha Louisa (Sanford) May Hughes died Apr. 16, 1926 in Leander, Williamson County, TX at the age of 93 years of respiratory failure. She and her husband, Lewis Cass Hughes, and several of their children are buried in Berry's Creek Cemetery (near Georgetown), Williamson County, TX.

HUNT-HARALSON, In 1835 Joseph Hunt of Franklin County, MS purchased land in his name and the name of his son James Marion Hunt. The land lies in Northeast Scott County in what is known as the Piketon Community. They moved to Scott County in 1836. James Marion married Nancy Sue Walters, daughter of John Walters and Lucretia Thomas of Scott County in the mid-1840s.

James Marion Hunt

Their first child was William Franklin "Babe" Hunt (b. 1846), followed by Sarah Elizabeth (b. 1847), Emanuel M. "Bud" (b. 1849), Lemuel Marion "Joe" (b. Jul. 27, 1855) and Martha (b. 1859).

James enlisted in Co. E, Lake Rebels on Aug. 24, 1861. This company was later made part of the Sixth Mississippi Infantry Regiment. His unit served in Kentucky, Battle of Shiloh, Vicksburg, Louisiana, Georgia and was in the battle of Nashville. In 1863 he was promoted to sergeant. While James was off at war, Grants troops moved East to Georgia along the Jackson Turnpike, which ran in front of the Hunt home place. While the troops forged for supplies along the way, usually leaving enough for women and children, Nancy cursed them. They took everything. The neighbors pitched in and helped Nancy and the children until James came home. James died about 1888 and was buried in Hunt Cemetery, located along the Jackson Turnpike. Nancy died in 1898, but had said she would not be buried with James. She is buried in the Summers Cemetery in the Piketon Community.

Lemuel Marion their 4th child, Joe as he was known, received a very good education for the time. He married Sarah Olivia "Sallie" Singleton, daughter of David Adam Singleton Jr. and Nepsa White of Scott County, on Dec. 23, 1879. He purchased some of his father's land, where he farmed and operated a general store. On Nov. 1, 1880 their first child, Pearlie D., arrived and died Nov. 4, 1880. She is buried in Summers Cemetery. Other children: Nancy

Maude (b. Apr. 12, 1882); James Singleton Hunt (b. Dec. 14, 1883); William Robert "Bob" (b. May 25, 1887); May Jewell (b. Jun. 9, 1889); Lilly Belle (b. Oct. 17, 1891); David Quincy "D.Q." (b. Nov. 12, 1893); Annie Clois (b. Sep. 15, 1896); Woods Eastland (b. May 17, 1899); and Drew Adam (b. Dec. 3, 1903). They moved to Forest, county seat of Scott County in 1910. He became a businessman and an influence in politics, although he never ran for office. They were members of the Baptist Church. Joe was a Mason as were all his sons. Joe died Mar. 27, 1926 and is buried in Eastern Cemetery in Forest. Sarah died Nov. 26, 1932 and is buried along side Joe.

Joe and Sallie Hunt

James Singleton Hunt became a mail carrier in Forest. William Robert owned and ran Hunts Frozen Food Locker in Forest. David Quincy, D.Q. as he was known owned Hunts Tourist Court. Woods Eastland, named after Senator James Eastland's father, became a Gulf Oil Distributor in Newton County. Drew Adam was one of Forest's City Marshals.

William Robert, May Jewell and Annie Clois were schoolteachers. Lilly Belle was deputy chancery clerk of Scott County for years. Nancy Maude climbed out a window, rode on a mule behind Tom Woods Haralson from Conehatta in Newton County and they were married the next day Jul. 7, 1900. On Apr. 2, 1901 their first child Allie Dee was born, the first of 11. Then came Leon, Annie Lee, Onabel, J.C., Hunt and French.

Tom and Maude lived in Newton County for a short time, then moved below Forest in Scott County. In 1914 they bought the old Hunt home place at Piketon, and Maude found herself looking out the same window she had slipped out in 1900.

Tom Haralson and sons

The old Hunt house burned and Tom and Maude built a new house where Sarah, Thomas, Ruby and Katie Maude (b. May 5, 1921) were all born. Their family was complete.

Allie Dee died at 6 years old with diphtheria. Leon married Sallie Bee Carson from Conehatta. They lived part time in Scott County and part time in Louisiana. Their first child, Leon Jr., died as a child, then Ida Maude, Ruth, Jack, Thomas and Keith were born. Keith married Carolyn Riser. They lived and raised their family in the Piketon Community, on part of the old Hunt homestead. Their children are Gordon, Peggy, Carl, Ronnie and Vicki.

Maude Haralson and daughters

Annie Lee married Howard Clark and had a daughter Dorothy Clark. Then she married Coyte Pearson and lived many years East of Forest on Hwy. 80.

Onabel married Lester Wolf and lived in the Ephesus Community. Their children were Theo, George, Eugene and Jerry. George lives at their home place with his wife Irene. They have four daughters.

J.C. married Mary Myers and raised his family in the Piketon Community, then moved to the Ephesus Community.

Hunt married Margaret Gouchie from New York and raised a son John and a daughter Margaret Ann. Hunt learned landscaping and tree surgery in C.C. camp at Vicksburg. He worked and owned his own business. He served in WWII and was in the Battle of the Bulge in Belgium. John joined the service fresh out of high school and served his country in many parts of the world. He and wife Sharon live in Virginia and he works for the State Dept. in Washington, D.C. Stacey and Derek are their children. Margaret Ann lives near John.

French married Tommie McDonald from Conehatta. French Jr. and Dudley Quincy are their children. French learned how to operate and mechanic on heavy equipment in C.C. Camp at Morton, what is now Roosevelt Park. He worked in many States and finally settled down near Fort Worth, TX. French Jr. lives at Bedford, TX, owns and operates Stonegate Pools. Dudley works for Delta Airlines and has lived in several states and in Germany. He now lives in Atlanta, where is an airline consultant. He and wife Virginia have two children, Holly and Dudley Jr. They have three grandchildren.

Sarah married Dwight Smythe. She was killed in a car accident at age 31.

Thomas left home and joined the Army at age 17. He was stationed in the state of Maine. After service he settled in New York, where he married Florence Kellor. They had two sons, Thomas Jr. and Donald. Thomas worked for his brother Hunt for a time, then went to work in a food service selling doughnuts. He worked his way up to manager of the business and later became district manager. His last days were spent in Tampa, FL. He was in WWII in the Navy.

Ruby was a beautician. She owned and operated a beauty shop in Newton, MS. Later she was manager of Mark Rothenburgs Beauty Salon in Meridian, MS. She married Walter Boykin from Demopolis, AL and lived most of her life there. She had one daughter Debra and lost a son a few hours after birth. Ruby has four grandchildren.

Katie Maude, the youngest of Tom and Maude Haralson's children, is the only one still living. She is the only one of the descendents of Joe Hunt that never left the old home place. She graduated Ringgold High School in March 1939, married James Matthew "Jack" Shelley from Kosciusko, MS and started her family. James Woods "Jimmy" was the first born, then Linda Darrell, Saralan Kay, Ruby Lee and Thomas Matthew. Jack farmed and helped his father-in-law operate a sawmill. He served in WWII. In later years he left the farm and worked in road construction. After Matthew started to school, Katie Maude went to work at Sunbeam Clock Company near Forest, where she worked for 19-1/2 years. After that she worked as clerk at a local clothing store. She is now retired and lives alone in the home where she raised her children.

Katie and Jack Shelley and family

Jimmy married Betty Lou Graham of the Sulpher Springs Community. They built a home and raised their family on the Graham homestead. Jimmy worked in maintenance at Sunbeam Clock Company and at US Motors in Philadelphia, MS while attending night school. He is an electrical engineer, owns and operates his own business, Shelley's Electric, near Sebastopol. Betty helps with the business and operates a large broiler farm. They have three children. Tammy has a doctor's degree in education. Pamela is a registered nurse and James Jr. is an electrician working with his dad. Jimmy and Betty have six grandchildren.

Linda Darrell married Robert Gardner from the Ringgold Community. They live on the site where her great-grandfather operated a country store and ran the Piketon Post Office. Linda Darrell has worked at several different factories over the years. Robert is now retired and is pastor of Pleasant Ridge Baptist Church. Their children are Joann, John and Sarah. Joann and husband live near Forest and operate a Broiler farm. Sarah and husband live at Petal, MS, and both are employed in Hattiesburg. John lives with his parents and is the 5th generation living on the Joe Hunt home site. John has a degree in poultry science and is employed as a chicken doctor. Linda Darrell and Robert have two grandchildren.

Saralan Kay married Charles Scott Brown from Sebastopol. They live in the Sulpher

Springs Community. Saralan works at Peavey's in Decatur. Charles is a sewing machine mechanic in a factory in Sebastopol. Their children, Bobby, Mary and Charles Jr. "Chuck," are married and all live near their parents. Katie is married and lives near her grandmother Shelley. She is in her 4th year of college to be a physical therapist. Saralan and Charles have four grandchildren.

Ruby Lee married Van Fortenberry from Harperville. They live on part of the Joe Hunt Homestead. Ruby works as a desk clerk at Day's Inn in Forest. Van works for Tyson Food Inc. They have two children, Tony and Joy. Tony is a Baptist Minister and lives near his parents. His son Daniel is the 6th generation living on part of the Joe and Sallie Hunt homestead. Joy is married and lives and works near Jackson.

Matthew first married Joan McCraw from Harperville. They had two children, Heather and Amon. Matthew then married Marsha Garvin from Louisville. Marsha is a schoolteacher at Scott Central. They have a son Mason Grant. Matthew built a house across the Old Natchez Trace Road from the very spot his forefather James Marion Hunt built one of the first houses in the Piketon Community. Matthew worked off shore and for Shelley's Electric. He is now employed as an electrician and a maintenance man at Lazy Boy in Newton. Heather is married and lives near Sebastopol. She is a beautician and is going to college to become a teacher. Amon is a junior at Scott Central School. Mason is in the third grade.

HUTSELL, Wilma was born on Feb. 1, 1932 in Jackson, MS to Audie Mae (Loper) and Len Floyd O'Shieles. When she was 2 the family moved to Texas. A brother Robert Len was born Jun. 22, 1934. Sisters, Mary Ann and Martha Jean, arrived on Nov. 21, 1938. Martha survived only two days.

Wilma and J.D. Hutsell Family

Wilma attended Robert E. Lee Elementary School and Lamar Consolidated High School in Rosenberg, TX, graduating in May 1950. Many summers were spent at the home of her grandparents, the Otho Davis Loper family in Forest, MS. Wonderful memories go back to those days.

In the fall of 1950 she enrolled at Southwest Texas State Teachers College in San Marcos, TX. Becoming a teacher had been her dream for many years. After completing her BS degree in education in 1954, she taught sixth grade in Port Lavaca, TX for two years. While there she met James David Hutsell who was in the Air Force stationed at Foster Field in Victoria, TX. They were married a year later on Aug. 19, 1956. Since J.D. was transferred to Shaw Air

Force Base in Sumpter, SC, Wilma resigned her teaching position in Port Lavaca, for the following school year to move to South Carolina. At the school near Shaw Air Force Base she taught second grade. After J.D. was discharged, they went into the retail shoe business in Texas, Oklahoma and Kansas. She continued to teach and helped with the bookkeeping at the stores. In 1964 they sold their business in Manhattan, KS and moved to J.D.'s "old home place" near Mountain Grove, MO where he raised beef cattle. Wilma began teaching in Mountain Grove schools in 1964 and continued for 31 years, retiring in June of 1995. In 1979 J.D. became the clerk of Wright County and served as clerk for 16 years, retiring in January 1995. They still live on the farm but many improvements have been made through the years.

Wilma and J.D. have three children: David Brett (b. in Corsicana, TX) Denise Ann (b. on Apr. 5, 1961 in Manhattan, KS); and James Derrick (b. Jun. 6 1966 in Houston, MO).

David and his wife Tamme live in Hartsville, MO. They have three children: Jennifer, Zachary and Jared.

Denise and husband, Curtis Richardson, live in Marshfield, MO. Ashley, Andrea and Angela are their daughters.

Derrick and Cindy, his wife, live near Mountain Grove. Their children are daughters: Kelsie, Kamryn, Kyla and son Jace.

The 10 grandchildren play a big part in Wilma's life today. She enjoys having them near as she gets to see them often. She and J.D. are very proud of them.

Wilma belongs to the Daughters of the American Revolution, Kappa Kappa Iota, and Missouri Retired Teachers. She substitutes in the local schools, teaches Sunday School, serves on the Wright County Library Board, Laclede Trust Board and judges exhibits at the Tri-County Fair. Making quilts, memory scrapbooks and crafts are pleasurable activities for her. She enjoys doing genealogy and loves to read.

IDOM, The 1880 Scott County Census lists 20 Idoms. Jackson J. Idom and his wife Nimer P. Turner are the oldest Idoms listed. They, and their parents, were all born in South Carolina. Some of their children are listed as having been born in Alabama and the younger ones in Mississippi. They are buried in the Carr Church Cemetery.

Absalom (b. Dec. 12, 1856, d. Aug. 20, 1919) was the fourth child of Jackson and Nimie. He married Thedosia Smith (b. Feb. 11, 1858, d. Nov. 13, 1905). They were both born in Alabama. They raised three sons and four daughters in the Lake and High Hill areas of Scott County. Two of the sons, Elbert Franklin and Ollie, raised their families in Scott County.

"Ab," as he was called, later married Nola Garner (b. Jan. 24, 1897, d. Jan. 13, 1977). Ab was a timber cruiser and rode a horse to do his job. He was on his way home on 19 Aug., 1919, when his horse went under a tree with a low limb that caught Ab's neck and threw him from the horse breaking his neck. He died the following day and is buried in the Springfield Baptist Church Cemetery.

Elbert Franklin (b. Nov. 30, 1883, d. Mar. 24, 1941) md. Pearly Celeste Garner (b. Aug. 25, 1902, d. Jan. 2, 1962). Celeste and Nola were

sisters. Frank's step-mother was also his sister-in-law and was always called "Aunt Nola" by their children. Frank and Celeste had five children:

Front: Willie, Mary. Middle Row: Celeste, Betty and Frances. Back: Louie

1) Frances Viola (b. Apr. 4, 1922) md. Lavelle Cooper. They had three children: Pamela, Janice and Jeff.

2) Louie Elbert (b. Nov. 30, 1924, d. Feb. 8, 1987) md. Norma Earle Alford (b. Jul. 7, 1925-) on Dec. 22, 1946 and had three children: Sylvia Claire, Michael Philip and Paul Winfred.

3) Betty Geraldine (b. Nov. 30, 1926-) md. H. Clayton Young. They had two sons: Douglas and Phillip.

4) Willie Garner (b. May 8, 1930, d. Jul. 13, 2000) md. Dorothy Ann Daniels and had three children: Frankie, Linda and Becky.

5) Mary Etta (b. May 7, 1934-)

Frank and Celeste are buried in the Springfield Cemetery. Betty Young and son Phil are the only members of Frank's family still living in Scott County. There are other descendants of Jackson and Nimmie still residing in Scott County. *Submitted by Sylvia Idom.*

JACK, Miss Bettye Mae Jack, a native of the Sand Hill Community in Rankin County, attended and graduated from Piney Woods High School. Bettye Mae received her BA degree from Southern Illinois University, her master's degree from the University of Chicago, and completed further post-graduate studies at Indiana University.

Miss Jack came to Forest about 1933 as a Jeanes Supervisor and worked with schools and children in the Midway, Morton, Sherman Hill, Ludlow and Forest communities. She worked in churches, civic, community and cultural affairs all of her life. She worked as assistant to the Scott County Superintendent of Education and when the new modern black school in Morton was built, it was named for her, the Bettye Mae Jack High School; later after integration it was known as Bettye Mae Jack Middle School.

Miss Jack was 82 when she passed away Dec. 1, 1992 at the Baptist Hospital in Jackson, after a fall in her home. She lived for years on Hill Street in Forest on the present site of Dominos Pizza.

JACKSON, William C. Jackson (b. 1845 in Georgia, d. 1907 in Forkville, MS) is buried in the Bethlehem Baptist Church cemetery. He has a Civil War grave marker. He married Winnie Williams (b. Sep. 8, 1845 in Maury County, TN), daughter of Billy Williams and Nancy Lane. She died Feb. 25, 1927 and is buried in Bethlehem

Baptist Cemetery. Her mother and Father are buried in the Old Ludlow Cemetery with a daughter Alice.

William C. Jackson and wife Winnie Williams Jackson

Children of William and Winnie: 1) Seletea Jackson (b. 1872, d. before 1900 in ScottCounty); 2) Alice Jackson (b. April 1874, d. in Groverton, MS [also called Beach Mail Route]); 3) Charlie "C.L." Jackson (b. April 1876, d. May 25, 1941), buried at Bethlehem Baptist Cemetery; 4) Nannie Jackson (b. March 1879) md. Otha Sumrall; 5) Allie Jackson md. Charlie Crapps; 6) Pearl Jackson md. Charlie Crapps after her sister Allie died; Charlie and Allie had three sons: Charlie, Ernest Oscar and Little Judge. Charlie and Little Judge died young; 7) William Felin "Judge" Jackson (b. Jan. 6, 1882, d. Mar. 2, 1967), buried at Bethlehem Baptist Cemetery, married Flossie Nutt (b. Dec. 24, 1893, d. Feb. 21, 1980), buried at Bethlehem Cemetery.

Jackson Genealogy

I. Isaac Jackson (b. ca 1745, d. 1793/1800) md. Pricilia Benedict (b. ca 1745, d. 1794/1840).

II. Henry Jackson Sr. (b. ca 1763) md. Sarah Mapp (b. 1763 d. 1850) (A) Henry Jackson Jr. (b. 1790/1804), wife unknown, 12 other brothers and sisters born between 1794 and 1820 (eight males and four females).

III. David Jackson (b. 1764 d. 1792).

IV. Isaac Jackson Jr. (b. ca 1790, d. 1817 in Georgia) md. Nancy Mapp. Children of Isaac Jr. and Nancy: (a) John Jackson (b. ca. 1806) and Fielding Franklin Jackson (b. 1809, d. ca. 1857) md. Elizabeth Sims (b. 1812, d. ca 1870 in Scott County). Children of Fielding Franklin Jackson and Elizabeth Sims: 1). Asher Henry Jackson (b. 1830) md. Maggie McElroy, served in Civil War Co. K 19th Inf. Co C, Pvt. 2). Enoch Jackson (b. 1832); 3). Nancy Mapp Jackson (b. Mar. 4, 1833 d. Nov. 9, 1880 in Forkville, MS) md. John William Kitchings (b. 1827, d. Sep. 30, 1869); 4) Mary Jackson (b. 1835); 5) Isaac Jackson (b. 1836); 6). Feilding Franklin Jackson (b. 1838); 7) Damarus Jackson (b. 1839), female; 8) Elizabeth Jackson (b. 1841); 9) Jasper Jefferson Jackson b. 1843 served in Miss Cav. Co A3 30th State Troops; 10) William C. Jackson (b. 1845); 11) Taylor Jackson (b. 1850); 12) Tobe Jackson; 13) Joseph J. Jackson served in several groups Co. G, 18th MS Inf., Co. F, 28th MS Cav., Pvt. (five months), Co. K Inf. (six months), Pvt. Partisan Rangers.

JEFFCOAT Some time before his marriage to Nancy Jane Baker on Jan. 12, 1876, Allen Henry Jeffcoat presumably joined his older sister Dorothy, who had married William E. Jeffcoat, a cousin, and whose family had come to Scott County. Allen and Dorothy, both born in Pike County, AL, were the children of Samuel Jeffcoat of Lexington District, South Carolina and D'Avis Sims of Columbus County, NC. After the deaths of their parents, the younger children were cared for by "Mammy Peg" Jeffre, who had remained with the family after the Civil War. In later years, Martha "Pattie" Jeffcoat Reeves, sister of Allen and Dorothy, also moved to Scott County from Pike County, AL, after the death of her husband, John E. Reeves. There is no evidence that four of the other five sons of Samuel and D'Avis Jefcoat lived in Mississippi, though the youngest son, General, resided in Yazoo County.

Allen Henry Jeffcoat was born Jan. 5, 1847. Nancy Jane Baker, the daughter of John Baker and Eleanor "Ellen" Adaline Smiley, was born Sep. 16, 1852, possibly in Santa Rosa County, FL. In Clarke County, MS, in 1864, Jane's mother had married as her second husband, the Rev. Jesse McKay, who owned land in the vicinity of Lillian in Scott County. A native of Amite County, Jesse McKay served in the War of 1812.

Children of Allen Henry Jeffcoat and Nancy Jane Baker:

Hattie Jeffcoat (b. Dec. 16, 1878, d. Jan. 1, 1933) md. Lee Troll Sessums.

Ernest Jeffcoat (b. Oct. 14, 1880, d. Apr. 3, 1937) md. Rebecca Page, daughter of James Polk Page and Sarah Margaret Bullard. About 1917 he moved his family to Jackson, where he lived until his death.

Mattie Jeffcoat (b. Jun. 30, 1882, d. Mar. 5, 1975) md. Hugh Donald and lived in Choudrant, LA.

Henry Long Jeffcoat (b. May 14, 1884) md. Mary D. Harvey and removed to Dubach, LA.

Ellen D'Avis Jeffcoat (b. Oct. 28, 1888, d. Oct. 26, 1984) md. first, Clifton Bustin and second, Barney Bishop. She lived in Harperville for many years before moving to Gloucester, VA where she died.

Zeddie L. "Bob" Jeffcoat (b. Mar. 9, 1891, d. Mar. 29, 1970) md. Lona Morgan. Bob lived in the Macedonia Community.

Allen Henry Jeffcoat died Mar. 4, 1926 and is remembered by a granddaughter as a devout Christian whose faith was evident to all who knew him. Nancy Jane Baker Jeffcoat died Dec. 10, 1939 in Lincoln Parish, LA. Both were buried in Macedonia Cemetery, and Allen's two sisters, Dorothy Jeffcoat and Pattie Reeves, were buried in Hillsboro Baptist Cemetery. *Submitted by Barbara Sudduth Lyle.*

JOHNSON, John Edward Johnson (b. 1880, d. 1951) was born near Clearwater, LA, his wife Hattie Mae Long Johnson (b. 1888, d. 1961) was born in Erath County, TX. John and Hattie had 13 children, 11 of these children lived in Scott County, MS at one time.

John was working at a sawmill in Eunice, LA when Frank L. Adams purchased the mill and offered John a sawyer job at his Morton, MS mill. John accepted and the family moved to Morton where John and Hattie lived until their deaths.

Ten of the Johnson children attended and graduated from Morton High School:

1) Roy Lee (b. 1906, d. 1999), a Navel Academy graduate married Margaret "Peggy" Gross and had two children. After a brilliant career in the U.S. Navy, Roy retired in 1967. He and his wife are buried at Virginia Beach, VA.

2) Floyd Everett (b. 1908, d. 1998) md. Ellen Swan Randel and had two children. Floyd retired from Mississippi Chemical Corp. in Yazoo City, MS then was elected mayor of Yazoo City and served for six years. Following his retirement he moved to Hattiesburg, MS.

3) Aldewin Theo (b. 1910, d. 1950) graduated from Morton High School in 1928. He married Laura Ellen Nutt, daughter of Samuel Robert Nutt and Nancy Elizabeth Kitchings of Forkville, MS. Aldewin and his family lived in Jackson, MS where he was superintendent of Life and Casualty Insurance Co. until the time or his death. His widow and two of his three children still live in the Jackson area.

4) Lois Inez (b. 1912) married first, Guy Max Williams of Forest and had three children. After Guy Max's death, Lois married Curt Mack Powell who has since passed away.

5) Irma Mae (b. 1914, d. 1979) md. Young Earl Turner and had two children. Irma and Earl are buried in the Morton City Cemetery near her mother and father.

6) Ruby Odessa (b. 1916) md. Howard Senseman and had two children. They moved to Edwards, MS in 1952 where they now live in retirement.

7) John "Son" Edward Jr. (b. 1917, d. 1992) made his home in Massachusetts after a career in the U.S. Navy. He died a year after his wife of 45 years passed away. They are buried in Winthrop, MA.

8) Fred Gilbert (b. 1921, d. 1997) married first, Elsie Nolan and had three children. He then married Chloris McGinty. A petroleum geologist, Fred had a successful career in the oil industry. Fred is buried in the Houston, TX area.

9) Infant female (b&d. in 1925) is buried at Eunice, LA.

10-11) Twins, Doris Elizabeth and Dorothy "Dot" Addelene were born in 1927. Doris married Frank W. Mize and now lives in California. Dot married Charles "Si" Laseter and had three children. Si died in 1983. Dot lives in Ellisville, MS.

12) Robert "Bobby" Max (b. 1930, d. 1965) md. Mary Louise Bright of Morton and had one child. Bobby was killed in an automobile accident and is buried near his mother and father in the Morton Cemetery.

13) Margaret Ann (b. 1936) md. Frank M. Donovan Jr. of Vicksburg. They had four children. Ann has a Ph.D. degree in music and now teaches in Savannah, GA.

JOHNSON, Oscar Leo Johnson and Minnie Lee Joiner were married Dec. 23, 1933. Leo (b. Jun. 15, 1915, in Sebastopol, MS) was the fifth child of William Oscar Johnson and Willie Mae Hartness Johnson. Minnie Lee (b. Aug. 17, 1916, in the High Hill Community of Neshoba County, MS) was the ninth child of Marion A. Joiner and Leita Gertrude Barber Joiner. Both Leo and Minnie Lee attended school at Sebastopol.

After they were married, they established their first residence with Leo's older brother and sister-in-law, Marion Douglas Johnson and Odessa Crocker Johnson in the community of Steele, located in Scott County, north of Forest and east of Harperville, on land owned by Leo's father. They worked as farmers until they moved to Forest, MS, in 1938.

Larry, Minnie Lee and Leo Johnson, 1955, at home of Oscar William and Willie Mae Johnson in Sebastopal

The couple rented a house on Longview Street where they were living when their first and only child, Larry Leo Johnson, was born on Oct. 2, 1941. The family continued living on Longview until Feb. 2, 1943, when they bought a house at 615 South Davis Street from Mr. Stites Liles. This was their residence for the rest of their lives.

Leo and Minnie Lee both worked to support their family. Leo worked at different times for Central Chevrolet Company, Lee Gray Chevrolet Company, the city of Forest and the state of Mississippi Parks and Recreation Department. Minnie Lee worked for the Thomas Great M Department Store, located on Main Street, and eventually established her own department store on Main Street, known as Johnson's Department Store. A successful businesswoman, she increased the size of her store and moved it to a new location at 252 East First Street.

Leo served in WWII with the U.S. Army as a member of the 1387th Engineer Base Depot Company in the Philippines. After the war he returned to Forest where he joined and became an active member of the American Legion Post and the Veterans of Foreign Wars. Minnie Lee was a dedicated member of the Ladies Auxiliary of both organizations. Both were faithful members of the Forest Baptist Church, attending all services with Minnie Lee and Larry members of the choir.

Larry Leo Johnson was born in the Scott County Hospital, Morton, MS, and grew up in Forest, graduating from Forest High School in May 1959. He attended the University of Mississippi on a football scholarship, earning an undergraduate and masters degree in business administration. Upon graduation he was commissioned a second lieutenant in the U.S. Army Ordnance Corps and served 27 months on active duty, one year of which was spent serving in South Vietnam, with the 74th Ordnance Company. Larry started to work in Jackson with Southern Bell Telephone Company and worked with them for 33 years, retiring in April 2000. Larry is the father of two sons, Frederick William Johnson (b. November 1967) and Scott Kornet Johnson (b. January 1971), and has one granddaughter, Evelyn Jane Johnson (b. September 1998), the daughter of Frederick William.

Minnie Lee died on Jun. 5, 1985 at Lackey Memorial Hospital and is buried in Eastern Cemetery in Forest. Leo died Apr. 11, 1995, in the

G.V. Sonny Montgomery Veterans Hospital in Jackson and is buried alongside Minnie Lee in the Eastern Cemetery.

JOHNSON, Paul Burney Johnson Sr. was born Mar. 23, 1880 on a small farm in Hillsboro, Scott County, MS. His parents were Thomas Benton Johnson and Jane Catherine McClenahan. Thomas Benton Johnson was born Jul. 4, 1836 at Monticello, Lawrence County, MS to Jourdan Johnson and Sarah Burney Johnson. Jane Catherine McClanahan was the daughter of William Hayes McClenahan, a native of Ireland, coming to America at age 14. He lived in New York for awhile, made his way to Mobile, then to Hillsboro where he was a tanner and saddler, then owned a general store sometime before the Civil War. Sarah Lawson Gray was born in Georgia and moved with her family as a teenager to Neshoba County in the early 1830s.

Thomas Benton Johnson praticed law, taught school and farmed while living at Hillsboro. In 1895 he moved his family to Hattisburg after the death of his wife. He was a Confederate Veteran having served in Co. B of the 16th Mississippi.

Paul B. Johnson's early education was received in a little frame lean-to at Hillsboro, and later he attended Harperville "College" where he completed a literary course. While teaching school, he studied law at night, later entering Millsaps College where he received his law degree. In 1903 he was admitted to the bar at Hattisburg, where he was appointed Hattisburg's first city judge. In 1910 he was appointed by Governor Edmond F. Noel, circuit judge of the 12th Judicial District, an office he held for eight years. In 1918 he was elected to the U.S. Congress where he served for four years. After running three times for governor in 1939 he was elected. He died Dec. 26, 1943 just four weeks before the end of his term of office.

An outstanding item of his term of office was the passage of the "Free Schoolbooks Law" that benefitted education in Mississippi.

Paul B. Johnson was married to Corrine Venable of Pike County, MS in 1915. They had three children: Paul B. Johnson Jr., who also became governor of Mississippi, 1964-1968; Patrick Hayes and Jane Catherine who died at a young age. Later, they adopted Peggy Elaine .

JOHNSON, It was in the year 1857 when William David Johnson, his wife Sarah Jane Slaughter Johnson, their young son, Andrew Robinson Johnson, along with his parents, William H. "Buck" Johnson and Mary "Polly" Wise Johnson, moved from Tallapoosa County, AL to Scott County, MS.

William David Johnson (b. Feb. 11, 1835 in Oglethorpe County, GA, d. Jul. 27, 1911 in Scott County, MS) md. Sarah Jane Slaughter on Nov. 15, 1855 in Tallapoosa County, AL. She was born Feb. 8, 1834 in Oglethorpe County, GA and died Dec. 28, 1899 in Scott County, MS. Both are buried at Damascus Cemetery in Scott County, MS.

William H. "Buck" Johnson (b. Jun. 3, 1808 in Georgia, d. Aug. 23, 1889 in Scott County, MS) md. Mary "Polly" Wise in March 1832. She was born Mar. 9, 1812 in Georgia and died Jun. 27, 1874 in Scott County, MS.

Both are buried in Damascus Cemetery, Scott County, MS.

William David Johnson and his father William H. "Buck" Johnson purchased a large tract of land when they came to Scott County. This tract of land began near Turkey Creek northeast and Sipsy Creek southeast along a ridge to Tuscolameta Creek northwest to Hontokalo Creek southwest. In about the center of this ridge is where the town of Sebastopol now sits.

William David Johnson and his wife Sarah Jane Johnson built their home on a hill overlooking Sipsy Creek just southeast of Sebastopol. His father and mother William H. "Buck" Johnson and Mary "Polly" Wise Johnson built their home in the Damascus Community near where the Damascus Church is now located.

They were what is known then as "Gentlemen Farmers." Unlike the wealthy Delta and Natchez area larger land owners, these farmers, nevertheless, were very successful in their farming. They raised row crops such as cotton, corn, peanuts, sugar cane and large vegetable gardens. They also owned large herds of cattle, teams of oxen and mules and were known for the fine riding horses they rode. The prominent William David Johnson's family was very successful in their farming efforts and they were very influential in local state and national politics. They married into the McClendon, Lang, Majure, Stribling, Austin, Blume and Pittman families, all prominent Scott, Leake and Neshoba County and Louisiana and Arkansas families.

William David Johnson was a Confederate veteran, Co. K, 2nd MS Cav. When he left home for the war he told his beloved wife Sarah Jane to load one of the big wagons with their valuables, silverware, china, good linens, the best livestock and go deep into Sipsy Swamp when and if word came that the Yankees were coming. She was to stay there until they left. She did just that.

Their oldest son, Andrew Robinson Johnson, born in Alabama, came with them to Mississippi that same year. In his early years he left Mississippi for Buckner, AR, and went into the timber business. He met and married Julia Pittman. In 1898 they moved to near Homer, LA continuing to be very successful in the timber business. Andrew R. "A.R." Johnson founded the town of Ashland, LA. He was a successful business man and was an influence in Louisiana business and politics. He was elected to the Louisiana State Senate in 1916 and served until 1924. His grandchildren live in Louisiana, Texas and Tennessee. One of his great-grandsons, Steven Johnson, lives in Madison County, MS.

Their second child, Lucy Frances, was born in March 1858 in Mississippi and died Jun. 22, 1934. She married Robert B. McClendon, Feb. 6, 1877. They lived on a large farm near the Damascus Community. Their grandchildren and great-grand children who still live in Mississippi are Frances Denton Watkins, Neshoba County; Jane Johnson Williams, Judge Tom Stewart Lee and Charles Austin, Scott County; and Horace Adair, Newton County.

Ripley Jefferson "Jeff" Johnson (b. Dec. 14, 1859, d. Jul. 7, 1920) md. Lucy Charlie Stribling Dec. 20, 1883. She was born Aug. 8, 1863 and died Aug. 8, 1939. They raised a large family on a large farm near Damascus where part of their farm was in Leake County. Their grandchildren who still live in Mississippi are Jeffie Lite Johnson Fairley, Grace Cockran Russell, Mattie Charles Reynolds Beasley, Dr. Willie Kermit Reynolds, Scott County, Dr. Ripley Jefferson "R.J." Reynolds and William Harvey "W.H." Johnson, Attorney-at-law, Newton County; and Sarah Nell Reynolds Ward, Rankin County.

Joseph Nicholas "Joe Nick" Johnson (b. Oct. 27, 1861, d. Aug. 1, 1936) md. Matilda Frances "Tilda" Lang on Oct. 10, 1887. She was born Nov. 23, 1869 and died Sep. 26, 1944. Their farm was on a hill just south of Sebastopol. The'ir home burned in 1910 and their grandson Billy Nick Johnson and his family still live in the home his grandparents rebuilt in 1910 after their original house burned. Their descendants who still live in Mississippi are Billy Nick Johnson, Scott County; Max Lindon Loper, Neshoba County and Tommie Jeannine Loper Hughes, Hinds County.

Mary Jane "Sweet/Mollie" Johnson (b. Nov. 1, 1864, d. Dec. 3, 1952) md. Dr. Richard Baker Austin on Dec. 20, 1882. Mary Jane was born while her father, William David, was gone to the Civil War. He mentioned her in a letter being so sweet and so she was called by her family her entire life, Sister Sweet or Aunt Sweet. This family has in its possession this very letter. Many fine doctors and fine business men and women are descendants of this family. Their grandchildren who live in Mississippi are Dr. Jesse William Austin, Charles Austin and Oulda Lowe Mitchell, Scott County and Reita Shepard Gibson, Newton County.

Nancy Eliza "Liza" Johnson (b. Nov. 6, 1866) md. Dewitt Majure, Jan. 31, 1887. They lived in Madden, MS in Leake County almost their entire lives and were one of the prominent and well known families of that area. Descendants of this family who live in Scott County are Joe Edward Majure, Harlon Parkes Majure and Carolyn Joyce Majure Dearman, Neshoba County.

Augusta "Gussie" Johnson (b. Oct. 11, 1867, d. 1949) md. William A. "Will" Hattaway Nov. 11, 1896. He was born in 1862 and died in 1939. He was a prominent businessman and landowner in Sebastopol. They built their beautiful home in the middle of Sebastopol. This house has been moved to Highway 21 between Forest and Sebastopol. Gussie and Will were the only childless couple in this family. However every child, grandchild and great-grandchild was always welcomed with open arms by this most beloved Aunt and Uncle.

William David Johnson (b. Aug. 12, 1869, d. Jul. 8, 1873). He is buried at Damascus Cemetery, Scott County, MS.

Henry Crofford Johnson (b. Jul. 27, 1871, d. Jun. 20, 1947) md. Alma Naomi Frances Stribling Jan. 12, 1895. Their farm was near his brother Joe Nick's farm, southeast of Sebastopol. They had all kinds of farm animals and yard fowl. Their beautiful home and fine barns would remind you of a "Currier and Ives" print. Their descendants are Henry Frank "Frankie" Johnson Tattis, Hinds County and William Crofford Johnson, Madison County.

Cordelia Virginia America "Delia" Johnson, a beautiful woman like her beautiful name, was born Feb. 25, 1873 and died Jul. 5, 1954. She married handsome Nicholas Marion "Nick" Lang Dec. 3, 1895. He was born Jan. 6, 1876 and died Nov. 30, 1947. Their gracious home was built on a hill overlooking their farm where they raised fine milk cows, pheasants and peacocks. Descendants of this family are Dorothy R. "Dot" Underwood Leonard, James Murry Underwood and Murry Lang, Scott County; Rachel Hudson Beeland and Jerry Lang, Newton County; Delia Lang Smith, Sadie Lang Brunson, Eliza Lang Freeman and Ruby Lang Weems, Rankin County; William Henry Hudson, Hinds.

James Colquit "Jim" Johnson, youngest son of William David and Sarah Jane Johnson, was born Nov. 26, 1874 and died Feb. 3, 1957. He was buried at Sebastopol, MS. He married Ollie Blume (b. Jan. 6, 1881, d. Sep. 5, 1919 in Lucky, LA). He attended Mississippi A&M College, was a member of the football squad and was Lightweight State Boxing Champion 1894-1895. He left school in 1896 and joined his eldest brother, A.R., in the timber business in Louisiana. His wife Ollie died in Louisiana and he moved his family back to Mississippi. He purchased a farm known as the Dollar Place near Sipsy Creek. His loving family helped him with the raising of his children. Jim and Ollie Johnson's descendants who live in Mississippi are Patsy Ruth Johnson Wilkerson, Scott County; Ollie Blume Johnson Johnson, Madison County and James Kenneth Ozborn, Newton County.

Susie Ida Johnson, their youngest child, was born Dec. 29, 1876 and died Oct. 13, 1878. She is buried at Damascus Cemetery, Scott County, MS.

After Sarah Jane Slaughter Johnson died in 1899, William David Johnson remarried to Annie Roberts in the early spring of 1901. Annie Roberts affectionately known in the Johnson family as "Ma Annie," was born around 1856 and lived to be close to 100 years of age. She died in 1952.

Annie Roberts Johnson was born on the island of Jamaica in the West Indies when her parents were en route to the United States. Her mother died at her birth and about three weeks later her father Richard Roberts brought her to America to live. Her father was railroad engineer of the first locomotive steam engine that came through Forest. Ma Annie and her son Alec S. McClendon were loved and respected by the entire Johnson family.

The William David and Sarah Jane Johnson family descendants remain to this day to be known as prominent citizens of the counties and states where they live and are active in business and politics, as were their ancestors.

JOHNSON, William Oscar Johnson (b. Nov. 12, 1880, in Sebastopol, MS) was the second child of Joseph Toliver Johnson and Nancy India Lang Johnson. Joseph Toliver was the seventh child of William H. "Buck" Johnson and Mary "Polly" Wise, who moved to Scott County after the territory was opened following the Treaty of Dancing Rabbit Creek.

William Oscar married Willie Mae Hartness and they raised a family farming land just south of Sebastopol on Hi-Way 21, next to land owned and farmed by his brother and sister-in-law, Clyde Johnson and Bonnie Wolverton Johnson. Oscar died on Dec. 7, 1962, age, and was buried in Scott County in the Damascus Cemetery, located behind the Primitive Baptist Church where he was a member.

Family of William Oscar and Willie Mae Hartness Johnson in Sebastopol in 1955

His wife of 55 years, Willie Mae Hartness Johnson (b. Feb. 18, 1890) was the 12th child of William Atialous Hartness and Sara Jane "Sallie" Quinn. William Atialous was a Confederate Veteran who fought with the 14th MS Inf. Regt. against Sherman and Grant's invading armies of the North. She died Jun. 16, 1972, and was buried alongside Oscar in the Damascus Cemetery.

There were 11 children born to Oscar and Willie Mae (eight boys and three girls). Two of the boys died as infants, but the others survived to adulthood. They were William Joe Johnson (b. Jul. 10, 1908, d. Dec. 9, 1980), never married; Marion Douglas Johnson (b. Mar. 5, 1910) md. Odessa Crocker (b. Jul. 19, 1916, d. Jul. 1, 1992); Roy Johnson (b. Jan. 12, 1912, d. Jul. 30, 1996) md. Florence Erkle Dodson (b. Sep. 5, 1917); Willie Una Johnson (b. Aug. 4, 1913) md. William G. Hamil (b. Aug. 5, 1906, d. Nov. 19, 1981). Oscar Leo Johnson (b. Jun. 15, 1915, d. Apr. 11, 1995) md. Minnie Lee Joiner (b. Aug. 17, 1916, d. Jun. 5, 1985); Cleveland Johnson (b. Nov. 6, 1916, d. Sep. 8, 1917); Elma Lois Johnson (b. Apr. 29, 1918) md. Denton Ray

Dukes (b. Apr. 16, 1912, d. Oct. 11, 1998); George Buck Johnson (b. Oct. 14, 1919, d. May 25, 1981) md. Jessie Lee Anthony (b. Mar. 16, 1922). Lawrence Fred Johnson (b. Mar. 3, 1921, d. Feb. 17, 1924); India Nola Johnson (b. Feb. 8, 1924, d. Aug. 8, 1999) md. James Harold Peoples (b. Jun. 26, 1922, d. Feb. 20, 1982). Jack Johnson (b. Jul. 13, 1927) md. Claudine Sharp (b. Nov. 12, 1930).

Joe lived at home with his parents, where he farmed. Douglas, Leo and Jack made their homes in Scott County where they worked and raised their families. After the Second World War, Roy located in Jackson, TN, and Buck located in Tuscaloosa, AL. Una lived in Sebastopol where she taught school for many years and then moved to Carthage after she married. Lois worked and lived in Jackson, MS, eventually moving to White Oak after she married. Nola and her husband lived in Montgomery, AL, and then Orlando, FL. There were 13 grandchildren born to the sons and daughters of Oscar and Willie Mae, only one of which was a grandson, Larry Leo Johnson.

JOHNSTON, Erle Johnston Jr., whose parents were the late Erle and Grace (Buchanan) Johnston of Hattiesburg, always knew he wanted a career in journalism. Despite having no formal education in the field (he was not financially able to attend college following his 1935 graduation from Grenada High School where he was selected class valedictorian) he landed a job with the *Clarion-Ledger.*

Although it was Johnston's dream to one day own his own weekly newspaper, he paid little attention to a classified advertisement appearing in the *Ledger* that publicized the sale of the *Scott County* Times newspaper in Forest.

However, while working on a story pertaining to Forest for the *Ledger*, Johnston had a conversation with Lewis Henderson, who at the time owned 60 percent of the weekly newspaper. Henderson and L.G. Agard, who owned the remaining 40 percent of stock, had established the *Scott County Times* in 1939.

During this conversation, Johnston casually asked Henderson if he had sold the paper. After replying that he hadn't, Henderson asked Johnston if he wanted to buy it. Johnston's first reply was a "no," he couldn't afford the purchase "for even five dollars."

The Erle Johnston family seated from left are Fay, Carol and Lynn. Standing from left are Erle and Erle III "Bubby."

But the two eventually reached an agreement by which Johnston would buy 50 percent of the *Times* stock, with the other 50 percent remaining with Agard, who would remain at the newspaper. With three mortgages against the *Times*, Johnston and his wife, the former Fay Martin of Edwards, and Agard worked "day and night" to keep their business going. Johnston and Agard each drew a salary of $35 per week when cash was available to make payroll.

After a year's operation, however, it became apparent that the newspaper was not big enough for two owners. So they discussed a deal whereby Johnston would pay Agard $300 for his half-interest and also assume the debt.

Johnston thought about the situation for a while and consulted friends in Forest who encouraged him to stay. But coming up with $300 to buy the paper was not going to be easy, Johnston first went to a local bank to borrow the money, but the bank turned him down claiming the loan was too risky, as the country was in the midst of what is now known as the Great Depression. Discouraged, yet still determined to raise the needed funds, Johnston approached Vern Lackey, a prominent businessman. Lackey wanted Johnston to remain in Forest, too, and agreed to loan him the money. In 1941, with finances in place, Erle and Fay Johnston officially established roots in Forest and Scott County (although Johnston admitted it took five years to repay the $300 to Vern Lackey!).

On Jun. 21, 1940 Erle married Fay Johnston, daughter of the late James Cornelius and Emma Chichester Martin of Edwards, and they continued operating the newspaper together until 1943, when Johnston was named director of the Office of War Information in Jackson. When the army sent him to Fort Ord, CA, Mrs. Johnston ran the newspaper until the end of WWII.

Erle Johnston served as publisher of the *Scott County Times* for 41 years, 1942-1983, when the paper was sold to Scott Publishing Company. Erle Johnston was credited with transforming the *Times* from a sleepy weekly newspaper to a guiding force in the growth and development of Forest and Scott County and a strong voice in Mississippi politics. His paper was a consistent winner in the Mississippi Press Association competition, and he was personally honored by the University of Southern Mississippi with the "Mississippi Medalist/Student Printz Award" for outstanding contributions to Mississippi journalism. After serving as the second youngest president in the history of the MPA in 1949 at the age of 32. Johnston was again honored by his peers in 1994 when he was inducted into the Mississippi Press Association Hall of Fame.

He also authored three books on Mississippi history: *I Rolled With Ross, Mississippi's Defiant Years: 1953-1973*, and *Politics: Mississippi Style*. He had completed two-thirds of a fourth book on Mississippi at the time of his death in 1995. The new book, which examined the history of the Republican Party, was titled *The Thunder of Elephants: From Bayonets to Ballots.*

Johnston was involved in numerous civic and community activities and served as mayor of Forest, 1981-1985. In recognition of his service to the community, especially his efforts in recruiting industry (including Hughes Aircraft of Mississippi, Inc., which later became the Raytheon Corporation), his successor, Mayor Fred Gaddis and the Forest City Council unanimously voted to name a street in his honor. Erle Johnston Industrial Drive is located off Hwy. 35 South.

Johnston served as director of the former Mississippi State Sovereignty Commission from 1963-68; he was public relations director of the commission from 1960-63. He also worked in several statewide political campaigns as publicity director of associate publicist.

When Johnston was on the campaign trail, Mrs. Johnston again took charge of the newspaper operation. She was also involved in various community activities and was recognized for her years of dedication to the Girl Scout program. She was awarded the Girl Scouts of America "Thanks Badge", the highest honor attainable for adult GSA leaders, for her role in helping found the Girl Scouts in Forest. She was also a charter member of the Scott County Chapter (Hontokalo) of the Daughters of the American Revolution (DAR).

Johnston's son, Erle E. "Bubby" Johnston III, succeeded his father as editor of the *Times* from 1979-1983. The younger Johnston, a 1971 graduate of Forest High School, had joined the family business in 1975 as associate editor, following his graduation from Mississippi State University. He married the former Janet Harris of Quitman and, at the time of this writing, serves as vice president for public information at East Central Community College in Decatur.

Both of Johnston's daughters were contributing writers to the *Times,* as well. For many years, Carol (Mrs. Bob Lindley of Hattiesburg) wrote a weekly column titled "Carollettes", a humorous tale of life with the Lindley family: Carol and Bob, and sons Scott, Brent and Walker. Carol graduated from Forest High School in 1959 and received her degree from the University of Southern Mississippi in 1963.

Lynn, who majored in journalism at Mississippi University for Women and graduated in 1970, contributed a column titled "From the Country of the Alps," while her husband Ben Catalina Jr., a Clarksdale native, was stationed at Aviano Air Base, Italy. The Catalinas have two children, Jeff and Jamie. Lynn is a 1966 graduate of Forest High School.

Erle Johnston died at age 77 on Sep. 26, 1995, following complications from heart surgery at St. Dominic Hospital in Jackson. His wife of 54 years lost her battle with lung cancer at age 80 on Feb. 27, 1999, at her residence in Forest.

JONES-CLARK, Jerrie Eugene Jones (b. 1942) is the son of Albert E. Jones (b. 1919) who is the son of Jeremiah Thomas "Jud" Jones (b. 1887, d. 1956). Jeremiah Thomas was the son of Thomas Nathaniel Jones (b. 1856, d. 1929), son of Jeremiah Jones (b. 1822, d. ?) b. Darlington, SC. Jeremiah was the son of Littleton Jones (b. 1797 in South Carolina, d. ?). He fought in the Civil War. Littleton came to Alabama from South Carolina, then to Mississippi. He is buried near Lumberton, MS. He was the son of Jeremiah Jones (b. 1759, d. 1848). (See History of Jeremiah Jones of Orangeburg District, South Carolina.) Jeremiah was the son of Thomas Jones (b. 1720, d. 1820) of Darlington, SC. Thomas was the son of Frederick Jones (b. 1670, d. *1722*). Frederick was born in England. He was the first

149

chief justice in North Carolina, and his first home near Williamsburg, VA was the source of an archaeological dig reported by Noel Hume in *Here Lies Virginia*. Frederick associated with Edward Teach - Blackbeard. (See Robert Lee's book, *Blackbeard the Pirate*.) Frederick's father was Capt. Roger Jones (b. 1641, d. 1702) of Nottinghamshire, England. (See L.H. Jones' book, *Capt. Roger Jones of London and Virginia*). Roger Jones was a noted mariner who made numerous trips between the colonies and England. It is from Capt. Jones' mother, Ellen Hoskins, that our family gained its coat-of-arms. (See *The Abridged Compendium of American Genealogy First Families of America, Volume II, 1926.*) Roger Jones was the son of another English mariner, Thomas Jones, no dates, but born in Limehouse, England.

Jerrie E. Jones (b. 1942) is the son of Flora Clark Jones (b. 1922) and the grandson of Mcnary "Mack" Clark (b. 1887, 1962). Mack Clark was the son of Warren Clark (b. 1874, d. 1966). Warren was the son of Richard Clark (b. 1844, d. 1915). Richard was the son of James Paulding Clark (b. 1804, d. 1891). James P. Clark was was born in Mercer (now Boyle) County KY and was instrumental in the building of the railroad through Scott County. He was the son of James Clark (b. 1759 in Mecklenburg County, VA) and emigrated to Kentucky with his father Francis in about 1783. Francis Clark (b. ?, d. 1799) came to Kentucky in about 1783 and was one of the first settlers in Kentucky. He was the first Methodist minister west of the Alleghenies and established several churches, notably, the Methodist church in Danville, KY, where a memorial to his honor hangs over the altar. There are also roadside historical markers to his honor. He was a noted tobacco farmer and raised prized horses. The first Methodist Bishop, Francis Asbury, mentions him his journals. Francis Clark's will can be found at the Harrodsburg Historical Society in Harrodsburg, KY.

JONES, Charley Quitman Jones (b. 1871, Walnut Grove, Leake County, MS, d. 1942, Harperville, Scott County, MS) was the oldest child of Isaac Jones (b. 1849, Coffee County, AL, d. 1907, Walnut Grove) and Francis Charlotte "Fanny" Harris (b. 1852 Leake County, d. 1920 Tuxedo, Jones County, TX).

Charley Quitman Jones

Isaac was the youngest child of Henry D.W. Jones (b. 1804 Georgia, d. after 1880 in Leake County) and Mary A. Simmons (b. 1803 North Carolina, d. after 1870 in Leake County). Fanny's parents were Thomas Sidney Harris (b. 1803 in South Carolina, d. 1874 in Leake County) and Matilda Henry (b. 1811 in Tennessee, d. 1889 in Union County, AR).

In 1895, Charley married Laura Agnes Langford (b. 1874 Neshoba County, MS, d. 1902, Walnut Grove), daughter of Henry L. and Caroline Langford (both born in Georgia). Children:

1) Laura Maye Jones (b. 1897, d. 1980) of Morton, married Joseph Harvey. Children: Joseph Euel Harvey (b. 1917, d. 1981), Spokane, WA; Charles H. Harvey (b. 1920, d. 1921); Agnes Elizabeth Harvey Cooper (b. 1923), Morton; Max Hilman Harvey (b. 1928, d. 1980), Morton.

2) Charles Carlton Jones (b. 1899, d. 1968) of Harperville, married Susie Matilda Warren. Children: Joe Fletcher Jones (b. 1920, d. 1984), Miami, FL; Charley Carlton Jones (b. 1922, d. 1983), Harperville; Lacy Loyd Jones (b. 1924, d. 1975), Forest; Robert Marion Jones (b. 1926), Harperville; Billy Austin Jones (b. 1928), Summit; Ollihu Jones (b. 1931, d. 1933); Loma Sue Jones Laney (b. 1933), Jackson; Laura Ann Jones (b. 1937), Slidell, LA; Mary Peggy Jones Whitmire (b. 1939), Louisville.

3) Almon Edward Jones (b. 1901, d. 1902).

In the mid-1800s, Laban Rushing bought the old Gilmer Place, 12-14 miles northeast of Forest, east of Tallabogue Creek, and south of Tuscameda Swamp, near Horseshoe. In January 1903, Charley Jones married his second wife, Rosanna Elizabeth "Bettie" Rushing (b. 1877, d. 1968 Scott County) and in 1915, he bought part of this land, with Lost Creek running through the pasture, from Bettie's father, who was Laban's son. Bettie's parents were Rev. Joseph David Rushing (b. 1850 Sumter County, AL, d. 1935, Forest) and Mary Edna Putnam (b. 1854, d. 1896 Scott County). Joseph's parents were Laban Rushing (b. 1812 North Carolina, d. 1880 Scott County) and Rosannah Harrell (b. 1814 North Carolina, d. after 1900, Scott County). Mary Edna's parents were Jeremiah Putnam (b. 1802 South Carolina, d. 1860 Scott County) and Elizabeth Smith (b. 1809 Kentucky). Children.

4) Hubert Harris Jones (b. 1903, d. 1979) of Forest, married Ollie Douglas Warren. Children: Elizabeth Irene Jones Brown (b. 1922), Forest; Eley Everette Jones (b. 1923, d. 1979), Las Vegas, NV; Emmitte Lee Jones (b. 1929, d. 1932); Laura Merle Jones (b. 1932, d. 1950), Forest; Hubert Harris Jones Jr. (b. 1939, d. 1987), Pearl.

5) Minnie Ethel Jones (b. 1904, d. 1996) of Harperville, married Horace Hall. Child: Bettie Jo Hall.

6) Mary Katie Jones (b. 1905, d. 1970) of Mobile, AL, married Homer Clifton. Children: Loy Naomia Clifton Ripley (b. 1929), Houston, Texas/New Albany, IN; Betty Nell Clifton Wall (b. 1937), Houston, TX.

7) Loy E. Jones (b. 1907, d. 1985) of Harperville, married Allen Tucker.

8) Troy Lee Jones (b. 1907, d. 1908).

9) Cecil Jones (b. 1909, d. 1983) of Harperville, married Trudie Brantley. Children: Andrew Quitman Jones (b. 1929), Forest; Joe Harold Jones (b. 1932, d. 2001), Forest; Aubrey Cecil Jones (b. 1934, d. 1995), Vermont; Kenneth Jones (b. 1936, d. 2001), Forest; Dorothy Marie Jones Reeves (b. 1939), Forkville; Rita Jones Waggoner (b. 1941), Forest; Lonnie Jones (b. 1942), Fort Worth, TX.

10) J.C. Jones (b. 1912, d. 1993) of Harperville and Pearl; married Catherine Beasley. Children: Autrey Doyle Jones (b. 1940), Pelahatchie; Linda Jones Thompson (b. 1945), Brandon. *Submitted by Betty Clifton Wall.*

JONES, John Hayes Jones (b. Nov. 18, 1912 in Newton County, in the Old White Plains Church of God Community), son of Joseph Alvin Jones and Mary Green Jones. He was the fourth child in a family of six. He attended Prospect School in Newton County where he met Lorene Thrash, from the Prospect Community. Lorene was the second child of James Oscar Thrash and Ota Grace Byram Thrash.

John Hayes Jones and Lorene Thrash Jones

Jones and his brother Elrie and two of his sisters, Onnie and Zelmer, formed a quartet while in their teens. They enjoyed singing gospel music at shaped note singings and singing schools, which were held at Old White Plains for two weeks every summer. The arrival of the new song books twice a year was an occasion when everyone would gather around the organ and spend the evening singing. The Jones' enjoyed traveling to gospel singing. A few years later, Lorene's father warned her that those Jones' were "going" people and she'd never stay home if she married John Hayes.

Lorene Thrash and John Hayes Jones were married on Oct. 22, 1932. They moved to Kemper County near Dekalb, where they operated a portable sawmill. They lived there for about one year, before moving to Scott County, where John Hayes purchased land on what is currently Highway 21, between Sebastopol and Forest, where John Hayes had hunted as a young man.

They moved onto their land and built their first home. Jones' father, Alvin, would come and stay a week at a time to help build their home, even though he warned Jones that he and Lorene would starve to death because a "pea wouldn't grow here."

Five children were born to Lorene and John Hayes: Opal Lee, Johnny Horval, James Harmon, Glenda Ann, and Pequita Lorene. Opal married Mack Amis (d. 1995). They are the parents of four children: Gail Strickler, Mack Amis Jr. Ricky Amis (d. 1984) and John Scott Amis (d. 1964). Horval married Betty Andrews. They are the parents of Kim Ervin, Stacey Gandy, Samantha Winstead and Johnny Jones. Harmon married Annie Sue McDill. They are the parents of Shelia Ware, Tammy Jones-Kersgaard and Bert Jones. Glenda married Donnie Earl McDill and they are the parents of Chris McDill, Jason McDill, and Tiffany Lathem. Pequita married Reverend Larry Duncan. They have two daughters, Nicole Smith and Natalie Duncan.

Jones was a farmer who grew corn, cotton, dairy cattle, hogs and timber. In later years, he and son Harmon and son-in-law Donnie owned a catfish farm, one of the first in the area. He was instrumental in organizing and assisting in various community fund-raisers. He ministered through a radio broadcast for 30 years to the people in Scott County and surrounding areas. He received nation-wide attention in the 1980s for his project, God's Love Letters, non-denominational signs posted along Mississippi and Louisiana highways that quote Bible verses.

Lorene was a homemaker who was like a second mother to her many grandchildren who lived nearby. She was a wonderful cook who never needed a recipe, but could make even simple foods special. She was a Christian lady who knew the power of prayer and prayed for her family and loved ones regularly. She would say that she prayed on her knees before her feet hit the floor every morning and before her head hit the pillow every night.

John Hayes Jones died on Apr. 8, 1997. Lorene Jones died on Mar. 25, 1998. They are buried at the Old White Plains Church of God in Newton County. Of their children Horval, Harmon and Glenda live near Sebastopol; Opal lives in Pascagoula; and Pequita lives near Lake.

KEENE-JOHNSON-LINDSEY, Willie Grace Lindsey (b. Jun. 28, 1914 at Rankin Station in Rankin County), daughter of Samuel William Lindsey and Mandy Fan Prestage, married Howard Earl Johnson on Oct. 20, 1937. Howard Earl Johnson was born in Rankin County. Grace had graduated from Clarksburg High School in 1936. Grace and Earl lived near Pelahatchie. On Mar. 4, 1946 Howard Earl Johnson was killed on the railroad not far from his home in Pelahatchie. After Howard Earl Johnson's death, Grace built a small house near her parents outside of Morton. Grace and Howard Earl had three children: Bobbie Jack Johnson, James Earl Johnson and Otto Mack Johnson.

L-R: Bobbie Jack Johnson Ray, Otto Mack Johnson, Willie Grace Keene and Ravis Lindsey Keene

L-R: Bobbie Jack Johnson Ray, Mickie Grace Keene Bounds, James Earl Johnson, Willie Grace Keene and Ravis Linsey Keene

On Mar. 25, 1950 Willie Grace married Ravis Curtis Keene. Ravis was from Polkville, MS in Smith County. He was the son of Joe Keene and Sarah Ann Phillips. Ravis served in the U.S. Navy during World War II. He was born Feb. 1, 1912 and died Mar. 5, 1973. They had two children, Ravis Lindsey Keene and Mickie

Grace Keene. All of Grace's children attended Morton High School. Bobbie Jack Johnson deceased, James Earl Johnson lives in Jackson, MS; Otto Mack Johnson lives near Morton, MS; Ravis Lindsey Keene lives near Meridian, MS; and Mickie Grace Keene lives near Lewisville, TX.

KING, Thomas Rivers King's father, Ira Eugene King, left Putnam County, GA and came to Scott County in the late 1800s. He settled in the Steele Community north of Forest. Ira Eugene King and Bessie Alice Madden had eight children. He supported this large family by farming and his sawmill operation.

Tiny and Melba King at an anniversary party in Texas

Thomas Rivers King received the nickname "Tiny" as a small infant. He had been very ill and was thin. The nickname remained throughout his life. Some called him simply "T.R." Mary Melba Shepard graduated from Walnut Grove High School in 1935. She was a bright student and was salutatorian of her class.

Sheriff Duff Austin gave Melba Shepard a job in his office at the Scott County Court House. He was her uncle and knew that her family needed help. She had lost her father in her teens to cancer.

Tiny enjoyed his trips around Forest. I'm sure he was thrilled to see the beautiful Melba Shepard in the Court House. He was a bachelor in his 30s. Melba was a petite lady with coal black hair. She had natural curls in just the right place. I'm sure he rushed to meet her.

I don't know how long they courted, but they were married on Sep. 18, 1938 in Meridian, MS. Rev. G.W. Griffin married the happy couple.

The newlyweds built one of the first houses on second avenue. They moved into the house on Aug. 4, 1939. I'm sure both were thrilled to have a house. The depression era had been extremely bad for everyone. Both survived those times.

Tiny was influential in Mississippi political circles throughout his life. He served for many years as chairman of the Scott County Democratic Party Executive Committee and served on the staff of several Mississippi Governors, including Ross Barnett and Paul B. Johnson Jr.

He also served on the Mississippi Forestry Commission during the Ross Barnett administration. The Barnett Reservoir was established during this time. He was best known for his loyal support of former U.S. Senator James O. Eastland. Their friendship dated back to 1942. Both men are buried in Eastern Cemetery in Forest, MS.

Melba King is a charter member of the Hontokalo Chapter of the DAR in Forest. She served as registrar at the first meeting held on May 26, 1976. She was also a member of several clubs over the years.

I must pay tribute to her skills as a south-

ern cook. She was one of the best in the entire Southland. She was talented in many areas. She could make heirloom quilts and anything she wanted to do. She could look at a dress and go home and make it. Melba and Tiny were longtime members of the Forest Methodist Church. We got to attend church at the first Methodist Church building. The new one stands today. They raised two daughters: Sandra King Bishop Howard and Kay Rivers King French. They have three grandchildren and four great-grandchildren.

KITCHINGS-MORGAN, Only by the providence of God could any mother of seven children live through such privations as Laura Morgan Kitchings passed through after the death of her 33-year old husband, Baskin. She lived in Scott County, one mile north of the post office of Forkville, MS. Today, known as "The Kitchings Place." To catalog her family hardships in full would tax the credibility of modern Americans. Many will say, "I do not believe it."

When Baskin died he had no insurance, no bank account, and no money saved for a rainy day. There was a mortgage on his team and wagon with which he made a living for his family. He was hardly cold in the grave when the wagon and team were claimed by the mortgage holder. Laura had to go through childbirth shortly after Baskin died. The oldest child, Slonia, was 9 years old and between her and the new born baby, Annie Bell, there were William Sanders "Bud," Atley Asher, Nancy, Johnnie and Fletta.

Some winters passed by before they had shoes to wear. The drinking water came from open cisterns in the yard, and often it was full of "wiggle tails." They lived in an open house, cracks in the floor below, cracks in the ceiling, boards on the sides, with no ceiling under the roof. Winter time was the hardest for them for their only heat was from a "stick and dirt" chimney. Houseflies and mosquitoes had free reign. It is a small wonder they reached adulthood in excellent health; however, Laura depended on her "home-made" remedies for all kind of illnesses. Some examples: croup was treated with onion poultices placed on the chest and throat while hot. Boils were also treated with warm poultices made of a leaf of cabbage. Sassafras tea was made, especially in the springtime, they drank to keep from getting sick. Poke Salad was a wild vegetable that was believed to ward off diseases. Did they eat it? Back then, they ate what was put on their plate—all of it!

A ball of asafetida on a string was tied around their necks to discourage germs. A good round of calomel was given them each spring, followed by a big dose of castor oil to clean them out and get them prepared for hoeing the garden and fields. Don't you wonder how they survived? Through it all, and in it all, Laura never wavered nor griped about her hard lot. She was a master economist, able to do the most with the least. Through the years she had one or two milk cows plus a few chickens. These plus some good-hearted relatives and neighbors, kept them from starving. Their transportation was walking and their reading was the Bible—no books or papers in the home. In dry weather they sometimes had to go to the creek, a half mile away, to do their laundry. They took with them a wash pot, tubs, rubbing board, dirty clothes and lye soap.

It took the whole family a whole day to do the laundry.

Laura lived to be 77 years old and was survived by sons, "Bud" and Dr. A.A. Kitchings, and daughters: Slonia Craig, Nancy Nutt, Johnnie Davis, Fletta James and Annie Bell Boykin.

KNOWLES-EDWARDS, William Limbert Knowles and Carolyn Sue Edwards-Knowles made Forest their home after their marriage in 1970. The couple had two children, Cory Limbert (b. Nov. 22, 1977) and Heather Shantay (b. Feb. 16, 1983).

William worked at Smith-Tarrer Wholesale, Mississippi State Highway Department and later became the maintenance supervisor for the Forest Housing Authority until his death Nov. 7, 1994. A park was named in his honor in July 2000. Carolyn worked as a teacher in the Scott County schools, North Scott and Morton Attendance Center for 16 years. In 1987, she was employed to teach science in the Forest School District at Hawkins Middle School. She worked until she retired in May 1999. She had taught school for 31 years.

William was born in Drew, MS (Sunflower County). He attended school at Hunter High School and after serving in the U.S. Navy and Navy Reserves, he attended Mississippi Valley State University. William was very active in the Forest Community. He worked with youth groups and was recognized as an outstanding work-site supervisor for the Summer Youth Employment Program during Governor William Winter's administration. He also served as a volunteer fire fighter and a deacon at his church.

Carolyn was born in Scott County and graduated from E.T. Hawkins High School. She attended Alcorn State University and received a master's degree from Fisk University in Nashville, TN. She is noted for her singing abilities. She has been an active person in the community serving as a Girl Scout leader, 4-H Club leader, and secretary for various organizations such as the Scott County Democratic Executive Committee, East Central Health Systems Agency and on the board of Mississippi Association of Educators, chairman of the East Central Community Action Agency Board of Directors.

Carolyn and both of their children were baptized in Concord Missionary Baptist Church. William was baptized in Drew at Holly Grove Baptist Church, but united with Concord Missionary Baptist Church after moving to Forest.

LACKEY, In 1901, Samuel Elmer Lackey and Mary Ellen Blevins Lackey moved from Lawrence County, IL, to Mississippi. They first lived in Rankin County near the Plains Community. It was in this place that Samuel began his first lumber venture. The beginning of S.E. Lackey Lumber Company in Forest was in 1904.

Mr. Lackey was one of the most prominent lumbermen and philanthropists in the state. He was the oldest shipper of lumber on the G&SI Railroad, and pioneer member of the Southern Pine Association. A long-standing deacon of the Forest Baptist Church, "Mr. Sam" was a benefactor of the Baptist Hospital in Jackson and started a fund to build a hospital in Forest. A Mason and a Shriner, he was also a director of the Jackson National Bank.

Front Row, L-R: Mrs. S.E. Lackey and Mr. S.E. Lackey. 2nd Row, L-R: Vern Lackey, Lida Lackey Felder, "Bus" Lackey, Letha Lackey Nelson, Eula Lackey Underwood, Sam Lackey.

Mrs. Lackey, wife of Sam and mother of six children, was a dedicated wife and mother. "Mayme," as she was called, was vitally interested in all activities of the Forest Baptist Church, especially Sunday school and WMU. It was Mrs. Lackey who made the initial gift of a hospital site in memory of her late husband.

Vera Wicker Lackey

Mr. Lackey died in 1943, and Mrs. Lackey died in 1962. Both are buried at Eastern Cemetery in Forest.

Children of Samuel and Mary Ellen were Vernon Roy (b. 1901), Lyda Margaret (b. 1903), Letha Elizabeth (b. 1905), Eula Bell (b. 1907), Claude Johnson (b. 1909) and Samuel Earl (b. 1912).

Vernon Roy Lackey

Vernon Roy, the oldest, was educated in the Forest Public Schools, Mississippi College Preparatory School and Bowling Green Business University. Graduating in 1921, he moved to Glendora, MS as a plantation accountant. Because of his father's ill health, he returned to Forest and began working with his family in the lumber business.

Vernon Roy Lackey married Vera Wicker (b. Jun. 6, 1903) on Feb. 17, 1927. The childhood sweethearts were always active in their churches and community. A member of the Forest Methodist Church, she was president of the Woman's Society of Christian Service, long-time member of the choir and served on the Board of Stewards.

A charter member of the Fortnightly Club, Vera served in every leadership capacity, as well as district and statewide officer ships. An ardent and devoted civic and social worker, Mrs. Lackey served over 25 years as Scott County Chairman of the National Foundation, benefiting polio victims and birth defects in children. The family's passion for good hospital care energized her to promote the organization of hospital auxiliaries in cities all over the state during the early 1950s.

Known for their hospitality, Vern and Vera Lackey shared their home with the entire community. The scene of weddings and receptions,

a resting place for visiting ministers and officials, their home was the stage for the annual farewell breakfast for the Forest High School seniors.

Abundant energy and the enthusiasm to do the impossible, Vera gave of herself. She died Feb. 15, 1993, at the age of 89.

Children of Vern and Vera Lackey are James Vernon Lackey, born Nov. 13, 1928 and Linda Joy Lackey, born Jan. 22, 1941.

James Vernon, known as Jimmy, attended Forest Public Schools and graduated in 1946. He attended Mississippi College and graduated from the University of Mississippi in 1950. After three years in the U.S. Army, Jimmy returned to Forest to join in Lackey Lumber Mills, Inc. and later Home Lumber Company, which now is Lackey Home Center.

On Jul. 12, 1953, Jimmy married Josephine Barnett. They were the parents of James Vernon Lackey Jr. (b. Dec. 12, 1954), Joy Lynn Lackey (b. May 26, 1956), Julie Ann (b. Apr. 20, 1961) and Jennifer Josephine (b. Dec. 16, 1967).

Following family tradition, Jimmy and Jo were active in all areas of church and civic life.

President of Lackey Home Center, Jimmy has served on business related boards, both in lumber and hardware business. For over 25 years he has been a member and officer of the board of S.E. Lackey Memorial Hospital. He has been a Rotarian for over 40 years. His interest and enthusiasm for Tennessee walking horses has made him a national director of Tennessee Walking Horse Breeders and Exhibitors Association.

Josephine Barnett Lackey, a native of Leake County, came to Forest in 1950 to teach first grade in the Forest Public Schools. Always active in her church, Jo served as Sunday School Teacher and WMU Chairman. She was a member of the DAR and president of the Forest Garden Club. Active in the family business, she touched the lives of many young people in our county. A dedicated lady, a beautiful, elegant woman, and a loving wife, mother and grandmother, Jo died on Mother's Day, May 14, 2000.

Jimmy married Carol Brunson Fleming, native of Baton Rouge, LA on Dec. 29, 2000.

Linda Joy Lackey (b. Jan. 22, 1941) attended Forest Public Schools and graduated in 1959. During high school and college, Linda was active against polio and birth defects. After serving as 1961 National Maid of Cotton, she graduated from the University of Mississippi in 1963.

On Jul. 12, 1963, Linda and Trenton Hughes Shelton married at Forest Baptist Church. They are the parents of Leah Lackey Shelton Wilkerson. Although Linda and Shelton reside in Jackson, MS, they maintain real estate interests in Forest.

LACKEY, Richard Stephen Lackey (b. Oct. 4, 1941, d. Jan. 16, 1983). At a time when emphasis in genealogical research had been on New England records and East Coast sources, Richard S. Lackey of Scott County was a leader in, and teacher of, scholarly research and the recording of it. His special areas of expertise were the states of the Old Confederacy and military, land and Indian records. In addition to genealogies of many ante-bellum Mississippi families and those of other parts of the South, he compiled much information on families of Indian countrymen in the Choctaw Nation, Choctaw-Cherokee-Chickasaw Indian claims. Researchers from all over the United States regularly visit the McCain Library and Archives, University of Southern Mississippi, to study Lackey's manuscripts. This recognized outstanding scholar, lecturer and organizer of workshops and classes pioneered in authoring, *Cite Your Sources and Write it Right with Donald R. Barnes*, manuals for writing and documenting genealogical records.

Richard was the son of Mr. and Mrs. C.J. Lackey. Richard, "Dick" as he was known, went to school in the Forest public school system His daughter Ellen teaches at Old Miss University in Oxford. He traveled all over the United States lecturing in genealogical and historical studies. He served on the facilities of several Universities and advisory boards. He was a member and held offices in many genealogical societies.

In spite of his untimely death at the age of 41, many scholastically superior books and articles published today are traceable to the high standards taught by Lackey. In addition, the growth of genealogical societies and the enthusiasm of their members in the Southern states reflect Richard Lackey's influence.

The Richard S. Lackey Memorial Genealogical Collection at the Forest Public Library is named in his honor.

LANG, William Jackson Lang (b. Apr. 7, 1837, Leake County, MS, d. Nov. 5, 1915, Scott County) was the son of John Lang and Elizabeth Kitchens. Married Mary Frances Kilgore "Fanny" on Jan. 2, 1868, Leake County. Fanny died Mar. 21, 1921, Scott County. Fanny (b. Jun. 6, 1843, Jones County, MS), daughter of Matthew T.G. Kilgore and wife Nancy Stafford. They are buried in Antioch Cemetery, Scott County.

William Jackson Lang and Fannie Kilgore Lang

Children of William J. Lang: Mollie Frances (b. Jan. 9, 1869, d. Jan. 4, 1901) md. Joseph Berry Gay (b. Feb. 23, Amite County, MS, d. Feb. 3 1945) on Mar. 7, 1889. Both are buried in Antioch Cemetery.

Nancy Louella (b. Feb. 6, 1871, d. Jul. 7, 1961) md. William Ellis Russell (b. Aug. 1, 1864, Neshoba County, d. Sep. 4, 1935 Hillsboro, MS) on Jul. 10, 1890. Both are buried in Antioch Cemetery, Scott County.

William Octavius (b. Apr. 12, 1873, d. Nov. 4, 1957) md. Mary Louella Hunt (b. Apr. 2, 1878, d. Feb. 2, 1977) on Dec. 24, 1895. Both are buried in Pleasant Ridge Cemetery, Scott County. Minnie Ida (b. Oct. 28, 1875, d. Apr. 29, 1954) md. Benjamin Marion Guthrie (b. Jul. 31, 1865, d. Aug. 24, 1945) on Dec. 23, 1891. Both are buried in Antioch Cemetery.

Exa Genettie (b. Feb. 24, 1878, d. Nov. 26, 1958) md. Walter Eugene Lay (b. Aug. 5, 1875, d. Jan. 26, 1921), both are buried Salem Cemetery, Scott County.

Florence (b. 1880) md. W.L. "Fate" Graham on Dec. 21, 1897. They moved to Monroe, LA between 1918-20 and are buried there.

Virginia "Jenny" (b. Aug. 1882, d. Dec. 14, 1969) md. Willie G. Wolf (b. Apr. 5, 1873, d. Dec. 26, 1960) on Dec. 21, 1898. Both are buried Ephesus Cemetery, Scott County.

W.J. Lang bought land from the McGowan Plantation in 1884 and moved his family from the Damascus Community to the Ringgold Community in Scott County. He lived out his life there. He acquired several cotton gins, saw mills and grist mills. A voting precinct was established at his grist mill in the Ringgold Community, and still goes by that name today. He gave each child 40 acres of land. He was quite a business man for his day and age. It is said that he only went to school six days in his entire lifetime. He served in the Confederate Army in the War between the States.

LANGFORD, Reverend Daniel Clarke Langford (b. Mar. 23, 1837 in Webster County, MS), son of Rev. Lorenza Dow Langford and Catherine J. Malloy. Rev. L.D. Langford was a circuit rider minister of the Methodist Episcopal Church for almost 60 years.

Daniel Clarke Langford spent most of his boyhood in Yazoo County, MS. On Nov. 16, 1865 he married Martha Foster, daughter of John Hugh and Rebecca Odgen Foster of Yazoo, MS. The following children were born to this marriage: Rebecca Amelia, Martin Lorenzo, Katherine Stella, Lucy Ella, Raiford Campbell, Mary Hannah, Agnes Mabel, Robert Hugh, Martha Elizabeth and James Clarke Langford.

When Daniel Clarke Langford was 37 years old he decided to preach the gospel. His license to preach was granted Feb. 3, 1872 and in 1873 he was received on trial in the Mississippi Conference. He was actively engaged in the ministry of the Methodist Church for 40 years. Both he and his father, Lorenzo Dow Langford, served the Mississippi Conference for 100 years.

After the death of his wife, Martha, in February 1883, Daniel Clarke Langford married Mrs. Fannie Laneir Bryant, widow of Henry Bryant. The family soon moved to Morton, Scott County, MS where he had a home built and spent the remainder of his life. On Mar. 22, 1912, Daniel Clarke Langford passed away and was buried in Morton City Cemetery along with his wife, Fannie, and daughters, Katherine Langford Bunch and Ella Langford Hester.

LASETER, The family of John Laseter (b. ca. 1819/20 in Georgia), wife Elizabeth (b. ca. 1824 in South Carolina) and children: Caroline, Martha and Frederick, all born in Georgia, appeared in the 1860 Scott County Census for District #3, Morton; occupation, farmer. Cemetery markers show that John L. Laseter, a native of Georgia, died Aug. 18, 1890. Elizabeth, wife of John L. Laseter, daughter of Frederick Gardner, died May 26, 1875.

Frederick Lemuel Laseter (b. Jul. 30, 1855), son of John L. Laseter, married Susan Emma Elizabeth Rushing (b. Oct. 8, 1858), daughter of

William Green and Mary Waggoner Rushing, on Aug. 12, 1875. They made their home on property around Independence Community where he farmed. They would later acquire a house and some acreage in Morton where they lived until Susan died Jan. 4, 1924 and Frederick Lemuel died Jun. 22, 1936, at 80 years of age. He was one of the oldest and most esteemed residents of Scott County. At the time of his death, he had made his home in Morton for 25 years. Both are buried in the Mount Olive Baptist Church Cemetery.

Frederick L. and Susan Elizabeth Laseter ca. 1901 and all their children

Fifteen children were born to this couple:

1) Mary Elizabeth "Lizzie" (b. Aug. 25, 1876, d. Mar. 11, 1967). She married William R. Neal (b. Aug. 27, 1871, d. Jan. 15, 1933). They are both buried at Independence Methodist Church. They had one son, W. Clemmons Neal (b. Feb. 26, 1909, d. Aug. 21, 1969) md. Sarah Elizabeth McGough (b. Nov. 4, 1911, d. Dec. 22, 2000) and they had two sons, W.C. Neal Jr. and Thomas Ellis Neal. The Neals purchased the F.L. Laseter Estate in Morton around 1943.

2) John William Laseter (b. Oct. 16, 1877, d. Dec. 5, 1930) did not marry and was a lifetime resident of Scott County. He is buried in the Mount Olive Cemetery.

3) Frederick Hansel Laseter (b. Feb. 11, 1879, d. Mar. 24, 1935) of a heart attack while leading the choir in the Morton Baptist Church. He married Audrey Milling who died Oct. 3, 1978 and had one daughter, Johnnie Sue Laseter Miller. He was appointed postmaster of Morton Sep. 1, 1924, and served throughout 1929. He is buried at the Mount Olive Baptist Church Cemetery near Morton and his wife and daughter are buried in Highland Memorial Cemetery in Knoxville, TN.

4) Martha Eula Laseter (b. Feb. 10, 1881, d. May 6, 1951) md. Robert Hardy (b. Nov. 8, 1880, d. Dec. 20, 1951) on Jul. 22, 1903. They had two sons, William Fred Hardy (b. Aug. 5, 1905, d. Dec. 9, 1946) and George Lamar Hardy (b. Mar. 19, 1912). Eula lived in Jackson at the time of her death. She is buried in Cederlawn Cemetery, Hinds County.

5) James Hue Laseter (b. Feb. 16, 1883, died Sep. 30, 1885) is buried at Mount Olive Cemetery.

6) Irvin Clark Laseter (b. Mar. 16, 1885, d. October 1957) md. Rosa Daisy Ueltschey (b. Feb. 27, 1891, d. February 1978) on Nov. 5, 1911. They lived in Scott County, near Morton until around 1926 when they moved to Raymond where they owned and operated a dairy farm. They had three children: Irma Laseter Godfree (b. May 8, 1913, deceased); Ueltschey Clark

Laseter (b. Mar. 12, 1919, deceased); Dorothy Ray Laseter Abel (b. May 5, 1921).

7) Carl Irwin Laseter (b. Nov. 5, 1886, d. Nov. 28, 1938) md. Carrie Bruce of Brandon, they had no children. They are buried in the Brandon Cemetery. He was a well known Jackson attorney associated with the legal firm of Chambers and Trenholm at the time of his death.

8) Susan Francis Laseter (b. Apr. 15, 1888, d. Aug. 10, 1888) is buried in the Mount Olive Cemetery.

9) Caley Booker Laseter (b. Sep. 1, 1889, d. Feb. 20, 1919) served as Sergeant Caley B. Laseter in France during WWI. The inscription on his monument reads: "His was a noble life given in France for a noble cause, the defense of his country." (Mount Olive Cemetery).

10) Samuel Baxter Laseter (b. Aug. 8, 1891, d. Jun. 18, 1938) was a lawyer and a lifelong resident of Scott County. He is buried in the Mount Olive Cemetery.

11) Daniel Emory Laseter (b. Aug. 6, 1893, d. Sep. 16, 1942) md. Allie A. Dobbs (b. Nov. 24, 1900, d. Feb. 14, 1950 at Stage, MS in Scott County) on Sep. 7, 1919. They made their home in Morton where they reared five sons. He was appointed postmaster in Morton in 1935. He served as mayor of Morton from Jan. 7, 1941 until his death, Sep. 16, 1942 without serving his full term. They are buried in the Mount Olive Cemetery.

Their first son, Daniel Emory (b. Jun. 6, 1920, d. Jul. 19, 1996) md. Ellen Anita Turnley Jul. 21, 1944. Children are Robert Douglas, James Daniel, Dianne Elizabeth and Denise Elaine (Laseter) Smith. He was a WWII Army Veteran and served with the Darby's Rangers unit. He is buried in Mount Olive Cemetery.

Their second son, Caley Booker (b. Jul. 11, 1922, d. Apr. 27, 1986) md. Neva Grace Sorey on Oct. 3, 1953. Children are Susan Gale, Wilson and Caley Booker Laseter Jr. Caley served in the U.S. Army from Dec. 15, 1941 until Aug. 10, 1942, when he was discharged because of poor health. He is buried in Morton Memorial Garden.

Their third child, William Frederick "Billy" (b. Dec. 4, 1924, d. Dec. 16, 1997) md. Mollie Annette Tadlock on Nov. 9, 1946. They had one daughter, Lea Annette Ferguson. Billy was a WWII veteran, served in the U.S. Army Air Force in England as a gunner on B-24s. He is buried in Morton Memorial Garden.

Their fourth son was Jack Wilber (b. Oct. 27, 1929, d. Jul. 17, 1981) md. Janelle Graham on Oct. 19, 1963. Children are Janet Marie Laseter Jones, Jack Graham Laseter, Jill Gaye Laseter Fairchild, Jennifer Anne Laseter Spears and Jason Dobbs Laseter. Jack served in the Mississippi National Guard, activated during the Korean Conflict. He is buried in Morton Memorial Garden.

Their fifth son, Charles Daniel (b. Jun. 19, 1931, d. Mar. 20, 1983), md. Dorothy Adeline Johnson of Morton on Sep. 5, 1951. Children are Charles Daniel Jr. "Chuck," John Emory, Jeffery Thomas. Charles was licensed as a Methodist preacher in December 1953. He served 25 years in the Mississippi National Guard where he held the rank of lieutenant colonel. He is buried in Ellisville Cemetery.

12) Emma Laseter (b. Aug. 11, 1896, d. Nov. 27, 1898) is buried in Mount Olive Cemetery.

13) Minnie Lou Laseter (b. Jan. 15, 1898, d. Apr. 7, 1987) md. Robert William Waldrip (b. Nov. 20, 1898 in Scott County, d. Aug. 24, 1956) on Feb. 7, 1918. Children were Robert Laseter Waldrip (b. Oct. 22, 1918, d. Jul. 5, 1943 over Sicily in WWII); Libbye Jean (b. Nov. 29, 1919, d. Sep. 21, 2000) md. James Andrew King (b. Aug. 14, 1916, d. Apr. 9, 1976) on Apr. 9, 1946. They had one son, James Andrew King Jr. Libbye and James are buried in Lakewood Memorial Garden. Caley Bryant Waldrip (b. Dec. 19, 1920, d. Jan. 7, 1994) md. June Carroll on Feb. 16, 1952. They had one son, David Bryant Waldrip (b. Nov. 16, 1954). Caley is buried in Lakewood Memorial Garden in Clinton,

14) Effie Laseter (b. Sep. 30, 1899, d. Jun. 13, 1900) is buried in Mount Olive Cemetery.

15) Edgar Ray Laseter (b. Dec. 4, 1900, d. Sep. 14, 1963) md. Lula Myrtis Dobbs (b. Dec. 4, 1907, d. Dec. 28, 1987). They made their home in Morton and operated the Laseter Department Store for 35 years. He was a partner in Laseter and Neal Butane Company. He was active in commercial, civic and religious activities. He served on the Board of Alderman. They had one daughter, Elizabeth Ann. She married Walter W. Blain on Aug. 17, 1958. Children are Walter William Blain Jr., Michael Ray Blain and Amy Elizabeth Blain, Edgar and Myrtis are buried in Mount Olive Cemetery.

LASSETTER, Benjamin Poole Lassetter was born in the Lillian Community of Scott County in the year 1893. His parents were Daniel Benjamin Lassetter and Molly Irene Lassetter (nee Poole). Three siblings: (John Madison (b. 1888), Myrtle (b. 1898) and Elizabeth (b. 1900), lived to maturity with him and like him married and produced families. Poole, as he was known, married Lola Louise Lyle in 1924. She with her family lived in the Flatwoods area of Scott County with postal address of Lena.

Poole and Lola produced seven children: Benjamin Poole Jr. (b. 1924), Clarence Ray (b. 1926), Dan William (b. 1928), Keith Madison (b. 1929), Robert Vernon (b. 1932), Nan Patricia (b. 1934) and Rose Marie (b. 1936).

During World War I Poole served approximately one year as a private in a cavalry unit of the U.S. Army in the state of California. Upon his discharge he received a small pension related to an ear infection disability.

Poole was born on a farm and spent most of his working years farming. He is reputed by some who knew him to be a hard and productive worker awaiting sunrise with his team to begin plowing. In the late 1920s he purchased the 360 acre Boss Farmer farm encompassing the banks of Shockaloo Creek 2-1/2 miles west of Harperville and 2-1/2 miles north of Hillsboro. While mules were the work stock, several black families occupied tenant houses as sharecroppers. When farm tractors arrived, wage hands provided field labor. As the five sons were growing up they became the primary work force.

Poole believed in diversified farming. He grew cotton, corn, sorghum, beef cattle and pork. Sorghum was cut into silage and stored in a trench silo which he dug with mule teams and dirt slips. Beef cattle were a source of needed cash from time to time and were sold singley or in small groups. The herd maximized at 100 head. Hams smoke-cured and hung in the smokehouse were in demand during year end holidays and were sold reluctantly to local persons for about $9.00.

Family foodstuffs came from a garden, wild blackberries and muscadines, truck patches of potatoes (Irish and Sweet), peanuts, popcorn, an occasionally slaughtered steer, and the cool weather hog killings.

During World War II Poole joined other locals working as a carpenter in the Mississippi coastal area of Gulfport and Biloxi building essential housing for military personnel. He did similar work on the diffusion plant in Oak Ridge, TN where radioactive atomic particles were separated for the burgeon-atomic energy needs of both the military and civilian power supply.

Poole sold the farm in the early 1950s after most of his children reached maturity and moved elsewhere. He lived briefly in several places, including Hazelhurst, before moving to Forest. Here, he did service station work for a long time friend, Travis Chambers, and met minimum requirements for social security. He died in 1969 from injuries sustained in a single car accident while returning home from an American Legion meeting. He is buried in the Harperville Cemetery.

Poole was a member of the Harperville Baptist Church and the American Legion.

As a young adult he is reputed to have driven two white horses on his buggy. On one occasion someone turned them loose, and they arrived home without him. He was a good if not great horseman. During depression years of the early/middle 1930s he rode Old Maud (a one-eyed mare with some smooth riding gaits) to Harperville daily when cash was not available to fuel the 1929 Chevrolet with gasoline. Attire for these riding trips consisted of jodhpurs and lace boots.

During the middle/late 1930s he was foreman of a work crew building bridges over local creeks and elevating roadbeds above wintertime high water levels to enable school buses to reach local schools daily. Most of this work was done with mule teams and dirt slips.

Poole contributed services to education (his maximum grade level was the 10th) as a trustee of the Harperville public schools during the late 30s and early 40s. Older buildings burned or were demolished to make way for a new building to house grades 1-12. He spent many long nights in trustee meetings at the local school and made multiple trips to Meridian to secure funding.

During pre-desegregation days on the farm he dealt honestly and courteously with black men and their families who supplied labor. A quote from some of them sums it up best: "Mr. Poole will give you his last nickel with a smile on his face."

LASSETTER, Clarence Ray Lassetter was born May 13, 1926 in his parents' farmhouse in the Harperville Community of Scott County. His parents were Benjamin Poole Lassetter and Lola Louise Lassetter (nee Lyle). The second of seven children his siblings were Benjamin Poole Jr. (b. 1924), Dan William (b. 1928), Keith Madison

(b. 1929), Robert Vernon (b. 1932), Nan Patricia (b. 1934) and Rose Marie (b. 1936).

Clarence grew up on his father's farm and participated actively in farm life. This included 4-H Club membership with pork and baby beef projects, Future Farmers of America (FFA) membership with fence building, gate construction and land terracing. Farm chores included, cutting firewood for winter warmth, hoeing the cotton, thinning the corn, driving the tractor, plowing the fields, milking the cows. He found summers hot and farm labor fatiguing.

As a growing child Clarence found role models in two professions he observed in the community, school teachers at school and preachers at church. He found that both seemed to know more than others within the community, and he wanted to know more. This led him to the contents of books from which they read and taught: school books, library books and the Bible. He thought that somehow both should go together, and this became a guiding quest for his future as he nurtured a non-vocal, unseen source taking him toward ordination as a Baptist clergyman.

World War II was raging during Clarence's high school years. During his senior year overtures were made to senior students to enter military service with some college/university experience upon entrance to active duty status. This seemed to fit Clarence's guiding purpose, and he traveled first to New Orleans and then to Atlanta where he was tested and enlisted in the U.S. Naval Reserve as an apprentice seaman. On Mar. 1, 1944 the call to active duty arrived, and he was first stationed at Mississippi College. Following two semesters of general studies, he was stationed at the University of Texas in Austin and assigned studies in electrical engineering. He went through the end portions of V-5 (aviation), V-12 (officer training), and NROTC (more officer training) and was discharged in June 1946.

Upon discharge from the Navy he returned immediately to the University of Texas and completed studies for the bachelor of arts with major in mathematics and minor in physics and the bachelor of naval science and tactics. He left the University in January 1947 and returned to his father's farm where he grew a field of cotton prior to enrolling in the Southern Baptist Theological Seminary, Louisville in September 1947.

He took a brief hiatus from the cotton field, took his first plane ride to Austin to spend a few days with D. Gean Spencer, whom he had met in the fall of 1945 upon her arrival on campus from Houston. He affirms she was his first serious love.

At seminary he earned master of divinity and doctor of philosophy degrees in the field of New Testament studies. During student days he served as pastor of the rural Raymond Baptist Church, Breckenridge County, KY.

He met Jean Elizabeth Rasco upon her arrival on campus to study voice and organ. She hailed from Coral Gables, FL from a family of educational and cultural standing—her father was Dean of the Law School, University of Miami. In January 1951 Clarence and Jean were married in Coral Gables, FL.

To this marriage were born four children:

Elizabeth Lee (b. 1953), Leslie Ann (b. 1955), Scott Austin (b. 1958) and Steven Lyle (b. 1960).

Clarence's church service following graduation from seminary was (1) pastor of Glen Allen Baptist Church, Glen Allen, VA, 1953-55; (2) pastor of Fort Mitchell Baptist Church, Fort Mitchell, KY, 1955-64; (3) Executive Secretary, Northern Kentucky Association of Protestant Churches, 1964-67.

Upon arrival in the Fort Mitchell Community Clarence became involved in the local mental health association. This set an altered direction for ministry within the community as he aided the formation of first a board of directors and subsequently a service delivery system first known as Comprehensive Care Centers Of Northern Kentucky. Within a few months of its origin in 1966 he was invited to join the professional staff and develop a program to benefit persons experiencing alcoholism problems. He guided the development of the community's first Half-Way House for the alcoholic male, educational schools for problem drinkers in several locations, group therapy for alcoholics, and outpatient care for alcoholics. When these were sufficiently established he turned to outpatient psychotherapy with the plethora of needs accompanying them.

Following 12 years in the mental health service delivery system Clarence was put on "loan" to a newly developed transportation system designed to aid mobility of elderly and persons with handicapping conditions. He spent 22 years here and retired at the coming age of 75.

Jean, Clarence's wife of 43 years, died in 1994. At this time D. Gean was a widow. In 1995 Clarence and D. Gean were married.

Clarence has lived with a healthy curiosity about all facets of life, has sought to explore them in productive and positive ways, has found meaning in all of them, and gives thanks to God for being with him along these diverse ways.

Additional ministries on a limited time basis include service as a Naval Reserve Chaplain which rounded out his naval career at 28 plus years and chapel minister at Panorama Apartments, Covington, KY through 26 plus years. In the latter he has sermonized in a devotional manner from almost every chapter in the Bible—portions of the Psalms and Isaiah alone remain at the time of this composition.

Throughout life Clarence sustained his love for the land with gardening and flower horticulture.

LASSETTER, Soon after their marriage on Jan. 12, 1879, Daniel Benjamin Lassetter and Molly Irene Pool (later members of the family spelled this name Poole) Lassetter settled in the Scott County community of Lillian. Both were, according to one of their daughters, "orphans." Daniel's father, John Lassetter, whose wife Ann had preceded him in death, had been killed in the Civil War. John joined the Confederate Army on Mar. 10, 1862 at the age of 30 as a private in Co. G, 28th Reg. of the Mississippi Cavalry. His military service was short-lived. After five months he was wounded in a skirmish in Bolivar County, MS at Carson's Landing and died on Aug. 19, 1862. Daniel and his siblings, Emily and John, were reared in the home of D.B. Odom, presumably a relative. Molly Irene Pool had lived

in Washington County and had lost both parents when she was young.

Records show that Molly and Daniel were members of the Mt. Olivet Baptist Church in the Lillian Community of Scott County. Daniel served the Mt. Olivet Baptist Church as both deacon and church clerk. After the family moved to Harperville, Daniel and Molly and their children became members of the Harperville Baptist Church where Daniel was also a deacon.

Daniel is remembered as a lover of fine horses and a lover of music. We are told that Molly dreaded seeing one of Daniel's friends from another community arrive in the afternoon, for she knew her husband and his friend would be up fiddling and singing until the wee hours of the morning. The Lassetters were the first family in Harperville to own a piano. It appears that life in the Lassetter home was a happy mixture of work and play. Visiting grandchildren remember the sweet smell of cape jasmine in the yard, the old well on the back porch, and the huge magnolia tree that seemed to be made just for them to climb.

Daniel and Molly became the parents of seven children. Two daughters died: Estelle in 1900 at age 15 and Nena in 1910 at age 31. A son died in August 1890 at age 14 days. Nena, Estelle and the infant son are buried in the Hayes Creek/Wright Cemetery in Scott County, as is Daniel's mother, Ann Hasletine Lassetter.

Their surviving children were John Madison "Matt" (b. 1888), Benjamin Pool (b. 1893), Myrtle (b. 1898) and Elizabeth (b. 1900. All lived productive and interesting lives. Matt, the oldest of these four, merits special attention.

John Madison "Matt" graduated from Mississippi College with a superior record in both academics and athletics (lettered in five sports) and later obtained a master's degree. Matt became an educator. He taught one term in the Philippine Islands and then came back to Mississippi to claim his bride, Annie McLean. The two of them returned to the Philippines where they taught for a total of six years. They later settled in Hinds County, MS where Matt was superintendent of the school at Tinnin. He later became superintendent of the Clinton Public Schools in which Annie taught primary grades. Mary Beth, a daughter, was their only child.

Matt's students affectionately called him "Prof Lassetter" and this name stayed with him throughout life. He is remembered by all whose lives he touched (and they were many) as a great teacher and encourager. An extraordinary individual, he exuded energy in all areas of life and was especially attentive to nephews born to Pool and Myrtle. The Lassetter boys and Marshall Beard Jr. were treated to a week at "Uncle Matt's" several consecutive summers before maturing enough to work on the farm. They enjoyed rollicking good times which included daily swimming trips to Livingston Lake in Jackson. A special bond existed between Matt and his nephews.

Annie died unexpectedly of a heart attack in 1941 at age 51. On Sep. 25, 1942, Matt married Genevieve Stuart, a teacher who lived in Clinton. They became parents to John Stuart, Nina Ruth, Gene Estelle and John Madison Jr. This happy marriage continued until Matt's death at age 100. Many family members and friends gathered at the First Baptist Church of Clinton in 1988 to celebrate Matt's 100th birthday. It was a great occasion!

Daniel Benjamin Lassetter and Molly Irene Pool Lassetter

Poole Lassetter married Lola Lyle, also of Scott County, and settled on a farm near Harperville. Seven children were born to this union (five sons and two daughters). The boys were Benjamin Poole "B.P.," Clarence Ray, Dan William, Keith Madison and Robert Vernon; the girls were Nan Patricia and Rose Marie. In their later years, Poole and Lola moved to Forest.

Myrtle Lassetter graduated from Hillman College, a two-year institution in Clinton for young ladies, and married Marshall H. Beard. They lived in Harperville where Marshall operated a general store. Their two sons were Marshall Beard Jr. and Joe Thomas Beard.

Elizabeth Lassetter also graduated from Hillman College. She married Herbert Lenoid "Slick" Herrington, a pharmacist. They first lived in Walnut Grove and later moved to Durant, where "Slick" had a drug store. They were the parents of two daughters, Jane Irene and Bettye Lenoice.

Daniel and Molly Lassetter, Poole and Lola Lassetter, and Myrtle and Marshall Beard are all buried in the Harperville Cemetery. Annie McLean Lassetter is buried in the Clinton Cemetery. Matt Lassetter gave his body to the University of Mississippi Medical Center for research purposes. His ashes are in the Clinton Cemetery. Elizabeth and Herbert Herrington are buried in the Mizpah Cemetery in Durant. Genevieve Stuart Lassetter resides in Clinton at the time of this composition. *Submitted by Jane H. Bailey.*

LEE, Henry Bryant Lee was born Mar. 15, 1806 in Edgecombe County, NC to Henry and Lettice Lee. His grandfather, Stephen Lee, is believed to have migrated to North Carolina from Virginia. The Lee family left North Carolina and settled in Wilkes County, GA where Henry Bryant Lee was married to Margaret Bell Lee in 1828. She was born May 29, 1813 in Wilkes County, GA to James Lee and Nancy Sanderson Foster. Although it has long been thought that Henry and Margaret Lee were cousins, no relationship has yet been found. Her paternal grandparents, John Lee and Margaret Bell, were natives of South Carolina.

Soon after their marriage, the Lees migrated to central Georgia, settling first in Twiggs County and later in Stewart County where they remained until the early 1850s. Settling in Ludlow about 1851, Henry Bryant Lee soon established his family as one of the most prominent in Scott County. In 1860 he owned 4,000 acres of land and 50 slaves worked his plantation outside of Ludlow.

Margaret B. Lee died in Ludlow Feb. 24, 1883 and her husband on Apr. 5, 1891. Both are buried near the former site of their plantation home outside of Ludlow.

Children of Henry Bryant Lee and Margaret Bell Lee:

1) James Henry Lee (b. 1829) md. Jane Henrietta Denson; 2) Susan Ann Lee (b. 1832) md. (1st) James L. House, (2nd) James Albert, (3rd) John W. Orman; John Lumpkin Lee (b. 1834, d. 1864) md. Elizabeth Cobb; 4) William Wallace Lee (b. 1836, d. 1911) md. (1st) Mariah Florence Beamon and (2nd) Josephine R. Gilbert; 5) Stephen A. Lee (b. 1818, d. 1905) md. (1st) Martha Whitehead, (2nd) Delilah DeMoss; 6) Mary Foster Lee (b. 1840, d. 1895) md. James Nathaniel Denson; 7) George Franklin Lee (b. 1843, d. 1886); 8) Andrew Jackson Lee (b. 1845); 9) Thomas Hugh Lee (b. 1848, d. 1924) md. Alethia Jane Denson; 10) Robert Augustus Lee (b. 1849, d. 1929) md. Mary Scott McCabe; 11) Richard Henry Lee (b. 1852, d. 1935) md. Mary Alice Denson.

James Henry Lee, eldest son of Henry Bryant Lee and Margaret Bell Lee, was born 1829 in Wilkes County, GA. The Lee family removed to Scott County from Stewart County, GA about 1851. Within two years of their arrival, James H. Lee was married to Jane Henrietta Denson. She was born 1834 in Rankin County, MS to Shadrach James Denson and Alethia Chambers of Ludlow.

James H. Lee was becoming like his father and father-in-law, a substantial planter and public servant of northwest Scott County. In 1860 he owned 10 slaves and a 400-acre farm. During the 1850s he served as justice of the peace and surveyor of Scott County.

During the Civil War he served in Co. F, 36th Regiment, Mississippi Infantry. His service being plagued by illness, he is believed to have died as a prisoner of war. The last record found for him was dated April 1864. In the 1890s Jane Denson Lee and children removed to Franklin Par., LA where she died about 1910.

Children of James Henry Lee and Jane Henrietta Denson: Henry Singleton Lee (b. 1854, d. before 1900) md. Martha E. Johnson; Elizabeth Lee (b. Mar. 5, 1855, d. Jun. 13, 1928) md. Charles Henry Gill; Doctor Denson Lee (b. 1857, d. Jan. 3, 1898) md. Frances A. Smith; Shadrach Hugh Lee (b. Aug. 16, 1859, d. Feb. 27, 1937) md. Josephine S. Richardson; Edna Alethia Lee (b. 1861, d. 1902) md. Benjamin Tolbert Johnson; James Henry Lee (b. 1863) md. Annice King Richmond.

LEE, Few families have contributed to Mississippi jurisprudence in as major a way, and for as many years, as have the Lees of Scott County. Former Chief Justice Percy Mercer Lee, retired Chief Justice Roy Noble Lee, and United States Chief District Judge Tom Stewart Lee are part of two generations of "The Lee Legacy."

Chief Justice Percy Mercer Lee of the Mississippi

Chief Justice Percy Mercer Lee

Supreme Court was a native and life-long resident of Scott County, MS. He was born Nov. 14, 1892, in Ludlow and died Feb. 6, 1969, at his home in Forest. He graduated from Mississippi College at the age of 18 years, studied law under Chief Justice Whitfield, and, after being admitted to the Mississippi State Bar, served as chief assistant to Attorney General Ross Collins. He began the practice of law at Forest in 1918 and distinguished himself in personal injury law.

Chief Justice Lee was elected district attorney of the Eighth Circuit Court District in 1929 (special election) and served in that capacity until his election as Circuit Judge in 1938. While serving as circuit judge, he was elected to the Mississippi Supreme Court and took office in 1950. Justice Lee served as Justice and Presiding Justice and retired as Chief Justice in 1965.

Chief Justice Lee was the father of 10 children, eight of whom survived him: Roy Noble Lee, Percy M. Lee Jr., James W. Lee, and Tom Stewart Lee became lawyers. Charles David Lee is a physician in Forest and Robert Edward Lee is a retired Federal Firearms Special Agent. Chief Justice Lee also has four grandchildren: Thomas D. Lee, Roy Noble Lee Jr., Elizabeth Lee Maron and Tom Stewart Lee Jr., who are lawyers.

LEE, Born Apr. 8, 1941, Tom Stewart Lee was the last of eight children born in the Judge Percy Mercer Lee family. Tom's mother was Claudia Stewart Lee, whose parents were Dallas Stewart and Sally Johnson Stewart. His paternal grandparents were Thomas Hugh Lee and Alethia Jane Denson Lee.

Tom attended Forest Public Schools,

Judge Tom S. Lee and Mrs. Norma Ruth Robbins Lee. Top: Elizabeth Robbins Maron and Tom Stewart Lee Jr.

where he excelled in academics and athletics. He was the valedictorian of Class of 1959. He graduated from Mississippi College in 1963, where he started on the basketball team and maintained a straight A record. He went to the University of Mississippi Law School where he graduated first in the Class of 1965. He returned home to Forest to join the Lee Law Firm. After 18 years of practice in Forest, Tom Lee was appointed U.S. District Court Judge for the Southern District of Mississippi. He has taught Sunday School at the Forest Baptist Church for 25 years and sings in the choir.

On Aug. 14, 1966 Tom married Norma Ruth Robbins at the Methodist Church in New Albany, MS. She was a 1962 graduate of Blue Mountain College where she served as SGA president. She received her master's degree from the University of Mississippi in 1965. She coaches drama students, directs weddings and is on the board of directors of Community Bank.

On May 17, 1969, Elizabeth Robbins Lee was born. Then on Oct. 5, 1975, Tom Stewart Lee Jr. was born. Elizabeth and Stewart had very successful experiences in the Forest Public Schools. They both graduated with perfect A averages. Elizabeth was outstanding in drama, music, tennis and track. She was the star student and was Scott County Junior Miss. Stewart excelled in sports, namely basketball, baseball and tennis. He holds a state record in tennis for winning six consecutive state tennis titles.

Pictured is the family of Justice Percy M. Lee on the day he was sworn in as a Justice on the Mississippi Supreme Court. Front row is Tom Stewart Lee, Claudia Stewart Lee, Justice Percy M. Lee, Jane Lee (Anderson). Back Row: Mercer Lee, Roy Noble Lee, James Walter Lee, Robert Edward Lee and Doctor David Lee. Tom Lee was 8 years old on the day of his daddy's swearing in, and 35 years later when Tom Lee was sworn in as a U.S. District Judge, his son, Stewart Lee, was 8 years old, also.

Elizabeth graduated from Mississippi College in 1991, where she played tennis and won the "Freshman Woman of the Year Award." She received a Master's Certificate from the University of Surry in Guildford, England, where she was a rotary scholar. She graduated from the University of Mississippi Law School in 1995.

Stewart graduated from Mississippi College in 1998. He was an All Conference basketball player, president of the student government and graduated with an all A average. Stewart was awarded a prestigious Eastland Scholarship to the University of Mississippi Law School and graduated in May 2001.

On Oct. 2, 1999, Elizabeth Robbins Lee married David Friedrich Maron. On Jun. 10, 2000, Stewart Lee married Heather Michelle Davidson.

The Lees list church and family as the top priority for activities. They all have great respect for the legal profession and have passion for sports. Tom plays tennis regularly and Norma Ruth enjoys painting as a hobby.

LEWIS, The Lewis family from Ludlow, Scott County, MS were of Welsh origin and our ancestor General Robert Lewis of Beacon, Wales arrived at Glouchester County, VA in 1650 with a land grant from the King of England. He brought with him his wife and three sons: John Jr., Edward and William.

Our line is descended from Edward Lewis. Edward married to Ruth had four children of whom William (b. Mar. 28, 1705) is our direct ancestor.

William's son Exum, a field officer in the Continental Army was born in 1732\33 in Virginia. He married Elizabeth Figures. Their son John Lewis and his wife Sarah had eight children: Luke, Eff, Mills, Phillip, John, Leuten, David and Molly. John of this line was born in North Carolina in 1780. He married Polly Eura on Mar. 23, 1801 in Cates County, NC. They

had five children: Exum, John, Celey, Sally and Peggy of whom John was born about 1810 in Cates County, NC and married Rachel Beeman on Dec. 20, 1833. The family moved to Leake County, MS in the early 1850s. Their children who had been born in North Carolina were Henery, Martha, William J., James Rufus and Mary.

L-R: Eugene Lewis, John W. Lewis, Catherine Lewis, Annie Lee Lewis, Bryant Lewis, Ella Willie Lewis (mother) and John William Lewis (father), Ludlow, MS ca. 1923.

James Rufus married Christian Thompson McDuff in 1867. Their children were John William, James Henry, Margaret, Estelle, Susie, Minnie, Bertie, Eddie Leon, Audie and Lillian. James Rufus is buried in Pearl River Cemetery.

John William (b. Nov. 22, 1872 in Leake or Scott County) was buried in Ludlow in 1947. He married Willie Ella Lee (b. Mar. 12, 1874 near Ludlow) in 1895. She is buried beside her husband. They had five children: Annie Lee, Catherine, Eugene, James Bryant and John W. All are deceased and all had children still living.

Annie Lee married William Edward Davis on May 30, 1926. Children were William Edward Davis Jr. and Catherine Ann Davis Marks.

Catherine married James Wright in 1929 and had two children Eloise (b. 1944) and Audrey (b. 1947).

Eugene Lewis married Mildred Carroll and had two children, Charles Eugene (b. 1947) and Linda (b. 1952).

John W. Lewis and May had four children: Paul, John W., Raymond and Ida Belle.

James Bryant and Nettie Mai had three children: Jimmy, Elaine and Lloyd.

Most of these people live near or in Scott County. *Submitted by Eloise Corley.*

LEWIS, This family came from Greene County in 1847. John Wesley Lewis (b. May 1864, d. January 1940) md. Mary Frances Hensley (b. January 1869, d. January 1959) in November 1884. In 1905 he purchased 153 acres of land from his brother W.W. Lewis. The land was located in Scott County in the Salem Community on Lewis Road. Their children were Ruby Ethel (b. December 1885, d. September 1906), Ernest (b. March 1888, d. 1978), Nettie Mae (b. March 1891, d. 1980), Olin Guy (b. August 1893, d. November 1976), Lillie Bell (b. July 1896, d. July 1995), William Coyt (b. August 1899, d. 1953), John Clark (b. October 1901, d. August 1955), Albert Hensley (b. May 1905).

The first school in the area was located on this land. Olin Guy Lewis served in WWI. When he returned he married Ava Colan Sharp (b. November 1901, d. July 1993). They purchased the property from his parents in January 1938.

Their children were Mary Mildred (b. January 1926), Margaret Cornelia (b. October 1927), Olin Guy Jr. (b. July 1934). They farmed this land, raised and educated their children.

The property now belongs to Mildred Lewis May and James M. May. Their children are Gwendolyn Mildred (b. April 1947), Wandalyn Jane (b. July 1949), James Morris Jr. (b. June 1952). John Wesley and Mary Francis Lewis are buried in the Salem Church Cemetery in Scott County. Olin Guy and Ava Colan Lewis are buried in Eastern Cemetery in Forest, MS.

LEWIS, Hugh and Elsie Lewis, better known as the owners of the Hwy. 35 North Fruit Stand, relocated to the Forest area from Raymond, MS. Hugh (b. Nov. 29, 1913) was one of the youngest of 14 children born to Brownie Lewis and Addie Grantham Lewis. Hugh was a veteran of WWII. He served Forest and surrounding areas as a plumber for many years and was community known as "Plumber Lewis."

H.L. Lewis and Elsie Adams Lewis

Elsie Adams Lewis, a native of Myrtlewood, AL was one of five children born to Strouder and Annie Dixon Adams on Apr. 4, 1913. While Elsie was not blessed with any children of her own, she gave her heart and shared her home with Joanne Grantham Macoy, her foster child.

Hugh and Elsie were well loved and respected in their community and were greatly known for their generosity and love for children. They loved their four grandchildren and spent considerable time with them. No child or grandchild was more cherished or nurtured than the Lewis. Before their deaths they saw the births of eight great-grandchildren and enjoyed more than 50 years together as husband and wife.

People visited the Lewis' at their roadside fruit stand for over 20 years. Children especially loved the Lewis'. No one ever left their establishment without a little "happy" from Bud or Mrs. Elsie. Nuts, apples, oranges, and bananas found homes in the pockets of smiling children. The Lewis' were equally generous to the local nursing homes and the poor of the area.

After a short illness, Elsie died on Dec. 31, 1993 in the home of her daughter, Joanne Macoy's. Hugh died after an extended illness in his home on Jun. 12, 1997.

LEWIS, Marshall was born the third of five children to John Terrance and Myrtle Lewis on Feb. 21, 1936 in the "Possum Hollow" area of Harperville. Living in the country, Marshall grew up helping with the gardening, cash crops, animals and all that was typical of farming in Scott County in the 30s, 40s and 50s.

Times were hard, but his childhood is remembered for the security of a large, happy family, good neighbors, church and the excellent school at Harperville. Besides brothers, J.W. (Thrash) and Ernest; sisters,

Marshall Henry Lewis

Nena, Una and Nancy, there were his grandparents, many aunts, uncles, and cousins. Baptized at the age of 12, Marshall was active in Union Baptist Church of the "Red Top" Community.

The classroom years were especially memorable for the many friends and good teachers. Among them Mrs. Mattie Charles Beasley, Mrs. Ray Hamilton, Mr. D.C. Smith and Mr. Autrey. During his senior year, Marshall drove a school bus. Basketball, FFA, and a job with B & E Feed Store of Hillsboro kept this young man very busy! At 17 he joined the Mississippi National Guard in Forest.

High school graduation in 1955 was a proud day. The end of childhood and the beginning of much that was new and interesting.

Marshall was invited to Florida to learn the cementfinishing trade by life-long friends of his family, Clifton and Martha Brown. In Hialeah, he lived with the Brown family, worked with Clifton and joined their church, North Hialeah Baptist.

South Florida was very different from central Mississippi! The wonderful climate, beaches, and tropical setting were all so new and lovely! Marshall made friends easily, worked hard and greatly enjoyed his new life. However, he was drawn home to Scott County and family and went there whenever he could.

He enlisted in the Army in 1957. Qualifying for military police, allowed him to experience many aspects of life and in various parts of the country. He was stationed in Texas, Georgia and Maryland, traveled to other states on duty and as far as Seattle, WA where he embarked for a one-year tour in Korea. There he visited the Baptist mission near Seoul being served at that time by Rev. and Mrs. Parkes Marler of Harperville.

Marshall returned to Florida in 1960 and resumed his work in concrete placing and finishing. He worked on condos, warehouses, bridges, sports arenas, office buildings, hotels, shopping malls and new home construction. He even worked a short-term job in Riyadh, Saudi Arabia.

At North Hialeah Baptist Church, Marshall noticed a girl who had grown up, somewhat, while he was away. He and Beverley Diane Martin were married Jun. 11, 1961. That same year Marshall was ordained a deacon and served in that capacity for many years. He also served on committees and taught Sunday School.

Three children were sent to bless their home: Marshall, Jr. (b. Jan. 6, 1964); Ivy Dianne (b. Dec. 28, 1965); and Holly Yvonne (b. Mar. 27, 1975). Their little home at 5490 West 1st Avenue, Hialeah was bursting at the seams with love and laughter. All three attended Dade Chris-

tian School graduating with the same commitment to Christian values as their parents.

Marshall Jr. (known to all as "Hal") joined the U.S. Air Force and is a master sergeant. He is married to Laura Lynn Slutz of Canton, OH. They are the parents of Thomas Marshall and Tyler Madison.

Ivy became a legal secretary and is married to Thomas Perchitti whom she met at church. Both are active at North Hialeah Baptist where Ivy is the organist. They also have two boys, Michael Joseph and Christopher Andrew.

Holly, too, is a legal secretary, and works in the same office with her sister. Holly and Timothy Carl Potts are raising his daughter, Carrie and expecting their first child in June 2001.

After 40 years in the same house, and with his retirement, Marshall and Beverley have decided it's time for a change. Feeling drawn to return to his roots, they will be moving to Harperville in the spring of 2001.

Home again, home again, Jigiddy-jog! *Submitted by Beverley Lewis.*

LEWIS, Jordan Lewis moved from Bullock County, GA to Greene County, MS in 1817 with his family, which included his sons: Stephen, Isaac, Seaborn, and daughter Susanna. With him came the John Futch Sr. family.

Stephen Lewis married Aletha Futch, daughter of John Futch Sr. in 1823. Jordan, along with Isaac, Seaborn and Susanna, moved to Mobile County, AL, where he died in 1838. Isaac married the granddaughter of the famous William Weatherford, better known as Red Eagle, Chief of the Creek Indian Nation. They had 17 children and this is a story in itself.

Stephen Lewis purchased land in Scott County in 1847 near Gum Springs and removed his family from Greene County, MS to Scott County along with a large number of slaves and is included in the 1850 census.

John Futch Jr. and his family, along with the Zachariah Murrell family, also moved from Greene County at this time. The Futches, another pioneer family, settled nearby Hontakalo Creek and the abandoned Futch Cemetery marks the location of their farm. The Murrells settled on the Hillsboro-Conehatta Road on the Tuscolameta Creek called Murrells Crossing near Newton and Scott County line.

Stephen Lewis's family consisted of Aletha, his wife, and the following children: Angus, Isaac, Stephen Jr., Aletha, John Jackson, Jefferson, Elizabeth and Louisa. Stephen's wife Aletha died in 1852 along with two grandchildren and was buried on the family farm off Highway 21 near Gum Springs there being no cemetery available. After the death of his wife, grandchildren and several slaves, which was attributed to their farm being in a low swampy area, Stephen purchased land and moved several miles to higher ground in the Salem Community on the Hillsboro-Conehatta Road near Lay's stagecoach stop. This route was primary road used between Hillsboro to Union to Meridian. After 1850, Stephen's son Angus moved to Texas. Stephen died in 1862. Prior to his death he had given each of his son's a farm. Stephen Lewis was considered a wealthy farmer and owned large acreage and many slaves. He also was well known for his blooded horses. As a result of the

Civil War Stephen lost sons: Isaac, Jefferson and Angus. Stephen Jr. moved to Texas about 1870. Isaac's widow moved to Pineville. John Jackson Lewis, who was in bad health from wounds received in the Civil War, remained on the original Stephen Lewis farm and married Mary Ann Graham, daughter of John Graham another pioneer settler. John Jackson died at age 33 in 1871 leaving his wife and minor children: John Wesley, William Wiley and Mary Ann. John Wesley, better known as Jack, remained on the original Stephen Lewis farm. A portion of this farm remains in ownership of John Wesley's descendants. John Jackson's sisters, Aletha and Louisa, were married and went to Texas. Few descendants of Stephen Lewis remain in Scott County. It was rumored that Stephen Lewis had buried a box around his house prior to his death. Numerous attempts have been made by many after his death to locate this treasure. As of this date no one has made a claim to finding it.

Descendants of Stephen Lewis with the name Stephen are found in numerous southern states. In fact, one of the Stephen Lewis' has a son named John Jackson Lewis. This information has been compiled by John Harry Lewis, a descendent of John Wesley Lewis, over a 35-year period. He has also researched the Murrell, Futch, Graham, Stroud, Everett, Clark, Hensley, Hollingsworth and Gibbs families associated with his family tree

LINDSEY, The Lindsey family came to Scott County, MS by way of Alabama, Tennessee, Kentucky and Virginia. In 1842 William Lindsey purchased 320 acres in what is now Scott County, MS. The property was purchased from Isaac Roberts, a business partner of William's brother, John Lindsey. He came to Mississippi from Marengo County, AL in about 1840 with his wife Rhoda (Varner) Lindsey, daughter of James and Martha Varner. William and Rhoda were married on Feb. 27, 1829 and lived near their parents in Alabama. Their parents were Abraham Lindsey and Martha Varner. They had both lost their spouses and had married on Jan. 24, 1827.

L-R: Mississippi "Mittie" Williams Lindsey, wife of John Wesley Lindsey; Nannie Virginia Lindsey; Ferbie Burgess Lindsey, wife of William Chesley Lindsey; Emma Francis Lindsey Burgess and wife of Carroll Dudley Lindsey.

It is believed that Abraham's first wife was Carroll or Francis Dudley. Abraham listed his place of birth as Kentucky and Martha listed her place of birth as Tennessee. Abraham (father) Lindsey had six children. They were William Abraham, Carroll Dudley, Louisa, Mary, Paminda, and John. William and Rhoda moved to Scott County after Abraham Lindsey (father) died in Alabama. The original log cabin was located on top of a high hill on property now owned by Johnnie Mitt (Lindsey) Moore. William and Rhoda died sometime in the mid-1860s and are believed to be buried in the Rocky Creek/Thorn-Lindsey Cemetery near old Highway 80.

Rhoda Varner Lindsey, wife of William Lindsey (b. ca. 1790 in Tennessee, d. 1866)

L-R: William Chesley Lindsey, Abraham Lindsey and John Wesley Lindsey

They had nine children: Barcenia (b. 1831), William Abraham (son)(b. 1834), Martha Jane (b. 1837), Emma R. (b. 1839), Mary E. (b. 1841), Louisa (b. 1844), Francis Carroll (b. 1847), William Chesley (b. 1850) and John Wesley (b. 1854). All Lindsey's living in the Morton areas of Scott County are related through three of the brothers: William Abraham, William Chesley and John Wesley. The three brothers and their parents lived on three hills approximately two or three miles outside of present day Morton, MS. The houses for these families were within sight of each other and located near a water source.

William Abraham(son) was married to Susan Tillman and they had 10 children. William Abraham Lindsey served the Confederate States during the civil war with the Morton Pine Knots (Co. H 20th Mississippi Regiment) at the battle of Franklin near Nashville, TN. Their children: William Abraham (Abram), Mary Sue, Priscilla, James Carroll, Sue Lauren, Kate, Minnie R., Emma, William and Hattie A.

William Chesley was married to Maude Ferbie Burgess on Jul. 3, 1892 and they had four children: William Lewis Jefferson, Marvin Francis, John Wesley and Eason Peek. John Wesley was married to Mississippi "Nettie" Williams on May 20, 1877 and they had nine children: Samuel William, Lillie Irene, Emma Francis, William Wesley, John Gale, Carroll Dudley, Henry Grady, Wiley Burton and Nannie Virginia.

Many of the original Lindsey family members are buried in the Line Creek Baptist Church Cemetery. There are several Lindsey family members still living on the original Lindsey property. They are Johnnie Mitt (Lindsey) Moore, Willie Grace (Lindsey) Keene, Zee (Edwards) Lindsey, Dora Nell (Latham) Lindsey, Elizabeth (Lindsey) Drummonds and others.

Note some names may have been left out or misspelled.

LIVINGSTON, In 1853 John P. Phillip Livingston migrated south to the Shongelo area of Smith County, MS from Newberry County, SC along with several other families including the "Barbers." John P. Phillip Livingston (b. Oct. 20, 1818 in Newberry County, SC, d. Apr. 25, 1862 in Smith County, MS) is buried in the "Old Zion" Cemetery in the Trenton Community, although no grave marker can

Elwin B. Livingston and Eunice Williams Livingston. Fall 1978

be identified for him. John P. Phillip's first wife was Ann Margaret Suber, who was born in 1818 in Newberry County, SC and died in Smith County. Ann's parent's names were George Suber and Christina Folk Suber. John P. Phillip Livingston purchased land in his name and proceeded to raise his family. This land lies in northern Smith County near the present day community of Trenton. Children born to his marriage to Ann: David Sligh md. Lucretia E. Westbrook; Sarah Wallace md. James Cooper; Francis E. md. Lemuel Davis; George Albert Burley md. (1st) Agnes Jane Muchelrath, (2nd) Annie Eliza Bell; and John P. Livingston Jr. md. Minnie Cooper.

The original ancestors of these Livingstons came over to the United States from Germany.

John P. Phillip Livingston's child, George Albert Burley, married Agnes Jane Muchelrath in Mississippi. Agnes Jane was born Nov. 28, 1848 and died Dec. 25, 1899. The following children were born to this marriage: Latisia Livingston md. Matthew Burns; Ella Monona Livingston md. Tom Gaddis; Emma Livingston md. Jerry Jones; Melvin Livingston md. Jewel Freeman; C. Ethel Livingston md. Otto Walter; Addie who died at age 4.

George Albert Burley married a second time after the death of his first wife, Agnes Muchelrath. His second wife was Nancy Ann Eliza Bell (b. Apr. 29, 1871, d. Jan. 29, 1945). Three children were born to this marriage: Elwin Burns Livingston (b. Nov. 1, 1901, d. Nov. 22, 1980); George Cohn Livingston (b. May 12, 1903, d. Feb. 8, 1971); Burley Suber Livingston (b. Nov. 8, 1905, d. 1964).

Their first child, Elwin Burns Livingston married Eunice Gertrude Williams in 1925 and raised a family in the "Stage" community in the old Livingston home place, which was located on Stage Road near where the old stagecoach was located. This land is located in Scott County; MS. Elwin also was public relations man for Southern Pine Electric Power, Dixie Electric and the State Forestry Commission. Elwin and Eunice lived for a brief time in Laurel, MS.

Elwin Burns Livingston was elected to the State Legislature in 1932 and served his country in the Mississippi State Legislature for over 20 years. Elwin enjoyed serving the people of

his district and was known for his compassion and generosity to his fellow man. Elwin was in the Navy as a young man and traveled the high seas. Although he only acquired an 8th grade education, he was well read and educated himself. When he finally retired from the legislature in 1971, one columnist, Jack Perkins wrote, "when he (Livingston) departs from the Capitol, the indigent and sick, the pulpwood haulers, small farmers and country school children will have lost one of their best friends at the State Capitol."

The following children were born to this marriage: Annie Ray, Bobbie Ruth, Elwin Arnette, Alice Nadine, Eva Grace, and Richard L. "Dick" Livingston.

Annie Ray Livingston married Milton Stroud and raised her family in Louisiana. She worked for over 30 years as a timber merchandiser for Georgia Pacific Timber Company. She died of pancreatic cancer in March 1996 and is buried at Independence Methodist Church alongside her husband Milton Stroud. She and Milton had three children: Charlie, Tanya and Randy.

1) Charlie Stroud, who is currently married to Linda Shipley Stroud. Charlie's first marriage was to Debra Wigginton and they had a daughter, Char'lee 'Sissy' Stroud and one son, Chris Allen Stroud. Sissy Stroud has four children, two of which are twins. The children's names are as follows: Ashton Victoria, Dakota Ann and twins-Megan and Michelle. Sissy is married to Randy Van Osdall.

2) Tanya Stroud married George Ripley White III and two children were born during their marriage: a) George Ripley White IV who married Robin Griffin and they have two children, Rachel and Joey. b) Mark Edward White who married Ashley Isbel and they have twins.

3) Randy Stroud married Karen and one son was born during this marriage, Daniel Livingston Stroud.

Alice Nadine Livingston married Edgar: "Pete" Herron and they had four children: Ed, Faye, Linda and John. Alice is and has been "election commissioner" for her district in Forest, MS for many years. Her husband Pete passed away on Jan. 19, 1999 and is buried at Homewood Methodist Church. He was an avid cattleman and forester. Alice still lives in the same home she and Pete raised their family in for over 30 years. The children are as follows:

1) Faye Herron Reed, who has a daughter, Melissa Reed. Faye is currently married to Roy Coward;

2) Ed Herron has one son Eric, who was born during his marriage to Kathy Harris. Ed and his wife Jeanette currently have a business just west of Morton, "Roosevelt Marine."

3) Linda Herron Guyse has one child, Marlee Thornton, who was born during Linda's marriage to Anthony Thornton.

4) John Herron has one child, Dana Leann Herron, who was born during his marriage to Teresa May. John now resides with Alice in Forest, MS.

Elwin Arnette Livingston married Cecilia Villano and they have one child, Daniel Burns, "Danny" Livingston, who is married to Lou Pritchard. Danny and Lou make their home in Tuscaloosa, AL. Elwin Arnette worked for the State Hwy. Dept. for many years and Cecilia retired from her many years of work at Sears Dept. Store in Jackson, MS. Arnette's hobbies include hunting, fishing and golfing.

Bobbie Ruth Duncan worked for the U.S. Postal Service as mail carrier for over 20 years inside Morton city limits. Her husband Frank worked for many years for the State Hwy. Dept. before dying at a young age from lung cancer. Bobby passed away in the Scott Regional Hospital of heart failure on Feb. 16, 1999. They had two children:

1) Vernon Crotwell is married to Linda Hudson Crotwell. Vernon has two children, Vernon Stanton Crotwell and Steven Ryan Crotwell, born during his first marriage to Donna Thompson. Vernon Stanton married Robin McDill and they have two children, Nicholas Stanton and Kimberly Michelle. Steven is married to Kristy Dees. Vernon and present wife Linda Hudson Crotwell have two children: Gera Hudson Bynum who is married to Vince Bynum and Dereck Hudson who has a daughter named Macy Brooke Hudson.

2) Becky Duncan Beard is married to Cooper Beard and they have three children: Jessica Leigh, who has a son Evan Derrick born during her marriage to Dewayne Derrick; Jeremi Lynn who is married to Jason Cale; and Marshall Duncan Beard.

Eva Grace Livingston married William S. "Billy" Noblin in 1955 and they had one child, Natalie Virginia Noblin. Eva Grace worked for the State Hwy. Dept. for many years. Billy was a rural mail route carrier for many years before retiring from the Postal Service in 1986. He passed away from a sudden illness in December 1998 and is buried at Independence Methodist Church. Eva still resides in the house in Pulaski they called home for over 35 years. She is and has been for many years a member of the State Democratic Executive Committee for the state of Mississippi. She is active in politics to this day. Their daughter Natalie Virginia is married to Christopher Lee Rhodes and they have two children: Rhianna Lee and Christopher Lee Rhodes Jr. "Buck." They make their home in Smith County, in the Wicker Mill Community.

Richard Lee "Dick" Livingston married Martha Anne Waggoner in 1963 and they have five children:

1) Lee Anne married Marcus Eugene Palmer and they are expecting triplets due in February 2001.

2) Marsha Grace married Robert Daniel Barnes and they have one son Blake Daniel.

3) David Blane Livingston, is unmarried (took Dick's place in the Legislature),

4) Rori Elizabeth is married to Bruce Bridges and they have a son, Blane Livingston Bridges. Rori also has a daughter, Bethany Leanna Barnes, born during her marriage to Mark Barnes,

5) Jennifer Ruth has one child, Abby Lee Miles, born during her marriage to Jimmy Miles Jr.

Richard L. "Dick" Livingston was a teacher and coach at Morton High School before being elected to the Mississippi House of Representatives in 1971. Dick was known for his compassion and concern for his constituents in his district. He was an avid supporter of hunting and fishing rights, and an avid conservationist. He served his district for over 28 years until in March

2000 he died of hepatic cancer. Martha still lives in their home in Pulaski. Their son David was elected to the legislature in May 2000 to finish out his father's term. Over 500 people attended Dick's memorial service held at the building named in his honor, Livingston Performing Arts) at Roosevelt State Park in Morton.

LOGAN, Bob Logan and his cousin, J.C. Buckley, bought the Logan & Buckley general merchandise building on Front Street in Lake in 1950. Mr. Buckley, a pharmacist, later sold his interest and moved to Athens, GA. Bob and wife Louvenia and family operated the store until their retirement in 1984, when the store was sold to Darvis Vance.

Bob and Louvenia Logan

Logan and Buckely purchased the store from Dewey Massey, who succeeded Floyd Loper as owner. The business was well-known for many years as a "furnishing store" for local farmers who bought their seed and fertilizer in the spring and paid when cotton was ginned in the fall. Some customers visited the store by horse and wagon as late as the 1960s.

Throughout its history Logan and Buckley sold everything from chicken feed to shoes. A few older customers knew Mr. Bob could be "talked down" on certain prices, and everyone enjoyed the game. Frank Wash's meat counter was the scene for many a tall tale, and politics was a frequent subject of conversation at the hot stove in front.

It is interesting to note that Floyd Loper served as state senator for Newton and Scott counties and that Bob Logan held the same post for the 1972-76 term. He also served as town alderman, Lake Attendance Center trustee and member of the Scott County School Board.

Bob and Louvenia still live in the house they bought from Dewey Massey. They have four children: Betty Kelly, Robert Logan Jr., Diane McMillan and Glenn Logan, and 11 grandchildren.

LONGMIRE, James C. Longmire was the ninth child of Malcolm and Maggie McFarland Longmire. He was married to Eleanor Boyd Longmire, our mother. He was a man of many talents. He was a great father and friend. Just ask my sisters and brothers: Neveland, James T. Woodrow (deceased), Kenneth, Charles D.,

James C. Longmire

Charles O., Bennie, Samantha, Brenda, Lamar and Cache'. I'm the youngest, Cache'.

From as far back as I can remember, daddy was the Superintendent of Union Grove Baptist Church Sunday School. He was very active in

church activities. He was also a terrific bass singer in the adult choir and he served on the deacon and trustee boards. Daddy had a playful sense of humor. He had nicknames for everyone and mine were "chebird" and "Hamburger." He also called the children who came into the store where he worked nicknames and they enjoyed the fun. Even now they tell my mother about him calling them names when they were little.

In the summer daddy would decorate the yard with beautiful flowers. In the garden he would grow turnips "just to watch them grow," and he would tell everyone to "come and get them." When he was unable to work the flowers in the yard he would call Cedric my nephew to come for a "few minutes" and daddy would keep Cedric all day putting out flowers. Mama would tell them where to put them.

Daddy loved children. He especially loved his grandchildren. He never wanted to see anybody, especially a child, hungry. Maybe that's why he kept so much food at our house. Or maybe it was just an old habit from his jobs at Sunflower and A&P Food Stores. He liked my mother's cooking, so he would call everyone to "come and have a sit down and eat," he would say. I can remember that before I started school we would go everywhere and see everybody. Before he stopped work he would carry me out to my Grandma Boyd's house. Daddy also loved to go to church. He went to church far away out of town and knew everyone there. How, is still a question?

He loved being the master of the lodge. He also loved his lodge members. I'll never forget daddy in his tall black hat, black suit, apron, and white gloves. He looked so strong and protective, I always thought he would live forever.

My mother says once after daddy had been sick they decided to have a small thank you ice-cream party for those who had been so nice to them. Their small party ended up with over 200 people on the yard. I do remember we had a family picnic and I think there was over our limit that time too. But, I know daddy enjoyed it. Daddy did love people.

Daddy went to Biloxi once because my brother Charles O. had been in a bad car wreck. The Army moved him to Keesler Air Base Hospital for surgery. As he looked out into the water his face brightened with amazement. He said, "look at all that water!" He said that one day he would go back and see it.

Like most men he loved football. He was a fullback at Hawkins High School. He later got a scholarship and went to Alcorn A&M College. while at Alcorn he was nicknamed the "mole" because of the way he ran with a ball. After a year he was drafted into the Army and sent to Korea. Sometimes when I would go into his room he would tell me about places he'd gone while he was in the Army. Daddy liked to tell stories about when he was in the Army or his younger life.

That's what I miss most about him. As I said before daddy was a man of many talents. When I was smaller I thought he was the strongest man in the world. He died of prostate cancer and a brain tumor on Apr. 5, 1999. May he look down on us in peace and happiness.

LOPER-DAVIS, William Perry Loper came to Scott County from Newton County, MS after the War Between the States. He had fought with the 39th Infantry of Decatur when he was only 15 years old. The "Bloody" 39th fought all the way to Atlanta (except Franklin, TN) and from Atlanta to Mobile Bay. They were taken prisoner at Fort Blakely, AL on Apr. 9, 1865 and imprisoned on Ship Island off the Mississippi Coast.

O.D. Loper Sr. and Emmitt Edwards Loper

Loper Home, Forest, MS

William Perry was the son of Captain Joel Walman Loper whom enlisted in Co. A, 5th Regiment of Minute Men on Aug. 24, 1862. He fought and was captured at Port Hudson. Paroled at Morton he returned to Decatur. He went to Vicksburg where he was captured again.

For 40 years William Perry Loper was a Justice of the Peace. He married Sarah Jane Hollingsworth, the daughter of Samuel H. Hollingsworth and Lenna Smith Hollingsworth. They lived in a log dogtrot house on his farm near Sebastopol. Their children were Newton A. (md. Emily Thomas), Otho Davis (md. Emmett Ross Edwards), Agnes Lee (md. Elihu Laster) and Matilda Jane (md. Abner McCann).

Otho Davis Loper attended Golden School, walking four miles each way from age 8-18. He taught in Scott and Leake County schools for several years. His wife Emmett Ross Edwards was the daughter of William Patrick Edwards and Sophonia Frances Hardage Edwards. William Patrick Edwards was a farmer, teacher and cotton gin owner.

Otho Davis and Emmett's children are Audie Mae (md. Len Floyd O'Sheilds), Etoile (md. Oliver Houston Hopkins), William Prentiss (md. Johnny Wilma Sevearinger), Otho Davis Jr. (md. Patricia Lucille Warren (Baker), Sarah Francis, Mildred Elizabeth and Opal (md. Lester Madison). O.D. Loper Jr. served in the Army and Prentiss Loper served in the Navy during WWII.

O.D. Loper was elected Scott County Superintendent of Education in 1913 and served for three terms. He was a staunch advocate of an education for every child. He furthered his own education by attending summer sessions at (then) Mississippi Normal College. He and his family were active members of the Forest Baptist Church where he was a deacon and Sunday school teacher for many years. Mr. Loper served two terms and an incomplete term as sheriff of Scott County. Following this he worked with the Mississippi State Tax Commission and then as sheriff's auditor with the state auditor's office.

On the local level he joined other community leaders in bringing educational attractions, historical movies and Chautauqua events to Forest. He believed that education was the key to advancement.

LOTT, William Landius Lott, son of Solomon Lott and Nancy Minerva Grogan Lott, had five boys: Landius, Howard, Grover, Abby and Valius, and three girls: Matt and Pat (twins) and Annie Laura.

Landius married Mammie Windham, daughter of Thomas Calvin and Mary Harvey Windham. They had four sons: W.L. "Dub," Jack, Billy and Robert and one daughter, Mozell Lott Warren.

Landius and Valius were range riders. They would ride the county lines on horseback wearing their pistols to check the cattle, making sure they had crosses painted on their hide. At this point in time, probably in the 1920s, cattle roamed the land freely and became badly infested with ticks. To get rid of the ticks, the cattle had to be dipped in a dipping batt. This was a hole in the ground, a little wider than a cattle shoot and about 25 to 30 feet long, filled with a water solution to kill ticks. The cattle were herded into the hole and out the other side. They were painted with a cross, meaning they had been dipped. The owners of the cattle were responsible for having the cows dipped. If the cattle had no cross, the range rider would confiscate them. The owner would have to pay so much per head to get them back.

Landius later became a deputy sheriff for Howard McCrory. He was also a constable for many years. He was a farmer and raised cotton and corn. He lived between Forest and Homewood most of his life and is buried in the Homewood Cemetery.

Mozell married Virgil Warren (deceased) of Homewood in 1931 and had four sons: Buddy, Johnny, Bobby and Donald, and four daughters: Geraldine, Peggy, Jean and Sandra. She has lived in Homewood all of her married life. *Submitted by Mozell Warren.*

LYLE-DODSON, John Floyd Lyle and Mary Susan Francis "Fannie" Dodson lived in the Cash Community near Lena, MS. John Floyd Lyle died of a heart attack at the age of 35 in about 1885. Family history says the heart attack was brought on by stress due to a disagreement with a teacher at a school board meeting. In 1894 his widow Fannie bought on contract 80 acres of farm land for $400 with eight years to pay, from a Mr. E. Creel who moved to

Mary Susan Francis "Fannie" Dodson Lyle

Texas. She farmed and continued to raise her children there on the land which was near the Heatherly Community, the residence now currently on Hattie Lyle Rd.

One of Fannie's son's, John Willie Lyle, also referred to as J.W. or Johnny and sometimes Big Red was the next to youngest child. He took care of his mother Fannie until her death in 1921. He and his brother Alfonso built a new house for their mother between 1912-15, when the price of cotton was about 40 cents a pound, a time when many cotton farmers were building new homes. This house still stands today while the first house has been gone for years, its' location was near an old cotton house that is still in existence.

Johnny was past the age of 40 and had never married when he began corresponding by mail with a young woman who was nearing

John Willis Lyle

John Willis Lyle and family. Standing l-r: Mrytle Estelle, Marshall Henry, Marion Christine; sitting: John Willis Lyle, son John Willis Lyle Jr. and 2nd wife Johnny Slay

the age of 30. She began to write him letters on the suggestion of a Miss Holladay, her relative that taught school in the community where John lived. Sophia Leona Graham and Johnny came to know each other through letters written to each other beginning about February 1918. They were married on Christmas Day 1918, at the Conehatta, Methodist Church, the church where Sophia and parents, Noah Randolph Graham and his wife, the former Nancy Rebecca Holladay, were members.

John and Sophia's first child was born in October 1919. They had three more children and an infant who died. Sophia died on Mar. 3, 1929 at age 40, in the Jackson Baptist Hospital suffering from complications of pregnancy. Her death left four children motherless.

Johnny later married a lady named Johnny Slay, who was a widow with children of her own, and together they raised their families. J.W. supported his family mostly through vegetable crops which he would load into a horse drawn wagon and drive to Forest, some 15 miles away, traveling back the same day. He also raised cotton with the help of his family and his close relatives in the community who helped each other pick cotton.

Presently only one child of John and Sophia is living, Marshall Lyle, who has lived in California since the end of WWII when his Army enlistment was over. The other children's names were Marion Christine Lyle, an RN for many years at the Choctaw Indian Hospital in Philadelphia, MS, Mrytle Estelle Eshee and John Willis Lyle Jr. Marion and John are buried at the Cash cemeteries.

Marion Christine Lyle came into possession of the land after her father died, and spent her retirement years in the old home place which she had renovated during the 1980s. Presently a granddaughter of John W. Lyle resides in the home with her family. *Submitted by Marcia Estep.*

LYLE, Lola Louise Lyle was born in the year 1894 in the Flatwoods of Scott County serviced by the Lena post office. Her parents were William Franklin "Doc" Lyle and Louvina Miranda Lyle (nee Rigby). She was the sixth child of Louvina. An older half brother, Henry Evans, lived in the household during his childhood and adolescent years. Her siblings were Mary Louvina "Molly" (b. 1880), James Franklin (b. 1882), Lawrence Wesley (b. 1887), Daniel Easom (b. 1889), Louis Vernon (b. 1891) and William Bryan (b. 1897).

William Franklin married Lilly Watson in 1900. This union produced six children thus enlarging Lola's siblings with Jerome Kenneth (b. 1901), Roger Brenton (b. 1902), Aubrey Enlow "Jack" (b. 1904), Marie Elizabeth (b. 1906), Fontaine Olivia (b. 1908), and Loree Erneze (b. 1911).

Lola married Benjamin Poole Lassetter in 1921 at the home of the Reverend Gary Parker in Harperville. They produced seven children: Benjamin Poole Jr. (b. 1924), Clarence Ray (b. 1926), Dan William (b. 1928), Keith Madison (b. 1929), Robert Vernon (b. 1932), Nan Patricia (b. 1934), and Rose Marie (b. 1936).

Upon graduation from the 8th grade Lola went to Forest, took an educational test, and was certified to teach school. During her teaching years she rode horseback to school.

Lola performed multiple household/farm chores in support of her family. She cooked, sewed, gardened, canned fruits and vegetables and sometimes meat, raised chickens, sold chickens and their eggs. When farm fertilizer arrived in 200 pound sacks she laundered these multiple times until all letters disappeared. The clean fabric then became bed sheets when stitched together and on one occasion became a white suit for her husband. When the source of this suit became known within the community, Lola received requests to make others for sale to neighboring menfolk. She declined all these and limited her sewing for family members only.

Lola started her small scale poultry production by putting eggs under "settin hens." This expanded with purchased baby chicks delivered by the rural mail carrier. She reached maximum production with several hundred laying hens. Feed was then purchased in multiple hundred pound lots, and eggs were packed in large egg cartons containing many many dozens. Chicken houses expanded from the small original with the "settin hens" to two others accommodating the larger flock. Production provided eggs and fried chicken for the family, payment for baby chicks and feed, and cash from sales to supplement farm income needed by a growing family. When feed sacks arrived in colorful floral patterns, Lola sewed shirts for her sons and dresses for her daughters. One son embarked on his last two college years with bed linens stitched from aforementioned fertilizer sacks.

Lola was widely recognized within the Harperville Community for her devotion to family, her brothers and sisters, her step-mother affectionately known as "mamma" by the children and "granny" by the grandchildren, her husband, and her children.

She showed a keen interest in her children's friends and welcomed them after church on Sundays to feasts of fried chicken and home-made

pies, both of which gained recognition as "unbeatable." Adult men visiting with family members as Lola awaited her funeral service spoke commendably of both.

When her children were grown and the farm was sold she lived in Forest in a modest home. Here she grew roses and a small vegetable garden. At this time Scott County was enriched by poultry production by the thousands on many farm sites. Packing plants sprang up in Forest to process chicken for shipment worldwide. Always industrious, Lola secured employment in one of the packing plants and "stuck it out" when younger fellow employees disbelieved she could do it. But she believed, and she did.

Lola's faith in herself, her family and others was a staunch character trait. This translated spiritually into church membership in Baptist Churches—Harperville, Forest, Jackson.

Several years after her husband died in 1969, she moved to Jackson and resided first with Rose and then Nan where she died in 1983. She is buried in Harperville Cemetery. Her children authorized and signed the following tribute to her and distributed it to friends and acquaintances.

To you we send our word of thanks for remembering us in our moments of grief; coming to us with your love and care; sustaining us with your gifts of food; bringing with you the beauty of flowers.

Words are inadequate when we express our gratitude for the life of Lola Lassetter. She was more than mother to us and more than grandmother to our children. She loved us, worked with us, hoped for us, prayed for us, believed in us, cheered us on.

She rejoiced in our successes, welcomed our friends and cherished our families. The spirit of her life blesses us yet when a bird sings, a flower blooms, a baby laughs, a church bell rings, a kind word is spoken, a good deed is done. *Submitted by B.P., Clarence, Dan, Keith, Bob, Nan and Rose.*

LYLE, Matthew Lyle, who served Scott County in both the Mississippi House and Senate, was born Sep. 29, 1818, probably in Jackson County, GA, before the formation of Walton County. The son of Matthew Lyle Sr. and Sarah Marshall McNab, he was reared in Walton and Troup counties in Georgia, and moved to Tallapoosa County, AL, where he became an attorney in Dadeville and served as Judge of Probate of Tallapoosa County. On Feb. 15, 1848, he married Mary Diana Caroline Pearson, who was born Jun. 15, 1831, in Jasper County, GA, and was the daughter of William Head Pearson and Mary White. Carrie had attended school in Cambridge, MA, when her brother James Madison Pearson was a law student at Harvard.

About 1855 Matthew Lyle purchased land in Leake County, MS and several tracts in Scott County in subsequent years. Other family members who came to Scott County were Matthew Lyle's brothers, Willis Lyle, Lewis Brown Lyle, John W. Lyle and one of his sisters, Sarah Ann Lyle Morgan. Jesse Marion Pearson and John Ewell Pearson, brothers of Mary D.C. "Carrie" Lyle settled near Ludlow, and her brother Micajah White Pearson lived in Leake County when he died in February 1860. After 1870,

Carrie's mother, Mary White Pearson, also moved to Scott County.

Mary Frances "Fannie" Lyle, the first child of Matthew and Carrie Lyle, was born Dec. 31, 1851 and died Feb. 19, 1903. She married Greene Washington Talbot, son of William B. Talbot and Nancy Haney Willis. William Henry Lewis Lyle (b. Aug. 4, 1856, d. May 30, 1921) md. Nancy Ellen Jones, daughter of James Jones and Delilah Barrier. Matthew Micajah Washington "Mike" Lyle (b. Sep. 2, 1857, d. Jul. 18, 1944) md. first, Elizabeth "Bessie" Slay, daughter of Drury Slay and Martha Jane Johnson; and second, Martha Susan Green, daughter of John Green and Sarah Oxner.

Mary Caroline Lyle was born Jun. 27, 1859 and died Jun. 12, 1863. Ann Elizabeth Jane "Lizzie" Lyle (b. Jul. 18, 1861, d. Dec. 18, 1921) md. Thomas Jefferson Meador, son of Robert Bunyon Augusta "Gus" Meador and Indiana Slay. James Madison Lyle (b. Mar. 1, 1863, d. Sep. 8, 1941) md. Sarah Hendrix, daughter of Henry Claiborne Hendrix and Susan Ella Young. Jessie Eliza Josephine Lyle was born Jan. 17, 1865 and died May 26, 1874.

John Willis White Lyle (b. Dec. 24, 1869, d. Sep. 16, 1948) md. Ouda Shellyne White, daughter of Gilbert Montier LaFayette White and Margaret Stevens Johnson of Scott County. John W.W. Lyle studied at the University of Tennessee and graduated from Baltimore College of Dentistry.

Matthew Lyle died Jun. 4, 1890 and Mary Diana Caroline Pearson Lyle died Jul. 31, 1895. Both are buried with many of the Lyle and Pearson family and friends in the cemetery established as the Lyle Cemetery circa 1860 on land patented by Matthew Lyle in 1859 in the Cash Community. Mike Lyle is buried in Woolmarket Methodist Cemetery in Harrison County; Lizzie Meador in Lena Cemetery and Madison Lyle in Ralls, TX.

The Lyle and Pearson papers, diaries, furniture, and other artifacts retained for more than 200 years attest to an appreciation of family heritage. *Submitted by Barbara Sudduth Lyle.*

MADDEN-CHESTER-ANDREWS, Josiah Madden, son of Elias John Madden I and Mary Plyler, was born ca. 1825 in Laurens County, SC, died ca. 1885 in Forney, TX. He married Margaret Isabel Chester on Nov. 18, 1849 in Tallapoosa County, AL. Margaret was born ca. 1831 in South Carolina and died ca. 1885 in Independence County, AR. Her exact ancestry is not known at this time, but several Chesters are found in Scott County in the 1860 Federal Census. Johnathan Chester, HH #331, may be her father.

This family moved to Mississippi soon after their first child, Mary N. Madden was born in 1850, as their second child, Martha J. Madden, was born in Mississippi in 1851/52. Josiah Madden purchased 120 acres of land in the Damascus/Sebastapol area in 1856. They appear on the 1860 Federal Census in Scott County, MS, HH #513. About 1869, the Josiah Maddens and several other families of Madden, Andrews, Nelson and Johnson moved on to the Independence/White counties in Arkansas area.

The other children born to Josiah and Margaret Madden are Emily S. Madden (b. ca. 1853 in Mississippi); Nancy Catherine Madden (b. Sep. 25, 1854 in Scott County, MS, d. Jun. 27, 1934 in Oklahoma City, OK) md. Oct. 15, 1873 to James Clinton Adams in Independence County, AR; Jesse C. Madden (b. ca. 1856 in Scott County, MS) md. Mary Molly Blancit; Frank M. "Fancy" Madden (b. ca. 1858 in Scott County, MS, d. Havanna, AR) md. Lula Hayes; Aldora Madden (b. ca. 1860 in Scott County, MS); Josephine Madden (b. ca. 1862 in Scott County, MS) md. Newton Woods; Aletha (Euretha) "Belle" Madden (b. September 1863 in Scott County, MS) md. B.F. Henderson; John W. Madden (b. ca. 1865 in Scott County, MS, d. 1936 in Moore, OK) md. Lelia Craig; Elias Calvin Madden (b. ca. 1869 in Scott County, MS, d. 1940 in Greer County, OK) md. Erma J. Cooper on Jul. 18, 1897 in Texas; Lelia Madden (b. ca. 1875 in Independence County, AR) md. Wess Miller on Oct. 3, 1895 in Texas.

Mary N. Madden married Daniel J. Andrews, son of Samuel W. Andrews and Annis Johnson, about 1865. Their first child, William Austin Andrews, was born in Mississippi ca. 1866/67. Daniel and Mary moved their family to Arkansas about 1869, along with Daniel's mother Annis, Mary's parents, and other Andrews, Johnson, Madden, and Nelson families. Additional children born to Daniel J. and Mary N. Madden Andrews were Margaret A. "Maggie" Andrews (b. ca. 1870 in Arkansas); Josiah "Joseph" Nelson Andrews (b. Feb. 24, 1873 in Oil Trough, Independence County, AR, d. Apr. 16, 1944 in Altus, OK); Jasper C. Andrews (b. ca. 1874/75 in Arkansas); John W. Andrews (b. ca. 1877/78 in Arkansas); Arthur Andrews (b. ca. 1883/84 in Arkansas). *Submitted by Bennett Nelson Andrews.*

MADISON, According to the 1900 Wayne County, MS census, the patriarch of the Madison family, Peter Madison (b. 1836 in Sweden) emigrated to the United States in 1857 and served an apprenticeship in New York before moving to Alabama. There he married Rebecca Jane (last name unknown). The "Journal of the Mississippi Conference of the Methodist Protestant Church" records that Peter joined the M.P. Church in 1887 as an elder from the Methodist Episcopal Church, South. He served as a minister of the Gospel in the Mississippi District until the year before his death in 1901. The obituary in the conference journal called him a good preacher and a master of dialect."

It is not known exactly when the Madison family moved to Scott County, but the 1900 census shows Charles, one of Peter's sons residing there. A farmer in the Kalem Community, Charles, affectionately known to the family as "Paw Charley," was a master story teller and was well known for his yarns. Among these were his claim of hitting a baseball from Homewood to Lorena. Paw Charley also passed on to the younger members of the family stories of Peter's Swedish accent which he apparently never lost.

The tradition of story telling is strong in the Madison family and many anecdotes have been passed down over the years. I have tried to avoid writing in the first person in this article, but I cannot, for it is extremely personal. Some of my fondest memories are of the many stories and humorous tales of the family which my fa-

ther told over and over, and of which I never tired. I confess that I cannot name all the descendants of Peter Madison and cite their place in the family or in the history of Scott County. To even try, I would slight someone. Truth be told, most of us know little of our family's history. Even the records are contradictory, and maybe that is as it should be with a family whose riches and values and contributions lie in the richness of the imagination and the ability to find humor in midst of hardship. Several of Charles's children, including my grandfather, William Oliver, and Uncle Capers and Uncle Dewey lived in the Kalem Community until their deaths. Now Peter's descendants are scattered, but wherever a story is recalled the family lives on. *Submitted by Larry E. Madison.*

MAPP, Charlie Howell Mapp (b. Jun. 21, 1890, Newton County, d. Apr. 14, 1965) moved to Forest from Newton County on Jan. 4, 1924. His wife, Lorene Harris Mapp (b. Mar. 6, 1896, Newton County, d. May 20, 1990) md. Nov. 14, 1915 at home of her father, William Hughes Harris, south of Decatur. His two sons, Raymond Lee Mapp (b. Dec. 15, 1916) and George Titus Mapp (b. Feb. 23, 1919, d.

Charlie Howell Mapp and Lorene Harris Mapp on wedding day Nov. 14, 1915

Sep. 18, 1976) accompanied him in the move. The family lived in rooms at the home of Mrs. Fanny Antley for about a year. In 1925 Charlie built a home at 312 E. 4th Street, which still stands today. A third son, Allan Hughes Mapp was born Jun. 3, 1929 in the home on 4th Street. Prior to moving to Forest, Charlie had been a farmer, built houses and put down water wells along with his father and worked in a lumber camp where he also learned the barber trade.

Charlie was a barber and worked for about a year at Oscar Sherman's barbershop on Main Street. In 1926 Charlie and Bill (W.W.) Yonce formed a partnership and opened the Yonce and Mapp Barber Shop, which operated until December 1958 when the business was sold. Charlie and his family were members of the Forest Methodist Church and he served on the board of trustees for many years. Charlie was active in many civic affairs of the town and served as chief of the Volunteer Fire Department from 1926-1960. He was a member of the Forest Separate School District Board of Trustees for about 12 years (about 1950).

On Oct. 25, 1939, Charlie was named as superintendent of water works for the city of Forest. He worked in this job for 21 years, until Jun. 20, 1960. During this time he operated the water filtration system, the water works system and the sewer system. He also supervised the addition of a fluoridation system to the water system. Under his supervision during this period the water and sewer systems had substantial growth and expansion.

Forest had 325 water customers in 1939 and

over 1,100 in 1960. In 1939 the city's only paved streets were Highway 80, Hillsboro Street, Main Street to the depot and around then Court House Square. During the time that Charlie was in charge of the Water Works, he also worked on Saturday's as a barber in his shop and others. On the day he died of a heart attack, Apr. 14, 1965, at age 74 years and 10 months, he was at work at Sherman's Barber Shop.

Charlie was affectionately known as "Pa Charlie," not only by family members but by his many friends, probably because of the many kindness and favors he had given to the people of the town over the years. Lorene was also affectionately known as "Ma Mapp."

Of the three sons of the family, Raymond lived in Forest, worked for Mississippi Power Company, married Francis Jones and had two daughters, Charlene and Elizabeth. Titus lived in Forest, worked for the U.S. Post Office, married Peggy Gibson and had one daughter Mollie. Allan lived in Clinton, worked for Mississippi Power and Light Company, married Shirley Ferguson and had one son Kenneth and one daughter, Lori. The immigrant ancestor of the family, John Mapp, came into Virginia in 1654. They migrated through the Carolinas to Georgia. William Foster Mapp (b. Jul. 22, 1807) was Charlie's Great-Grandfather and migrated from Jasper County, GA to Newton County, MS, in the spring of 1857 along with his family, including his son James Allen Mapp (b. Dec. 1, 1835), Charlie's Grandfather; and Cosrow Fincher Mapp Charlie's father (b. Oct. 20, 1867).

The Harris family migrated through the Carolinas to Mississippi probably in the 1820s. William Harris (b. Oct. 7, 1801) was Great-Grandfather of Lorene and married Cynthia Everett on Oct. 19, 1826, in Lawrence County, MS. His son, R. Oliver Harris (b. Apr. 24, 1839) was Grandfather of Lorene, and William Hughes Harris (b. Dec. 5, 1861, in Newton County) was Lorene's father.

MAPP, Marcus Mills Pomeroy "Fritz" Mapp (b. Feb. 4, 1878) was one of 13 children of Jeremiah and Susan B. Reeves Mapp. He married Martha Ann "Mattie" Sessums in 1898 and moved from Newton County to Beat One in Scott County where they purchased property for farming purposes and also acquired a general store in the community of Harperville. In

Mr. Marcus Mills "Fritz" Mapp, 1938

this area they found people who were congenial, hard working and close knit. They built a home in Harperville and reared their six children in whom they instilled strong ties of family, community and church. Myrtle married Edgar Marler and they lived in Forest all of their married life. Jerry married Ruby Mason of Neshoba County. They lived in Harperville until buying property north of Forest where they raised cattle. Jesse Rae married Myra Bailey of Harperville. Claire married Ben Alford and they resided in

Harperville until moving to Oak Ridge, TN during WWII. Excell married Lucille O'Bannon of Harperville and Marcus married Elise Dearman of Forest.

The Mapps are descendants of educators and churchmen and they realized a dream by sending all of their children to institutions of higher learning. All have served in their churches as musicians, deacons, elders and lay ministers.

"Fritz" was a rural mail carrier who began by riding horseback. He then carried the mail by horse and buggy until purchasing the first Model T in that part of the county. He was always happy and smiling and singing. Those on his mail route declared that they could tell how close Mr. Mapp was to their house just by listening for the verse of the hymn he was singing.

He taught singing schools in the days of shaped notes and was a song leader of great renown. All six children enjoyed music. Mrs. Mapp was known for her beautiful needlework. She appliqued beautiful quilts and grew show stopping flowers. She was productive in her tireless effort of making a wonderful home and rearing happy children. Mr. Mapp was one of the founding fathers of the Methodist Church of Harperville which recently celebrated its 100th anniversary. A host of descendants of "Fritz" and "Mattie" Mapp were in attendance Jul. 28, 1998 and their youngest child, Marcus Mapp, was the speaker for the event.

Fritz and Mattie built a second house closer to Harperville. It had a large windmill in the back yard and became a landmark. Although the wind mill is no longer in existence, the home is still occupied.

Of the 10 grandchildren, only one still lives in Scott County, James Archie Marler and his wife, Mary Jo, reside in Forest.

Red hair and freckles are a trait of the Mapps. Good nature and music comes next to Godliness with the descendants of this couple who gave of themselves to their church and community. *Submitted by Mrs. Marcus Mapp.*

MAPP-NAILS, Grady Mapp was one of six children born to Will Mapp and Donnie Kirkland Mapp. Grady was born Mar. 4, 1902 in Ludlow, MS. Grady's brothers and sisters were Atlee, Sam, Jack, Mae Mapp Stewart (all deceased) and Donnie Mapp Ormond of Carthage, MS. Grady's mother, Donnie, died when he was an infant. After Donnie's death, Will met and married Rosa Ella Horne. They had four children: Birdie Lee, Frenchie Lee, Willie Lee and Augusta.

After becoming an adult, Grady married several times. The children from these marriages were Sam (deceased), Burnham and Deonie Mapp Blouin. He was also the father of Lodell Ware.

Clemmie Nails was one of the daughters of LeBraska and Nettie Woods Nails. They also had another daughter, Jessie Mae.

While working for the GM&O Railroad Company Grady met Clemmie and they married in November 1945. Grady and Clemmie later moved to Walnut Grove, MS. Clemmie loved children and often had her nieces, Jo Ann and Sarah Rebecca Tittle, come to her home for long visits. She also had a nephew, George Tittle. Grady and Clemmie had their first son, Grady Douglas Mapp born on Sep. 8, 1947. After living in Walnut Grove for a short period of time, Grady and Clemmie moved to Forest, Scott County, MS.

Four years after moving to Forest on Mar. 25, 1951, Grady and Clemmie had Clemmie Dianne. Douglas and Dianne would be the only two children for the next six years.

Grady became a cafe operator in downtown Forest and Clemmie became a cook for the cafe. She also sewed for others to supplement the family's income. As the years passed, Grady became a night watchman for the cotton compress. He also worked as a butcher for Hunt's Frozen Foods.

Mickie Joe was born Sep. 16, 1957); Michael Timothy (b. May 9, 1960); Marion Frank (b. Sep. 13, 1962) and finally, on Oct. 18, 1968, Clemmie and Grady had another girl, Margaret Melissa.

Clemmie and Grady knew the importance of getting an education. All of their children finished high school. Some of the children went on to graduate from a two year or four year college program.

Grady Douglas resides in Milwaukee, WI and has a son, Grady Douglas Mapp Jr. and a daughter, Monique Mapp. Grady also has a grandson, Grady Kordell Mapp.

Clemmie Dianne is married to Eddie James Rigsby and they have three sons: Keith Douglas, Kevin James and Kelton Nicholas. Clemmie and her family live in Jackson, MS.

Mickie has five children: Tony, Quinteshia, Brooke Nicole, Meikai and Mickie Joe Jr. Mickie resides in Forest, MS.

Michael and his wife Alice have a son Michael Dylan. They reside in La Mesa, CA.

Marlon is unmarried and lives in Forest, MS.

Margaret lives in Forest, MS with her three children: Justin Kevon, Mark and Denzeana.

Grady and Clemmie Mapp both lived a long and fruitful life. Grady departed this life on Sep. 21, 1978 and Clemmie on Jul. 29, 2000. They are greatly missed.

MARLER-MAPP, Benjamin Edgar "B.E." and wife Myrtle Mapp Marler moved to Forest in 1925. He worked at Central Chevrolet Company for 20 years. They had two children, James Archie (b. 1926) and Bobbye June (b. 1928). Both graduated from Forest High School. James Archie served in the Navy two years and graduated from Mississippi State University in 1949. He married Mary Jo Hubbard and has lived in Forest since then. They have three children: Brenda, Martha and Dave. Bobbye June married Dr. Roy Brinkley. They have lived in North Little Rock, AR since 1947 and have four children: Gwyn, Ann, Diana and Judy.

In 1945, B.E. Marler opened a new automobile dealership on Hwy. 80 (Marler Auto Company) on the site where the Jitney Jungle stands. James Archie began working there after college in 1949. This business operated until 1987.

Parents of B.E. Marler were John Capers Marler and Carrie Noel Marler. They had six children: Edgar, Lois, Elizabeth, Wilson, Ruth and John Davidson.

Parents of Myrtle Mapp Marler were Marcus Mills Mapp and Martha Sessiums Mapp.

They had six children: Myrtle, Jerry, Claire, Jessie Ray, Excell and Marcus. Myrtle Marler died in 1982 and Edgar Marler died in 1985.

MATHIS-VANCE, On May 11, 1985, Joe Marzene Vance and Dorothy Lee Mathis were married in Taylorsville, MS, in the home of Reverend and Mrs. Steve Mooneyham. Mrs. (Tammy Weger) Mooneyham, cousin of the groom and Nathan Mooneyham, son of Steve and Tammy witnessed the small ceremony. The newly married couple made their home in Jackson and attended Northside Baptist Church in Clinton, where Joe, a licensed and ordained minister, was Minister of Music. Jennifer "Jennie" Elizabeth Vance was born to the couple on Dec. 27, 1985.

Joe, Dorothy and Jennie Vance

The family moved to Hattiesburg in 1986 for Joe to attend University of Southern Mississippi, where he earned a master's of music education. After graduation the family moved to Opelousas, LA, where Joe was the head of the Music Department at Westminster Presbyterian Church and Academy.

Jennie celebrated her third birthday in Pasadena, TX. The family had moved in July 1988 to the suburb of Houston for Joe to take a teaching position in Pasadena. Joe was also Minister of Music at Thomas Avenue Baptist Church where the family worshiped.

The family was to make one more move in 1991 to Morton, Scott County, MS, where the position of band director at Lake Attendance Center was waiting for Joe. Jennie started school and the family settled in close to friends and relatives. Dorothy, employed by Central Mississippi Regional Library System, worked at several libraries in the four county system over several years and is, now technical services manager for the system. Jennie, now in the ninth grade, loves music, reading, working and performing in church groups and spending time with family and friends.

Joe (b. Jan. 26, 1958, in Jackson, MS) is the son of Marzene Clark Vance (b. Sep. 29, 1936 in Newton County) and Marguerite Viola Smith (b. Nov. 11, 1935 in Scott County). He is the grandson of Robert Talmadge Vance (b. Mar. 23, 1912, d. Feb. 26, 1959) and Adelia Ruth Clark (b. Jul. 20, 1910, d. Dec. 30, 1982) and James Elmer Smith (b. Apr. 13, 1909, d. Aug. 29, 1999) and Elizabeth Bernice Rube (b. Oct. 1, 1910, d. Feb. 29, 1988).

Dorothy (b. Dec. 1, 1958, in Roanoke, VA) is the daughter of Glenn Dean Mathis (b. Jun. 15, 1934, Watertown, Codington County, SD) and Clyda Jean Tedstrom (b. May 21, 1933, Labette County, KS, d. Jul. 12, 1994, Scott County). She is the granddaughter of Aaron Dewey Mathis (b. Feb. 10, 1899, Monmouth, Crawford County, KS, d. 1959, Parsons, Labette County, KS) and Arlie Bernice Hall (b. Jun. 10, 1911, Ames, Story County, IA, d. October 1983,

Parsons, Labette County, KS) and Clyde Eugene Tedstrom (b. Sep. 9, 1912, Mound Valley, Labette County, KS, d. Feb. 10, 1969, Mound Valley, Labette County, KS) and Hazel Evalena Munday (b. Dec. 15, 1913, Severy, Greenwood County, KS).

MATTHEWS, The family of T.L. "Lonnie" Matthews and spouse Tressie Gardner Matthews have roots back to Scotland. John Matthews, came from Glasgow, Scotland in the 1700s and with wife Jane produced eight children. In 1799 he is credited with naming the newly formed Kentucky Barren county seat, Glasgow. John owned the first tavern and blacksmith shop in Glasgow. Son James married Elizabeth Strawther in 1801. Their union produced 12 children.

George and Emma Matthews and children

Lonnie and Tressie Matthews and family

He had extensive land holdings, race horses and a mill on Skagg Creek near Glasgow. Son, Jordan Winston (b. 1809 in Barren County), with his first wife, Sarah Williams, produced four children. Sarah died and at the age of 45 Winston married Elizabeth Rivers (age 17) in Marango County, AL. Their union added four more children. From 1860-67 they were in Lauderdale County, MS on their land in what is known as the Bailey Community in Meridian near Gum Log Cemetery and church. In 1881 their children sold that property to a person named Bailey.

Their son George R. Matthews (b. 1852 in Alabama) md. Emma Pettey in 1875 in Scott County by Rev. W.R. Butler, brother of Emma's Mother, Mary Ann Butler Pettey. Emma's grandfather, Landon C. Butler, owned many acres in the Steele Community in sections 35 and 36 until 1856, then sold his holdings to Geo. W. McCabe and moved to Texas. George and Emma Matthews union produced nine children. The last two, my father Lonnie and his younger brother Jim, were born on the present day Matthews place in Scott County which George and Emma bought in 1890 and built their home. George died in 1922 and Emma in 1947, Both are buried in the Antioch Church Cemetery. The home place

was left to son Lonnie (b. 1892) who married Tressie Gardner in 1919 and to them were born five children. One (a girl) died after birth; Melvin, a retired Marine, lives at Hillsboro, MS; Lucille M. Sessums, a retired state employee, resides in Vicksburg, MS; George Rufus, killed in action in Iwo Jima, 1945 and buried at Ephesus Church Cemetery; Mitchell, the writer of this brief, a USAF retiree is presently living with his spouse on the old home place.

Lonnie was a diversified farmer involving dairy, truck and regular farm products. He also was a professional trainer of bird dogs and in summer months sold commercial fertilizer for a local Forest dealer. He was one of the prime movers in establishing Ringgold High School in 1929, serving as president of the first local board of trustees. Active in community affairs and served on the county board of education for many years, he was instrumental in the location and building of Scott Central High School presently used today, this after considering himself retired, accepted another term on the board to speak for the communities education concerns. He was fair and honest, with the ability to get things accomplished. Tressie, a devoted wife and loving mother, died in 1984 and Lonnie in 1985. Both are buried in Ephesus Church Cemetery. *Submitted by Edwin M. Matthews.*

MAY, Ezra May (b. Dec. 24, 1893 in Smith County, MS) was the son of John Wesley May and Martha Coverson. They moved to Scott County when Ezra was a small child. They lived in the Usry Community on Old Hwy. 80, east of Forest. Ezra met and married Lula Mae Myers (b. Dec. 11, 1900), daughter of John S. Myers and Annie B. Chambers. They married Jun. 3, 1917, at the home of Sam Clark in Scott County.

Ezra Elija May and Lula Mae Myers

To this union was born 10 children: Annie Lucille (b. Apr. 14, 1918, d. Jan. 15, 1969); Bertha Codile (b. Feb. 5, 1920, d. Jun. 30, 1999); Hazel Ruth (b. Oct 14, 1921); Ezra Junior (b. Feb. 3, 1923, d. Jul. 5, 1976); James Marice (b. Dec. 11, 1924); Dealie Orlena (b. Sep. 26, 1926); Edward Leon (b. Apr. 26, 1928); Clara Joyce (b. Nov. 20, 1934); Robert Arnold (b. Nov. 7, 1937) and Harry Raburn (b. Jan. 21, 1939).

Ezra bought his first property in October 1916 from his father, and in September 1923 bought adjoining property from Mrs. Sallie Usry and J.E. Usry and his wife. This land is located in Scott County in the Usry Community east of Forest on old Hwy. 80. Ezra farmed this land and raised his family. He was a big supporter of getting an education. He made sure all his children went to school and got a good education. Ezra died Jul. 13, 1963 and is buried in the East-

ern Cemetery in Forest; Ms. Lula Mae followed on Mar. 29, 1996, and is buried alongside Ezra. Both of Ezra's parents are buried in the Liberty Baptist church cemetery in Scott County. Lula Mae's mother is buried in the Hillsboro Baptist Church Cemetery in Scott County. Her father was killed in Stutgart, AR while working in the logging woods. He is buried in Arkansas.

MCCABE, George W. McCabe (b. 1814 in TN), son of James H.L. McCabe and Rebecca Baines. In 1844, he was married to Obedience Julia Denson, eldest daughter of Shadrach James Denson and Alethia Chambers of Ludlow. She was born 1828 in Rankin County, MS. Prior to their marriage, George McCabe had joined his future father-in-law in the operation of a mercantile establishment. In 1843 the firm of Denson, McCabe and Chambers was taxed on $653 worth of merchandise sold. Another of their joint businesses was a sawmill, which they operated near Ludlow. In his history of northern Scott County, Dr. A.A. Kitchings wrote that Shadrach J. Denson and George W. McCabe, "...found a mill seat on Tallebogue creek (sic) a mile from Harperville. Here they erected a grist mill, maybe the first in the county."

George McCabe, like his father-in-law, was a substantial planter of northwest Scott County. In 1850, he owned 600 acres, which was valued at $5,000. From existing, records it can be seen that his fortunes grew with the years. At his death, his estate was put into trust for his minor heirs. It consisted of real estate valued at $6,000 and a personal estate (slaves, etc.) of $20,000.

Sometime between May 1855 and January 1859, George W. McCabe and Obedience J. (Denson) McCabe died. Their five orphaned children lived with their guardian and uncle, Thomas J. Denson. Children of George W. McCabe and Obedience Julia Denson: Sarah Irene McCabe (b. Aug. 3, 1845, d. Nov. 6, 1918) md. Newton Edney Burnham; Mary Scott McCabe (b. Jan. 17, 1847, d. Mar. 27, 1929) md. Robert Augustus Lee; Henry Clay McCabe (b. Jan. 31, 1850, d. May 20, 1907) md. Flosse Jack; Florence Antoinette McCabe (b. April 1852) md. George W. Butler; Harriet Theresa McCabe (b. Jul. 5, 1854, d. Mar. 2, 1923) md. John Nathaniel Robbins.

MCCABE, By 1837 Silas McCabe was buying property in Scott County, MS. He had migrated from Smith County, TN to join his brother George. Later in 1853 they would be joined by their father James Harrison McCabe.

Silas McCabe married in 1841 to Ann Smith whose father, John Jackson Smith, was the first sheriff of Scott County. They had seven children born in Scott County and four born in Texas.

Children: Antoinette McCabe married Waddy Thomas Hunt; Byron Lloyd McCabe served in the Confederate Army and married Martha Frances Taylor; James H. McCabe died unmarried; Albert McCabe died young; Emily Ann McCabe died young; Matilda Murry McCabe died unmarried; Franklin Seaborne McCabe md. Emma Hayes; Delina McCabe md. William Pope Bonds; John Quitman McCabe md. Sarah Ann King; Elizabeth McCabe died unmarried; Nellie Helen McCabe md. James Edman Gouldman.

Silas appears with his family on the 1850 Census for Scott County, MS. There are many deeds recording the land Silas sold before he moved to Bosque County, TX.

Brother George W. McCabe became an attorney. He married Obedience Denson, daughter of Judge Shadrach Joseph Denson and Althea Jane Chambers. Their children were all born in Scott County, MS. Sarah Irene McCabe md. Newton Eddy Burnham; Mary S. McCabe md. Robert A. Lee; Henry C. McCabe md. Flossy Jack and he became a well-known attorney in Vicksburg and was once a candidate for the governor of Mississippi; Theresa M. McCabe md. John Robinson. *Submitted by Doris Maxwell Dell.*

MCCORMICK,

Peter S. McCormick (b. Apr. 24, 1830 in Newton County, d. Aug. 17, 1898) was a one-eyed schoolteacher, having, lost one eye as a child while cutting kindling with an axe. A splinter from the wood struck him in the eye and the blow caused him to lose the sight in that eye. He later married Mary Jane Nicholson of Newton County. She was a student of his. Their marriage produced three children: Ellie E. McCormick, never married; Sallie E. McCormick married Perry Monroe Simmons on Dec. 27, 1887. They resided in Lake. Ms. Marshall William McCormick (b. Mar. 31, 1867, d. Sep. 3, 1941) md. Tressie Lyle Talbot, daughter of Washington Green Talbot, the first mayor of Lena, MS, on Oct. 13, 1894. The family moved to Scott County around 1885 and purchased 1100 acres of land along Futches Creek northeast of Forest, MS.

There were nine children born to Marshall and Tressie McCormick. Three of which died before they were 5 years old.

The oldest daughter Elvie Elizabeth (b. Jun. 21, 1897, d. Oct. 15, 1983), md. James Coley McMurphy of Harperville, MS and they produced two sons, Hugh McMurphy of Forest, MS and Horace McMurphy of Madison, MS. They were both born in Scott County.

Talbot Green McCormick (b. Jun. 6, 1899 d. Feb. 23, 1985) md. Laura Gaines of Decatur, MS and they produced two sons. Talbot Green McCormick II of Hobbs, NM and James Marshall McCormick of Marietta, GA. Both were born in Scott, County.

Fannie Lyle McCormick (b. May 20, 1903 d. Sep. 16, 1927) md. Bartley Fikes of Scott County. They had no children.

Lois Jane McCormick (b. Sep. 6, 1906, d. Aug. 14, 1992) md. Robert McAlister of Tennessee and they produced three children: Mary Jane Lupberger of New Orleans, LA; Teresa Adams, New Orleans, LA; and Robert of Mandeville, LA. All children were born in Memphis, TN.

Hardy Ferrell McCormick (b. Jan. 26, 1909 d. Feb. 16, 1988) md. Thelma Lucas of Newton County. They produced three children: Francis, Hardy Ferrell, and Cheri Bess. Hardy Ferrell McCormick II married Betty Comans of Scott County on May 28, 1983 and they have two children, Kyle and Candice.

Marshall William McCormick (b. Feb. 4, 1912, d. Mar. 10, 1977) md. Virginia Woods of Gadsden, AL. They have one son Danny Marshall who lives in Fletcher NC. Virginia Woods McCormick lives in Henderson, NC.

All deceased members of this family are buried in Eastern Cemetery in Forest, MS.

MCCRAVEY,

James Richard "Jimmy" McCravey was born Apr. 6, 1866 on a farm near Tyro, MS. He was the youngest of 10 children born to Richard Holmes McCravey (b. Feb. 27, 1809, d. Jan. 20, 1867) and Mary Ann Holland (b. Jan. 22, 1824, d. Mar. 27, 1903). Less than a year old when his father died, the deaths of his two brothers in 1873 and 1878 left Jimmy the man of the house before the age of 12. He worked on the farm until he was 22 when he began clerking in a country store, where he slept in a room above the store and made $16.67 a month. The first money of his own that he ever earned he loaned to another farmer on farm real estate security. "I was born on a farm, but I was born a banker." In about 1895, he left Tyro for Senatobia where he obtained his first bank employment.

Martha Lytle Myers McCravey and James Richard McCravey Sr.

In 1901 Jimmy McCravey moved to Forest pursuing a job opportunity offered him by Major R.W. Millsaps, President of the Capital State Bank, Jackson, MS. Major Millsaps and his associates were acquiring the Bank of Forest, established in 1900, from its original shareholders, who had voted to dissolve it after four discouraging months of operation. Major Millsaps wanted to reopen in February 1901 with J.R. McCravey, whom he had met at a bankers' convention, as cashier. Mr. McCravey had saved $2,500. He borrowed $1,000 from a sister and bought $3,500 of the stock of the Bank of Forest. On Feb. 6, 1901, the Bank of Forest reopened as planned. When Mr. McCravey arrived in Forest he did not know a single resident of the town and there was not a single local stockholder. But with hard work and the advice and support of Major Millsaps, Mr. McCravey and the Bank of Forest were able to succeed.

In 1902, J.R. McCravey brought his bride, Martha Lytle Myers, to Forest. He had met Miss Myers in Senatobia where she was a schoolteacher. They married in Nashville, TN on Jun. 26, 1902. She was born Jun. 2, 1869, the sixth of 10 children of William Talbert Myers and Mary Jane Davidson of Wartrace, TN.

"Jimmy" and "Mattie" McCravey were members of the Forest Presbyterian Church where he was a deacon and she was active with the youth group. She was also active with the Girl Scouts and called herself, "the oldest Girl Scout in Scott County." They had three children: Mary Lytle McCravey (b. Jul. 4, 1904, d. May 30, 1985); md. Oliver Beaman Triplett Jr. on Jun. 19, 1930; James Richard McCravey Jr. (b. Mar. 5, 1908, d. Feb. 13, 1974); md. Mary Lilla Irwin

on Jan. 19, 1937); and William Davidson McCravey (b. Sep. 14, 1910, d. Dec. 6, 1993) md. Mary Katharine Knoblock Layocono on Sep. 14, 1967.

Although Mr. McCravey's own formal schooling had been limited, he was an avid reader and a great believer in the benefits of education, and his children were all well educated. He was both generous and careful with his money, meticulously researching purchases. When time came for him to buy his children a bicycle, he wrote to Western Union asking their recommendation. Telegrams were delivered by bicycle, so he judged their advice sound and ordered the bicycle from England.

In 1921 Mr. McCravey was elected President of the Bank of Forest. His faith and steady hand brought the bank through the Great Depression. In 1939 his son, William Davidson "Bill" McCravey, succeeded him as President, and Mr. McCravey assumed the position of Chairman of the Board of Directors. J.R. McCravey died Feb. 27, 1947 and Martha Lytle Myers McCravey died Jul. 19, 1963. She and Mr. McCravey are buried in Eastern Cemetery.

MCCRAVEY,

Mary Katharine Loyacono McCravey, artist and teacher, was born on Apr. 1, 1910 in Forest, MS where she lives and works today. She is the daughter of Mr. Reuben Julius Knoblock (b. Dec. 21, 1885, d. Feb. 3, 1972) of Lafayette, IN and his wife, who was before her marriage, Miss Mary Belle Tillman (b. Dec. 19, 1889, d. Aug. 18, 1975) of Magnolia, MS. In 1910 the Knoblocks moved to Forest, where Mr. Knoblock was instrumental in bringing Forest into the age of electricity. He also served on the volunteer fire department and was known throughout the town and county as the best man to have around in any kind of emergency. "He could do anything, fix anything, and he wasn't afraid of anything." The Knoblock home was on the site of the current Bank of Forest.

Reuben J. Knoblock, Mary Tillman Knoblock, Mary Katharine Knoblock

An example of the many paintings Mary Katharine McCravey has donated to charitable causes

Mary Katharine's artistic gifts were encouraged by her mother, Mary Tillman Knoblock, who was also an accomplished artist. Upon occasion their work has been exhibited together. Mary Katharine's younger sister, Doris Virginia Knoblock Edmondson (b. May 28, 1918, d. Feb. 14, 1999) taught for many years in the Jackson schools, notably the Little Red Schoolhouse, the Mississippi School for the Deaf, and the Mississippi School for the Blind. She was the mother of seven daughters and two sons.

Mary Katharine studied art and Spanish at Belhaven College in Jackson, MS, graduating in 1932. When she returned to Forest, she was employed as the city's first librarian, and the first library was housed in the first floor of her parents' home. As the depression deepened, and the town could no longer pay a librarian, Mary Katharine continued to work without pay.

In the late 1930s Mary Katharine began her career as an art teacher in Jackson public schools. During her summer vacations she continued her education at the Chicago Art Institute, the University of Colorado, and art colonies in Taos, NM, and Rockport, MA. She also made five trips to Europe and several trips to Mexico. In 1945 she married Joe Loyacono and many of her paintings are signed under that name.

Her reputation as an artist in her own right began to develop during her teaching tenure at Central High School. From there she moved to Provine High School from which she retired in 1968 and returned to her native Forest. On Sep. 14, 1968, she married William Davidson "Bill" McCravey, the son of Mr. and Mrs. James Richard McCravey Sr.

Mary Katharine has exhibited her paintings in solo and group exhibitions for over 25 years. In recent years her works have been included in numerous benefit art auctions, helping to raise funds for cultural, medical and social service organizations. She continues to have the pleasure of seeing many of her students embarked on flourishing careers in the arts, and she continues to be an encourager of and mentor to developing Mississippi artists.

Blue Cross Blue Shield nominated her one of its first "Ageless Heroes" In May of 2000 she was awarded a Doctorate of Humane Letters from her Alma Mater, Belhaven College.

MCCRORY, Howard B. McCrory was born Sep. 4, 1896 to James Love McCrory and Susan Etta Noel McCrory in Raworth, MS, a railroad flag stop six miles west of Forest. On Jul. 9, 1916 he married Ellis Merle Rowe (b. Jan. 5, 1894 in Dorchester NE), daughter of Dr. Ellis J. Rowe and Dr. Alma L. Rowe. The Doctors Rowe moved to Mississippi in 1906 into a small house near Forest. They were the first married couple to practice medicine in Mississippi. Dr. Ellis made his house calls in a two-wheeled horse-drawn cart and Dr. Alma rode horseback.

Howard and Merle had five children. Marion Ellis (b. Jun. 28, 1917); Elizabeth Earl (b. Feb. 21, 1921); Howard Jr. (b. Jun. 27, 1924); Mary Alice (b. May 18, 1926) and Robert Glenn (b. Apr. 18, 1930).

The family moved to Forest in January 1925 into a house on Banks Street, at the time there were no street signs. Howard was employed by the city as night Marshall. He was a lawman for 50 years starting even before he moved to Forest. He wore a .45 Cal pistol at all times, so the street became known as Pistol Street or Pistol

Ave. Even though he was known as Big Pistol he never had to shoot anyone. In 1927 he was shot in the leg by a prisoner he was transporting. He was known far and wide as a smart and efficient lawman. He knew most every local crook's modus operandi which helped him solve many cases.

Standing, L-R: Marion E. McCrory, Howard B. McCrory Jr., Robert G. McCrory. Seated: Mary A. McCrory, Merle Rowe McCrory, Howard B. McCrory Sr., Elizabeth E. McCrory Bassett

Marion married Charlie Ann Alexander (b. Sep. 21, 1920) on Mar. 2, 1944. They had one son Michael Alexander McCrory (b. Apr. 26, 1947). Charlie Ann died Jan. 24, 1955. Marion married again on Jul. 30, 1955 to Thelma Izard Patterson. Thelma had two boys, Donald P. (b. Jun. 14, 1947) and Kenneth M. (b. Apr. 18, 1949) whom he adopted. Marion worked as City Housing Officer and managed real estate. Thelma died Jan. 12, 1999.

Elizabeth married James B. Bassett (b. Aug. 2, 1920) on Apr. 27, 1942. They had three children: James B. Jr. (b. Mar. 2, 1944); Robert D. (b. Dec. 24, 1947) and Betty (b. Nov. 23, 1948). James and Elizabeth live in Dallas, TX where he operated a used car lot.

Howard Jr. married Lida Wasson (b. Apr. 4, 1930) on Apr. 15, 1949. They had four children: Dea (b. Mar. 30, 1953); Krisan (b. Sep. 3, 1956); Howard B. III (b. Aug. 17, 1958) and Alex (b. Oct. 12, 1961). Howard was a lawyer and cattleman. He died Jun. 2, 1998.

Mary Alice married Carl H. Rogers (b. Aug. 23, 1926) on Oct. 16, 1946. They had four children: Bryant (b. Apr. 24, 1948); Glen (b. Jan. 15, 1953); John C. (b. Sep. 6, 1950) and Susan (b. Aug. 10, 1957). Carl owned and operated furniture stores until he retired. Mary is a registered nurse.

Robert G. married Linda Stone (b. Dec. 23, 1934) on Sep. 1, 1956. They had two sons and an adopted daughter: James M. (b. Jul. 8, 1957), Scott Dean (b. Jan. 14, 1960), Marion E. (b. Jan. 5, 1970). Robert is a veterinarian in Benton, KY.

MCDILL, Victor Lee McDill was featured as "The Highway Gardener" in the Jul. 12, 1978 issue of the *Scott County Times.* He was renowned for gardening every nook of yard at his Highway 80 home in Forest, MS, although his eyesight was very poor. He often used string to guide him to the far end of the row when planting. Victor was 88 years old when featured.

Victor was the son of Thomas James McDill and Annie Ideliah Edwards. His grandparents were Thomas Alexander McDill and Sarah Jane Callahan; maternal grandparents were William Lindsay Edwards and Amanda Parlee Boxx. He

was born Oct. 1, 1889 in Conehatta, Newton County, MS and had 13 younger brothers and sisters.

Victor had a logging business at Lake, MS for 17 years and also worked as a carpenter. During WWI, he helped build an airport at Lake Charles, LA and he worked at the shipyard in Mobile, AL.

Victor Lee McDill

On Jan. 2, 1910, Victor married Sussie E. Carson. Their son John Singleton (b. Apr. 22, 1911) md. Sarah Corinne Singleton on Dec. 24, 1932 and had two sons, John Donald and James Lee "Jimmy." Asa Dan died at one week old. Sussie died Sep. 19, 1915.

Victor married Clara Lee Allen of Meehan, Lauderdale County, MS on Jan. 8, 1919. Their first child Frances Earlene (b. Dec. 10, 1919) md. Owen Freeman McMillan on May 5, 1938. They have three sons: Steve Owen, Terry Neal and Van Earl.

Walter James McDill (b. Apr. 8, 1921) md. Marie Kirksey and they have a son, Walter James McDill, Jr. Marie died Sep. 4, 1944. Walter then married Helen Freeny. They have two daughters: Sonya Katherine and Tonya Jean.

Rebecca Lee McDill (b. Jun. 9, 1928) is the third child. Reba married Walter Emanuel Hatch of Hillsboro. They have two children: Janice Rebecca and Walter E. Jr.

Victor Lee McDill died Jun. 23, 1984.

MCGEE, Roy Odom McGee was born to Malcolm Daniel McGee and Eula Lee Westerfield. His mother and father were the parents of 12 children (nine boys and three girls). His oldest brother died at 13 months of age, so 11 children reached adulthood. They were a large family, but a very good and decent family. They always lived in the country and raised cotton, corn, peas and other vegetables and always preserved lots of fruits and vegetables. They took their corn to the gristmill for corn meal. They raised and butchered a couple of hogs each winter. Mom milked one or two milk cows, for plenty of milk and fresh butter. Believe me, you can't beat good country food, raised and prepared on the farm and cooked on an old wood stove.

His dad usually worked in town at a lumber company or someplace at very low wages. They did not have very much cash money but they had parents that cared and took care of their family. There weren't any jobs available and they didn't have much education. All of the boys left home as soon and as fast as they could. They had folks in the military from 1940 forward and now the nephews are serving. They all managed to get a high school diploma or equivalency and some college, some with degrees. They all learned trades, married and raised decent, tax paying citizens. They are a very fortunate and thankful family for every opportunity.

Roy made a living working with the data processing machines and the big mainframe computers for many years. He then retrained and worked in law enforcement. Currently, he work for the Hunt County Judge doing special projects and is looking forward to retirement in a few years.

Roy married in 1961 to Glenda Kay Robinett. They have twin sons, Jeffery Linn McGee and Robert Kevin McGee. Glenda Kay and Roy divorced after some years. Jeff married Connie Wallace and they have two fine sons, Connor and Cameron. Kevin is divorced and has a fine son named Robert Michael. Both families are still young.

Roy remarried to Anna Lynn Flower and has five children and seven grandchildren. He has always believed in God and the Protestant religions. He was baptized as a Presbyterian but he attended other faiths more often. He is a member of the Masonic Lodge, Scottish rite and Shrine. He served as the Master of a Masonic Lodge in Dallas, TX, 1975-76

His parents and four brothers are deceased. He believes there are 27 grandchildren and about 40 great-grandchildren. To his knowledge all are sane, welldeveloped and solid citizens and take responsibility for their actions.

They mostly live in Scott County and farmed, as share croppers most of his life. He always liked raising livestock and living in the country. He currently owns a small cow-calf operation near Greenville, TX. He is very interested in genealogy and Civil War history and always likes to encourage and help people to be good citizens and set a good example for their children.

His great-great-grandparents were Phillip McGee and Martha Warren. They were also farmers and had a large family. His great-grandparents were Robert McGee and Catharine Jones. They too were farmers and had a large family. Grandparents were Jay Hugh Jackson McGee and Emma Narcissi Harvey. They had a large family and worked the land and timber.

Roy's mother's parents were Ausborn Thomas Westerfield and Eliza Smith. Her grandparents were David Westerfield and Maranda Gamble and her great-grandparents were Casperaus Westerfield and Rebecca Billingsley.

MCGEE, Vernon McGee Sr. was the son of Malcolm Daniel McGee and Eula Lee Westerfield McGee. This family lived in Scott County MS for many years. There are 12 children born in this McGee family (three girls and nine boys).

Vernon was born Apr. 1, 1933 in Jackson, MS. He was the seventh child of 12 children and attended school in Scott County until his enlistment in the military service.

Vernon McGee

Vernon McGee married first Shirley Ann Jones of Flint, MI, born to this union were two children, Vernon McGee Jr. and Charlotte Bernice McGee.

Charlotte McGee grew up in Houston, TX and is married to Dan Walsh. They resides in Houston, TX and are in the oil and gas business.

Vernon McGee Jr. grew up in Houston, TX and served in the U.S. Navy. He passed from this life at the veterans hospital in Houston, TX in October 1992.

Vernon Sr. adopted two of his brother's grandchildren, Patricia D. McGee and Heather B. McGee, both are married and live in Houston, TX.

Vernon Sr.'s second marriage was to Doctor Nancy Phipps. They live in South Dakota where they own and operate a large cattle ranch. Nancy is a medical doctor with the veterans hospital and Vernon is an investigator for the State's Attorney General in Meade County, SD.

Vernon McGee served in all five branches of the military service. His last service was with the Texas Air Guard. He served as a reservist or on active duty from Dec 12, 1950 and retired as an officer in 1998. He is most proud of his years in the U.S. Coast Guard and his assignment in Europe.

He was a secondary education teacher in Texas for 20 years. After retirement from the teaching profession, he re-entered active duty military service and retired from the military.

After retiring a second time, he earned a jurist doctorate, board certified in criminal law and a doctor of philosophy in Biblical studies.

Vernon is a life member and a past master of Baytown Masonic Lodge number 1357, Baytown, TX as well as all of the associated bodies of that organization. He is the Grand Orator for the Grand Lodge of South Dakota for the year 2000-2001.

He was commander of Group 13 Civil Air Patrol, Ellington Air Force Base, TX and retired from that organization after 25 years volunteer service.

Vernon McGee is a life member of the following organizations: Texas State Teachers Association, U.S. Coast Guard Chiefs Association, Non-Commissioned Officers Association, Reserve Officers Association, Retired Officers Association, Disabled Veterans Association, American Legion, Navy League, Marine Corps League, Masonic Grand Lodge of Texas; The Scottish Rite Valley of Houston, TX; Shriner NAJA Temple, Deadwood, SD; Iota Lambda Sigma Fraternity and York Rite College of North America.

Vernon has worked in law enforcement with the city, county, state and federal agencies.

MCILHENNEY, George Neal "Jockey" McIlhenney (b. 1895, d. 1968) was born in a farm house built in 1857 near the present location of Scott Central School. The house was located in the NW 1/4 NW1/4 Section 15 Township 7 N Range 8 E. The original location is given in notes written by Jockey in 1948. He indicates a early name of what today is called Old Jackson Road was the old Brandon to Livingston Road stage coach road. The nickname "Jockey" came from his riding horses as a young man.

Viva and "Jockey" McIlhenny. Camp house in background

Jockey's father was Dr. George A. McIlhenny (b. 1859, d. 1938). He was a dentist that traveled in a horse drawn buggy to practice and carried a wooden dental chair in the buggy. Dr. McIhenny later moved to Forest and established a practice until it became easier for patients to come to an office.

Jockey graduated from Mississippi Agricultural and Mechanical College (today Mississippi State University) Jun. 3, 1914 with a degree in electrical engineering. He was interested in science and history all his life.

Jockey married Viva Brooks (b, 1895, d. 1978) who graduated from Mississippi State College for Women (today Mississippi University for Women). Viva's parents were George A. and Martha Olive Brooks of Lake. Viva was a long time member of the Lake Garden Club and pianist for the Lake Baptist Church.

Jockey and Viva did not have children, but they were adored by their nieces and nephews. Many of the children in Lake called them Uncle and Aunt even though they were not actually related.

Jockey was employed as an engineer and executive in the ship building industry. He worked in Newport News, VA and Mobile, AL. He and Viva were in Mobile during WWII.

He invented a formula for paint that prevented barnacles from attaching to the bottoms of ships. This solved a serious marine problem. His paint was the best solution for the problem for a period of time. He established the McIlhenny Paint and Varnish Company at Lake in 1929. A complete line of paints and varnishes were produced including marine, house paints, and tree marking paint. A laboratory was built to conduct research.

Jockey and Viva moved back to Lake after WWII. He built a race track for horses, a bird dog kennel, tennis court, camp house, and ponds. He became interested in nuclear energy and Dr. Edward Teller once visited with him.

The old farm house was moved to Lake in 1946 to house the McIlhenny Museum of Science and Industry. A story connected to the old house was that Gen. Sherman spent the night in it when he came through Hillsboro. The museum housed a number of exhibits including marine, natural science, old guns, a civil war cannon ball, books, artifacts, and implements.

Jockey and Viva McIlhenny are buried in the Forest Cemetery. *Submitted by Paul F. Tadlock.*

MCLAUGHLIN, Lillie Ann Mize Mclaughlin was born in Scott County, MS near Cooperville on May 20, 1882. Her parents were James Claxton Mize and Nancy Josephine Duckworth. They moved to Forest in 1890 and built a two story house on Davis Street. They had five children: Lillie Ann, Joseph Henry, Francis Floyd, Emmitt

Lillie Mize McLaughlin, a teacher in the Forest School from 1915-52

Ross and Sidney Carr. All of the children except Lillie became lawyers. Lillie became a school teacher and was known to all as "Miss Lillie."

Miss Lillie graduated from Hillman College in 1902. Hillman College is now part of Mississippi College. Her first teaching position was in Mt. Olive, MS. In 1915 she began teaching in Forest and except for four years when her own children were small, continued there until she retired in 1952. Her love of learning was imparted to her students. She followed their careers and felt great pride at their successes in life. Her career spanned generations and she often taught children of her former students. She always had great faith in the younger generation. She usually taught in the grammar school but during WWWII taught math in the high school. Many of the math teachers had gone into service. The students who wanted to go into special programs (V-12, etc.) had to have more advanced math than the school offered. She had had these courses when she was in college and took on the task of teaching them. She studied and worked as hard as the students did. The ones in those classes successfully entered the various programs in service and she was delighted.

During the depression years people had very little money and some had little food. Her class read a news booklet called the *Weekly Reader*. Each year this booklet offered vegetable seeds for sale for a few pennies a packet. She got parents interested and urged them to plant a garden to supplement their food. Many parents did and later told her what a help it was. She also was aware that some children needed warmer clothes, a coat or shoes. She used the outgrown clothes of her family and friends and quietly saw that they were passed on to someone needy.

In 1925 she married Patrick Henry Mclaughlin. He was born in New York and grew up in Missouri. He was known in Forest as "Mr. Mac." He had come to Forest to drill an oil well. He was a widower and had a college aged daughter, Elizabeth Katherine "Betty." He and Miss Lillie had two daughters, Patricia Ann (Mrs. George Fell) and Edith Josephine (Mrs. Maxie Scott). They built a house at 709 Raleigh Street. Mr. Mac died in 1950.

Miss Lillie retired in 1952 but continued to tutor children. She often said she would like to live on a college campus and be a perpetual student. She led an active life after retirement. She taught Sunday School in the Presbyterian Church, planted roses, visited her children, kept up with five grandchildren, etc. She was young at heart all of her life and died peacefully in her sleep in 1965. *Submitted by Patricia McLaughlin Fell.*

MCMILLAN, John Wade McMillan was born in Newton County, probably not a stone's throw from the Piketon Community. He was born July 21, 1885, the fourth of seven children of Robert Mose and Lyda Futch. On May 19, 1907, John married Effie Leona Myers, daughter of Henry R. "Dick" Myers and Ida Haralson.

John and Effie moved to Ellisville, MS. He cut wood, carried it to town, and would bring food home that evening. He soon returned to Scott County. John could not read or write, but could calculate the board feet of a wagon load of logs after having the log diameters called to him. Later he operated a taxi in Forest.

John W. and Effie McMillan

Nine children were born to John and Effie. The first born, twin daughters, died at birth on Aug. 10, 1908.

Gladys Estelle (b. Mar. 15, 1910, d. Mar. 22, 1984) never married.

Eula B. (b. Jan. 23, 1913, d. Jan. 8, 1974) md. Gettis M Sanderson on Oct. 26, 1939. The family lived in California and everyone gathered for food and fellowship on their visits back home. Their son is Wallace "Wally" (b. Nov. 21, 1940).

Owen Freeman (b. Apr. 23, 1916, d. Mar. 29, 2000) was a farmer and a road construction foreman in Scott and Covington counties. He married Frances Earlene McDill on May 5, 1938, daughter of Victor Lee McDill and Clara Lee Allen. He was paralyzed in a farm accident in 1983. Frances was born Dec. 10, 1919. Children are Steve Owen (b. Dec. 20, 1942); Terry Neal (b. Sep. 12, 1950); Van Earl (b. Aug. 6, 1955).

Mable Ruth (b. Nov. 27, 1918) md. Willie Doyle "Bill" Weaver on Mar. 30, 1940. Mable owned a cafe in Sebastopol, MS and worked at the Skyway Hills Shopette. Their daughter Judy, Julia Ann, was born Feb. 10, 1944.

Myra Christine worked at WJTV in Jackson where she had the opportunity to meet a number of entertainment stars and take nieces and nephews on the local kids cartoon show. Christine married Lee Sanderson on Aug. 21, 1939. Their child Patricia Lee died at birth on June 29, 1941.

Andrew Johnson served in the Pacific during WWII and retired from the U.S. Navy. He was born Sep. 13, 1924 and married Ina Pearl Usry Feb. 7, 1947. Their children are Avis Dale (b. Jun. 26, 1950); John Andrew "Johnny" (b. Jun. 16, 1953). Johnson died Apr. 1, 1992.

Wayne was born Apr. 9, 1927 and died Feb. 21, 1998. For much of his career, Wayne worked at a Service Station in Jackson. This, at a time when auto service was provided at gas stations rather than food and snacks as at today's "convenience" stores. He married Margaret Lewis on Dec. 29, 1950. Their children are Margaret Anne Kurst (b. Dec. 20, 1946); Linda Sue (b. Oct. 23, 1954); Patricia Wayne (b. May 29, 1957); Guy Wade (b. Nov. 1, 1960).

Gaynell (b. Nov. 13, 1933) worked for the Mississippi Military Department, but returned to the Scott County homestead after the death of John and Effie. She married Harry Butler on Jan. 22, 1954. Their child is Harrolyn Denise (b. Jan. 10, 1955). Gaynell later married Carrol McNeil on May 31, 1957. Evelyn Carol was born Mar. 3, 1960. Gaynell died Nov. 21, 1978.

MCMILLAN, On Aug. 6, 1876, Robert Mose McMillan, son of Dan and Mary McMillan, was married to Lyda A. Futch, daughter of Wade H. Futch and Nancy Stewart. This union will grow to settle in most communities of east Scott County, Piketon, Goodhope, Salem, Ursytown, and the Singleton Settlement.

Robert Mose McMillan

The first two of seven children died very young. Lyda B. (b. Nov. 1, 1877, d. at age 6 on Dec. 5, 1883); Clinnie (b. Dec. 26, 1876, d. Oct. 20, 1881).

Ephram Abner (b. Feb. 1, 1882) md. Rhoda Parks (b. May 1891) on Sep. 6, 1905. Their children are Robert Clifton (b. Dec. 7, 1907); Abner Emmit (b. Feb. 3, 1910); Velma Agnes (b. Jun. 8, 1912); Clarence Newson "Buster," (b. Jul. 5, 1914). Rhoda died Jul. 6, 1914 in West Monroe, LA.

Ephram returned to Scott County and on Jan. 22, 1919 married Lydia Pearl Williamson (b. Oct. 15, 1893). Children are J.T., (b. Nov. 3, 1919); O.Z. (b. Jun. 21, 1921); Mammie Ruth (b. Jul. 20, 1923); Minnie Lee (b&d. Nov. 18, 1925); Clois Rebecca (b. Nov. 24, 1926); Irma Jewel (b. Dec. 29, 1929); Molly Blanche (b. Nov. 12., 1932); Maude Elizabeth (b. Dec. 8, 1936). Ephram died Apr. 19, 1961 and Lydia died Aug. 31, 1975.

William Oscar (b. Jul. 13, 1893, d. Nov. 15, 1962) md. Bessie L Barnes on Dec. 27, 1914. Bessie was born Sep. 27, 1899 and died Dec. 27, 1978. Children: Addie Doris (b. May 19, 1919); Clyde; Marjorie (b. Feb. 3, 1917); Louise (b. Feb. 23, 1923); and William Felton (b. Oct. 28, 1915).

John Wade, the fourth child, was born Jul. 21, 1885. John married Effie Leona Myers on May 19, 1907, daughter of Henry R. Myers and Ida M. Haralson. Effie was born Aug. 13, 1891. John and Effie are buried at Salem Cemetery. He died Mar. 19, 1964 and she on May 15, 1964. Other than a short time in Ellisville, this family lived in east Scott County. Ten children were born to John and Effie: twin girls, (b&d. Aug. 10, 1908); Gladys Estelle (b. Mar. 15, 1910); Eula B. (b. Jan. 23, 1913); Owen Freeman (b. Apr. 23, 1916); Mable Ruth (b. Nov. 27, 1918); Myra Christine (b. Jan. 4, 1922); Andrew Johnson (b. Sep. 13, 1924); Wayne (b. Apr. 9, 1927); and Gaynell (b. Nov. 13, 1933).

Minnie Lee (b. Jul. 20, 1888) md. Doncie Perminter on May 19, 1907. Doncie was born Jun. 20, 1885 and died Dec. 7, 1962. Minnie died Aug. 18, 1963. Children: Nola (b. Dec. 22, 1922); Ollie (b. Mar. 23, 1909); Eula Lee (b. Dec. 14, 1914); Coniel (b. Aug. 13, 1920).

Fannie Ola (b. Feb. 6, 1892, d. Dec. 10, 1975) md. Jacob Benjamin Hollingsworth on Dec. 15, 1907. Jacob was born Jun. 23, 1888 and died Mar. 21, 1969. Hoye Clarence was born Apr. 20, 1909; Chloteal (b. Oct. 16, 1912); Thelma Meridian (b. Jul. 1, 1914); Floyd Benjamin (b. Jun. 10, 1917); Harold Clyde (b. Jun.

10, 1920); Fletcher Jacob (b. Dec. 25, 1921); Florence Pauline, Apr. 2?, 1924; Fanny Everne (b. Apr. 26, 1928); Benny Gene (b. Apr. 22, 1930); Nina Joyce (b. Oct. 17, 1932

MCMULLAN, Milton Rolfe McMullan entered the world in January 1904 as the third child of Dillard Mc-Mullan and Minnie Ola Huff. Milton graduated from Mize High School in 1920 at the age of 16 and moved with the family to Lake in 1921. He worked for a year in his father's bank before enrolling at Ole Miss.

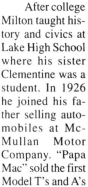

Thelma McMullan early 1950s

After college Milton taught history and civics at Lake High School where his sister Clementine was a student. In 1926 he joined his father selling automobiles at Mc-Mullan Motor Company. "Papa Mac" sold the first Model T's and A's

Milton McMullan at Lake Bank

and later sold Pontiacs, Chryslers, Dodges and Plymouths.

There at McMullan Motor, he met Thelma Boozer, daughter of James Strother Boozer and Ida Inear Russell. Thelma was his father's beautiful young secretary/bookkeeper, recently graduated as valedictorian of her class. They were married May 13, 1928. From this marriage has come four children, 11 grandchildren and 10 great-grand children. Milton served as vice president of the Lake Bank and managed the motor company after his father's death. In the early 1940s he relocated to Newton. He has written several short stories about Lake. Profiles from Lake in the Silver Age and Lake Chronicles... True Tales of a Mississippi Boyhood. His wife Thelma has written a small poetry book titled *The Slender Volume.*

Time (Mine)
I give to the sands of time,
All that my heart can hold,
Of love and friendship this hour
And Tomorrow and on until I'm old-
Too old to see or to perceive
The Gleam of the sunset's gold
That bedims my eye as I pass
Fragile and lilting things:
Words that break into song
And stories new but still old.
I ponder them as I wish
I had more to give each day
To the sands of time as I pass
On my way to the realms of new and old.
Submitted by Thelma McMullan

MCMURPHY, Colon McMurphy (b. Sep. 21, 1841 in Wilcox County, AL) was one of six chil-

dren. After serving in the Confederate Army as a young teenager, he later moved to Tuscola, Leake County, MS, and married Ida Jane Denson on Feb. 21, 1877. There were 11 children born to this couple, three of which died as infants in a span of four years. Two of the children died within two days, Aug. 24 and 25, 1886.

After the loss of the children it was believed that the "damp night air" in Tuscola caused their illness. The family sold out and moved to Harperville, MS. It was thought at that time the hilly terrain at Harperville afforded a healthier climate.

There were only two male grandsons that were born to James Coley McMurphy and Elvy Elizabeth McCormick. The oldest is James Hugh McMurphy (b. Feb. 12, 1926) and Horace McCormack McMurphy (b. Aug. 28, 1929).

Hugh McMurphy of Forest, MS, married Jonnie Jo Upton on Nov. 17 1951. She is a native of Bay Springs, MS. Two children were born to this couple. Lea Ann McMurphy who is married to Robert Burns. They have two boys, Allen McMurphy Burns and Graham Bucklin Burns. They reside in Houston, TX. The second child is Patrick Hugh McMurphy who is married to Janet Lynn Woods of Eupora, MS. The children Justin Coley McMurphy, Anna Lora McMurphy and Jenna Lynn McMurphy. They reside in Grenada, MS.

Horace McCormick McMurphy of Madison, MS married Ann Marie Linderman of San Antonio, TX on Feb. 20, 1954. One son James Martin McMurphy is married to Kay Brown of Camden, SC. They reside in Greenville, TN with their two daughters, Adrianna and Emily. All deceased family members are buried in the Harperville Cemetery or in Eastern Cemetery in Forest, MS.

MEASELLS, The name is also spelled Measles, Measels and Mizell. Some researchers believe the name was originally Meisel (German) and Maisel (French), as they lived in the Alsace-Lorraine region on the border of Germany and France.

Martha Jane Measles Peagler was born around 1805 in the Charleston area of South Carolina. The names Measles and Peagler are recorded in the Goose Creek area of Charleston, SC in the archives. She moved to Mississippi about 1841 in oxen drawn wagons. She located her second husband and family in the Clarksburg Community on the Rankin and Scott County Line in east Rankin County (also referred to as the Line Creek Community). They also lived in the Leesburg Community. She married Mr. Thomas Measles of South Carolina and they had three sons.

Her second husband was Peter Washington Peagler and it was he who accompanied her to Mississippi along with a daughter Jane Peagler who had been born to them in South Carolina. Mr. Peagler was born around 1815 in the Charleston area.

Members of the family remembered they were related to the Valentines in South Carolina who are also listed in the Goose Creek area. They also remember two members of the family not moving to Mississippi. Henry Measles and his sister Mary who married a Mr. Rudd. These two members are possible brother and sister to Tom

Measles and Liza Measles who members believe were cousins to Jessie David, Lewis Robert (Robert Lewis) and Madison Measles. These family members (Mary and Henry) visited the family after they moved to Mississippi.

The following children were brought to Mississippi: (1) Tom Measles (b. ca. 1825) md. Eliza Harrell (b. 1825 in Georgia); (2) Elizabeth Measles (b. ca. 1826) md. first, Mr. Moore (CSA Pvt. Co. B 48th Reg. MS Inf.) and second, Mr. Wilson; (3) Jesse David Measles (b. Apr. 7, 1833, d. Jan. 2, 1896), buried Spring Hill Cemetery, Rankin County, MS, married Mariah Harrell (b. ca. 1833, d. 1926); (4) Lewis Robert Measles (b. Oct. 27, 1837 d. Oct. 11, 1913) Pvt. Co. C, 39th Regt., MS Inf., buried in Mexea TX, married first, Susanne Davis (b. Aug. 8, 1838 d. Jul. 23, 1902), married second, Carrie Tennessee Alexander (b. Aug. 17, 1833 d. Aug. 1, 1904); (5) Madison Measles (b. ca. 1840, d. Jun. 22, 1862) Pvt. Co. C., 39th Regt. MS Inf., died of measles during Civil War when he walked to Pelahatchie from his army post and died at the train station); (6) Jane Peagler (b. 1840) md. Dempsey Smith, moved to Arkansas; (7) Bluford Telfair Peagler (b. 1847, d. 1889) md. Mary Callum (b. 1844) moved to Livingston, TX; (8) Georgiana Peagler married Jim Callum; (9) Becky Peagler married first, Nick Moore and second, Jack Harrell; (10) Martha Sarah McElroy married Jasper Jefferson Jackson. This family moved to Groverton, TX.

MEASELS, William Berry "Bill" Measels Sr. and Mary Tennessee "Tennie" Williams were married in 1881. They were together for 54 years, until his death in 1934. They had five children and 21 grandchildren, all of whom were born in Scott County. Mary Tennessee died in 1948. She and her husband are buried in Grovetan Presbyterian Cemetery, north of Morton.

Bill was born in 1859 to Jesse David and Mariah Harrell Measels. While still a young boy, Jesse David had moved with his mother, Martha Measels Peagler, from South Carolina to Rankin County. Tennie Williams was born in 1854 in the state for which she was named.

The family of William Berry and Mary Tennessee Measels, probably in 1902. The two women seated on the left are Tennie's sisters, Fannie Williams and Mat Williams Phipps. Tennie is seated between her nephew Willie Green Phipps and her youngest son, Jim Lane. Jesse is standing on the other side of Bill. In the back row are Nonie, Berry Jr. and Tennie's sister, Carrie Williams. Unfortunately, time has destroyed the faces of Mitchell Measels and of Bill's niece, Pearl Thompson Crapps.

Bill and Tennie raised their children in the community now known as Branch. Mitchell (b.

in 1882) md. Alice Gordon; he was followed by William Berry Jr. who married Jessie Massey; Nonie married Robert Massey; Jesse David married Mary Irby; and Jim Lane married Emma Gordon. Jim (b. 1895) was a veteran of WWI. Seven grandsons: Billy Jack and James Earl, the sons of Jesse; Fred, son of Berry Jr.; Mitch, son of Mitchell; and Lawson, Ray, and Warren, the sons of Nonie Massey, were veterans of WWII.

All of Bill and Tennie's children reared their families in or near Branch. Their son Berry built a general store that was operated by three generations of his family. Berry's grandson, W.J. Measels Jr., was supervisor for Beat 4, Scott County, for 32 years.

Bill's grandsons remember their Grandpa Bill as a man who loved to talk, a trait inherited by many of his grandchildren. *Submitted by Kay McCullough.*

MEASELS-JACKSON, Margaret Muriel
Jackson and Frederick Dudley Measels were married in 1942 at the Baptist pastorium in Morton. Fred was in the Army at the time, and they made their first home in La Mesa, CA, where he was stationed. While they were in California, Muriel worked as a bookkeeper at a defense plant.

They had met in 1938 when Muriel came to Branch to teach high school math. Originally from Moscow, a small community in Kemper County, she was the daughter of Thomas and Annie McDonald Jackson.

Because there was no high school in her community, she boarded with cousins and attended the high school at Coldwater in Neshoba County. She attended East Mississippi Junior College in Scooba and graduated from Millsaps with a bachelor of science degree in mathematics.

Muriel Measels and Fred D. Measels

Fred was the son of Berry and Jessie Massey Measels of the Branch Community. After graduating from high school at Branch, he worked for his daddy on the farm and at the family's general merchandise store until he was drafted into the Army. As a staff sergeant in the infantry, he fought in France and Germany during WWII. While in Europe, he was awarded the Purple Heart. He was discharged from the Army in October 1945, and returned home to Branch.

Muriel began teaching at Branch again, and the couple built a home on land Fred had inherited. Fred farmed and assisted his brother in managing the store their daddy had built. Fred and Muriel had two daughters, Sandra and Kay. The entire family was active at Branch Baptist Church, where Muriel taught Sunday School and was church clerk for 22 years. Fred served on the building committee for the present church.

Except for short breaks when her daughters were born, Muriel continued to teach at Branch until the county schools were consolidated in 1958. Then, she began teaching at Morton. When she retired in 1979, she had taught for more than 40 years.

Fred died in 1979 and Muriel in 1986. Their two daughters continue to live at Branch, Sandra in the home her parents built. Sandra Measels teaches English composition and literature at Holmes Community College in Goodman. Kay, who is married to Joe Harlon McCullough, has been teaching third grade at Morton since 1977. The McCulloughs have two children, David and Janice.

MILNER, Pate Wills Milner (b. 1734, d. 1788)
was born in Scotland or England, moved from the Tidewater area of Virginia to Bute County, NC, ca. 1765, and served as captain in the county militia during the American Revolution. In 1779 he deeded 100 acres to establish the town of Louisburg, NC, the county seat of Franklin County (created from a division of Bute County).

Pate Wills Milner had five sons and six daughters. Before 1840 his youngest son, Benjamin Wills Milner (b. 1786-c. 1845) moved from North Carolina to Wilkes County, GA to the same area where John Milner, his uncle, owned land and lived with his family. Benjamin had six sons and three daughters.

In 1850 or 1851 Benjamin's youngest son, Oswald Ely Milner (b. 1825, d. 1876), moved westward to available farm land in central Mississippi, following his brothers, Wilson and Matthew Dickinson, who had settled in Leake County, MS, between 1840 and 1850. The three brothers were probably attracted to that area because some of the Eley family (their mother's relatives) had earlier moved to Leake County. Oswald settled in the Cash Community in Scott County near the Leake-Scott County line, living there for the remainder of his life. Many of the children of the three brothers left Scott and Leake counties to live in Attala, DeSoto, Simpson, Smith, and Yazoo counties in Mississippi as well as in Ennis, TX.

Oswald fought in the Civil War, taking the place of an Eley, a relative, in exchange for 40 acres. A farmer and freight hauler, Oswald was robbed and killed while transporting cargo to Canton in 1876, leaving behind nine children, the youngest five to be cared for and reared by his oldest daughter, Huldah.

Three of Oswald's nine children (all born in Cash) remained in Scott County throughout their lives: Huldah L. Milner Rasco (b. 1851, d. 1906); William Council Milner (b. 1857, d. 1930), who lived in Cash, and Thomas Edward Milner (b. 1871, d. 1943), who lived in Balucta and Lillian near Hillsboro.

Six of William Council's 11 children (all born in Cash) spent their lives in Scott County. Horace Earnest Milner (b. 1889, d. 1956) lived in Contrell and Morton except for 10 years in Yazoo County. Mittie Bell Milner Brooks (b. 1894, d. 1962), Benjamin Clifton Milner (b. 1899, d. 1968), James Lafayette "Fate" Milner (b. 1901, d. 1983) and William Council "Dub" Milner (b. 1909, d. 1958) lived in Cash. William Alton Milner (b. 1896, d. 1973) lived in Cash and Forest.

Four of Thomas Edward's five children (all born in Balucta) resided in Scott County all their lives: Lessie Estell Milner Sessums (b. 1894, d. 1978) in Clifton and Ringgold; John Lyle Milner (b. 1896, d. 1959) and Zebb Thomas Milner (b. 1899, d. 1967) in Lillian near Hillsboro. Elvie Odell (b. August 1900, d. October 1900) died in Balucta; A.L. Morris Milner (b. 1902, d. 1981) spent his working life outside of Scott County but returned to live his last 10 years in retirement on the site of his father's home place in Lillian. That Milner home site is now owned by John Edward Milner of Jackson, the great-grandson of Thomas Edward Milner, the grandson of John Lyle Milner, and the son of William Edward Milner.

MIZE, Francis Floyd Mize, always called
Frank, was born Jan. 23, 1885 in the southwest corner of Scott County near Cooperville, was son of James Clackston Mize and Nancy Josephine Duckworth.

Always interested in cultural, religious and political life of the community, he enjoyed practicing law from 1905 until he suffered a stroke in the courtroom in 1959. He had a long career in public service. He served as sheriff, chancery judge, special judge, district attorney, and two terms as State Motor Vehicle Comissioner.

His wife Bessie Lee Morse (b. Jan. 8, 1888 at Montrose, MS) was the daughter of Rev. William Webb Morse and Mary Ann "Manie" Coleman Lanier. He was pastor of Forest Methodist Church.

Frank and Bessie always lived at 668 Raleigh Street in home built before their marriage in Methodist personage May 15, 1907.

Children: James Floyd Mize (died in infancy); Webb Morse Mize (attorney in Gulfport, MS); Joseph Sidney Mize (attorney); Frances Virgene Mize (Mrs. Jack Olson); Betty Lee Mize (Mrs. Raymond Conner).

The Mize family moved to Forest in 1890 when James Clackston Mize became chief deputy sheriff as result of tied election between Mize from southern part of county and a Mr. Stephens from northern part of the county. Due to widespread interest, a handbill circulated throughout the county telling terms of their mutual agreement - flip a coin to decide the election, winner—sheriff, loser—chief deputy. Mize was elected sheriff the next term and later chancery clerk.

The family built a two story house on Davis Street. Children: Joseph Henry Mize, attorney, Gulfport, MS; Lillie Ann Mize (md. F.H. McLaughlin) and is a teacher; Francis Floyd Mize is an attorney; Sidney Carr Mize, attorney, Gulfport, MS and US District Judge, Southern District Mississippi, 1937-1965; Emmette Ross Mize (md. Colbert Dudley), a teacher and attorney.

About 1930 a first cousin, Robert Madison Mize, and wife, Marsha Miller, bought the E.E. Butler house on South Raleigh next to Frank and Bessie. Their son, Frank Warren Mize, chemical engineer grew up here.

Later Lillie Ann Mize and P.H. McLaughlin built a house on South Raleigh Street. Children: Patricia Ann McLaughlin md. George Fell and Edith Josephine McLaughlin md. Maxie Scott.

Sometime later Joe Sid and wife, Virginia

Alice Cohen, built a garage apartment further down Raleigh Street. Joe Sid practiced law with his father until his untimely death Mar. 14, 1947. Their daughter, Sidney Louise Mize, md. Jerrald Nations and Virginia lived there until they moved to Brookhaven following death of Virginia's Mother.

Virginia pioneers were Jeremiah Mize and wife Tabitha, their son Henry who settled in Banks County, GA. Henry Mize Jr. came to Rankin County, MS after 1850 from Banks County, GA and Greene County, AL. Henry's son, James Clackston Mize, homesteaded in southwest corner of Scott County with wife Nancy Josephine in 1878.

MOORE, Lodwick Moore (b. Jul. 24, 1821 in Greene County, AL) was the third child of Robert Moore of Kentucky and Theodoria Ladocia Hamilton Moore of North Carolina. The family moved to Marengo County in 1821 then to Sumter County and on to Kemper County, MS where his father died in 1836. Lodwick returned to Alabama with his mother and grew to manhood there. His mother married Robert Allison of North Carolina. Lodwick married Elizabeth Thompson Nov. 15, 1847 near Livingston, AL. She was born Dec. 4, 1823 to Daniel and Sarah Thompson.

Lodwick and Elizabeth with their two children, Lou and John, stopped at old Berryville in Scott County to spend the night. They left their home in Alabama searching for a place that suited their fancy, in which to build a permanent home. The journey was overland. The husband, wife and babies had ridden in an old shay and the household goods and two Negro slave women were driven in an ox wagon by Uncle Adicus with the cattle and livestock following. The next morning they journeyed a mile and were arrested by the beautiful country. Lodwick with the slow precision that characterized his Irish decent halted his caravan to see Yockey Abbey Hill. They both realized this was the place they were looking for and set up "camp" in a small log cabin. The beautiful hill was then occupied by Indians and it took several years to get possession and build a log house adequate for the growing family for another son had been born to them. The logs for the new house were hewn by hand and the home was finally finished.

Nine other children were born to this worthy couple. Their children were Louisa Jane (b. Nov. 8, 1843, d. Jun. 2, 1902); John Roderick (b. Dec. 21, 1845, d. Nov. 16, 1916; Charles Henry (b. Mar. 5, 1848, d. Nov. 11, 1937); William Walker (b. Jan. 29, 1850, d. Jan. 24, 1936); Sarah Ladocia (b. Apr. 7, 1852, d. Jan. 20, 1944); Francis Mozelle (b. Apr. 4, 1854, d. Jun. 23, 1936); Margaret Ann (b. Jan. 11, 1856, d. Jun. 22, 1947); Colin Black (b. May 26, 1858, d. Aug. 26, 1948); Ellen H. (b. Jul. 29, 1860, d. Sep. 18, 1877); Robert Daniel (b. Aug. 18, 1862 d. Dec. 17, 1900); Donnie Etta (b. Feb. 6, 1865, d. Dec. 21, 1963); Katherine Elizabeth (b. Dec. 21, 1867, d. Jul. 26, 1960). Their daughters were educated at Whitworth College, MS.

In 1863 Lodwick enlisted in the state militia under Cart. J.C. Harper and served until the close of the war. He returned home and engaged energetically in planting and business operations. He owned 2,000 acres of land and three store buildings in Forest. He was interested in the mercantile establishment of the local Farmer's Alliance and was one of the first depositors of the Bank of Forest.

William Walker's sons, Mac and Lod, enjoyed telling about the hay fields on their grandfather's farm. "He ordered seed to improve his hay for the cows and horses. The grass grew large and tough. He wrote the company to find out what kind of seed and how to control it. The company wrote back, 'You planted Johnson grass and the only way to control it just move off and leave it.'"

Another home was built on the crest of Yockey Abbey Hill by Pat Henry who dressed every plank by hand. The brick was made from the clay off the place. This home known as Amomoor was finished Aug. 11, 1871. It still stands today near the Forestry Lod Moore Tower.

Lodwick and Elizabeth Moore

100th anniversary of Lodwick Moore Home, Aug. 15, 1971

The A&V Railroad through Scott County was put through land owned by Make Graham, Andrew Gatewood and Lod Moore. It was his slaves that constituted the major part of the labor used in this undertaking. Warren Clark, Lod Moore's son-in-law, was one of the contractor's on the railroad.

Elizabeth died Apr. 9, 1909, several days after falling and breaking her hip. Twenty days later on Apr. 29, 1909 Lodwick died after gradually growing weaker in grief. She had been his loving companion for 66 years. They are both buried in the family cemetery near Amomoor. Compiled from: *Memoirs of Mississippi; News Register,* Scott County; members of their family, Elsie Moore, Charlotte Comans, and Mable Carr.

MOREMAN-MCKENNEY: Henry Jefferson Moreman (b. 1819, d. 1910) md. Nancy McKenney (b. 1821, d. 1877). Both are buried at the Baptist Cemetery in Hillsboro, MS. They had two children, John M. Moreman (b. 1838, deceased) and Mary Frances "Mollie" Moreman (b. 1839, d. 1923).

John Moreman married Mary B. Smith (b. 1844, deceased). They had six children: Lizzie, Sarah Eulalae, Mary Nancy "Missie," Henry, Nigil A. and Aola.

Sarah Eulalae Moreman (b. 1866, d. 1950) md. Wilber Willis Cochran in 1889. Eulalae and Wilber had three children: Wilber John, Zola and Thelma. Wilber John Cochran married Sula Cordelia Johnson and they lived in Harperville, MS. They had two daughters, Eula Anne and Mary Grace.

Henry Jefferson Moreman after his accident jacking up a house—here clearing some land (early 1880s)

Mollie Moreman married Alexander Cecil "Mart" Farmer (b. 1835, d. 1912) (see Farmer-Moreman information).

Henry Jefferson Moreman was known as Marster (Master) back in those days and owned a large amount of property on the ScottLeake County lines. He mortgaged his plantation during the Civil War and after the war he lost his plantation. He then went to live with his daughter Mollie and her husband, Mart Farmer, at Harperville.

It was said that during the Civil War period, there was a place called "Sullivan's Hollow" where people would go and trade horses. Usually, people who went to Sullivan's Hollow never returned, but Marster would always go and return. The slaves would not dare venture into Smith County unless they knew for certain they would be back before nightfall.

MORGAN, Marvin Morgan was born Jan. 27, 1929 at Forest, MS to Alberdia and Doss Morgan. They had one other child, a son, T.J. Morgan. Marvin attended Scott County Training School in Forest and served a term in the U.S. Army before continuing his education at Alcorn State University. He then taught school at Sherman Hill High School in Scott County where he met his future wife, Viola Cotton (b. Oct. 16, 1933 in Kemper County). She was one of nine children. Viola attended school at Stevenson's Vocational High School at Toomsuba, MS. She received her teaching degree from Jackson State University before beginning her teaching career at Sherman Hill. Viola and Marvin were married at Forest in May 1959. One son Vince was born of this union. Vince lives in Forest and is employed by Cataphote, Inc. in Flowood.

Marvin Morgan

After teaching school at Sherman Hill for several years, Marvin and Viola taught at East Scott School where Marvin was the assistant principal, the girls' basketball coach, and assistant football coach. In 1966 he became principal. In 1970 Marvin and Viola began teaching school at Lake Attendance Center where Marvin was employed as assistant principal, class room teacher and assistant football coach. While performing their duties at Lake they both continued their education: Marvin earning his master's degree in education administration from Southern Mississippi and Viola receiving her master's degree from Mississippi State University. During this period Marvin was appointed by Gov. Waller to serve on the State of Mississippi Welfare Board.

Marvin and Viola Joined Lynch Chapel United Methodist Church where Marvin served as Sunday School Superintendent, taught Sunday School and was an active member of the choir. Viola also taught Sunday School and sang in the choir. Marvin was a frequent speaker in area churches, especially during February, Black History month. He also stayed busy with civic work, serving on the city election commission and promoting fund drives for charitable organizations. Marvin retired from his career in education due to health problems in December 1983. Viola retired in June 1990.

Marvin was always a favorite with the young people. He remained faithful to the athletic program at Lake where he was a constant participant at the pre-game pep talks. Young athletes he was associated with will remember him best for his Victory song. An award was established in his name and honor by Granville Freeman, with whom he coached many years. This award is presented to a deserving individual each year at the athletic banquet. Since Marvin's death in 1997 this award is presented by Viola and his son, Vince.

MYERS, John A. Myers, son of George Myers Sr., married Hulda Killingsworth about 1844/45 in Kemper County, MS. In 1860 John and Hulda, along with seven children and his mother Mary, were living in Neshoba County, MS. Two more children were born between 1860 and 1863.

John entered the Confederate Army on Oct. 18, 1863 at Philadelphia, MS. He enlisted as a private in Co. D 26th Regt. MS Volunteers. He was killed in the Battle of the Wilderness on May 6, 1864. His burial place is unknown. By 1870 Hulda and children were living in Beat 5 Scott County.

Their children were: Mary Jane md. Elias Theodore Clark; John Matthew md. Lucrecy Moore; Matilda C.; George W. md. Angie; James Melton md. Mary Jane Gardner; Henry; Richard md. (1st) Jane, (2nd) Martha Haralson (3rd) Ida Haralson; Andrew.

Hulda died Dec. 24, 1901 and is buried in Salem Cemetery, Scott County. Their son James Melton (b. Jan. 4, 1854) md. Mary Jane Gardner, daughter of John and Isabella (Hickman) Gardner, on Jul. 2, 1877, in Scott County. They lived their married life in Beat 5, Scott County. James was a farmer.

Their children were Matilda Ellen md. Ida Kitt Hall; Hulda F. md. James B. Moreland; J. Lee md. Nancy Annie Harrison; Jeff Davis md. Cora Belle Creel; Neely L. died at age 5; James J. md. Mary Elizabeth "Molly" Waltman; J. Floyd md. Mary Jane Myers; Mary married Ira

Theodore Creel; George md. Alma Harrell; Alma md. William Edward Harrell; Ephie md. Alex A. Harrell.

James Melton died Sep. 23, 1909 and Mary Jane died Dec. 30, 1932. They are both buried at Salem Cemetery in Scott County.

MYERS-HARRISON, J. Lee Myers (b. Aug. 20, 1883), son of J.M. and Mary Jane Gardner Myers, married Nancy Annie Harrison (b. Dec. 5, 1885), daughter of Bill Harrison and Lucy Sims, on Nov. 2, 1900 in Scott County. They had the following children: Oldest child, a daughter, died at birth Dec. 24, 1903; Leona "Onie" md. Neal Bradford; Mamie md. Milton Walters; Virgie md. Deloss Warren; Mary Lucille md. J.C. Haralson.

J. Lee Myers

J. Lee died May 4, 1918 of Brights disease and is buried in Salem cemetery. With four small girls to raise Nancy Annie met and married a widower W.T. Hales on Mar. 21, 1922. They had two children: Lodena md. Jessie Walker and B.E. md. Lorene Wallace.

Nancy Annie lived a full life raising her children and watching grandchildren come along. She died Oct. 9, 1963 and is buried in Salem Cemetery beside J. Lee Myers, her first husband.

MURRELL, Rev. Lee P. Murrell (b. Sep. 25, 1808, in Bladen County, NC) was the son of Zachariah Murrell Jr. and Emma White Murrell and the grandson of Zachariah Murrell Sr. While young, he came with his parents to Mississippi, living in several different counties. He eventually settled in Scott County, where he lived for most of his life.

In 1840, Mr. Murrell professed

Rev. Lee Powell Murrell

faith in Christ and was baptized into the fellowship of Antioch Church in Scott County, by Elder Stephen Berry. Mr. Murrell was licensed to preach by the Antioch Church in 1842, and in 1844, was ordained to the gospel ministry.

Rev. Murrell was called to Pleasant Hill Church in Conehatta in 1846 and served a total of 44 years there. He also served Bethel Baptist Church, Newton County, MS, beginning May 1847 through October 1862. He was called again to serve there in 1865 and 1866.

On Aug. 4, 1848, Friendship Baptist Church

in Leake County, MS, was organized. Lee P. Murrell, John M. Chambers and William Denson formed the presbytery with 12 charter members.

In 1864, Salem Baptist Church, Scott County, was organized and he was one of the first pastors there. In 1867, along with Rev. Dan Fore and Nathan L. Clark, Bro. Murrell organized Lake Baptist Church, Scott County, with eight charter members. In 1882, Goodhope Baptist Church was organized and Brother Murrell and Rev. Dan Fore were the first two ministers there.

Brother Murrell became a much loved preacher. He was an untiring worker in the gospel ministry. He was a gifted speaker and his labors were much appreciated by the churches. He arose to great influence and usefulness which continued with growing force while he lived. His faithfulness and devotion to the cause of Christ will be held in grateful remembrance.

Rev. Murrell married Nancy Taylor, daughter of Alfred Taylor. They had the following children: Franklin; Margaret Zelpha; Sophronia Elbridge (b. Jan. 6, 1839, d. Jul. 18, 1920) md. first, Enoch Walton and had five children, md. second, Henry Clay Emmons and had eight children; Alfred Taylor (b. Mar. 29, 1841, d. May 31, 1863 in Vicksburg during the Civil War) md. Elizabeth Pace; Elizabeth (b. in 1843) md. Dempsey Pace; Susan Eliza (b. Nov. 13, 1849) md. Wesley Graham.

Rev. Lee Murrell married second to Tabitha Bell and had the following children: Nancy Ann (b. 1853); John Lee (b. 1854) md. Mollie Smith; James Lafayette (b. 1856) md. Ida Grisham; Sarah Ann (b. Feb. 5, 1858) md. John V. Thornton; Mary Alice (b. 1859); Nathaniel Clarke (b. Aug. 14, 1860, died Aug. 17, 1933) md. Emma Roberta Day, daughter of Charles Day and Parizade Amis; Tabitha Bell.

Brother Murrell, "Uncle Lee" as he was called, closed his life in great peace on Jan. 22, 1892. He is buried at the Old Pleasant Hill Cemetery at Conehatta, MS, beside his father Zachariah Murrell Jr. He leaves many descendants in Scott County, MS.

NICHOLSON-MUSE, George Edward Nicholson Jr. and Patsy Muse Nicholson, both Newton County, MS natives, made Forest, MS home in 1988. The couple came from Newton with their two young sons, Austin Chandler Nicholson (b. Jun. 25, 1985) and Cameron Brady Nicholson (b. Mar. 9, 1988).

The Nicholsons came to Forest when George went to work at then Farmers and Merchants Bank. The family built a house on McCormick Road in Scott County and moved there in September 1990. The house was built by local contractor Bill Blossom.

Malcolm Nicholson, great-great-grandfather to George, migrated to America in 1803 from the Isle of Skye, Scotland. He settled in Wilmington, NC. His son, John Malcolm Nicholson moved to Newton County, MS as an adult and raised his family there.

Patsy's family has thus far been traced to the Mewes family in 14th century England.

George was born in Newton, MS and graduated from Newton High School. After graduation from Mississippi State University, he returned to Newton to begin his banking career at then First National Bank of Newton.

Patsy was born in Union, MS and graduated from Union High School. She also graduated from Mississippi State University and began her work in communications in Meridian, MS in 1978. She and George were married at Merrehope in Meridian in 1980 and made their home in Newton.

Both of their sons were born in Meridian, MS. Chandler was baptized in the Newton Presbyterian Church. Cameron was baptized in the Forest United Methodist Church.

NOBLIN, Robert Holmes Noblin md. Dec. 24, 1834 in Granville County, NC to Sarah Martha Adams, daughter of Richard and Sarah (Allen) Adams. She was born Dec. 24, 1834 in Granville County, NC. They are buried in Carr Church Cemetery, Smith County. Issue:

1) Louesa Marie Noblin (b. Oct. 22, 1835, Virginia, d. Sep. 12, 1859 in Pineville) md. Robert Franklin Wilkins Jan. 6, 1853, Smith County, and died a few days after her third son was born and is buried in Carr Church Cemetery. In the 1860 census the three boys were living with Robert Holmes Noblin.

2) Cephas Hardy Noblin (b. Sep. 8, 1837, Virginia, d. Sep. 30, 1897), Edwards, Hinds County, MS during a Yellow Fever outbreak. He married Margaret E. McCollum.

3) Frances Jane Noblin (b. Nov. 8, 1839 in Mississippi, d. Mar. 19, 1897 in Edwards) md. Burwell B. Boling.

4) Robert Holmes Noblin Jr. (b. Sep. 30, 1841, d. Sep. 26, 1897, Edwards) md. Sarah Ann Catherine Wilkins (b. May 15, 1839, d. Jun. 17, 1900) on Jan. 5, 1868.

5) Emily Ann Noblin (b. Dec. 18, 1844, Mississippi, d. Jun. 15, 1907), single.

6) Josephine Adalia Noblin (b. Jun. 22, 1846, d. Dec. 25, 1876, Smith County) was the first wife of Thomas Edward Anderson. They married Jul. 15, 1867.

7) Margaret Emma Loretta Noblin (b. Jul. 25, 1848, Smith County, d. Oct. 8, 1920, Edwards, MS) md. George Wm. Howie on Nov. 17, 1868. He died Nov. 24, 1911, Marion, Perry County, AL.

8) Drusilla Melina Noblin md. John Easley Anderson on Sep. 22, 1870. They are buried in Mt. Carmel Cemetery, Smith County.

9) Eramus Kannon Noblin (d. Oct 17, 1897, Edwards, MS) md. Margaret L. Howie.

10) Martha Beatrice Noblin md. Pleasant Henry Anderson. Both are buried Carr Church Cemetery, Smith County.

11) Henry Adolphus Noblin (b. Aug. 26, 1859, Jan. 25, 1863).

12) Lee Andrew Noblin (b. Nov. 4, 1861, d. Sep. 15, 1862).

13) Lazrus Crawford Noblin md. Frances J. Daniel. Both buried Homewood Methodist Cemetery, Scott County, MS. Issue: (a) Charles Rufus md. Mary Jane Dearman. Both buried Eastern Cemetery, Scott County, MS; (b) Connie Hugh md. Cornelia Barnes. Both buried Eastern Cemetery; (c) James Robert md. Ollie Ladonia Moore. Both buried Homewood Methodist Cemetery, Scott County.

NOBLIN, Thomas Noblin I was born in Mecklenburg, VA and came in a caravan with his family (ancestors of Acie Noblin) Robert

Noblin and Sarah Martha Noblin and Sarah Martha's family, the Adams, from Mecklenburg County, VA about the year 1838 (the year the stars fell).

They settled at what is now known as Homewood and at the time was occupied by a tribe of Choctaw Indians.

At this time Tom I was 11 years old. His son Tom II married Rebecca (Rasberry) Noblin (b. Aug. 1, 1829 in Alabama). To this union was born seven children: (twin) Robert Lafayette Noblin married Frances Elizabeth Wicker, died Mar. 17, 1922; (twin) Roberta Noblin married Elbert Youngblood, died Apr. 22, 1943; Ellen Noblin married William Youngblood, died Feb. 7, 1943; Jane "Jennie" Noblin married Tim Anderson, second C.A. Barnes, died Apr. 13, 1939; Pamelia Noblin married R.H. Rolf Stokes, died between 1943-48; Mollie Noblin (d. January 1974 at age 17); John Thomas Noblin married Maggie Pryor (Jan. 20, 1895), died Sep. 16, 1958.

Tom Noblin II was born Oct. 23, 1824, died Jan. 24, 1874 (50 years old). Rebecca (Rasberry) Noblin born Aug. 1, 1829, died Jan. 2, 1874 (age 45). Their 6th child Mollie died the same month as her parents. All died of typhoid fever and are buried in the Noblin Cemetery.

Children of James Thomas Noblin III and Maggie Estelle Pryor Noblin: James Otis Noblin (b. Oct. 8, 1895, d. 1913); infant son (b. Mar. 8, 1898); Jewelle Noblin (b. Jan. 24, 1900) md. Hines Winstead; Irma Noblin (b. Feb. 24, 1903) md. Guy Singleton; Myra Noblin (b. Jan. 1, 1906) md. Alton Singleton; Ercelle Noblin (b. Oct. 1, 1908) md. Paul D. Singleton; Eva Noblin (b. Dec. 18, 1912) md. Dave Franklin, Margaret "Peggy" Noblin (b. Jul. 25, 1915) md. Spinks Singleton.

Robert Lafayette "Bob" Noblin was a merchant at Homewood, afterwards a long time merchant at Forest. He died Mar. 17, 1972 and was buried at Homewood.

John Thomas Noblin's father, mother and sister Mollie died when he was 6 years old. His elder brother took him to live with him. He lived with brother Bob until his sister Jennie's first husband Tim Anderson died. Then John Thomas went to live with her and helped her rear her three children: Tom, Anna and Walter Anderson. When Jennie married Charley "Dosh" A. Barnes, John Thomas married Maggie Estelle Pryor and bought the old home site "Bumpers Place" on Tallabougue Creek in Scott County.

The Noblins, Pryors, Youngbloods and Rasberrys were among the very first settlers of Homewood.

Rufus Noblin, brother of Tom Noblin II, was gored to death by an ox in the year 1848 and was the first grave in the Noblin Cemetery which is located about one mile south of the old Homewood site.

NOEL, The Noel name has been spelled as Noel, Noell, Nowel, Nowell, Noal, Nole and possibly other ways. The Scott County family spells the name with only one "l", but our direct ancestor spelled the name Nowell. Following is the beginning of the Scott County Noels from *Our Noel Heritage* compiled by George and Alice Noel and published in July 1978.

Four of Beverly Noell's children migrated

to Mississippi from Oglethorpe County, GA in the mid-1800s. One son, William Andrews Noell settled in Vicksburg. Two sons, Robert Garnett Noell and George Washington Noell, and a daughter, Mary Catherine Noell, settled in Scott County.

Robert Garnett Noell married Susan J. Fambrough in Georgia and four children were born to this union. Susan died in Georgia and her brother raised the children. Robert and his sister, Mary Catherine Noell Michael, migrated to Scott County, MS in 1858. In Mississippi Robert married Judith Ann E. Pate.

They were parents of six children. Judith died and Robert married Cynthia Beavers. Robert is buried in Lillian Cemetery.

Mary Catherine Noell married William "Billy" Michael in Oglethorpe County, GA, and they migrated to the Lillian Community in Scott County. The Michaels were the parents of five children.

Apparently, George Washington Noell migrated to Scott County before Robert and Mary Catherine, since he married Mary Ann Meador in 1849 in Scott County. Six children were born to them. Mary Ann died in 1862 or 1863, and George married Caroline Ruth Ann Dodson Eure, a widow with two children. To this union six children were born.

A Noel Family Association was organized in 1967 and holds an annual meeting in Forest in July each year.

If you are a descendent of any of the Noels you are cordially invited to join us.

NORDAN, Council Mancel Nordan (b. Oct. 25, 1850, d. Jan. 21, 1940) with his wife, Elmira Jane Palmer, and family moved from Rankin County to Scott County in the late 1800s and purchased a farm near Morton, MS on the Old Wire Road. When no longer able to farm, they moved to Forest, MS and were there until their deaths.

Council and Jane Nordan are shown in front of their Forest Home during a family reunion in 1922

Their first child, Walter Owen Nordan (b. 1876, d. 1947) md. Annie Howard and was assistant postmaster of Forest for 26 years. Next, was Mamie Nordan who died of Flux at the age of 2; Eula Jane Nordan (b. 1885, d. 1956) md. Solomon Abner Dearman; John Elisha Nordan (b. 1886, d. 1981) md. Emma Elizabeth Dearman and was postmaster of Forest for 26 years; Eva Roberta Nordan (b. 1889, d. 1983) md. Clifton Clay Cooper, world war veteran; twin—Lolly Ann Nordan (b. 1892, d. 1979) md. Barney Otis Myer, Scott County Sheriff; Lemuel Alonza Norton (b. 1892, d. 1941), Navy veteran and mail carrier in Scott County, md. Sara Hightower.

Council and Jane were also the parents of two sets of twins and one set of triplets who were stillborn. Council was not old enough to join the Confederate Army but served as water boy for the troops.

As legend has it two Nordan brothers were fisherman of the North Sea. They sailed to the British Isle of Wight and from there, crossed the Atlantic Ocean to the East Coast of North America.

NUNLEY-MOORE, Ceasar Nunley and Ella Green came to Forest, MS as slaves. Ceasar came from Atlanta, GA and Ella From Birmingham, AL. After the slaves were freed they met, married and had seven children: Georgia, Staton Baker, Dave, Lucy, Elizabeth, Mamie and Will.

Laura Gatewood was born a slave in Demopolis, AL. After the slaves were freed her parents brought her to Forest. She was 5 years old. Laura married Baker Moore and three children were born: Tinnie, Mamie and Frank.

Staton Baker Nunley (b. Nov. 11, 1874, d. Jan. 25, 1959) and Mamie Moore (b. Apr. 14, 1884, d. Sep. 5, 1957) were married in Forest in 1900. To this union 14 children were born: Kermit, Baker, Janie, Ceasar, Richard, Albert, Hattan, Lucile, Eddie, Elizabeth, Dave, Frank, Mamie Laura and Sammie Louise. Three sisters are still living, Elizabeth Nunley Reed, Los Angeles, CA; Mamie Laura Nunley Crudup, Westland, MI; and Sammie Louise Nunley Rigsby, Forest, MS.

Staton Baker was a good provider. Even during the Great Depression he had a job at the compress. He helped to build it and was hired as a night watchman and a fireman when there was cotton to be pressed. In the winter when it snowed, Baker's footprints were the first ones up the road. He did not have a car and had to walk. Of all the years worked, he was late only once. The men were standing around waiting. He said to them, "There's one thing about it, you can't come to work in your sleep. If you wait a few minutes I'll have the steam ready?" He loved his boiler and took good care of it. There was never an explosion. He knew just how much coal to put into it to keep the steam at the proper gauge. He didn't learn this from a book. This was a God given talent.

In 1939 Staton Baker became 65 and had to retire. He was the first black person in Forest to draw social security benefits. He received $21.03 per month. His children, Mamie Laura and Sammie received $7.01 each. This was the talk of the town.

Mamie was a wet nurse. She would nurse white babies whose mothers didn't have enough milk for their babies. Since Mamie had a baby almost every year, she always had plenty of milk. These babies grew up to be lawyers and doctors and never forgot about Mamie. They came back to visit and thanked her for nursing them. She boarded many teachers and students who came to Forest to live and work.

Staton Baker and Mamie were God fearing and law abiding citizens. They tried to raise their children that way. They always said, "Let your word be your bond. If you make a debt, pay it. If you borrow something, return it. If you move something, put it back where you found it." They believed that "excuse me, thank you, and please"

would open many doors. They were very active members in Lynch Chapel Methodist Church.

NUTT, The Nutt family has been in this country for over 250 years beginning, with William Nutt of Augusta County, VA in the 1740s. This family followed the Great Wagon Road migration route from Philadelphia, PA to Augusta, GA as they moved into Georgia.

The Nutt family consisting of William and Eleanor Nutt and children: Eleanor, John, Andrew and William Jr. lived in the Waxhaw and Twelve Mile Creek area of Anson County, NC, then moved in 1766 to present day Kershaw County, SC where they lived until about 1810. During this period of time Andrew (son of William and Eleanor) and his wife Margaret had four children: Andrew Nutt Jr., Samuel Nutt Sr., Mathew Nutt and William Nutt Sr.

Samuel Nutt Sr. and wife Jennett Mackey Nutt had nine children, two of which moved into Marion County, GA with their families. Samuel Nutt Sr. died in Marion County, GA at age 88 years while his wife Jennettt Mackey Nutt was more than 84 years when she died.

Andrew Nutt, son of Samuel and Jennett, married Jane Curry and had eight children, while Samuel R. Nutt had three children.

Children of Andrew Nutt and Jane Curry Nutt were William Christopher Nutt (b. 1811, d. 1857 in Marion County, GA) md. Desdemonia Ann Newberry and had 10 children; Samuel M. Nutt (b. 1816, d. 1869 in Scott County, MS) md. Damarious Jackson (Fielding Franklin Jackson's sister) and had four children; John C. Nutt (b. 1817); Carolina Jane Nutt (b. 1819, d. 1875 in Scott County, MS) md. Enoch Jackson (Fielding Franklin Jackson's brother) and had seven children; Elizabeth J. Nutt, (b. 1820); Harriet Missouri Nutt (b. 1828).

Samuel Nutt Sr., Andrew Nutt, Samuel R. Nutt and their children owned land and farmed in Marion County, GA near the town of Buena Vista, GA.

In 1858 Samuel M. Nutt's family, Desdemonia Nutt's (Samuel's sister-in-law) family, Enoch Jackson's (Samuel's brother-in-law) family sold their holdings in Marion County, GA and moved to Mississippi.

The Samuel M. Nutt family and Enoch Jackson family settled in Scott County around the Forkville area. Desdemonia Nutt and her 10 children settled in Leake County, MS around the Good Hope area.

The children of Samuel M. and Damarious Jackson Nutt were Nancy George (b. 1842, d. 1928); Andrew (b. 1845, d. 1865); William C. (b. 1847) md. Willie Williams; Fielding Franklin (b. 1849, d. 1927) md. Martha Jean Champion and had three children.

Martha Jean Champion Nutt died in childbirth in 1887. Fielding Franklin never remarried but raised his three children with the help of his sister Nancy George Nutt. Children from this marriage were Augusta Jean "Gussie" Nutt (b. 1880, d. 1903); Samuel "Sam" Robert Nutt (b. 1883, d. 1944); William M. "Bill" Nutt (b. 1884, d. 1941). Gussie and William never married.

Samuel Robert married Nancy Elizabeth Kitchings and had 11 children, all married and had families of their own. Many descendants of this Nutt family still live in Scott County.

ORMOND, The J.R. Mitchell Family, Joe Reat and Cora Alice Mitchell, better known later as Papa Joe and Mama Mitt and three sons: Loren C., Harry L. and Chester came to Scott County, Forest with the opening of Bienville Lumber Company. Loren came first, along with Rob Boyter and Evan Allen. Their parents and many others: Howells, Davenports, Williamsons, Hoods, Coopers, Franklins, Neills, Parkers moved from Alberta, LA in 1914.

Loren met Fannie Crook, daughter of Claude William and La Una Culley Crook of Forest. Papa was a cotton buyer and moved his family to Athens, GA. When war was declared, Loren, Harry Banks, Marion Christian and Ned Rew enlisted and were sent to Camp in Louisiana.

Loren and Fannie Crook were married in Atlanta, GA Feb. 28, 1918 and lived at Camp Beauregard until he and his buddies were sent to France. Fannie then went back to Georgia, where MayBeth Mitchell was born Mar. 29, 1919. When the Troop Train came through Athens, they made a short trip stop and Loren saw his daughter for the first time—she was six weeks old. He carried her all through the train for the soldiers to see. They were discharged in Louisiana and Loren came to Athens and worked in the cotton business for several years. When MayBeth was ready for third grade they moved to Forest where she graduated from Forest High School in 1936 and Belhaven College in 1940.

In 1942, Oliver Ormond, son of Ida Eastland Ormond and the late Robert Fletcher Ormond, and MayBeth were married. Oliver, a graduate of Forest High, Delta State and Cumberland School of Law, was honorably discharged from Air Corps. In 1941 he began training as a special agent in the FBI and served for 11 years. During WWII he was undercover agent in Mexico. MayBeth and daughter, Loren, lived in Forest with parents. When the war ended, they were sent to Weslaco, TX where Beth was born in 1947. Other offices included, Detroit, Newark, Washington, DC, San Antonio, TX, and New Orleans. From there they went to Arlington-Alexandria to work in the CIA. Jan was born in Alexandria, VA in 1954. That fall, Oliver went to Anaco, Venezuela to work for Socony Mobil. The girls and MayBeth joined him in the spring of 1955; we loved living in the oil camp.

On Sep. 3, 1957 Oliver, along with five other Americans, was killed in a plane crash in the mountains of Venezuela. It took days to find the bodies. Again they came back to Forest and her parents. They just added more rooms! All three girls graduated from Forest High. Loren and Beth both from Belhaven College and Jan from Mississippi College.

Loren served as Mississippi's Miss Hospitality in 1962 and traveled over the U.S. She taught school in Jackson, met and married Ben McKibbens of Laurel. They have lived in Harlingen, TX for 22 years and have four grown children: Kib, Missy, Merridy Sims and Woods. All are college graduates.

Beth taught school in Jackson before going to Washington, DC for a summer job in 1976 and remained there until her death with breast cancer in 1995.

Jan also went to Washington for a summer job in 1976 and stayed. In 1986 she married Larry Sherman of Connecticut. They have two children, Charlie, 13, and Cory, 11 and live in Clearwater, FL.

They tell me I've been writing for the *Scott County Times* for 30 years it does not seem possible.

O'SHIELES, Audie Mae was born in Madden, Leake County, MS on Jul. 18, 1907 to Otho Davis Loper and Emmett Ross (Edwards) Loper. Her sister, Etoile was born on Jun. 14, 1910 followed by William Prentiss (b. Apr. 12, 1912); Otho Davis Jr. (b. Feb. 21, 1914); Sara Frances (b. Nov. 9, 1916); Mildred

Audie Mae (Loper) O'Shieles

Elizabeth (b. Feb. 18, 1920); and Opal Jackson (b. Dec. 27, 1921). An infant sister (b. in 1905), William Prentiss and Otho Davis Jr. are deceased.

Audie's family moved to Forest where she attended public school, graduating in 1925. She went to Mississippi Woman's College in Hattisburg for two years and then to Draughn's Business School. Returning to Forest she worked in the Scott Count Courthouse.

In 1925 she met Len Floyd O'Shieles from Texas who was drilling an oil well near Forest. On Sep. 19, 1929 they were married in her parent's home. In the next few years the couple lived in Shreveport, LA and Jackson, MS. While living in Jackson a daughter Wilma was born on Feb. 1, 1932. In 1934, Len Floyd moved his family to Rosenberg, TX where he had grown up. A son, Robert Len, arrived on Jun. 22, 1934 followed on Nov. 21, 1938 by twin daughters, Martha Jean and Mary Ann. Martha lived only two days.

For many years Audie worked in retail businesses. Floyd worked for Humble Oil Company then later went into business for himself.

Starting in the 40s and continuing for 30 years, Audie and Floyd enjoyed working with the youth and young adults in their church. Many get togethers were held in their home. Although it has been years since she did this, several from these groups still drop by to visit with her. Floyd passed way in May 1993. They had been married for 64 years.

Audie continues to live in her home in Rosenberg. Her son Robert Len and his wife Sue live close to her and check on her daily. Daughters Mary and her husband Ken Stuart are located in Atlanta, TX and Wilma and her husband J.D. Hutsell in Mountain Grove, MO.

Audie enjoys visiting with her friends and family, walking about a mile a day, and working in her yard. She is still very active and looks much younger than her 93 years. *Submitted by Wilma O'Shieles Hutsell.*

PACE-HARRIS, George Alfred Pace (b. Mar. 12, 1878) was the son of George Washington Pace and Laura Ellen Erwin. George Alfred's father, George Washington Pace was born in the spring of 1852 on May 21 in Connehatta, MS as the tenth child and youngest son of Thomas Jefferson Pace and Jincy Ann Touchstone. At age

17, George Washington Pace traveled to Henderson County, TX with his widowed mother to where his brother Tony and two sisters, Mrs. Wiley Thornton and Mrs. John "Jake" Thornton, lived. While in Texas he married Laura Ellen Erwin and became a farmer.

George Alfred Pace (known as Alfred) was the third of four children born of this marriage. Shortly after the birth of their fourth child, Laura Ellen died in 1881 and was buried in Caleen Cemetery near Athens TX. Following her death, George Washington Pace returned to Scott County and in 1882 married Sally A. Finlayson. This marriage produced five children. In the town of Forest, MS, the Pace Street is named in honor of George Washington Pace.

George Alfred Pace married Sarah Naoma Harris, age 24, on Apr. 12, 1903. Their two daughters, Blanche Ruth (b. Jan. 13, 1904) and Margaret Ellen (b. Jan. 12, 1907), were both born in the Piketon Community. Alfred Pace was the first mail carrier for Route 1, Forest, including the Ringgold Community and surrounding areas as far north as the Piketon area. This mail delivery was from the Forest postal office and a buggy was used for delivery. Later, Alfred was employed as a supervisor at a spoke and stave mill in the Piketon Community which shared an artesian spring water supply with the local Choctaw Indian Community. He purchased timbered land in the Ephesus School Community and moved into a small house. He sold the timber and hauled logs to a dummy line leading to a saw mill near Lake, MS.

After clearing the land, he built a larger house and became a farmer again. He loaned money to the less fortunate to be paid back as they were able. He was active in church and community affairs, with the three-room school being the center of the community at that time. He was known for his honesty and integrity.

Naoma taught in a one-room school near Chunky, MS for a year before she married. She was a true help-mate and quite thrifty, making clothes for herself and their two girls. She re-trimmed hats to look like new. Naoma's greatest possession was a new organ which she learned to play by the instruction book, and taught her daughter Margaret Ellen to play.

Alfred and Naoma lived by, and reared their girls by the Golden Rule, "Do Unto Others As You Would Have Them Do Unto You." Sarah Naoma Pace died Mar. 10, 1965 and George Alfred Pace died Oct. 15, 1966. Both were buried at Antioch Cemetery.

PAGE, James Polk Page, one of four Page brothers to live in Scott County, was born Nov. 19, 1849, in Oktibbeha County, MS, the son of William H. Page of Bedford County, VA and Sophronia Busby, of Madison County, AL. He married Sarah Margaret Bullard (b. October 1848, in either Coosa or Tallapoosa County, AL), one of three daughters of Thomas J. Bullard and Elizabeth Amanda McEwen.

Often erroneously referred to as "Poke" or "Pope," James Polk Page had an older sister, Mary Frances Page, who married Robert Jasper McEwen, uncle of Sarah Margaret Bullard. The McEwens moved to Scott County, as did brothers Davis Page, Charles M. Page and Emmett Page. Alonzo Page lived in Lamar County, TX

and was buried in Caviness. Sallie B. Page married John Calhoun Bishop and was buried in Webster County, MS. Anna Eliza Page, rescued by Polk Page from abusive foster parents in Oktibbeha County, married James Morris Buntyn and was buried in Newton County.

James Polk Page and Sarah Margaret Bullard's first child, James Henry Page (b. Dec. 30, 1871, d. Sep. 3, 1954) md. Mary Virgie Lyle; second child, Dora Elizabeth Page (b. Dec. 21, 1873, d. Jun. 4, 1960) md. William Thomas Lyle; Aldon Page (b. September 1877, d. Aug. 27, 1921) was a murder victim; Clementine Virginia Page (b. Oct. 19, 1879, d. Mar. 20, 1950) md. Robert Elonzie Waggoner. William Page (b. February 1882, d. Jun. 2, 1966) md. Willie Brassfield Bryant.

Rebecca Page (b. Mar. 15, 1884, d. Feb. 17, 1982) md. first, Ernest Jeffcoat and second, Ben Strong. She was buried in Lakewood Memorial Park, Jackson, MS. Josie Page (b. Aug. 25, 1885, d. Apr. 13, 1971) md. James Everett Bailey. Sarah Almeda Page (b. Dec. 24, 1887/9, d. Oct. 29, 1976) md. first, Rice Latimer and second, William Russell Pettigrew.

Thomas Arthur Page (b. Aug. 15, 1891, d. Feb. 28, 1958) was never married. Claude Verton Page (b. Nov. 16, 1894, d. Aug. 27, 1937) md. Earline Harrell.

James Polk Page died May 16, 1904 and was buried in Bishop Cemetery, Morton, MS, beside his brother Emmett. Sarah Margaret Bullard Page died Mar. 5, 1921 and was buried in Morton City Cemetery in an unmarked grave. *Submitted by Barbara Sudduth Lyle.*

PAGE, Peyton Page was born in Carolina County, VA about 1776 and married there in 1801 to an unknown lady. They had three or four children, but there is no worthwhile information on a fourth one. William Humphrey Page born in Bedford County, VA, a twin sister Tabitha Page and John Guthrie Page.

William Humphrey Page married first (name unknown) and had three children: John C., age 6 in 1840 Bedford County census; William H. Jr., age 3; and Emily age 1.

James Henry Page, 1906

William married second, Saphronia Busby and had six more children: Mary Page (b. 1846 in Madison County, AL) and moved with family in 1847 to Oktibbeha County; James Polk Page; Alonzo Page married (name unknown) and lived in Texas; Davis Page married first, Grogan and second, Melinda Lang Walter; Charlie Page married first, Martha McLemore and second, Ann Herring; Emmett Page married Sallie Robinson Miles; Sallie Page married Calhoun Bishop and lived in Oktibbeha County, MS, Ann Page married J.M. Buntin and lived in Neshoba County, MS.

James Polk Page (b. in 1849) md. Margaret Bullard and had 10 children; James Henry Page md. Mary Virgie Lyle; Dora Elizabeth Page md. William Thomas Lyle; Jasper Alton Page never married; Clementine Virginia Page md. Robert Elonzo Waggoner of Scott County, MS;

William Caley Page md. Willie Brassfield Bryant and had one son Billy G. Page and one step-son J.E. Bryant; Josie Morton Page md. J.E. Bailey; Sarah Alameda Page md. first, Rice Latimer and second, William Russell Pettigrew; Thomas Arthur Page never married, Claude Verton Page md. Erline Harrell; and Rebecca Leona Page married first, Earnest Jeffcoats and second, Benjamin Strong.

The above named James Henry Page was a naturalist and his ability to clearly observe all that he saw whether it was animal or plant form. He was well informed in geography and history. He was a landowner and farmer and had timber interest. He also enjoyed hunting and fishing and was an expert marksman with a firearm.

PAINE, Bernice McGee Case Paine, tenth child of Eula Lee Westerfield and Malcolm D. McGee. They were encouraged to work hard and put God first in their lives. It was their decision to teach them values that would be life changing for their family. They were quality parents and wonderful people.

Bernice McGee Case Paine

Bernice had many aunts, uncles and cousins in Mississippi. She had a great life and two wonderful sons, John A. Case Jr. and Malcolm D. Case, and three wonderful grandchildren: Stephanie, Tanis and Johnathan. Life is 10% what happens and 90% what I do with it.

They were happy because her mom had what it takes. Happiness doesn't come from one's position, but from one's disposition. Her most special times as a child were with her parents, brothers and sisters. Bernice had special times shared with her dad. He would tell her all about his mom and dad and they would drive in the country at Forest, MS where his boyhood home was. Even though she never knew her grandparents, her dad through stories brought them to her, so in her heart, she felt like she knew them. Because of the love her dad had for his folks, they each had great respect and love for one another.

Bernice is now a Grandmother herself. They were all alike, they wore second-hand clothing, played Button, Button, Who's Got The Button. But think of this, all their life they had a child in hand, just think of the joy when after all odds they reached for a hand and found it was God.

History is brief, but it does reveal changes we all make everyday. Our greatest triumph is rising every time we fall. *Submitted by Bernice Paine.*

PALMER, Bobbye Ruth Palmer, daughter of Homer Stanton Palmer and Johnnie Ottice Palmer, was born Oct. 17, 1923. Her great-great grandfather was James Benjamin Palmer (b. ca. 1799 in North Carolina and died in Smith County, MS). He married twice, and Bobbye's father and mother are descendants of half-brothers from these two marriages.

James Benjamin served in Beauchamp's Company, 42nd Alabama Militia during the Creek Indian wars.

His first wife was Lovie Wise, probably of North Carolina. Their only child was James Lemuel (Jeems) Palmer, born in Eufaula, AL, and died in Scott County. MS.

He served in the 54th Alabama Regiment during the Civil War, the only one of four brothers to return home after that conflict. When his unit surrendered he was in the hospital in Mobile, suffering from a hernia, therefore he was never paroled.

During the war he was sent to Florida to make salt for the troops by boiling seawater in pots. Apparently it was not known then about the huge domes of salt under the soil in south Louisiana and Mississippi.

He married Mary A. Bullock, born in Eufaula, AL, and died in Scott County, MS. They are buried in Line Creek Church Cemetery, southwest of Morton. Their children were Jane P. Norden, George Washington and James Westley.

George Washington was Bobbye's grandfather. He was born in Eufaula, AL. He was 16 years old when he moved with his family to Kemper County in 1876, then to Scott County.

He married Jessie Eunice Tibbs, daughter of James Anderson Tibbs, formerly of Tennessee, and his second wife, Virginia Corinne Bennett of Morton. They are also buried in Line Creek Cemetery. They had seven children who lived to grow up: James Clyde, a train engineer for a lumber company in Morton; Homer Stanton; Verna Ray Lindsey; Lois P. Hodges; Ethel, a registered nurse who worked in Morton many years; and Nell P. Wiggins.

Homer Stanton Palmer married Johnnie Ottice Palmer, who was also descended from James Benjamin Palmer through his second wife, Nancy Ann Jones, born in Georgia and died in Smith County, MS. They are buried in the old "Ditch Cemetery," better known as "Bezar" near Liberty Church at Raleigh, MS.

William Alexander "Billy" was the ninth of their 12 children, born in Eufaula, AL and died in Scott County, MS. He married Julia E. Russell of Smith County, MS, and is buried in Line Creek Church Cemetery. They had a store in the Homestead Community near Cooperville.

Their oldest son John Benjamin married Ida Belle Cooper, both of the Springfield Community south of Morton, she being the daughter of Richard "Dick" Cooper and his wife Harriet Ann Edwards. John and Ida are buried at Line Creek Church Cemetery.

Harriet's parents were Jackson J. and Annbery Drummond Edwards of Polkville, MS.

This Edwards family is descended from Morgan Edwards, a pioneer Baptist minister and author of North Carolina.

The Drummonds are descended from James Drummond, first provincial governor of North Carolina.

Dick Cooper's family first came to America when James immigrated from Stratford-on-Avon, England to Trenton, NJ. after hearing William Penn's great story of the opportunities in America. He first bought land in New Jersey, then in 1683, he purchased a lot in Philadelphia, PA. He was a second cousin to James Fenimore Cooper.

James' son William moved to Virginia where his son Fleet was born. Fleet was a Revolutionary War patriot.

Below is an insert from *The Cooper Family* by Murphy Rowe Cooper.

Revolutionary Oath Of Fleet Cooper, Senior

The following is from Wheeler's *History of North Carolina*, pages 138, 139. "By Act of Assembly, passed at New Bern, Nov. 15, 1777.

"I, A.B., do solemnly and sincerely promise and swear, that I will be faithful and bear true allegiance to the state of North Carolina, to the powers and authorities which are or may be established for the government thereof, not inconsistent with the Constitution. And I do solemnly and sincerely declare, that I do not believe in my conscience, that neither the king of Great Britain, nor the Parliament thereof, jointly with the said king or separately, or any foreign prince, person, state, or potentate, have or ought to have any right or title to the dominion or sovereignty of this State, or to any part of the government thereof. And I do renounce, refuse and abjure any allegiance or obedience to them, or any of them, or to any person or persons put in authority by or under them, or any of them. And I will do my utmost endeavors to disclose and make known to the Legislative or Executive powers of the said State, all treason and traitorous conspiracies and attempts whatsoever, which I shall know to be made or intended against the said State. And I do faithfully promise that I will endeavor to support, maintain, and defend the independence of the said State, against him the said king and all other persons whatsoever. And all these things I do plainly and sincerely acknowledge and swear, according to these express words by me spoken, and according to the plain common sense and understanding of the same words, without any equivocation, mental evasion, or secret reservation whatsoever. And I do make this acknowledgment, abjuration, renunciation and promise, heartily, willingly and truly, so help me God."

There were 25 signers to this oath of obligation. Fleet Cooper's name was 17th on the list. This Fleet Cooper was the ancestor through whom the applicants for membership in the Daughters of the American Revolution qualify.

Fleet's third son was William Cooper, born in Duplin County, NC. He enlisted in the Revolutionary War, Apr. 20, 1776, and was given an honorable discharge 2-1/2 years later in order that he might become a minister.

He was a pastor in several Baptist churches in North Carolina, then in 1814, he and his second wife, Martha Thames moved with some of his sons and their families by covered wagon along the Chickasaw Trail to Monticello in the Mississippi Territory.

William and Martha settled in Bogue Chitto where he was a pastor of several Baptist churches, wrote hymns, and helped to organize the Pearl River Baptist Association. He is buried just outside of town, dying in 1821.

His son James was 8 years old at the time. He and his mother moved to Smith County, then when he grew up he had a store near Homewood in Scott County, where he married Celia Rasberry, daughter of Benjamin Rasberry of Smith County.

James' mother, Martha, later married Colonel Dias, a veteran of the Battle of New Orleans, and is buried at Polkville. James is buried at Springfield and Celia in Hinds County.

James and Celia's oldest son, Richard "Dick" Cooper was 18 years old when the Civil War started. He joined Co. D, 6th Mississippi Regiment, Lowery's Division, Adam's Brigade, General Hood commanding, where he became a corporal. He was a mule driver.

His first battle was at Shiloh, TN, where 300 of the 425 men of his regiment who were present were killed.

He also fought in the battles of Corinth; Port Gibson (where his brother, Joseph, and an uncle were killed); Vicksburg; Baker's Creek; Jackson, MS; Chattanooga; Nashville and Franklin, TN.

The night of Jul. 3, 1864, Dick's commanding officer told his company that Vicksburg, would surrender the next day, that they were at liberty to make their escape that night if they cared to take the risk, that they could rejoin the company if they succeeded. This Dick Cooper did.

There were two battles at Nashville. In the last one, Major Pat Henry, Rock Searcy, and Dick Cooper were the last to leave the ditch.

It was December, very cold, and they were almost naked. Dick was barefooted, so he "borrowed" a pair of shoes from a Yankee. He was never captured, wounded or sick.

When he returned from the war, he and Harriet started farming near Springfield Baptist Church, south of Morton. He also had a water mill, cotton gin, sawmill and store. Later he had a general store on Main Street in Morton, where his youngest son joined him in the business.

He was elected County Supervisor for two terms, serving one as President of the Board. He and Harriet are buried in the Baptist Church cemetery at Springfield.

Note: Richard "Dick" Cooper was not given a middle name, but when his mail and business papers kept getting mixed up with another Richard Cooper, owner of a newspaper in Jackson, he added the middle initial "C" to his own name, thereby solving the problem.

Born to their union were Alva Warner Cooper, a lawyer and public defender of Forest; Emma C. Hall; Rodolphus "R.D." Cooper, a lawyer and police judge of Meridian; Mattie C. Morehead; Minnie C. Livingston; Nettie C. Campbell; William Richard Cooper, a Baptist minister; Ida Belle C. Palmer; Murphy Rowe Cooper, a Baptist minister and author of Richmond, VA; Della C. Williams Jarvis; Phenie C. Davis Hartsel; Addie Lucy C. Leonard Sterling and Albert Taylor Cooper, a merchant of Morton who served several terms as mayor.

Ida Belle Cooper married John Benjamin Palmer and they became the grandparents of Bobbye Ruth. They are buried in Line Creek Church Cemetery.

Born to them were Willy Livingston, Etoile P. White, Richard Miley, Lona Mae P. Walters, Marvin Major, Ottice P. Palmer, Emma Lee P. Stegall, Christine P. Doyle, Spurgeon Lee Palmer, Lozine P. Stegall and Roby Daniel.

John and Ida owned several farms in Scott County during their married life. At the time of Bobbye's birth they lived in the Homestead Community near Cooperville.

Ottice and Homer had a farm next to theirs. In the spring of 1920, John and Ida still had five children living at home as well as Ottice and Homer, who were staying with them while their own house was being built, when a tornado came one night and completely destroyed their house and scattered the livestock.

Their youngest daughter, Lozine, age 6, was blown, along with her bed, across the road, however no one was seriously hurt. Sometime after that Homer almost died from the bite of a black widow spider.

In 1929, Ottice, Homer and Bobbye moved to Caldwell Parish, LA, where Homer worked for a lumber company, managing a sawmill at Kelly, LA, where their son, John Aubrey, was born Mar. 20, 1930.

John Aubrey Palmer married Marzelle Kelly. Her parents were Reuben and Lucy Pace Kelly of Lake, MS. Their daughters are Deborah Lucy and Kimberly Joyce.

The business transferred Homer to Sicily Island, LA, in 1935, but in 1939 he decided to leave the sawmill and return to farming. He was too young to fight in WWI, he would have been called in the next draft, and in WWII he was too old, but like many men in like circumstances he worked in construction of military installations, including Camp Shelby, MS; Ft. Hood, TX and Oak Ridge. TN. He would come home from Oak Ridge telling about building big buildings then other workers would come along and cover them up with soil so they only looked like part of the landscape, but no one knew why.

Then after the atomic bombs were dropped that ended the war with Japan, we found out that Oak Ridge was where they were produced.

At Ft. Hood he fell 30 feet from the roof of a building, landing on his knees and elbows on a concrete floor, suffering multiple broken bones and other injuries, but before the war was over he was able to go back to work.

Ottice and Homer are buried in Eastern Cemetery at Forest.

Bobbye Ruth Palmer married Perry Franklin Gibson. *Submitted by Bobbye P. Gibson.*

PALMER, In 1939 Homer Stanton, his wife Johnnie Ottice and daughter Bobbye Ruth (Palmer) Gibson moved to Scott County from Louisiana. Their son John Aubrey went to school in Forest and Morton, and graduated from Forest City High School, Forest City MO.

In 1947 John Aubrey enlisted in the U.S. Navy and remained until retirement in 1967. During his watch in the Navy he served on many and with ships, naval stations and the U.S. Marine Corps. He was involved in many battles in Korea, in the Bay of Pigs Invasion of Cuba and the Cuban blockade. His last duty station was the U.S. Naval and Marine Corps Training Center, Gulfport, MS. He retired with the rank of Chief Petty Officer in 1967.

On Nov. 12, 1949 he married Marzelle Kelly of Lake, MS, in Vallejo, CA. They have two daughters, Deborah Lucy and Kimberely Joyce.

Deborah Lucy Patton was born in Oakland, CA and now lives in Saucier MS. She works for Pacific and Orient Ports, Gulfport, MS, a company that is responsible for loading and unloading most of the ships that come into Gulfport.

Kimberely Joyce Palmer who was born in Beaufort, SC and now lives in Gulfport, MS and is employed with Resource Consultant Inc. as a counselor supervisor at Gulfport Job Corps Center.

Since retiring from the U.S. Navy John has worked for Gayfer's Dept. Store, Biloxi, MS, then with Mississippi Power, Watson, Generating Plant, Gulfport, MS until retiring in 1992. *Submitted by John Aubrey Palmer.*

PARKMAN, Thomas Marion Parkman (b. Oct. 5, 1840 in Scott County, MS) was the second child of Edmondson Parkman and his wife Phebe Richardson, the daughter of Elijah and Patsy Guion Richardson. Edmondson had moved to Scott County some time before 1840 from Lawrence County, MS, where he had married Phebe Mar. 10, 1827. Edmondson died by 1850 and Phebe was left to raise their children alone.

The Thomas Marion Parkman Family in 1904. Back Row: Alvin Parkman (Charlie's son), Barney Traxler, James Leon Parkman, Luther Preston Parkman, Dave C. Parkman, Sarah Hawkins Parkman.
Charlie E. Parkman, Thomas Jefferson Parkman, George Ben Parkman. Front Row: Leila Parkman Traxler, Leroy Parkman (James's son), Mary Jane Hawkins Parkman, Shelby Parkman (Charlie's son), Thomas Marion Parkman, Henrietta J. Brown Parkman, Minnie Belle Parkman, Fannie Lingle Parkman, Clyde Parkman (Charlie's son), Nancy Dora Lingle Parkman, Emma Elizabeth Parkman (George's daughter), Delta Parkman (Charlie's daughter).

During the Civil War Thomas Parkman enlisted in the Army on Apr. 1, 1862 and was assigned to Co. C, 39th Regiment of the Mississippi Infantry also know as Johnston's Avengers. He served under Captain M.V. Collum and left for Grenada where it was recorded that they had only 41 defective flint lock muskets. From there they were sent to Vicksburg, MS; Baton Rouge, LA; Tennessee; Corinth, MS; Oxford, MS; and finally to Fort Hudson in Louisiana. On Jun. 8, 1863 after much fighting the fort surrendered and Thomas was taken prisoner. He was paroled in July 1863 from a prisoner of war camp in Port Hudson, LA.

Shortly after the war Thomas married and had two children: Lucy Anne Parkman (b. 1867) md. Ben M. "Letha" Hawkins and Charles E. Parkman (b. 1869) md. Fannie Lingle. Research has failed to discover a marriage certificate which would identify their mother's name and no tombstone has been located for her. In the Scott County, MS 1870 census, Thomas is a widower and living in the household with his mother, his brother Eddy, his sister Martha, and his daughter Letha. His youngest child Charles is shown living with his sister Susan and her husband Thomas Lard (Laird).

Thomas was married for the second time to Henrietta J. Brown on Sep. 12, 1878 in Scott County, MS. Of this union was born eight children.

Their first child was Dave C. Parkman (b. Nov. 12, 1879) who married (1) Sarah Hawkins and (2) Lizzie Lingle; George Ben Parkman (b. Nov. 19, 1881) md. Nancy Dora Lingle; James Leon Parkman (b. Aug. 8, 1884) md. Mary Jane Hawkins Nov. 15, 1903 in Scott County, MS. He died Sep. 23, 1951 and is buried at Searcy Cemetery in Pulaski, Scott, MS; Leila S. Parkman (b. December 1887, d. October 1912) md. Barney Traxler; Thomas Jefferson Parkman (b. December 1890, d. June 1947) md. Era Westbrooks Nov. 24, 1917; Luther Preston Parkman (b. Feb. 28, 1895) md. Adelaide Drummonds Feb. 6, 1915 in Scott County, MS; Minnie Belle Parkman (b. Jun. 30, 1901) md. Clyde Thomas and moved to Wynne, AR. Their last child was Bernice Josephine Parkman (b. Jun. 20, 1905). Bernice later married a Mr. Champion and resided in Arkansas.

Thomas spent his life in Scott County farming. He and Henrietta are buried side by side at the Old Hardshell Baptist Church Cemetery south of Pulaski, MS.

James Leon "Jim" and Jennie Hawkins Parkman had three sons: Leroy, Lamar and Wayne. Lamar was this author's daddy and his only son. He married Peggy Sue Warren from Homewood and they have a daughter, Cheryl, and three sons: Louie Jr., Brian and Phillip. Louie Sr. also has a daughter, Anita, by a previous marriage. Her mother is Earlene Harvey of Ludlow. After retiring from Pearl River Valley Water Supply District, Peggy and Louie Sr. have moved back to Pulaski and live on the original Parkman land. *Submitted by Louie Parkman.*

PEAGLER-DENSON, Peter Marion Peagler (b. 1883) and Bessie Kate Denson (b. 1902) were married in 1923. Marion and Kate were born in the Branch Community where they established their home. They were dedicated Baptist, good parents, prosperous farmers and citizens of vision who supported progress and goodwill.

Their son, Marion Wayne Peagler (b. 1924) and Annie Marie Calcote were married in 1947. Marion Wayne and Annie Marie's two sons are Donald Wayne and Marion Lee. Their daughter Katie Ethel (b. 1928) md. W.J. Measells Jr. in 1948. Their children are Dr. Clark Measells, Mrs. Melodie Measells Pickett and Mrs. Rebecca Measells Moss. Katie and W.J. were divorced in 1990.

Peter Marion Peagler was the fifth child of 10 children. His father, Peter Washington Peagler Jr., was born in Madison County in 1848. Peter Jr.'s father, Peter Washington Peagler Sr., was born in South Carolina in 1805. Peter Jr.'s first wife was Martha Jane Measells and she died soon after they married. Peter Jr.'s second wife was Elizabeth "Liza" McElory, the mother of Peter Marion Peagler. After the death of Elizabeth McElory, mother of six of the 10 children, Peter Jr. married Rebecca Lyle and they had four children.

Bessie Kate Denson Peagler, wife of Peter Marion Peagler, was the third of 11 children. Her parents were Shadrick James Denson (b. 1868) and Bessie Webb Denson (b. 1879). Shadrick's father was the Rev. William Denson. William's father, Nathaniel Denson, moved in 1811 from Ashboro, NC to near the Pearl River in Rankin County. This place is known as Denson Landing.

Rev. William Denson was known as "Parson Billy." He was well educated, very successful in farming, prominent in leadership, and the builder of churches. He served in the Mississippi Legislature, pastored several churches and helped to establish the Mississippi Baptist Convention.

Bessie Webb Denson, wife of Shadrick James Denson, was the daughter of Henry Webb and Annie Moore Webb.

PEARCE-BISHOP, John David Pearce (b. Jul. 27, 1932 in Amory, MS, Monroe County) md. Ouida May Bishop (b. Aug. 4, 1932 in the Frogtown Community, southwest of Forest) on Jun. 9, 1952 in Vicksburg, MS. They moved from Columbus, where John was with the IRS, to Forest in 1973 with their son Pete and daughter, Judy Melanie. John communted to Jackson until he retired in 1990. Ouida worked for Meridian Production Credit until 1985 when she went to work for the Post Office and retired in 1994. When they moved to Forest they lived in a mobile home while their home was being constructed. They moved into their completed home, which was built by local contractor Cecil Bailey, in February 1976.

John's father, Pete Pearce, was a native of Tilden, MS in Itawamba County and his mother, Maggie Brown Lee, was the first white child born in Amory after it was incorporated in July 1889. After graduating from Amory High in 1950, John attended Itawamba Junior College in Fulton and Mississippi College in Clinton. After a two year stint in the Army, John went back to M.C. and graduated in 1957. He went to work for the IRS in 1957 and was stationed in Clarksdale where he remained until moving to Columbus in 1968. Ouida graduated from Forest High in 1950 and went to Mississippi College where she met John.

Ouida's father, Robert Murphy Bishop, was from the Frogtown Community. Her mother, Eula May Windham, was from Homewood, Ms. John and Ouida had four children. Sarah Gayle (b. Jul. 20, 1956 in Jackson at the old Baptist Hospital) md. Kenneth McDill in 1975. They had one daughter, Kimberly Michell (b. Jul. 12, 1976). Gayle and Kenneth divorced and Kimberly lived with her mother. Gayle was killed by a drunk driver on Sep. 23, 1989 and Kimberly came to Forest to live with John and Ouida. John David Pearce Jr. (b. Nov. 22, 1957 in Jackson, MS at the old Baptist Hospital) had Muscular Dystrophy and died May 17, 1973. Pete Pearce (b. Jan. 22, 1963 in Clardsdale, MS) md. Leslie Dukes from White Oak, MS. They had three children: Thomas Pete (b. Aug. 31, 1987); Tamara Leann (b. Oct. 1, 1989) and Taylor Brooke (b. Aug. 10, 1992). Judy Melanie Pearce (b. Mar. 19, 1964 in Clardsdale, MS) md. Robert Denton and they had one child, Brandi Nicole (b. Aug. 22, 1981). Melanie and Robert divorced and she later married Grady Austin. They had two children, Jon Charles (b. Jun. 20, 1991) and Abby Christina (b. Dec. 18, 1993).

Kimberly has four children: Twin girls Randi Gayle Carter and Shelby Leigh Carter were born May 17, 1993. Kimberly and Randy Carter divorced and she later married Alex Harrell. Kimberly and Alex have two children, Devin (b. Apr. 28, 1998) and Samuel E. (b. Jun. 29, 1999).

PEARSON Rev. Jesse Marion Pearson (b. Mar. 23, 1821 in Jasper County, GA, d. Aug. 24, 1905 at Ludlow, Scott County, MS) was the son of William Head Pearson and Mary White. He married (1) Elmira Black on Dec. 12, 1843, Tallapoosa County, AL, the daughter of Judge John Black and Eliza Lawrence. At her death in 1885 he married (2) Mrs. Lucy Emma (Waggoner) Rushing on Apr. 29, 1888 at Ludlow. Jesse Marion Pearson, his wife Elmira, his mother Mary, and other family members are buried at Cash Cemetery in Scott County.

Back: William Lawrence Pearson and William Rushing. Front: Rev. Jesse Marion Pearson and Lucy (Waggoner) Rushing. Photo taken Mar. 29, 1888, Ludlow, MS.

He was ordained to the full ministry on Aug. 20, 1868 and served at Jerusalem Baptist Church, organized the New Hope Church, and preached at others in the area. He first appears on the 1859 Scott County Tax Rolls but was in the county by 1857, coming from Macon County, AL directly to Scott County where his mother had purchased a large tract of land on Coffee Bogue Creek. He served as Justice of the Peace for Scott County from 1879 through 1892. The family is enumerated on the Scott County census for 40 consecutive years (1860-1900). During the Civil War he and his brother John Pearson were captured by the Yankees and carried to Camp Chase, OH in 1864 and kept there for 14 months.

Jesse Marion and Elmira (Black) Pearson were the parents of the following 10 children, four of whom were born in Scott County: William Washington Pearson (b. 1844, d. in the Civil War); Mary Eliza Pearson (b. 1846) md. William M. McKenzie; Sarah Elizabeth Pearson (b. 1848) md. John Hodge Vineyard of Arkansas; Jesse Marion Pearson Jr. (b. 1850) md. Annie Elizabeth Lloyd; John Lawrence Pearson (b. 1853, d. 1854); John Thomas Pearson (b. 1854) md. Martha Lucy Buckner; Tallula Caroline Pearson (b. 1858) md. Shadrach James Denson; Elmira Buenna Pearson (b. 1861) md. her cousin John Marion Pearson; Charles Ewell Pearson (b. 1864) md. Margaret Spinks; and William Lawrence Pearson (b. 1866) md. Neva Eliza Waggoner. *Submitted by Charles P. Phillips.*

PETTEY, The Petteys were among the first settlers in Scott County. Thomas M. Pettey (b. 1800) and Louisa Roberts Pettey (b. 1808) came into Scott County around 1830. In the same year, Louisa's father, Robert Whyte Roberts, brought the rest of his family to Scott County from Alabama. Robert W. Roberts served Scott County as circuit judge, the state of Mississippi as a representative and served as a Democrat to the 28th Congress of the U.S. from 1843-47. Thomas M. Pettey served as postmaster of County Line Post Office 1841-48 when the post office moved to Newton County.

Mr. and Mrs. Thomas Landon Pettey on their 50th wedding anniversary, Nov. 5, 1946

Thomas M. Pettey's son, Robert L. (b. 1826 in Tennessee) md. Mary Ann Butler (b. 1832). Her parents, Landon C. Butler and Elizabeth Byrn Butler owned what is now known as the Burnham Plantation. In 1856 the Butlers sold the property to John McCabe, left Scott County and settled near Palestine, TX.

On Nov. 5, 1896, Robert L. and Mary Ann's son Thomas Landon Pettey (b. 1868) md. Mary Ann Rebecca Saxon (b. 1875). Her parents were John H. Saxon (b. 1832 in Georgia) and Martha Sant Saxon (b. 1832 in Tennessee). They were also early Scott County settlers.

Tom and Becky had nine children: Orin Columbus (b. Oct. 3, 1897, d. Sep. 7, 1899); James Gleen (b. Sep. 21, 1898, d. Oct. 10, 1989); Andrew Woods (b. Nov. 25, 1900, d. Sep. 25, 1970). These three were born at the Saxon home, known as the Wood's place near Steele. Mary Eva (b. Sep. 2, 1903, d. Aug. 3, 1992); Martha Iva (b. Apr. 27, 1906, d. Aug. 7, 1928) were born at the McElhaney place near what is now Scott Central School. In 1906, Thomas L. Pettey bought a place from Will Hamilton in the Pea Ridge Community, three miles north of Harperville. The house on this place had been used as a school. When the Pettey family bought the place, the school was moved further down the road. The name of the school was Oak Grove, later known as Pea Ridge School. The remaining four children were born at this place. Bertha Mae (b. May 23, 1909, d. Dec. 15, 1995); Merle Amanda (b. Feb. 13, 1911); Thomas Wright (b. May 17, 1913); and Clyde Austin (b. Jul. 11, 1918).

The Petteys never moved again. Thomas L. served as supervisor and Justice of the Peace for Scott County for many years. He was church clerk for Ridge Baptist Church. The family raised cotton, corn and cattle on this farm. Eight of Tom and Rebecca's children grew up and attended school in Scott County. Orin died at age 2. Thomas Landon Pettey died at age 91 after a long life of service to his family and community. Rebecca died at age 87, a quiet loving wife, mother and grandmother who loved and appreciated her home and family. "Miss" Becky was at her best cooking and keeping her home. They are both buried at Harperville Cemetery.

Janette Leach Sawyer and her sister Rebecca Leach Baldwin submitted this family history in memory of their grandparents, Thomas and Rebecca Pettey, and their mother Bertha Pettey Leach, who was called home on Dec. 15, 1995. She, her husband Ernest Leach, and son CWO James W. Leach (killed in Vietnam)

are buried in the Beulah Cemetery in Simpson County.

PETTIGREW John Newton Pettigrew (b. Jan. 14, 1838), son of Thomas M. Pettigrew and Elizabeth B. Elliott in Tuscola, Leake County, MS, married Mary Jane Smith, daughter of Robert Palmer and Nutty Newton Alverson Smith of Scott County.

John N. and Mary Jane Smith's oldest child, Mary Newton "Mollie" Pettigrew (b. Sep. 17, 1863 in Leake County) md. George W. Anderson, son of Charles C. Anderson and Nancy Ann Bolling. She died Dec. 20, 1953 and was buried in Ludlow Cemetery. William Russell Pettigrew (b. Oct. 15, 1865, d. Jul. 30, 1953) md. first, Emily Florence Britt and second, Sarah Almeda Page Latimer.

Samuel Pettigrew (b. Sep. 7, 1867, d. Sep. 8, 1868) was buried in Lena Cemetery. John Thomas Pettigrew (b. Jul. 24, 1869) married first, Cora Farmer Parrish and second, Sarah Estella Keahey, whose family had moved to Rockwall County, TX, from Scott County. His third wife was Geneva Flowers and the fourth, Daisy Mable Webb. John Thomas Pettigrew died Feb. 16, 1949, in Rockwall, TX.

Robert Pettigrew (b. Nov. 14, 1871, d. Sep. 14, 1872) was buried in Contrell Cemetery. Henry Franklin Pettigrew, M.D., was born Jul. 16, 1873 in Ludlow, his death record states, and died Mar. 23, 1937, in Malakoff, TX. He married Amanda Pearl Wilkie in Rockwall County, TX.

Minnie Josephine Pettigrew (b. Feb. 18, 1876, in Hinds County, according to her Bible records, d. Jun. 21, 1959 in Kosciusko, MS) md. first, Felder William Sudduth of Attala County, whom she had met when he was visiting his relatives Richard Angus and Cynthia Herring Sudduth. Richard's father and Felder's father were first cousins; Cynthia's mother and Felder's father were sister and brother.

Minnie Pettigrew Sudduth married second, James Brown, in Danville, IL.

Claudia Pettigrew (b. Aug. 3, 1878, d. Jan. 19, 1912) md. Charles M. Day, son of Robert M. Day and Olivia Fairchild. Claudia's four young children were cared for by their Pettigrew grandparents and later moved to Texas with their father, whose second wife was a Pettigrew cousin of their mother. Eva Pettigrew (b. Nov. 16, 1880, d. Aug. 15, 1883) was buried in Lena Cemetery.

Mary Jane Smith Pettigrew (d. Feb. 6, 1917) and John Newton Pettigrew (d. Sep. 11, 1928, in Kosciusko, MS) were both buried in Contrell Cemetery. *Submitted by Barbara Sudduth Lyle.*

PULLEN, Henry Pullen (b. 1769 in Delaware, d. 1851 in Newton County, MS) md. Sarah in Georgia where their first six children were born. The Pullens arrived in Lawrence County, MS about 1818 but they lived there only a few years. They were in southern Hinds County between Terry and Utica in the 1820s. Some of their neighbors were John B. Stewart, James Weaver, Thomas Futch, Elizabeth and William Goodson and James and Richard Stewart. They, along with some of their neighbors, sold their land and moved to Newton and Scott County in the mid-1830s.

Their children were John (b. 1798 in Geor-

gia, d. 1860 in Texas); Ruby (b. ca. 1802 in Georgia); Stephen (b. 1804); Charity (b. Feb. 25, 1806 in Georgia, d. Sep. 7, 1893 in Louisiana) md. James Henry Weaver in January 1828 in Hinds County; Edward (b. 1810 in Georgia); Henry (b. 1813) md. Louisa Stewart Dec. 27, 1831; Loid (b. before 1815 in Mississippi, d. before 1866 in the Civil War) md. Louisa Ray on Jul. 4, 1833; Matilda Pullen (b. Mar. 10, 1815, d. Mar. 6, 1893) md. Joseph Stewart Apr. 7, 1831. Wiley was born in 1823. He married Lydia Stewart. Lydia was probably related to Joseph and Louisa Stewart, who also married Pullen children. James was born about 1826 in Hinds County. Several of these children along with their families migrated to Texas and Louisiana after the Civil War.

RANDALL-CLARK, Frederick B. Randall (b. 1793 in Virginia) md. Sarah Ann Clark (b. 1809), daughter of a Georgia farmer, on Jan. 7, 1827 in Forsythe, GA.

Edward Franklin Randall

In an interview made by Kaaran Martin of Pasadena, TX, with Call Randall, a grandson of Frederick and Sarah dated Jul. 10, 1973, Frederick died Jun. 24, 1876, in Newton County, MS and is buried at Bufkin Cemetery in Newton, County. Sarah died after 1880 and is buried beside him.

The children of Frederick and Sarah were Franklin, a mechanic who went to Texas; Samantha md. Wes Hosea; James B. md. Deliah Ann Hammons; John B. md. Virginia Boswell; Mary md. Joseph Warbington; Rudolphus C. married Martha A. Ott; Charles W.

They moved from Georgia Jan. 29, 1852 and bought 80 acres of land from E.A. Durr and wife Martha H. located E 1/2 SW 1/4 Section 20-Township 7 Range 17E Lauderdale County, MS.

They lived there for 10 years and Apr. 14, 1862, Frederick sold his land for $800 to W.P. Andrews.

Frederick, James B., John B., and Rudolphus moved to Newton, County near what is now Caney Creek Road according to land deeds. In the 1870 census Frederick and Sarah were living with James Benton.

Frederick filed for a pension from the War of 1812 on Oct. 21, 1874. He filed again in 1875. He was 84 years old at this time. Sarah filed several times before her death too.

James B. enlisted in the Confederate States Army at Enterprise, MS Aug. 22, 1862. He was with Co. K 1st Regt. Inf. He was temporarily attached to Co. D. 39th Regt. MS Vol. It was told when he came home from the war, he was riding an ox.

James' brother John B. was with Co. H. 8th MS Regt. Inf. He enlisted at Marion, MS Apr. 27, 1861 at the age of 23. Rudolphus C. was with Co. I, 37th Regt. MS Inf.

James Benton Randall married Deliah Ann Hammons Jan. 3, 1856 in Lauderdale County, MS, the daughter of Jobe and Deliah Hammons.

Their children were Sarah A.; William; Eugenia Alice married William T. Monk; James Warren married first, C. Hollingsworth and second, Emma Perritt; Deliah married Jules J. Roberts; Willia; Edward Franklin married first, Ella Loper and second, Bertha Rainey.

James Warren was a farmer and blacksmith. Edward Franklin (b. Mar. 11, 1885, d. Aug. 27, 1950), the youngest son was a sawmill operator and farmer. He married Ella Loper on Jul. 2, 1914. They had two children, Jesse Ozro Randall (md. Mary Louise Edwards) and Lillie Bell Randall (md. Henry Lee Jones). Several years later Edward Franklin married Bertha Rainey and they had three daughters: Ruth (Randall Harper Ferrell); Annie Mae Randall Hinton and Mary Katherine McSwain. *Written by Sylvia Ann Randall Roland, GG-granddaughter of Frederick and Sarah.*

RASBERRY, Benjamin Rasberry, son of Benjamin and Sarah Rasberry, was born in Georgia on Jun. 4, 1797. He married Mary Ann Tullos in September 1818 in Pike County, MS. She was born Dec. 10, 1802. The family moved to Smith County, MS by 1825 and between 1834 and 1841 were living in Homewood in Scott County. Their children were Martha Rasberry md. Shadrack Thames; Richard "Dick" Rasberry md. Mary Bradshaw?; Celia Rasberry md. James Cooper; William Green Rasberry md. first, Jane Noblin and second, Mary Ann Gibson; Rebecca Rasberry md. Thomas Noblin, Purity Rasberry married Wilson I. Russum and Elizabeth Rasberry md. a Mr. Rhyne/Rhymn. Other children were Emily Rasberry, Ben Rasberry and Sarah Rasberry.

William Douglas Rasberry Family ca. 1903. Standing l-r: Green David Rasberry, William Douglas Rasberry, Tiny Rasberry, Bryan Rasberry, Tilman Rasberry, Bessie Rasberry. Sitting l-r: Mary Ann "Polly" (Gibson) Rasberry, Millie Ann (Bradshaw) Rasberry, Sallie Rasberry. (another son, James Dolan Rasberry had not yet been born when this photo was taken).

By 1850 the Benjamin Rasberry family had moved to Louisiana and in 1852 Benjamin died at his residence in Morehouse Parish, LA. On Aug. 22, 1860 Benjamin's widow Mary Ann sent a letter from Lafayette Parish, LA to her son William Green Rasberry and a daughter (probably Celia Rasberry Cooper) in Mississippi encouraging them to move to Louisiana:

"...Well Green me and Allen made a very good crop this year and we have tended 50 acres land ... load up your wagon and come here. There is corn enough made here for you and Cooper ... me and Dick have enough land for you..."

William Green Rasberry and his first wife, Jane Noblin had four children: Philadelphia

Rasberry, Mary Rasberry, Rufus Rasberry and Martha Jane Rasberry. Jane died in 1855 and is buried in Homewood Cemetery, Scott County, MS. On Jan. 14, 1858, William Green Rasberry married Mary Ann "Polly" Gibson, daughter of Ambrose and Lucinda Gibson, both formerly of South Carolina. They were the parents of three sons: James Newton Rasberry, Simeon A. Rasberry and William Douglas Rasberry. During the Civil War, William Green Rasberry served in Co. D, 6th MS Vol. He was killed at the Battle of Little Bayou Pierre near Port Gibson, MS on May 1, 1863 when he was struck in the leg by a cannonball. This left Polly to care for their three little boys, all under the age of 5. In December 1879 their first son, James Newton Rasberry, was killed in a horse race near Morton, MS. Simeon A. Rasberry married Malissa Caroline "Callie" Myers in 1884. The third son, William Douglas Rasberry married Millie Ann Bradshaw, daughter of David Autrey and Sarah (Easterling) Bradshaw in Scott County, MS on Nov. 1, 1888. They had seven children: Tiny May Rasberry md. Ben Everit, Green David Rasberry md. Lela Mae Liles, Thomas Tilman Rasberry Luna Echols, Henry Bryan Rasberry md. Timmie Fortenberry, Bessie Eular Lee Rasberry md. Schley Varner, Sally Velma Rasberry md. Willie Johnson and James Dolan Rasberry md. Anna Lucille Liles. William Douglas Rasberry died on Feb. 7, 1907 and his wife Millie Ann died Sep. 11, 1942. They are both buried in Concord Cemetery.

RICKS, William Ricks (b. 1780 in South Carolina), son of John Ricks, married 1808 in Sumter County, SC to Martha Ward, daughter of Benjamin Ward, a Revolutionary War soldier, and Patience Ricks. William moved his family to Washington County, AL in 1820. After several other moves they settled in Scott County, MS in 1834 where William bought land and was elected the county's first probate judge.

William and Martha Ricks had four children:

1) Robert Eldridge (b. 1809 in South Carolina) came with his father to Scott County where he bought land in 1835. In 1836, Robert married Martha Smith, daughter of John J. Smith and Margaret Butler, daughter of John Butler and Mary Ann Jones. Elizabeth Smith, Martha's sister, married Hiram Eastland and they were the great-grandparents of Senator James Eastland of Scott County. Robert and his family went to Karnes County, TX in 1852 with the Burnall Butler family. Robert died there in 1865.

2) Sarah Ann (b. 1811 in South Carolina) md. Burnall Butler. (See Burnall Butler)

3) William W. (b. 1814 in South Carolina) md. Lucinda Sullivan in 1833 in Hinds County, MS. After Lucinda's death William married Frances. He bought land in Scott County in 1837, sold it in 1839 and moved into Newton County. From here he and his family accompanied Robert Ricks and Burnall Butler to Texas. William settled in Live Oak County, TX.

4) Mary (b. 1820 in Alabama) md. first Mr. Butler in 1835, Scott County. Candasa Ware Butler, their only child, was born 1836. In 1839, Mary and Candasa moved with William W. to Newton County. Here in 1841, Mary married Powell Taylor, son of James Taylor of Scott

County. After they moved back to Scott County in 1845, Powell joined his father as member of the Antioch Primitive Baptist Church. In 1852 Candasa Ware Butler married in Scott County to Hiram Pullin, son of John and Mary Pullin of Scott County. In 1856 Powell and Mary Taylor, Hiram and Candasa Pullin, and Levin, Thomas and Henry Pullin traveled to Karnes County, TX. John Pullin followed later. He died there in 1867. Mary Taylor died in 1869. Hiram Pullin was killed in a shoot-out at Daileyville in 1886. Candasa died in 1916.

William Ricks and Martha Ward were divorced 1830 in Hinds County. William and his second wife Mary had Elizabeth (b. 1832), John (b. 1834) and Richard (b. 1836) who went to Karnes County; Stephen, Suzanna and Landon.

Martha Ricks's second husband was Mr. Payne. As Granny Payne she walked from Mississippi to Karnes County, TX to visit her children. Visit over, she walked back home. She died in Bosque County, TX in 1870 on a return trip home. William Ricks died in Scott County 1855.

John Wofford, a teacher in Scott County in 1850, went to Karnes County, TX in 1851. Here he established Wofford's Crossing on the San Antonio River. He married Nancy, daughter of Powell and Mary Taylor, and became the grandfather of the Wofford family in Texas.

RIGSBY-NUNLEY, E.J. Rigsby, the eldest of two sons of John Rigsby and Minnie Graham Rigsby, was born May 5, 1925 in Forest, MS. The other son to this union was John D. Rigsby.

Sammie Louise Nunley, the 14th child of Staton Baker Nunley and Mamie Moore Nunley, was born Oct. 7, 1926 in Forest, MS. The other children to this union were Kermit, Baker, Janie, Ceasar, Richard, Albert, Hattan, Lucile, Eddie, Elizabeth, Dave, Frank and Mamie Laura.

E.J. and Sammie grew up, fell in love, and married in Forest, MS. To this union three children were born: Jeriece (b. Mar. 3, 1945), Joyce Marie (b. Oct. 28, 1947), and Eddie James (b. Nov. 16, 1949).

E.J. was a loving husband, father, and a good provider. He worked for the Illinois Central Railroad, Scott County Co-Op, Lewis Plumbing Company, Carruth Pipeline Company that bought natural gas to Forest, United Gas Company, and helped to build Interstate 20. He was a veteran of the U.S. Army and served during WWII. E.J. died Mar. 13, 1997.

Sammie Louise was a loving wife and is a loving and devoted mother. She instilled in their children good moral values and continues to support them in the things they need to succeed in life. She is a loyal and active member of Lynch Chapel United Methodist Church where she holds many positions. Sammie was one of the first three black females to be hired by Sunbeam in Forest. She is very active in community services. Their children graduated from E.T. Hawkins High School in Forest, MS and graduated from college.

Jeriece Rigsby Hill graduated from Tuskegee University (Tuskegee, AL) in 1964 with a BS degree in social studies. After graduation, she moved to Chicago and met and married Richard Hill. To this union two children were born, Richard Hill II and Jeriece DeLynn Hill. Jeriece moved to Los Angeles, CA in 1976. She now resides in Lancaster, CA where she is employed by the state of California Employment Development Department as a program manager.

The Rigsbys from l-r: Eddie James, Jeriece, Joyce Marie, Sammie Louise and E.J., 1966

Richard Hill II graduated from Quartz Hill s High School (Quartz Hill, CA). He attended the University of California, Santa Barbara, Harold B. Washington College (Chicago, IL), UCLA, University of Southern California, and Tuskegee University (Tuskegee, Alabama). He is a senior computer software engineer and lives in Atlanta, GA.

Jeriece DeLynn Hill graduated from Quartz Hill High School (Quartz Hill, CA). She received a BS degree in civil engineering with a minor in environmental engineering from UCLA. She attended Howard University School of Law (Washington, DC) and received a juris doctorate.

Joyce Marie Rigsby graduated from Jackson State University (Jackson, MS) in 1970 with a BS degree in elementary education and a minor in social studies. She furthered her education at Mississippi State University (Starkville, MS), and the University of Southern Mississippi (Hattiesburg, MS). She married Alnard Lovelady and Billy George Handford (Forest, MS). She is a loving and devoted aunt to her niece and nephews. Joyce has devoted 30 years of her life to educating children in Forest and Morton, MS. She is currently employed as an elementary school teacher at Forest Elementary School (Forest, MS). She lives in Forest, MS.

Eddie James Rigsby graduated from Jackson State University, Jackson, MS in 1971 with a BS degree in chemistry. He has been employed by the U.S. Food and Drug Administration for 29 years as a chemist and investigator. He married Clemmie Dianne Mapp of Forest, MS. They currently reside in Jackson, MS.

Clemmie Dianne Rigsby attended Jackson State University and The University of New Orleans (UNO). She graduated from UNO with a BA in elementary education. She is employed by the Jackson Public School District (Jackson, MS) as an elementary teacher.

Eddie and Dianne have three sons: Keith Douglas and Kevin James (twins), and Kelton Nicholas. Keith and Kevin graduated from Eleanor McMain Magnet High School (New Orleans, LA). They received a BS degree in biology from Jackson State University (Jackson, MS) in 1998. Keith attends The University of Tennessee School of Medicine (Memphis, TN). Kevin attends The University of Tennessee School of Pharmacy (Memphis, TN).

Kelton is currently a junior attending Morrah High School in Jackson, MS.

RISHER, Charles Ray Risher (b. Jan. 20, 1937) and Minnie Jean Cooper (b. Sep. 18, 1938) were married on Jul. 7, 1962 in the Springfield Baptist Church, Morton. His parents were Jack and Sue Risher and her parents were Spurgeon and Roberta Cooper. Both were graduates of Morton High School. He attended East Central Community College and Mississippi State. She graduated from Mississippi College. They have lived in Scott County most of their life and on Blossom Hill Road for 33 years.

Charles and Minnie Jean have been members of the Forest Baptist Church most of their married life where he has served as a deacon and she taught 3-year-old Sunday School Class for several years. Shortly after they married Charles began working, in the automobile business with Morton Motor Co. He has worked for the Lee Corporation and Ed Davis Motors for a total of 37 years serving as parts manager or service manager. Minnie Jean has worked for the U.S. Forest Service for 16 years both at Raleigh and Forest.

First Row: Kimberly Ann Risher Harrison, Minnie Jean Cooper Risher, Charles Ray Risher. Second Row: Paul L. Harrison, Janet Lynn Risher Reeves, Michael Blair Reeves

Their first child Charles Cooper was born premature on Feb. 19, 1964 and died shortly after birth. They have two daughters, Kimberly Ann (b. Dec. 18, 1968) married to Paul L. Harrison and Janet Lynn (b. Nov. 17, 1971) who is married to Michael Blair Reeves. Kim and Paul are graduates of University of Southern Mississippi and are both teachers. Janet graduated from Mississippi University for Women in Commercial Music and works for a performing arts company. Blair is a graduate of Mississippi State University with a degree in aerospace engineering and is employed with Southwest Airlines in Dallas, TX. Kim and Janet graduated from Forest High School where both participated in the band. They were active in the youth activities at the Forest Baptist Church.

After living in the city for three years, Charles and Minnie Jean were glad to get to move to the country. They have enjoyed the quietness of country life. The community is called "Frogtown." They do hear a lot of frogs during the summer months. Charles has enjoyed gardening and for many years, like his dad, planted enough in his garden to feed the community. He enjoys riding his ATV on the farm and just having a small garden if he can keep the deer from getting the harvest first. Minnie Jean enjoys tracing family history when time allows. Another past-time is watching the birds in the backyard. During the winter they enjoy feeding the birds and during the summer seeing the hummingbirds and other birds who love the birdbath.

RISHER, Mark Ray "Jack" Risher (b. Aug. 2, 1912, d. Aug. 28, 1998) was the youngest son of James Garrett and Josephine Alabama Chestnut Risher. On Feb. 15, 1934 he married Ena Sue Searcy. They have lived in Scott County all their life and mostly in the Pulaski Community.

Jack was in farming partnership with his brother Mack until his brother died. They raised mostly cotton and some corn. After his brother's death the farm was divided but he continued to see about Mack's children making sure they had what they needed as long as they were at home. Jack continued to farm on his property for many years. Later he worked many years with the Scott County Cooperative in Forest where he learned many people. The customers would go to him for advice on farming problems: the best pesticide, herbicide, fertilizer, seed, etc. He loved his work but health problems caused him to retire.

Mark Ray and Ena Sue Searcy Risher. Picture taken about two months before his death on Aug. 28, 1998.

Jack was very good in math. He did not have to use a calculator to get totals and within seconds he could give you a total. He had a good memory as long as he lived, always giving information you needed about family and neighbors, who they married, type of work, a lot of background history.

Sue was a housewife. She was always there for her children. She enjoyed doing special things for others. They both enjoyed giving from their garden. They always had a garden big enough to feed the community. After Jack died Sue's health declined and she went to live in the Scott County Nursing Home.

Jack and Sue were active members of the Pulaski Independent Methodist Church. They raised their children in a Christian home. He was a steward in the Methodist Church. They had two children, Charles Ray Risher (b. Jan. 20,1937) and Sybil Jean Risher (b. Nov. 14, 1944). Charles married Minnie Jean Cooper and they had two daughters, Kimberly Ann Risher and Janet Lynn Risher. Jean married Russell Wayne Ferguson and they had one son, Kevin Wayne Ferguson. They really loved those grandchildren and looked forward to their visits. Both of their children have lived close by which meant a lot to them.

There will always be fond memories of both Jack and Sue for those who knew them both - family and friends.

ROBERTS, Fred and Jerry Roberts moved to Morton, MS Feb. 9, 1956 with five children: Freddie, Wanda, Kaye, John David and Ronnie. They were enrolled in church and school the following week.

Fred was a pharmacist at OTT Drug Company.

Jerry stayed home and chauffeured the children here and there.

Christmas 1978, back row l-r: Bobby Joe, Ronnie, John David, Kaye, Wanda, and Freddie. Front: Fred and Jerry Roberts.

On Sep. 25, 1958 a new baby was born named Bobby Joe. All the children graduated from Morton Attendance Center with high honors.

Freddie and John David are graduates of Ole Miss. Ronnie and Bobby Joe are graduates of Mississippi College. Wanda and Kaye went to Jackson Commercial College.

Fred and Jerry were married 49 years and 7 months before Fred died in 1990. They had 11 grandchildren and five great-grandchildren.

ROLAND, Jesse Roland was born on Nov. 2, 1909 in Clifton, MS. His parents were William Jefferson Roland (b. 1861, d. 1931) and Mary Bailey (b. 1872, d. 1937). Jesse was born and raised on a farm in the Clifton Community. While in school, he played basketball and met Flora Denson in the Branch Community. They were married in 1932 and made their home with his mother in Clifton. He did various jobs to supplement the farm income including driving the school wagon (talleyho). He also worked as a barber in the Hillsboro Community. They have three children, eight grandchildren and four great-grandchildren.

James L. Roland (b. Mar. 27, 1933 in Clifton, MS) md. Nancy Nutt in 1958 and they have two children. Tammie Ann Roland (b. Nov. 6, 1959) is married to Tim Tabor and they have two children, Tyler and Taryn. Tim Roland (b. Sep. 8, 1964) and his wife Stephanie have two children, James and Jacob. Both Tammie and Tim live in Tupelo, MS with their families. James lives in Morton, MS.

Melvin T. Roland (b. Aug. 3, 1937 in Clifton, MS) md. Franceska Loeb on Jul. 5, 1957 and they live in Morton, MS. They have four children: Harold Melvin "Hal" Roland (b. May 16, 1958) md. Bobbie Ditcharo in 1983 and they live in New Orleans, LA; Franceska Kyle Roland (b. Mar. 17, 1961) and now lives in Seattle, WA; Alben David Roland (b. Jan. 8, 1966) lives in Cincinnati, OH; Brian Jess Roland (b. Nov. 10, 1970) lives in Morton, MS.

Shirley Fay Roland (b. Oct. 31, 1941 in Hillsboro, MS) md. James C. Sawyer Jr. in 1959 and now lives in Morton, MS. They have two children and one grandchild. Tommy Ray Sawyer (b. Oct. 31, 1960 in Jackson, MS) md. Stephanie Johnson of Monroe, LA in 1988. They live in Cropwell, AL. Suzanne Sawyer (b. May 12, 1963 in Jackson, MS) md. Ray Meador of Forest, MS in 1988 and they have one child, Bryan. They live in Forest, MS.

In 1942, Jesse moved his family to the Branch Community near Flora's family. Jesse farmed and worked at the local saw mill in the winter. In the late 1940s, they moved to Morton. In the early 1950s, Jesse and Flora went to work for the Morton School System. Jesse retired in 1961 from the school due to ill health and Flora retired a few years later. Jesse died in 1968 and is buried in the Morton Cemetery. Flora now resides in the Mississippi Care Center in Morton, MS.

ROWLAND (ROLAND), By an act of the U.S. Congress in the year 1798, the "Mississippi Territory" was formed of virginal wilderness sparsely inhabited by Indians. It included the lands which comprise the present-day states of Alabama and Mississippi. The news of this development created excitement among would-be colonists on the eastern seaboard as a golden opportunity to procure new, untouched lands upon which to build a prosperous future.

According to the late Howard Roland of Lake, MS, who did extensive research on the Rowland/Roland family history, three young Rowland brothers from Robeson County, NC, were among the eager youngsters seeking their fortune in the new territory.

When they arrived in what is present day Marion County in 1815, Samuel would have been 23 years old, Allen would have been 20, and Charles would have been 19. They settled for a time near Columbia in Marion County which is where they were when Mississippi became a State in 1817.

Charles and Allen acquired property, wives and children in their new homeland, but Samuel disappeared from family records. It is assumed that he ventured further north or west, and all family contact was lost.

When Scott and Smith Counties were formed in 1833, Charles and Allen decided to relocate into this new territory. They moved their families in the year 1834 into the Scott/Smith County area and formed the Rowland Plantation about 15 miles south of present-day Forest. It contained some 1280 acres of land. (The O.T. Gilbert property is part of that old plantation).

The surname Rowland was changed in Mississippi to Roland sometime in the mid-1850s, presumably by census takers. The families prospered and grew until the Civil War, after which time the land ownership slowly eroded to accommodate the demands of hard times, lack of slave labor, and to make provision for the new families formed by married children. The last of the land was sold in 1897.

During the turbulent years of 1870-1880, Allen and Charles Roland moved back to Marion County for a time. Allen died there sometime between 1870 and 1876. Josiah Roland, son of Allen, returned to the Scott/Smith County area and again settled on the Roland Hills, the place which his father had settled years before.

Over time, a large number of the Roland families who were descendants of Charles and Allen migrated to the Clifton, Hillsboro, Norris and Pulaski, communities in Scott County. The expanded families of the Roland line now include not only Rolands but also, Baileys, Waggoners, Milners, Hogues, Davises, Russums, Durrs, Alsobrohs (Alsobrooks?) and many, many

others. The Rowland/Roland descendants now live all across Scott County, the state of Mississippi, the south, and the nation.

RUSHING-JONES, Archibald "Archie" Douglas Rushing was born in Scott County, MS, Jan. 18, 1880, near an area known as Red Top, East of Tallabogue Creek. Lost Creek ran through the property that is 10 to 15 miles northeast of Forest in Scott County and near Walnut Grove in Leake County. It was known as the Old Gilmer Plantation before his grandfather Laben Rushing bought it. Archie's father Joseph "Joe" Rushing (b. Apr. 9, 1850, near Montgomery, AL, d. Apr. 1, 1935) was the son of Laben Rushing. He married Mary Elizabeth Putnam (b. Mar. 18, 1856, d. Sep. 24, 1896). Rushings still live on parts of that land on Rushing Road, in Scott County. Joe Rushing sold most of the plantation to his son-in-law Charley Quitman Jones after he married Joe's daughter Roseanna Elizabeth Rushing.

Minnie Matilda Jones (b. May 19, 1854 in Walnut Grove, Leake County, MS) was the daughter of Isaac Jones (b. Dec. 12, 1849, near Selma, AL, d. May 10, 1907 in Walnut Grove) and Charlotte Francis "Fannie" Harris (b. Jul. 24, 1852, in Leake County, d. 1918 in Tuxedo, Jones County, TX and is buried there). Isaac is buried in Walnut Grove. After his death, Fannie moved to Texas to live with one of her daughters.

Archibald "Archie" Douglas Rushing and Minnie Matilda Jones on their wedding day Dec. 24, 1905

Archie and Minnie married Dec. 24, 1905, in Walnut Grove. They had eight children, seven of whom are deceased. All died in Fort Worth, Tarrant County, TX. The first five were born in Forest, Scott County, MS. They were Fannie Lois "Francis" (b. Feb. 26, 1907, d. Dec. 21, 1983) md. Melvin L. McCarty. Archie Verna (b. Jul. 9, 1908, d. Apr. 22, 1982) md. Hazel Noblett. Trichelle Charles "T.C." (b. Jun. 6, 1911, d. Oct. 8, 1967) md. Lola Angeline Dragoo. Hazel Eva (b. Apr. 2, 1913, d. Jan. 20, 1988) md. William Albert Atherton Jr. Their children, both born in Fort Worth, are Barbara Jean (b. Jan. 27, 1939) md. Donald Lee Williams and William Albert Atherton III (b. Aug. 14, 1944) md. Betty Lou Greeney. Minnie Gladys (b. Sep. 14, 1915) md. first, Octave Stiles, second, Ollie Kent and third, Charles E. "Chuck" Sternenberg. The last three children were born in Texas. They were Lee Eutus (b. Aug. 3, 1919, Tuxedo, Jones County, d. Feb. 10, 1999) md. Ida Ruth (Bootz) Brawner. Joseph Everitt (b. Oct. 26, 1922, Buffalo Gap, Jones County, d. Jan. 2, 1994) md. Betty Erwin Mulkey. Auda D. (initial only) (b. Oct. 1, 1925, Buffalo Gap, d. Jul. 23, 1984) md. first, Doris Neace, second, Doris Price and third, Bettye R. Cook.

Archie farmed in Scott County until 1918 when Minnie's doctor advised her to leave the damp conditions of Mississippi and move to a drier climate. Archie packed up his family and moved to the West Texas town of Tuxedo. A brother and two sisters of Minnie had already moved there. He farmed there for a number of years, moved to Buffalo Gap to farm for a while and finally to Abilene, Taylor County, TX, for his last effort at farming.

By 1933 the family had moved to Fort Worth. Archie, also an accomplished carpenter, started work at A. Brandt Furniture Company and was employed there many years.

In his earlier years Archie was an Ordained Southern Baptist Deacon and had many Bible passages committed to memory and quoted them often. In his later years he lived with the family of his daughter Hazel Eva Rushing Atherton. In a return to his farming days, he planted a garden every year. He loved gardening almost as much as reading his Bible. He continued planting and working his garden until a stroke and ill health no longer permitted it.

Minnie died Jan. 24, 1943 and Archie died May 25, 1972. They are both buried in Mt. Olivet Cemetery in Fort Worth. *Submitted by Bill Atherton.*

RUSSELL, William Ellis Russell was born Aug. 1, 1864 Neshoba County, died Sep. 4, 1935, Scott County and is buried Antioch Cemetery. Married first Mollie Crecelius Dec. 23, 1885 Leake County. She was born Feb. 15, 1867, died Mar. 23, 1887 and buried Antioch Cemetery.

William Ellis, Nancy Louella, Mary and Martha (twins), May Ade in papa's lap

Second wife was Nancy Louella Lang (b. Feb. 6, 1871 Scott County, d. Jul. 7, 1961) md. Jul. 10, 1890, buried Antioch Cemetery.

First baby (b. Jul. 8, 1893) was stillborn. Twins were born Mar. 26, 1895. Martha Odell died Sep. 25, 1984, buried, Antioch Cemetery.

Mary Odessa died Feb. 26, 1940 and is buried Hillsboro Baptist Cemetery.

Married Dec. 23, 1916 to Ernest Leon Carpenter. May Odee was born Feb. 4, 1897, died Jan. 16, 1972, buried Coy Cemetery, Neshoba County. Married Apr. 3, 1918 to James David Fulton of Neshoba County and lived the rest of her life there.

William Duffie (b. Dec. 31, 1902 at Hillsboro, Scott County, d. Apr. 14, 1980 at Hillsboro) md. Elizabeth Waldrip on Mar. 21, 1923, Scott County Both are buried Hillsboro Cemetery.

Octavius Ray (b. Jul. 13, 1912 at Hillsboro, d. May 27, 1980 Hillsboro) md. Sep. 16, 1940 to Ruby Verne Simpson, Scott County. She was born Feb. 2, 1924 in Seattle Washington and died Sep. 30, 1981 in Scott County. Both are buried Antioch Cemetery.

RUSSELL, William H. Russell (b. Nov. 9, 1840 in Alabama) and wife Martha Sylvester Franks Kennedy moved to Scott County ca. 1897/98. Martha was born in Alabama on May 10, 1836. William died in Hillsboro Aug. 30, 1917 and Martha died May 30, 1930 in Forest, MS. Both are buried Hillsboro Baptist Cemetery. They were married Dec. 26, 1860 in Neshoba County. Their only daugh-

William H. Russell. Martha Sylvester Russell: daughter Alice: and grandchildren. Mary, Martha and Odee in Grandpa's lap.

ter, Alice moved with them. Alice (b. May 30, 1871, d. Dec. 16, 1947) md. James Francis Gardner on Aug. 19, 1900. He was born Nov. 3l, 1845 and died Mar. 31, 1924. Both buried Salem Cemetery, Scott County.

William H. Russell served in Co. F, 27th Regt. 33rd Inf. during the Civil War. After Williams death Martha lived with her daughter Alice Gardner until she died. Martha lived through a lot of changes in her lifetime. Her first husband died leaving her with a 4-year-old son and a 1-year-old daughter, James and Savannah Kennedy. Savannah died around age 2. She and William were the parents of four sons and a daughter. John Wesley, William Ellis, Charles Cicero, Edward C. and Alice. John Wesley was born 1861 and William Ellis 1864. She lived through the Civil War with two babies. She and sister Hannah Tucker lived together during the war. Hannah's husband joined the Union Army. William said he could not have any respect for a man who would fight against his wife and child. Martha lived 94 years.

RUSHTON/RUSTIN, Henry Rushton/Rustin Sr. (b. 1780 in Randolph County, NC) moved his family to Williamson County, TN, around 1806-1812. Henry Rushton/Rushtin/Rushing moved his family to Bond County, IL, around 1835 and died around 1844. Henry married Market McCain Feb. 25, 1802, in North Carolina. Henry and Market Rushton/Rushtin/Rushing had eight issues. A son, Henry Rushton/Rushing Jr., moved to Scott County, MS, around 1840. Their oldest son, James L., was born in Scott County, MS, in 1842; that is about the time the family changed the spelling of Rushton to Rushing.

Henry Jr. and Sarah E. had nine issues. A daughter Elizabeth Rushing (b. 1849) had two issues. A son, John L. Rushing (b. Aug. 27, 1867, in Morton, MS) md. Lula Cynthia Coward in 1894 in Scott County, MS. Johnny and Lula had five issues. They reared one son, Needham Bruce Rushing (b. May 1900) in Scott County, MS. He married Maggie Lee Champion in December 1925 in Scott County, MS. Bruce and Maggie had two issues. Their son John Paul Rushing was born Aug. 15, 1927. On Jul. 17, 1965, in Jackson, MS, John married Gloria Ann Ocain, who was born in 1937. They had no issues. Bruce and Maggie's daughter, Maxine Rushing, born in September 1931, married Thaddeus Homer

Davis in September, 1951. Maxine and Thaddeus had three issues, two daughters and a son. John L. and Lula remained in Scott County, MS, and reared their children.

Elizabeth's second son, Frank Willis, and Mamie had nine issues, four sons and five daughters. Frank and Mamie moved their family to Louisiana after 1907 and finally established residence in Lake Providence, LA, East Carroll Parish, where they remained until their deaths.

The photograph of Frank Willis and Mary Josephine (Mamie) Hollander was taken some time in the early 1930s in Louisiana. Frank Willis Rushing, son of Elizabeth Rushing and unknown. (Mamie) Mary Josephaine Hollander daughter of unknown Hollander from Switzerland. and Minerva McLemare from Ireland.

Frank and Mamie's oldest son, Claude Rushing, was born Aug. 18, 1897, in Morton, MS, Scott County. On Feb. 3, 1923, in Tallulah, Louisiana, Claude married Ola Mae Hall (b. Feb. 24, 1905), the daughter of John Robert Hall and Minnie Isabel Mitchell from Livingston County, KY. Ola Mae was visiting an aunt in Louisiana when she was introduced to Claude Rushing. She never returned to Kentucky to live. Claude and Ola Mae Hall Rushing had 10 issues, six sons and four daughters. All children were reared in East Carroll Parish, Louisiana. Claude and Ola Mae remained in East Carroll Parish until their deaths. Ola Mae Hall Rushing died in March 1998, at the age of 93.

From the union of Claude and Ola Mae Rushing came 10 children. From these ten children and their spouses came 30 grandchildren, 50 great-grandchildren, and nine great-great-grandchildren—what a legacy from Scott County, MS, and Smithland, KY, Livingston County! *Submitted by Patsy Adkerson.*

SANDERS, In November 1968 Jimmy Harold "Jim" and Delores Estelle (Pickering) Sanders moved from Texas to Scott County. Jim is a Baptist minister and shoes horses. He was born Dec. 5, 1939 in Lufkin, TX and graduated from Baylor in August 1964. He pastored churches in Texas and Smith, Newton and Scott County, MS.

Delores (b. Nov. 20, 1938 in Kilgore, TX), daughter of Roy Mervyn Pickering of Jones County, MS and Salba Estelle Tally of Smith County, MS. They both are buried in Hebron Cemetery, Jones County, MS. Delores graduated from Sam Houston College in May 1961. She taught school some and then decided to be a full-time mom. As the children grew older, Delores discovered genealogy.

The three boys were born in Texas and daughter Nicole in Jackson. All graduated from Lane High School. Nicole graduated from Mississippi College with a business degree, then decided to go into nursing. She graduated with that degree from Mississippi Southern.

Jim Lane (b. Oct. 5, 1962) married Cadi Ann Howe Feb. 12, 1992. She was born Oct. 8, 1973. Two girls were born, Laci Anne Sep. 12, 1993 and Rachel Elizabeth May 24, 1995. Lane married secondly, Dawn Renee Crass. Jonny Lamont, second son, came Dec. 7, 1963. Marrying Melissa Gail King, they had a daughter Victoria Shasta (b. Apr. 12, 1982). Third son, Jason Lance (b. Jan. 6, 1967) married in Lake Baptist Aug. 14, 1987 Connie Jana, daughter of Fletcher Rooney and Zelma Cornelia "Connie" (Massey) Hollingsworth. Jana was born Jul. 9, 1969. They have a daughter Alana Holli (b. Oct. 13, 1995) and a son Landon Massey Sanders (b. Mar. 3, 2000).

Nicole (b. Oct. 14, 1971) was the fourth Sanders' child and married Cameron Wayne Polk on Aug. 6, 1994 in McComb. They have a son Colton Wayne Polk (b. Aug. 2, 1999 in Hattiesburg).

SANFORD-MAY, Barry B. Sanford and Ruby W. May Sanford were married on Jan. 18, 1969 at Forest in the home of Judge Blant Breland. They made their home in Harperville, MS. They have three children and one grandchild. Rhonda E. Haralson Alford, lives in Harperville and works as a cashier at Harperville General Store. She has one son Tony Ladell Alford (b. Mar. 8, 1991, at Anderson's Hospital in Meridian). He is a student at Scott Central School in the fourth grade.

Dell Sanford, son, lives at Harperville and is a service technician at Killen's Motors in Forest. Dell attended Scott Central School. He was later regional manager of Refrigerated Food Express of Harperville, MS.

Tony Sanford married Hope Shumaker of Hillsboro, MS. She is the daughter of Bobby and Faith Shoemaker. They live at Coal Bluff Park. Hope works at Union Planters Bank in Jackson. Tony works for the Reservoir Patrol, and is currently in the police academy in Pearl. They married in June 1998 while Tony was still serving a 4-year tour in the Marine Corps.

Ruby's parents were Herman L. May and Ruby E. Hollingsworth May. Herman was the son of William N. and Maggie Ann Creel May of Ringgold. They had 10 children. The Mays migrated from North Carolina and started settling in Newton County. Ruby E. was the daughter of William J. Hollingsworth and Ina Mann of the Piketon Community. They had five children.

Barry's parents were T.O. Sanford and Stella Barnett from Madden, MS in Leake County. They moved to Harperville in the early 1960s and Mr. T.O. owned and operated the Harperville Garage and Stella was a schoolteacher. They had eight children.

The Sanfords have lived in Harperville since marrying in 1969. Barry is the Service Manager at Killen's Motors in Forest. He is an avid hunter and sportsman. Ruby is a housewife, mother and grandmother.

SAWYER, James Chester Sawyer Jr. (b. Dec. 14, 1937 in Scott County), son of James C. Sawyer Sr. and Cleo V. Sawyer. They are both de-

ceased and buried in the Faulkner Cemetery in Morton, MS. He married Shirley Roland on Nov. 26, 1959 at East Morton Baptist Church. They have two children.

Tommy Ray Sawyer (b. Oct. 31, 1960 in Jackson, MS) attended high school in Forest, MS and later

Seated: Shirley Roland Sawyer and Chester Sawyer. Standing: Tommy Ray Sawyer and Suzanne Sawyer

attended Hinds Jr. College in Raymond, MS. He married Stephanie Johnson of Monroe, LA in 1989. He is employed by El Paso Gas Co. and lives in Birmingham, AL.

Suzanne Sawyer (b. May 12, 1963 in Jackson, MS) attended high school in Forest, MS and later attended Hinds Jr. College in Raymond, MS. She received a degree in fashion merchandising from the University of Southern Mississippi in Hattiesburg, MS. She married Ray Meador of Forest, MS in 1988 and they have one child, Bryan Raymond "Dude" Meador. She owns and operates S&R Clothing in Forest, MS. They live in Forest.

James Chester Jr., commonly called Chester, attended Forest High School and graduated in 1957. While in high school, he played football for the Bearcats and lettered for three years. He received Honorable Mention All Little Dixie in 1956. In 1957-1958 and 1958-1959, he attended East Central Jr. College where he played football and lettered both years. He started to work for the U.S. Dept. of Agriculture in 1961.

Shirley Roland Sawyer (b. Oct. 31, 1941 in Hillsboro, MS) attended Morton High School and graduated in 1959. She also completed a business course at Draughn's Business College in Jackson, MS in 1959. She attended East Central Jr. College and received an associate degree in 1980. She later attended Belhaven College in Jackson, MS and graduated cum laude in 1988 with a BS degree in accounting and business administration. She started to work for the Bell System in 1964 and held many titles there over the years.

Chester retired from the USDA in 1994 where he had worked in the meat inspection service for 33 years. Shirley retired from BellSouth as an electronic technician with 33 years of service in 1997. They live on Blossom Hill Rd., Morton, MS.

SAWYER, James Chester Sawyer (b. Sep. 27, 1907), son of William John Sawyer (b. in Kentucky) and Mary Robertson "Molly" (b. in Toomsuba, MS), married Cleo V. Risher (b. Oct. 10, 1911 in Morton, MS). She died on Aug. 22, 1989 and is buried in the Faulker Cemetery in Morton, MS. Her parents were William Henry Risher (b. Oct. 30, 1868, d. Mar. 10, 1942) and Nannie Smith Risher (b. Feb. 25, 1877, d. Jun. 23, 1953). Her parents were buried in the Faulkner Cemetery in Morton, MS. Chester and Cleo have seven children.

1) Mary V. Sawyer "Molly" (b. Oct. 28, 1933 in Scott County) ms. Duke E. Sanders and

they have four children: Maria, Patty, Duke Jr. and Joe. Molly and Duke divorced and she is now married to Richard Walker. They live in Chicago, IL.

2) Fredna Jean Sawyer (b. Oct. 2, 1935 in Scott County) md. James E. Hood in 1961 and they have three children: James Jr., Sylvia and Keith. They live in Clinton, MS.

3) James Chester Sawyer Jr. (b. Dec. 14, 1937 in Scott County) md. Shirley Roland in 1959 and they have two children, Tommy Ray and Suzanne. They live on Blossom Hill Rd. in Morton, MS.

4) Nancy Ann Sawyer (b. Nov. 8, 1941 in Scott County) md. Marvin A. Milner and they have two children, Donna and Marvin Jr. They live in Ridgeland, MS.

5) Betty Jane Sawyer (b. Jan. 25, 1944 in Scott County) md. Ralph Sirois and they have one child, Cheryl. They live in San Antonio, TX.

6) Gloria Francis Sawyer (b. Apr. 17, 1947 in Scott County) md. Roy Love and they have two children, Cindy and Doug. After they divorced, she married Tom Schletch and they live in Long Beach, CA.

7) Wanda Dorene Sawyer (b. Oct. 28, 1949 in Scott County) md. Ronnie Howell and they have two children, Danny and Amanda. They divorced and Wanda now lives in Terry, MS.

James Chester Sawyer, commonly called Chester, was born in Meridian, MS and lived there until he was about 12 years old. His parents died in Meridian from all accounts during the flu epidemic of 1919 and he moved to the Blossom Hill Rd. Community to live with his sister. Chester died in 1995 and is buried in the Faulkner Cemetery in Morton, MS.

SAXON-KNOWLES, our earliest known Saxon and Knowles ancestors were Archilaus Saxon (b. Jul. 17, 1797 in Georgia, d. Oct. 20 1867) and his wife Elizabeth "Betsy" Knowles (b. 1802, d. 1873), both are buried in Antioch Primitive Baptist Church Cemetery on Highway 21N. They raised a family of at least 10 children: John, Anthony, Samuel, William Harrison, Elvira Morgan, Polly Hood, Eliza Kight, Francis, Adeline Collins

William Harrison and Mary Ann Knowles Saxon

and Matilda Callaway. William Harrison, John and Anthony were Confederate soldiers. In 1853 Archilaus purchased land in Scott County and settled there.

William Harrison Saxon (b. 1841, d. 1920) md. Mary Ann Knowles and had Alfonso, Sidney Eugene, Martha Ina Belle Robinson and Eliab Crecelius. On the death of his first wife Mary Ann, he married her sister Martha who had always lived with them. William deeded land to his surviving children, Eliab and Ina Belle. William and both wives are buried in Antioch Cemetery.

My husband's grandparents, Eliab

Crecelius (b. 1878, d. 1963) and Mary Gertrude, daughter of Confederate veteran Daniel Noonan Knowles, and themselves first cousins, lived on the farm he inherited from his father adjacent to Ephesis Baptist Church and extending to the corner of what is now Riser and Ephesis Rds. They reared five children: my father-in-law Dovie Wood, Gertrude Gill, Flora McDill, Roy Anderson and Lanora Leach, all born in Ringgold Community. Eliab and Mary Gertrude lived on their land until their deaths, when they were buried in the Antioch Cemetery.

Dovie Wood Saxon (b. 1900, d. 1981) md. Trudy Gill of Conehatta, while his sister Gertrude married Trudy's brother Tommy Gill, a WWI veteran wounded in France. Dovie and Trudy lived in the old Levi Robinson place where their two children, Evelyn Walters and D. William were born in 1923 and 1928. They later built a house on the SE corner of what now is Ephesis and Greer, where they farmed. During WWII, Dovie worked in a N.O. shipyard from 1941, moving the family there in 1943, and moving to Pascagoula in 1945 where Dovie worked at Ingall's shipyard. They moved to New Orleans again where he became the chief carpenter on the paddlewheel steamboat *The President* for about 17 years. In 1966 they retired to Scott County and settled across the road from the church and Eliab's property until Trudy's death in 1976 and his death in 1981; they were buried in the Ephesis Cemetery.

Their son, D. William, attended Ringgold School, working first on the family farm and when his family moved to NO, in a grocery store. While in Pascagoula as a shipyard welder, he met Rubye Lee Smith (of Sidon and Greenwood) and were married there. D enlisted in the Army-Air Force in 1947. During his 28-year career as an administrative specialist, we lived in N.O. where our first two children, Scharlotte Saxon and Stephanie Purvis, were born, then New Jersey, France (birthplace of Kenneth), SDakota, Taiwan (birthplace of Deborah Telemeco), Biloxi, Vietnam and Hampton, VA, until his retirement in 1975. We settled in Gulfport, but frequently visit D's property where his parents spent their retirement years, across the road from his grandfather Eliab's place, and just around the corner from the homeplace on which he was raised. *Submitted by Rubye Smith Saxon.*

SAXON, Archibald/Archelaus Saxon was the first Saxon to migrate to Scott County, MS. To jump backward in time and place ancestrally, Samuel Saxon, born in England in 1698, was reared in New Kent County, VA and died in 1766 in Halifax County, NC. His son, Samuel Jr., was very active in the Revolutionary War and, along with his brothers and kinsmen, survived the massacre at Hayes Station. Samuel Jr. and his son, Davis, both died about 1805 in Wilkes County, GA.

Davis was married to Polly Edge. After his early death, Polly lived with her father, Obediah Edge, who helped rear the three sons: Archelaus, James and Benejah. Archelaus followed the migration westward along with brothers and several other families. By 1830, they were in Henry County, GA and by 1840 in Chambers and Tallapoosa County, AL. In 1854 Archelaus bought land from Rufus West in Scott County,

MS. Once more he moved with his wife Elizabeth Knowles and the younger children. Their oldest daughter, Elvira, married Henry Morgan and lived in Scott County for a time but moved back to Georgia.

Their other children were Eliza Saxon Kight, Francis Saxon Jones, Nancy Saxon Moffitt, Mary Saxon Hood, Fannie Saxon Pharr, Sarah Matilda Calloway, John H. Saxon married Martha Sant, William H. Saxon married first, Mary Ann Knowles and second, her sister Martha Knowles, Anthony H. Saxon married Saphronia Kight, Samuel Saxon and two other children died as babies.

In the Antioch Primitive Baptist Church of Scott County, MS minutes of the church, A.H. presented his letter and was received into fellowship on Mar. 15, 1873. On Sep. 20, 1879 he was granted a letter of dismissal from Antioch. Anthony H. was able to apply for newly released Indian land in Yazoo County, MS by inserting a "t" in his name, as he was a Civil War veteran, too proud to apply for a pension or pardon. Anthony Saxon, Joseph Hood and Henry Morgan also were in the Civil War.

Mary Saxon Hood, Fannie Saxon (married to Henry H. Pharr who was killed in the CW), and Francis all moved to Yazoo County with Anthony. Samuel Saxon married Nancy Ann Smith and lived a while in Scott County before moving to Polk County, TX.

In January 1885 Samuel Saxon gave power of attorney to William H. Saxon (his brother) to any interests he had in Mississippi. This document was signed in Polk County, TX and recorded in Book EE on Page 229. John H., William H., Eliza Saxon Kight, Sarah Matilda Calloway and Nancy Saxon Moffitt lived out their lives in Scott County, MS. John and Martha Saxon bought SW/NW Sec. 2 T7N R9E on Aug. 3, 1857, 40 acres. William Calloway and Sarah Matilda were living in Scott County, MS when William left to fight in the Civil War. After the war, they moved to Texas. William died Sep. 13, 1912. William and Sarah had eight children.

SCHWAB-HARALSON, Peter Schwab (b. Nov. 2, 1943 in Bay City, MI) was the youngest of three sons born to Selwyn Schwab and Margaret Helen Maus.

After Peter graduated from Central High School in 1961, he joined the Navy. Serving during the Vietnam conflict on the USS *Hancock* (CVA-19), *Oriskaney* 38, *Shangri-La* 34 and The *F.D. Roosevelt* 42. After serving a little over nine years he received an honorable discharge from the Navy. A friend talked him into moving to Alaska, where he worked as a chemical technician at a pulp mill and as a tour guide. He moved to Minnesota where he returned to school to get a degree in engineering, then went to work for Honeywell.

In February 1989 Hughes Aircraft of Forest, MS called Peter for an interview. When he

Peter and Mary Grace Schwab

came to Mississippi, he fell in love with the south. Peter took the job at Hughes and in 1992 he met and fell in love with a fellow employee and Forest native, Mary Grace Haralson (b, Feb. 14, 1952), daughter of the late Robert Clinton Haralson and Mary Helen Jones Dudley. They were married April 1993.

Hughes transferred Peter and Mary back to Minnesota for a year, but his heart was firmly rooted in Scott County. In May 1994, Peter and Mary Grace moved back home to Forest. They live on Old Hwy. 80 in the house where Mary was raised.

Peter says he will never leave Forest, this is his home and he intends to stay. He now works at Craft-Co Enterprises of Morton, as a quality engineering supplier supervisor. Mary Grace is a homemaker and member of the Scott County Genealogical Society and The Bay County, MI, Genealogical Society.

Peter has three children by a previous marriage: Ta, Joshua and Zach, and several grandchildren. They live in Minnesota. Mary has a son Robert Earl who lives in Forest. *Submitted by Peter Schwab.*

SEABERRY, Daniel Mattison Seaberry (b. Jun. 19, 1851 in Scott County, MS), son of Raleigh Seaberry and Rebecca Altman Seaberry, and grandson of Susan Seaberry who owned the property designated as the NE 1/4 of NE 1/4 Section 2, Township 8, Range 8. She sold this property to Green B. Clark in 1856. Susan died Oct. 25, 1862. We find no record of her grave and assume she was buried on the land on which she was living since she died during The War Between The States.

Frances "Fannie" Rebecca Thompson Seaberry and Daniel Mattison "Matt" Seaberry

Matt married Frances "Fannie" Rebecca Thompson on Nov. 24, 1870. They were married by Rev. W.M. Butler at Harperville. On the 1870 census Matt's occupation is listed as carpenter. Matt and Fannie's first child, Delia Ann "Nannie" was born in Scott County on Mar. 24, 1873. The family moved to Texas around 1875. Fannie's brother W.H. "Bill" Thompson came with them. He later married Matt's sister, Martha Ann Seaberry. On Nov. 24, 1875 a second child, Carrie Rebecca, was born to Matt and Fannie in Dallas County, TX. This was my grandmother. Then the family moved to Poolville, TX. Gippy M. was born Jun. 22, 1878; William in July 1881; Beulah June in June 1882 and Dove on Dec. 14, 1885. Fannie died of pneumonia on Feb. 14, 1886, leaving behind six young children. She is buried in the Poolville Cemetery.

On Feb. 5, 1887, Matt married Lucy Anice Carter. To this union were born: Daniel Mattison

Jr. (b. Apr. 10, 1888); Louis Poindexter "Dyke" (b. Oct. 13, 1889); Tintie Bonna (b. Sep. 13, 1891); James Guy (b. Feb. 16, 1894); Amy Belle (b. Mar. 27, 1896); Dewey Monroe (b. Jun. 03, 1898); Harper Allen (b. Oct. 21, 1901); Pernie L. "Kitty" (b. May 01, 1903); William Elic "Bill" (b. Apr. 26, 1905); Ozella Fay (b. Nov. 07, 1906); Jesse Jackson (b. Jul. 13, 1909) and LaRaine Ruth (b. Aug. 03, 1912).

Matt farmed in the Poolville Community and was a member of the Baptist Church. He died of pneumonia following an attack of influenza on Jan. 12, 1919. Due to the influenza epidemic, his funeral was held in the home. He is buried in the Poolville Cemetery at Poolville, TX. Lucy died Dec. 07, 1930 and is buried beside Matt.

SEABERRY, Most mystery stories begin "On a dark and stormy night....," but this one began in Alabama, continued in Mississippi, and remains unsolved. In 1837, Susan/Susannah (b. Feb. 4, 1808) Seaberry bought land in Alabama, in her name only, for which she paid cash. In 1850, Susan Seaberry settled in Scott County, MS, in the Hillsboro-Harperville area where she bought 44.27 acres of land in her own name and paid cash on Dec. 1, 1849, from Columbus Land Office, Document No. 33507. Susan had 10 children. Here's the mystery: Who was the father of these 10 children? How did she obtain the cash with which to buy property in her own name? Do you know the answers to these questions?

In 1850, five of Susan's 10 children were living in her household: Nancy Maria "Pace," Ruth A., Robert, Pamela Ann and Alexander.

Nancy Maria "Pace" (b. Nov. 21, 1836, Alabama) md. Tom Oglesby in Red River Parish, LA.

Ruth A. (b. Jun. 22, 1842, Mississippi) md. James Madison Yates in Mississippi on Jun. 4, 1866. The Yates family moved to Texas. Mr. Yates died and Ruth A. married Rev. W.D. Hammack in Kaufman County, TX on Jan. 5, 1893. Ruth died in Kaufman County Apr. 29, 1925.

Pamela Ann (b. Oct. 6, 1846 in Mississippi) md. Orren McCarty Feb 2 1864 in Jackson, MS and had three children: Orren (b. Nov. 27, 1864, in Ben Wheeler, Van Zandt County, TX, d. 1906) is buried in McCarty Cemetery, Coalgate, OK; Robert J. McCarty (b. Feb. 7, 1875, Shitefield, Haskell County, OK) and Artho Ann McCarty (b. Jan. 17, 1877, Yell County, AR).

It is said that Alexander never married but migrated to Texas and died in Comanche County, TX about 1875.

Susan Seaberry (whose maiden name may have been Harper) had five other children: Avea (b. 1825, Alabama, d. Sep. 3, 1841); Raleigh (b. Jan. 6, 1827, Alabama, d. Dec. 26 1908, Parker County, TX) served in the Confederate Army as private in Co. F, 36th Regt. MS Vols., Mar. 5, 1862 to Jul. 4, 1863, when he was captured at Vicksburg, MS. On Dec. 20, 1863, he was one of the men in the prisoner exchange.

Raleigh and his wife, Rebecca Altman, were married in 1850 in Mississippi and listed as the family "next door" to Susan on the 1850 census. Raleigh and Rebecca had 10 children: Daniel Mattison md. Francis Rebecca Thompson and second, Lucy Anise Carter; George Anderson

md. Mollie Rebecca Kornegay; Martha Ann md. William H. Thompson; Henry James md. Nancy Louisa Voyles; Exer Catherine md. Milton M. Webb; Raleigh Poindexter md. Mary Ann Voyles and second, Annice Jennie Nelson; Mary Cleopatra md. Warren Tennell Baggett; John Briscoe md. Lucy Elizabeth Taylor; Minnow Rebecca md. George William McLeary Taylor; and William Robert md. Nancy Caroline McCurry.

Raleigh and Rebecca Altman Seaberry

Raleigh Seaberry, his wife, and children came to Texas from Mississippi about 1878, settled in and around Poolville, Parker County, TX. Many of them are buried in the Poolville Cemetery.

Polly (b. Jun. 25, 1830, Alabama) md. Irvin Clark; Helen (b. Jun. 27, 1832, d. Oct. 20, 1838); and Henry Robert (b. Jun. 17, 1845, d. Dec. 15, 1931, Crandall, Kaufman County, TX), never married. Robert served in the Confederate Army in MS State Troups Ruth's Scouts.

So, it is at the end as it was in the beginning. The mystery of the father of the children of Susan/Susannah Seaberry is still unsolved. Do you have a clue?

SESSIONS, The Sessions family was originally from South Carolina. They came to Mississippi by way of Georgia and Alabama.

Franklin Sessions moved from Alabama to Newton County, MS around 1850. His first child, Joseph Wesley Sessions, moved to Scott County around 1880 settling in the Clifton Community near Hillsboro. Joseph's brother, Allesberry Sessions moved to the Morton area around the same time.

Joseph Sessions married Mary Ellen Dollar and they had nine children. Their first child, Calvin C. Sessions, married Martha "Mattie" Robinson. There were 11 children in their family.

The second child of Joseph and Mary Ellen was Cornelius Franklin "Neal" Sessions. Neal was named after his grandfathers, Cornelius Dollar and Franklin Sessions. Neal was murdered on Christmas Eve 1905. His throat was slashed, and he was left to bleed to death. *The Scott County Register* reported the crime in the Jan. 3, 1906 edition. The paper stated Governor Vardaman of Mississippi had offered a reward for the arrest and conviction of the murderer. For many years after Neal's murder his brothers would ban together to search for the murderer to no avail. The murder was never solved.

The third child of Joseph and Mary Ellen Sessions was Georgia Ann Mary Ellen Green Sessions. She married Josiah Carl Roland. They had 10 children.

John Wesley "Johnny" Sessions was the fourth child of Josiah and Mary Ellen Sessions. He married Ida Lashley. She died of typhoid fever in 1907 leaving four children under the age of six years. Johnny never married again.

Joseph George Washington "Jodie" Sessions was the fifth child of Joseph and Mary Ellen. He married Leanna Nicholes and had five children. Jodie was killed in a train accident in 1944. Sarah J. "Sally" Sessions was the sixth child of Joseph and Mary Ellen. Sally never married.

Patrick Henry "Pat" Sessions was the seventh child. He married Jessie Lashley, a sister of Johnny Session's wife. She, like her sister, was stricken with typhoid fever and died in 1907. Jessie and Pat had been married two months when she passed away. Pat would later marry Minnie Lee Mott. They had three children.

Martin Luther Sessions was the eighth child. He married Ozie Jones and they had five children.

The ninth child of Joseph and Mary Ellen was Baxter Clyde (Brack) Sessions. He married Neva Bishop and they had three children. Brack Sessions served as night marshal in Forest, MS for many years.

The Sessions' descendants have traveled and resided in foreign countries and throughout the United States. The wanderlust of their ancestors remains even today.

Professions chosen have been many and varied: teachers, scientists, auto mechanics, psychologists, farmers, nurses and postmen. Their laughter, friendship and storytelling personalities are well known. *Written by Patricia Wynell Crane Parrish, great-granddaughter of Joseph and Mary Ellen Sessions. Her grandfather was Patrick Henry "Pat" Sessions.*

SESSUMS, James Thomas "Jim" Sessums (b. Apr. 8, 1857, d. Jul. 28, 1925), son of William Oliver Sessums (d. Mar. 23, 1879) and Mattie Vance, and Roxanna "Roxie" Smith (b. Aug. 15, 1848, d. Aug. 18, 1914), daughter of James C. Smith and Mary A. Rentz, were married at home in Leake County in 1875 by

J.T. and Roxanna Sessums

a Rev. Sones. Five children soon followed. William (b. Mar. 21, 1877, d. age 2); Martha Ann "Mattie" (b. Jun. 19, 1879); Jim "J.C." (b. Feb. 1, 1881); Nolia (b. Dec. 8, 1882); and Maude (b. Oct. 1, 1884). In the family Bible in her father Jim's handwriting, Nolia is written "may nolia." Is this a double name, or is Nolia merely a diminutive of May nolia? (Note: None of the names in Jim's writing is capitalized.)

On Jun. 16, 1879, their second child, Mattie, married M.M. "Fritz" Mapp. The wedding was held in the Jim Sessums' home. A Rev. Milling performed the ceremony. After this marriage and sometime between 1898 and 1900, Jim, his wife Roxie, and the remainder of the children moved from Leake County to Scott County, west of Harperville on the Lillian Road, to a farm owned by Fritz. The Sessums lived across the road from the Mapps. (See article on the M.M. Mapp Family.)

Jim "J.C." married Zella (or Stella) Coleman. They had three daughters and one son. He raised his family in Walnut Grove and is buried there.

Nolia married Lemuel Sigrest (b. Sep. 23, 1895, d. Nov. 30, 1940). They lived in the Clifton Community. Their son Junior, his wife and child, and Mayola Sigrest (not Junior's mother) were killed in a car-train wreck at Morton on Dec. 15, 1937. Nolia's other children were James Malcom (md. Effie Mae Calhoun) and Marquain.

Maude married Clarence Calhoun (b. Sep. 13, 1881, d. May 12, 1945). Maude and Clarence had one son, Vonceil, who married a Sullivan and had two daughters, Geneva (md. Ralph Pope) and Bessie L. (md. Earl Brewer Bailey).

Jim had a niece, Sallie Ann Sessums Dumas, and a nephew, Will Sessums, who both raised families in the Harperville area on the Lillian Road.

Nolia and Maude are buried in the Clifton Baptist Church Cemetery. James Thomas and Roxie are buried in the Lebanan Cemetery on Lillian Road west of Harperville.

There are descendants of their families still in the area.

Information for this article came from the M.M. Mapp Family Bible and Delores Sanders book, *Remember Me*. J.T. Sessums and Roxie were my great-grandparents on my mother's side. *Contributed by Norma Earle Alford Idom.*

SHARP-JOHNSON, Woodley Sharp (b. Oct. 18, 1895 in Scott County near Sebastopol), son of Marshall Baxter "Bay" Sharp and Addie Cordelia Jones. Bay and Addie lived near Sebastopol with their eight children at the place that now belongs to Nolan Sistrunk and the subdivision was his farm. He carried the mail from the depot to the post office for many years. He was a Christian man, had prayer every night and the blessing before each meal, witty and liked fun but never had anything bad to say about anyone and never harmed anyone.

Bay Sharp

Woodley Sharp was named after a Mr. T.L. Woodley a friend of the family. He died on Jul. 21, 1948 and is buried in Sebastopol Cemetery.

Woodley, Lessie and Henry Sharp

Lessie Lee Johnson Sharp was born Mar. 27, 1897 in Scott Co. near Sebastopol to Henry Crawford Johnson and Alma Eugenia Francis Stribling Johnson. Henry and Alma Johnson lived most if not all their married life just East of Sebastopol, at what is known as the Hi Eastland Johnson place and his farm just past, with their eight children. He was a farmer and a very prominent family in Scott County.

Lessie and Woodley were married Aug. 29, 1916. They were Baptist. To this union were born five children. They lived in several places near Sebastopol and in 1930 bought the "Hotel" and boarded teachers, drummers and travelers in the 1930s and 1940s during WWII. They moved to several places like Duck Hill, MS and helped build Army camps at Camp McCain. Then Biloxi where they were building Keesler Air Force Base, Jackson as they were building Jackson Air Force Base. They boarded moneymen from Sebastopol and

Johnson family reunion

Johnson family reunion

Workers on Army base

Sharp family

Johnson family

around here as many as 25 at one time. Later Woodley Sharp was employed for a number of years until shortly before his death at the U.S. Post Office.

In Lessie Sharp's early adult life she taught school in the public school system and taught private piano lessons in her home for over 50 years. She died Jul. 2, 1987. Lessie Sharp married John Burdette (b. Jul. 2, 1968, d. Mar. 28, 1977). Children:

1) Woodley Coba Sharp (md. Lillan Laverne Gardner, Jun. 30, 1939), children: Coba Julian Sharp (md. Jean Harrison); Margaret Ann Sharp (md. Jerome Rush; Travis Milton Sharp (md. Wanda Comans).

2) James Calquette Sharp (md. Helen Grace, Jul. 15, 1951), children: James C. Sharp Jr. "Jimmy" and John Thomas Sharp "Tommy."

3) William Francis Sharp (md. John Carl Amis, Mar. 15, 1942), children: (a) James Carl Amis (md. Sharon Gilmore), children: Melanie Amis (md. Chris Pope), Lance Amis (md. Linda Eurbo) and April Amis; (b) William Edward Amis (md. Patsy Nester), children: Bethany Amis (md. Ken Crosby) and Stacy Amis; (c) Robert Eugene Amis (md. Sandra Dickerson), children: Alishia Amis (md. Arthur McMillian), Deidre Amis (md. Charles Maxie) and John Oliver Amis (md. Amberly Bounds); (d) Valrie Amis (md. Terry Thrash), children: Stephanie Thrash (md. Kenneth Morris) and Julie Nechole Thrash (md. Mark Rabun).

4) Lessie Rejeania Sharp (md. Marshall Lamar Gardner, Aug. 15, 1945), children: (a) Wanda (md. Leon Mabry then Ted Hardin), children: Roxanne Mabry (md. Greg Oakley) and Ted Gene Hardin II); (b) Randall Marshall Gardner (md. Lyndell Crawford), children: Angela (md. Robert Keeton Jr.) and Jason Randall.

5) Henry Johnson Sharp (md. Anita Gouchy).

SHEARON, Helen Burke Shearon (b. Jul. 28, 1901, d. Jun. 18, 1996) was the daughter of William Warren Shearon and Emma Leona Nordon. She had one brother Willie Nordon Shearon (b. Jun. 24, 1908, d. Oct. 31, 1983). Helen never married but Willie married Neva King and had five children: Emma Kathryn, Bobbie, Freda Jo, Beri Lynn, Lawrence and Buddy deceased.

Helen Shearon

Helen Shearon graduated Morton High School and attended Ole Miss and graduated Pharmaceutical School in 1928. The era of time that Helen graduated and being a female trying to obtain a job in the work force was impossible because women were not accepted.

She purchased a truck and operated a rolling store dispensing RX and general merchandise to area customers.

In 1941 she purchased property and a building in Lake, MS and started Shearons Drug Store for 41 years, closing in 1982.

On Oct. 24, 1946, along with C.E. Noblin, Helen purchased the Kidd estate from Eugene Vinson. Jan. 26, 1952 the Noblin heirs conveyed their 1/2 interest in and to the land in Scott County to Helen.

Helen was a member of the first Baptist Church of Lake, and took her religion serious. She never missed Church, Sunday school or Prayer Meeting, unless out of town or sick.

She enabled a number of Newton and Scott County residents to own their home by co-signing notes. She also loaned down payments for land with no collateral.

Many a night Helen would be awakened by a rapping on the door by persons needing help for a child with high fever. Adults, animals or whatever the cause, she always went and even though she knew they could not pay, she felt she had relieved their pain.

SHELTON, In 1951, Trenton Garfeild Shelton and Gladys Hughes Shelton moved to Forest. The couple came to this city when Mrs. Shelton, a native of Smith County, accepted the position as Director of Nurses for Lackey Memorial Hospital.

Having grown up in Calhoun County, Mr. Shelton graduated from Derma High School. He attended Mississippi College from 1926-30, majoring in math and education. A teacher/coach for many years, he became affiliated with an engineering firm as accountant. Mr. Shelton died in June 1958.

Gladys Shelton, known to all who were fortunate to receive her care. She retired from nursing, celebrating 50 years of dedicated service. After the death of Mr. Shelton, she married J.C. Johnson of Pulaski. Gladys continued to give herself to her church, community and family. She died Jan. 15, 1995.

The Shelton's had one son, Trenton Hughes Shelton (b. Sep. 28, 1938.). Trenton was in the eighth grade when they moved to Forest. He attended Forest, Public Schools and graduated in 1956. After graduation from Mississippi College in 1960, he joined Dixie Portland Flour Mills. In July 1963,

Trenton married Linda Lackey. After their child, Leah Lackey Shelton (b. 1967), they moved back to Jackson from Memphis, where Trenton began his insurance career.

SIGREST, Most families have a history that begins: "Two brothers came to America, one went to Virginia and the other went to Georgia." Just like this legend, Sigrest brothers came to America, some went to Pennsylvania and other directions, but one went to Virginia.

Two Sigrest boys, Frederick and Henry, began their wanderings

Margel Sigrest (b. Feb. 28, 1842, d. Jun. 16, 1905)

around Frederick, County, VA in the 1740s. This can not be verified because, like our Scott County Courthouse at Hillsboro, MS, the Frederick County Courthouse burned.

Henry decided to check out the Carolina scenery with brother Fred. Soon Henry headed out again, eventually stopping in Macon County, AL. His clan hung onto the name Segrest with an "e." Frederick seemed to have been lost in North Carolina, but his handsome son Martin married the lovely Lyddia Thomas (of course she was lovely because she was our great-great-great something or the other she had to be). "Marty" and "Lyddy," with their brood of eight, loaded up the wagons and headed south to Wayne County, MS. Alas, by this time, Papa Martin was just "wore out" and was buried there. Eldest son, McKager Thomas, given his mother's family name, moved to Scott County in 1826. Unlike Henry's clan, who went by "Segrest," the first record of the name spelled "Sigrest" was in the 1836 Scott County Census.

In 1835, Grandpa Tommy and his charming wife, Christian (Graham), moved to Hales Crossing Community, recognized now as Clifton. Like many of the Sigrest, he was a builder and the first county jail in Hillsboro was built by Grandpa Tommy. Until the 1960s the bars from the jail were still in use on the Cochran Grocery Store, right in the center of Hillsboro.

Unfortunately, the courthouse that he helped construct in Hillsboro went up in flames in Sherman's "March to the Sea." After that divisive war the county seat was moved to Forest.

A reflection of future generations helped "put up" the first Methodist Church just North of Hillsboro in the county. Grandpa Tommy's grave site at the Hillsboro Methodist Cemetery is surrounded by graves of other generations of his family.

Once in Scott County, it was hard for the Sigrest clan to wander anywhere. Margel, the fourth child of Thomas and Christian, stopped

the family wanderings and homesteaded some land there. He married Isabella Chambers. This is noteworthy since he and "Belle" are responsible for the present generations of Sigrest in Scott County. Among their heirs are family names like Waggoner, Lum, Rigby, Benton, Sessums, Burkes, Noel, Bustin and Sigrest (with apologies to those omitted). They became farmers, builders, teachers, preachers, nurses, doctors, homemakers and skilled managers in business.

Maybe the wandering Sigrest feet will send more Sigrest family members back to Scott County to help proliferate those remaining family names.

SIGREST, Doctor Ernest Americus Sigrest (b. Jan. 6, 1875 in Scott County, MS) was the fourth child in a family of 11 children born to Jasper Gunning Sigrest and Mary Elizabeth Manning. Dr. Sigrest was 12 years old when he and his family moved to Madison County, MS and settled on a farm out from Flora, MS. For over 50 years he served the town of Flora and the surrounding communities. He began his practice after receiving his diploma from Tulane University May 4, 1904.

On Feb. 28, 1864 his father Jasper Gunning Sigrest (b. Jan. 14, 1844 in Hillsborough, Scott County, MS) married Mary Elizabeth "Lizzie" Manning in Morton, Scott County, MS. She was the daughter of Milburn Edward Manning and Martha Marion also of Morton, MS. Of this marriage 11 children were born, namely: Jasper Franklin, Florence Lorreta, John Milburn, Martha Emma, Ernest Americus, Otho Randolph, George Henry, Connie Rufus, Harley LeEstrange, Lauren Alda, Willie Gunning and Bob Sigrest.

Martin (b. about 1775) and his wife Lydia Thomas Sigrest were the ancestors of the Sigrest of Scott County, MS. In the 1820 census of Wayne County, MS one can find record of this family and their eight children. They were listed on the 1825 tax roll of Wayne County as having 80 acres on Ucutta or Eucutta. By the 1830 census of Wayne County, Martin Sigrest was deceased and his wife Lydia had remarried a Mr. Pennington. She was listed as head of household with four male children and one female child.

According to early tax records of Scott County, MS, John B. and his brother Thomas "M.T." Sigrest were present on the 1837 tax list. On the 1850 census of Scott County, MS, John B. Sigrest was listed with his wife Martha G. and seven children, namely: George M., Lydia M., Maloy Gaines, Joseph or Jasper Gunning, Zedra Ann, Amanda J. and Mary M. Sigrest. Other Sigrest families listed on the 1850 census included Micajah or McKager Thomas and his wife Christian Graham Sigrest and their children, Robert Martin, Ethelbert E., Celina E., Margel V., Marion H., Charles N., and Thomas M. Sigrest. Also listed in this household was Edward M. Sigrest, probably a younger brother of M.T. Sigrest. The only other Sigrest household listed on the 1850 census was William M. and Louisa Alsobrook Sigrest and their children, Mary P., Joab and Susan M. Sigrest.

I have been told that there was a twin brother to John B. Sigrest named John G. Sigrest, but I have found no records that prove this. According to census records and family records, I only find the four brothers: McKager Thomas Sigrest, John B. Sigrest, William N. Sigrest and Edward M. Sigrest. John B. Sigrest and his wife are buried in the Brassell Cemetery in Pulaski. Their daughter Laura R. Wackter is also buried beside her parents. McKager Thomas Sigrest and a lot of his descendents are buried in the cemeteries located at the Methodist Church and Baptist Church in Hillsboro.

SIMS, John Sims (b. 1813, Laurens County, SC) and his wife Martha had eight children: James H. (b. 1846), Drew (Drury) R. (b. 1844)), Pennelia J. (b. 1846), William T. (b. 1841)), Sarah (b. 1851), Francis (b. 1853), John (b. 1855) and Benjamin (b. 1858). All were born in Alabama except Benjamin who was born in Mississippi. John was a farmer and he and Martha died in Smith County, MS.

Drew Sims with his medal awarded by the Daughters of the Confederacy

Their sons, John and Drew, served in Co. G, 46th MS Regiment (Singleton's Guard) in the War Between the States and both were captured at Vicksburg Jul. 4, 1863. Drew went on to the Battle of Peach Tree near Atlanta where he was wounded. He lay "in the field of glory" two days before medical help arrived.

Drew came back to Mississippi and married Alabama Buford Singleton, daughter of David Adam Singleton and Nepsa White of Scott County, MS. They had 11 children all believed to born in Scott County:

1) John David (b. 1874) md. Martha Warren. Their daughter Ella Mae md. Marshall Durbin of the chicken industry.

2-3) Marietta (b. 1876) and Nannie (b. 1878) both died young of malaria.

4) Drucilla (b. unknown) md. William Duckworth.

5) Annie Adella (b. 1880) md. Harvey Lavander Thornton of Newton County.

6) James Elbert (b. 1887) md. Cora Brown and they lived in Monroe, LA.

7) Helen Lee (b. 1891) md. Wayne William Weger and they lived in Birmingham, AL.

8) Ella Mae (b. 1893) was called "Bamie" after her mother Bama). She married Sam Herbert Owens and had four children: John Drew (md. Alice Ruth Carr and they reside in Jackson, MS); Sam Herbert Jr. (md. Karon Brumfield and resides in Magnolia, MS); Betty and Kitty.

9. Julia (b. 1894) md. Wheeler Jacobs.

10) Willie (b. 1898) md. Mr. Harper

11) Merle Miller (b. 1902) md. Eric Scott Palmer and raised two children in Forest: Charles Webber (md. Jean) and Doris Marlow (md. Willis Greer).

Drew's war wounds plagued him through his life. He owned land northeast of Forest near the Singletons. In 1909 Drew and Alabama "Bama" opened a boarding house in Forest east of the depot.

The Sims family (spelled Sims, Symes, Simms) came from a long and glorious pedigree. William Symes (b. 1490) was known as the Merchant of Poundsford, Sumerset, England. His son John (b. 1515) owned Barwick Manor, son William (b. 1540), son John Symes Esquire (b. 1572) married Amy Horner. Her family was of the "Little Jack Horner" rhyme. Her mother Jane Popham has a family line that goes back through all the Kings and Queens of England and many of France, Italy and Spain, back to the year AD 0060 to Rathaerius, King of the Franks, totaling 71 generations to date.

John Symes (b. 1572) and Amy had a son Thomas Symes "Esquire" (b. 1621) who married Amy Bridges, their son George "Captain" (b. 1643) sailed from England to Antiguia, British West Indies and married Dorothy Everard, their son George (b. 1670) came to America at Hanover County, VA, married Elizabeth Sherwood, had son Adam (b. 1689), Surry County, VA, married Mary Isham, their son Charles (b. 1721), Brunswick County VA, married Esther Murry, their son Drury "Drew" (b. 1755), Laurens County, VA, married Ruth and their son John (b. 1813) came to Mississippi to bring us our heritage. *Submitted by John Drew Owens and Betty Owens Allen, daughter of John Drew.*

SINGLETON, The Singletons came to the United States in the 1800s and landed in North Carolina. David Adam Singleton Sr. (b. Oct. 11, 1793, Beaufort County, NC, d. Oct 17, 1863, Beaufort County, NC) md. Mary Cherry Jun. 30, 1817 and they had 10 children.

David Adam Singleton Jr. (b. Jan. 25, 1829, Beaufort County, NC, d. Jan. 1, 1905 in Scott County, MS) md. Nepsa White in 1858. She was born Sep. 23, 1833 in Bladen County, NC, and died Nov. 15, 1905 in Piketon, Scott County, MS). They had worked their way through South Carolina, Georgia and on into Alabama. Their children were David James Singleton (b. 1858 in Alabama, d. in Alexandria, LA); Alabama Beaufort (b. Jan. 25, 1859 in Alabama, d. Jul. 31, 1931); Sarah Olivia (b. Apr. 22, 1861, Scott County, MS, d. Nov. 26, 1932 in Scott County); Sidney Savannah (b. 1865, d. Oct. 15, 1948, Memphis TN); Otho Robert (b. 1868 at Singleton Settlement near Forest, d. Sep. 1, 1934); William White (b. Oct. 6, 1870, d. Jun. 9, 1944); Asa Adam (b. Aug. 26, 1875, d. Mar. 1, 1952).

David Adam Jr. had purchased a lot of land and his farm was called Singleton Town.

They didn't have a church to worship in so they built a brush arbor. Later he gave three and a half acres of land and built a one-room church in 1893. It was called Liberty Missionary Baptist Church. The black people also worshiped with them. Liberty Baptist Church is still on the land donated by him. He built the first black school in the county and also donated land for a white school and some of the grandchildren attended that school before attending Forest School. A jail was built on his land and the prisoners worked the land.

SINGLETON, David Adam Singleton Jr. was the son of David Adam Singleton Sr. and Mary "Polly" Cherry of Beaufort County, NC. He married Nepsa White, daughter of William White

and Sarah Robertson of Bladen County, NC, sometime in the 1850s. David and Nepsa along with their two oldest children came to Scott County in 1859. They settled and built a home on what is now old Hwy. 80 east of Forest.

The 1860 census lists David as a miller and machinist. Their third child, Sarah Olivia (b. 1861 in

David Adam Singleton Jr.

Scott County), was the first of their children to be born in Mississippi. Sarah or Sallie as she was known married L.M. "Joe" Hunt. Her older brother David James (b. 1856 in Alabama) md. Mae Hemmenway and moved to Louisiana. Their older daughter Alabama Beaufort (b. 1859 in Alabama) md. Drew Sims. Their other children were Sidney Savannah (b. 1865) md. William Asa Abbett; Otho Robert (b. 1867) md. Molly Lewis and after her death married Ruby Jones; William White Singleton (b. 1870) md. Laura Spinks; Asa Adam (b. 1875) md. Ina Ott.

In 1873 during the controversy of the county seat being moved from Hillsboro to Forest, David had the contract to build the new building. In 1876 Liberty Baptist was organized in a schoolhouse on David's land. In 1893 David deeded three acres to the trustees of Liberty Baptist Church. In 1875 David Singleton planted 15 acres of rice on his land in Scott County. During his life he was well respected by the whites, as well as the blacks and Choctaw Indians. The Indians held ball games on his land several times.

David died in January 1905 with Nepsa following him in November 1905. They are both buried in Liberty Baptist Cemetery. All of their children became prosperous citizens of Scott County.

SITRUNK-COOPER, William Larry Sitrunk and Leslie Carol Cooper were married on Jun. 12, 1970 at Springfield Baptist Church. After living in Jackson for several years, they made their home at 2386 Cooperville Road in March 1976 on the old Sheeley Place. Larry is the son of the late Willie Gene "Pete" Sistrunk and Bobbie Nell Gainey Sistrunk. Larry had one brother, Curtis Dwayne, who died at age 27 of complications from neurofibromatosis, and one sister Deborah Ann Robinson who lives near Larry. He also has one half-brother, Dennis Ray Sistrunk and one half-sister, Pamela.

Larry is a builder, having started his business in December 1977. He has built or remodeled many homes for individuals in Scott, Rankin and Hinds counties. Larry also enjoys deer hunting and fishing. In the early 1970s when quail were still plentiful, he and his best friend Ronnie Frith of Wynndale spent many hours walking the hills and hollows around Crystal Springs quail hunting together. He also spent many enjoyable hours rabbit hunting with his friends and neighbors, Leon Stuart and Lavon and Mark Purvis. Dennis Marlett (his cousin Ramona's husband) and Carol are his fishing partners. Howard and Leon Stuart have fished with Larry many times in years past.

Carol is the daughter of James Malcolm

Cooper and Audie Mae Stegall Cooper both of Morton. On Jun. 1, 2001 she will celebrate her 30th year of employment as Chief of Library Service at the G.V. (Sonny) Montgomery VA Medical Center in Jackson. She has served as organist at her church (Springfield Baptist Church) for about 18 years, having also served as a pianist for quite some time during her grade school years. In addition to serving as organist, she has taught a ladies Sunday School class for 15 years. Carol enjoys deer hunting with Larry and has just this year killed her first 8-point weighing over 200 pounds. She thinks that she came by her interest in hunting honestly, since her two grandfathers, Argie Lee Stegall and James Leslie Cooper, hunted together for many years.

Carol also enjoys working with flowers like her grandmother Nona Cooper and cooking like her grandmother Effie Stegall. When their girls were small, she spent time reading to them and making their dresses, smocked and French handsewn styles (by machine). Their home is decorated with a number of counted cross stitch projects that she has completed including one of the 23rd Psalms which took more than three years to complete. Carol plans to do much more flower gardening (and much less cooking) after she retires sometime in the next couple of years.

Larry and Carol have two daughters who are the joy of their lives: Wendy Carol (b. Apr. 4, 1978) md. Doug Stuart on Jun. 5, 1999 and Amanda Elaine (b. Jan. 12, 1981), now a student at Hinds Community College. Both Larry and Carol are looking forward to the prospect of spoiling grandchildren, taking them fishing and hunting when they get older.

SMITH, John Lane Smith, prominent merchant of Ludlow, Scott County, MS, was born Aug. 9, 1821 in Tennessee to Francis C. Smith Sr. He was married about 1847 to Mary Denson, second daughter of Shadrach James Denson and Alethia Chambers. She was born Mar. 4, 1830 in Rankin County.

Spending the first years of marriage in Madison County, they moved to Ludlow in the early 1850s where he took over management of his father-in-law's store. Sometime thereafter, John L. Smith opened his own mercantile establishment, which in 1855 sold over $10,000 worth of goods. During the Civil War invading Union soldiers burned his store.

A substantial planter, John L. Smith owned in 1860 $4,000 worth of real estate and a personal estate valued at $20,000. Much of this personal estate consisted of his 23 slaves, three of which belonged to his wife. He had a large home built in 1858, which was located one block west of the present site of Ludlow Baptist Church. This house was still standing in middle part of this century and belonged to Mrs. L.B. Bilbro.

Mary (Denson) Smith died Jan. 6, 1876 and John Lane Smith nine years later.

Their children include Sarah Alethia Josephine Smith (b. July 1848) md. William S. Morgan; Thomas P. Smith (b. Jul. 31, 1850, d. Aug. 26, 1870); Jane G. Smith (b. April 1852) md. Ronald M. Kincaid; William Josiah Smith (b. Mar. 7, 1854, d. May 16, 1882; Mary Elizabeth Smith (b. 1856, d. before 1898) md. Josiah Buchanan Denson; Lula Margaret Smith (b.

March 1857) md. Joe B. Madden; Jonnie Lane Smith (b. Jun. 13, 1859, d. Oct. 28, 1939) md. Samuel Burnham Riddick; Solia Martha Smith (b. Aug. 13, 1863, d. Mar. 23, 1948) md. Jeff D. Williams; Fannie E. Smith (b. May 1865) md. E.H. Bailey; S. Coleman Smith (b. 1866, d. 1897) md. Nora L. Porter; Edna Omega Smith (b. May 16, 1870, d. Oct. 13, 1952) md. Newton Franklin Wallace; James R. Smith (b. Dec. 10, 1871, d. Aug. 4, 1886).

SMITH, John Smith (b. 1796-98 in Moore/Montgomery County, NC, d. after 1880) moved to Franklin County, GA then Lawrence County, MS near Fair River before 1820. This family then moved into Copiah County, Hinds County and then Newton County, MS by 1840.

John C. Smith and Annie Everett Smith (1948)

John Smith married three times and had seven children from each of his wives. His second wife was Jeminia Hollingsworth, daughter of Isaac Hollingsworth Sr. and Dorcas Smith. John's third wife was Eliza Graves.

Some of his 21 children names are Cindariller Jane Smith (b. 1822) md. Robert Hollingsworth; Joshua Smith (b. 1834); Ruben Anderson Smith (b. 1835, d. 1927) md. Narcissus Ann Stephens; Johan Smith (b. 1838); Mary Smith (b. 1840, d. 1863); Isaac Smith (b. 1842); Bailey Smith (b. 1844) md. Rachel Katherine Bounds; Huldy Smith (b. 1846); Jane Smith (b. 1848); James Smith (b. 1849), Sarah "Cilia" Smith (b. 1854, d. 1919) md. Joseph Arron Bounds; Jackson Smith (b. 1857); Elizabeth Smith (b. 1858).

John Smith's son Ruben Anderson Smith was a church Elder and served in the 6th MS Inf Co. D, 36th MS Inf CSA. Ruben Anderson Smith and Narcissus Ann Stephens children were Sarah "Sallie" Francis Smith (b. 1862, d. 1945) md. Charles A. Huddleston; William Anderson Smith (b. 1864, d. 1946) md. Julia G. Atkinson, daughter of Abner Atkinson and Henrietta McDaniel; Henrietta "Hattie" Smith (b. 1868, d. 1957,) md. Joseph Berry "Joe" Gay; Margaret Smith (b. 1871); John S. Smith (b. 1873) md. T.M. Volentine/Valentine; Narcissus L. Smith (b. 1875) md. W.B. Volentine/Valentine; Lena Leota "Mittie" Smith (b. 1878, d. 1967) md. Virgil Isaac Pennington; Mary Alice Smith (b. 1880, d. 1920) md. Walter Maxwell; Edward "Edd" Smith (b. 1882, d. 1961) md. Margaret "Maggie" Vesta Russum; Samuel Smith (b. 1886, d. 1902). Ruben Anderson's son William Anderson Smith was born while his father was serving in the Confederacy.

By 1900 William Anderson Smith and his wife Julia had moved from Newton County, MS into beat five, Scott County, MS area. With them were their five children: Henrietta Smith (b. 1887, d. 1967) md. James "Jim" M. Gibbs; Mammie Renald "Nallie" Smith (b. 1891, d. 1971) md. Jessie Richard "Dock" Gibbs; Robert "Ruben" Anderson Smith (b. 1896, d. 1972)

md. Katie Ethel McGee; William Conelious "Neal" Smith (b. 1898, d. 1982) md. Lida Alma Usry; John Clark Smith (b. 1900, d. 1950) md. Annie Myrtle Everett; Allie Mae Smith (b. 1902, d. 1943) md. William Claude Myers.

Although John Clark Smith and Annie Myrtle Everett are buried at Pine Ridge Baptist Church Cemetery in Newton County, MS, they were born, lived and died in the beat five area of Scott County, MS. Their six children were John Mavis Smith (b. 1923) md. "Deaner" McCully had three children and now live in Louisville, MS; Julia Evelyn Smith (b. 1924, d. 1958) md. Basil Marquel Porter and had five children: Herron Aron Smith (b. 1927, d. 1928); Clyde Alvis "Buddy" Smith (b. 1929) md. Nancy Iwana Nutt, have two children and now live in Citronelle, AL; Margaret Ann Smith (b. 1933) md. Aldewin Theo Johnson Jr., have two children and now live in Brandon, MS, Peggy Frances Smith (b. 1940) md. Guy Junius Howard, have two children. Peggy now lives in Meridian, MS.

SMITH, John Jackson Smith was part of a 12-man commission that organized Scott County in 1834. He was selected as the first sheriff.

His father was John Smith who served as a private in the Revolutionary War with Colonel William Thompson's Regiment in the Line of the state of South Carolina. His mother was Martha Jones the daughter of a Welshman with a Choctaw wife. The Smiths were part of the migration of about 12 families from Edgefield District, South Carolina to Mississippi.

In 1818 in Hinds County, MS John Jackson Smith married Margaret Katherine Butler. Her father John Landon Butler (b. about 1763 in Richmond, Henrico County, VA) was the son of William Butler (b. 1736 in Goochland County, VA), who migrated to North Carolina then to Edgefield District, SC where he died in 1790. John's widow, Mary Ann Jones, became a member of the Antioch Primitive Baptist Church in Scott County.

1) Martha Smith married 1838 in Scott County, Robert Eldridge Ricks, who worked as an overseer for the Smiths. The couple migrated to Kenedy County, TX, with her Uncle Burnell Butler who had married Robert's sister Sarah Ann Ricks.

2) Ann Smith married in 1841 Silas McCabe who had come to Mississippi from Smith County, TN. After the death of her brother Burton Smith, they moved to Bosque County to settle on Coon Creek.

3) Seaborne Jones Smith married Delina Wilson Eastland in Hillsboro, Scott County, and served two terms in the Mississippi Legislature in 1854 and 1856. After the Civil War they migrated to Texas.

4) Anderson B. Smith, though born four years before the county was formed, was said to be the first white child born in Scott. Anderson had a successful legal practice, died 1879 and is buried in the Eastern Cemetery, Forest, Scott County. He married first Lucy Fennel Graham and second Maggie S. Horn.

5) Elizabeth Smith married Hiram Eastland in 1849 and died in Scott County.

6) Most tragic was the 1856 death of 24-year-old C. Burton Smith on his father's newly

acquired land in Bosque County, TX. When his mother arrived, Margaret selected the most attractive part of the tract for a cemetery. Burton, his parents and six of his siblings are buried in the Smith Bend/Coon Creek Cemetery.

7) Thomas Jefferson Smith married Jane Byrn in Mississippi and Lodimia Herring in TX.

8) Emily Smith married Benjamin Franklin Burks, son of James Lyons Burks of Hillsboro, Scott County.

9) Martin Van Buren Smith married Aileen Ham in Texas.

10) Gipson Smith married Elizabeth Jones Bonds in Texas.

11) Laura Smith was born in 1847 in Scott County.

Fourteen deeds were recorded in Scott County for land, between 1839 and 1846, bearing the name of John J. Smith. Because of his knowledge of the Choctaw language, John Jackson Smith participated in the removal of some of the Choctaws from Mississippi. His Sister Anne Smith married Bryant McCartny from another of the families in Edgefield District. They migrated to Oklahoma to live on Indian land. *Submitted by Doris Maxwell Dell.*

SMITH, Robert Palmer Smith, who lived for many years between Lena and Contrell, was born in Union County, SC, on Oct. 31, 1809. His parents were Samuel Smith and Nancy White of the Hughes Creek area near Mount Tabor. Family tradition states that the mother of Robert Palmer Smith was a sister of Wylie White of Leake County, whose original will is in the handwriting of R.P. Smith.

After his marriage to Nutty Newton Alverson, who was born in Union County to Benjamin Alverson and Polly Addis(?) on May 29, 1819, Robert Palmer Smith moved his family to Pickens County, AL, before 1840 along with his brother George W. By 1850 they were living in Leake County but eventually purchased land in Scott County.

Robert Palmer Smith's father died in Union County, SC, in 1838; between 1844 and 1850 his mother and five of his siblings moved to Madison County, where his older brother owned adjoining land in Madison and Leake counties. About 1853 these relatives relocated to Neshoba County near Arlington. One sister of Robert Palmer Smith remained in South Carolina. George W. Smith moved from Pickens County to Choctaw County, MS, before 1860, after which time his family has not been located.

The first Smith child, Nancy Ann, was born May 25, 1839, and died Nov. 13, 1839, probably in Pickens County, AL. Russell P. Smith, was born Sep. 22, 1840. As a divinity student at Cumberland University in Lebanon, TN, he left the university after the Civil War began and died Apr. 19, 1863, in Clinton, MS, in service to the Confederacy. Samuel Feemster Smith (b. Sep. 12, 1842, d. Mar. 18, 1863) died as a Federal prisoner in Alton, IL, where his name is inscribed on the Confederate memorial.

Mary Jane Smith (b. Nov. 18, 1844, Pickens County, AL, d. Feb. 6, 1917) md. John Newton Pettigrew on Jul. 3, 1861. He was the son of Thomas M. Pettigrew and Elizabeth B. Elliott, who were early residents of Tuscola in Leake County.

Robert Palmer Smith Jr. (b. Feb. 8, 1847, d. Jun. 26, 1943) attended Cumberland University and became a Presbyterian minister. He married first, Mittie Elizabeth Nucknis and second, Alice McGaw. Elvira Mahala Smith was born Oct. 7, 1848, and died May 29, 1862. Her burial site has not been located.

Benjamin Franklin Smith (b. May 28, 1850, d. Feb. 3, 1934) md. first, Rose Morris, daughter of William Morris and Susan Glaze, sister of Anderson Glaze of Scott County. His second wife, Carrie Lee Orman, was the daughter of Stephen Lee and Martha Whitehead.

Berry Alverson Smith (b. Apr. 17, 1852, d. Sep. 30, 1938) md. Dollie Orman, daughter of John Orman and Susan Lee. Rebecca White Smith (b. Nov. 1, 1854, d. Jul. 2, 1938) md. Albert Jefferson Henkel, son of William Henkel and Mary White(?). Sarah Elizabeth Cuba Smith (b. Sep. 6, 1855, d. Apr. 3, 1932) md. James Alpheus Albertson, son of James Albert and Susan Lee and half brother of Dollie Orman. Josephine Newton Smith (b. May 7, 1859, d. May 8, 1943) md. George W. Gann, son of James M. Gann and Elizabeth Franks.

Robert Palmer Smith died Aug. 20, 1889, and Nutty Newton Alverson Smith died Oct. 21, 1884. Both are buried on the west side of Lena Cemetery. *Submitted by Barbara Sudduth Lyle.*

SMITH-LOVETT, In 1948 John B. and Myrtice Smith bought some land and built a house and a one-room grocery store on Hwy. 35 south about three miles from Forest.

John was from Comer, GA and was the son of Charles Henry and Gena Smith. He had three brothers: Hoyt, B.B., Dozier, and two sisters, Minnie Belle and Lilborn. His brothers and sisters all lived around Macon and Atlanta, GA.

Myrtice Smith by her store (1980)

Myrtice was the daughter of Tom F. and Patty Lott Lovett. Her grandparents, Solomon B. and Nancy Lott and William H. and Rebecca Lovett were all from Scott County. She had two brothers, Bill and Floyd Lovett, and three sisters: Vera (Moore), Margie (Carlisle) and Pattie Mae who died at three months. They were all raised on the road that is now the old Hwy. 35 south loop and lived close around that area most all their lives.

John and Myrtice had three children: Dr. Charles B. Smith who married Cheryl Rasco of Lena, MS. They have three children: Chris, Amy and Stephan, and now live in Fairhope, AL. Dr. John Smith Jr. is their second son and he married Diane Nations of Gulfport, MS. They have three sons: Tyler, Thomas and Taylor. They live in Forest, MS. John and Myrtice's daughter is Linda Warren. She was married to Jimmy War-

ren of Lake, MS and they have one daughter Debbie Gliddon. Linda has three grandchildren: Misty, India and Candy of Forest, MS.

John and Myrtice made a living from the little grocery store. John also bought and sold used cars. The store was a place where people could buy a week's groceries or just come to sit and talk. We kids were partly raised in the store and have wonderful memories of the times we spent there. We would sit in the back and parch peanuts on the wooden stove and listen to the grown-ups talking, and many times we helped out by bagging groceries. When our father died in 1964 our mother continued running the store until she was almost 80 years old. Mother died in June 2000 at 91 years of age and the little store still stands today.

SPARKS, The trek of the Sparks family began in the mid-1600s as new lands were opened and made available for settling. These pioneers settled in Virginia, the Carolinas, Georgia, Alabama and Mississippi. William Thomas and Mary (McMurray) moved from Alabama to Scott County in 1871 and settled on land that became known as Sparksville. Mary McMurray Sparks died in 1871 and later William Thomas married Caroline Graham. They are buried in the Hillsboro Methodist Cemetery where a Confederate marker was placed on his grave.

From the marriage of William and Mary, four children were born: Elizabeth, Mary, Jim, David Henry and Jessie. David Henry kept the land and acquired more. He married Mary Elizabeth Gann in 1852. Both are buried in the Hillsboro Methodist Cemetery. From this marriage eight children were born: Carrie Sparks Simmons, James "Jim" Sparks, George Sparks, Erana Sparks Eure, Josie Bell Sparks Sanders, Cecil Sparks, Leon "Bill" Sparks, Beulah Mae Sparks Kern. Descendents of these families are now scattered all over the world.

The Sparks family lives centered around farming and for over a hundred years the eight families continued to live in the Sparksville Community. Records indicate that at one time there was a post office and store, which served the Sparks family and neighbors as well. A large, hardworking family, the Rascos, lived nearby and often helped with the farming activities.

Memorable were the occasions when people from all over Scott County came to the cane mill at syrup making time and the Christmas breakfasts that were served with plenty of eggnog. State and local politicians were made welcome at the table. Social life consisted of attending church, going to town and having company.

The large families continued to expand and today descendents of the Sparks family are found in most professions and have made a name for themselves by contributing to the good things of life.

The Sparksville Community has undergone drastic changes and today very little can be seen of the earlier community. Poultry houses now exist where crops were raised and cattle grazed. Modern techniques, better roads, and a new generation indicate the changes that time has brought to a once thriving, family owned, progressive community. Most of the original land is now owned by a descendent of the Sparks, and the community is identified by a road sign on old Hwy. 35 showing the road that goes to Sparksville. Surrounding the Sparks land is the vast Bienville National Forest.

Sparksville can be located on the old maps of Scott County but not on the new maps of today. Nevertheless, Sparksville still exists with its proud heritage, rich in values that will continue on and on.

SPARKS, When my father, Jim Sparks, opened his store in the early 1900s in Hillsboro there was one other store there owned by Taylor Tadlock. His brother Turner Tadlock operated a grist mill in the back of Tadlock's place. Dave Stallings and son Martin operated an auto repair shop and service station with one gasoline hand pump out front. Mr. and Mrs. Calvin Cochran were the post office operators. There was no electricity or running water, all roads were mostly clay which made them very stick when they were wet. Very few people had cars anyway. Most travel was by horseback, wagons and a few had buggies.

Hillsboro was a farming community, and Dad saw the need for a store where the farmers could buy all their farming needs at one place. We had a well stocked store; my mother Georgie McCrory Sparks was in charge of the fabric department and often cut out a garment for a customer using one of her newspaper patterns.

Saturday was our busiest day. The farmers would come in their wagons and some would bring their families and stay all day. Sugar, rice and coffee beans would come in 100 pound sacks. We would have to re-bag this into five cent, 10 cent and 25 cent bags. Flour came in 24 and 48 pound bags and wooden barrels containing 96 pounds. We sold oil sausage from a wooden barrel and also soda crackers loosely by the pound. We had a cheese cutter and sold cheese by the slice We had a tobacco cutter where we could cut 5 cent or larger slices for the customer. The favorites were Brown Mule and Days Work. Prince Albert smoking tobacco was 15 cents a can. Golden Grain and other small sacks of tobacco were 5 cents a sack, and cigarettes were 15 cents a pack, cigars were 10 cents each. We sold men's overalls for 75 cents a pair and children's for 50 cents. Dad took orders for tailor made suits also. We sold sardines for 5 cents a can and we furnished crackers and home made pepper sauce for the customer to eat them with. In the winter our store was heated with a pot bellied stove fired with hard wood.

We had lots of loafers who came early in the morning to sit around the stove and tell tall tales all day, chewing tobacco and spitting on the hot stove. I always looked forward to Christmas season because we had nice apples, oranges and raisins that came in wooden boxes as well as hard candy and chocolate drops. Mother would buy hickory nuts from children to make cakes as there were no pecans around. When we got electricity times changed some. Daddy bought a radio for the store and a 6-inch oscillating fan to sit by it. Electricity also brought cold drinks and ice cream at 5 cents a cone. On Saturday nights the whole community would come to the store to listen to the Grand Old Opry. Moon shine whiskey was cheap and plentiful and many took a drink as the bottle was passed

around. Our main source of news was over a party line telephone that many in the community owned. When the phone rang regardless of the coded ring, everyone ran to listen to all conversations. When I was about 9 or 10 I started helping in the store, the good times were gone. There was little money, many of our customers would bring eggs, chickens, syrup and corn to trade for groceries. Daddy bought a truck so he could take produce to Jackson, soon other stores were sending their produce by him. Soon he was making two trips a week to the city. Mother took charge of the store. Later Daddy got allergic to feathers and had to give up handling chickens. We then sold chickens to Hugh Haralson of Harperville. At one time a cotton gin was operated out back of the store by Edgar Waggoner and Earl Rigby.

The store closed when WWII was brewing and my uncle H.B. McCrory Sr. was elected sheriff of Scott County. My mother went to work for him in his office.

I want to say thanks to my brother Dallas Sparks and my cousin Marion McCrory for helping with this story of the Sparks Friendly Store of Hillsboro. *Story by Dorothy Sparks Lackey.*

SPARKS-ROWE, Janice Matilda Rowe and Leon "Bill" Sparks married August 1922 and made their home in Sparksville with Bill's parents, where they helped on the farm until January 1923. Then they moved in with her father, Dr. Ellis J. Rowe, at their Hillsboro home which was also his office. They shared chores with tenants who lived in a house on their 80 acre farm, which was one of a few that General Sherman did not burn on his march to Georgia.

The Depression took its toll on the area but people on the farms were perhaps better able to feed their families, some help finally came from government programs. In 1932 Janice helped set up the first Welfare Dept. At Hillsboro, by going around to see what was most needed. The Red Cross also helped by giving underwear and stockings for the children, fabric and cotton for making clothing and bedding.

Later Bill and Janice bought a 127 acre farm and a livable house for $1,500. With help from Bill's daddy (Pa Sparks) they mainly farmed cotton, corn, sugar cain, peanuts and a large garden. As children continued to come Bill was appointed to a county committee for the Farmers Home Administration. It wasn't long before hogs, chickens and cattle helped raise the standard of living for the Sparks family. Eight healthy, happy children were prepared for life by the sacrifices of Bill and Janice and many friends and relatives as they worked, played and worshiped together.

Ellis, Frances, Delbert, Leon Jr., Richard, Gene, Daniel and Janet will attest to a job well done.

STEWART, Buck Stewart arrived in Scott County in the mid-1800s and homesteaded a section of land. Buck's three sons, William Lewis "W.L," Dick and P.H., were also in Scott County. His son W.L eventually inherited the land and added more acres to the farm. W.L. Stewart (b. 1824 in Georgia, d. 1893) md. Rebecca J. (b. ?, d. 1895). They are both buried in the Damascus Cemetery in Scott County.

Their children were Charles J., Sarah Catherine, Martha F., Thomas Ashberry (twin), W.L. Jr. (twin), Malissa, and Mary Elizabeth.

Martha F. Stewart md. William Crecilius. Malissa Stewart md. Bill Goodwin. Mary Elizabeth md. O.I. or O.E. Williams, W.L. Jr. md. Colista Hammock.

Sarah Catherine Stewart (b. Sep. 27, 1848) md. William Andrews, son of Samuel and Annis Andrews. Sarah died June 1897 and William February 1914. They are buried in the Damascus Cemetery in Scott County.

W.L. and Rebecca Stewart were my great-grandparents. My grandparents were Sarah Catherine Stewart and Wiliiam Andrews. Their son Robert was my father. Robert (b. Mar. 2, 1884 in Scott County) md. Alma Burns on Sep. 8, 1912 in Scott County.

Samuel and Annis Andrews

Robert Andrews, grandson of W.L. Stewart

Art Goodwin and family. He is the grandson of W.L. Stewart

Both sets of my great-grandparents, the Stewarts and the Andrews, settled in Scott County, where many of their descendants still live. *Submitted by Josie Grantham.*

STEWART, Benjamin Stewart (b. about 1815 in Louisiana) was the youngest child of John B. Stewart. Benjamin married Rebecca Jane Taylor, daughter of Powell Taylor, and they Spent the remainder of their life in Scott County. Their children were William, John Benjamin, Eveline, Lee Pullen, James J., Susan and Melissa Elizabeth. Lee Pullen Stewart married his first cousin, Sarah Ann Stewart, and James J. married Susan S. Williams.

STEWART, Fredrick B.L. "Fed" Stewart (b. Aug. 31, 1858 in Newton County, MS, d. May 13, 1934 in Hillsboro, Scott County, MS) was the son of Joseph W. Stewart and Matilda Pullen. On Aug. 29, 1878 he married Laura Emma Smith in Scott County, MS. Laura was the daughter of Jefferson Smith. She was born Jun. 30, 1859 and died Mar. 25, 1946 in Hillsboro. Both are buried at Hillsboro Baptist Church Cemetery. Their children are as follows:

1) Birdie Laura Stewart (b. Jun. 7, 1878, d. Jan 15, 1929 in Lawrence, MS) md. Benjamin Franklin McCoy on Dec 24, 1898 in Scott County.

2) Ernest Fredrick (b. Nov. 13, 1880, d. May 4, 1945 in Hillsboro) md. Elizabeth Bell Cole, daughter of Albert Cole and Margaret Nicholas, on Nov. 11, 1903 in Scott County.

3) Cora Dell (b. Oct. 6, 1882, d. Jun. 13, 1954 in Lawrence) md. Joseph Lloyd Stewart, son of James T. Stewart and Mollie Gibbs, in December 1899.

4) Minnie (b. Aug. 8, 1884, d Mar. 29, 1944 in Hillsboro) md. Rudolph Hatten.

5) Stella (b. Nov. 9, 1886) md. Rex Erick Reeves. They are both buried at Antioch Baptist Church Cemetery.

6) Nellie (b. Jan. 20, 1889 in Hillsboro, d. Jan. 9, 1968 in Rio Vista, TX) md. Levi Putnam from Newton County.

7) Eunice Carl (b. Jun. 21, 1892, d. Jul. 23, 1970) md. Cora Lee Simmons on Nov. 1, 1911. They are both buried in Hillsboro.

8) Otho Roger (b. Feb. 14, 1894 in Hillsboro, d. Jan. 7, 1972 in Madison County, MS) md. Nannie Leona Johnson, the youngest child of Leonidus Printus Johnson and Nannie Floy Culipher, on May 9, 1914 in Scott County.

9) Bailey Glen (b. Mar. 24, 1896, d. Jan. 25, 1973 in Hillsboro) md. Maude Viola McDonald, daughter of Ross McDonald and May Wallace. Bailey and Maude are both buried at Hillsboro Baptist Church Cemetery.

STEWART, Joseph W. Stewart (b. Feb. 5, 1805 in Louisiana, d. Jan. 10, 1875 in Newton County, MS) was the oldest son of John B. Stewart from South Carolina. Joseph married Matilda Pullen, daughter of Henry and Sara Pullen (b. Mar. 10, 1815 in Lawrence County, d. Mar. 6, 1893 in Newton County, MS) on Mar 29, 1831 in Hinds County, MS.

Both Joseph and Matilda Pullen Stewart's families lived in Hinds County, MS along with several other families that would all migrate to the Newton/Scott County area during the 1830s. Some of their Hinds County neighbors were James Weaver, Thomas Futch, Elizabeth and William Goodson, James and Richard Stewart.

Joseph and Matilda Pullen Stewart had 13 children:

William Wylie (b. Apr. 22, 1832 Hinds County, d. Apr. 14, 1865 Camp Chase POW Camp, OH) md. Catherine Althea Ware on Oct. 4, 1850, daughter of William Ware and Leah Price. Catherine Ware Stewart, along with her children and many other Scott/Newton County families, left by wagon train for Texas in the late 1860s.

2) Harold Charles (b. Feb. 15, 1834, d. abt. 1836).

3) Henry Pullen Stewart (b. Jan. 20, 1837, d. May 23, 1890) md. Martha Jane Smith on Sep. 5, 1854, daughter of Elijah Smith and Martha Brown.

4) Benjamin J. (b. Apr. 27 1838, d. May 2, 1921) md. Margaret M. Futch Jul. 4, 1860, daughter of John Futch and Elizabeth Cook.

5) Jessie M. (b. Mar. 24, 1839).

6) Nancy Jane (b. Sep. 25, 1841) md. Wade Hamilton Futch on Oct. 29, 1859, son of John Futch and Elizabeth Cook.

7) Louisa M. (b. Jan. 6, 1843) md. Albert G. Futch on Dec. 14, 1858, son of John Futch and Elizabeth Cook.

8) Lydia Ann Elizabeth (b. Jul. 30, 1844, d.

1891) md. John L. Loftin, son of Fredrick Loftin.

9) Joseph W. (b. Jul. 4, 1846, d. before 1850).

10) John Wade H. (b. Mar. 24, 1848, d. Jul. 10, 1870).

11) Sara Ann (b. Aug. 19, 1850) md. Lee Pullen Stewart, son of Benjamin Stewart and Rebecca Taylor.

12) Matthew Lafayette (b. Mar. 23, 1853, d. Sep. 5, 1921) md. Cornelia Frances Smithon Dec. 26, 1871, daughter of Elijah Smith and Martha Brown.

13) Fredrick B.L. (b. Aug. 31 1858, d. May 13 1934) md. Laura Emma Smith on Aug. 29, 1878 in Scott County, daughter of Jefferson Smith and Barbara Brown.

STEWART, Louisa Stewart (b. about 1813 in Louisiana), daughter of John B. Stewart, married Henry Pullen Jr., son of Henry and Sara Pullen, on Dec. 26, 1831 in Hinds County. They had 11 children. The two oldest were born in Hinds County and the two youngest were born in Bienville Parish, LA. All of the other children were born in Scott/Newton County.

The children were Henry III (b. 1832); Harvey B. (b. 1833) md. Mary Emily Graham Feb. 26, 1860; Francis M. (b. 1836, d. 1864) md. Eugene A. Bates; Sarah (b. Feb. 18, 1837, d. Feb. 15, 1915) md. John Monk Jun. 21, 1861; Elizabeth Matilda (b. Apr. 29, 1840, d. Mar. 5, 1878) md. Mabry Nathaniel Bates Oct. 21, 1858; Wiley Alexander (b. Nov. 12, 1842, d. Sep. 6, 1908) md. Caldonia Graham Dec. 5, 1867; William R. (b. 1845) md. Rebecca Vaughn; Nehemiah (b. ca. 1847); Lee M. (b. Apr. 25, 1850, d. Oct. 1, 1921) md. Mary A. Hadwin; Robert J. (b. Mar. 24, 1853, d. May 16, 1943) md. Camellia Graham; Rosena (b. 1856 in Louisiana) md. Edward Alonzo Mixon.

STONE, Abner Miller Stone (b. Dec. 18, 1864 in Scott County, d. Mar. 27, 1921 in Texas), son of David and Mary Stone, married Hester Ann Caldonia "Dony" Taylor on May 9, 1889 in Gatesville, TX. She was born Feb. 24, 1874, the daughter of Rev. Isaac and Amanda Francis E. Taylor. She died on Jan. 11, 1925. They are both buried at Hillscrest Cemetery in Temple, TX. Their children are as follows:

Abner Miller Stone

1) Charley David Stone (b. Dec. 14, 1890, d. May 27, 1958) md. Lella May Bowers, daughter of Robert and Georgia Russell Bowerson, on May 31, 1910. Charley and Lella are buried in Waco, TX. Their children were Clois David, Geneva Meryle, Charles Abner, Edna Earle and Lena Bessie Ruth.

2) Oscar Wesley Stone (b. Feb. 7, 1892, d. Jun. 19, 1925 at Orange, TX) md. Cleria Elizabeth Wilkinson, daughter of Tom and Mary Lou Wilkinson. They had three children: Toddler (deceased), Bernadine and Ernestine. Oscar is buried at Hillcrest Cemetery, Temple, TX.

3) Herbert Lafayette Stone (b. Dec. 24, 1893, d. July 1968) md. Audie Gilliland, daugh-

ter of Weldon and Bell Gilliand. Their children were Flora Maxine, Dony Belle, Alta Oleta, Nella Faye and Herbert Losson. Herbert is buried in Woodlawn Cemetery in Houston, TX.

Abner Miller and Dony (Taylor) Stone and grandchild

4) Bessie Leona Stone (b. May 15, 1899, d. Mar. 13, 1986) md. first, Charley Embry and had one son, Ulric R.; married second, L.L. Saurage and had one daughter, Betty Jo; married third, Richard Grigg.

5) Abner Earl Stone (b. Sep. 21, 1896, d. Sep. 21, 1978) md. Sarah Flossie Embry. She died Apr. 4, 1992. Both are buried at Greenlawn Memorial Park, Groves, TX. Their children were Richard Lee, Lucy Earl and Edgar Romney Stone.

6) Edgar Wood Stone (b. Dec. 2, 1901, d. Aug. 18, 1983) md. Gladys Leona Hay. She died Dec. 23, 1995. They are buried at Woodlawn Cemetery, Houston, TX. Their children are Jessie Miller Stone who married Loraine Still. Their children are Gale Ann and Jeanne Beth Stone.

7) Alta Margie Stone (b. Jul. 28, 1906, d. Sep. 15, 1988) md. Richard K. Caraway. He died in December 1995. Both are buried at Hillcrest Cemetery, Temple, TX.

8) Clyta Stone (b. Dec. 16, 1909, d. Apr. 16, 1999) md. Garvin Marion Shotwell. He died Jul. 27, 1967. They had one child Garva Lou Shotwell.

9) Dony Eugenia Stone (b. Aug. 26, 1912, d. Jun. 6, 1952) md. Rudolph L. Clark. They had twin boys, Donnie and Gary Clark.

10) Cal Culbert Stone (b. Mar. 1, 1915) ms. Flavia Breaux. Their children are Darlene Kay, Larry Wayne and Jeffrey Dale Stone.

11) Culbert is the last surviving child of Abner and Dony Stone.

STONE, Caroline Liberty "Ebb" Stone (b. Jun. 7, 1861 in Mississippi, d. Sep. 30, 1942 at Waco, TX) was the daughter of David and Mary Johnson Stone. She married Alfred Eastland Battle in Mississippi. He was a master carpenter. They later moved to Texas. Many of their descendents live in the Waco area. Their children were:

1) Albert Edward Battle (b. Oct. 14, 1879, d. Sep. 18, 1951) md. Minnie Mae Standridge Aug. 2, 1900. She was the daughter of John Wesley and Mary Caroline (Whatley) Standridge of Blevins, Falls County, TX. Their children were Beatrice Thelma Battle (b. Apr. 28, 1901, d. Nov. 28, 1902); Albert Clarence Battle (b. Nov. 7, 1903, d. Nov. 14, 1963); John Wesley Battle (b. Sep. 25, 1906, d. Aug. 6, 1991) md. Ethel Keeton in 1934. She died in 1990. They are both buried at Waco Memorial Park, Waco, TX; Mildred Inez Battle (b. Aug. 14, 1909, d. Mar. 6, 1969) md. John Bone; Katherine Fay Battle (b. Feb. 3, 1912) md. Manuel Hill. He died Oct. 18, 1985. Katherine is in a nursing home; Luna Mae Battle (b. Sep. 20, 1916) md. James Maurice Pace Sep. 5, 1936 at Marlin, TX.

After the death of Minnie Mae Ed Battle married Inez (Bertrand) Rickett. They had two children, Dollie Elizabeth and Albert Edward Jr. He married third, Lillie (Ingram) Jackson. They had no children.

2) Bessie Emma Battle (b. Mar. 28, 1882, d. Mar. 28, 1916) md. Bruce Standridge on Jan. 2, 1899. He was the son of John Wesley and Mary Caroline Standridge.

3) Katie M. Battle.

STONE, Edgefield District, South Carolina 1850 Census shows David Stone with his family as follows: David Stone age 32, his wife Mary age 21, James male age 2 years, John R. age 6 months, Patsey Stone age 63 (female). By 1860 they were in Scott County, MS. David Stone is not shown in the 1870 census in Scott County. He apparently died between 1860-1870. Mary Stone is shown as head of household. David and Mary are listed in "Minutes of Antioch Primitive Baptist Church 1835-1920 Scott County MS.

Their children were: 1) James Presley Stone (b. Aug. 1, 1848 in South Carolina, d. Feb. 19, 1921 in Scott County, MS) md. first, Susan Walters and second, Martha "Mattie" Olive Crecelius.

2) John Wesley Stone (b. Sep. 8, 1850 in South Carolina).

3) Mary Elizabeth Stone (b. Oct. 28, 1851).

4) Thomas Moses Stone (b. Apr. 28, 1852 in South Carolina).

5) Susan Savannah Stone (b. Aug. 13, 1853 in South Carolina) md. J.T. Waldrip Jul. 12, 1891 in Scott County, MS.

6) Georgeanna Sarah Stone (b. Nov. 8, 1856).

7) Robert David Stone (b. Dec. 20, 1857 in Scott County, MS, d. Jan. 12, 1936 at Lake, MS) md. Ella Cornelia Saxon;

8) Emma Stone (b. Nov. 21, 1859).

9) Caroline Liberty Stone (b. Jun. 7, 1861, d. Sep. 30, 1942).

10) Abner Miller Stone (b. Dec. 18, 1864 in Scott County, MS, d. Mar. 27, 1921 at Chadwick Mills, TX) md. Hester Ann Caldonia "Dony" Taylor May 9, 1889 at Gatesville, TX.

11) Henry Lafayette Stone (b. Jul. 3, 1866 in Scott County, MS, d. Apr. 12, 1932 at his home in Bomarton, TX). He is buried in Brushie Cemetery. He was a farmer and married Phedora "Dodie" Parker. She had one son from a previous marriage named Guy Parker. In 1930 he had a sheep ranch in Montana. Henry and Dodie have one natural son Henry Lafayette Stone Jr. (b. Jun. 12, 1904, d. Jun. 12, 1930 from typhoid fever). Place of residence Goree, TX. He is buried in Rowden City cemetery.

12) Margaret Conbry Stone (b. Jun. 25, 1868).

13) Savannah Abnery Stone (b. December 1873).

STONE, James Presley Stone Sr. (b. Aug. 1, 1848 in South Carolina) was the son of David and Mary Johnson Stone. He married first, Susan Walters and their children were:

Benjamin Franklin "Frank" Stone (b. ca. 1873, d. Nov. 6, 1934) md. Levi Roberts on Jun. 4, 1910. He is buried at Antioch Cemetery in Scott County, MS.

Ida Catherine Stone (b. Feb. 7, 1878, d. May 27, 1961 in Forest, MS) md. Ernest Grenada Burkes.

James Presley Stone Sr. married second, Martha "Mattie" Olive Creclius on Dec. 7, 1884. She was the daughter of E.C. "Cline" and Mary (Fleming) Creclius. Martha (b. Jun. 15, 1869 in Alabama, d. Oct. 21, 1943 at 74

James Presley Stone Sr. and Mattie Crecelius Stone with family ca. 1904

years of age). James died Feb. 19, 1921. He was a farmer. They are both buried at Antioch Cemetery. Their children are as follows:

James Presley Stone Jr. "Jack" (b. Mar. 31, 1885, d. April 18, 1972) md. Minnie Ponder on Mar. 8, 1915. James Jr. is buried in the Forkville Baptist Cemetery.

Abner Malcom Stone (b. Jan. 21, 1887 at Hillsboro, MS, d. Dec. 12, 1956) was a farmer. He married Virgie Morgan.

Clifton Lenwood Stone (b. Aug. 5, 1889, d. Feb. 25, 1920) never married

Elmer Herd Stone (b. Oct. 22, 1893, d. Mar. 3, 1970) md. Cleo Estelle Sessums. He was a WWII veteran.

Eva Patricia "Pat" Stone (b. Aug. 13, 1896, d. May 16, 1993) md. Percy William Gordy (b. Jul. 15, 1896 in Scott County, MS, d. Jun. 28, 1978 at Baptist Hospital) on Apr. 20, 1922. They are buried at Morton Memorial Garden Cemetery. They had no children.

Ella Belle Stone (b. Oct. 4, 1898, d. 1972) md. William Hewie Roberts. She is buried in Morton Memorial Gardens. They had no children.

Ola Louise Stone (b. May 25, 1901, d. 1989) md. Clyde C. Myers on May 24, 1924 in Scott County. They had one son Bobby Stone Myers who married Lodena Townsend.

Henry Cline "Henry C." Stone (b. Oct. 27, 1903, d. May 12, 1991 at Scott County Nursing Home at age 86) md. Frankie Lee Watkins. She died on May 19, 1991. They are buried at Morton Memorial Gardens. He was a farmer, poultry and livestock trader until his retirement. Their children were James Cline and Elaine. Elaine married Dick Warwick and they live in Dallas, TX.

Dionie Stone (b. May 11, 1906 at Hillsboro, MS) md. Charles Beaven. Their children were Patricia, Christy and Charles Beaven Jr.

Jessie Clois Stone (b. Nov. 1, 1912 at Hillsboro) md. Ruby Marie Williams on Oct. 9, 1935 at Ludlow. Ruby Marie (b. Oct. 2, 1917) was the daughter of Floyd and Willis Virginia Williams. Their children are Joe Earl, Philip Clois and Sara Elizabeth.

STONE, Robert David Stone (b. Dec. 20, 1857, d. Jan. 12, 1936 at Lake, MS) was the son of David and Mary (Johnson) Stone. He married Ella Cornelia "Nelia" Saxon on Mar. 21, 1913. She was born Nov. 21, 1859 and died Jan. 12, 1918. They are both buried at Antioch Cemetery, Primitive Baptist Church, Scott County, MS.

Their children were: 1) Henry David "Dave" Stone (b. July 1881, d. Jun. 19, 1935 at Morton) md. Martha "Mattie" Putnam. He is buried at Antioch Cemetery.

2) Tressie Stone (b. Dec. 29, 1882, d. Mar. 12, 1908) md. W.P. "Pat" Warren Dec. 27, 1899 in Scott County. She is buried at Antioch Cemetery. In 1936 they were living in Forest.

3) Birdie Stone married J.H. White Sep. 6, 1903 in Scott County.

4) Clifton F. Stone married Neva Williams Feb. 12, 1913. In 1936 he is living in Shelby, MS. Their children were C.F. Stone Jr., Taylor M. Stone and Nelson Stone.

5) J. Benton Stone (b. December 1890, d. Jan. 20, 1926) is buried at the Shelby Cemetery, Shelby, MS.

6) Viola Rebecca Stone "Bess" (b. November 1893) md. __ Hunt. In 1936 she and her family were living in Temple, Bell County, TX.

7) Malcolm G. Stone (b. March 1897) never married. He was living in Tunica, MS in 1936.

8) Cora Stone (b. March 1899) md. Otha Massey. He died in 1970).

9) Velma Stone.

SULLIVAN, Monroe Sullivan was born Apr. 20, 1836 in Perry County, AL. His father was Dunklin Sullivan, an attorney, magistrate, state legislator and planter in Marion, AL. His third great-grandfather was John Thomas O'Sullivan who arrived in Virginia from Ireland in 1655. Monroe married Mary A. Griffin, daughter of Hardy Griffin and Elizabeth Boyles, on Jun. 19, 1858. Mary was born Oct. 18, 1842 in Perry County.

Monroe Sullivan

Monroe enlisted in the 40th Alabama Inf. Div., Co. H, CSA, in 1862 and served in the Vicksburg campaign where he was taken prisoner when the city surrendered. His company was paroled and reassembled several months later in Demopolis, AL and participated in battles at Lookout Mountain, Missionary Ridge, and Rocky Face Mountain, GA. Monroe was taken prisoner again at the battle of Noon Day Creek (Big Shanty, GA) Jun. 15, 1864 and spent the remainder of the war at Rock Island, IL, prison camp.

Monroe returned to Perry County, AL, following his release Jun. 22, 1865 and lived there until 1871 when he acquired 80 acres of land in the Hillsboro Community of Scott County on Jan. 18, 1871. The property was exchanged for 80 acres in an adjoining Section in 1907 and this property is still in the family.

Monroe died Dec. 3, 1909 and Mary died Jan. 29, 1917. Both are buried in Hillsboro Methodist Cemetery.

Monroe and Mary had four children: Mary Judson "Juddie" (b. Apr. 22, 1859 in Alabama, d. Mar. 8, 1886), buried in Mt. Zion Cemetery, Perry County, AL); James Monroe "Jim" (b. Dec. 5, 1864 in Alabama, d. Jan. 26, 1940), buried in Clifton Cemetery); Willie (b. 1872 in Scott County, d. 1881), buried in Hillsboro Methodist Cemetery; and Tolbert Boyles "Tollie" (b. Aug. 18, 1877 in Scott County, d. Mar. 23, 1947), buried in Clifton Cemetery).

Juddie married Marion Frances Crawford Nov. 9, 1876 in Scott County and moved to Perry County, AL. She died a few months after the birth of her son Marion Raymond. Raymond, who moved to Scott County as a youth,

Tollie Sullivan, his wife Lula, and son O.B.

married Mary Lavenia Walker and they had Jettie Lee and Francis Henry, both born in Scott County.

Jim married Mary Rebecca Hearn Dec. 9, 1896 in Holmes County, MS. He received a Homestead Certificate for 40.5 acres next to his family's property on Jan. 5, 1915. Jim and Mary had three sons: James Wyatt (b. Oct. 9, 1901, d. Feb. 20, 1923, buried in Clifton Cemetery); Chesley Glynn (b. Jan. 28, 1907, d. Dec. 31, 1976, buried in Clifton Cemetery); Lester Lloyd (b. Aug. 17, 1909, d. Mar. 14, 1997, buried in Clifton Cemetery). Glynn married Lillian Voncil Calhoun in 1927 and they had two sons, Gerald Glynn and Truitt Almond. Lloyd married Loye Alene Patrick Oct. 19, 1945. No issue.

Willie died in 1881 in Scott County on his ninth birthday.

Tollie acquired a Homestead Certificate for 121.3 acres of land Jul. 23, 1908. He began working the property about 1903. Tollie married Lula Leona Latham, daughter of Henry Clay Latham and Martha Louise Aycock, Jan. 24, 1906. They had five children, all born in Scott County: Otis Beamon "O.B." (b. Nov. 20, 1906, d. Apr. 6, 1989, buried Borger, TX); Bertha Lavern (b. Dec. 2, 1910); Ollie Marion (b. Sep. 23, 1914); Mary Lou (b. Jan. 4, 1917, d. Apr. 21, 1980, buried in Floral Hills Memorial Gardens, Pearl); Lois Merle (b. Jan. 2, 1921).

Tollie was a successful farmer who also operated a dairy farm and raised mule colts and cattle. He served on the board of trustees of Clifton Schools for many years. He and his family were members of Mt. Zion Methodist Church.

O.B. moved to Texas about 1926 and married Velma Mary Phy in Borger in 1927. They had two children, Wayne Tolbert and Shirley Ann. O.B. was employed by Phillips Petroleum. He was a Mason and a member of the Baptist Church.

Bertha graduated from Harperville Agricultural High School, then attended Mississippi State Teachers College for two years. She married Robert Oliver Hannah, son of Edward Eugene Hannah and Vallie Tadlock, Oct. 2, 1933. They had four children, all born in Scott County: Robert Oliver Jr., Ray Eugene, Thomas Edward, and Ted Sullivan. Robert Oliver Sr. became the first superintendent of Roosevelt State Park in 1940 and Bertha managed the food service operations. They remained at the Park until they retired to their Newton County farm in 1960 and, after selling the farm in 1965, moved to Forest. They are members of the Methodist Church.

Ollie joined the Civilian Conservation Corps in Vicksburg in the early 1930s. He was sent to Camp Beauregard in Alexandra, LA. He first married Iva Mae Dehaven and they had one son, Ronald Lee, born in Alexandra. He then married Willow Lee Reeves in Pineville, LA in 1952. They had one daughter, Sarah Jane. Ollie owned Pineville Tire and Appliance for many years before selling the business. They are members of the Methodist Church.

Mary Lou married Theron Bazil Wallace, son of Charles Henry Wallace and Mary Robinson, Oct. 12, 1932 in Scott County. A few years after the marriage they moved to Texas where Theron worked for Phillips Petroleum. Later they returned to Mississippi and Theron eventually worked for Valley Mills, later acquired by Ralston Purina. They had four children: Retha Malverene, Loys Joan, Henry Tolbert, and Russell Cleveland. Retha and Joanie were born in Scott County and Tolbert and Russel were born in Jackson, MS. Mary Lou and her family were members of the Baptist Church.

Lois married Claude Dee McDonald, son of Claud McDonald and Christian Coward, Mar. 10, 1943 in Scott County. Dee served aboard the USS *Hazelwood* and was stationed in Hawaii when Pearl Harbor was attacked. After the war he worked for Chicago Bridge and Iron Co. and the family moved from construction site to construction site for several years. They eventually settled in Scott County on the farm that Lois's father homesteaded. The marriage produced four children: Seglenda Merle, Betty Sue, Michael Dee and Harlen Dwayne. Seglenda and Sue were born in Scott County, Mike in Paducah, KY and Dwayne in Jackson, MS. Lois and her family are members of the Methodist Church.

TADLOCK, Elisha Turner Tadlock (b. Jul. 21, 1850 in Perry County AL), son of Albert Green Tadlock and Malinda Boyles. He moved to Scott County in the mid-1800s where he married Clemmie Virginia Gardner, daughter of Dr. William Wilford Gardner and Mary Hunter. Clemmie was born Apr. 12, 1852 in Scott County MS.

Elisha and Clemmie had six children: Magnolia Belle (b. Dec.

Elisha Turner Tadlock and Clemmie Virginia Gardner.

9, 1874 in Homewood, MS) md. Karl Thomas Wardell; Mary Neal (b. Jan. 27, 1877 in Scott Co MS) md. Benjamin Franklin Gray; William Marvin Oliver (b. May 26, 1881 in Scott County) md. Ida Ora Brown; Albert Hunter (b. Mar. 19, 1886 in Scott County) md. Mary Rebecca Madison; Turner Roscoe (b. Feb. 11, 1889 in Scott County); and Josephus Penn (b. Jul. 20, 1891 in Scott County) md. Nannie Belle Moore, daughter of John Moore and Jeannie Carmichael. Elisha and Clemmie lived out their lives in the Homewood area of Scott County. Elisha died Apr. 7, 1920 and Clemmie died Feb. 15, 1925. They are both buried in the Homewood Methodist Cemetery.

TADLOCK, James Albert "Jim" Tadlock (b. Jul. 18, 1871 in Scott County) was the son of Rev. John Webster Tadlock and Margaret E. Ann "Maggie" McCraw. He grew up in Hillsboro where the family owned a store and farm. He spent some time in Texas with relatives.

On Dec. 25, 1910, Jim married Eva Mae James (b. Jan. 22, 1886), daughter of Daniel P. James and Mollie P. Lovett of Scott County. His father, Rev. John Webster Tadlock, officiated. Jim was 15 years her senior, having first been a hunting friend of Mr. James. When speaking of her husband Eva referred to him as "Mr. Jim." They began their married life in Forest where they owned and operated a boarding house and livery stable with his brothers, John and Cleve.

Eva James, wife of Jim Tadlock and James Albert "Jim" Tadlock

After Rev. Tadlock's death, Jim purchased his home place and acreage in the Sparksville Community. He and Eva reared eight children, four boys and four girls, in the farmhouse they built on the Morton-Hillsboro Road. He provided for his family by farming, raising cattle and logging. Eva was a pioneer in the poultry industry, raising broilers from chicks ordered by mail.

Jim was very political minded, but he never sought a public office. He followed the Methodist religion of his father and grandfather.

The first child, Nova Douglas "Billy," graduated from Clifton High School and attended an electrical college in Chicago. He worked with his cousins, Jack Bustin and Robert Lovett, in the oil fields in Texas for some time, where he met and married Lorraine Watson in Kilgore, TX, on Dec. 21, 1937. They had a daughter, Maureen, and a son Jimmy Douglas, who died as an infant and is buried in Sardis, TX. The family returned to Scott County and later made their home in Jackson where Billy was employed and retired from General Electric Corporation. Maureen married Edward M. Watt on Oct. 9, 1970. Lorraine died Nov. 27, 1999 and is buried in Lakewood Cemetery in Jackson.

The Jim Tadlock house on the Morton-Hillsboro Road in Sparksville Community. The front and side porches were shaded in summer by a grapevine that Eva planted.

James Albert Tadlock Jr., second child, graduated from Clifton High School and worked for some time in Forest for Walter Sharpe. He worked at the military base at Alexandria, LA, joined the U.S. Coast Guard and served in the Pacific Theater during WWII. After the war he followed construction work as a millwright. He married Nellie Mae (Downing) Brooks on Dec. 22, 1951. They had a son, James Albert III. J.A. suffered a heart attack and retired from public work, returning to the home place in Scott County where he died on May 20, 1980. Nellie Mae died Feb. 4, 1990. Both are buried in the Hillsboro Baptist Church Cemetery. James Albert III "Jim" married Janice Renee Thompson on Mar. 4, 1981. As of this writing, they live on the Tadlock home place in Sparksville.

Buron Harwell Tadlock, third child, attended Clifton and Forest High Schools. He stayed on the farm until WWII. He served in the U.S. Army, was employed at Keesler Air Force Base in Biloxi until he retired. He married Mildred Mae (Watermullon) Bond on Oct. 3, 1954. He had two stepchildren: John Marion Bond who married Geraldine Holbrook Feb. 9, 1962 and they had three sons; John Marion Bond Jr.; James Eugene Bond, and Jeffery Michael Bond and Laverne Mae Bond who married Albert Kisner, they had two children, Adam Kisner and Leeja Marie Kisner. They made their home in Ocean Springs, MS, where Harwell died Oct. 10, 1965; his wife, Mae die Oct. 12, 1991, having been preceded in death by her daughter Lavern Mae Kisner on Dec. 11, 1988. They are buried at Crestlawn Cemetery, Ocean Springs, MS.

Dextal O'Neil Tadlock, fourth child, attended Clifton High School. She married Wayne S. Davis, a native of Springfield Community in Scott County, on Dec. 23, 1934. They had two children, Ruby Jewell and Wayne Reginal. They made their home in Pelahatchie (Rankin County) where Wayne and his three brothers owned and operated a very successful poultry business. The family later moved to Jackson. Ruby Jewell married James Lavoy Martin on Jun. 9, 1957; they had two sons, Michael Wayne Martin and Kenneth Lavoy Martin. She married a second time to Samuel Yates on Dec. 31, 1976. Wayne Reginal married Shirley Ann Ainsworth on Oct. 25, 1956 and they had three children: Elinor Lorraine, Wayne Reginal Jr. and Stephen Lee. Wayne Reginal married a second time to Peggy Hollingsworth Puckett. Wayne S. Davis passed away on Jul. 10, 1973 and is buried in Floral Hills Memory Garden in Pearl. As of this writing O'Neil Davis lives with her daughter, Ruby Jewell Yates in Jackson. She has five grandchildren and eight great-grandchildren.

Herbert Waldris Tadlock, fifth child, attended Clifton and Forest High Schools, farmed with his family, and went to work with his brother J.A. at a military base in Alexandria, LA where he met his future wife. He volunteered to join the U.S. Air Force immediately after Pearl Harbor. He married Mary Ollie Slayter of Pollock, LA, on Sep. 2, 1942, in San Antonio TX, where he was stationed. He served overseas in the European Theater of WWII and in Korea. He retired from the Air Force after 20 years. He came back to Scott County and built a home in Forest where he worked for Fountain Hardware about

four years. He later moved to Jackson and was employed by Miller Ace Hardware for several years, and when he retired he moved to Dry Prong, LA near his wife's family. Herbert died Jun. 26, 2000 after a long illness. He is buried in Frazier Cemetery, Dry Prong, LA. They had one daughter, Mary Anita, who married Medford Ross Kellum on Mar. 11, 1966. They have three children: Mairi Catherine Kellum Rennolds, Erin Danielle Kellum, and Jonathan Evan Kellum. Mary Anita has two grandchildren.

Mattie Elizabeth Tadlock, the sixth child, attended Clifton High School, married Wilber Lee Weems, a Scott County native, on Aug. 4, 1937. They first lived south of Forest on Wilber's father's farm. During WWII Mattie and Wilber moved to Sparksville and Eva deeded Mattie her portion of the land so they could make a home and farm there. They had three sons: 1) Billy Brooks married Judith Ann Teske on Mar. 31, 1962. They had three children: Mark Adam, Brenda Bridgette and Kimberly. 2) Curtis Sheldon married Georgette Saab on Jun. 4, 1967 they have one son, Shane. William Larry, who at this writing lives in his mother's home in Sparksville. Wilber Weems died Aug. 1, 1996 and is buried in the Homewood Methodist Cemetery. Billie Brooks Weems died Aug. 15, 1997 and is buried at Morton Memorial Cemetery.

Lillie Mae Tadlock, seventh child, graduated from Morton High School and worked in Jackson, where she met Denver E. Idol in the U.S. Army stationed near Jackson. When Denver returned from a tour of duty in the Pacific they married on Feb. 23, 1946. They made their home in Knoxville, TN, near Denver's home. They had two sons, James W. Idol and Walter Darek Idol. Denver died Sep. 4, 1986 and is buried in Greenville Cemetery in Knoxville. On Apr. 22, 1995 James married Lois Donauer (Peterson). They have a daughter Leslie DeAnn (b. Mar. 18, 1999).

Molly Annette Tadlock the eighth child graduated from Morton High School and married William F. "Billy" Laseter on Nov. 9, 1946. Billy served in the U.S. Army Air Force in England during WWII as a gunner on B-24s. They made their home in Morton where Billy worked for Laseter and Neal Butane Company; he later worked at Vickers, Inc. in Jackson, where he retired. Molly worked in the State Department of Education for Chevron Oil Company, and retired from Magnolia Federal savings Bank as branch manager of Crossgates Bank. They had a daughter, Lea Annette, who married Michael V. Fegerson Oct. 10, 1992 and they have two daughters, Molly Ree Fegerson and Margaret "Maggie" Rose Fegerson. William F. Laseter died of a heart attack on Dec. 16, 1997 and is buried in Morton Memorial Gardens. Mollie continues to live in their home in Morton.

TADLOCK James Oliver "Jim" Tadlock and Myrtle Irene Wilkerson were married in 1925 and made their home one mile north of Homewood, near Jim's boyhood home. He was the son of Robert Koger Tadlock and Mattie Carolyn Craig (Robert's second wife). Robert was a farmer. Robert's father and siblings had moved to Scott County from near Marion, AL following the Civil War. Prior to marriage Jim helped his father farm. He worked on road and

"dummy line" construction. He used mules and a slip or grader to move dirt. Myrtle was the daughter of Francis Sheppard "Shep" Wilkerson and Mary Elizabeth "Betty" Youngblood. Shep Wilkerson was a Justice of the Peace, farmer, logger and sawmill operator. Myrtle grew up in the High Hill Community near the intersection of Hwy. 501 and Sherman Hill road. Myrtle graduated from Scott County Agricultural High School and taught school prior to marriage. Myrtle's paternal grandfather, Dr. William H. Wilkerson, served in the 53rd Alabama Regiment during the Civil War. He moved to Scott County in 1866 and later to Smith County.

Jim and Myrtle bought land and established a farm. Jim grew crops, cattle and also traded livestock. Jim always kept a horse to work cows or ride for pleasure. Jim ran an ice route where he delivered ice to homes in rural Scott County before electricity was available.

Jim and Myrtle had five children. Mary Elizabeth Tadlock married C.T. Bailey of Forest. Their children are James Thomas "Tommy" and David Randal "David" Bailey. Mary Elizabeth made her home in Pearl and Richland. She maintains a second home at the house site of Jim and Myrtle.

Jack Shepherd Tadlock married Evelyn Bailey of French Camp. Their children are Ronald Shepherd "Ronnie," Randal Oliver "Randy," and Richard James Tadlock. Jack moved his family to Forest prior to his retirement from the Air Force. He was a Vietnam veteran and awarded the Bronze Star with one cluster. After retirement from the military he began a second career as a USDA poultry inspector and farmer. He grows beef cattle on the land that once belonged to Shep Wilkerson, his grandfather.

James Paul "Paul" Tadlock married Viva Francis Brooks of Lake. He was a naval veteran during the Korean War. After service he attended Clark College and Mississippi State. He then moved back to Lake to operate a dairy farm which was eventually converted to beef cattle. He was employed at Lazy Boy and later retired from Lazy Boy. Viva was the town clerk for 28 years at Lake. Their children are Paul Franklin and George Neal Tadlock.

Fleeta Tadlock married Norvel R. Middleton of Smith County. Their children are Johnny Robert Middleton and Beverly M. Kaseman. Norvel was wounded while serving in the Navy during WWII. Later he was an aircraft mechanic until his medical condition necessitated an early retirement. After his retirement Norvel and Fleeta moved to Forest and lived there the remainder of their lives. Fleeta was employed by local banks.

The youngest child of Jim and Myrtle was Francis Irene Tadlock. She was killed in a car accident during her senior year in high school.

TADLOCK, John Webster Tadlock (b. 1844 in Perry County, AL) was the son of James Albert Green Tadlock and Malinda Boyles. They married in Perry County, AL in 1832, where they settled. Albert Green was a Methodist, an officer and classleader of his church. He was successful as a farmer and accumulated property; however, the Civil War swept much of it away, and he died in 1874 at the age of 61, having very little estate. His wife died two years later.

Children of James Albert Green Tadlock were Adaline (md Henry Herran); Cynthia A. (md. James A. Atherton); Flavelia M. (md. William M. Manley), William B.J. (d. 1862 in Confederate service); James Hendon (d. in Texas); Malcolm. Demas Cannon;

Margaret A. McCraw Tadlock, wife of John Webster Tadlock

John Webster of this writing; Martha (md. Nathaniel Chestnut); Elisha Turner; Josephine Teatus (md. William Moore); and Robert Koger, all of Scott County.

John Webster enlisted in Co. K, 11th AL Inf. Regt. of CSA, Aug. 20, 1863, Marion Alabama at age 18. He was present at the battles of Wilderness, Spotsylvania Court House, Hanover Junction, Turkey Ridge and was wounded at Wilcox Farm Jun. 22, 1864, and was listed as a POW belonging to the Army of northern Virginia. He was surrendered by Gen. Robert E. Lee, CSA to Lt. Gen. U.S. Grant, U.S. Army at Appomattox Court House, VA, Apr. 9, 1865. He returned to Perry County, AL and married Margaret Easter Ann McCraw, daughter of William A. McCraw and Lucinda C. Bennet on Nov. 30, 1865. He was a farmer.

Between 1870-1880 the Tadlock brothers and families came to Scott County, MS in Oxen wagons. Most of the families settled around the Homewood and Pulaski communities. James H. moved on west to Kansas then to Wise County, TX.

John Webster purchased a store and property in Hillsboro in the name of John W. Tadlock and Sons. He later acquired land in the Sparksville Community on which there was a pre-Civil-War log house.

John Webster was received into the Mississippi Conference of the Methodist Protestant Church and ordained as a minister in 1889. He served faithfully throughout his life as pastor of various churches, including Liberty, Morton, Chickasawhay, Meridian, Philadelphia, Hillsboro, and at McLain at the time of his death on Oct. 15, 1912. He served as Conference President in the year 1898.

The children of John Webster and Margaret "Maggie" were Mattie Elizabeth (md. W.R. Bustin); James Albert (md. Eva M. James); Norah O. (md. Gary T. Gilbert); Minnie (md. Rufus Bradley); Mary Alice (md. William H. Hall); John Webster Jr. (md. Naomi Askin); and Grover Cleveland (md. first, Pearl Askins and second. Ora Lee Sessums).

Maggie made her home with her daughter, Mattie Bustin, in the Sparksville Community after Reverend Tadlock's death. Although almost completely blind, she loved to visit her kinfolks and was always welcome because of her happy disposition. In her latter years, the Sunday nearest her birthday, May 19th, became a day of celebration and reunion for a the kinfolks, friends and neighbors at the Mt. Zion Methodist Church in the Sparksville Community.

John Webster died at age 68 on Oct. 15,

1912. Margaret died Jul. 14, 1939 at 90 years old. They are buried in the Hillsboro Methodist Cemetery in Scott County, nearby Maggie's mother Lucinda C. McCraw.

TADLOCK-GRAY, Malcolm Demas Cannon Tadlock, born May 6, 1843 in Morgan Springs, AL, son of Albert and Malinda Tadlock. M.D.C. as he was known served in the Civil War in Co. K, 11th AL Inf. He was wounded in the left leg at Chancellorsville and was at Appomattox when Lee surrendered.

On Nov. 4, 1865 in Selma, AL, he married Silena Gray, daughter of Williamson and Winny Gray. They are shown in Scott County by 1880.

They were the parents of 11 children, seven of whom survived to adulthood: 1) Etta Minerva (md. Henry Westberry); 2) Lula (md. C.S.C. Horn); 3) Malcom Turner remained single; 4) Roland Lee (md. Laura McEwen); 5) Virgie Elizabeth (md. John H. Burkes); 6) Mattie Jo (md. Otha A. McEwen); 7) Calop Taylor (md. Clara Sigrest); 8) Mary (died in early childhood).

M.D.C. and Silena lived in the Frogtown Community of Scott County until they died, him on Mar. 24, 1908 and Silena on Feb. 13, 1929. They are both buried at Sims Cemetery in Scott County.

THOMPSON, Prior to 1850, two Thompson brothers left Missouri making their way to Mississippi. The younger brother, Hiram A.S. Thompson (b. ca. 1825 Missouri, d. Jun. 7, 1899) md. Kessiah Harrell (b. ca. 1825, d. before 1891) on May 20, 1850 in Hinds County. She was a sister to Eliza Harrell who married Thomas Jefferson Measells. These two families would continue to be joined through marriage throughout the years. Hiram and Kessiah had no children.

In 1861 Hiram purchased land from Andrew J. and Matilda Ann Barker in Scott County, later purchasing adjoining land from John R. and M.A. Burk. In 1869 he sold this land to Samuel Otto Williams and purchased 960 acres from Charles H. and Susan Hodges of Falls County, TX where Hodge Hill Cemetery is located.

He served in the CSA 39th Inf., Co. C. After Kessiah's death, Hiram married Georgianna Peagler Collum (b. Sep. 18, 1843, d. 1923) on Jun. 19, 1890. She was the half sister to Thomas Jefferson Measells mentioned above.

The older Thompson brother, Joseph Henry Thompson (b. ca. 1821, d. Jan. 27, 1905) md. prior to 1851 to Catherine Williams (b. ca. 1833, d. ca. 1916). In the 1860 census, they are living in Hinds County. During the Civil War, Joe Henry served in Ham's Regiment, CSA Calvary. Soon after the war, he and Catherine separated. She took all but one of their children to Texas where she married Martin Van Buren Abernathy. The children that went to Texas were James W. (b. 1853); Felix G. (b. 1855); Belle; Lula; and Bedford Forrest (b. Aug. 1, 1866, d. Jul. 2, 1953). Wiley S. (b. 1857, died young in Mississippi).

The eldest child left in Mississippi was Joe Buford. He and his father moved to Scott County to live with Hiram and Kessiah Thompson. Joe Buford (b. Jan. 5, 1851, d. Nov. 29, 1935) md. Martha Jane "Fannie" Measels (b. Oct. 23, 1856, d. Nov. 20, 1941), daughter of Jessie David and Mariah Ann Harrell Measels. Jessie David and Thomas Jefferson Measels were brothers.

The family of Joe Burford and Fannie Measells Thompson around 1900: Seated, l-r: Cos Thompson, Odell and Bud, Great-Grandma Mariah Harrell Measells, Lizzie Thompson Lum, Grandma Fannie Measells Thompson, Grandpa Joe Buford Thompson Sr. and Willie (died age 5), Great Grandpa Joe Henry Thompson, Odie Thompson Henry, Charlie Thompson and Lennie Thompson Peagler. Standing, l-r: Hettie Fortenberry Thompson, Ivy Belle, Pearl Thompson Crapps, Burl Thompson (was deaf), Lummie Belle Thompson Brassfield, Joe Thompson Jr. (was deaf), Ollie Thompson McCurdy, Lucy Renfroe Thompson and Fannie. Another son, Jimmy Thompson, was born later and was deaf.

To Fannie and Joe Buford were born 12 children, as follows:

1) Charles Henry Thompson (b. Sep. 1, 1873, d. Feb. 19, 1956) md. Mary Lucy Renfrow. Their children are Estelle Thompson Hollingworth, Fannie Kate Thompson, Ora Ethel Thompson Bates, Jennie Lucy Thompson Coward and Lennye Gertrude Thompson Peagler.

2) Burl Thompson (b. Aug. 5, 1875, d. Apr. 1, 1915 as a young man).

3) Cosmo Thompson (b. Mar. 9, 1877, d. Nov. 3, 1939) md. Hettie Olivia Fortenberry (b. Dec. 6, 1880, d. Oct. 5, 1960). Their children are Odell Thompson, Joe Cosmo "Bud" Thompson Jr.; Ivry Bell Thompson, Vada Elizabeth Thompson Denson, Albert Thompson, J.B. Thompson, Lee Thompson, Claude Clay Thompson, Clyde Clayton Thompson, Levie Oleta Thompson Franklin, Bill Joe Thompson, Ruby Thompson Pruitt and Eva Dee Thompson Irby.

4) Felix Thompson (b. May 23, 1880, d. Sep. 1, 1893 as a young boy).

5) Pearl Thompson (b. Jan. 23, 1883, d. Sep. 5, 1953) md. Mack Crapps Sr. (b. Dec. 16, 1879, d. Dec. 20, 1945). Their children are Willie Ray Crapps, Ola Crapps Gordon, Myrtle Pearl Crapps Lum, Sarah Elizabeth "Lizzie" Crapps Peagler, Fannie Louise Crapps Kersh, Woodrow Crapps, Mack Crapps Jr., Johnnie Crapps, Joe Crapps and Jenny Crapps.

6) Joe Buford Thompson Jr. (b. Apr. 1, 1885, d. Sep. 7, 1941) md. Mary Alma Parker (b. May 23, 1900, d. Nov. 5, 1995). Their children are Felix Thompson, Jimmie Joe Thompson, Martha Catherine Thompson Shoemaker, Francis Oleta Thompson Cooper, William Edward Thompson, Shelby Ray Thompson, Julius Carter Thompson, Laura Sue Thompson Barnes and Peggy Ann Thompson Huggins.

7) Lummie Thompson (b. Jun. 12, 1887, d. Aug. 12, 1932) md. Walter Brasfield.

8) Ollie Estell Thompson (b. Aug. 22, 1889, d. Aug. 19, 1972) md. Willie Lane McCurdy, Sr. (b. Aug. 22, 1887, d. Jan. 2, 1972). Their children are Lucy McCurdy Davis, Annie McCurdy Sumrall, Johnnie McCurdy Cooper, Fannie Jo

McCurdy Thames, Floyd McCurdy, William Napoleon McCurdy, Ollie McCurdy and Burnice Lane McCurdy.

9) Sarah Elizabeth "Lizzie" Thompson (b. Feb. 19, 1893, d. Aug. 11, 1971) md. Daniel Garner Lum (b. Mar. 17, 1890, d. Oct. 28, 1977). Their children are Morris Lum, Gilbert Lum, Mary Frances Lum Bula, William Clinton Lum, Charlie Lum, Hubert "Pete" Lum, Lula Bell Lum Risher and David Lum.

10) Odie Thompson (b. Sep. 25, 1895, d. Apr. 19, 1986) md. Earl Henry (b. Mar. 20, 1894, d. Sep. 4, 1961). Their children are Ola Estelle Henry Carroll, Joe Henry, Mable Earlene Henry Munn, Jack Bedwell Henry and Charlie Henry Sr.

11) Willie Thompson (b. Apr. 17, 1898, d. May 14, 1902 as young boy).

12) James Lewis Thompson Sr. (d. 1945) md. Lorene Robinson. Their children are Clara Bellezola Thompson Renfrow, Rachel G. Thompson Renfrow, Lucille Thompson, Betty Jean Thompson Ivy, James Lewis Thompson Jr., William Hilton Thompson, Helen Marie Thompson Shumaker, Bobby Ray Thompson; Jimmy Buford Thompson and Patsy Ann Thompson Massey.

The Thompson family has been an integral part of the Leesburg/Branch Community in Scott County since the 1860s. In 1881 the founding fathers of the Leesburg Baptist Church included Hiram and Kessiah Thompson, Thomas Jefferson and Eliza Measels, and Jim and E.C. Measels Williams. Members of this family continue to be leaders in their community, many serving as pastors, teachers, attorneys and politicians in Scott and surrounding counties.

For further information on this family, see "Our Family Tree, Thompson/Abernathy/ Measels/Peagler," compiled by Jan Thompson Harrell and Peggy Thompson Huggins.

THOMPSON (Joseph Henry and Hiram A.S. Thompson family): Prior to 1847, two brothers made their way to Mississippi. The younger brother, Hiram A.S. Thompson (b. 1825 in Missouri, d. Jun. 7, 1899) md. Kessiah Harrell (b. 1825, d. before 1891) on May 20, 1850 in Hinds County. Her sister, Eliza Harrell, married Thomas Jefferson Measels. These two families would continue to be joined through marriage throughout the years. Hiram and Kessiah had no children.

In 1861 and 1862, Hiram purchased land from Andrew J. and Matilda Ann Barker and John R. and M.A. Burk in Scott County. In 1869, selling this land to Samuel Otto Williams, he purchased 960 acres where Hodge Hill Cemetery is located, from Charles H. and Susan Hodges of Falls County, TX.

During the Civil War, Hiram served in the CSA 39th Inf., Co. C. After Kessiah's death, he married Georgianna Peagler Collum (b. Sep. 18, 1843, d. 1923) on Jun. 19, 1890. She was the half-sister to Thomas Jefferson Measels above.

The older brother, Joseph Henry Thompson (b. Apr. 17, 1821 in Tennessee, d. Jan. 27, 1905) married first, Elizabeth Luellen "Ellen" Lee, daughter of Sherod and Rachel Carnes Lee in Hinds County, on Nov. 4, 1847. In 1848, Ellen died in childbirth leaving one son, Charles N. Thompson, who died in 1849. Joe Henry inherited this son's share of the Sherod Lee estate.

Buying out the other Lee children, he acquired the 400 acre plantation, believed to have been at Edwards. On Jan. 14, 1850 in Hinds County, he married Keziah A. "Kitty" Williams (b. 1833, d. ca. 1916), daughter of James and Lucinda Williams and granddaughter of John and Fanny Williams.

He and Kitty sold the Lee Plantation in 1858 to R.O. Edwards, founder of the town of Edwards and the King Edward Hotel in Jackson, and acquired the 240 plantation in Raymond that had belonged to Kitty's father.

During the Civil War, Joe Henry served in Ham's Regiment, CSA Cavalry. While he was gone, the Yankees came through their home at Battle Hill Plantation in Raymond, tearing up bedding and pillows to be used for bandages. After the war, they sold the plantation to her mother.

Later, Kitty divorced Joe Henry and left for Texas where she married Martin Van Buren Abernathy. She took all of the Thompson children except the oldest, Joe Buford. The children that went to Texas were James W. (b. 1853), Felix G. (b. 1855), Belle, Lou and Bedford Forrest (b. Aug. 1, 1866, d. Jul. 2, 1953). Wiley S. (b. 1857) died young. In Texas, the Abernathys had Annie, John R. and Van. Two others, Frank and Martha, died young. John R. was appointed the first U.S. Marshall in the Oklahoma Territory by President Teddy Roosevelt, his hunting companion. John was called "Catch-em-Alive" Abernathy due to his prowess in catching wolves and outlaws with his bare hands. His two sons, Temple and Louie, became famous for taking cross county trail rides as small boys on horses, in a brush-run-about-car and on an early model motorcycle. They rode in a parade in New York with President Howard Taft. Newspaper articles and books have been published and a movie has been made about John and his sons' escapades.

Meanwhile, Joe Henry and Joe Buford moved to Scott County in 1870 to live with Hiram and Kessiah. Joe Buford (b. Jan. 5, 1851, d. Nov. 29, 1935) md. Martha Jane "Fannie" Measels (b. Oct. 23, 1856, d. Nov. 20, 1941), daughter of Jessie David and Mariah Ann Harrell Measels and granddaughter of Martha Jane Measels Peagler (wife of Peter Washington Peagler). Jessie David and Thomas Jefferson Measels were brothers. Joe Buford moved his father and family to land acquired from the Measels family by the old railroad "dummy line" in Leesburg. Our family still resides here today.

To Fannie and Joe Buford were born 12 children, as follows:

1) Charles Henry Thompson (b. Sep. 1, 1873, d. Feb. 19, 1956) md. Mary Lucy Renfroe. Their children are Estelle Hollingsworth, Fannie Kate, Ora Ethel Bates, Jennie Lucy Coward, and Lennye Gertrude Peagler.

2) Burl Thompson (b. Aug. 5, 1875, d. Apr. 1, 1915).

3) Cosmo Thompson (b. Mar. 9, 1877, d. Nov. 3, 1939) md. Hettie Olivia Fortenberry (b. Dec. 6, 1880, d. Oct. 5, 1960). Their children are Odell Thompson, Joe Cosmo "Bud" Thompson Jr., Ivry Bell Thompson, Vada Elizabeth Denson, Albert Thompson, J.B. Thompson, Lee Thompson, Claude Clay Thompson, Clyde Clayton Thompson, Levie Oleta Franklin, Bill Joe Thompson, Ruby Pruitt and Eva Dee Irby.

4) Felix Thompson (b. May 23, 1880, d. Sep. 1, 1893).

5) Pearl Thompson (b. Jan. 23, 1883, d. Sep. 5, 1953) md. Mack Crapps Sr. (b. Dec. 16, 1879, d. Dec. 20, 1945). Their children are Willie Ray Crapps, Ola Gordon, Myrtle Pearl Lum, Sarah Elizabeth Peagler, Fannie Louise Kersh, Woodrow Crapps, Mack Crapps Jr., Johnnie Crapps, Joe Crapps and Jenny Crapps.

6) Joe Buford Thompson Jr. (b. Apr. 1, 1885, d. Sep. 7, 1941) md. Mary Alma Parker (b. May 23, 1900, d. Nov. 5, 1995). Their children are Felix Thompson, Jimmie Joe Thompson, Martha Catherine Shoemaker, Francis Oleta Cooper, William Edward Thompson, Shelby Ray Thompson, Julius Carter Thompson, Laura Sue Barnes and Peggy Ann Huggins.

7) Lummie Thompson (b. Jun. 12, 1887, Aug. 12, 1932) md. Walter Brasfield

8) Ollie Estell Thompson (b. Aug. 22, 1889, d. Aug. 19, 1972) md. Willie Lane McCurdy Sr. (b. Aug. 22, 1887, d. Jan. 2, 1972). Their children are Lucy Davis, Annie Sumrall, Johnnie Cooper, Fannie Jo Thames, Floyd McCurdy, William Napoleon McCurdy, Ollie McCurdy and Burnice Lane McCurdy.

Sarah Elizabeth "Lizzie" Thompson (b. Feb. 19, 1893, d. Aug. 11, 1971) md. Daniel Garner Lum (b. Mar. 17, 1890, d. Oct. 28, 1977). Their children are Morris Lum, Gilbert Lum, Mary Frances Bula, William Clinton Lum, Charlie Lum, Hubert "Pete" Lum, Lula Bell Risher and David Lum.

10) Odie Thompson (b. Sep. 25, 1895, d. Apr. 19, 1986) md. Earl Henry (b. Mar. 20, 1894, d. Sep. 4, 1961). Their children are Ola Estelle Carroll, Joe Henry, Mable Earlene Munn, Jack Bedwell Henry and Charlie Henry Sr.

11) Willie Thompson (b. Apr. 17, 1898, d. May 14, 1902).

12) James Lewis Thompson Sr. (d. 1945) md. Lorene Robinson. Their children are Clara Bellezola Renfroe, Rachel G. Renfroe, Lucille Thompson, Betty Jean Ivy, James Lewis Thompson Jr., William Hilton Thompson, Helen Marie Shumaker, Bobby Ray Thompson, Jimmy Buford Thompson and Patsy Ann Massey.

The Thompson family has been an integral part of the Leesburg Community in Scott County since the 1860s. In 1881 the founding fathers of the Leesburg Baptist Church included Hiram and Kessiah Thompson, Thomas Jefferson and Eliza Measels, and Jim and E.C. Measels Williams. Members of this family continue to be leaders in their community, serving as businessmen, ministers, teachers, attorneys and elected officials in Scott and surrounding counties.

THOMAS, Daniel McMillan Thomas and Marilakin Key Howard Thomas moved to Forest, and Scott County, MS on Aug. 31, 1958, from Montgomery, AL. He bought the veterinary practice of Dr. Bob Henry Mayo on Sep. 8, 1958. Dr. Thomas, the third of five siblings, was born and reared on a farm west of Tupelo, MS. Dan is the son of the late Dan Thomas and Myrtle Irene Compton. After graduating from Tupelo High School in May 1949, he attended Mississippi State College, then transferred to Alabama Polytechnic Institute, Auburn, AL in the fall of 1951, and graduated Jun. 4, 1955, with a degree in veterinary medicine.

During the summer of 1955, he worked with Dr. Bob Mayo, Forest, and entered the U.S. Air Force on September 17 of that year. While he served two years in the Veterinary Corps, he was stationed at James Connaly Air Force Base, Waco TX. From there he was discharged from active duty on Sep. 17, 1957, with the rank of captain. After the Air Force, he was associated with Dr. Guy J. Phelps Jr. in a small animal practice in Montgomery, AL, for 11 months.

Dan and Marilakin met while students at Alabama Polytechnic Institute and were married in Montgomery, AL on Dec. 28, 1955.

Marilakin was born and reared in Montgomery, AL and was the daughter of the late Milo Barrett Howard and Mary Josepha Key. After graduating from Sidney Lanier High School in June 1950, she graduated from Alabama Polytechnic Institute, Auburn, AL, on Jun. 5, 1954 in home economics, with a major in foods and nutrition. After serving a one-year Dietetics Internship at Duke University, Durham, NC, she accepted a position with the Veterans Administration in Waco, TX as a staff dietitian and worked there until their first daughter was born.

After purchasing Dr. Mayo's practice, Dr. Thomas practiced from Dr. Mayo's office (where the present Choctaw Farms Processing Plant parking lot is located) until December 1967, when he moved into his new office and clinic, located further out U.S. Highway 80. The practice and property was sold to Dr. Michael J. Walker on Jun. 14, 1976.

After practice he worked as a counselor for Weems Mental Health Center, Meridian, MS and later as supervisor of the Quality Assurance Department of Chef Pierre of Forest. He returned to his profession and joined the U.S. Department of Agriculture in 1981, as Station Epidemiologist for the state of Mississippi, stationed in Jackson, MS. In October 1984, he transferred to the Meat and Poultry Division of USDA and was inspector in charge at the McCarty Farms Processing Plant in Forest. He retired from USDA Sep. 4, 1996 as circuit supervisor of the Forest Circuit.

Marilakin was a full time mother and wife until 1967, when she returned to her profession and accepted a position with Leake County Memorial Hospital as a consultant dietitian. Later, she accepted a similar position with Lackey Memorial Hospital and the Scott County Hospital in Morton. She then accepted the position as director of the Dietary Department at Lackey Memorial Hospital. In January 1984, she accepted a position as a nutritionist with the state of Mississippi, working at the Scott County Health Department in Forest. She retired from this position in April 1996.

Marilakin served as president, as well as other offices, of the Mississippi Veterinary Medical Association, secretary/treasurer of the Mississippi Dietetic Association, chaired committees of the Forest United Methodist Church and United Methodist Women.

Dr. Thomas served as president of the Mississippi Veterinary Medical Association, president of United Methodist Men of the Mississippi Conference, president of the Forest Chamber of Commerce, and was a member of the Forest City Council. He has served as Chairman of many committees of the church, including lay leader,

chairman of the Administrative Board and delegate to the Mississippi Annual Conference. He also served as delegate to the Southeastern Jurisdictional Conference.

Dr. and Mrs. Thomas have also been quite active in retirement life, volunteering help to many charitable organizations and the Forest United Methodist Church. Some of their interests are United Methodist Men, Trinity Mission Center, which he was quite instrumental in helping to organize, and Habitat For Humanity, which he served as its first president.

Her special interests are time with grandchildren and assisting Dan with his interest. Dr. and Mrs. Thomas have four children, two daughters and two sons.

Daniel McMillan Thomas Family. Standing: William Lakin Thomas, Linda Carol Thomas Tucker, Martha Key Thomas Smith, Daniel McMillan Thomas Jr. Seated: Daniel McMillan Thomas, Marilakin Key Howard Thomas

The oldest, Martha Key Thomas (b. Jul. 19, 1957 in Waco, TX) attended public schools in Forest, and received her pre-nursing at Mississippi State University and a bachelor's degree in nursing with honors, from the University of Mississippi. She married Charles Leonard Smith, son of Esther Irene Koonce and Joe Carroll Smith of Morton, MS on Feb. 20, 1982, and they have two daughters, Josie Carol Smith (b. Dec. 16, 1985) and Martha Irene Smith (b. Jul. 26, 1988). Leonard received a bachelor's of science degree in business administration from Mississippi College and a master of business administration degree from Wake Forest University, in Winston-Salem, NC. The Smith's reside in Clifton, VA.

Their second child Linda Carol Thomas (b. Apr. 5, 1960 in Forest, MS) also graduated from Forest High School and Mississippi State University in foods and nutrition, with honors. She did graduate work at The University of Alabama, at Birmingham and received her master's degree and a certificate of dietetics internship. She married William Bryan "Bill" Tucker, son of Virginia Joyce Bennett and James Hiram Tucker Jr. of McComb, MS, on Aug. 11, 1984. Bill received a bachelor and master's degree from Mississippi State University in dairy science and a doctor of philosophy degree from the University of Kentucky. Bill and Linda have a daughter Amanda Joyce Tucker (b. Apr. 7, 1988) and a son William Bryan Tucker Jr. (b. Oct. 29, 1990). Prior to moving to McComb, MS in July 2000 to help manage the family dairy farm, the Tuckers' lived in Starkville, MS, where he was a professor in the Dairy Science Department and herdsman of the dairy at Mississippi State University.

Their third child, Daniel McMillan Thomas Jr. (b. Jul. 18, 1962 in Forest, MS) graduated from Forest High School and Mississippi State

University with a bachelor's of professional accountancy. He married Leigh Kirby Graves, daughter of Nancy Taylor Kirby and Clinton Hannibal Graves of Starkville, MS, on May 30, 1987, and they have a daughter and two sons: Kirby Elizabeth Thomas (b. Jul. 4, 1990), Daniel Lakin Thomas (b. Apr. 16, 1993) and William Taylor Thomas (b. Feb. 22, 1995). Leigh received a bachelor's of science degree in horticulture from Mississippi State University. Danny, a certified public accountant, is employed as an accountant for KLLM Transport Services, Inc. of Jackson, MS, and they live in Jackson.

The fourth child, William Lakin Thomas (b. May 10, 1966), also graduated from Forest High School and Mississippi State University with a degree in chemical engineering with honors. He is not married and lives in Atlanta, GA. He is employed as a sales representative for Shell Chemical Company.

THORNTON, Harvey L. Thornton Jr. and Onzell Goodson married on Christmas Day in 1932. Both had roots in Scott County, MS. He graduated from Forest High School and she attended the Good Hope Schools. They settled in Lake, where the families operated a grocery, appliance and butane business from 1940-1970.

Harvey and Onzell Thornton in 1974 with son Larry, grandson Matthew and granddaughter Leigh Ann

Their first child, Lavonne Thornton Weaver (b. 1935) was followed by Larry Lee Thornton (b. 1937). Lavonne graduated from Lake High School, married and had a son Jim and a daughter Lori. She has continued to live in nearby Newton County her entire life.

After graduating from Lake High School in 1955, Larry attended Mississippi College, the University of Southern Mississippi, the New Orleans Baptist Theological Seminary, Harvard University and the International Baptist Theological Seminary in Ruschlikon-Zurich, Switzerland. He has spent most of his adult years as a professor of psychology at Delta State University in Cleveland, MS.

His son, Matt A. Thornton, is a senior vice-president of AmSouth Bank in Jackson and daughter, Leigh Ann Thornton Dauler serves in the medical profession. Daughter, Pam Alexander is a homemaker in Atlanta, GA.

The Thornton family has deep roots in Scott County, but most have moved to other locations. The Liberty Baptist Church of Forest is the home church of the Thorntons and most family members are buried in the Liberty Cemetery.

At this time, there are six grandsons in the family, all baptized in the United Methodist Church. Harvey and Onzell married life-long Baptists. After Mr. Thornton's death in 1976 of cancer, Mrs. Thornton moved to Newton and has remained there since that time.

TOUDT, Gordon Lee Toudt (b. 1926 in Minneapolis) moved from Berwyn, IL to Scott County in 1964 when Sunbeam Corporation was operating the Forest Industries Company. Gordon was promoted to quality control manager to replace the previous manager. Gordon arrived in Forest in October 1964 and was able to move his family there later. It was a beautiful day on Jan. 1, 1965 that he arrived in Forest with his wife Mae, daughter Diane and son Gordon Jr. Having just arrived from the snowbound area around Chicago, it seemed to Mae that she had arrived in Paradise.

The family settled into Forest through school, community and church activities and was soon a part of the local scene. Gordon became a member of the Kiwanis Club where he served as club president and later as regional chairman for public and business affairs for the Louisiana, Mississippi and Western Tennessee area. He was a substitute teacher of his men's class at the Forest Baptist Church. Gordon served as Scoutmaster for the local Boy Scout troop. At the state level he served two years as chairman of the Economic Education Committee for the Mississippi Manufacturers Association.

Mae served as Scott County Chairman for the March of Dimes for two years during which she arranged for all Scott County children to be vaccinated for Rubella to guard against birth defects. She was teacher of her ladies class at the Forest Baptist Church. In her community service she was affiliated with the Federated Women's Clubs serving on the Conservation Committee. Mae also served as Girl Scout troop leader.

In 1970 Gordon was transferred back to Sunbeam headquarters where he became chief engineer of product statistics dealing with quality of all Sunbeam products and later became chief lab engineer. During his tenure at Sunbeam he received a certificate from the School for Middle Managers at Illinois Benedictine College.

Upon retirement from Sunbeam Corporation, Gordon became director of Quality Assurance for Glenwood Range Company in Ohio and later Quality Assurance Manager for Hamilton Beach/Proctor-Silex Company in North Carolina from where he retired and lives with his wife in Greenville. They are members of Peoples Baptist Church where Gordon is Sunday School Superintendent and Mae is teacher of the Ladies Bible Class.

Their two children attended the Forest Public Schools where Gordon Jr. played cornet in the band. During his few years there he was so impressed with the Band Director, Doug Harvel, that he decided that was what he wanted to be. While in Forest, he took piano lessons that augmented his playing of wind instruments. He has a bachelor's degree in music education from Elmhurst (IL) College. He went on to teach as band director in Kansas schools and in North Carolina where he now lives with his wife and two sons. While currently engaged in teaching computer classes in the public schools in Pitt County, NC, he is director of the Tar River Community Band, has acted with community groups, has composed Christian songs for choir and most recently composed a Christmas Cantata.

Diane (Toudt) Robertson has been married but does not have children and lives nearby.

Since leaving Forest, Gordon and Mae became the parents of another son, James. With a communications degree from East Carolina University, he was employed as disk jockey at radio stations in eastern North Carolina and as assistant manager of a music store.

TRIPLETT, The Oliver Beaman Tripletts of Forest, Scott County, MS descend from Moses Washington Jackson Triplett (b. May 8, 1829, Chester County, SC, d. Aug. 15, 1905). His wife was Elizabeth Johnson of Chester County, SC. He was a farmer from Plattsburg, Winston County, MS. They are both buried in the Triplett plot at the old Baptist Cemetery, Louisville, Winston County, MS.

They named their son Oliver Barnett Glen Triplett (b. Sep. 17, 1860, d. Apr. 4, 1946). He was a 1886 graduate of the Harperville Collegiate Institute at Harperville, Scott County, MS. He met Emma Elizabeth "Lizzie" Beaman (b. Aug. 2, 1868, d. Feb. 18, 1947) and married on Apr. 1, 1888. They bought her father's home, the George Gray Beaman Sr.'s home in Harperville, Scott County, MS. He owned the G.G. Beaman Mercantile Store, Harperville, Scott County, MS. In June 1902 they moved to Oak Street, Forest, Scott County, MS where he was serving as chancery clerk of Scott County. On Mar. 28, 1908, he was licensed to practice law in the state of Mississippi. On Jan. 29, 1910 he acquired the deed for the second Forest Methodist Church and served as trustee. He served as a Forest school trustee. In 1919-1920, he served as the mayor of the city of Forest. The Triplett family served as Sunday school teachers, and one daughter, Mary Evelyn "Eva" Triplett, served as church organist in 1914 for six years. Elizabeth and Oliver Barnett Glen Triplett Sr. are buried at the Triplett plot at Eastern Cemetery, Scott County, MS.

Their third child was Oliver Beaman Triplett Jr. (b. Nov. 4, 1902, d. Apr. 12, 1980). He was educated in the Forest Public School. In 1924, he received a bachelor of arts degree from Millsaps College, with honors, and was a member of Kappa Alpha fraternity, and was the editor-in-chief of the Purple and White Millsaps College newspaper. He served twice as president of the Millsaps College Alumni Association: 1937-1938 and 1957-1958.

From 1924-1925, he taught Latin in the Forest Public School. He attended the University of Florida at Gainsville, FL. On Jun. 20, 1928, he received his law degree with honors from Yale University at New Haven, CT. In 1929, he began practice of law at the Triplett Law Office, 238 Main Street, Forest, MS.

On Jun. 19, 1930, he married Mary Lytle McCravey (b. Jul. 4, 1904, d. 30 May, 1985), Forest, Scott County, MS. She was educated in the Forest Public Schools, Scott County, MS and Belhaven Preparatory School, Hinds County, Jackson, MS.

In 1926, she received a bachelor's of arts degree as an English major and served as president of her senior class at Belhaven College and was the business manager of Kinetoscope, the Belhaven College Yearbook. After her college graduation, she taught English at the Scott County Agricultural High School at Harperville, Scott County, MS. She was a member of the Forest Presbyterian Church.

In 1929, Oliver Beaman Triplett Jr. was admitted to the Mississippi State Bar Association. On Aug. 30, 1960 he became a member of the Supreme Court of the United States of America. At an early age, he became a member of the Forest United Methodist Church and taught the Beaman Triplett Sunday school class for 40 years.

On Jan. 27, 1953, he was presented the Silver Beaver Award from the Andrew Jackson Boy Scout Council of America for distinguished service. He was a member of the Forest Rotary Club, the state of Mississippi Library Commission, attorney for the city of Forest. He was a prominent trial lawyer and respected citizen of Forest. He died in an automobile accident on Apr. 12, 1980 in Forest, Scott County, MS and is buried with his wife, Mary McCravey Triplett, at the Triplett plot, Eastern Cemetery, Scott County, MS.

They had two sons: Donald Gray Triplett and Oliver Beaman Triplett, III of Forest, Scott County, MS.

TRIPLETT, DONALD GRAY, of Forest, Scott County, MS, unmarried (b. Sep. 8, 1933), was named for Donald Lycurgus McKay, unmarried (b. Nov. 5, 1876, d. 1930). Donald McKay is buried in the McCravey plot, Eastern Cemetery, Forest, Scott County, MS. He was a nephew of the late James Richard McCravey

Donald Gray Triplett

Sr., formerly president of the Bank of Forest of Forest, Scott County, MS. Donald McKay was employed by the Railway Mail Association, Memphis branch. In 1930, the year of his death, he was clerk-in-charge of the Memphis Terminal.

Donald Gray Triplett is the first son of Mary Lytle McCravey (b. Jul. 4, 1904, d. May 30, 1985) and Oliver Beaman Triplett Jr. (b. Nov. 4, 1902, d. Apr. 12, 1980) both of Forest, Scott County, MS. He was educated in the Forest Public Schools and attended Goodhope Public School, Scott County, MS. In 1953, he graduated from the Forest High School and was a member of the cast for the senior play, *The Monkey's Uncle*, member of the Future Farmers of America and the Forest High School Chorus.

In 1954, he served as treasurer of his freshman class at East Central Junior College, Decatur, Newton County, MS. He was song leader of the Young Men's Christian Association, member of the Student Christian Association, President of Westminister, a Presbyterian Fellowship and their representative, Treasurer of the Liberal Arts Student Association, member of the Drama Club, member of the East Central Junior College Mixed Chorus, member Phi Theta Kappa, a Junior College National Honorary Scholastic Fraternity, Treasurer of the Student Body Association, Executive Council, member of the Future Business Leaders Association. In

1955, he received a liberal arts degree from East Central Junior College.

In 1958, he received a bachelor of arts degree as a language arts major at Millsaps College, Jackson, Hinds County, MS, where he was a member of Lambda Chi Alpha fraternity, the Millsaps Singers, the German Club and the Westminister Presbyterian Fellowship.

In June 1958, he became an employee of the Bank of Forest as a bank teller. In 1970, he worked in the loan department of the Bank of Forest and became a world traveler during his annual vacations. In 1980, he began work in the bookkeeping department of the Bank of Forest.

In 1998, he received a 40 year appreciation certificate as an employee of the Bank of Forest. He is a member of the Forest Country Club, where he is an avid golfer. He is an active member of the Forest Presbyterian Church, and has served in several offices of the Forest Kiwanis Club. He resides at 344 North Hillsboro Street, Forest, MS 39074.

TRIPLETT, OLIVER BEAMAN III. of

Forest, Scott County, MS (b. May 22, 1938) was named for his father Oliver Beaman Triplett Jr. (b. Nov. 4, 1902, d. Apr. 12, 1980). He is the second son of Mary Lytle McCravey (b. Jul. 4, 1904, d. May 30, 1985) of Forest, Scott County, MS. He was educated in the Forest Public Schools, Scott County, MS. In

O.B. Triplett III and Carolyn East Triplett

1956, he graduated as Salutatorian of his Forest High School class and was a member of the Forest High School Band; the Beta Club and the Latin Club. He was an active member of Forest Troop 63 Boy Scouts of America. He summer camped at Kickapoo Boy Scout Camp, Pocahontus, Hinds County, MS; Alpine Camp for Boys, Mentone, Alabama and the McCallie Sports Camp, Chattanooga, TN. He served on the Alpine Camp for Boys staff as a counselor and instructor in the crafts department.

In 1960, he received a bachelor of arts degree in English at Millsaps College, Jackson, Hinds County, MS; where he was a member of Lambda Chi Alpha fraternity, the Millsaps Singers, Dean's List, Millsaps College Band and Intramural Sports.

In May 1963, he received his law degree from the University of Mississippi at Oxford, Lafayette County, MS. On May 27, 1963, he was licensed to practice law by the Supreme Court, state of Mississippi. He became an associate with his father, Oliver Beaman Triplett Jr., known as Beaman Triplett at the Triplett Law Firm, 238 East Main Street, Forest, MS.

In 1962, he married Carolyn Grant East (b. Apr. 12, 1936) at Trenton, Mercer County, NJ. She was educated in the public schools of Jamesburg, NJ, Oxford, Lafayette County, MS, Augusta, Georgia, The Matthew Whaley School, Williamsburg, James River County, VA, Spencer, Roane County, WV. In 1954 she graduated from Spencer High School and was a member

of the Thespians Drama Club and performed in the senior play and was a member of the Spencer High School Band. In 1953, she completed senior course of the American Red Cross instruction in Life Saving and Water Safety, and was the assistant instructor and life guard at Spencer Swimming Pool, Spencer, Roane County, WV. From 1950-52, was member of the Matthew Whaley Chorus, Matthew Whaley Majorettes, studied ballet, tap, modern and ballroom dance, member of Williamsburg, Virginia Girl Scout troop, member Williamsburg Inn Country Club. In 1950 completed Junior Course of the American Red Cross instruction in Life Saving and Water Safety. In 1954 was swimming instructor and counselor at Camp Kirby, a Girl Scout Camp, Cleveland, OH. In 1954 attended the University of Kentucky, Lexington, KY, member Alpha Ki Delta Sorority, and the Blue Marlin Swimming Club. In 1955 was waterfront instructor and counselor at Ogontz Camp for Girls, Lisbon, NH. In May 1963 she received a bachelor of arts degree with a major in sociology and anthropology and minors in French and history at the University of Mississippi. Later, she assisted in establishing an Alpha Xi Delta Sorority at the University of Mississippi, Oxford, Lafayette County, MS.

In May 1963 they moved to Forest, Scott County, MS where she taught French and History at Morton High School, Morton, Scott County, MS. On Oct. 20, 1963, she organized the Forest Arts Association at the Bank of Forest Art Gallery with the assistance of local artist, Mary Katherine Loyacano. In 1964, Director Girl Scout Day Camp at Moore Tower, Forest, Scott County, MS; a girl scout troop leader, and Forest Girl Scout neighborhood chairman, Middle Mississippi Girl Scout Council.

On Jun. 30, 1976 assisted in establishing the Dr. George Gray Townsend Scholarship Fund at the University of Mississippi with the Scott County Ole Miss Alumni Association. They are active members of the Forest Presbyterian Church and reside at 108 Janwood Circle, Forest, MS 39074. They had two sons, Oliver Beaman Triplett IV and Cooper East Triplett; one grandson George Beaman Triplett (b. Sep. 15, 1996) and one granddaughter Olivia Jane Triplett (b. Oct. 2, 2000).

TRIPLETT OLIVER BEAMAN IV, of

Forest, Scott County, MS, (b. Dec. 29, 1962) was named for his father, Oliver Beaman Triplett, III (b. May 22, 1938) who was an Attorney-at-Law, Triplett Law Office, 238 East Main Street, Forest, MS; and was the first son of Carolyn Grant East Triplett (b. Apr. 12, 1936) and Oliver Beaman Triplett, III, both of Forest, Scott County, MS. He was educated in the Forest Public Schools, Scott County, MS and attended the McCallie School, a preparatory school at Chattanooga, Hamilton County, TN. In 1981, he graduated from Forest High School and was chosen a

O.B. Triplett IV and Ingrid Burnham Triplett

senior class favorite; and was a member of the Forest Junior High Band, the Forest Junior High School football team, and the Forest High School Golf team. He was an active member of Forest Troop 363 Boy Scouts of America. On Jun. 3, 1981, he was presented the Eagle Scout Award. He summer camped at Kickapoo Boy Scout Camp, Pocahontus, Hinds County, MS; Alpine Camp for Boys, Mentone, AL, and the McCallie Summer School, Chattanooga, TN; and attended several Boy Scout training camps, Camp Brownlee, Boy Scout Leadership Camp for patrol leaders; in 1977, he attended the International Boy Scout Jamboree and in 1979, the Philmont Scout Ranch.

In 1973, he recited the Child's Catechism as an introduction to the Westminister Shorter Catechism, and in 1979, he became a member of the Forest Presbyterian Church.

In 1981-1982, he attended East Central Junior College, Decatur, Newton County, MS. In 1984, he received an associate of arts degree from Hinds Junior College, Raymond, MS. In 1987, he received his bachelor's degree in public administration from the University of Mississippi, Oxford, Lafayette County, MS. He is a licensed state certified general real estate appraiser, GA-101. In 1987, he was employed by Morrow Realty Incorporation, 158 West Government Street, Brandon, Rankin County, MS, as a real estate appraiser. In 1992, he began the Triplett Realty Services, 238 East Main Street, Forest, MS.

In 2000, he was president of the Mississippi Forestry Commission. He became a member of Ducks Unlimited, as an avid sportsman and conservationist; and was a member of numerous fishing and hunting clubs in Scott County, MS.

On Sep. 30, 1998, he began the Wildlife Habitat Improvement Program with the U.S. Department of Agriculture Natural Resources Conservation Service, Forest, Scott County, MS. In 1999, he was vice-president of the Scott County Forestry Association and served as president in the year 2000, and he served on the Board of Directors of the Mississippi Forestry Association.

On Aug. 21, 1995 he married Ingrid Elizabeth Burnham (b. Mar. 25, 1958, Fort Rucker, Coffee County, AL). She was educated in the Puckett Public Schools, Puckett, Rankin County, MS and Brandon Public Schools, Rankin County, MS. In 1976, she graduated from Brandon High School, where she was 1973 Freshman Homecoming Maid, a member of the Brandon High School Pep Club, and secretary of the Brandon High School Bible Club. In 1975, she was chosen a Beauty from her Junior Class at Brandon High School. In 1976, she was chosen a Beauty by her senior Brandon High School class. During her high school years, she was employed by Murphy's Drugstore, Brandon, Rankin County, MS.

The summer of 1976, she visited her maternal grandmother, the late Mrs. Hans Christian Buhur (ne Elizabeth Oma Buhur) who resided in the Basque region of France; formerly of Stuttgart, Germany, where she deceased. Her maternal grandfather, the late Hans Christian Buhur, known as "Opa" was an aeronautical engineer, and a graduate of Stuttgart University, Stuttgart, Germany. His hobby was watercolor painting; which became the hobby of his daughter, Felcites "Faye" Buhur Burnham (b. Feb. 7,

1932, d. Nov. 9, 2000), mother of Ingrid Elizabeth Burnham of Brandon, Rankin County, MS. In 1977, she attended the University of Mississippi, Oxford, Lafayette County, MS. In 1978, she was a member of the Phi

George Beamon Triplett

Mu sorority at the University of Mississippi. In 1981, she received a bachelor of science degree in business administration, from Belhaven College, Jackson, Hinds County, MS. She was employed by the Wilson Company and McRae's Department Stores of Jackson, Hinds County, MS.

In 1992, she received an Elementary Education degree from Mississippi College. In 1993, she began teaching at Stevens Elementary School Kindergarten, Brandon, Rankin County, MS and continues teaching at the Rouse-Boyce Elementary School, Brandon, Rankin County, MS, Year 2000. She became a member of the Scott County Junior Auxiliary. They are active members of the Forest Presbyterian Church and reside at 1578 Old Highway 80, Forest, MS, 39074. They have one son, George Beaman Triplett (b. Sep. 15, 1996); and one daughter, Olivia Jane Triplett (b. Oct. 2, 2000).

George Beaman Triplett (b. Sep. 15, 1996) of Forest, Scott County, MS was named for his maternal grandfather, the late Rufus George Burnham (b. Sep. 13, 1918, d. Apr. 28, 1989) where he is buried at the Burnham Plot, Puckett City Cemetery, Puckett, Rankin County, MS. and who was sergeant first class in the U.S. Army, and was a civil engineer for the state of Mississippi Highway Department and his paternal great-grandfather, the late Oliver Beaman Triplett (b. Nov. 4, 1902, d. Apr. 12, 1980); known as Beaman Triplett, where he is buried at the Triplett Plot, Eastern Cemetery, Forest, Scott County, MS. He was a prominent trial lawyer and practiced law at the Scott County Bar Association, the Mississippi State Bar Association, the Supreme Court of the state of Mississippi and the Supreme Court of the United States of America.

The Beaman name descends from George Gray Beaman Sr. (b. Aug. 27, 1829, d. May 15, 1880) of Macon, Noxubee County and Harperville, Scott County, MS; where he owned the G.G. Beaman Mercantile Store and was a farmer. In 1851, George Gray Beaman Sr. received a bachelor of arts degree from the University of Alabama, son of Whitmill Beaman of Plattsburg, Winston County, MS, who was the principal of the Plattsburg, MS High School.

He is buried at the Lebanon Cemetery, Harperville, Scott County, MS with his wife, Susan Jane "Jennie" McCoy Beaman (b. Nov. 5, 1841, d. Dec. 3, 1912).

Olivia Jane Triplett (b. Oct. 2, 2000) of Forest, Scott County, MS was named for her father, Oliver Beaman Triplett, IV (b. Dec. 29, 1962) and who is a real estate appraiser at Triplett Realty Services, Forest, Scott County, MS. The Jane name was from a family name.

Olivia Jane Triplett

TRIPLETT, COOPER EAST , of Forest, Scott

County, MS, unmarried was named for his maternal grandfather, the late Isaac Cooper East, M.D. (b. Dec. 13, 1905, d. 21 Oct., 1991). He is buried in the East Plot, St. Peter's Cemetery, Oxford, Lafayette County, MS.

Cooper East Triplett was the grandson of the late Isaac Cooper East, M.D. former staff psychiatrist at Mississippi State

Cooper East Triplett

Hospital, Whitfield, Rankin County, MS; and was the second son of Carolyn Grant East and Oliver Beaman Triplett III both of Forest, Scott County, MS. He attended the Forest Public Schools; where he was a member of the Forest High School Band, the French Club, and the Forest High School Tennis Team. He was an active member of Forest Troop 363 Boy Scouts of America. He summer camped at Kickapoo Boy Scout Camp, Pocahontus, Hinds County, MS; Alpine Camp for Boys, Mentone, AL and the McCallie School, Chattanooga, TN.

In 1985, he graduated from the McCallie School where he was a member of the track and cross country teams, and began his travels abroad to Europe with his classmates.

In 1989, he received a bachelor of science degree in business administration and economics from Belhaven College, Jackson, Hinds County, MS; where he was in the 83rd Regiment and a member of the Men's Christian Club. He was an avid stock and futures investor for over 20 years. Upon graduation from Belhaven College, he formed his own corporation titled, Standard of Mississippi, as a private investor in the stock market and futures trader and was a member of the Forest Presbyterian Church.

TUCKER-WOLF, James Edward Tucker and

Claudette Wolf Tucker, Scott County natives, were married at Ephesus Baptist Church near Forest, MS in 1980. The couple built a house on Line Creek Road near Morton, MS in Scott County. Adjoining property was located in Rankin County near Pelahatchie MS.

James (b. Jan. 20, 1947 in Jackson, MS), son of William Lee Tucker and Frances Winstead Tucker. His sister Virginia Lee Tucker (b. Jun. 8, 1952) was followed by his brother Charles Rochester Tucker (b. Jul. 28, 1953).

Graduating from Morton High School in 1965, he attended east Central Junior College

and Mississippi State University. After graduating from Mississippi State with a bachelor of science degree in agricultural economics, he accepted a position at Mississippi State, MS where he was employed with the

Joe and Claudette Tucker

Agricultural Aviation Board of Mississippi for five years.

In 1980, James co-authored a publication entitled Aerial Application of Pesticide Sprays.

Returning to Scott County in 1980, he continued his agricultural career by focusing on poultry and cattle farming. With a continued interest in pesticides, James organized his own pest control company. Jet Pest Control, in 1986, which he operated in the local areas.

Mariea Claudette Wolf was born in Newton MS to parents Jesse Lang Wolf and Stella Posey Wolf on Apr. 1, 1948. Her family included two sisters and one brother: Jessie Burnette Wolf (b. Sep. 18, 1949); Brenda Barcell Wolf (b. Jul. 30, 1952) and her only brother, Rockey DeWest Wolf (b. Jul. 9, 1955).

Residing with her family in the Ringgold Community near Forest, MS, she graduated from Scott Central High School in 1966. She graduated from East Central Junior College and Delta State University with a bachelor of science degree in education. Later she attended the graduate school of Mississippi State University and obtained a master of education degree.

Claudette began her teaching career in Bolivar County at Pace Elementary School in 1970.

Returning to Scott County in 1971, she became a teacher in the Scott County School District and later, in the Forest Separate School District. After 25 years of dedication in the field of educational instruction, she retired to pursue a career with her husband in his established pest control business.

James and Claudette accepted Jesus Christ as their personal savior at an early age and became members of Morton First Baptist Church where James served as deacon. Both were involved in the Gideon's International.

UNDERWOOD, Ripley C. Underwood was

living in the household of Thomas Underwood during the 1850 Jasper County federal census. Ripley was a 30-year-old laborer born in Alabama. Ripley married Bethany and moved to Scott County before the 1860 federal census.

Ripley served as a private in the Confederate 36th MS Inf., Co. D. He enlisted on Mar. 7, 1862 at Meridian, MS for a period of 12 months. He is present on muster roll calls through February 1863. There is no record of his discharge.

Ripley and Bethany had at least eight children: Catherine (b. ca. 1851); Susan (b. ca. 1852); Sarah (b. ca. 1855); Martha (b. ca. 1856); Harriett (b. ca. 1857); George W. (b. May 2, 1858); Margaret (b. ca. 1862) and Frances (b. Aug. 24, 1863). George W. Underwood married Almanza Helen Day on Dec. 3, 1879 in Leake County.

George died on May 4, 1899 in Pike County, MS and is buried in East Union Cemetery in Pike County. Frances Underwood married Daniel Comans on Dec. 23, 1879 in Leake County. Frances died on Sep. 9, 1898 and is buried in High Hill Baptist Church Cemetery in Neshoba County beside her husband.

Ripley was living in Newton County during the 1870 federal census and in Leake County during the 1880 federal census. Since Ripley lived close to the boundaries between three counties it is unknown whether Ripley moved from county to county or the census taker was unsure of the county boundaries.

Ripley and Bethany are buried in a private family cemetery in Scott County. There are no dates on either of their headstones.

USRY, John Baxton Usry and Mahaley Gordy Usry moved to Scott County, MS in the late 1850s. In 1877 John Baxton purchased 160 acres of land in the NW 1/4 and 160 acres in the SW 1/4, Section 4, T6N, R9E, Scott County, MS. John Baxton paid for this land by clearing the land and delivering the timber to the government. A two-story home was built off the road going to Salem between Irving Clark's and Howard Clark's place. There was a small store and a one-room schoolhouse called the "Usry School." Alice Warren was the teacher. She later married Henry Abner Usry, son of Allen Thomas Usry, John Baxton's 7th child. Years later the Usry School was moved to Goodhope and the two schools combined. The two-story house built by John Baxton burned. Allen Thomas Usry built the big house on what we grew up knowing as Noblin Hill.

After John Baxton's children were grown, he decided to return to Georgia. He deeded each son a portion of his land. John Baxton had 11 children. They are as follows: 1) Mary Ann (md. to John Pickard); 2) Octavia Ann (md. George Massey); 3) William Franklin md. first, A.L. "Vicey" Pickard and second, Josie Permenter; 4) Sarah A. (md. W.J. "Jasper" Stewart); 5) John Robert (md. Salena Pickard; 6) Elizabeth; 7) Allen Thomas (md. Sarah Permenter); 8) Henry J. (md. Mary Elizabeth Permenter); 9) Hasty Ann (md. William J. Permenter; 10) Dexter B. (md. Lida Futch); and 11) Betty Jo (md. J.B. Ducksworth).

Travis Usry, owner of the Back Forty Seafood Restaurant, is descended from William Franklin's first marriage to Vicey Pickard and he is the great-great-grandson of John Baxton Usry.

WADE, Marion Lee Wade (b. Jan. 29, 1875, d. Mar. 11, 1970) was married to Betty Cornelia "Nelia" Stuart (b. Jul. 25, 1886, d. Jul. 4, 1976) on Oct. 4, 1903 at the home of the bride's parents in the Homestead Community. They are both buried in the Springfield Baptist Church Cemetery. They were the parents of

Marion Lee and Betty Cornelia Stuart Wade

11 children. Marion was working for Nelia's father when they met.

Marion Lee was a farmer. He bought a farm in the Springfield Community in 1920, but during the depression he lost the farm because he was unable to pay for the money borrowed to plant his crop. It was hard times trying to raise a big family. In those years there was no electricity in the country. They used oil lamps to see at night. They did not have a car so they either walked or rode in a wagon when they went some place. There were very few roads with gravel.

One of their daughters wrote in remembering her growing up days that we knew that we were loved not only by our mother and father but also our brothers and sisters. They were a very close family. Another daughter said that some of the things she heard her mother and father talking about was that in the past they wore clothes that were all made of cotton, the dresses were long down to their ankles and long sleeves, long hair—all the women and girls wore their hair platted or balled up in a bun. Their shoes were high top with little round buttons to fasten. They wore aprons around the house and wore bonnets outside. Some of the women wore bonnets to church— pretty white ones with ruffles and lace. They cooked on wood stoves and had iron pots and skillets. Since this was a large family they did not have a lot of money to spend on Christmas gifts. Most of them said that they remembered getting an orange and an apple along with some little something else. They were happy with what they received.

In 1941 he bought land and built a home on Hwy. 13 south of Morton. They lived there until his death. Nelia was in the Scott County Nursing Home several years before her death. They were married for 66 years. On Jun. 15, 1968 on Father's Day, the Springfield Baptist Church honored the Wades as the oldest members of the church and also on the occasion of their 65th year as members of the church. The pastor presented a brief resume of their life "This is your Life Mr. and Mrs. Lee Wade."

A fond memory of Marion Lee is that he enjoyed sitting on the front porch watching the traffic go by while chewing his tobacco. They enjoyed having family visiting with them. Their twin daughters and their family were next door neighbors so they were able to see those grandchildren grow up.

WALDRIP, The known history begins with Hillan Waldrip (b. 1792 in South Carolina). By about 1830, the family had migrated westward to Sumpter and Choctaw counties in Alabama. They were farmers and apparently moved west searching for new farmland as the Indians were relocated out of a territory. With no fertilizer available, nutrients in the soil would be depleted after a few years farming; therefore, the need for new farmland.

Hillan Waldrip's family included wife, Elizabeth M. (b. ca. 1800), and sons: James P. (b. ca. 1827); William B. (b. ca. 1829); Benjamin C. (b. ca. 1831); Thomas P. (b. ca. 1835) and Wallis L. (b. ca. 1839). There are indications there were more sons and at least one daughter, but no specifics are known at this time.

During the 1850s, Hillan and part of his family migrated to Scott County, MS, first settling in the Lake area, then moving to the Hillsboro area. This move again occurred shortly after the Indians had been moved out of the territory per the treaty of Dancing Rabbit in 1830. Members of the family known to have moved to Scott County were Hillan and his wife Elizabeth, and sons William B., Benjamin C., and Wallis L. They were apparently pretty prosperous farmers with a number of slaves. The Civil War was very shortly to change this though. Two of Hillan and Elizabeth's sons, William and Wallis, both joined Co. H, 38th MS Regiment in the Confederate Army. Wallis was killed Oct. 4, 1862, in the Battle of Corinth. William served throughout the war, including the Battle of Vicksburg where he was captured and paroled in July 1863, and was later captured at Citronelle, AL, and paroled again in May 1865.

Hillan and Elizabeth remained in Scott County until their deaths—Hillan in the 1860s and Elizabeth in the 1870s. The exact location of their graves is not known, but it is probably in the Lake area. Wallis Larkins Waldrip married Narcissa Burge about 1860, and they had one son, Thomas B. Waldrip (b. May 10, 1861), before Wallis was killed in the war. Narcissa remarried another Waldrip, William H., a cousin who was born 1841 in Sumpter County, AL. Narcissa and her second husband, William H. Waldrip, moved to Texas. William B. Waldrip appears to have been the only child of Hillan and Elizabeth that permanently remained in Scott County.

In the mid-1850s, Hillan and Elizabeth's son, William Benjamin, married Mary Jane Patrick who was born in Selma, AL in 1836. Their first child, Marylan Elizabeth "Bettie," was born in 1858 followed by James T. "Jim" (b. 1859), William H. (b. 1864), Dora (b. 1867), Loula "Lou" (b. 1868), Charley Benjamin (b. Dec. 13, 1870), Robert William "Bob" (b. 1873) and Harriet E. (b. 1876). William B. and Mary moved with their children from the Lake area to the Hillsboro area about 1880, and remained in Scott County until their deaths (in the early 1900s). They are both buried in the Hillsboro Baptist Cemetery (no headstones).

William B. and Mary Jane's first child, Marylan Elizabeth "Bettie," married William Mathison Crye from Pulaski on Nov. 15, 1871. William M. and Bettie's known children were James Benjamin, Curtis, John and Clara. On Mar. 19, 1899, James Benjamin married Betty Miles, daughter of Robert Miles and Nancy Stuart Miles. James Benjamin and Betty had three children: Myrl, Ianthe and Bennye. Bennye (b. Nov. 25, 1907) md. Harold Loeb and still lives in Morton. Bennye and Harold had one daughter, Franceska "Frisky" Loeb. Frisky married Melvin T. Roland and they also reside in Morton.

William B. and Mary Jane's second child, James T. "Jim," married Susan S. Stone in 1881. Nothing more is known about this family.

William B. and Mary Jane's third child, William H. married Martha "Mattie" Miles from the Pulaski area on Nov. 19, 1895. Martha was born in October 1870. They lived in the Hillsboro area until William died (between 1900 and 1910), at which time Martha moved back to the Pulaski area and lived with her twin sister, Mary. William H. is buried in the Hillsboro Baptist Cemetery, and Martha is buried in the Brassell Cem-

.lery between Homewood and Pulaski. They had two children, Robert William "Robbie" and Libbie. Robbie married Minnie Lou Lassetter in 1918, and they had three children: Robert Lassetter, Libbye Jean and Caley Bryant. Robert Lassetter was killed Jul. 5, 1943, when his plane was shot down on a bombing mission to Gerbini, Sicily; his body was not recovered. Libbye Jean married James Andrew King and they had one child, James Andrew Jr. (b. November 1949). James Andrew Jr. married Veleta Woods and they had one son, Jeffery Scott born in 1974, Caley Bryant married June Carroll and they had one child, David Bryant (b. 1954). This family moved to Jackson in the 1920s and still live there.

William B. and Mary Jane's forth child, Dora, married James W. "Jim" Weems from the Lena area on Jan. 9, 1895. They had four sons: Leroy, Alex, Arthur and Hilton, and one daughter, Mary. Mary married Gordon Bennett. Dora and James remained in the Lena area throughout their lives, but some or all their children apparently moved to the Jackson area. Nothing more is known about this family except that "Uncle Jim" was a small man that visited Charlie (Dora's brother) and Lina Waldrip quite often and really loved to eat.

William B. and Mary Jane's fifth child, Loula "Lou" married J.C. Weems (maybe James W.'s brother) on Dec. 13, 1894. They apparently moved to Texas. Nothing more is known about this family.

William B. and Mary Jane's sixth child, Charley Benjamin, married Salina Keeton from the Pulaski area on Dec. 22, 1897. Charley met Salina during visits to his sister Bettie's who lived in Pulaski after marrying William Mathison Crye. Salina was the daughter of Austin Keeton and his wife Amanda Stewart, and was born May 28, 1881. Charley had a farm at Hillsboro (just north of Scott Central School on Old Jackson Road), but he moved to Pulaski and lived on the farm that Salina's father had given her. They built a house on it near Ben and Bettie Crye. Most of their children were born during the time they lived in Pulaski. Sometime in the early 1900s, Salina got sick with rheumatic fever and was near death for weeks, maybe even months. This disrupted the normal activities, and they lost that year's crop and eventually the farm. They moved to the farm in Hillsboro, but never regained the success and prosperity they had in Pulaski. Most of the time the children were growing up, the family "sharecropped" the McElhaney place directly across Old Jackson Road from Scott Central School, and it included the land where the school is located. Charley and Salina's first child, Taylor Percy (b. Feb. 11, 1899) was followed by Lilla May "Aunt Sister" (b. Aug. 31, 1900); Ben J. (b. Jul. 11, 1902); William Austin (b. Sep. 4, 1904); Mary Elizabeth (b. Nov. 10, 1906); Erbin Bates (b. Aug.

Salina Keeton, circa 1897, age 16, daughter of Austin Keeton and Amanda Stewart and wife of Charles Benjamin Waldrip

21, 1912) and Woodrow Wilson (b. Nov. 22, 1918). Charlie and Salina lived at several places in the Hillsboro area until their deaths: Charlie on Dec. 21, 1955 and Salina on Feb. 27, 1961. They are both buried in the Hillsboro Baptist Cemetery

James W. "Jim" Weems, husband of Dora Waldrip; Salina Keeton Waldrip, daughter of Austin Keeton and Amanda Stewart; and Charley Benjamin Waldrip, son of William Benjamin Waldrip and Mary Jane Patrick circa 1950.

On Jun. 7, 1930, Charlie and Salina's first child, Taylor Percy, married Winnie Alma Rochester from Morton who was born Apr. 17, 1904. Winnie graduated from Mississippi Woman's College in 1927 and met Taylor while teaching in Homewood and Taylor was working there with the County Road Dept. Their first child Paul Ray (b. Jan. 7, 1932) was followed by Ruth Carolyn (b. Apr. 30, 1933); Winnie Ellen (b. Oct. 12, 1934); Lena Percy (b. Jun. 21, 1937) and William Taylor (b. Nov. 13, 1939). They both lived in Scott County until their deaths: Taylor on Jul. 24, 1985 and Winnie on Mar. 13, 1981, except for short periods when Winnie taught elsewhere (at the Choctaw Indian Reservation near Philadelphia and at Lucedale). They managed to send all five children to college even though their resources were rather limited. They are both buried in the Hillsboro Baptist Cemetery.

Taylor and Winnie's first child, Paul Ray, married Edna Blanche Clair on Oct. 16, 1959. Edna (b. Oct. 24, 1937) was from the Ringgold area. Paul had a career in retailing and Edna remained at home while raising the children. Their first child Ray (b. Oct. 18, 1960) was followed by Joe (b. Mar. 11, 1962); Pat (b. Oct. 11, 1964) and Desirre (b. Jul. 29, 1994). Pat married David Bryon Rushing from Forest and they have one child, Laura Ashley, born Jun. 4, 1998. After graduating from Mississippi State, Pat passed the CPA Exam, which may be the highest academic achievement in the Waldrip family. This family has basically remained in Scott County continuously.

Taylor and Winnie's second child, Ruth Carolyn, married Robert J. "Bob" Summerlin Jr. on Jun. 4, 1954, and they had four children: Rhonda, Theresa, Ricky and Tammie. During their working career and while raising their family, the family lived in Jackson; upon retirement, Ruth and Bob moved to their farm in Canton. Ms. Ruth went to East Central and Hinds Junior Colleges and her career was in medical records and medical transcription, and Bob's was in equipment sales.

Taylor and Winnie's third child, Winnie Ellen, married Edward "Ed" M. Hargrave Jr. and they lived in Richmond, VA. Ellen graduated from Mississippi College and worked for the Southern Baptist Missions Board, and Ed was a

physical therapist. They had two daughters, Kellie and Kristen. Ed died Mar. 16, 1999.

Taylor and Winnie's fourth child, Lena Percy, married Fred Marchioni Jr. from Biloxi on Jul. 3, 1960. Lena graduated from Southern Mississippi University and taught school a few years before staying at home to raise their family. Fred's career was in the family dry cleaning business in Biloxi. They had four children: Margaret Lynn (b. Jun. 4, 1962); Fedele (b. Oct. 1, 1963); Karen Frances (b. Dec. 7, 1964) and Gerald Keith "Jerry" (b. Nov. 2, 1972).

Taylor and Winnie's fifth child, William Taylor, married Jean Harvard from Lucedale on Aug. 19, 1966, and they remained in Lucedale. They both graduated from Southern Mississippi University. William taught school his whole career, semi-retiring in the late 1990s, and Jean remained at home raising the children. They had two children, Penny Suzanne and Jeffrey William.

Charlie and Salina's second child, Lilla May, married Albert Otho Putnam (b. Jul. 22, 1896) on Jul. 3, 1920 at Gum Springs (near the family home) while they remained in the buggy. Lilla May was known to the family as "Aunt Sister," because her siblings always called her sister, and their children (her nieces and nephews) knew no other name for her. Otho was a teacher and farmer, and they lived on a farm in the Steele Community. Otho was a Private in the U.S. Army in WWI. Their first child Charlene (b. Aug. 21, 1924) was followed by Lilla Lols on July 25, 1926. Otho died Jan. 8, 1975, and is buried in the Eastern Cemetery in Forest. Aunt Sister celebrated her 100th birthday Aug. 31, 2000. She is the only known Waldrip to reach the century mark.

Lilla May and Otho's first child, Charlene, married James Edward Tanner Jr. on Jun. 11, 1950, and they make their home Newton. Charlene graduated from Mississippi State College for Women (MSCW), and taught school; James operated a retail meat market. Their first child was Nancy Elizabeth (b. Aug. 14, 1952), followed by James Otho "Jimmy" (b. Dec. 11, 1954) and Amy Lois (b. Mar. 7, 1957). James E. died on Aug. 13, 2000.

Lilla May and Otho's second child, Lilla Lois, graduated from Mississippi State College for Women (MSCW) and worked in medical research for many years. Lois married Orris George Tillman Jr. in 1947, and they made their home in the Raleigh-Durham, NC area. Lois and George later divorced, and Lois married John Raymon Derway on Aug. 27, 1972. Lois and John later divorced, and she moved back to Scott County after retiring in the late 1970s or early 1980s.

Charlie and Salina's third child, Ben J., did not marry and lived in the Hillsboro area all his life, except for a short time while working on the Oak Ridge project in Tennessee in the late 1930s, and while serving as a private in the U.S. Army during WWI. Ben J. worked as a carpenter, at sawmills, sharpening saws, and other jobs during his life. Ben J. died Jan. 9, 1975, and is buried in the Hillsboro Baptist Cemetery.

Charlie and Salina's fourth child, William Austin "Austin," was born in Pulaski, and lived there until about the age of 6. At this time, he moved with the family to "East" Hillsboro. As discussed above, his mother's sickness put the family in a bad financial condition. They had lost the farm in Pulaski and apparently were in debt when they moved to "East" Hillsboro. They lived on the McElhaney place, just north of Scott Central School, in a "share cropping" arrangement. Theirs was a subsistent existence throughout his childhood. Austin's education ended at about the sixth grade, because of financial reasons. His father "Charley" hired Austin and his brothers out as laborers to area farmers to bring in a little money for the family. During his late teens and early 20s, he was involved in logging timber and hauling it to the sawmills, first with mules, horses and wagons, then with trucks.

William Austin Waldrip, Lilla May Putnam, and Taylor Percy Waldrip, children of Charley Benjamin Waldrip and Salina Keeton.

About 1927, he migrated to Gary, IN, to find job opportunities. He got a job with U.S. Steel Corporation, and worked for them until he came back to Scott County in 1943. During the Depression years, he only worked a very limited amount, but said that was much better than most peoples' situation. While he was in Gary, he sent money to help the family, including helping Erbin and Wilson go to college.

Austin married Alice Rose Wilkinson on Sep. 12, 1942, in Crown Point, IN. Alice was the widow of Raymond Leir and had two children at the time of the marriage: Betty Marie (b. Jan. 3, 1924) and Raymond "Jack" (b. Jun. 30, 1926). Alice was born Dec. 31, 1906 in Glasgow, MO. Austin and Alice had migrated to Gary, IN, during the late 1920s and early 1930s in search of job opportunities. They met while both were working in the Payroll Office at U.S. Steel Corporation. After they married, they lived in Alice's house at 4008 W. 10th Avenue in Gary.

About a month after they were married, Austin was drafted into the Army on Oct. 19, 1942. He served as a private until Mar. 10, 1943, at which time he was discharged to return to his job at the steel mills, which were "necessary to the defense industry." In addition, he was getting close to the maximum age of 40 to serve in the Army. He served as a cook while in the Army.

Austin and Alice moved to "East" Hillsboro in 1943. Betty also moved to Mississippi (Jackson), but Jack joined the Army. Austin bought and operated a general store in "East" Hillsboro, then a restaurant in Forest. After a few years, he bought the remaining part of the family farm still owned by the family (his father) and the part of the McElhaney farm north of Old Jackson Road. He sold the restaurant, and began farming fulltime about 1950. He also acquired about 400 acres about a mile south of Scott Central School and bordering the west side of Tallabogue Creek. His farming activities included corn, hay, a little cotton, cattle, chickens, and timber.

Austin and Alice's first child, William Austin Jr. "Bill" (b. Jul. 3, 1944) was followed by Linda Gail (b. May 23, 1947). Bill and Linda grew up in the family home at the intersection of Highway 35 and Old Jackson Road, and participated in all the numerous farm jobs. The country was just coming out of the depression and times were pretty tough financially. They went to school in Forest and Bill went on to East Central Junior College and Mississippi State getting a BS degree in accounting, while Linda went to Ole Miss getting a MS degree in music and education.

Alice and Raymond Leir's first child, Betty, lived and worked in Jackson as a secretary for several years upon moving to Mississippi. There she met James Roy Howell (b. May 16, 1925) from Philadelphia, and they were married in June 1951. They made their home in Meridian. Betty stayed at home raising their children and Roy was self-employed as a structural architect. Their first child, Alice Angela (b. Dec. 12, 1951), was followed by Benjamin "Ben" (b. Jun. 29, 1954). Roy died in December 1988 and is buried in Philadelphia. Betty died Jan. 26, 1992 and is also buried in Philadelphia.

Alice and Raymond Leir's second child, Jack, made a career out of the army. He was in the Special Services most of his time in the army and served in the Korean War where he was wounded by shrapnel, and Vietnam where he was involved with the guerrilla forces in Laos. After retiring from the army, he moved to Meridian and married Pauline (last name unknown). They were divorced after a few years. He moved to Folsom, LA and lived in that vicinity near his niece, Angie, the rest of his life. Jack died Jul. 21, 1997, and is buried in Glasgow, MO next to his father.

Austin and Alice's first child, William Austin Jr. "Bill," faced a major choice as he neared graduation from Mississippi State in 1965; his military obligation at the height of the Vietnam War. He took advantage of a rare opportunity at that time to join the National Guard. He served six years in the Guard, first in a Military Police unit in Brandon, MS, then in an Armored (Tank) unit in Knoxville, TN.

Upon graduation in January 1966, Bill went to work for the Tennessee Valley Authority (TVA) in Knoxville, TN. He worked for TVA as an auditor and budget analyst his entire career, retiring in 1994. He met Diana Jane Deatherage of Knoxville in 1968, and they were married May 17, 1969. Diana won the Miss Knoxville Pageant shortly after they met, and served as Miss Knoxville most of the time they were dating. Diana was born Aug. 7, 1946, received a master's degree in elementary education from the University of Tennessee, and taught school her entire career with Knoxville City Schools which was later consolidated with Knox County School System. After many years of trying to have a baby, their only child, Brandon Adair, was born on Feb. 23, 1982. Bill and his sister, Gail, bought all the family farm, including the original Waldrip home site (circa 1870) in "East" Hillsboro, which is located about a quarter of a mile north of Scott Central School.

Upon graduation, Austin and Alice's second child, Gail, started teaching in Memphis, and was involved in taking students to Europe on musical tours during the summers. While in

Memphis, she met and married Randall "Randy" Clint Howard on Mar. 23, 1974. After marriage, Gail stopped teaching and worked with Randy in their personnel consulting business. Their first child, Parker Waldrip (b. Jan. 23, 1975), was followed by Ashley on Oct. 6, 1976. Gail and Randy were divorced in 1987. Gail then worked in the food catering business in the Memphis area and for a short time in Louisiana with her niece, Angie. She moved back to the farm in Mississippi in 1998, and operated different business ventures.

Charlie and Salina's fifth child, Mary Elizabeth, married William Duffie Russell about 1923. Duffie (b. Dec. 31, 1902) worked at sawmills for a living. They lived in the Hillsboro area until about 1950, then moved to Texas for about 20 years, coming back to Hillsboro about 1972. Their first child, William Duffie Jr. "W.D.," was born Jan. 14, 1924.

The birth dates and order of birth for their other seven children are not known. The known info about these other children is James A. (b. Jul. 10, 1927), Charles Kenneth (b. Jan. 16, 1929), Lamar, Janice, Merideth, Woodrow and Mrs. Bob Smith (her given name is not known).

Elizabeth died Oct. 4, 1970 and Duffie died Apr. 14, 1980. They are both buried in the Hillsboro Baptist Cemetery. W.D. died Feb. 24, 1976, and is also buried in the Hillsboro Baptist Cemetery. Charles died Jan. 16, 1972 and James Oct. 15, 1977; it is not known where they are buried. Most of the children remained in Texas when Duffie and Elizabeth moved back to Hillsboro.

Charlie and Salina's sixth child, Erbin Bates, went to East Central Junior College and the University of Alabama, receiving a degree in education. Erbin married Helen Romera Navarro on Dec. 21, 1938 in Meridian. Helen (b. Apr. 27, 1915) was from New York City (don't know how she ended up in the Meridian area). They lived in Birmingham for a short period then moved to the Mobile, AL, area about 1941 and remained there. They were both teachers all their careers. Their first child, Helen Robey (b. Jan. 24, 1940), was followed by Michael Austin on Nov. 8, 1942, and Frederick "Fred" Arthur on May 12, 1944.

Helen Robey married Edward Kenneth Callahan. Michael married Alice Newton and Fred married Sarah Baker. All the children have made their home in the Mobile area. Erbin died May 1, 1977, and is buried in the Montrose, AL, Cemetery.

Charlie and Salina's seventh child, Woodrow Wilson "Wilson," attended East Central Junior College and the University of Alabama. Wilson married Ruth Etalene Stamper from Stratten, MS on Mar. 9, 1940. He served in the U.S. Navy during WWII from 1940-1944. They lived in Birmingham, AL, for a short period, then moved to the Mobile area where they remained. Wilson operated a pest control business as a career. Their first child, Nancy Carolyn (b. Oct. 7, 1940), was followed by Barbara Ann (b. Sep. 18, 1942). Nancy and Barbara have continued to live in the Mobile area. Nancy married Howard Maherg on Oct. 19, 1964, and Barbara married John William McKellar Jr. on Apr. 16, 1965. Wilson died Dec. 3, 1976 in Mobile and is buried there.

William B. and Mary Jane's seventh child,

Robert William "Bob," was born in Lake, later moving to "East" Hillsboro with the family. Bob was killed as a young man (date unknown) by a falling tree limb while robbing a honey tree. He is buried in the Hillsboro Baptist Cemetery (no headstone at the present time).

William B. and Mary Jane's eighth child, Harriet E., apparently moved to Texas with Lou and J.C. Weems, but according to relatives (mainly Aunt Sister) is buried in the Hillsboro Baptist Cemetery with no headstone. She married a Bobbit, but nothing more is known about her.

WALLACE, William Wallace (b. 1825, d. Feb. 15, 1905) and Margaret Beasley came from North Carolina and he was living in Sharon, MS when he died. His family brought him in a covered wagon to Contrell Cemetery to be buried. He had a second wife, Frances Mary Smith, who is buried in Wesson, Copiah County.

One of the descendants of William Wallace and Margaret Beasley was John Calvin (b. Feb. 19, 1847, d. Sep. 11, 1931). He married Clara Frances Patrick (b. Oct. 6, 1855, d. Aug. 4, 1922). They settled three miles northeast of Forkville off Road 483. To their union were born 12 children. John Calvin was a farmer and one day while he was cutting hay, he switched the mule who jerked causing an accident and the loss of his leg. Ironically, Maude (youngest child) had to have leg amputated after a 1966 tornado destroyed their home in Forkville.

John Calvin Wallace Family

During the time John Calvin and Clara Frances were living in Forkville, living in their home was Clara's mother, Ann Lucretia Banks (b. 1837, d. 1929). Her husband, John Patrick, who served in Co. C, No. 39th Inf. had died in a Camp David, IL, prison during the Civil War.

Children of John Calvin and Clara Frances:
1) Beulah Virginia (b. Apr. 4, 1874) md. Joseph Lawson Latham and settled in Beach.
2) Walter Wallace (b. 1876, d. 1888).
3) Lou Della (b. Dec. 8, 1877, d. Apr. 10, 1947) md. Sephus Leon Waggoner and settled in Ludlow.
4) Robert Lee (b. Nov. 18, 1879, d. July 1961) md. Minnie Zell Myles and they settled in Raymond, MS. He served as a Baptist minister.
5) Ona Pearl (b. Nov. 14, 1881, d. Mar. 14, 1967) md. George Benton Coward and settled in Branch.
6) Minnie Myrtle (b. Sep. 30, 1883, d. Oct. 25, 1941) md. William Franklin Duncan and settled in Beach and later in Ludlow.
7) John Wiley (b. Oct. 23, 1886, d. Feb. 22, 1956) md. Molly Day. After her death he married Hattie Stone and they settled in Forkville.
8) Simon Charles (b. Sep. 27, 1888, d. Nov.

23, 1968) md. Valeria Williams and settled in Ellisville. He served as a professor at Jones Co. Junior College.
9) William Denson (b. Nov. 30, 1890, d. Nov. 21, 1969) md. Mamie Rigby and settled in Hughes, AR, serving as Baptist minister.
10) Annie Laurie (b. Feb. 14, 1892, d. Feb. 19, 1953) married John Rushing and settled in Forest.
11) Jodie Thomas (b. Sep. 29, 1894, d. Jun. 18, 1970) md. Estelle Iona Husbands and settled in Forest.
12) Maude (b. Dec. 9, 1896, d. Sep. 11, 1978) md. William "Gip" Waggoner and settled in Forkville. "Gip" lived to 105 years.

We the children, grandchildren, great-grandchildren thank this family for our Christian heritage and we have "precious memories" of the family.

WALTMAN, Elijah Waltman, son of Oliver Felix Waltman and Amanda Gould Waltman, was born at Lake, MS on Jun. 6, 1881. He was the grandson of Elijah and Harriet Skinner Waltman. He married Eliza Elizabeth Baggett on Oct. 16, 1901. Elizabeth (b. Feb. 19, 1879) was the daughter of John Wesley and Sarah McCants Baggett. Elijah and Elizabeth are buried at Salem Cemetery, Scott County, MS. She preceded him in death, Feb. 7, 1933, and Elijah died Dec. 14, 1951.

Elijah Waltman with the vehicle he used as a school bus for Goodhope School, Scott County, MS.

The nine children of Elijah and Elizabeth are as follows:
1) Sarah Mary Emmaline "Emma" (b. Sep. 16, 1902, d. Mar. 18, 1984) md. Lon Hendry.
2) Elijah Felix "Sige" (b. Dec. 28, 1903, d. Feb. 3, 1978).
3) John Wesley (b. May 6, 1906, d. Jul. 17, 1987) md. Eva Mae "Susie" Myers.
4) Benjamin Hogan (b. May 6, 1906, d. Jul. 23, 1974) md. Agnes Sanders. He and John Wesley were twins.
5) Salome Florence "Lome" (b. Apr. 22, 1909, d. Dec. 25, 1941) md. Marion Adolph Henderson.
6) William Frank (b. Feb. 19, 1913) md. Velma Moreland.
7) Thomas Edward (b. May 24, 1916, d. Jan. 10, 1979) md. Juanita Gipson.
8) Oliver Freeman (b. Apr. 6, 1920, d. Oct. 6, 1976) md. Evelyn Emmons on May 18, 1945. She was the daughter of Tad Emmons and Eula Clark Emmons.
9) Alton Monroe (b. Aug. 16, 1923) md. Frances Elizabeth Baverschmidt.

WALTMAN, Oliver Freeman Waltman (b. Apr. 6, 1920 Lake, MS) was the son of Elijah and Eliza Elizabeth Baggett Waltman, and the

grandson of Oliver Felix and Amanda Gould Waltman.

He attended Goodhope School where he lettered in basketball. After graduation he went to East Central Junior College for two years. At Mississippi State College he studied agriculture and received a bachelor of science degree. He also received a certificate of graduation from the Illinois Central Forestry School at Forest, MS.

He served during WWII and was a member of the American Legion.

Oliver Freeman Waltman Family. Back, l-r: Freeman, Larry, Carolyn, Phillip. Front, l-r: Billy, Evelyn and Ricky

On May 18, 1945, he married Evelyn Emmons, daughter of Tad and Eula Mae Clark Emmons. They had five children as follows: 1) James Phillip Waltman (b. May 10, 1946) md. Martha Morgan in 1986; 2) Larry Dean Waltman (b. Jan. 24, 1948) md. Linda Wehmeier; 3) Carolyn Ann Waltman (b. Oct. 21, 1950) md. W.D. "Red" Stroud; 4) Ricky Lee Waltman (b. Sep. 8, 1953) md. Sherry Gunn; 5) Billy Roy Waltman (b. Mar. 1, 1957), married Sue Simmons.

Freeman lived in the Goodhope Community all of his life. He raised poultry and was later a poultry inspector. He worked also at the Sunbeam clock factory for several years.

He attended Salem Church where he was a deacon and he and his wife were both active members. He was an avid sportsman and loved to attend the basketball and football games at Lake.

L-R: Larry Dean Waltman served in the U.S. Navy and James Phillip Waltman served as paratrooper with the 82nd and 101st Abn. Divs.

Two of his sons, James Phillip and Larry Dean, served during the Vietnam War. Phil was in the 82nd and 101st Abn. Div. and Larry was in the Navy. He was very proud of them. Freeman died Oct. 6, 1976 and is buried at Salem Cemetery, Scott County, MS.

WARDELL-TADLOCK, Karl Thomas Wardell, son of Thomas Daniel Wardell and Elizabeth Halsel, was born Jul. 1, 1877 in Scott County MS. He married Magnolia Belle Tadlock, daughter of Elisha Turner Tadlock and Clemmie Gardner, on Dec. 13 1896 in Pulaski, MS. She was born Dec. 9, 1874.

Karl Thomas Wardell and Magnolia Belle "Maggie"

Karl was a minister in the Primitive Baptist Church in Pulaski/Pelahatchie/Walnut Grove/ Morton Charge. He patented (homesteaded) 160 acres of land in Smith County on Oct. 19, 1905. Karl and Magnolia had 11 children: Louie Glenn, Nola Virginia, Edwin Thomas, Lois Obie, Magnolia Belle, Karl Turner, unnamed infant, Burnice Pailine, unnamed infant, Mary Neal and Willie Mildred. Karl died Mar. 5, 1941 and Magnolia died Dec. 9, 1950. They are both buried in the Homewood Methodist Cemetery along with their two unnamed babies. *Submitted by Andy Miller.*

WARREN, Henry Hunt Warren established headquarters in Forest, Scott County, MS in 1941. Buying and selling pulpwood for Brown Paper Mill of Monroe, LA, he was dubbed "Dean of Pulpwood Operators" by the *Scott County Times.*

Henry and Myrtice Warren at their 50th wedding anniversary celebration

Henry (b. 1882 in Tensaw, Baldwin County, AL), son of Lee Ford Warren and Lilla Jane Hunt. In 1914 he married Myrtice Louise Maxwell (b. 1888), daughter of Carrol Winston Maxwell and Martha Louise Wylie of Lincoln County, MS. Until they settled in Scott County, they lived in several timber communities in Louisiana. Myrtice died in 1973 and Henry in 1975.

Their children were Patricia Lucille "Pat" (b. 1915 in Bogalusa, LA); Henry Hansel (b. 1918 in McNairy, LA); and Martha Carolyn (b. 1922 in Fal, LA).

Pat married Roy Baker of Alabama in 1938. Their only child, Patricia Carolyn "Patsy" was born 1941 in Montgomery, AL. They moved to Forest in 1943 and Roy died in 1944. Pat married Otho Davis Loper Jr., son of O.D. Loper Sr. and Emmet Edwards of Forest, in 1950. O.D. Jr. died in 1971. Patsy married Austin Lee Waggoner, son of Barney Waggoner and Tommie Dee Robinson, in 1962. Their children were Cynthia Leigh (b. 1964), Pamela Susan (b. 1966) and Patricia Dee (b. 1972).

In 1940 Henry Hansel married Lillian Janelle Edwards, daughter of Josh Edwards and Bertie Bailey of Walnut Grove. Their first child was Henry Carrol "Skipper" (b. 1942), followed

by Gerald Wayne (b. 1949). Henry died in 1967 and Janelle in 1994. Skipper married Linda Dean Johnson, daughter of Charles Rolph Johnson and Willie Mae Pigg of Lena, in 1965. Their children were Henry Carrol "Scotty" Jr. (b. 1966), Gregory John (b. 1968), Todd Maxwell (b. 1970) and Amanda Elizabeth (b. 1979). Wayne married Cheryl Dolan, daughter of Bill Dolan and Adeliah Harris, in 1978. Their daughter, Lora Janelle, was born in 1980. Wayne died in 1994.

Martha Carolyn married Lucius Arthur Davis Jr., son of L.A. Davis Sr. and Katie Mae Werner of Georgia, in 1940. Their daughter, Linda Marilyn, was born in 1941. Carolyn later married Harvey Hill "Git" Wallace Jr., son of H.H. Wallace Sr. and Mary Elizabeth Bowie of Carthage. Their son, William Warren, was born in 1949. "Git" adopted Linda in 1950. "Git" died in 1976 and Carolyn died in 1986. Linda married Terry Keith Long, son of William Arnold Long and Pearl Vanderford of Carbon Hill, AL, in 1963. Their children were Terry Keith Long Jr. (b. 1964) and Laurie Ann (b. 1967). Terry Sr. died in 1984. Linda married William Louie Dobbs Jr., son of W.L. Dobbs Sr. and Hattie Mae Fairchilds of Forkville, in 1992. Warren married Pamela Elaine Pryor, daughter of Waldo Pryor and Zola Mae Morrow of Homewood, in 1970. Their children were Christie Carol (b. 1970), Wendy Renee (b. 1975), William Warren II (b. 1977) and Lisa Lynn (b. 1981). *Submitted by Pat W. Loper and Linda W. Dobbs.*

WEEMS, The American family of Weems originated in the Parish of Wemyss in Fifeshire in Scotland. When the adoption of surnames began (at the close of the 12th century), the family with the largest land holdings adopted the parish name as their own. The first Wemyss to immigrate to America was David (b. 1706, d. 1779) and his two brothers, John and James (b. 1707, d. 1781). All adopted the English pronunciation of the Wemyss name Weems. David was the father of 19 children—one was a reverend (Episcopal) and author, Mason Locke Weems (b. 1759, d. 1825) of Dunfries, VA. He wrote biographies of several of our founding fathers (Marion, Penn, Franklin, Washington), but is most well known for originating the story of Washington and the cherry tree in his book, *The Life of Washington.*

Seven of E. Luther Weems' 10 sons at the Tallabogue Creek farm homesite (l-r): Bob Frank, Eugene Clements, Wilbur Lee, Luther Brooks, Lovett Hayes, William Lenford and Hilton Thurman

The Scott County, MS branch of the Weems' are descended from a John (possibly named James) Weems (b. 1741?) in Maryland. This John/James, second cousin of Mason Locke Weems and a Revolutionary War soldier under

Washington, emigrated to southern Virginia with his wife, Margaret Rosemond. They had six children: John II (b. 1762, d. 1840), Samuel Rosemond, James (b. 1775, d. 1827), Bartholomew (b. 1774?, d. 1850?), Margaret and Helen. All sons emigrated to Smith County, MS, in 1824, except Samuel Rosemond.

Bartholomew married Catherine Jones in 1808 in Abbeville, SC. Their children are Joseph S. (b. 1809, d. 1850), James S. (b. 1812, d. 1900), Samuel Rosemond (b. 1814, d. 1915), and Samantha (b. 1825, d. 1904).

Joseph S., believed to be the first to live in Scott County, married Elizabeth Ann Mallard in 1830. Both are buried near Sherman Hill in Scott County. He was a farmer southeast of Forest. Their eight children, all born in Mississippi, are Joseph J. (b. 1831, d. ?), Mary Anna (b. 1835, d. 1923), Minerva (b. 1840, d. ?), Louise Elizabeth (b. 1841, d. 1928), William Jefferson, John Melton, Milissa (b. 1854, d. ?) and Martha (b. 1854, d. ?).

William Jefferson Weems (b. Dec. 19, 1845 in Scott County) md. Lennie Harvey (b. 1843, d. 1914) before 1867. A blacksmith and farmer living south of Forest, he died Jul. 23, 1930. They are buried in High Hill Methodist Cemetery. Their children were E. Luther, Lee C., Annie, Eugenia and Emma.

John Melton Weems (b. Feb. 28, 1850, d. Dec. 20, 1914) was buried in Dennis Cemetery in Scott County. He married Mary Alice Dennis and they had one child, Isaac Eutevee.

William F. married Emma Doolittle in 1886 in Scott County. James S. Weems was born Jul. 12, 1812 in South Carolina and died Nov. 10, 1900. He married Sarah Flowers and their children are Mary J. (b. 1853, d. ?), John J. (b. 1854, d. ?), William F. (b. 1855, d. 1910).

E. Luther (b. Aug. 27, 1870, in High Hill, MS, d. Aug. 27, 1959), son of William Jefferson Weems, was buried at Homewood Methodist Cemetery. He owned and farmed 120 acres on Hwy. 35 south of Forest on Tallabogue Creek. He married first, Essie Hellen on Feb. 27, 1894 and second, Lucie J. Lovett, Jan. 29, 1912, in Scott County. Lucie was the daughter of William Lovett and Rebecca Roberts.

Children of E. Luther Weems and Essie Hellen are Eugene Clements (b. 1895, d. ?); John Talmadge (b. 1897, d. 1899); Henry Gibson (b. 1898, d. 1923); Luther Brooks (b. 1903, d. ?); Hilton Thurman (b. 1907, d. 1961); William Lenford (b. 1907, d. 1972); and Mary Lemina (b. 1901, d. 1914).

Children of E. Luther Weems and Lucie Lovett are Annie Lois (b. 1912); Wilbur Lee (b. 1914, d. 1996); Lovett Hayes (b. 1915, d. 1970); Kenneth Clayton (b. 1917, d. 1974), Bob Frank (b. 1920, d. 1996), and Ozelle (b. 1922, d. 1992). All children were born in Forest.

Eugene Clements Weems married Pearl Mangum. Their children are Willie (b. 1919, d. 1995), and Lillie Mae (md. Gatewood). They owned property south of Forest on Hwy. 35. Willie married Ozella Millings (b. 1918) in 1940 (no children). They lived in Forest where Willie was a long-time announcer for the radio station.

Luther Brooks Weems married Frances Elizabeth "Lizzie" Peterson (b. 1906, d. 1986). Their children are Luther Brooks Jr., Joseph, Edgar Lea, John Frances (b. 1930, d. 1982), and

Mary Hellen (all are deceased except Mary Hellen who resides in Texas).

Hilton Thurman Weems married Etta Irene Sorrey of Smith County in 1927. He farmed his father's Tallabogue Creek farm south of Forest. Their children are Richard Thurman (b. 1927), Alice Jean (b. 1932, d. 1981), and Julia Maxine (b. 1940). Hilton, his daughter Alice Jean, and one grandson Michael are buried at Homewood Methodist Cemetery.

William Lenford Weems married Floy Riley (b. 1908, d. 2000). Both are buried at High Hill Methodist Cemetery. In 1999, at the age of 92, Floy was crowned Mississippi Nursing Homes "Most Beautiful" resident (her beauty secret was a daily cup of water with apple cider vinegar). Two sons, Timothy (b. 1933, d. 1954) and Joe (dates unknown) are deceased. Their other children: Ouida Joyce (b. 1931) lives in Crystal Springs; James Henry (b. 1938) md. Ada Ruth Risher (b. 1942) in 1962 and they live in Harperville. Their children are Vicki Lyn (b. 1960) and Angie (b. 1962), Paul Luther (b. 1945) and wife Patricia Crimm and daughters, DeLyn and Jason, live in Forest.

Anne Lois Weems married Elvin Hugh Hall in 1939. They now live in Rock Hill, NC. Their children, Hughlene (b. 1942) md. Robert Lucas; Brenda (b. 1943) md. William Murril Telpig; and Julia (b. 1949) md. Robert Booth.

Wilbur Lee Weems married Mattie L. Tadlock (b. 1921). They had three sons: Billy Brooks (deceased) and wife Judy had three children: Mark (b. 1962), Brenda (b. 1963) and Kimberly (1967); Sheldon had one son, Shane; Larry (never married); Wilbur was a career state game warden living between Forest and Morton.

Lovett Hayes Weems married Harriett Lou Vaughn. He was owner and proprietor of Weems Cash Grocery, on Hwy. 35 south of Forest, until his death. They had one son, Lovett Hayes II, a Methodist minister. He and his wife, Emily, have four children: Lovett III (b. 1970), Cynthia (b. 1972), Elizabeth (b. 1975) and Lawrence (b. 1980).

Kenneth Clayton Weems married Ola Mae Possey, and is buried in Homewood Methodist Cemetery. Bob Frank Weems (deceased) lived in Phoenix, AZ, and married first, Anita and had one child, Bobette. He married second, Mildred. Ozelle Weems married Joe Aylor and lives in Knoxville, TN. They have four children: George, Libby, Jozelle and Huey.

Richard Thurman, son of Hilton Thurman, married Beulah Elaine Duncan (b. 1929) in 1948. He was a mechanic and proprietor of Weems Cash Grocery for many years. He purchased 117 acres of the Tallabogue Creek farm after his father's death. They have two daughters, Judy Ann (b. 1948) and Rita Coleen (b. 1952).

Judy married first, Robert Wayne Parkman in 1966 and they had two sons: Robert Jason (b. 1971) and Richard Janssen (b. 1976). She married second, George Vardaman Moore Jr. in 1992. They own the old Eugene Clements Weems homesite south of Forest. Rita married first, Carl James Leslie of Newton in 1971. One child, LaDonna Allison, was born in 1976 (her surname was changed from Leslie to Williams in 1984). Rita married second, John Davis Williams (b. 1947) in 1983. They reside in Madison, MS and Allison resides in Memphis, TN.

Robert Jason Parkman married Lori Lea Chambers (b. 1972) in 1991. They have two children, Shelby Lea (b. 1992) and Jason Mitchell (b. 1995), and reside in Homewood. Richard Janssen Parkman married Felicia Scott in 1997. With their two children, Faith (b. 1999) and Janssen Scott (b. 2000), they reside in Smith County.

Alice Jean Weems married Halbert "Pat" Patterson in 1952. Their children are Sandra Irene (b. 1958), Halbert Thurman (b. 1960), Alecia Rose (b. 1967), and Michael (b. 1968, d. 1987). Sandra and husband Eugene Odom (b. 1954) have two daughters, Hope (b. 1976) and Heather (b. 1978). All reside north of Forest. Hope is married to Brock Rhodes (b. 1975) and has one child, Hunter Brock (b. 2000). Heather is married to Kevin Polk (b. 1974) and has one daughter Emilee Nichole (b. 2000). Halbert married first, Wanda Smith in 1981 (no children) and second, Sherri McMillan Bell in 1990. They have one son Shelby McMillan (b. 1993) and reside in Harperville. Alecia married Ricky Pearson and they have two sons, Dustin and Brandon. They reside in Brandon.

Julia Maxine Weems married James Ellis Mitchell (b. 1936) in 1958. They reside south of Forest and have three children: James Jeffrey (b. 1958), Renita Jan (b. 1961), and John Hilton (b. 1962). They own the General Services Air, and MMS companies in Forest.

Jeffrey married first, Cathy Little of Forest and they had two children, Clay (b. 1975) and Corrie Leigh (b. 1976). He married second, Susan Ezell (b. 1967) in 1994 and they reside in Enterprise, AL. Clay married Heather N. Copeland (b. 1979) and they reside in Jacksonville, FL. They have one child, Angela (b. 1998). Corrie resides in Forest. Renita Jan married Tony Lyn Maner (b. 1960) in 1979. Their children are Jennifer Nachole (b. 1982), Jamie Lyn (b. 1986), and Jordan Ellis (b. 1992). Jennifer married Jason Gibson (b. 1982) of Forest in 2000 and they reside in Enterprise, AL. John Hilton married first, Anita Walters and second, Lisa Harrison Harrell. They have one child, Anna Gabrielle (b. 2000). They reside south of Forest.

WICKER, The Wicker's blew into the New World from Germany on Sep. 14, 1751 on the ship *Upton* in the midst of a hurricane. The destination was Charles Town, now Charleston, SC. Matthias Wicker and three sons lived and prospered there upon leaving Germany. They were originally from England. Our descendent, Henry Wicker, decided to move west in 1857 joining a wagon train heading west and it took two months to reach the timber rich lands that sold for 25c an acre in Mississippi. They fought in the American Revolutionary, War of 1812 and the Civil War.

The Coopers arrived from Ireland to the New World in the mid-1700s. Following the government treaties or movement of Indians, they moved west arriving in Mississippi in the early 1800s. The Coopers fought in the Revolutionary War, War of 1812 and the Civil War.

The Tadlocks arrived in the New World in the 1600s. After settling in Virginia, North Carolina, South Carolina, Tennessee and Alabama moved to Scott County, MS after the Civil War. Our great-grandfather, Malcolm Dumas Cann Tadlock, after serving in the 11th Alabama Infantry and late in the war, guarding Robert E. Lee, moved to Scott County from Marion, AL sometime after 1870. The Tadlocks also fought in the Revolutionary War. During an interview with one of the oldest living Tadlocks, she told of her grandmother telling tales of how they crossed the mountains and how they were not so much afraid of the Indians as they were the bears. Another gentleman said that there were five brothers who arrived from Ireland and traveled west heading for Texas; one became ill so another brother stayed behind to help an Indian woman heal him, and the others continued on.

The McEwens arrived in the New World from Scotland in 1685 after losing in a battle of Bothell Bridge against the British. John was a foreman for Penn's Land which belonged to William Penn. Their ship was blown off course and landed in New Jersey. They settled in Pennsylvania and moved to Georgia, Alabama, and to Mississippi in 1855. We had always heard about someone marrying an Indian and not until recently found photo evidence of it. They fought in the Revolutionary War, War of 1812 and the Civil War.

Ransom Oliver Wicker and Sarah Arminda Cooper married in 1904 in Smith County and moved to Scott County in 1917. Arminda Cooper was born in the Monterray Community in Mississippi. She and our aunts would regale us of tales about early Scott County living. In a newspaper article from the 60s, Grandpa states that "they could see the fire and smoke from 14 miles away when the Forest courthouse burned in 1890." He was known all over the southeast for his stock of pecan trees.

Milton Roy Wicker (Wicker, Cooper) and Beulah Tadlock (Tadlock, McEwen) married in Scott County on Dec. 08, 1933. They had three children who still come back to visit friends and relatives in Forest. Hilda Roy Wicker Ryberg, Sandra Lee Wicker Penniston, and Minda Ann Wicker Grasman.

Remembrances of our childhood include visiting the sawmill and another mill that ground sugarcane into juice in order to make sugar and syrup, living at Moore's Tower during WWII, going to "camp" meetings, all day dinner on the ground with our Tadlock and McEwen cousins. We were always told laughingly by our father, that we were kin to all of Scott County and half of Smith County. It wasn't until I became avidly interested in genealogy that we found that true.

WILKINSON, Since we were in the Marine Corps, we passed through Forest so many times and called it the town with pretty houses. In November 1966, we acquired Forest Finance Company. Charles Palmer showed us several houses. At one house, we met Ouida Mitchell and Mary N., our daughter, met Muriel. These were our first friends in Forest. Later, Charles came to North Pine Ridge, he turned around in the driveway of a house that had a sign that said, FOR SALE by Owner. We went back to see the house facing Highway 21. We moved from Florence at semester break.

In May 1966 we lost a son, I.E. Jr. "Butch," who was in the Air Force. He was killed by a drunk driver. We thought moving would help, but, of course, we brought our happy memories of him with us. When we visited Forest Methodist Church, Brother Hunt announced that we had come to join. Our former Pastor, Rev. M.L. McCormick Jr., had let him know that we had moved here. Rev. McCormick was a dear friend, and his family helped us so much during our grief laden days.

Sarge did not stay with the finance business very long, it gave him bleeding ulcers. Later he got a job with *The Scott County Times*, and he enjoyed working with Earle Johnston and his crew. He made life-long friends. In the meantime I worked at Kenwin Dress Shop, as our daughter helped open it. She went to Mississippi State, so we alternated and kept the job. Linda Risher was the manager, and she was great to work with.

After opening Modern Loan here in Forest, Sarge again gave it up, and had surgery for bleeding ulcers. Thanks to Dr. J.P. Lee who sent him to Dr. James Griffin in Jackson for surgery. After the successful surgery, he went to work as a director for the WIC Program sponsored by the Federal Government. They had three warehouses in Mississippi. When he retired in February 1988, there were 82 warehouses in Mississippi distributing food to anemic and pregnant women, and children up to six years of age.

Mary N. had been busy with high school, and later met Ronny Asa Jones, who went on to Mississippi State to play football, so of course she had to go. During that time, we had been going to games in Forest on Friday Nights. Those Forest seniors went on to East Central, so on Thursday nights we were at East Central, Friday nights-Forest, and on Saturdays we were at Mississippi State. Our gang usually consisted of Reta Waggoner, Roy and Dot Sumrall, Pope and Glenda Godfrey, also Mr. and Mrs. Asa Jones to the Mississippi State games.

Mary married Ronny Jones. They had four children: Mary Kristina (b. Jan. 4, 1974); Ronda Audi-Nichol (b. July 1975); Amy Machell and Ashley Dawn were born 15 minutes apart, otherwise they are very opposite.

I worked at Gibsons in the office with Mrs. Rushing and loved all of the clerks. Then I worked the county agents office for Mr. Charles Sanders, Curlee Green and Deborah Bennett Harris. After eight years, I had to retire because of health problems. I had to much time on my hands, so I got involved with church work and spent time with our mothers who lived in Jackson. Now we enjoy people, family, and friends that are all over North Carolina, Illinois and California. When our day comes, we will be carried to Lakewood Cemetery in Jackson, to be buried by our son, Butch, and Aunt May. We gave her the extra grave space for her going away present. *Submitted by Mr. and Mrs. I.E. "Sarge" Wilkinson.*

WILKERSON-PARKER, In 1921 two sons were born to Ben and Gertie Weeks Wilkerson, sharecroppers in the Forkville Community. These twins were named O.B. and J.B. One of these twins, J.B., died shortly after his birth.

O.B. grew up in a time when life was hard. As a young man he became part of the Civilian Conservation Corps. This group of young men cleared the land for Roosevelt State Park.

About this time O.B. met a young girl in what is now the Leesburg Community. Her name was Geroldean Parker, oldest daughter of Walter and Willie Robinson Parker. The daughter of a farmer, Geroldean learned at an early age how to take care of everything on a farm, from milking cows to tending a garden, or how to plow with a mule. As the oldest daughter she was often called on to take care of the younger children in her family. She had 10 siblings, nine younger than she.

The romance between the couple was interrupted by WWII. O.B. joined the Army to serve his country on the field of battle. He was in many campaigns. He saw much hand-to-hand combat and was wounded in battle as was evidenced by the Purple Hearts in the medals he brought home. Also there were medals of marksmanship.

While he was away Geroldean continued to work at home. Her mother was having children so Geroldean became as a mother to her younger siblings. She saw some of them marry before she did.

O.B. came home from the war and on Geroldean's 18th birthday they became husband and wife. They stood in the home of Mr. Ruby Lee Cross and exchanged vows.

To this union was born six children: Billy, Linda, Fletcher, Deborah, Sandra and Teresa.

Years went by and O.B. and Geroldean soon saw a need for a church in their community. They donated the land for a church and Two Mile Baptist Church was born. The couple, along with several others, became charter members of this church.

In 1983, Geroldean passed away after a length illness. O.B. and Billy, his oldest son, lived at home. In 1989 tragedy struck. Billy passed away suddenly in August. In 1991 O.B. passed away at the age of 70.

WINDHAM-MARTINDILL, was born Apr. 19 1925, in Forest, MS to Henry Roy Windham and Flossie Dee Combs. Roy (b. Jul. 13, 1900 in Forest) was the son of John Houston Windham and Alice Lenora Barnes. John Houston (b. May 1, 1871, in Pulaski, Scott County, MS, d. Jan. 19, 1944) is buried in Homewood. Alice Lenora (b. May 17, 1892 in Homewood, d. Mar. 13, 1919) is buried in Homewood.

John H. and Alice Lenora had four sons and two daughters, Victor Raynor, William Houston, Henry Roy, Sarah Mable, Flora Miller and Thomas Graham Windham, all born in Scott County.

John Houston Windham was the son of William Franklin Windham (b. Dec. 24, 1850 in Smith County, d. Sep. 11, 1901 in Scott County, buried near Pulaski). He married Mary Elizabeth "Bettie" Thompson May 11, 1870, in Scott County. She was born Apr. 11, 1851.

John Stanley Windham (father of William Franklin Windham) was born Sep. 22, 1827 in Wilcox County, AL and died Mar. 4, 1905, in Homewood. He married Martha Elizabeth Marlar on Dec. 7, 1849 in Smith County. She was born Jan. 28, 1832 in Georgia, died Feb. 19, 1908 and buried in Homewood.

My g-grandfather, William Henry Barnes, was the son of Calvin Barnes of Echo, AL. He was born Sep. 5, 1845 near Echo, Dale County, AL. On Nov. 12, 1865 he married Sarah Jane Miller (b. Jun. 18, 1847, Coffee County, AL), daughter of Rev. David Laughlin Miller and Isabella. Sarah died May 19, 1920 in Homewood. William died Mar. 18, 1924, Homewood. Dr. Barnes served in the CSA Co. D, 57th AL Regiment, Schoots Brigade, Lorings Division, TN Army. He practiced medicine in the Homewood area for many years, delivering many of the families there.

After Roy and Flossie married, they returned to Forest and rented a room from Blanche Adcock. Her home was on RR Street, located behind the old Southern Hotel. I was born in Blanche's home, and lived there until I was 7 months old, when Roy and Flossie moved back to El Dorado, AR. Roy worked for years for Standard Oil Co., during and after the oil boom in that area, then moved to Baton Rouge, LA area for a while. Roy left Std. Oil, returning to El Dorado to open a hardware store and began to drill water wells.

Roy and Flossie had three sons: Charles Houston Windham (b. May 19, 1926, d. Oct. 2, 1984 in Silsbee, TX); Henry Horace Windham (b. Feb. 3, 1928); Forrest Dewitt Windham (b. Jun. 31, 1930); two daughters: Geraldine (b. Apr. 19, 1925) and Alice Lenora Windham "Shug" (b. Mar. 16 1932). All, except Geraldine "Jerri" were born in Union County, AR.

Geraldine "Jerri" Windham married Herman Young Martindill on Dec. 28, 1948, at First United Methodist Church, El Dorado, AR, and had two sons, Wyck Young Martindill (b. Dec. 11, 1951, El Dorado) and Mark Dean Martindill (b. Jul. 1, 1954, d. Apr. 12, 1992, El Dorado).

Wyck married Nell Bearden of Camden, AR Mar. 8, 1974, and they have a son Keith Young Martindill (b. Oct. 17, 1977). Keith married Sep. 27, 1996 in Camden, AR. Christie Lynn Poindexter (b. May 29, 1979, Pine Bluff, Jefferson County, AR) and they have a son Joshua Young Martindill (b. Apr. 25, 1997, in Ouachita County Hospital, Camden, AR).

WILKERSON-YOUNGBLOOD, These families are very familiar to Scott County. The Wilkerson family has been a part of Scott County from its start and it will forever remain a vital part of its existence. The Wilkerson family has certainly contributed to society by producing its share of medical personnel, war heroes, educators, judges, farmers, and most of all positive contributors to the success of Scott County.

Francis Shephard "Shep" Wilkerson (b. Oct. 7, 1861, d. Oct. 20, 1946) md. Dec. 29, 1881 Mary Elizabeth "Betty" Youngblood (b. Nov. 29, 1862, d. Apr. 5, 1948).

Shep was the son of Dr. William Harrison Wilkerson (b. Sep. 4, 1836, d. Dec. 3, 1902) and Lucinda Ursula Wilkerson (b. Nov. 29, 1843, d. Nov. 22, 1907). He was born in Alabama, but moved to Scott County when he was 6 years old. Betty was the daughter of James Albert Youngblood (b. Sep. 9, 1825, d. Feb. 4, 1904) and Lucy Ann Noblin (b. 1838, d. 1918). Her family was in Scott County prior to 1842. Shep and Betty's home was what is now where Sherman Hill Road intersects Hwy. 501. Shep made his living in the Norris Community for the rest of his life. He farmed, had a sawmill, cotton gin and gristmill. He was justice of the peace for his district for many years. As service commissioner, he supervised the building of roads in this community. He had a dipping vat for cattle and provided humanitarian services for the community. Eight children were born to this marriage. One son moved to Lake and one daughter moved to Homewood. The other six stayed in the Norris Community. Most of the family lands are still owned by the families.

The eight children to this marriage are as follows:

1) Minnie Ona Wilkerson (b. Mar. 4, 1883, d. May 15, 1965) md. in 1900 to Wardie Gatewood (b. Oct. 12, 1876, d. Mar. 5, 1968).

2) Connie Cleveland Wilkerson (b. Jul. 19, 1885, d. Feb. 14, 1955) md. Dec. 23, 1914, Ione Elizabeth Tadlock (b. Sep. 27, 1891, d. Mar. 15, 1984).

This photograph is part of Shep and Betty Wilkerson's family. It was made about 1908. Front row, l-r: Shep, Betty, Myrtle. Second row l-r: Will, Ed, Guy and Hi

3) Henry Rufus Wilkerson (b. Sep. 10, 1887, d. Jul. 6, 1971) md. Jan. 25, 1915, Mary Christian "Mollie" Duckworth (b. Apr. 22, 1888, d. Sep. 17, 1943.)

4) Willie Harris Wilkerson (b. Jun. 21, 1889, d. Oct. 1, 1975) md. Dec. 11, 1910, Ruby Putnam (b. Jul. 16, 1887, d. Jan. 1, 1973).

5) Edward Clinton Wilkerson (b. Mar. 24, 1892, d. Mar. 18, 1978) md. Jun. 17, 1921 Mary Lou Weems (b. Feb. 11, 1895, d. Jul. 24, 1984).

6) Guy Wilkerson (b. Apr. 28, 1895, d. Oct. 16, 1967) md. Dec. 2, 1915, Gertrude Ethel Crout (b. May 7, 1897, d. Feb. 6, 1977).

7) Hi Wilkerson (b. Sep. 19, 1897, d. Aug. 27, 1956) md. Gussie Lane (b. Jan. 10, 1905, d. Sep. 20, 1992).

8) Myrtle Irene Wilkerson (b. Sep. 28, 1899, d. Jan. 29, 1983) md. July 5, 1925, James Oliver "Jim" Tadlock (b. Jun. 29, 1898, d. May 3, 1987).

These eight children gave Shep and Betty 34 grandchildren. The families remained close and on December 7 when Pearl Harbor was attacked many of us were at Shep and Betty's for our regular Sunday gathering. It was a solemn occasion because there were 11 grandsons of age to fight for their country. They were Robert Francis Wilkerson, Aubrey Wilkerson, James Wilkerson, Woodrow Wilkerson, Major Wilkerson, Jerry Wilkerson, John Shep Wilkerson, William Edward Wilkerson, Marvin Wilkerson, Howard Duckworth Wilkerson and Sam Ray Wilkerson. Seven of these were in the Army, two were in the Navy, one was in the Merchant Marines and one was in the Air Force. They were involved in active combat duty in Europe, Africa, South Pacific and Asia. Unlike many families across the county, all of the Wilkerson boys survived the war and came

home! The Wilkersons have been a close family for all of these years, and the family ties are still felt within the many ancestors who travel the roads of Scott County today. It has always been a prideful feeling to be a "Wilkerson" from Scott County.

WOLVERTON, On a cold November morning in 1934 in the Damascus Community, identical twin brothers, Otis and Ottis, were born to Lee Buck Wolverton and Lillian Murtle Haralson Wolverton. For identical twins, Otis and Ottis, one aspect of their lives has been one laugh after another, usually at the comical expense of unsuspecting customers and friends who mistook one for the others.

As babies, even the family was dismayed when the twins were switched and they lost track how to tell who is Otis and who is Ottis? As young adults, the twins lived in Jackson, and became known as the "Toddle House Twins" because both worked as short-order cooks in that restaurant. The people they worked with could not tell them apart.

Both Otis and Ottis remember their 150-year-old-roots which run deep in the Damascus Community near Sebastopol. It all began when James Wolverton (b. 1815 in Louisiana) moved to Damascus. James' father was born and reared in Germany and his grandfather in Ireland. He married Martha Oglesby in 1855 and had nine children.

Ottis Dee Wolverton (left) and Otis Lee Wolverton (right), twin sons of Rev. Lee Wolverton and Murtle Haralson Wolverton.

Otis Lee Wolverton married Shelby Jean Moore of Leake County on Jun. 4, 1954. They made their home in Jackson. Their first daughter, Deborah Anne, arrived and died on Sep. 10, 1956 of heart failure. Then Jennifer Anne (b. Aug. 29, 1958) md. Micheal Crowell of Forest in May 1984; Lynda Lee (b. Oct. 9, 1959) md. Marty Killen of Sebastopol in February 1978; and last, Donna Jean (b. Mar. 12, 1961) md. Brian Nunnery of Liberty in July 1984).

After living several years in Jackson and Hillsboro, Otis Wolverton moved his family back to Damascus in 1965. There he lived until his death on May 5, 1997.

Otis Wolverton worked for Borden in Forest and the surrounding area for many years. Then he served as the Scott County Land Surveyor for 17 years. At the time of his death, he was serving his second term as Scott County Tax Assessor/Collector. Otis was a member of Sebastopol Baptist Church for 32 years and served as a deacon and Sunday School director. He was a member of the Forest Masonic Lodge, the Forest Rotary Club, and Sebastopol Achieve-

ment Club. He was very active in the Hispanic ministry at the Sebastopol Baptist Church.

Otis and Shelby Wolverton had seven grandchildren: Billy Davis Killen (md. Silje Aadensen of Egersund, Norway on Aug. 14, 1999); Rebecca Lee Killen, Leanne Marie Killen, and Martin Cole Killen, all of Sebastopol; Jessica Anne Crowell of Quitman; Natalie Jean and Nathan Brian Nunnery of Louisville.

Ottis Dee Wolverton married Laverne Corley on Dec. 31, 1957. They live in Covington County. They have two children: Ottis D. "Buddy" Wolverton Jr. (b. Nov. 3, 1958), who married Lynn Chandler in October 1989, and daughter Sherri Lynne (b. Jan. 21, 1961). Ottis and Laverne have three grandchildren, Leslie, Sam and Daniel Wolverton, all of Covington County.

Ottis served as Covington County Land Surveyor for 20 years, and was owner of WKNZ radio station for 17 years. Ottis is a deacon at Calhoun Baptist Church at Hot Coffee. He is a member of Taylorsville Masonic Lodge, Collin Rotary Club and Covington County Chamber of Commerce. Ottis Wolverton is president of Wolverton Engineering, Inc. at Collins, MS.

WRIGHT, Costello H. Wright (b. Apr. 15, 1815 in Franklin County), son of Hiram and Elizabeth Brockman. Hiram Wright's father and grandfather, William Wright Jr. and William Wright Sr., had removed from Fauquier County, VA to the area of Bedford County, VA that became Franklin County in the mid-1700s. Costello H. Wright's mother was born in Amherst County, VA, and was a descendant of the prominent Brockman family of Orange County.

In the 1830s Hiram and Elizabeth Wright left Virginia and moved their family to northwest Georgia. In 1841 Costello H. Wright was married to Elizabeth J. Ware in Floyd County. She was born 1825 in Madison County, GA to Hamilton Ware and Nancy Sorrells. Her parents were both members of prominent north Georgia families whose roots run deep in Colonial Virginia.

Shortly after their marriage, Costello H. and Elizabeth Ware Wright removed with their parents to Coosa County, AL. There they remained until the late 1860s when they migrated to Mississippi. First settling in Pontotoc County for a short time, the Wright family moved south into Scott County in the early 1870s. Upon their arrival Costello H. Wright purchased a large tract of land from the Banks Family in the Hayes Creek Community of north central Scott County.

Costello H. Wright died Jan. 26, 1881 and his widow in 1902. Both are buried in the Hayes Creek Cemetery on the Wright property. Children of Costello H. Wright and Elizabeth J. Ware are as follows:

Mary Frances Wright (b. 1842, d. 1915) md. John F. Lauderdale; Louisa W. Wright (b. 1845); Hiram Hamilton Wright (b. 1848); James M. Wright (b. 1850) md. first, Willie Ann Pettigrew and second, Julia Ann Adaline Myers; Anna Elizabeth Wright (b. 1852, d. 1882) md. Henry J. Thornton; Ophelia H. Wright (b. 1857) md. Henry J. Thornton; Costello Richardson Wright (b. 1859, d. 1923); Neal Baker Wright (b. 1862, d. 1905) md. Claudia Eugenia Patrick; Ada Jane Wright (b. 1868, d. 1951) md. Alonzo Huddleston.

213

Main Street Forest looking North 2000.

Printed in the USA
CPSIA information can be obtained
at www.ICGtesting.com
JSHW060051150824
68134JS00032B/2712

9 781681 625348